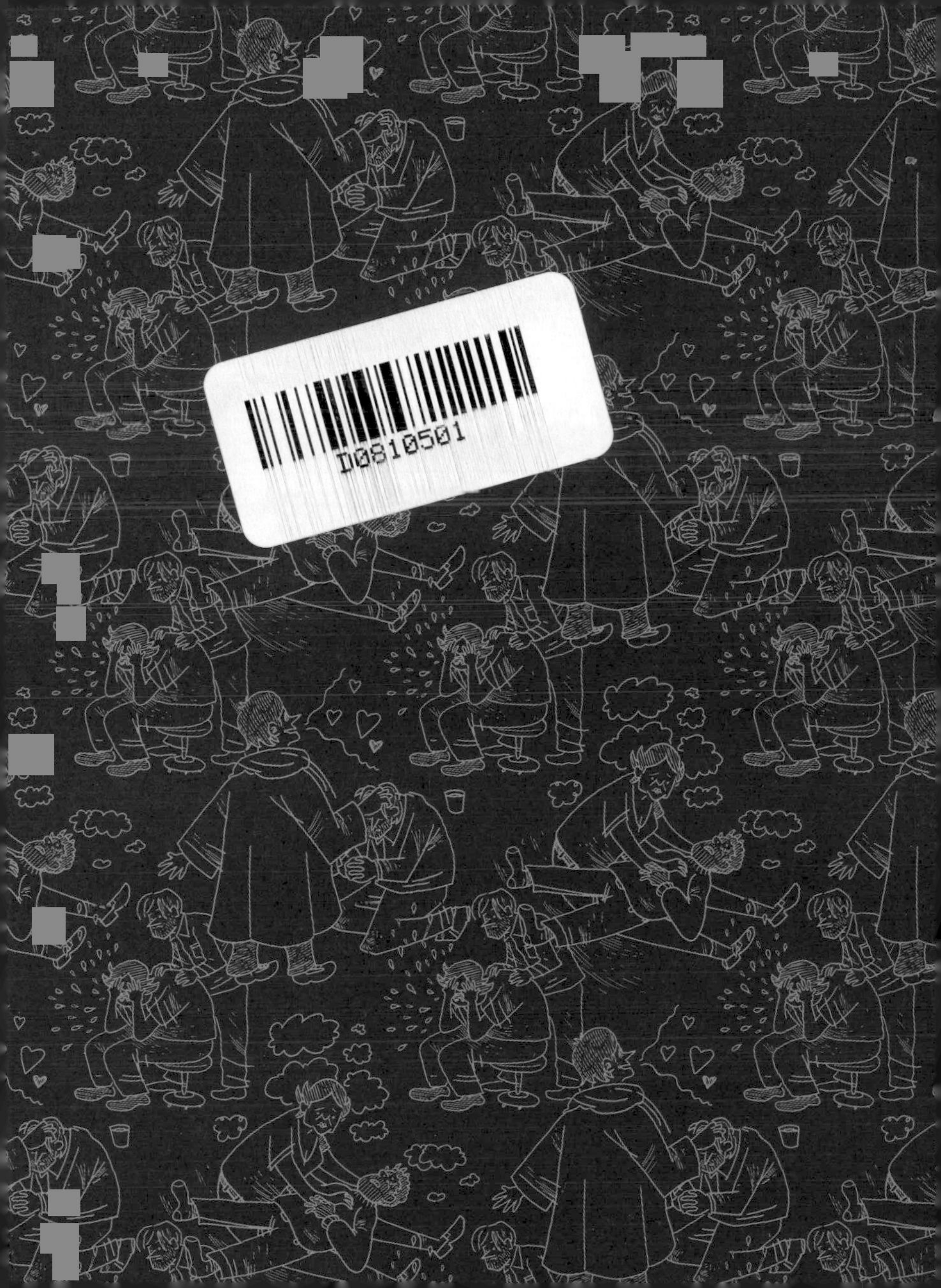

Holy Hannah

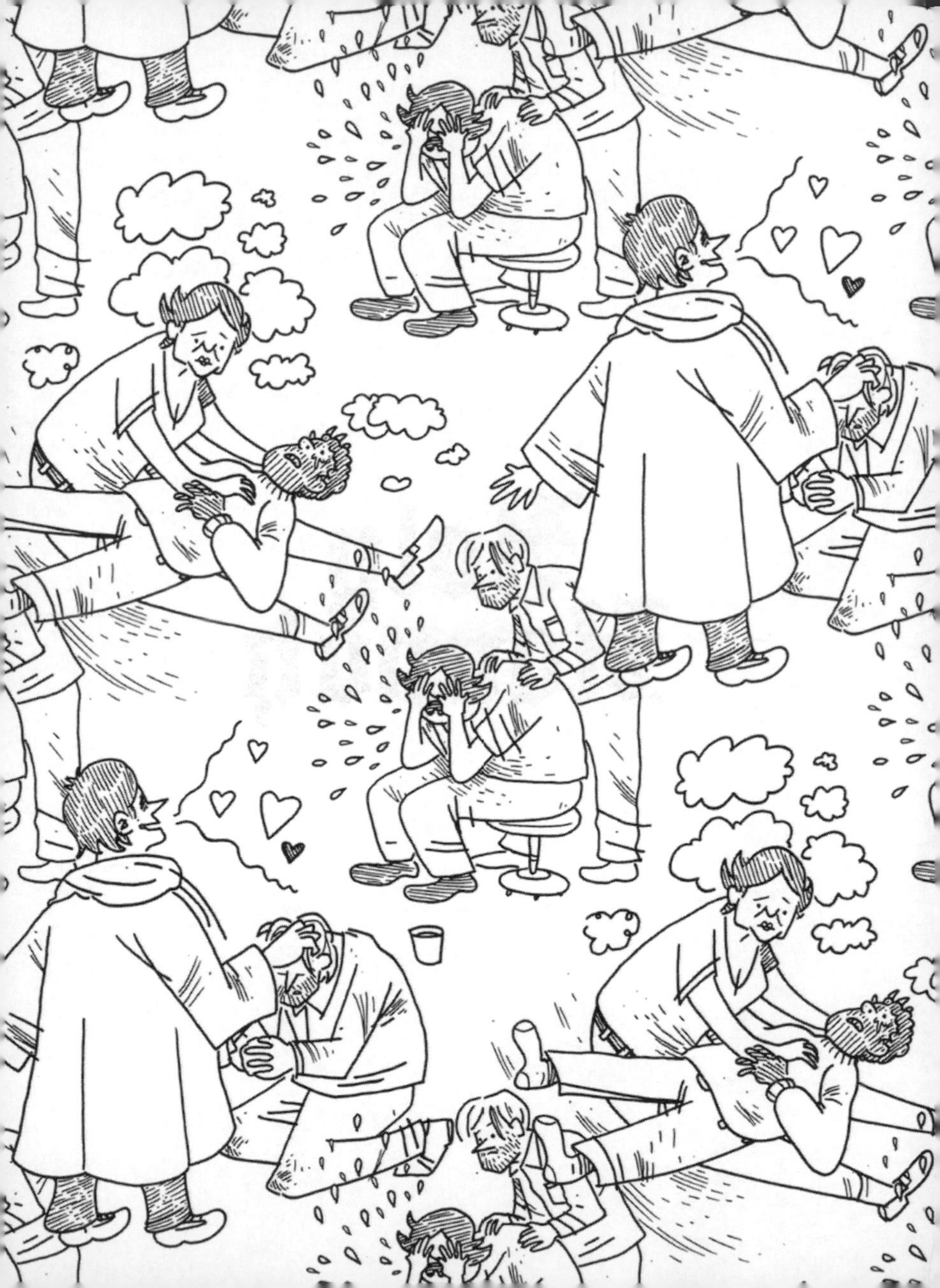

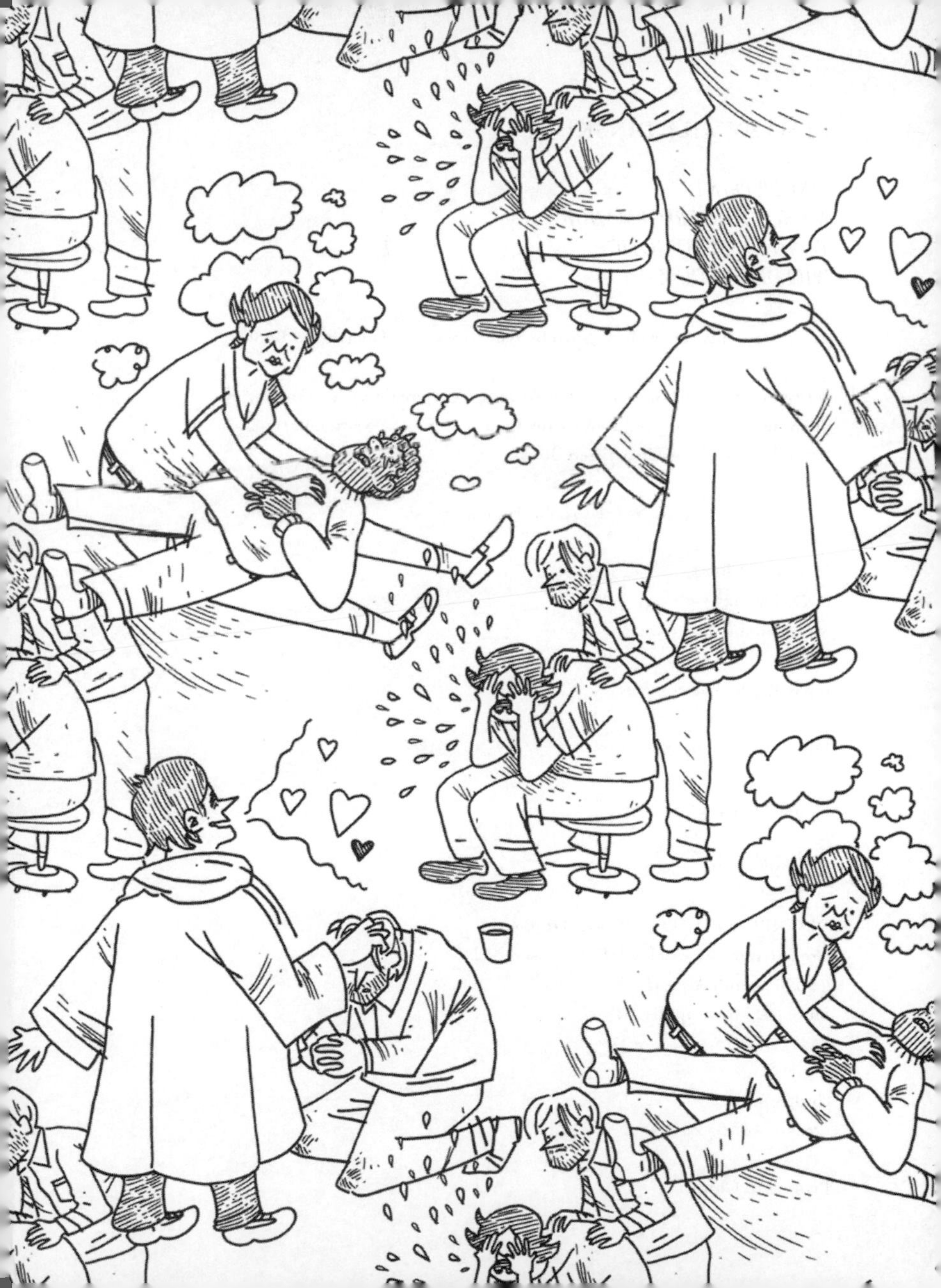

ALSO BY WILL DINSKI:

FINGER PRINTS
AN HONEST PERFORMANCE
TRYING NOT TO NOTICE
WILLDINSKI.COM

Design & Production: Will Dinski & Tom Kaczynski

Uncivilized Books
P. O. Box 6534
Minneapolis, MN 55406
USA
uncivilizedbooks.com

First Edition, October 2019

10 9 8 7 6 5 4 3 2 1

ISBN 978-1-941250-36-5

DISTRIBUTED TO THE TRADE BY:
Consortium Book Sales & Distribution, LLC.
34 Thirteenth Avenue NE,
Suite 101 Minneapolis, MN
55413-1007

cbsd.com
Orders: (800) 283-3572

Printed in China

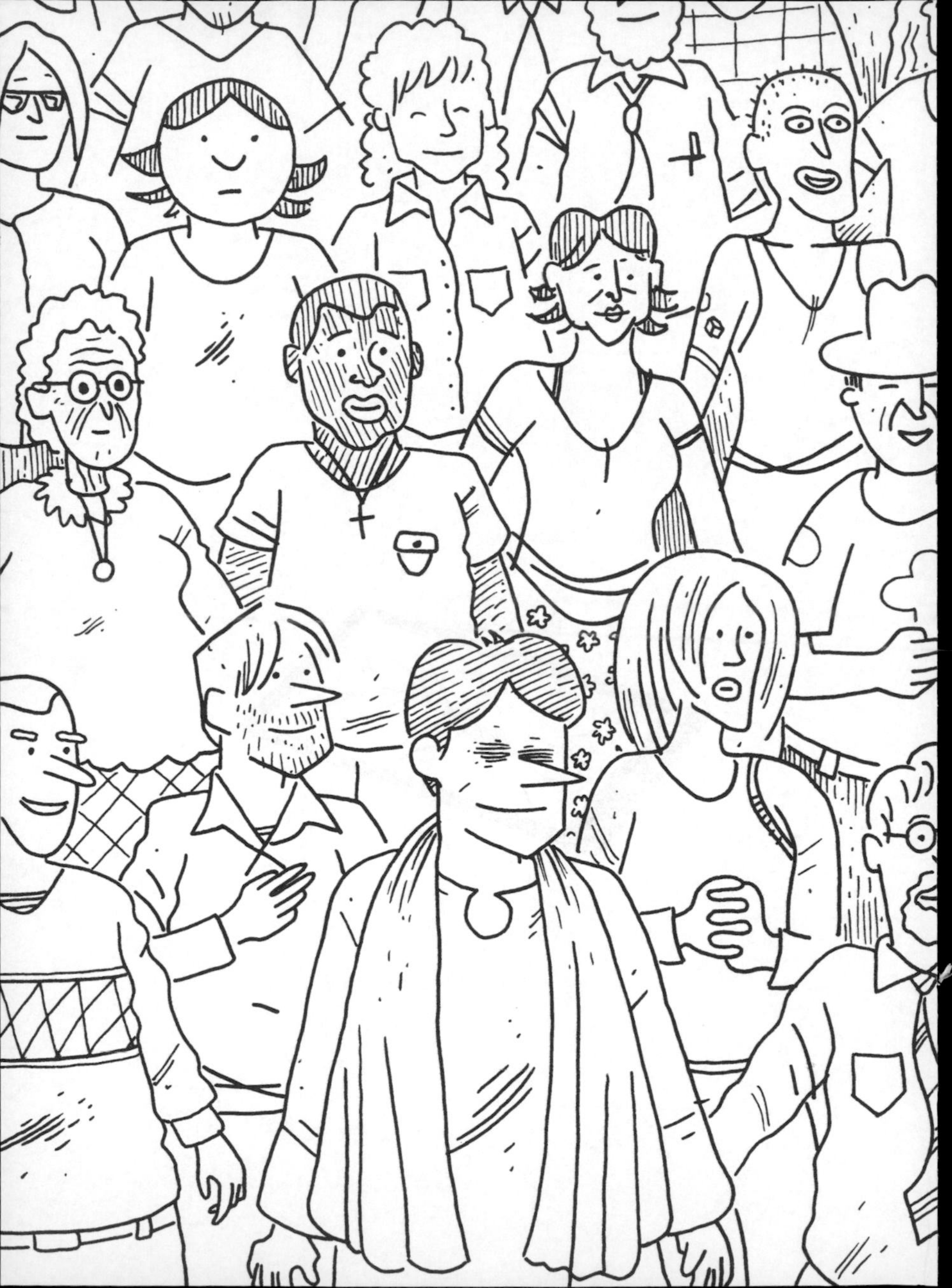

Holy Hannah

By Will Dinski

UNCIVILIZED

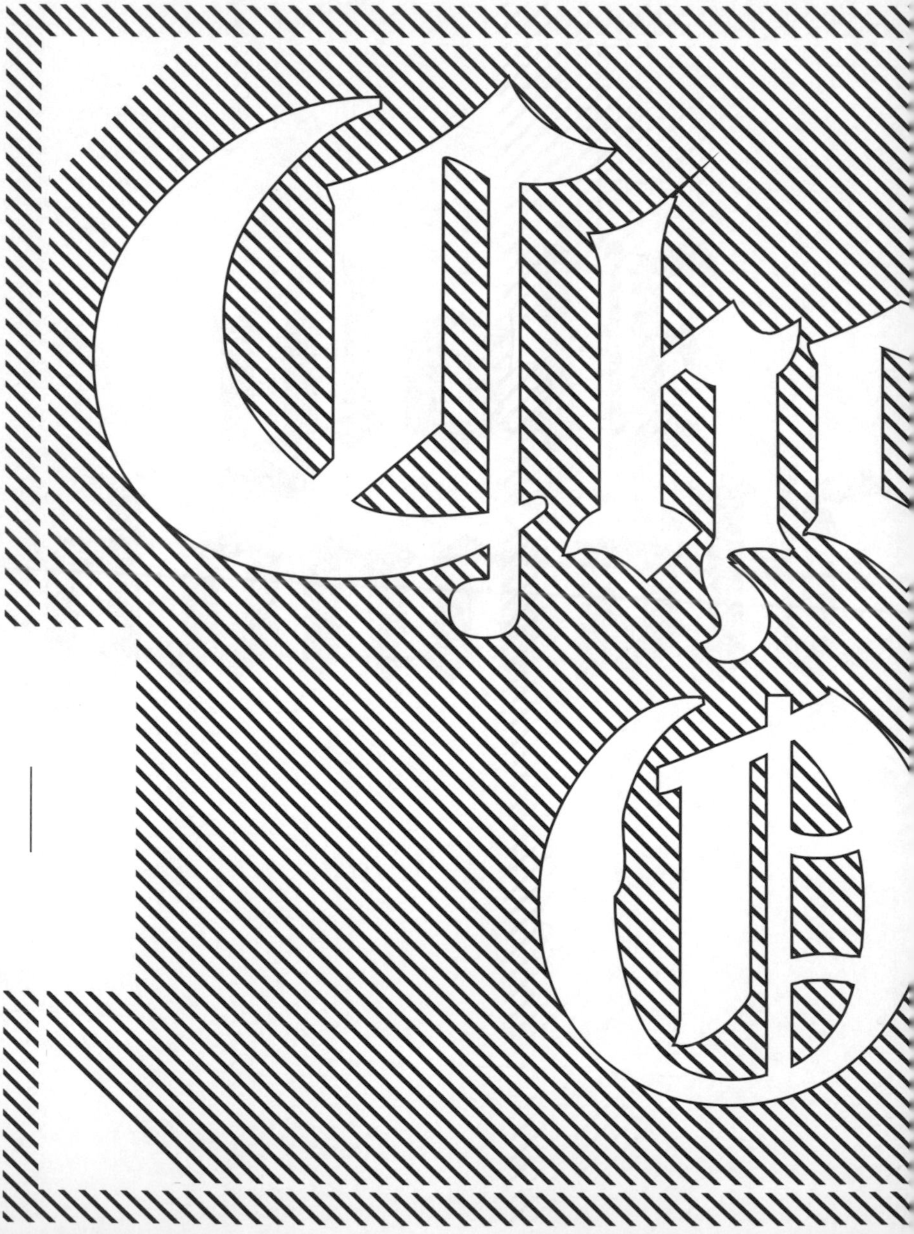
Chr
O

pter

ne

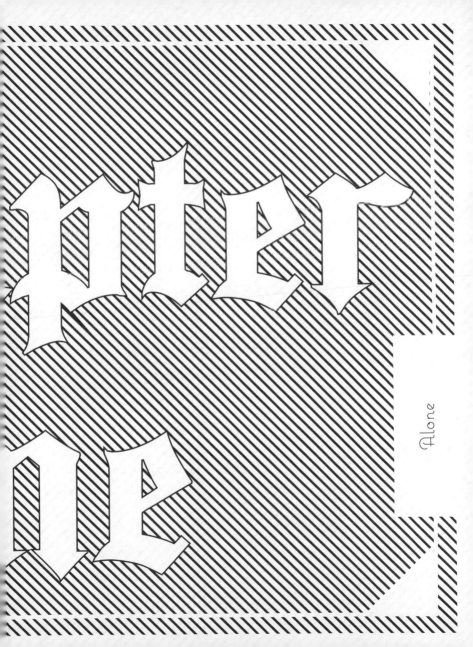

Alone

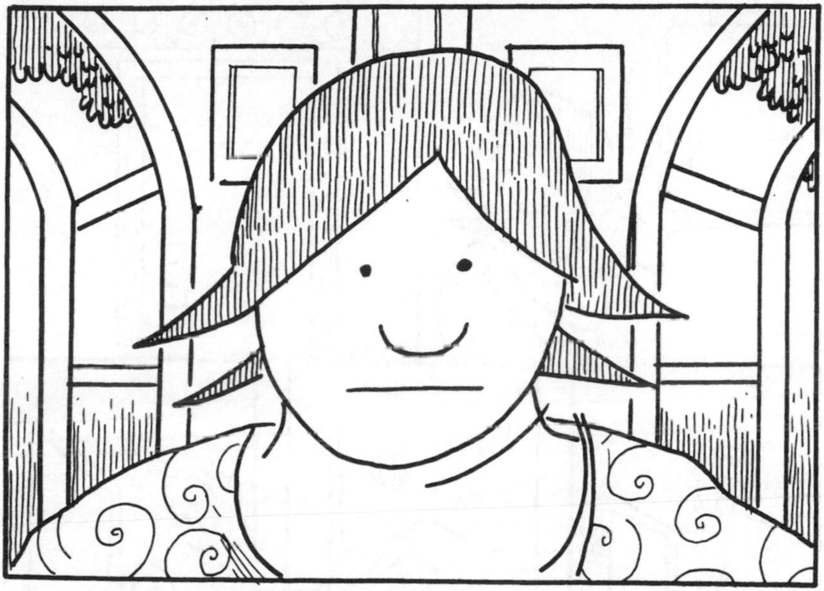

I don't expect you to relate to much of my life. A lot of it, I think you would run from in fear. For me, it was almost all paradise.

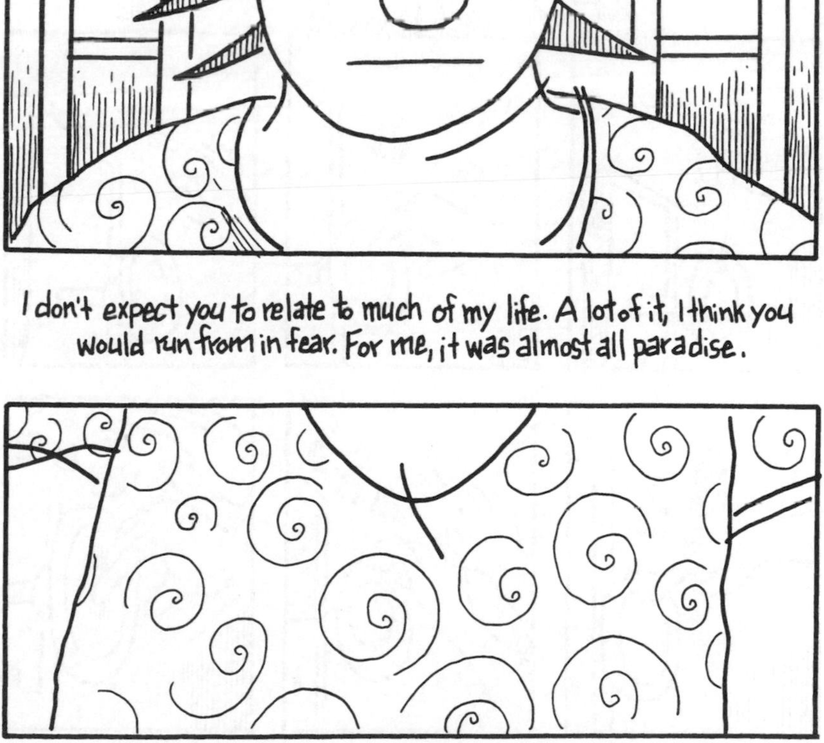

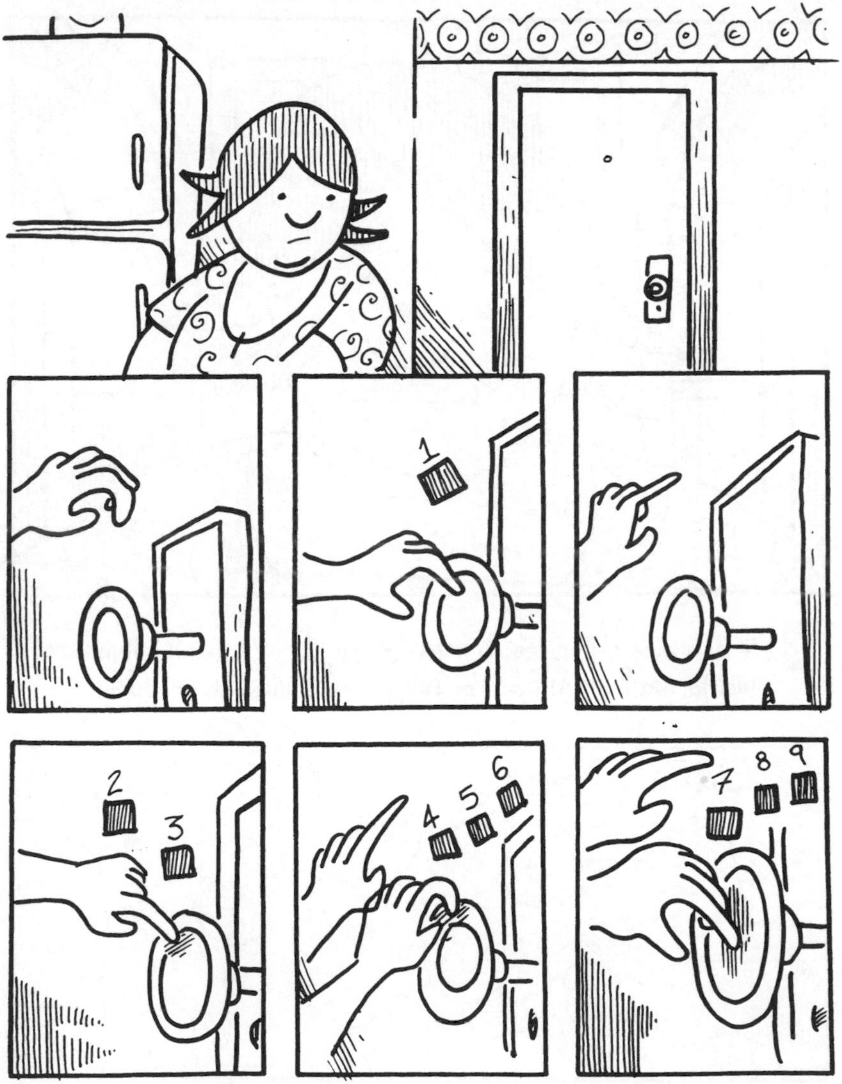
1
2
3
4
5
6
7
8
9

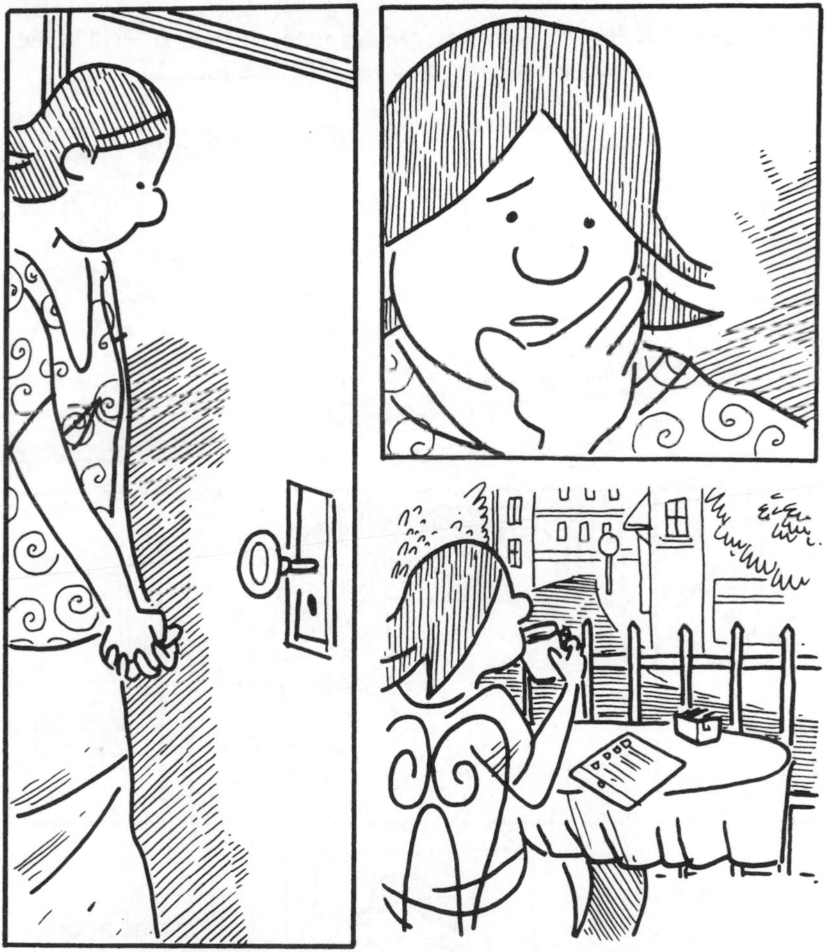

The trick to most things is figuring out how to limit your options.
So, if the world is your oyster, only eat oysters.

I only ate what the restaurant downstairs made for me. A table in the small patio was on reserve, and I dined there every evening.

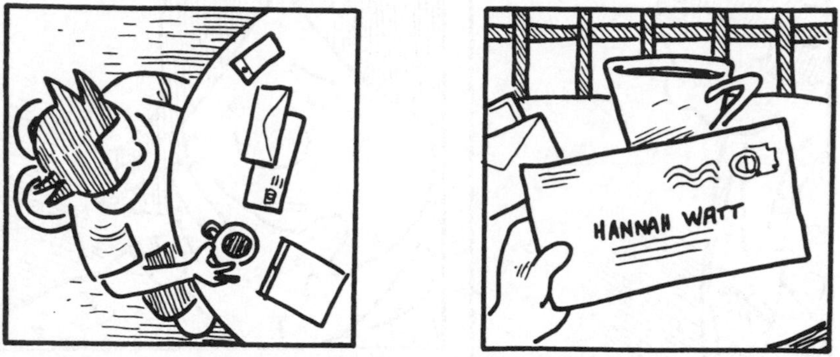
HANNAH WATT

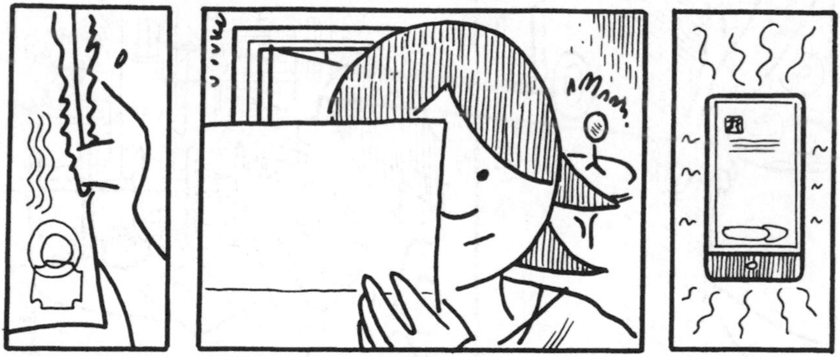

That table was as far away from my room as I permitted myself to go.

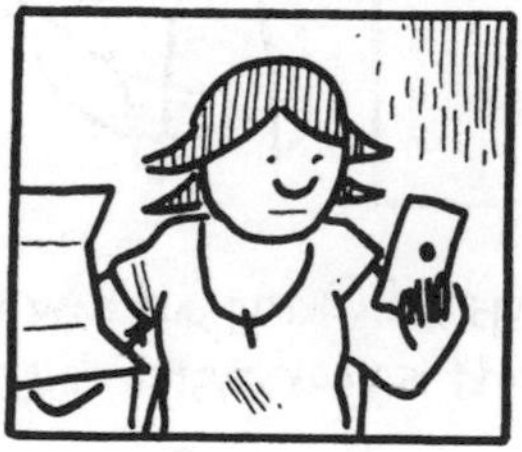

It served as an invisible fence that I never crossed.

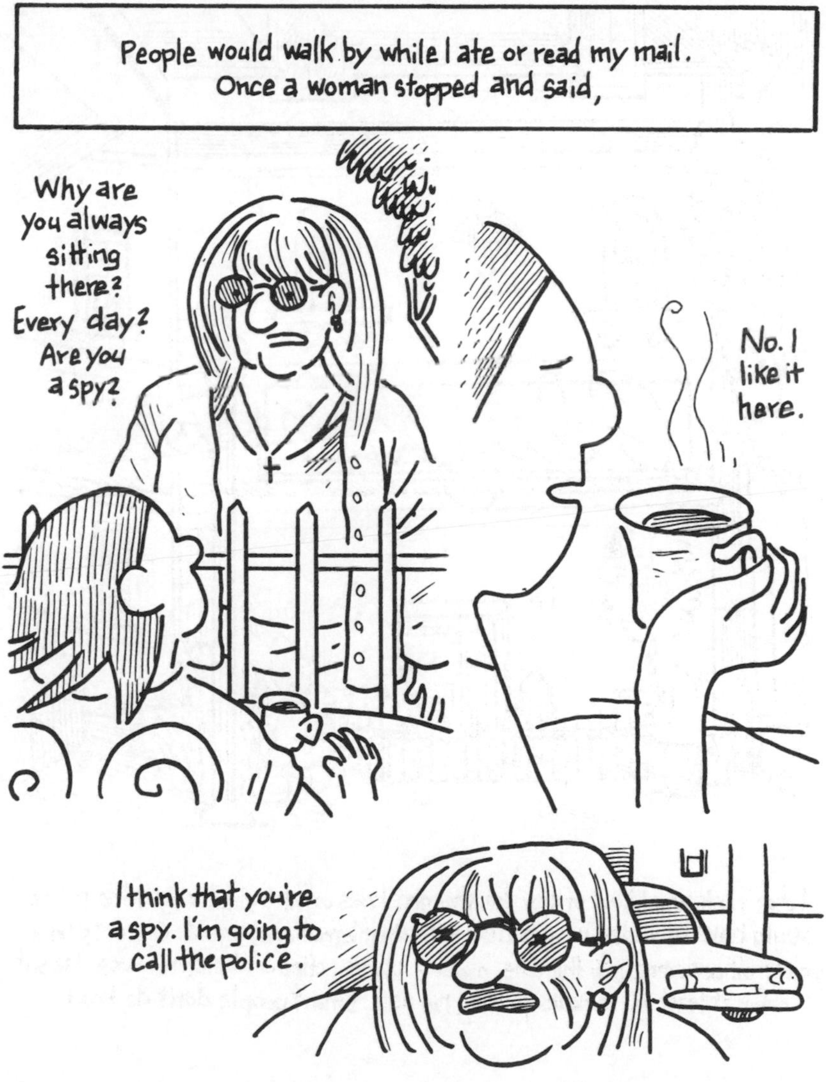
People would walk by while I ate or read my mail. Once a woman stopped and said,
Why are you always sitting there? Every day? Are you a spy?
No. I like it here.
I think that you're a spy. I'm going to call the police.

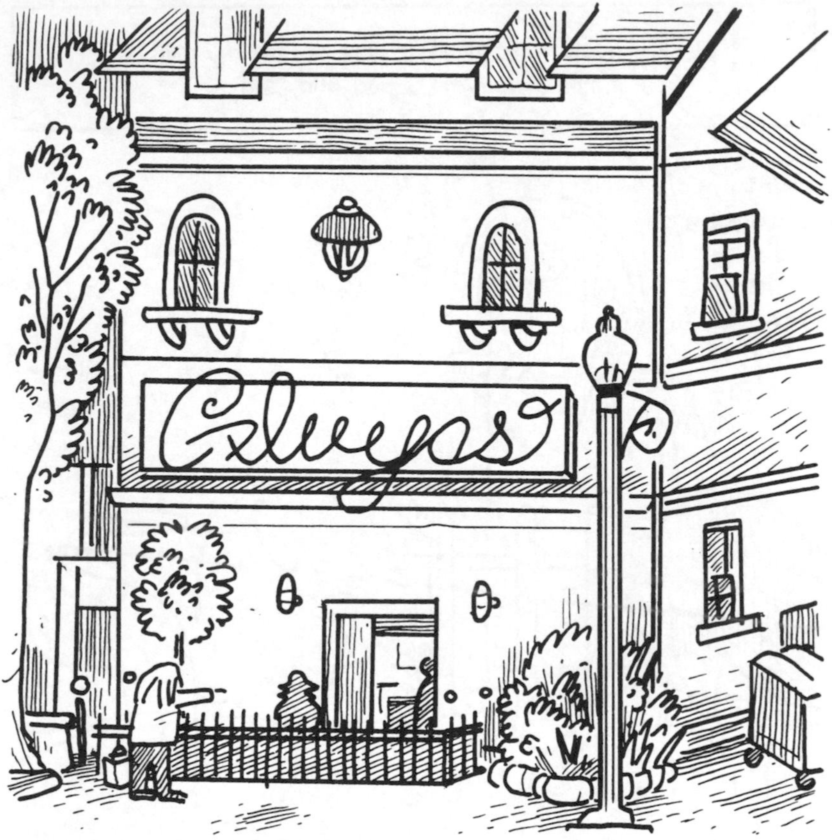

I didn't ask what kind of spy she thought I was or why she thought the police would have any idea how to deal with an international agent. Once, I saw a police officer come into the cafe, order a black coffee and pick his nose. He sat for at least 20 minutes picking his nose. Smart people don't do that.

What allows me to live this way is a computer program
I wrote when I was still in high school.

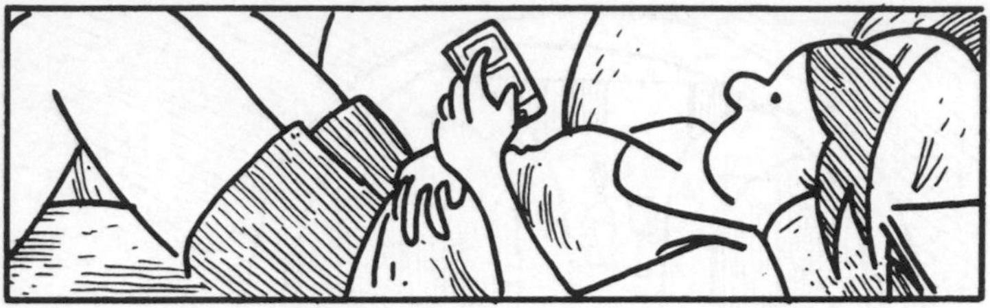

You know how you can buy crap online? I wrote the software that lets you pay and allows the merchant to take your money. Doesn't sound like much, but it was a big deal at the time. I became very rich and a little famous.

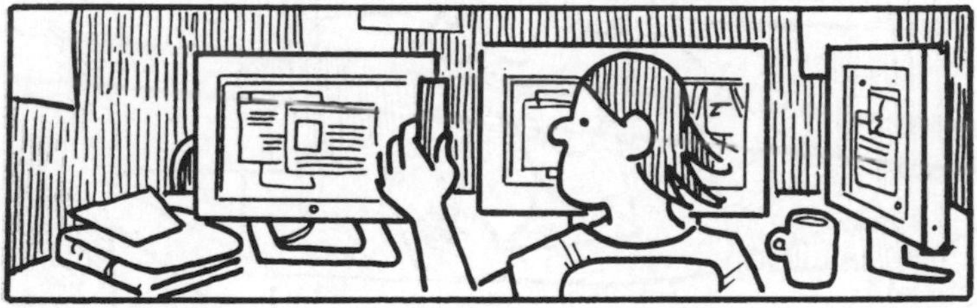

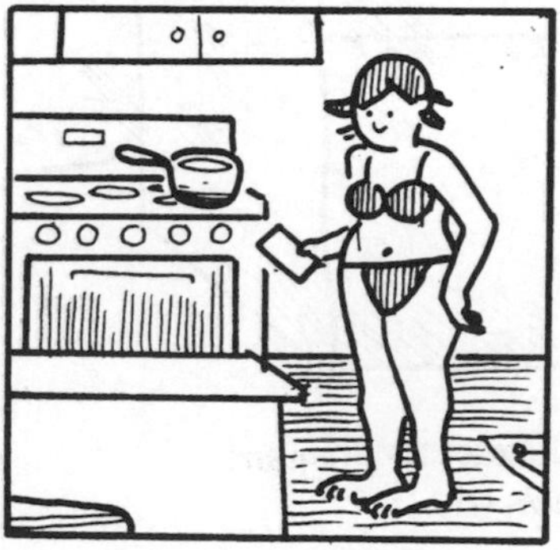

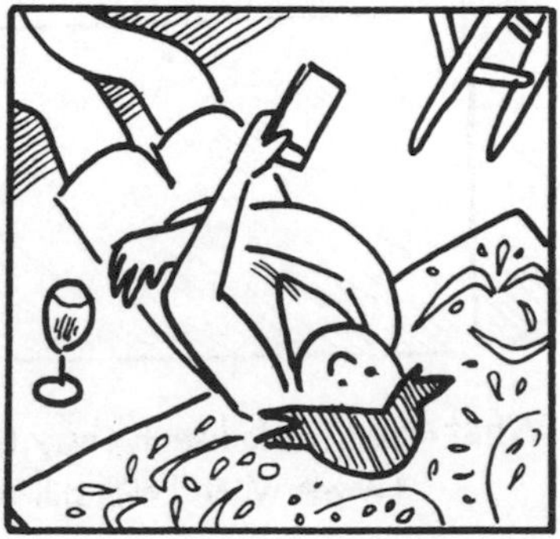

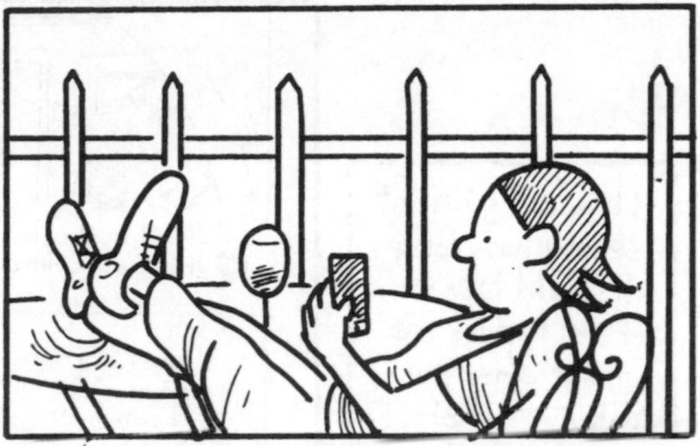

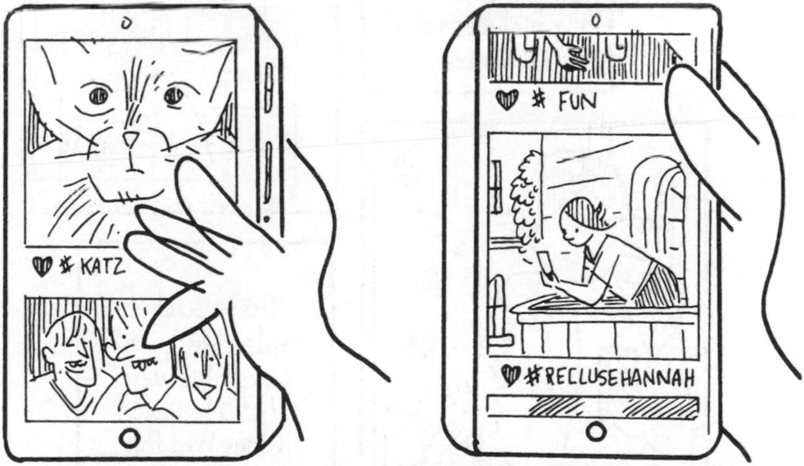

KATZ
FUN
RECLUSEHANNAH

For a while I could see people taking pictures of me from the street. Around the apartment, there wasn't much for me to photograph myself, but I liked to look at other people's photos.

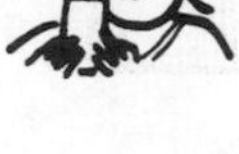

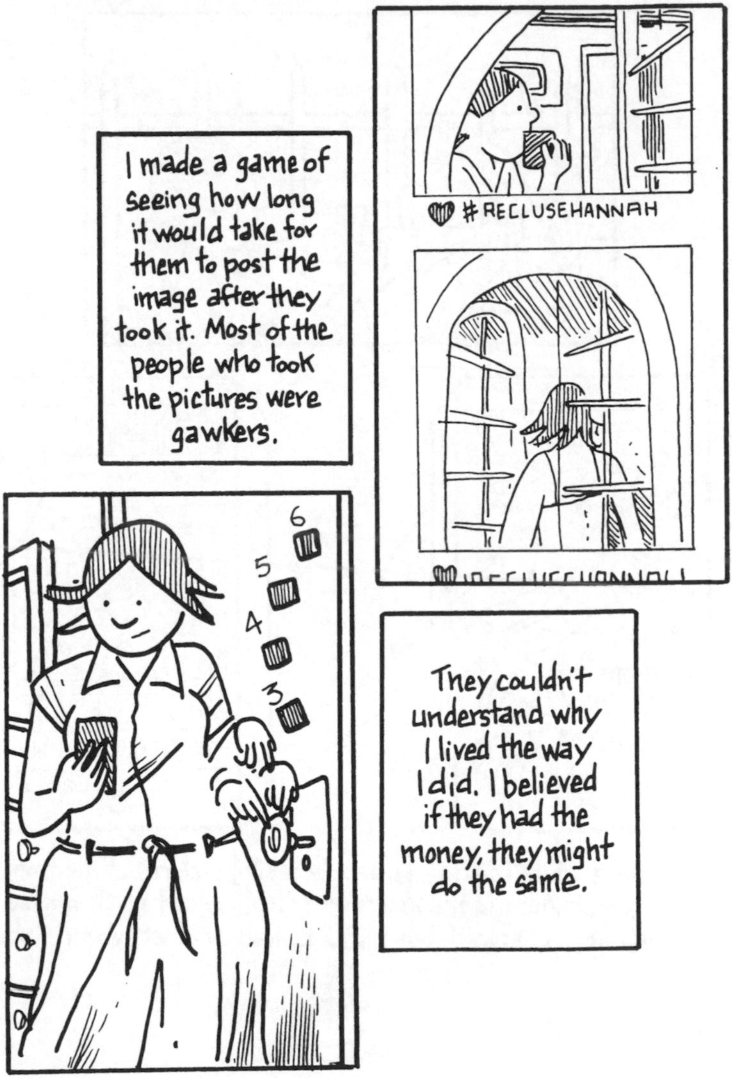
#RECLUSEHANNAH
I made a game of seeing how long it would take for them to post the image after they took it. Most of the people who took the pictures were gawkers.
6
5
4
3
They couldn't understand why I lived the way I did. I believed if they had the money, they might do the same.

It wasn't individuals that I was avoiding.

Groups of people worried me.

I grew tired of the sect of people who photographed me.
The style and content of the images failed to mature.

You want it right outside your window?
Yes.
It will block your view.
Very well. We will do this for you.

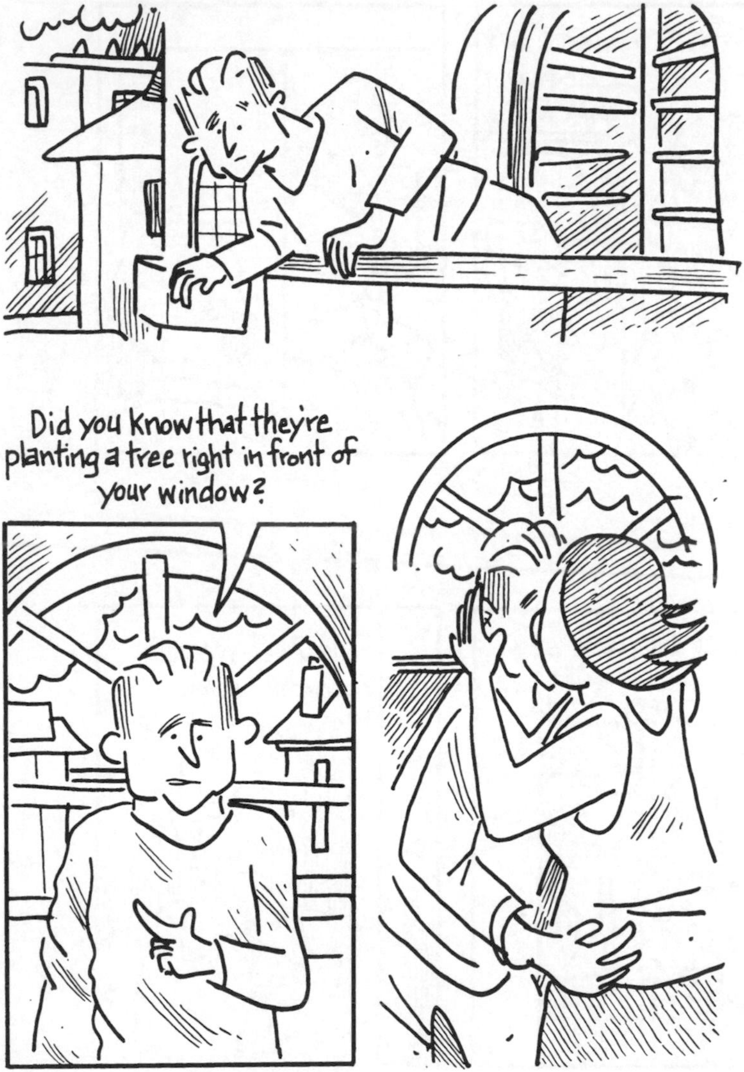
Did you know that they're planting a tree right in front of your window?

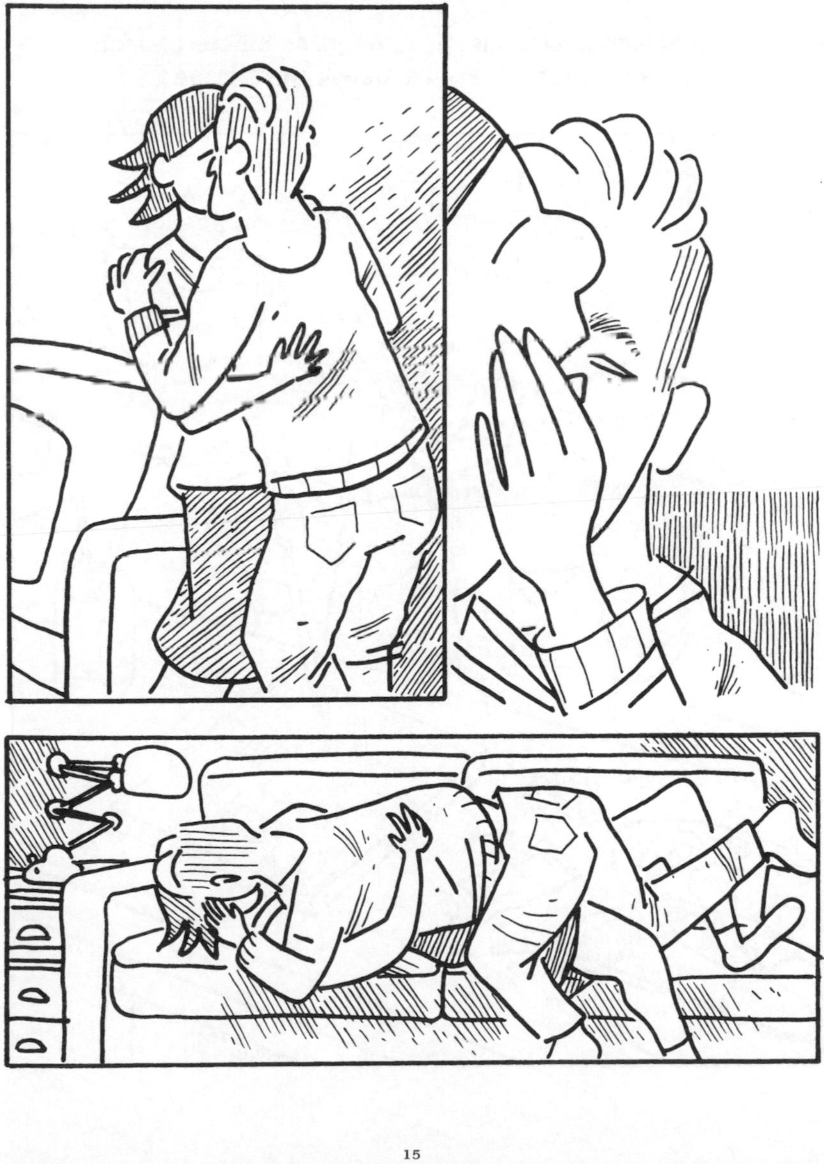

Nicholas was good to me. He never made me feel strange for never leaving, and he always came to me.

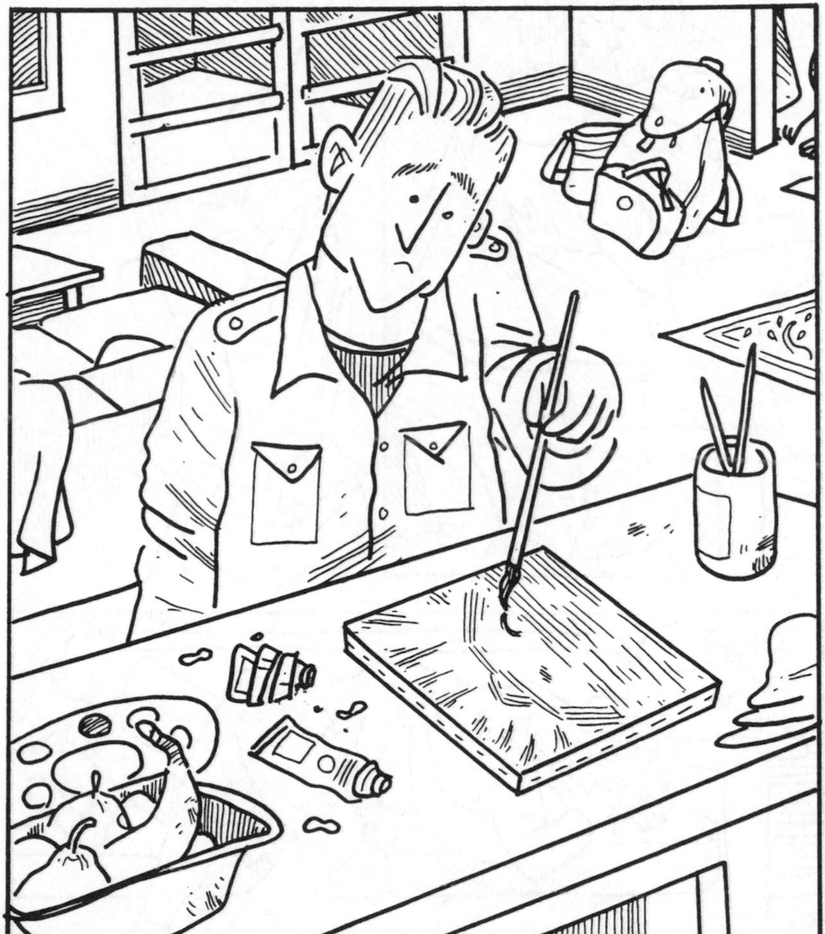

Made this for you.

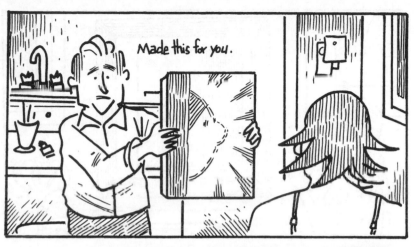

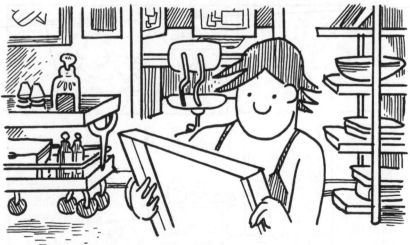

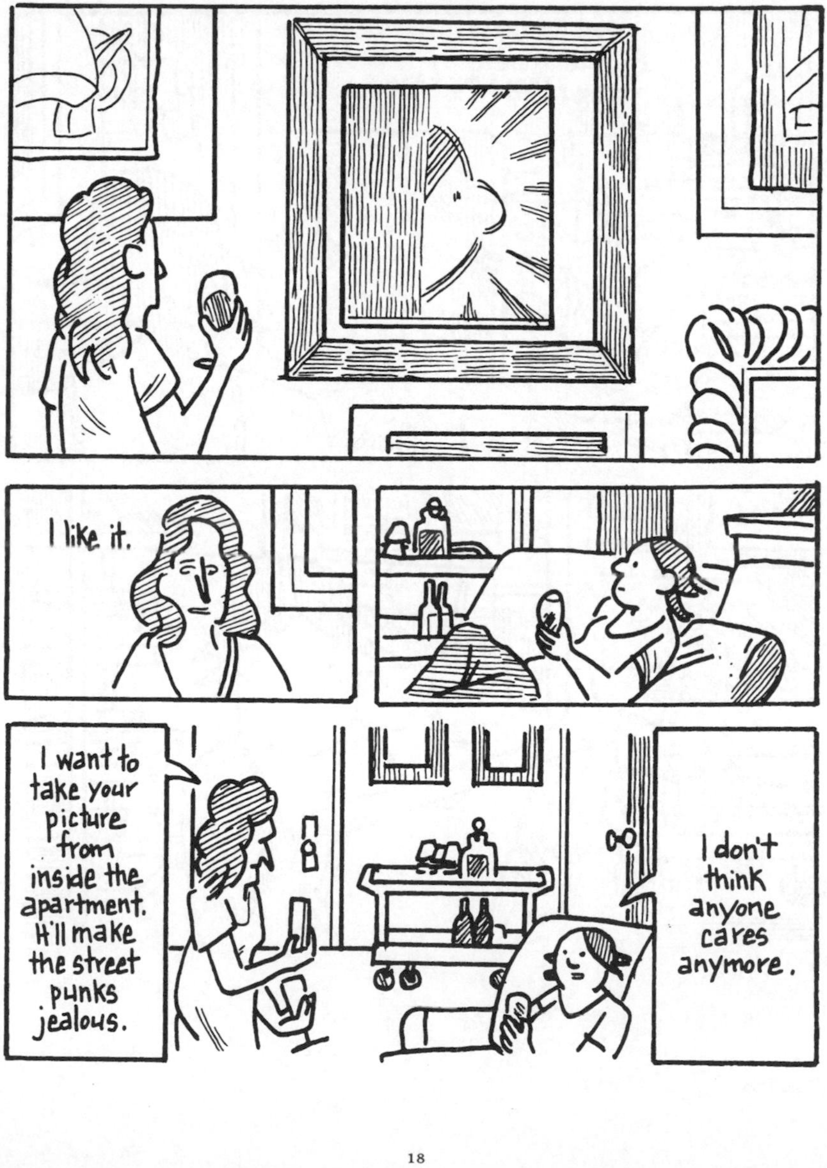
I like it.
I want to take your picture from inside the apartment. It'll make the street punks jealous.
I don't think anyone cares anymore.

The tree blocked the view as well as I'd hoped, and photos of me stopped appearing online. Without the distraction, I was able to spend my days focused on a new project.

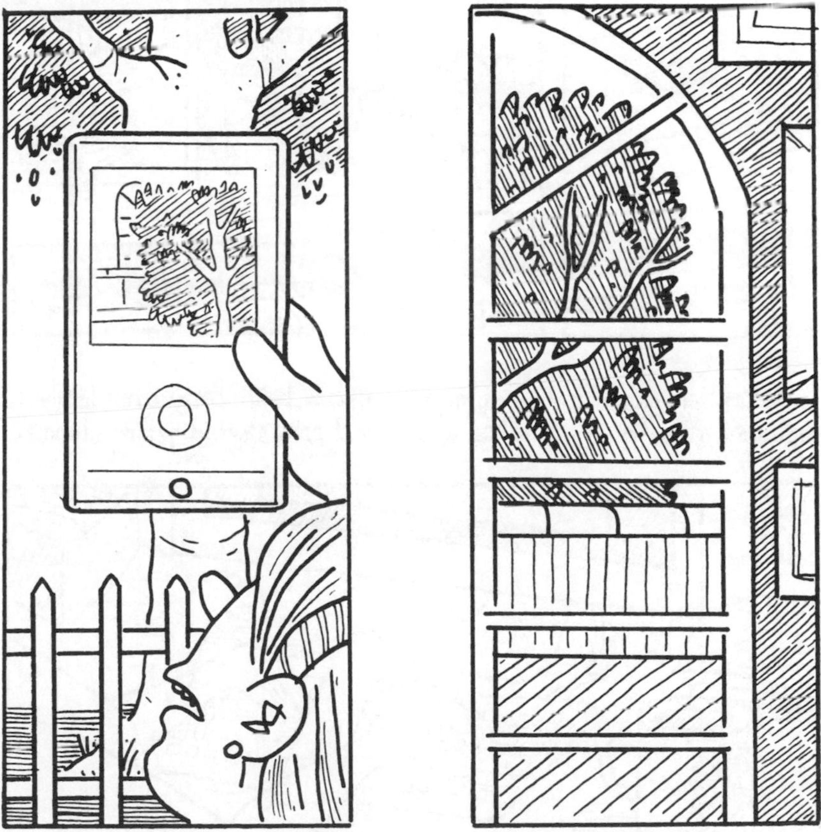

It's good to always be working on something new.
You never know when you'll need it.

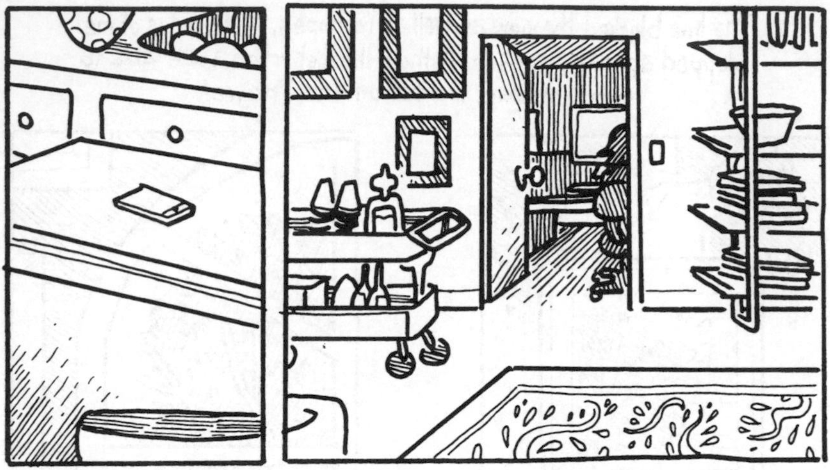

Better versions of my e-commerce software had nearly completely replaced my own. I took notice when my checks started getting slimmer.

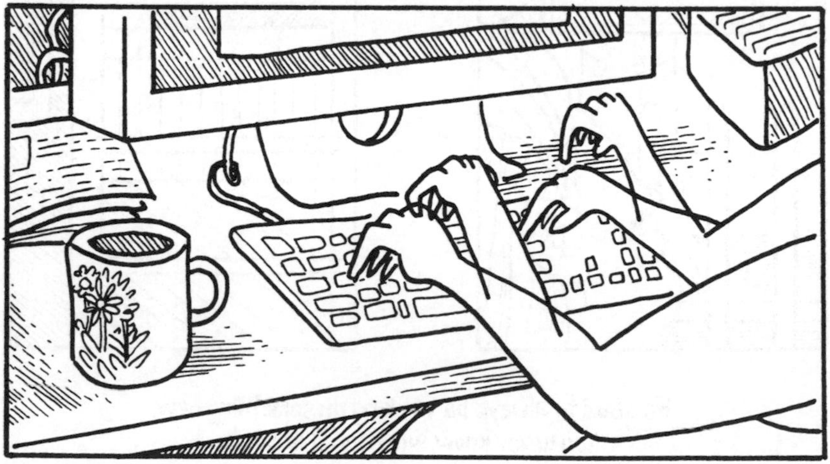

Also, my visitors started to thin out.

Susan, at least, used to come by twice a week.

She didn't even bother to tell me that she was moving.

There were long stretches where I spoke to no one.

It was lovely.

There was a time that I'd speak to anyone who approached me in the cafe.

I'd have my dinner interrupted constantly by strangers who wanted to know my story.

It was fun at first, but eventually everyone had to go through José.

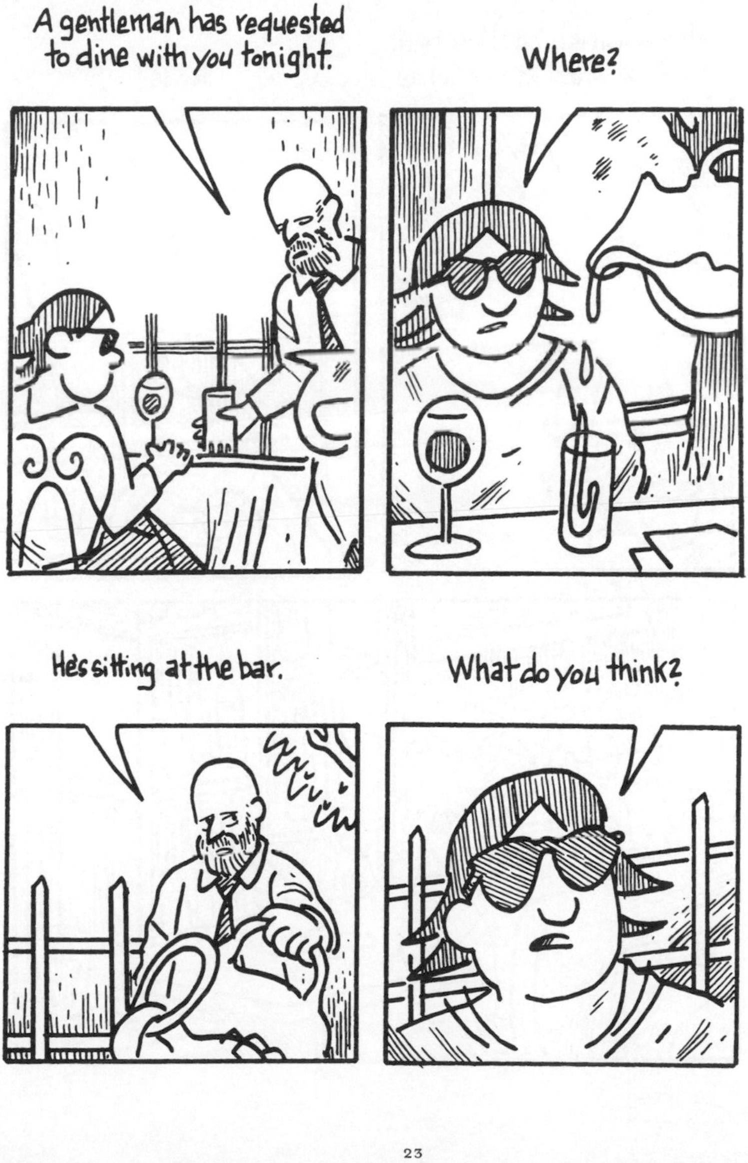
A gentleman has requested to dine with you tonight.
Where?
He's sitting at the bar.
What do you think?

He's a tourist, but I like him. He laughed at my jokes.

Jokes?

For a while, my life was perfect.

26

I think I'm finished.
Do you want to try it?

Nicholas left me in the fall.

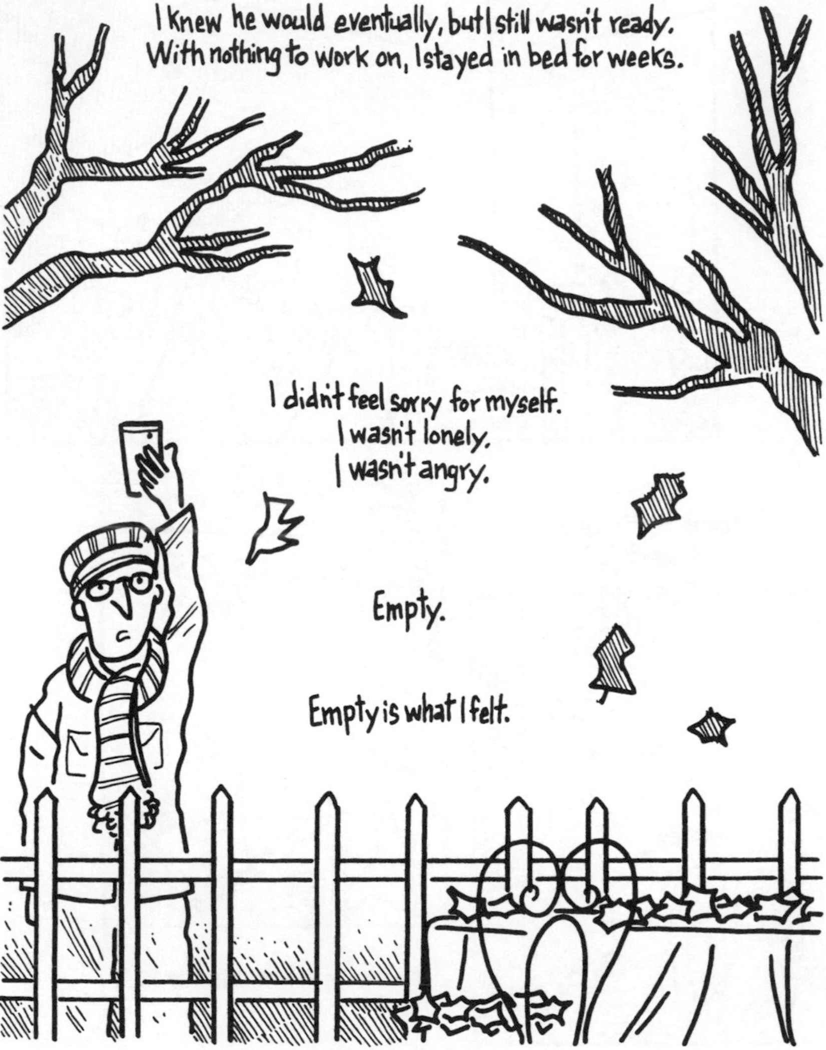
I knew he would eventually, but I still wasn't ready.
With nothing to work on, I stayed in bed for weeks.
I didn't feel sorry for myself.
I wasn't lonely.
I wasn't angry.
Empty.
Empty is what I felt.

By December, I was out of bed and
making changes to the new program.

Even though it was finished, there were a
few final touches that I wanted to make.

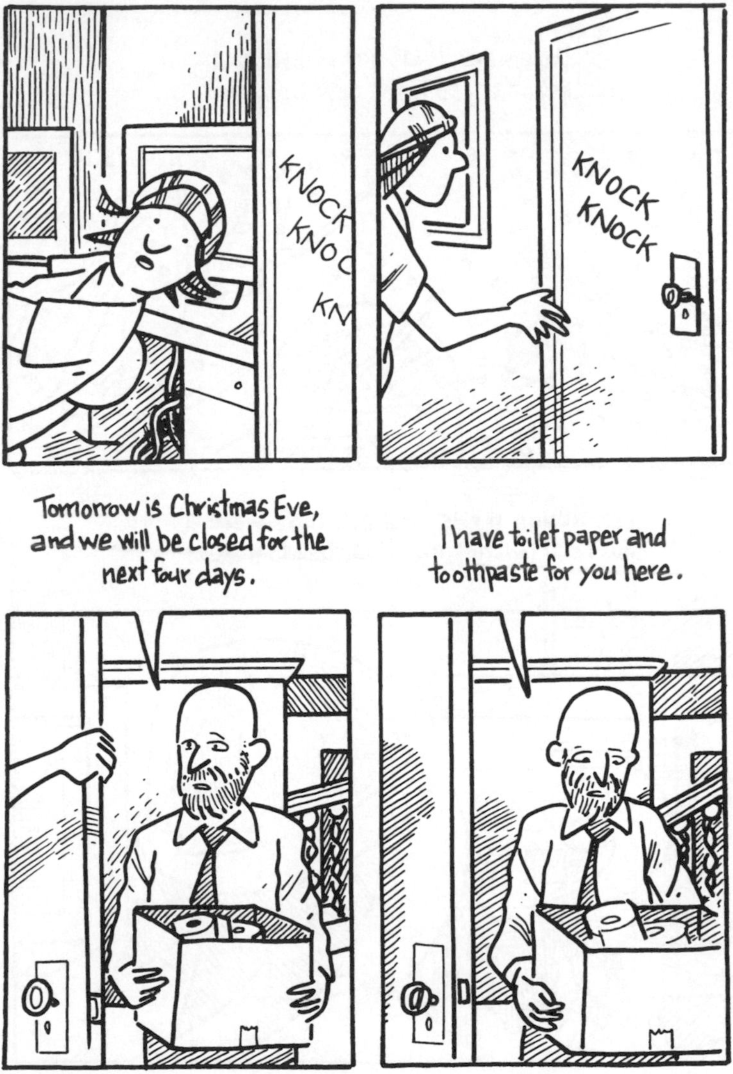

KNOCK
KNOCK
KN
KNOCK
KNOCK
Tomorrow is Christmas Eve, and we will be closed for the next four days.
I have toilet paper and toothpaste for you here.

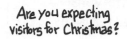

Also, you may go into the kitchen. I have all your meals prepared for you with instructions.

Are you expecting visitors for Christmas?

Had the world changed that much?

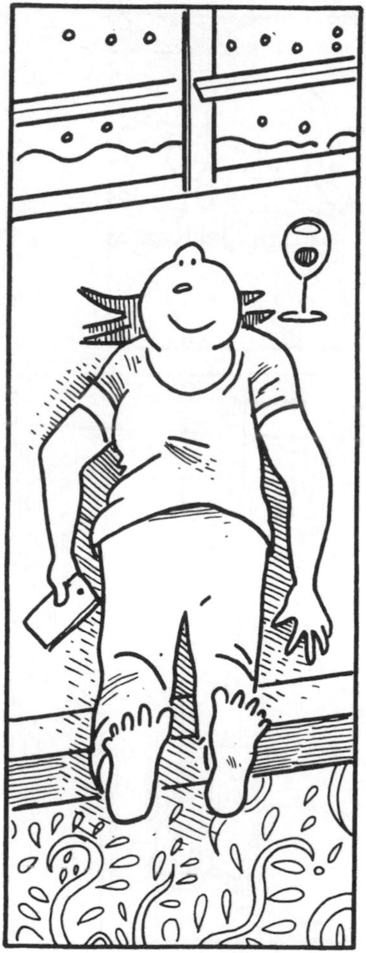

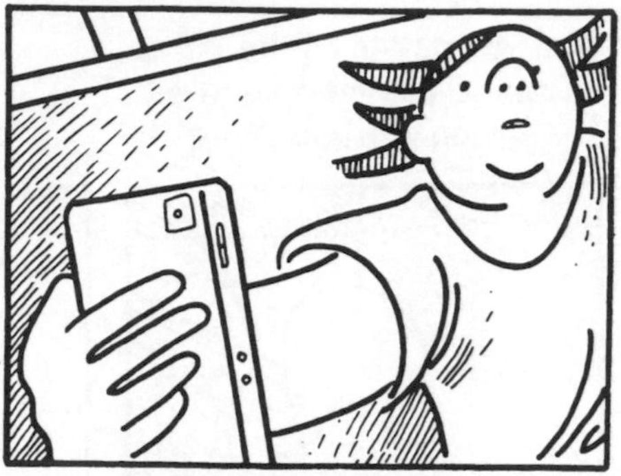

It didn't look like it. Although, even my online networks had been more silent lately.

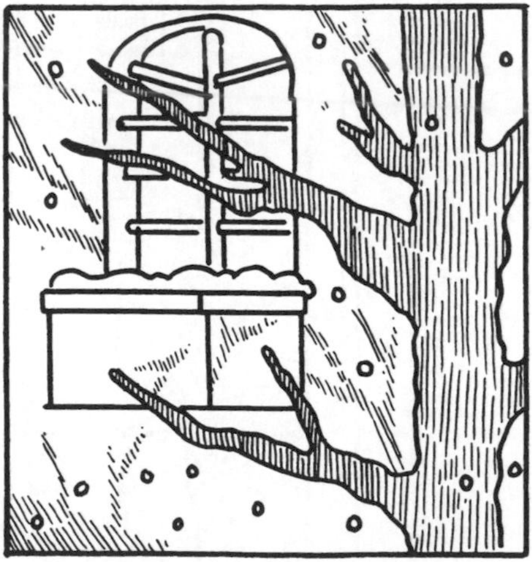

Where did everyone go?

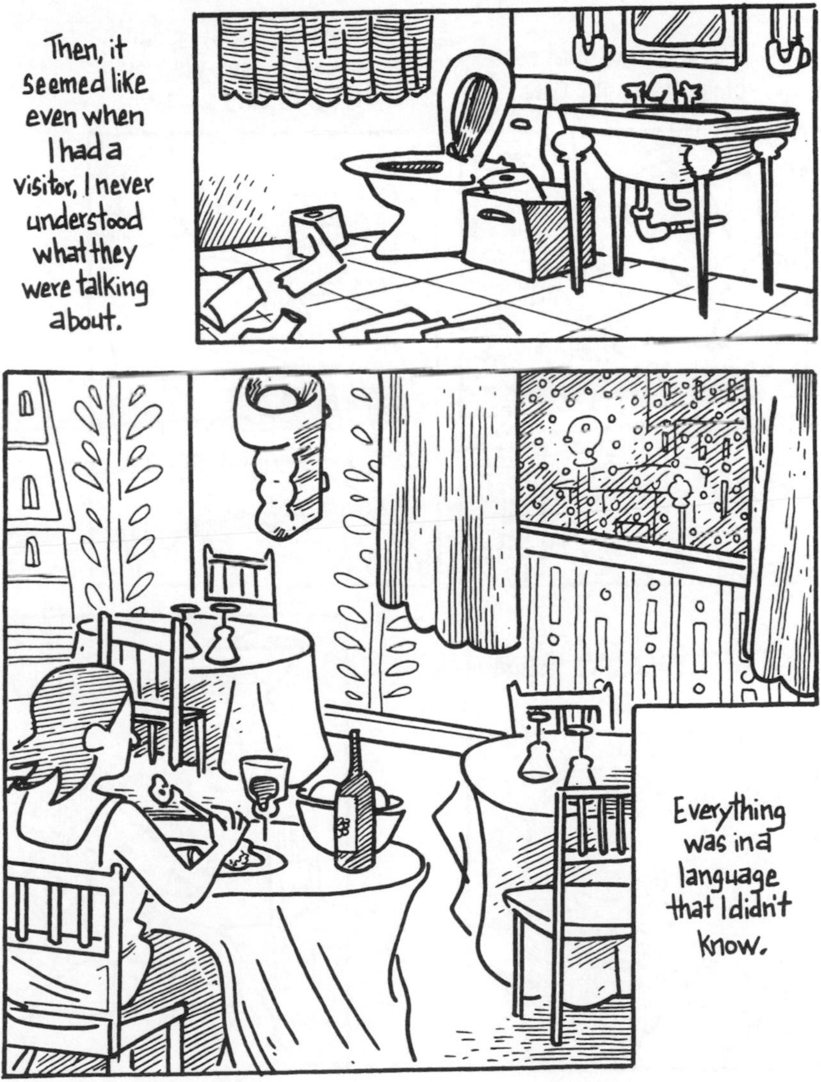
Then, it seemed like even when I had a visitor, I never understood what they were talking about.
Everything was in a language that I didn't know.

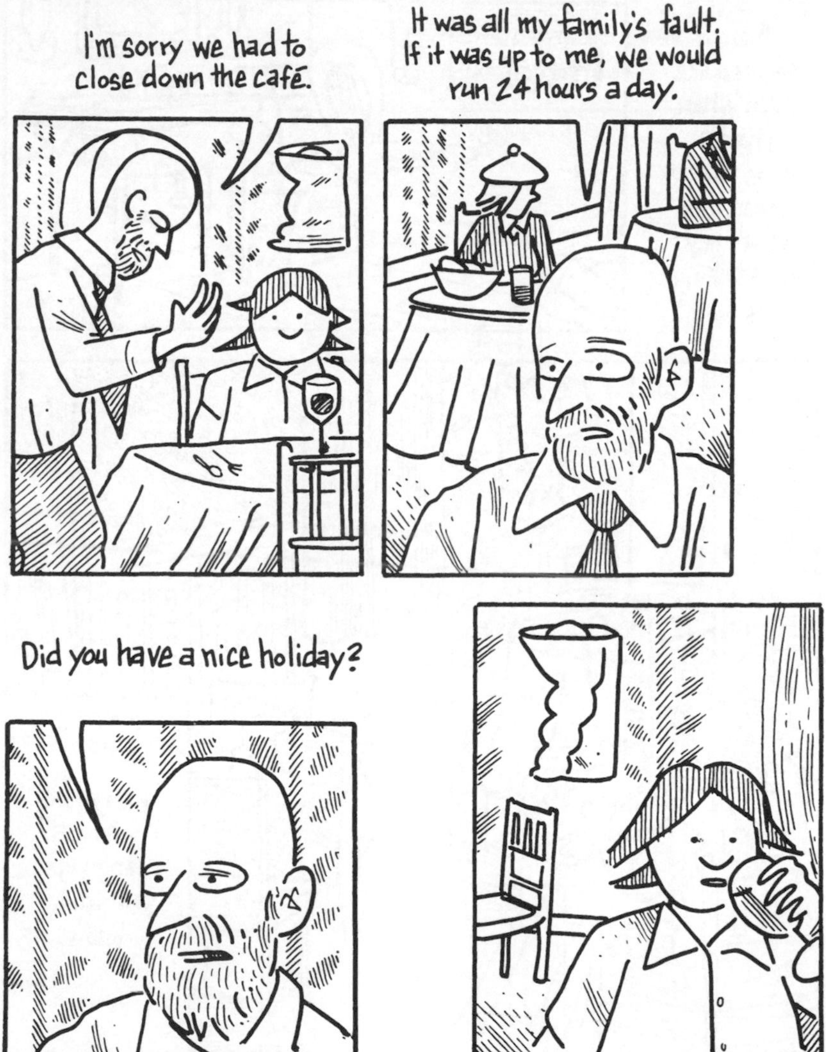
I'm sorry we had to close down the café.
It was all my family's fault. If it was up to me, we would run 24 hours a day.
Did you have a nice holiday?

Reverend Carpenter used to say that the third excuse a person gives is always the real excuse.

So, when a student didn't finish their homework, they would say something like, "I had a family issue last night and I wasn't sure if it was due today, and I just didn't feel like doing it."

I had grown tired of that apartment and its same four walls.

I realized that a person needs to be part of a community if they're to thrive.

Also, my money had run out.

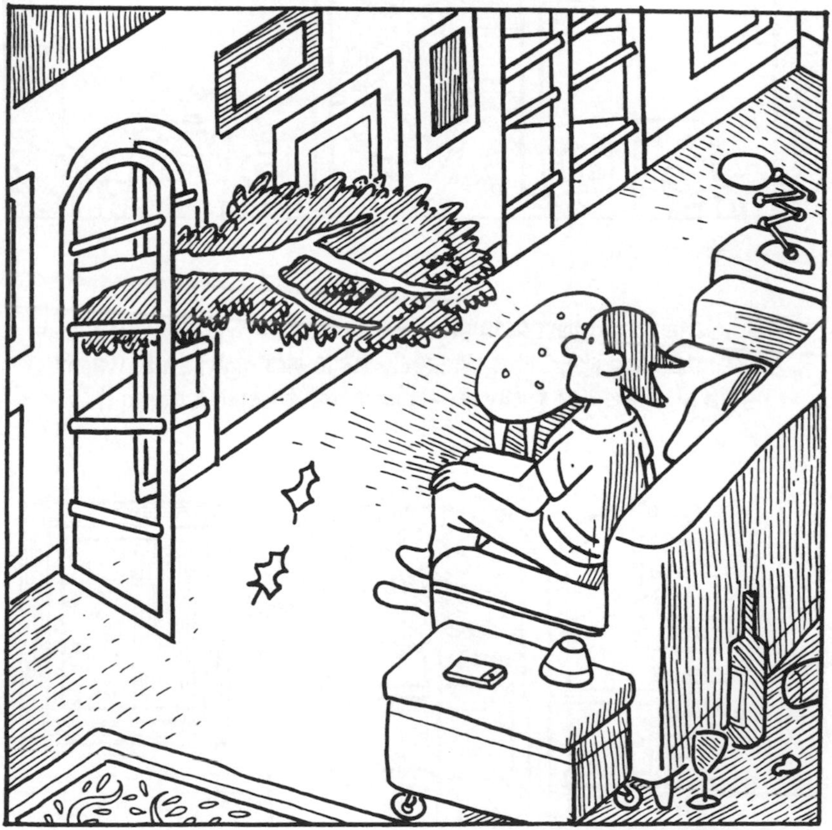

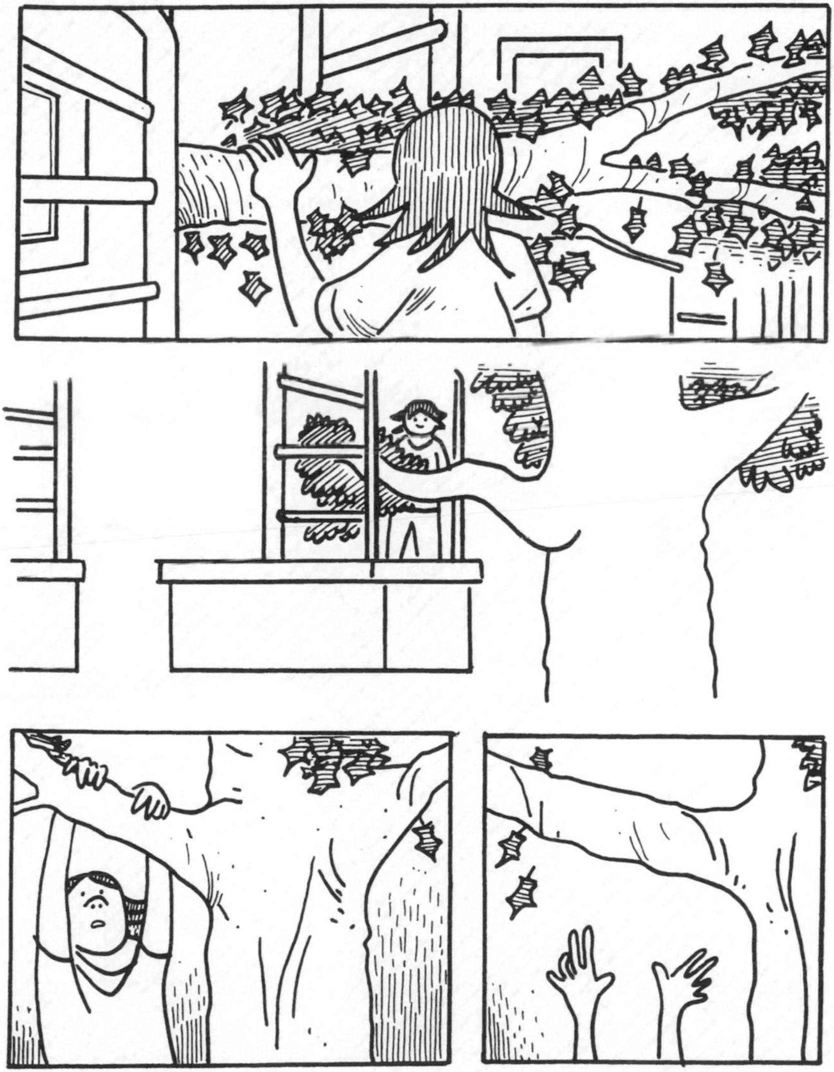

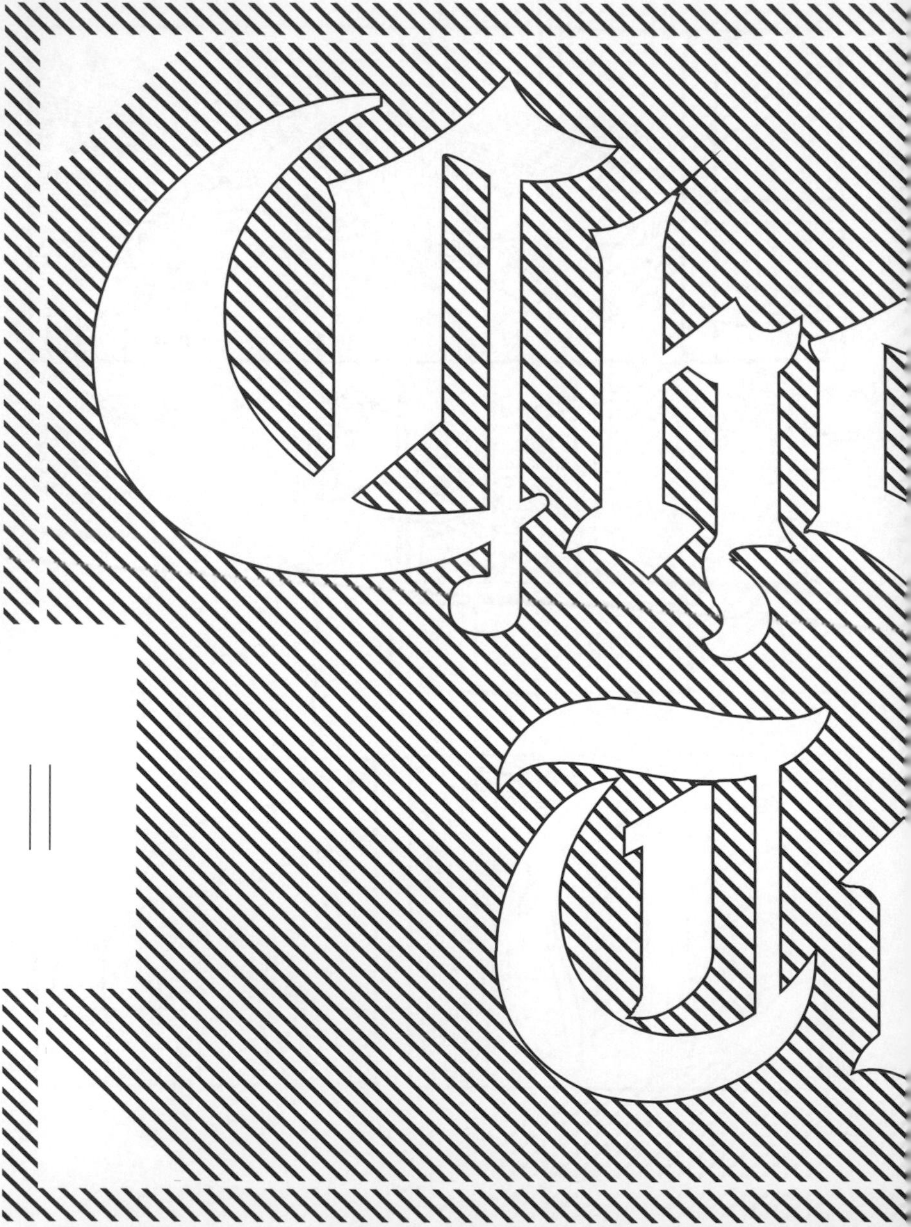

pter 10

Noah

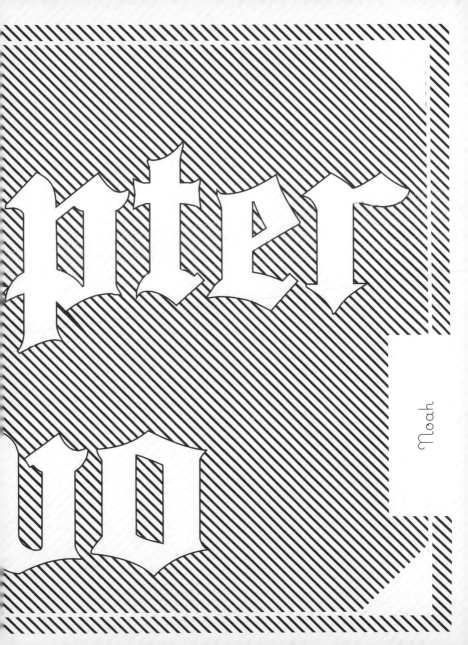

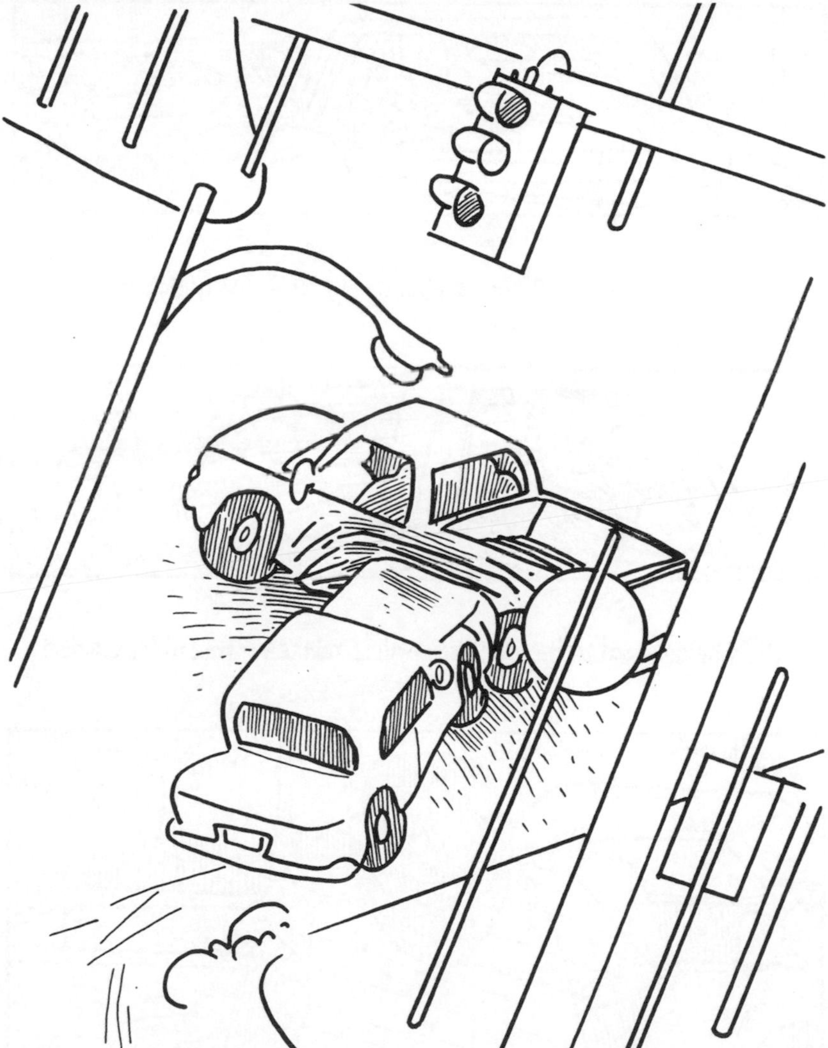

He looks like his name is T-Bone, but it's actually Robin.

When he gets out of the car, the vehicle relaxes — free of its burden.

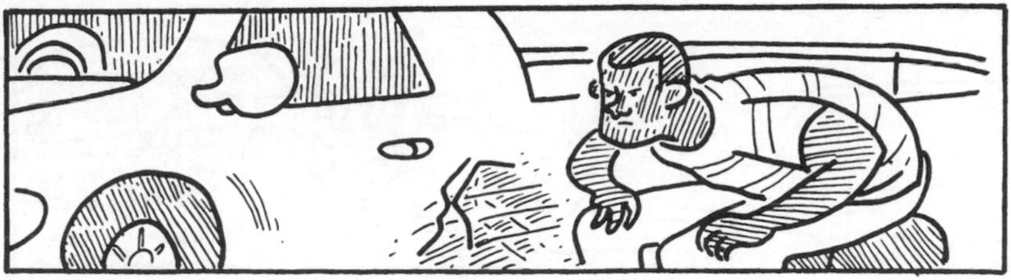

The car is only a year old.
Over that year 2,362,000 people were injured in car accidents.

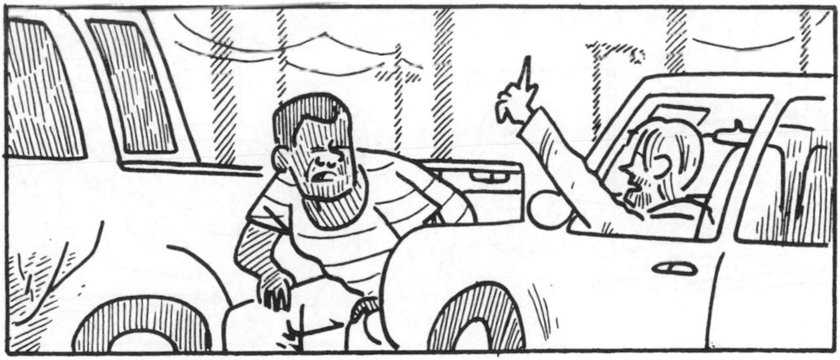

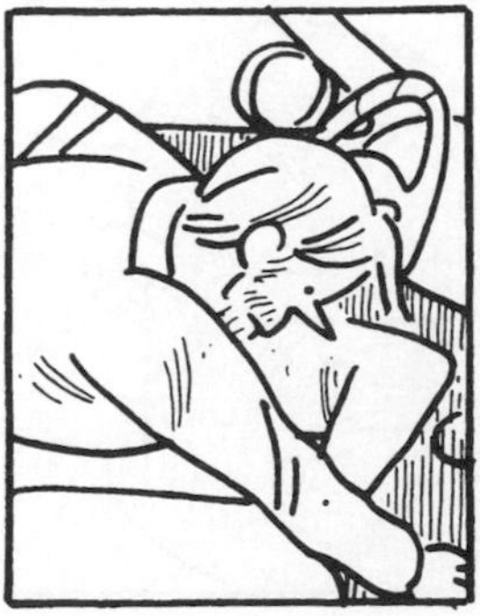

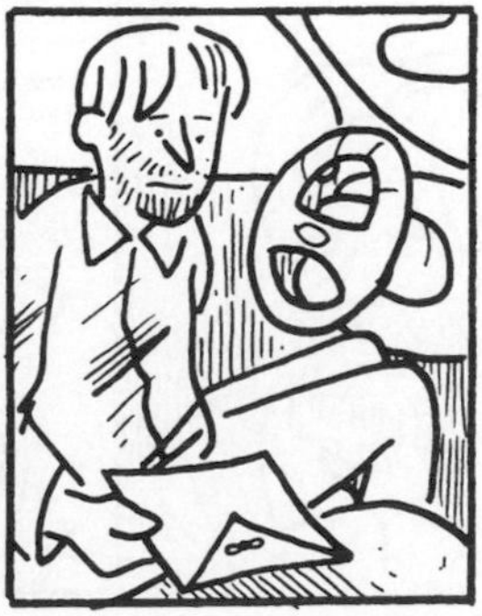

There is an average of 90 vehicular fatalities a day.

We're both lucky not to be hurt. Robin is sore only about his truck. He looks at me to take responsibility for the crash.

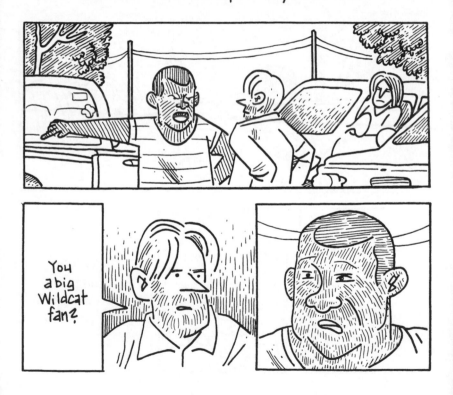

You a big Wildcat fan?

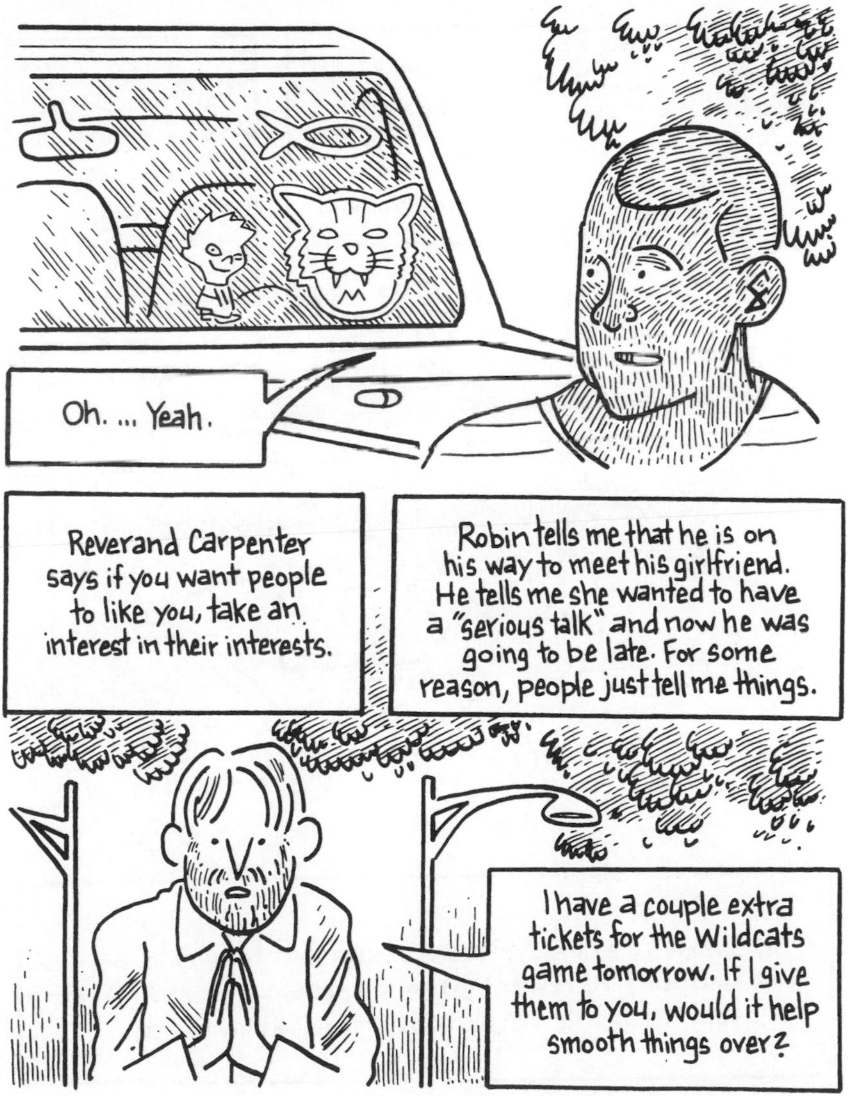
Oh. ... Yeah.
Reverand Carpenter says if you want people to like you, take an interest in their interests.
Robin tells me that he is on his way to meet his girlfriend. He tells me she wanted to have a "serious talk" and now he was going to be late. For some reason, people just tell me things.
I have a couple extra tickets for the Wildcats game tomorrow. If I give them to you, would it help smooth things over?

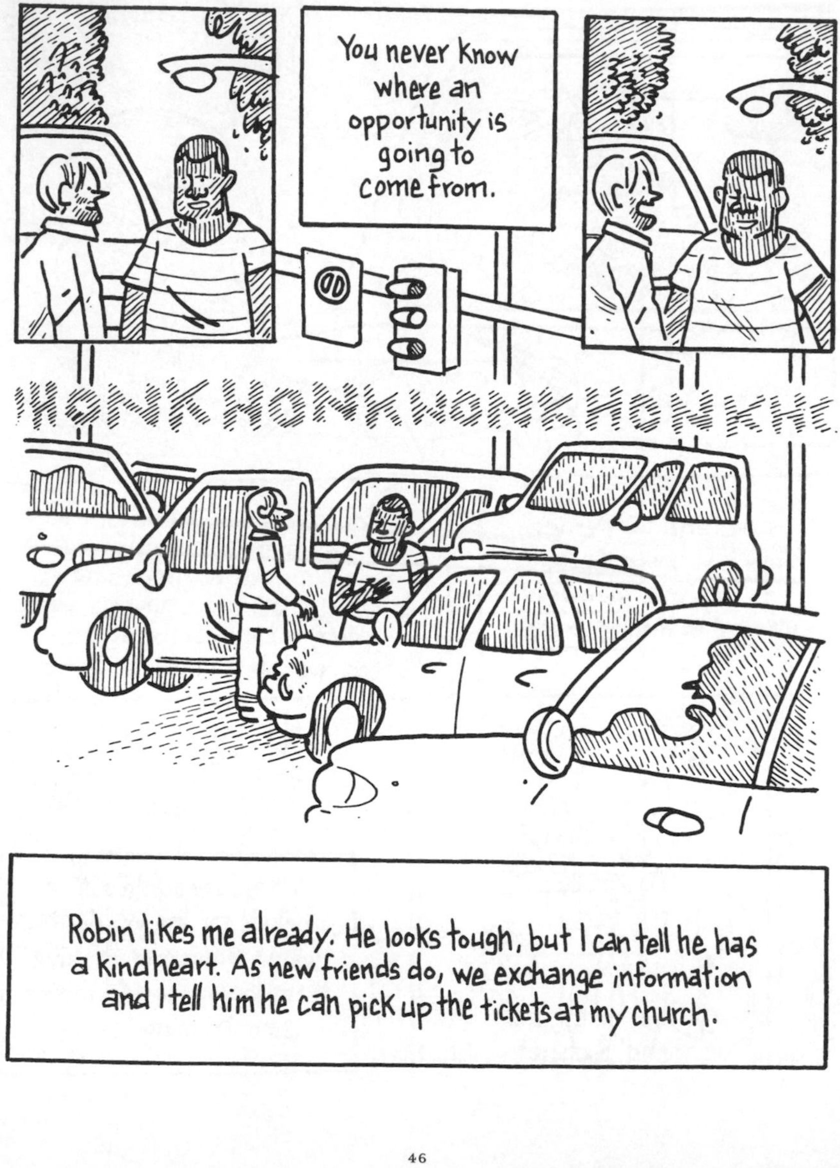
You never know where an opportunity is going to come from.
HONK HONK HONK HONK HO

Robin likes me already. He looks tough, but I can tell he has a kind heart. As new friends do, we exchange information and I tell him he can pick up the tickets at my church.

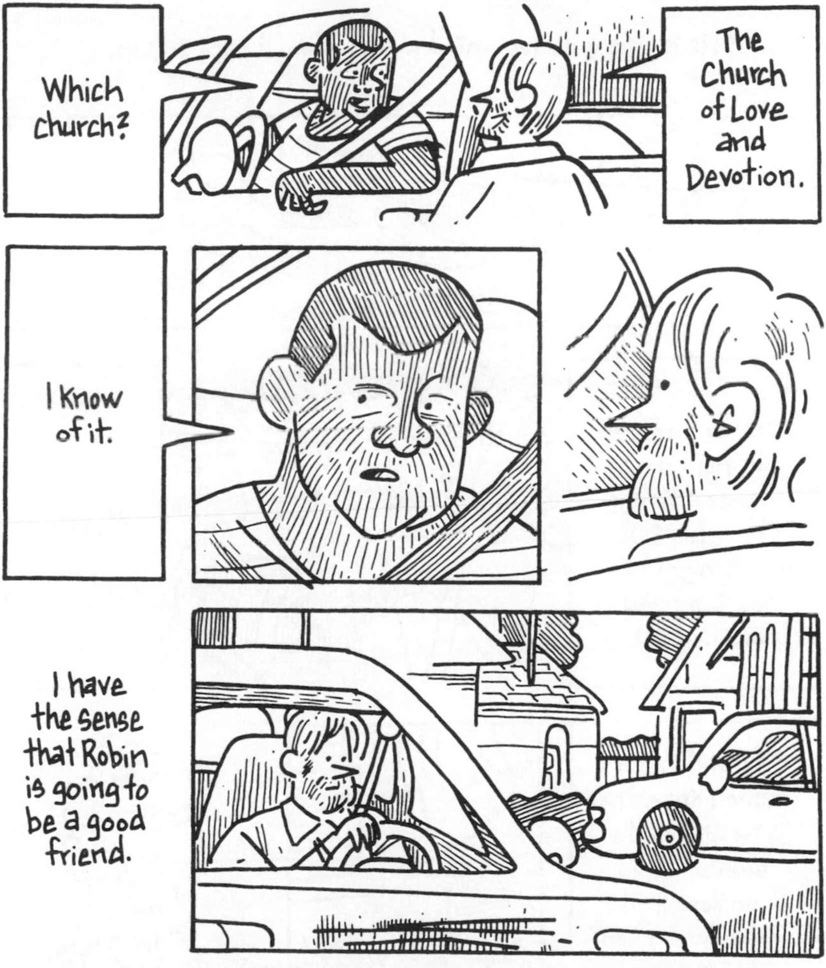
Which church?
The Church of Love and Devotion.
I know of it.
I have the sense that Robin is going to be a good friend.

Through the church, I've made many friends that I can rely on.
One friend, Richard, was kind enough to lend me his car.

He is visibly disappointed when I bring it back to him.

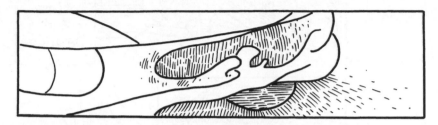

Don't worry. We'll get it fixed. But right now, you and Kathy have to pack an overnight bag. You two need a vacation.

Noah...

I'll watch the baby. I know that you and Kathy wanted to go on Reverend Carpenter's retreat. I saved you both a spot.

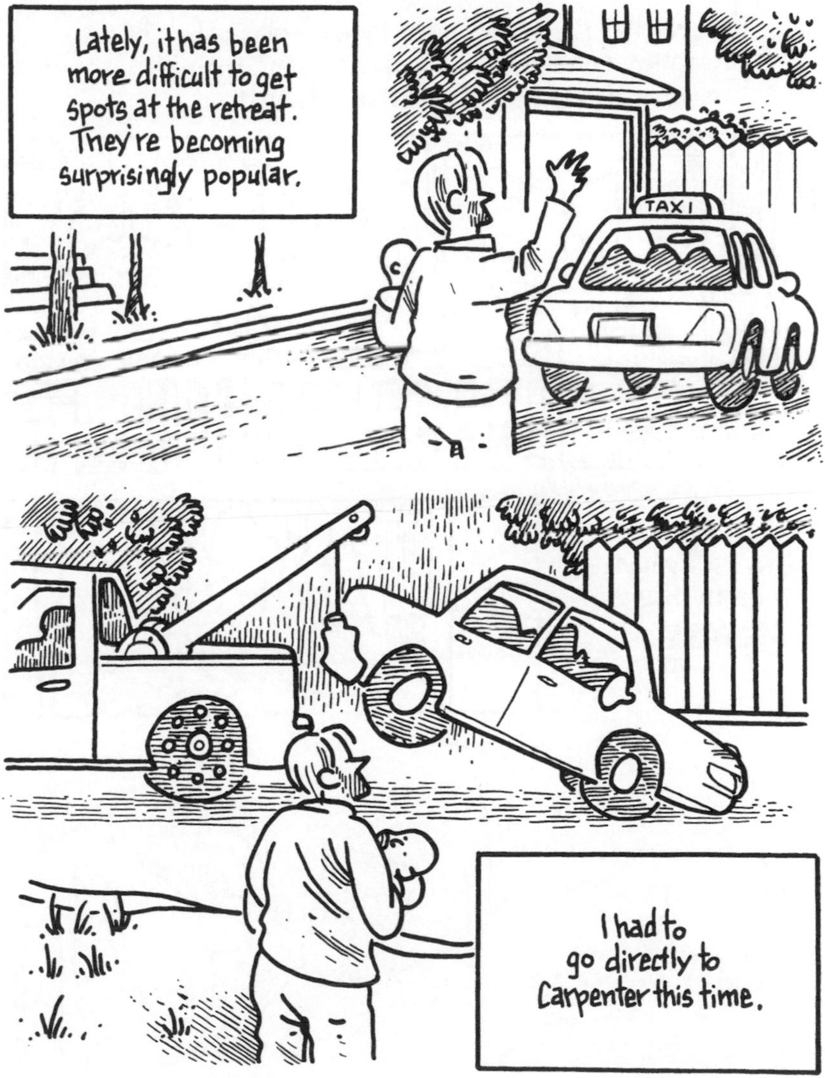
Lately, it has been more difficult to get spots at the retreat. They're becoming surprisingly popular.
TAXI
I had to go directly to Carpenter this time.

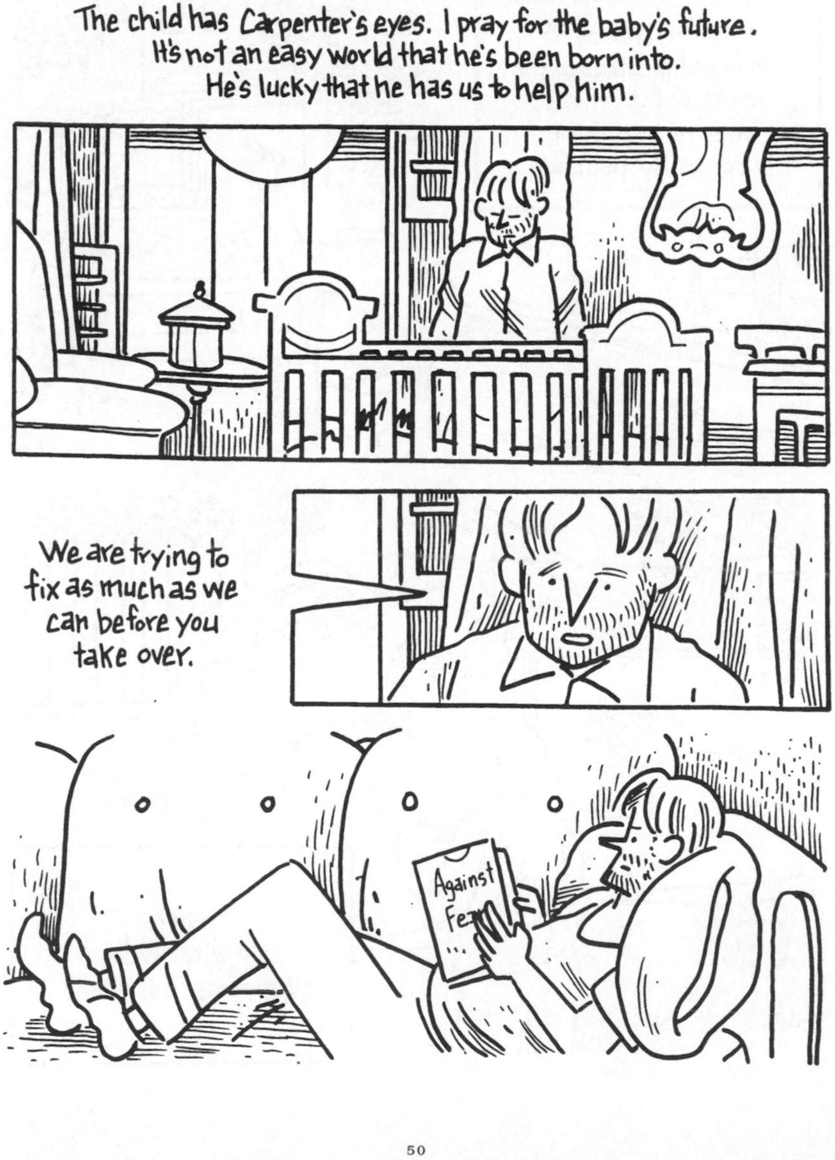
The child has Carpenter's eyes. I pray for the baby's future.
It's not an easy world that he's been born into.
He's lucky that he has us to help him.
We are trying to fix as much as we can before you take over.
Against Fear...

He sleeps all through the night. I wish that I could say the same.

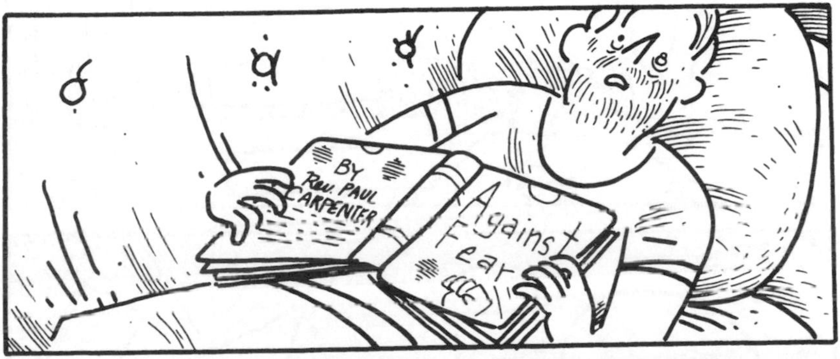
By Rev. Paul Carpenter
Against Fear

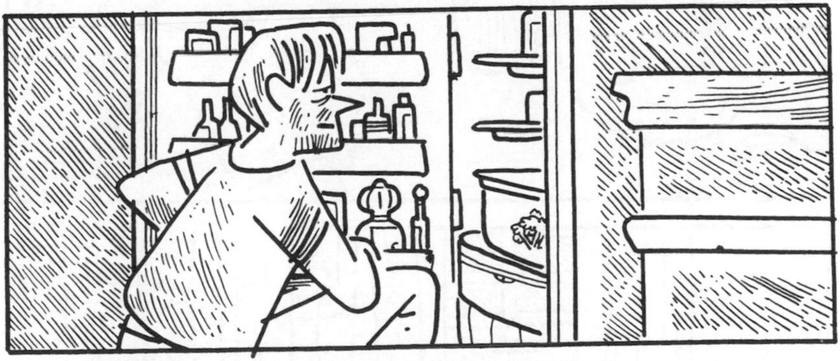

Some people have trouble sleeping and some people have insomnia. I like to think of myself as a patient man, but I get very annoyed when people confuse the two.

I'm not tired. I'm in pain.

I get Kathy to drive me to the church when they return because I couldn't drive right now even if I wanted to. I can barley see straight I'm so tired.

53

She's in high spirits after spending the night with Reverend Carpenter, and doesn't mind the inconvenience of being my chauffeur.

Carpenter has that effect on everyone, so when I call the church there is an excitement on the other end that tells me he is there.

I'm on my way now.

Is Madeline working today?

Give her a couple of the Wildcats tickets and have her meet me in 10 minutes. Traffic is light this morning.

A car crash slowed us down so I'm right on time instead of being 3 minutes early.

As expected, Robin is already there looking a little lost. When he sees me we hug like old friends. He tells me that his girl broke up with him last night and he won't be needing the tickets anymore. She got sick of him and she said he was a little addicted to the internet. People just tell me things.

Madeline walks up, right on cue.

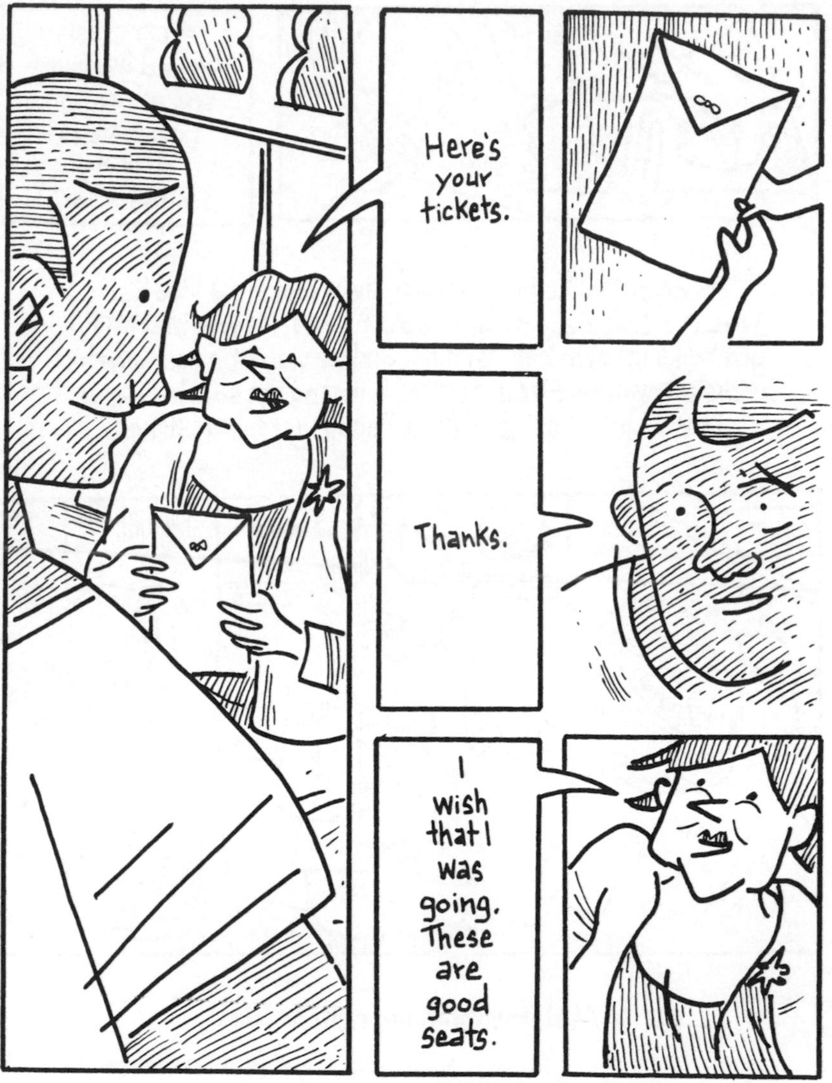
Here's your tickets.
Thanks.
I wish that I was going. These are good seats.

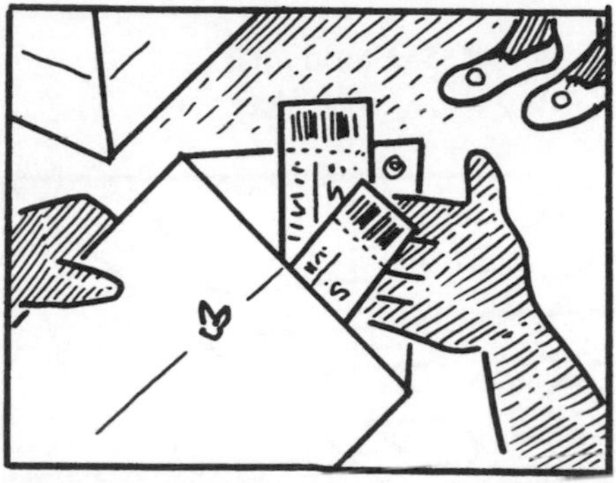

The church has season tickets, and Madeline goes to pretty much every game and always sits in the same place.

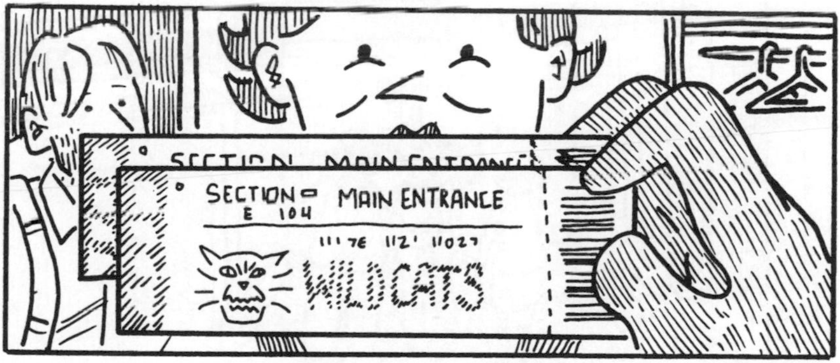
SECTION MAIN ENTRANCE
E 104
WILDCATS

I introduce her to Robin so she can find a way to accompany him to the match.

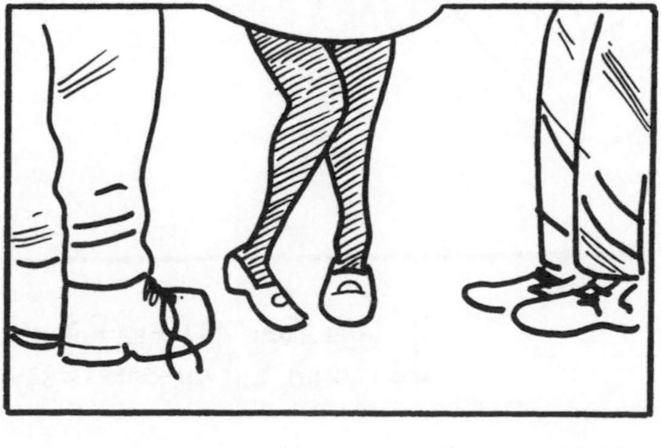

Madeline knows that she makes a good first impression, but has to play it safe after that.

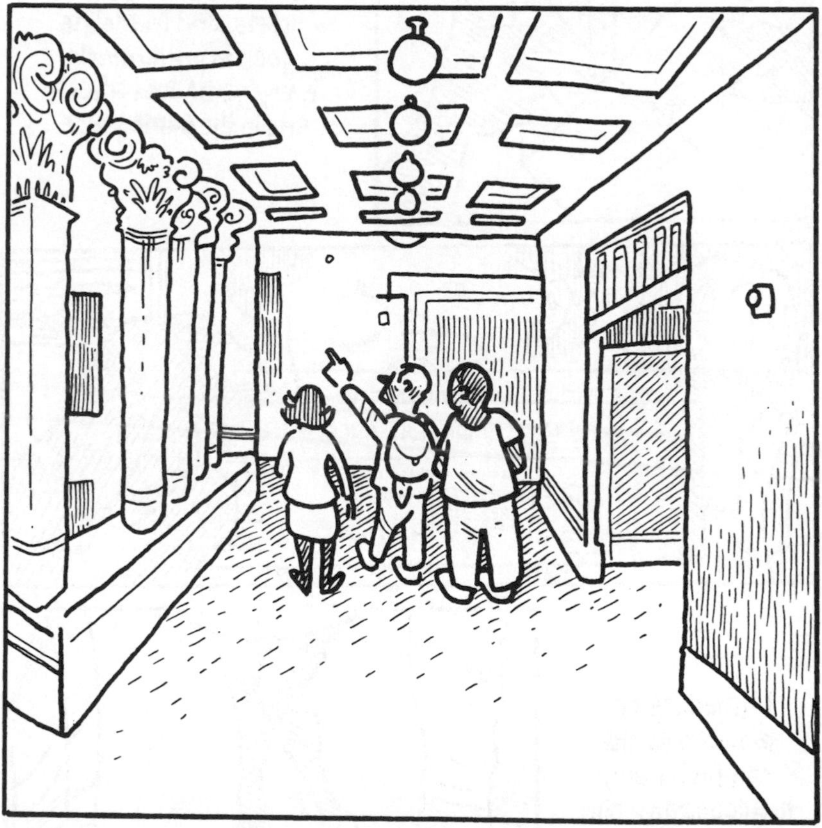

She tags along as I give Robin a tour of the church, but she doesn't say much.

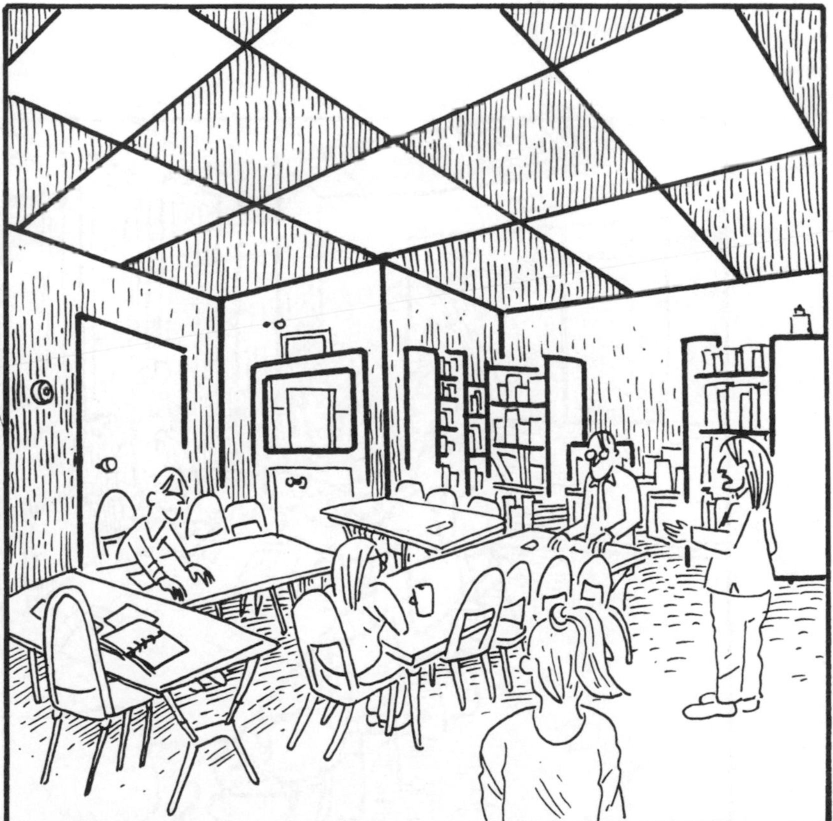

We have ten classrooms that teach various skills to our members. Mostly life skills and how to better understand our world.

No one pays for the classes, but they need to volunteer in some way. Most like to work in the kitchen feeding the homeless in the area. We feed nearly 5,000 people a week. Looking at the meals, I realize that I haven't eaten since last night.

My growling stomach echoes through the worship space. This room is where you can usually find Reverend Carpenter.

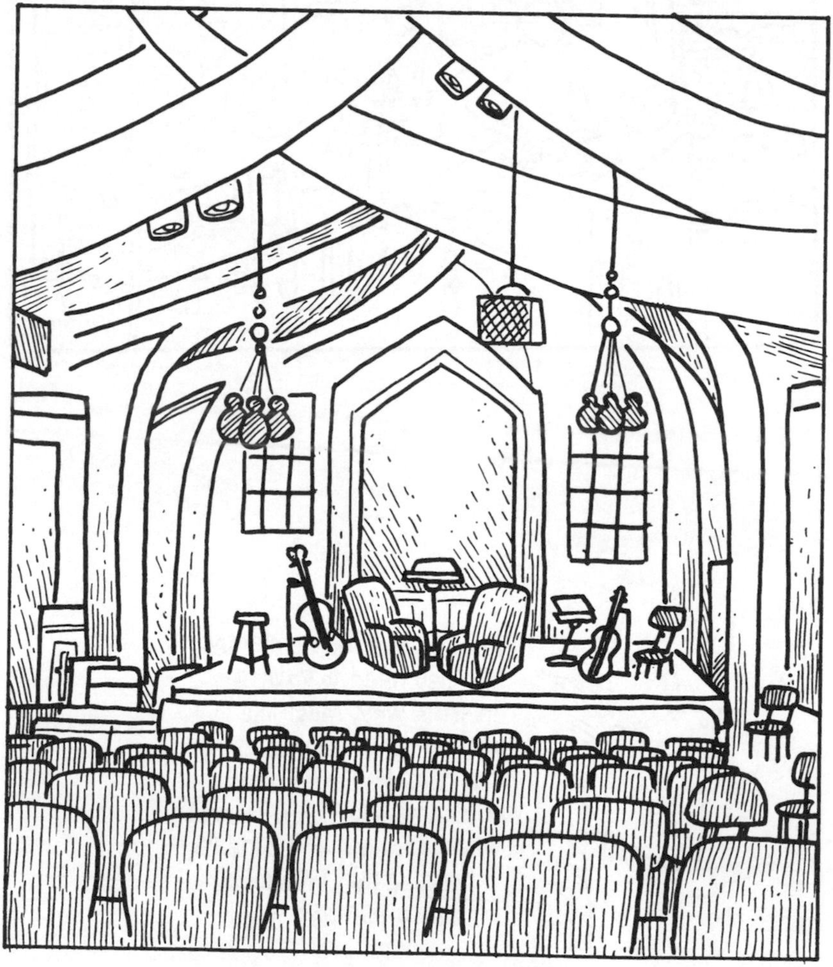

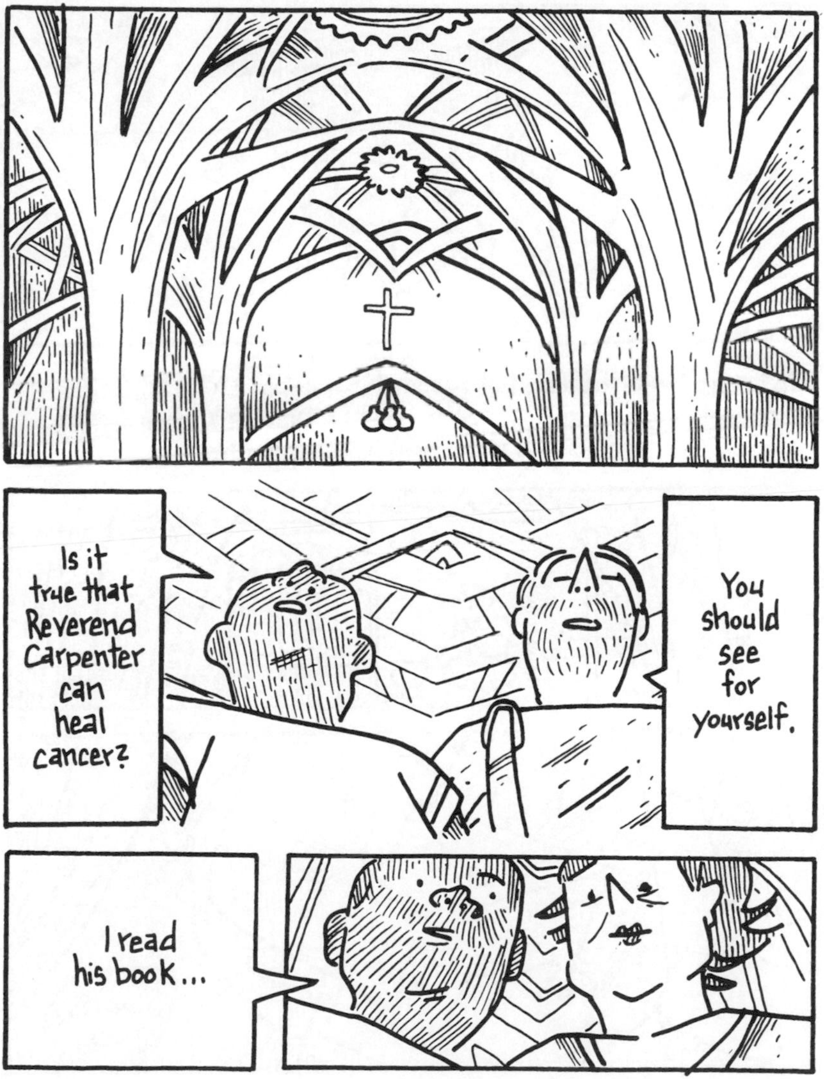
Is it true that Reverend Carpenter can heal cancer?
You should see for yourself.
I read his book...

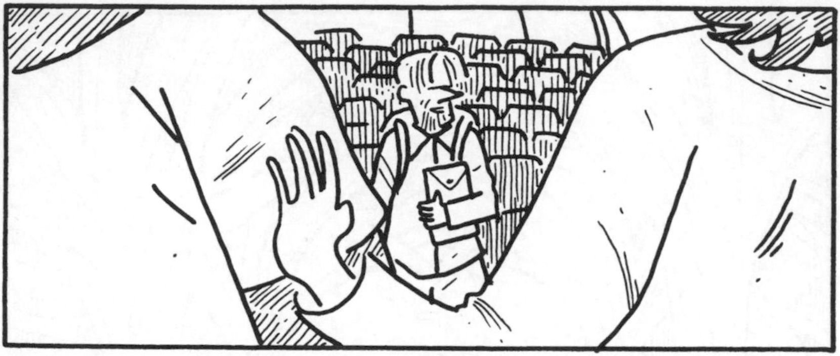

I'm finished with the tour, but I can tell that Robin isn't ready to leave. Madeline sees it also and offers to show him the kitchen again. Maybe they need help packing lunches?

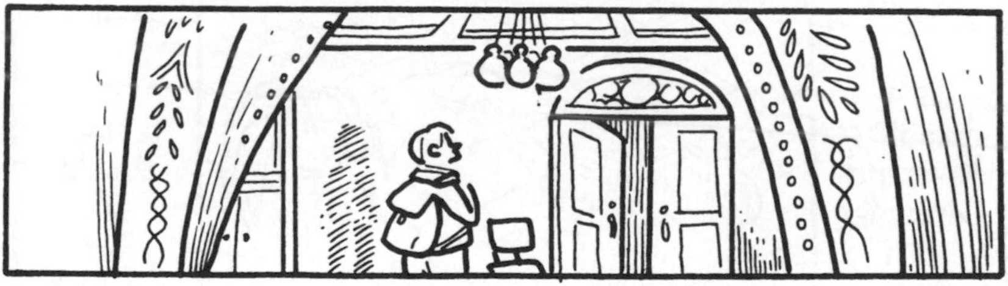

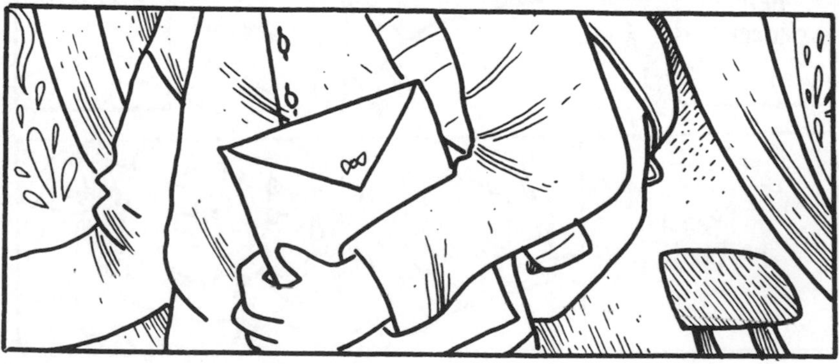

I want to go along and grab a sandwich from the kitchen, but I also need some fresh air.

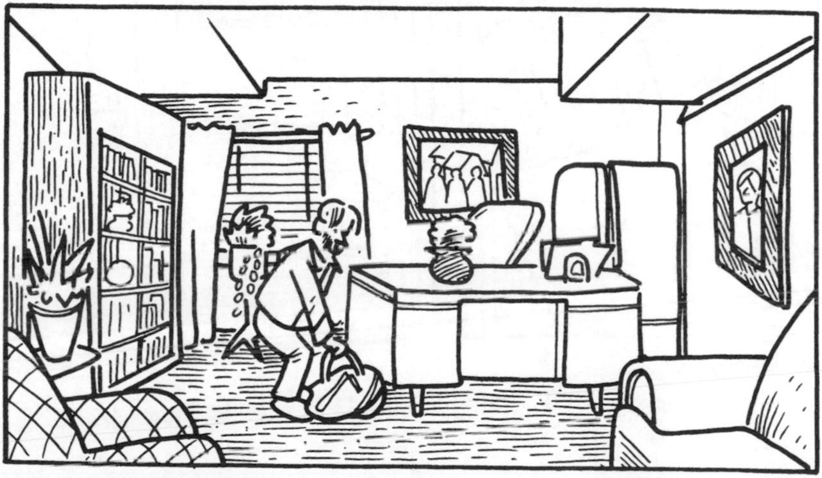

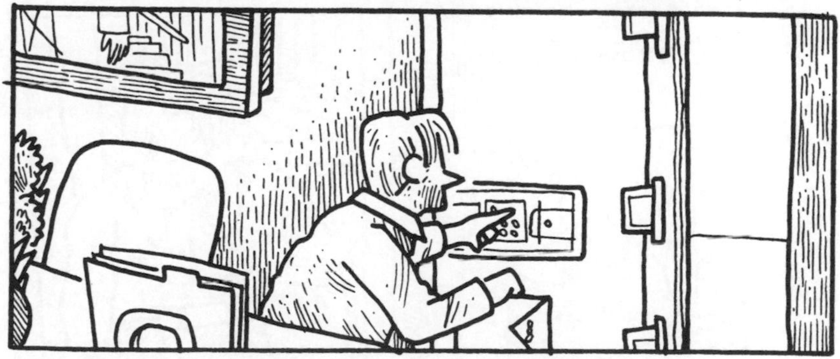

It's too bad that modern life requires that so much of our time is to be spent inside stuffy structures.

Sometimes I think that if I could live outside, I would.

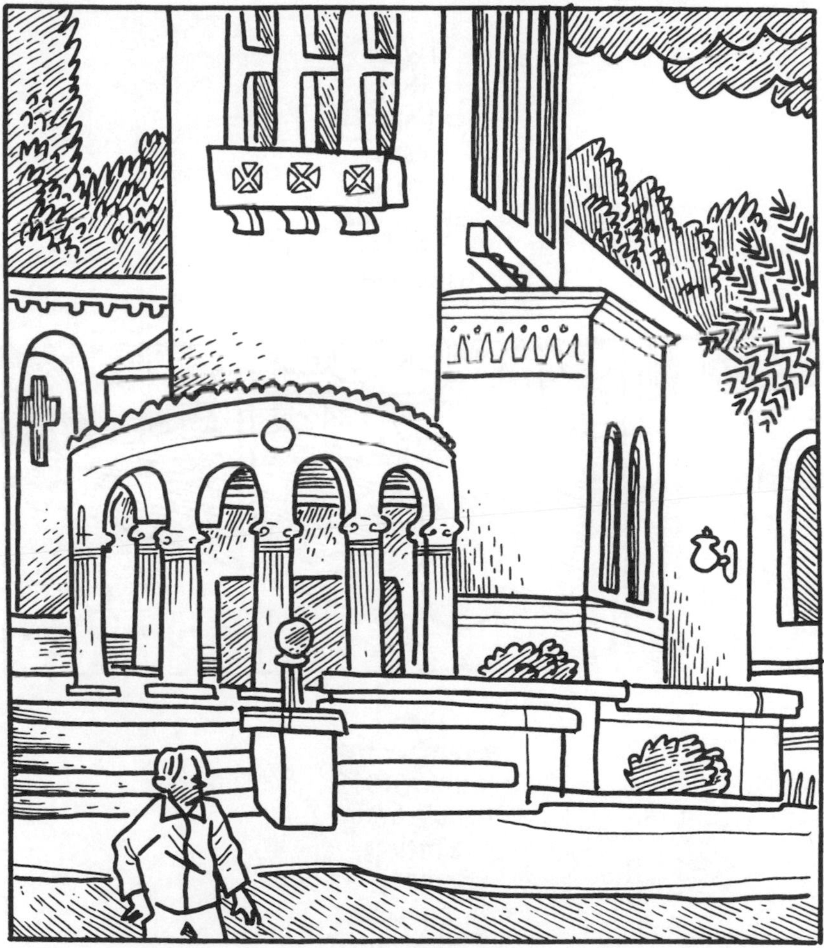

I love when the clouds are big and dark blue, like it's going to rain, but there are waves of light orange spotted throughout the sky.

I wish
that
I had
more
time to
appreciate
God's
handiwork.

Then I
remember that
with 610,042
people living
homeless
on any
given night,
fantasizing
about living
outside is cruel.

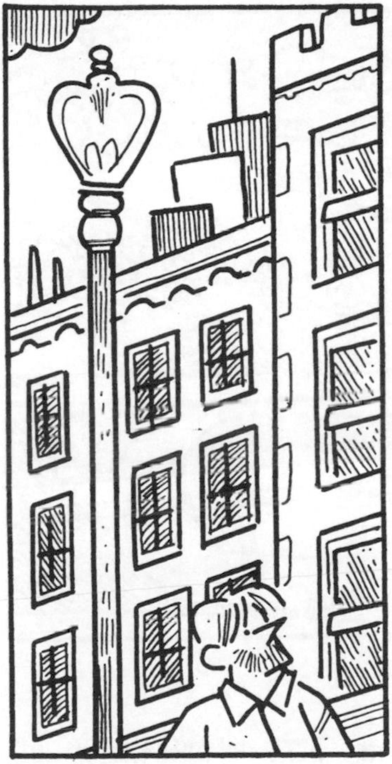

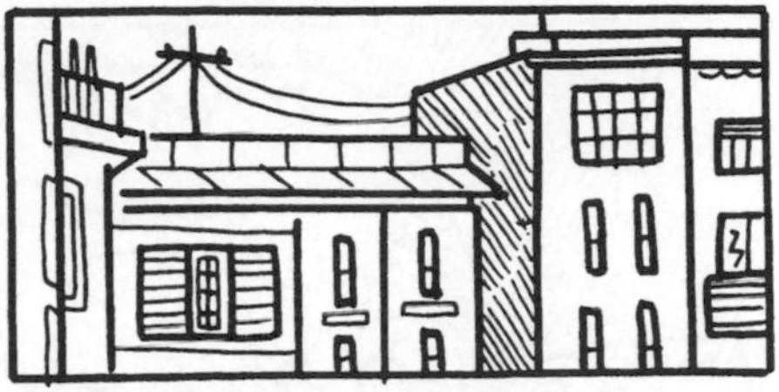

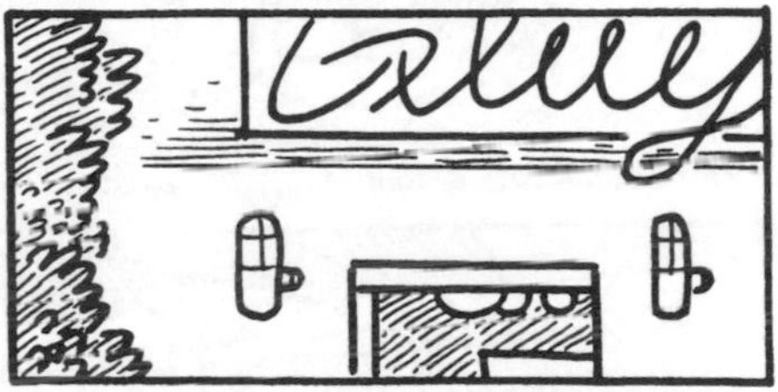

There are two new homeless men that I haven't noticed before hanging around the neighborhood. I need to stop by and say hello on my way back from the cafe.

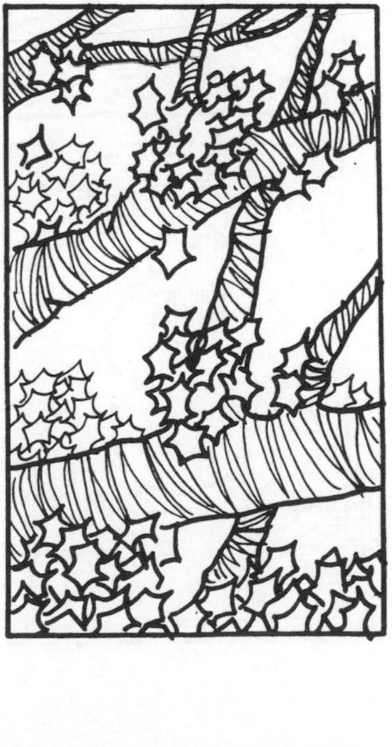

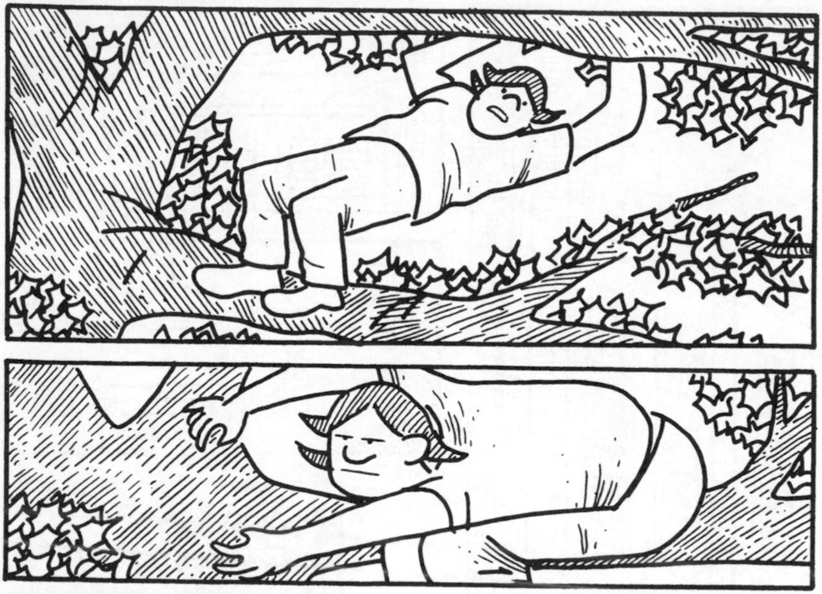

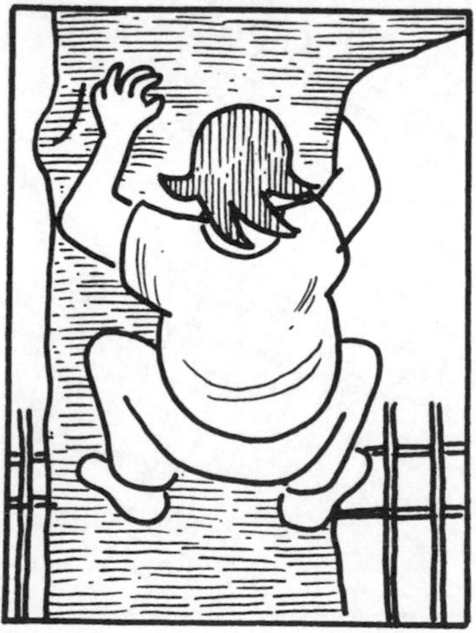

Gluyas is a small cafe that is in walking distance from the church. I'm friends with the owner, José, who has yet to let me pay for a meal.

I overheard once that the restaurant is well funded by a single guest who lives alone in the apartment upstairs.

She sounds like a
very generous person.

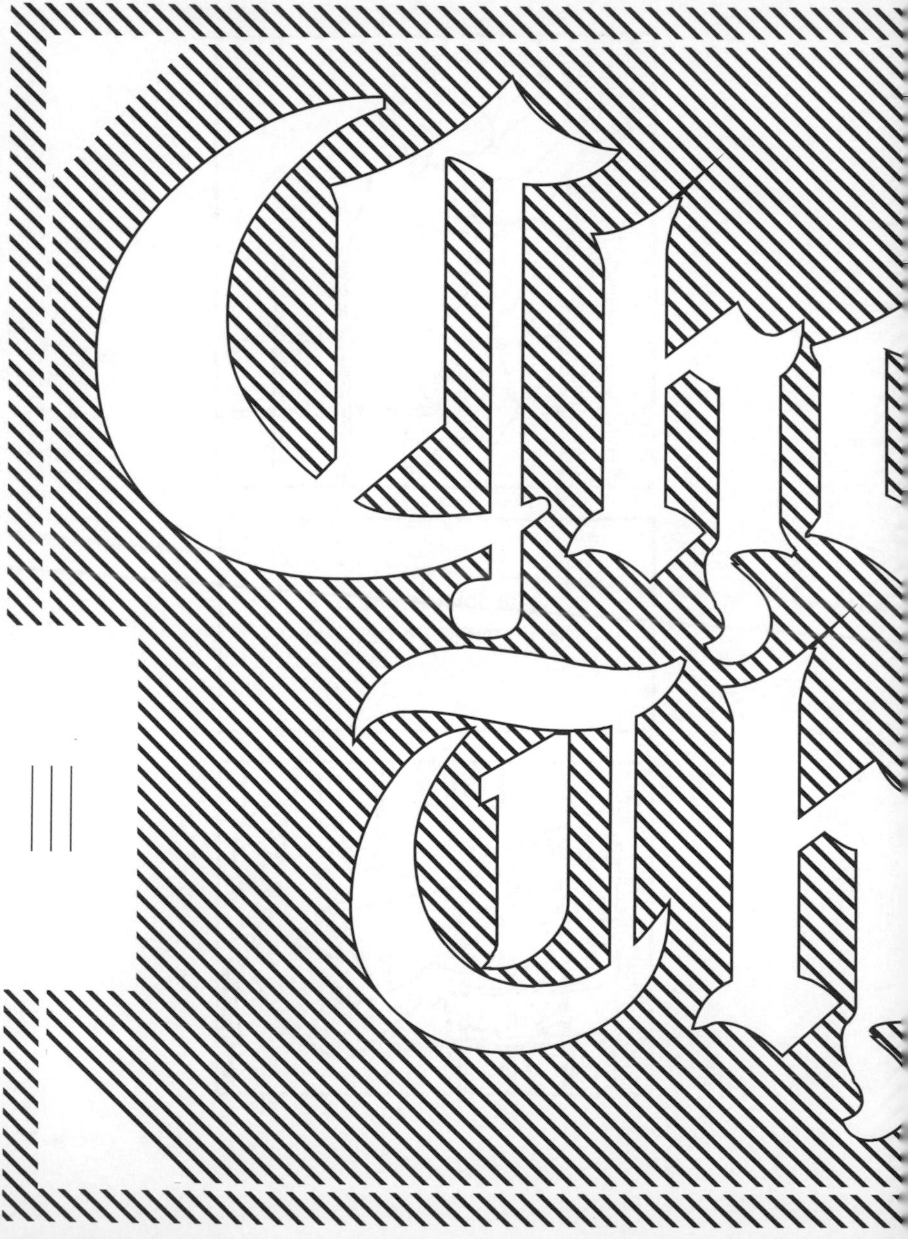

pter
ee

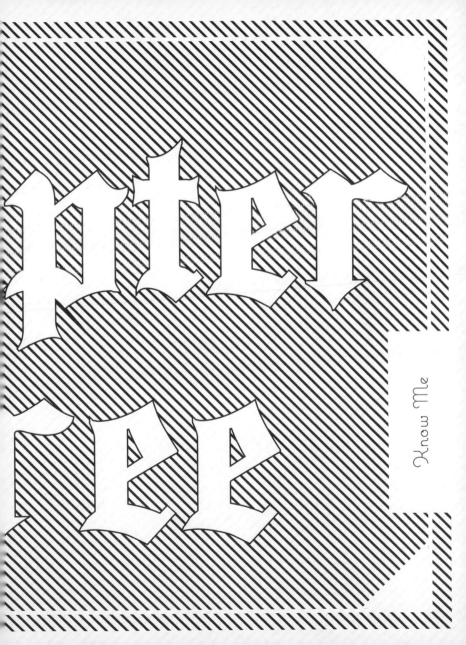

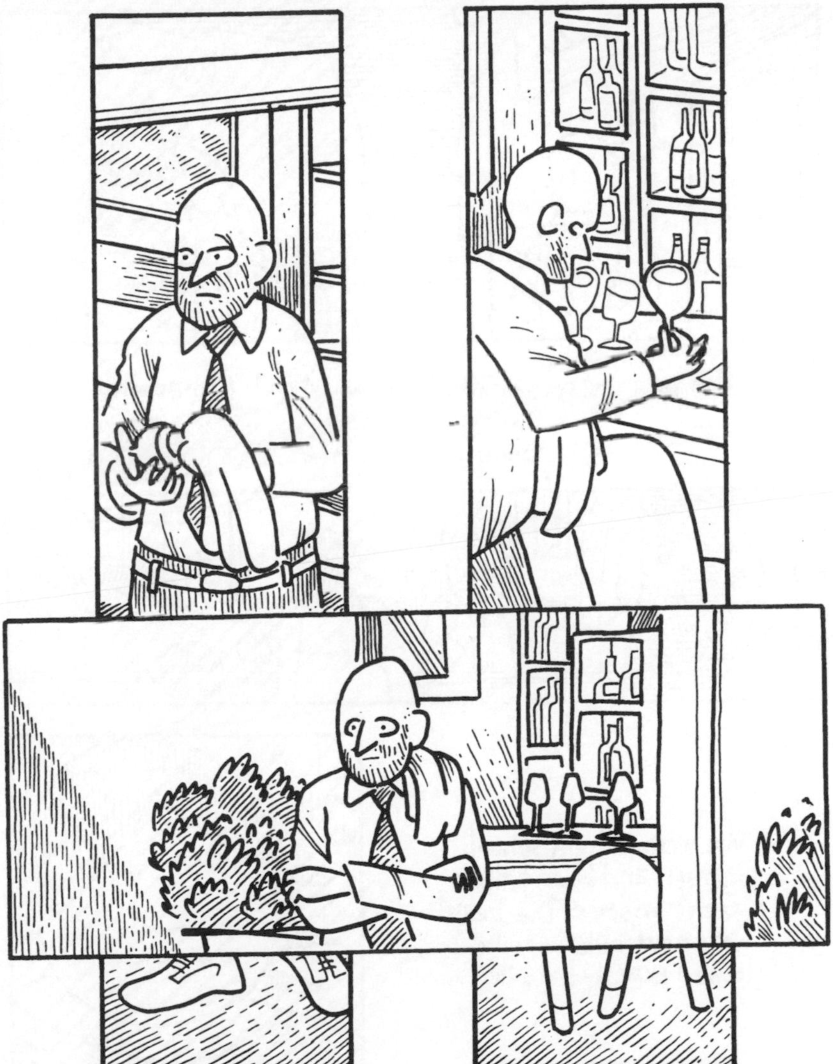

The very first person that I saw was Noah Ganapathy.

Noah, of all people.

We were in high school together, and I don't think I'd seen him since. The beard was new, otherwise he looked exactly the same.

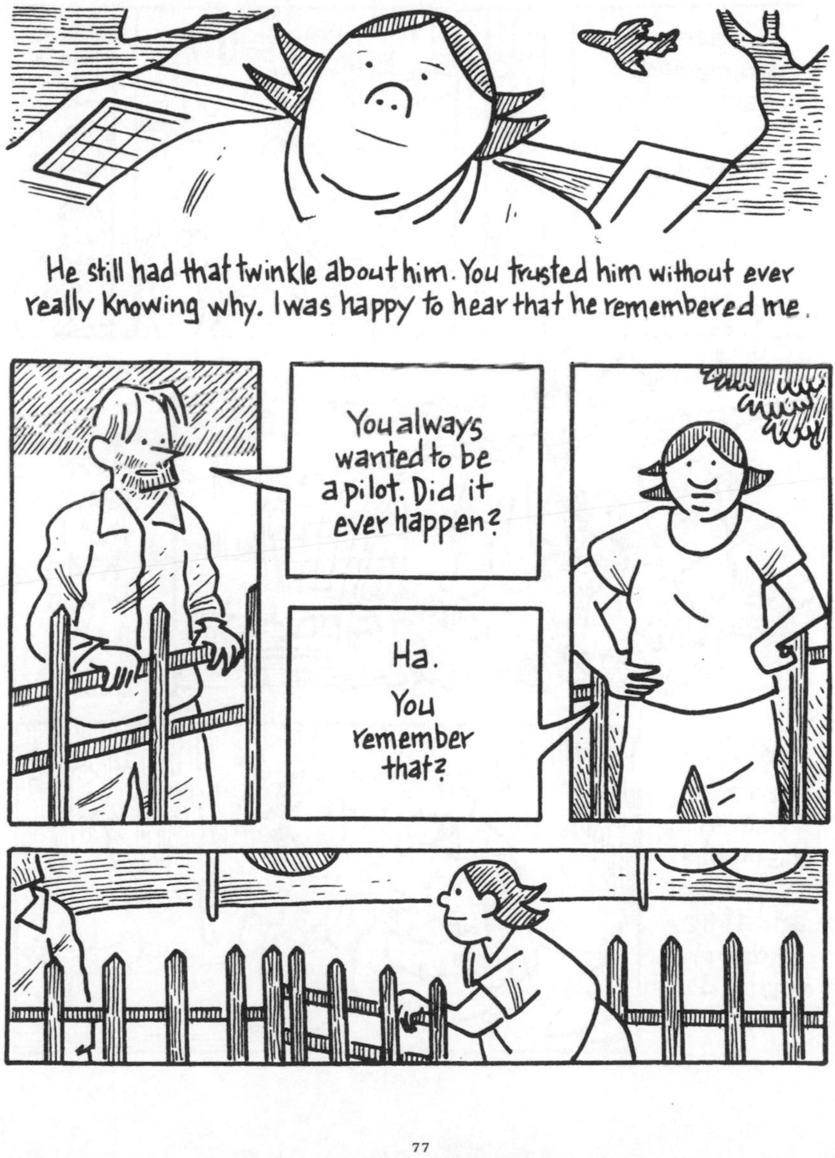
He still had that twinkle about him. You trusted him without ever really knowing why. I was happy to hear that he remembered me.
You always wanted to be a pilot. Did it ever happen?
Ha. You remember that?

I barely remember wanting to be a pilot. Yet Noah didn't recall that I left high school without graduating.

He also didn't know that I had struck it rich.

Well, I used to be rich. At this point, I was broke and a little unsure of what to do next.

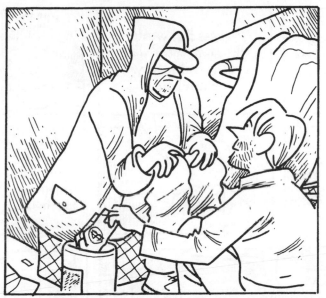

Noah must have been able to read "aimless" on my face because he invited me to visit his church. It was just down the block.

You've been staying in that cafe this whole time?

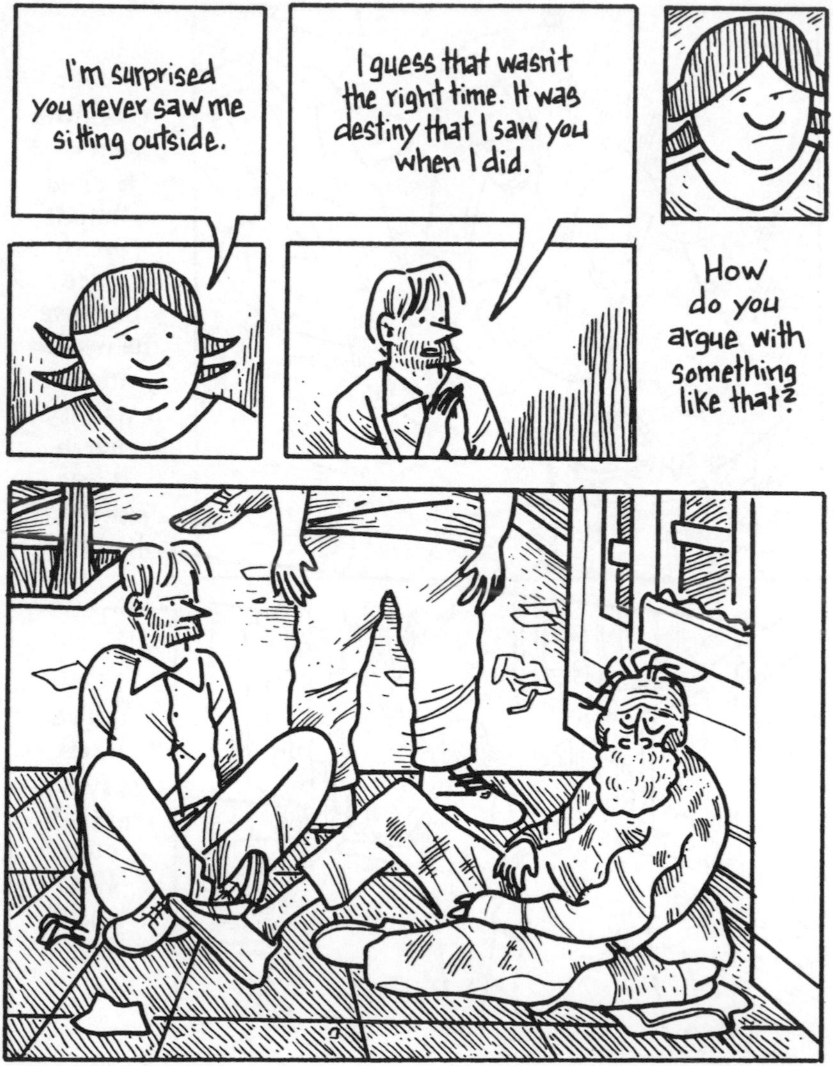
I'm surprised you never saw me sitting outside.
I guess that wasn't the right time. It was destiny that I saw you when I did.
How do you argue with something like that?

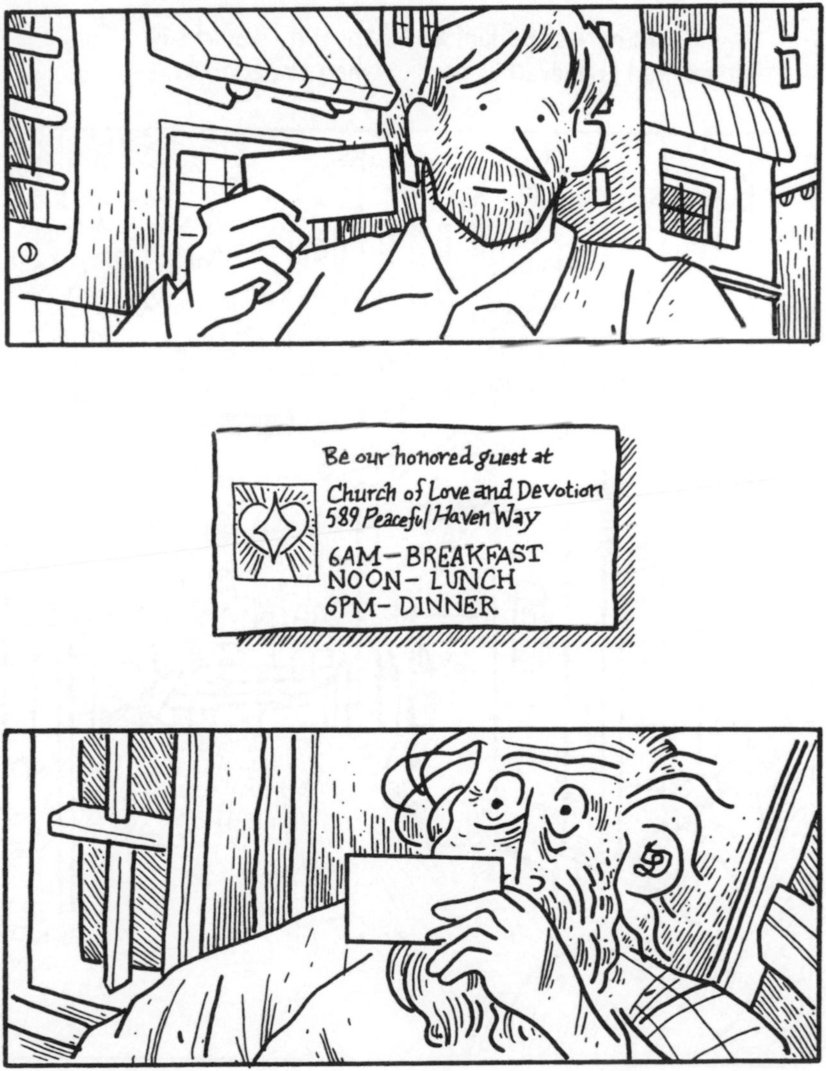
Be our honored guest at
Church of Love and Devotion
589 Peaceful Haven Way
6AM— BREAKFAST
NOON— LUNCH
6PM— DINNER

I was not as spiritual as Noah, but I would say that I believed in destiny when I needed to.

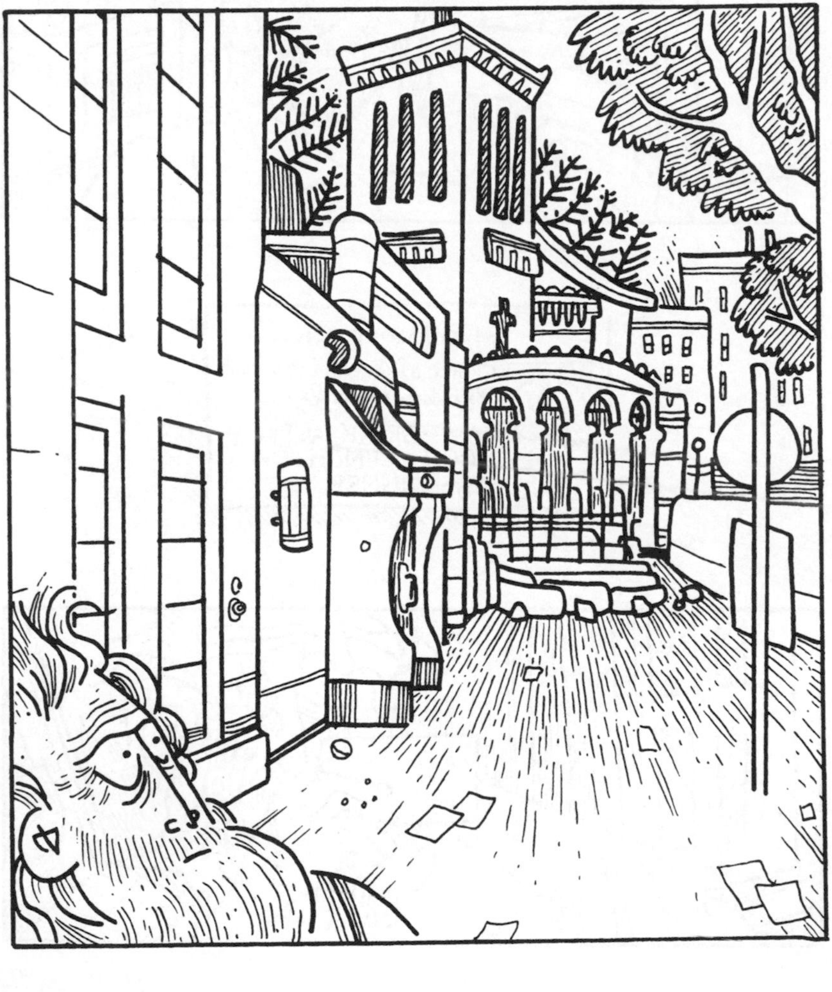

I'm an all or nothing kinda woman, and terrible with moderation. Point me in a direction, and I'm all in. 100%. Whether it's destiny or luck, I walked with Noah because I needed a place to stay for the night.

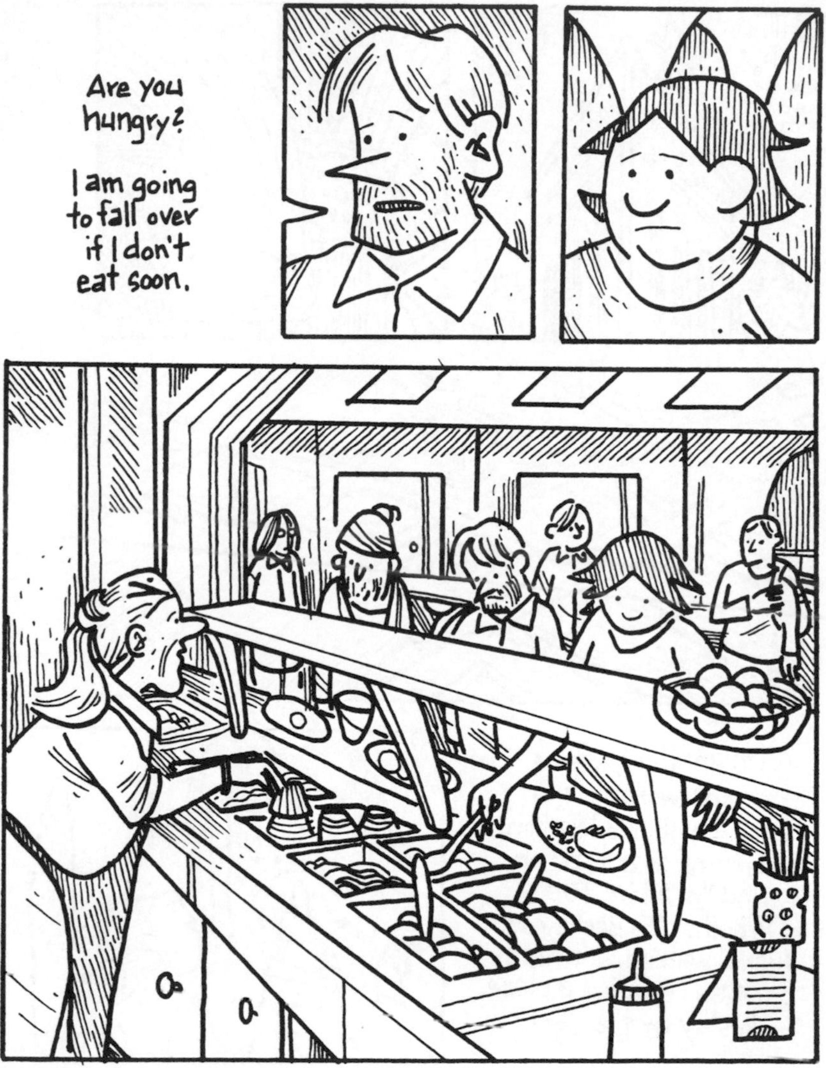
Are you hungry?
I am going to fall over if I don't eat soon.

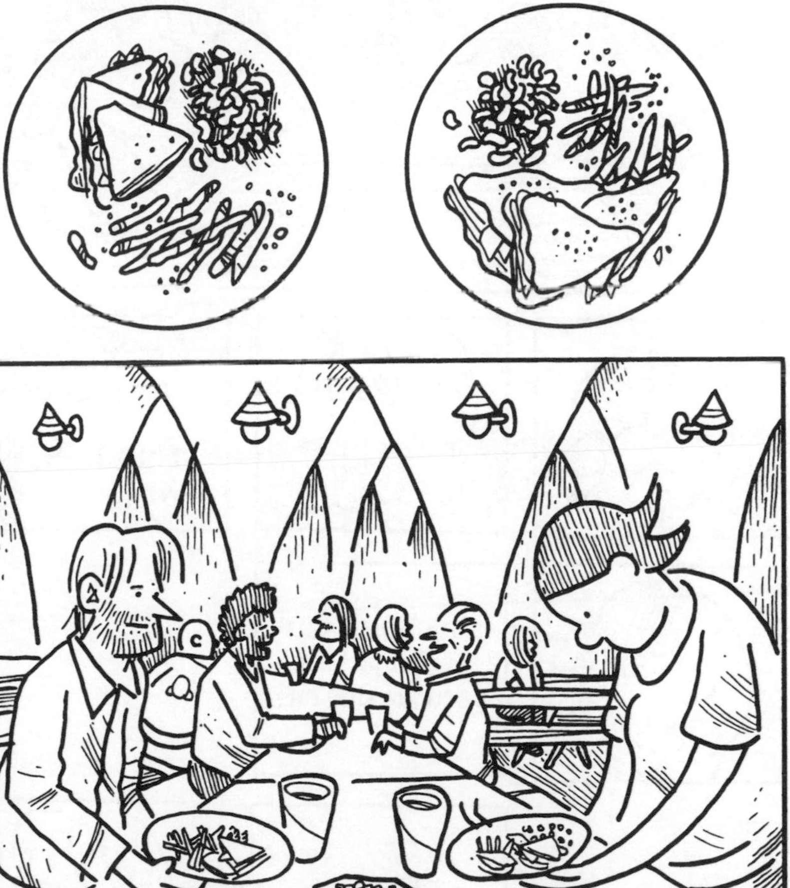

It had been a while since I had a successful conversation over a meal. It was hard to know what to talk about.

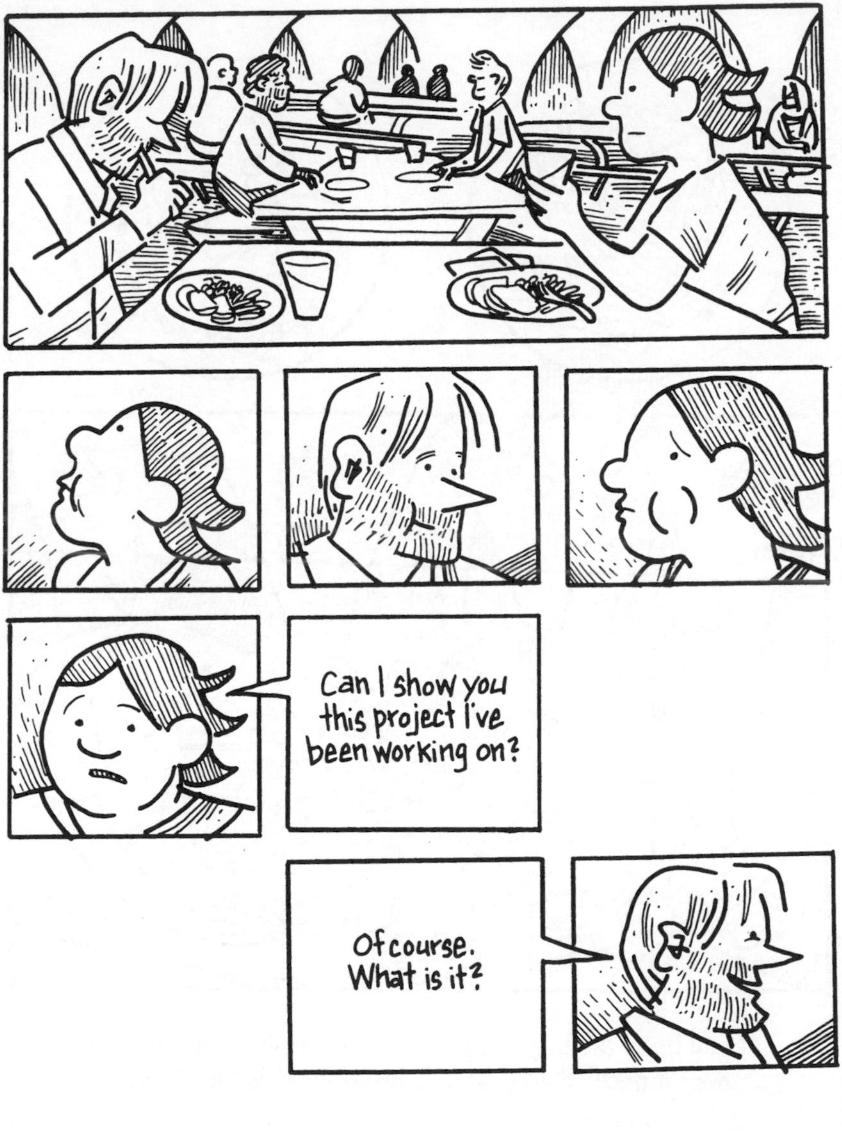
Can I show you this project I've been working on?
Of course. What is it?

It's an app. You open it up and you're asked a question. A personal question.

See?

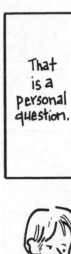

That is a personal question.

You answer the question, and then go to the next screen.

Oh my. Who is that?

You don't know for sure. Someone in the network.

You can invite people, but you can't know who's answer you're viewing.

So the more questions that you answer for yourself, the more answers you see by other people within your network.

Interesting.

Very interesting.

Thanks.

Will you send me a copy of the app?

Noah was a good guy. He somehow knew that I didn't have anywhere to go and offered me a room.

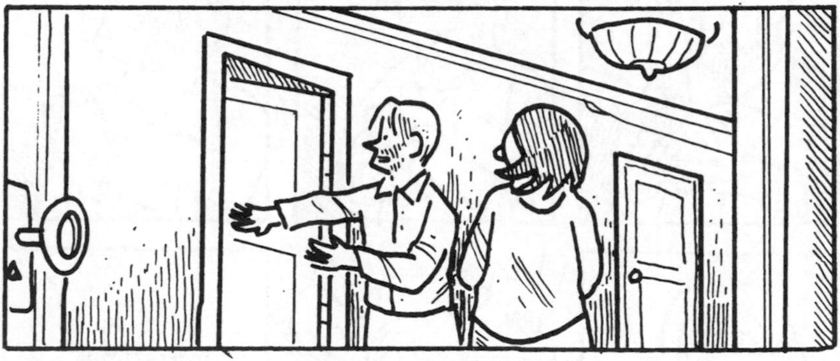

It was like a hotel in those days. My room was one of many.

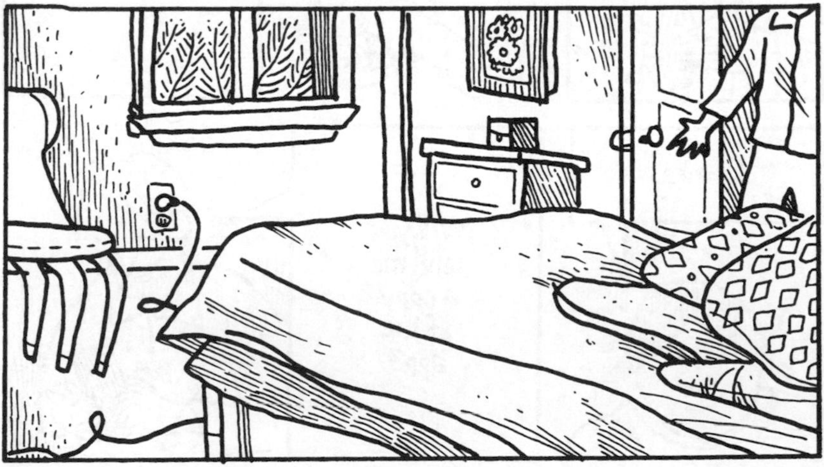

Laying down on the bed, I closed my eyes and realized it was the first time I'd slept in a different bed in a very long time. Mostly it was the smell that I noticed. Clean bedding.

I fell asleep immediately.

It's when I woke up that I felt like I was dreaming. The ceiling in the breakfast hall is the most ornate thing I'd ever seen, and I couldn't take my eyes off it.

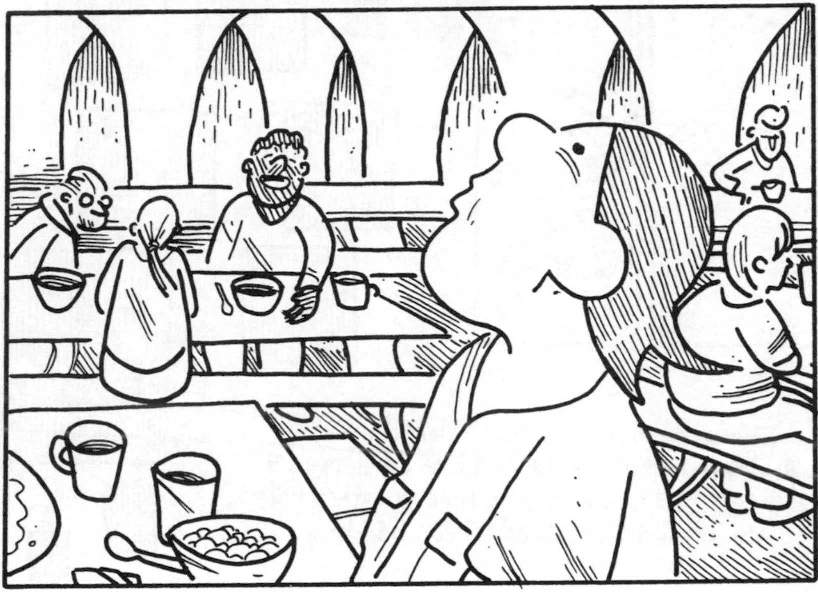

The detail was unbelievable.

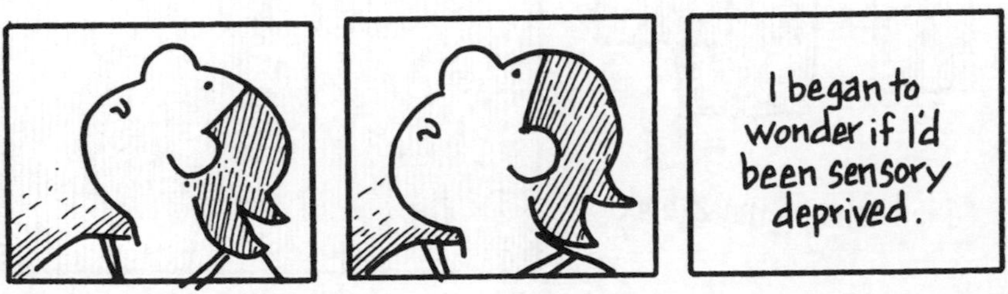
I began to wonder if I'd been sensory deprived.

I could barely pay attention to the conversation around me.
Noah was talking about something.

I showed Reverand Carpenter your phone application.

He thought you might want to test it out with our congregation?

We could all load the application and give you feedback.

Somehow I had fallen into the perfect environment to test the new project. I try not to rely on luck. In my experience, it's never there when you want it.

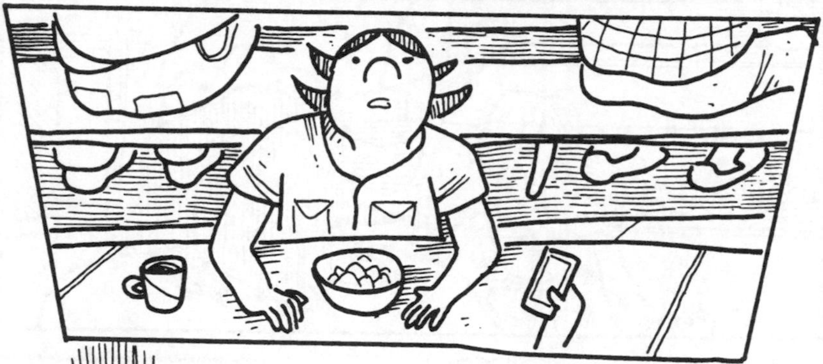

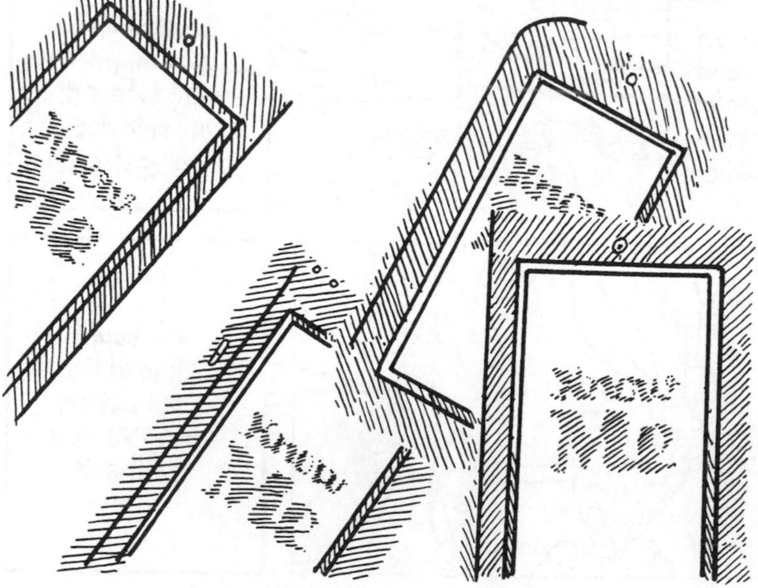

Luck didn't find me when I was kicked out of my parent's house.
Luck didn't find me when I had to sleep outside.

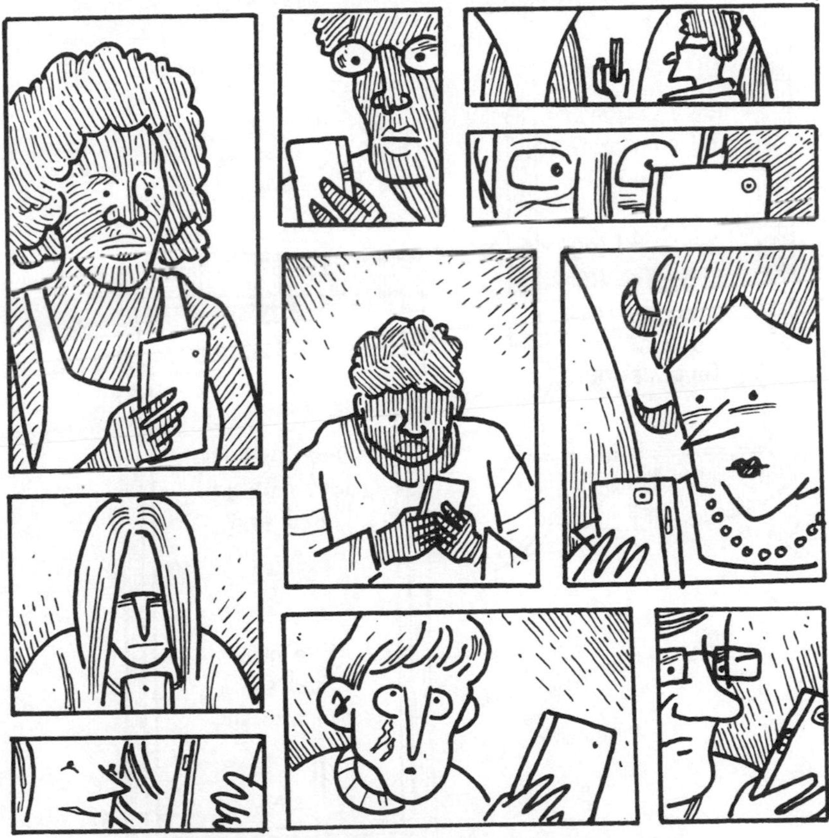

Most of us make our own luck to get us out of bad situations. The people here understand that. They understand how the app works.

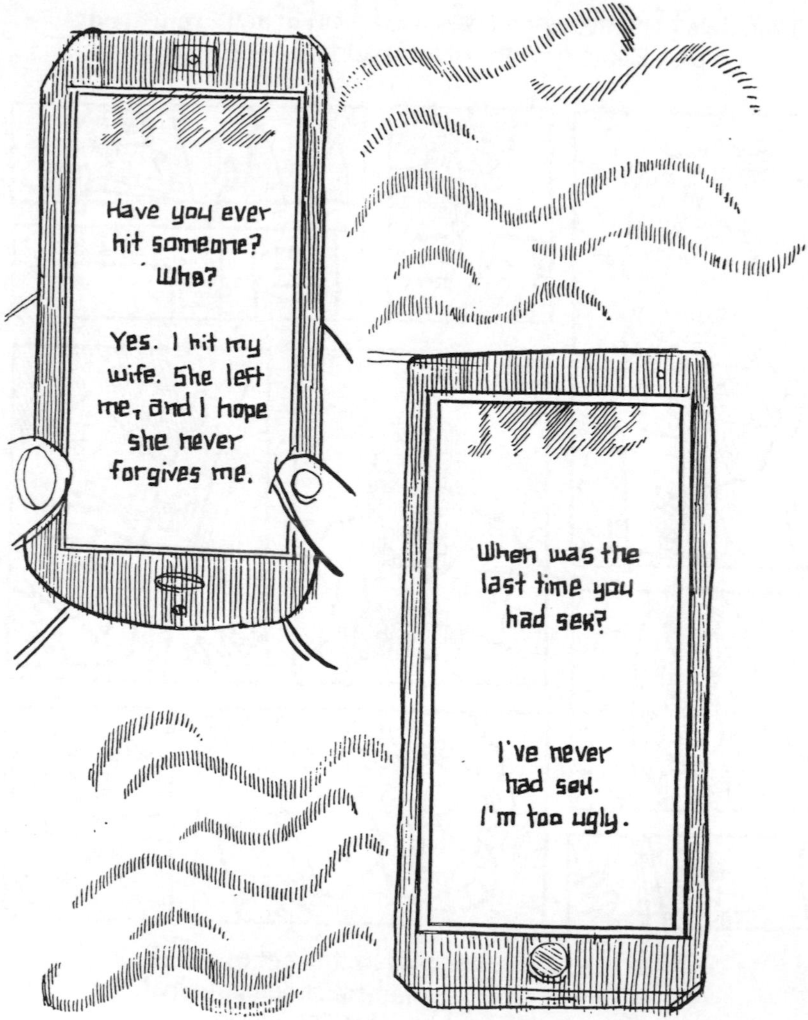
Have you ever hit someone? Who?
Yes. I hit my wife. She left me, and I hope she never forgives me.
When was the last time you had sex?
I've never had sex. I'm too ugly.

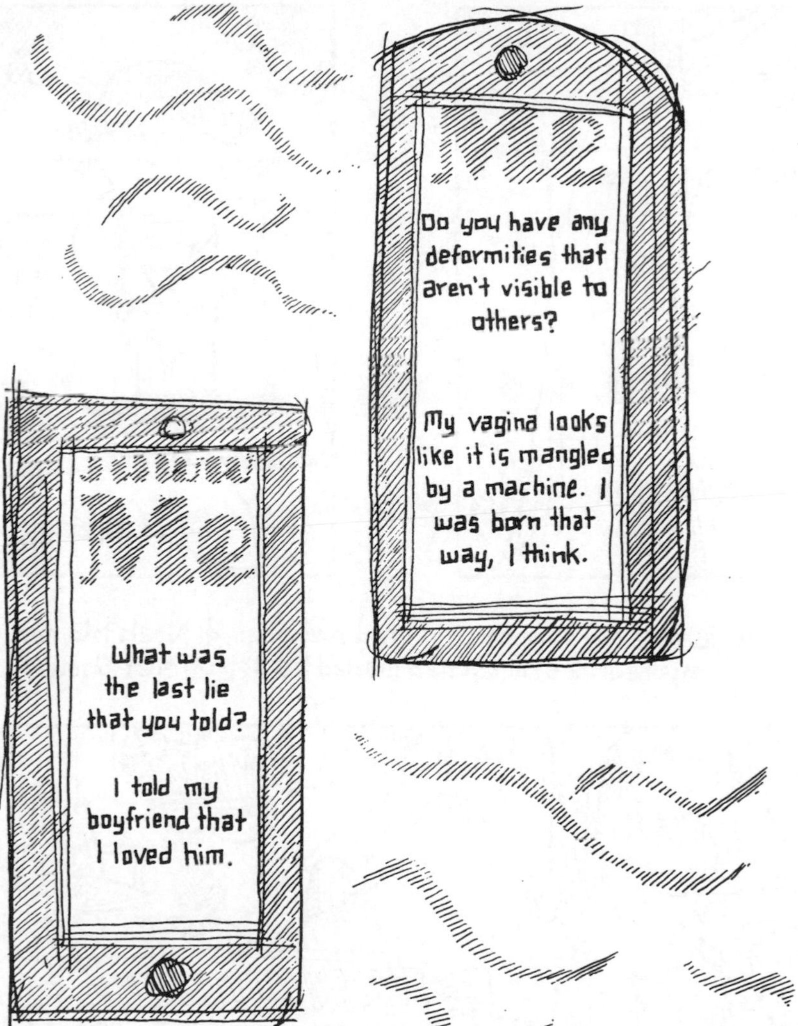
Me
Do you have any deformities that aren't visible to others?
My vagina looks like it is mangled by a machine. I was born that way, I think.
Me
What was the last lie that you told?
I told my boyfriend that I loved him.

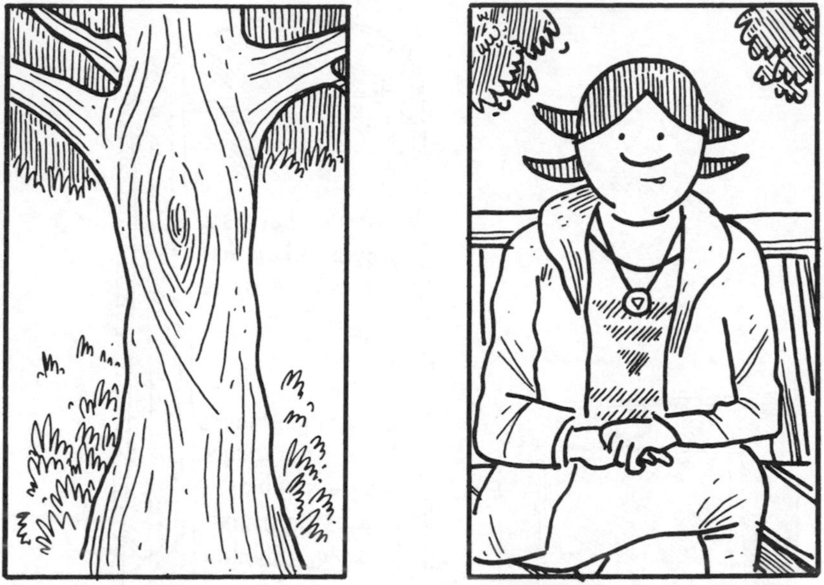

People were more honest than I had even hoped. Noah told me that everyone in the church had loaded the app on their phones.

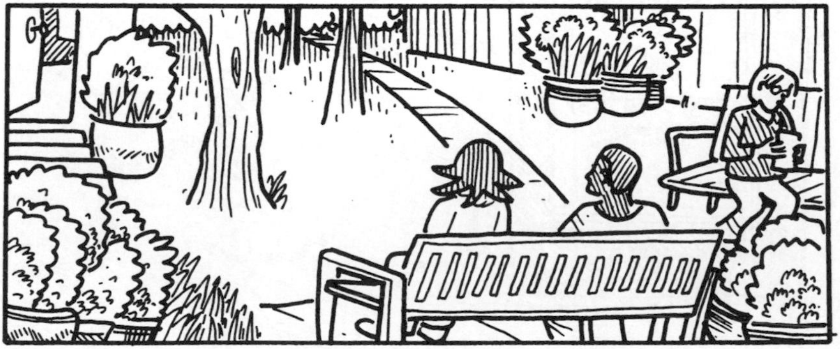

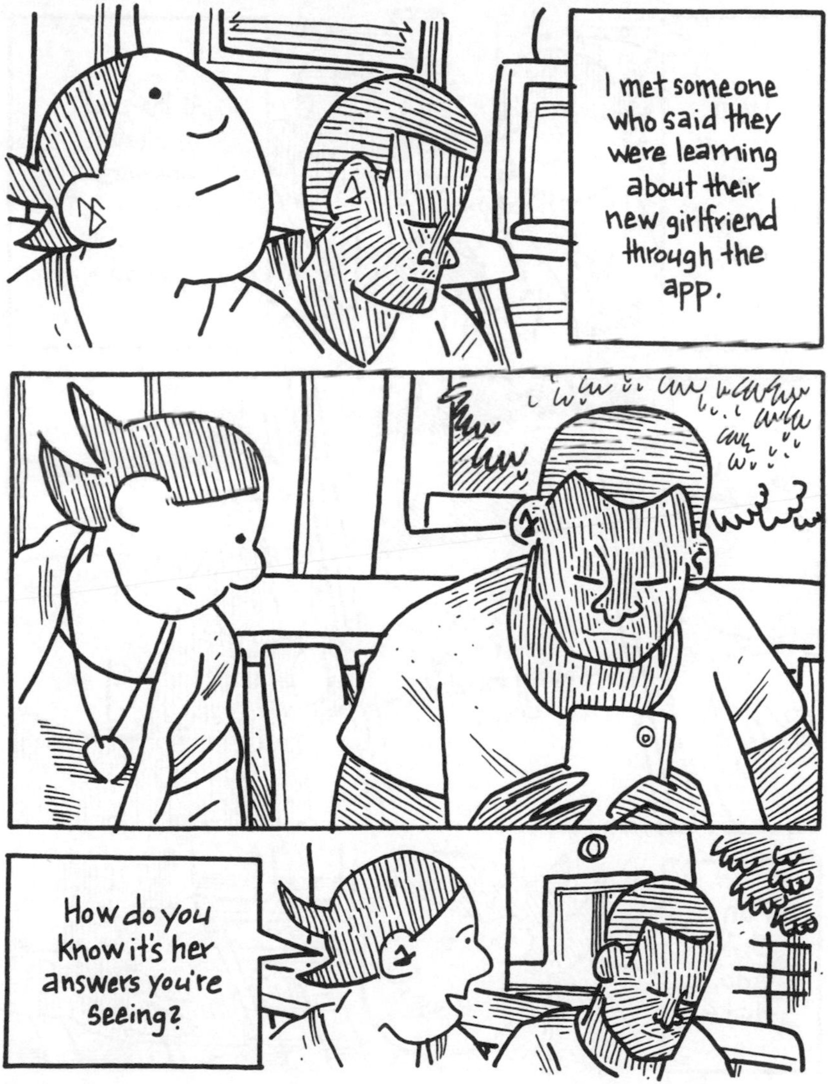
I met someone who said they were learning about their new girlfriend through the app.
How do you know it's her answers you're seeing?

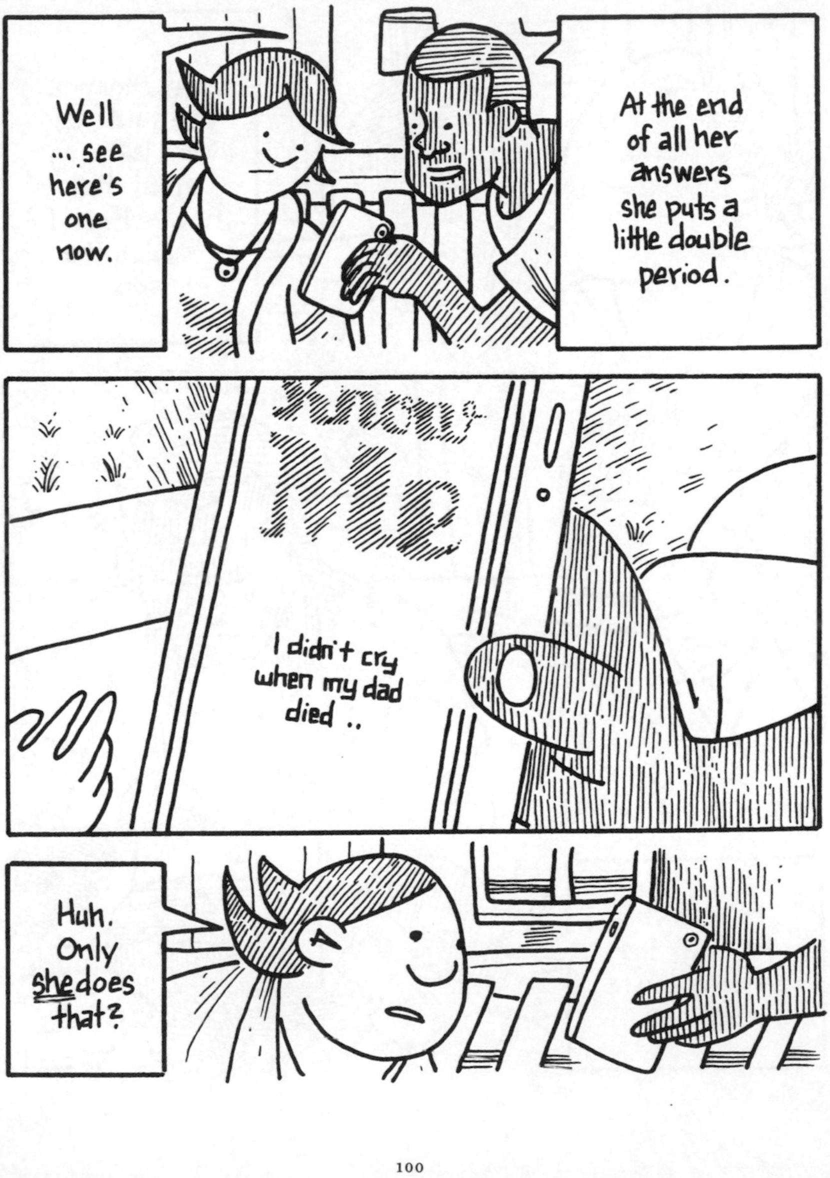
Well ... see here's one now.
At the end of all her answers she puts a little double period.
Know Me
I didn't cry when my dad died ..
Huh. Only she does that?

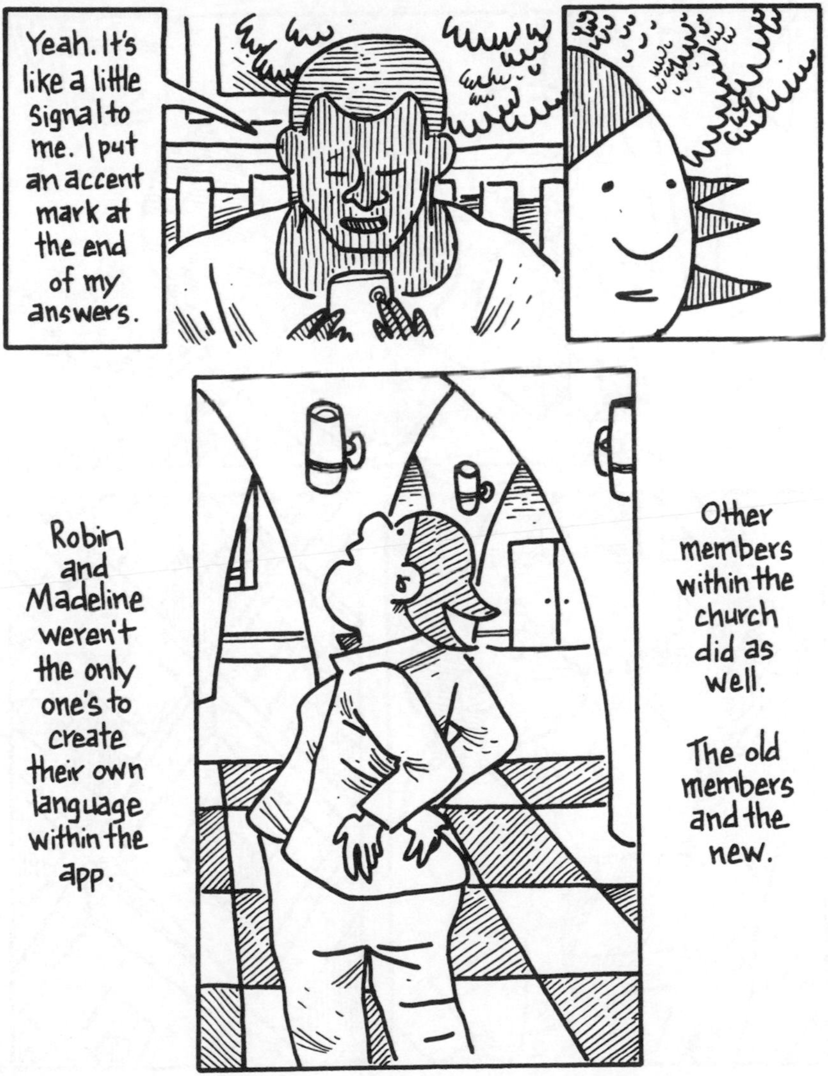
Yeah. It's like a little signal to me. I put an accent mark at the end of my answers.
Robin and Madeline weren't the only one's to create their own language within the app.
Other members within the church did as well.
The old members and the new.

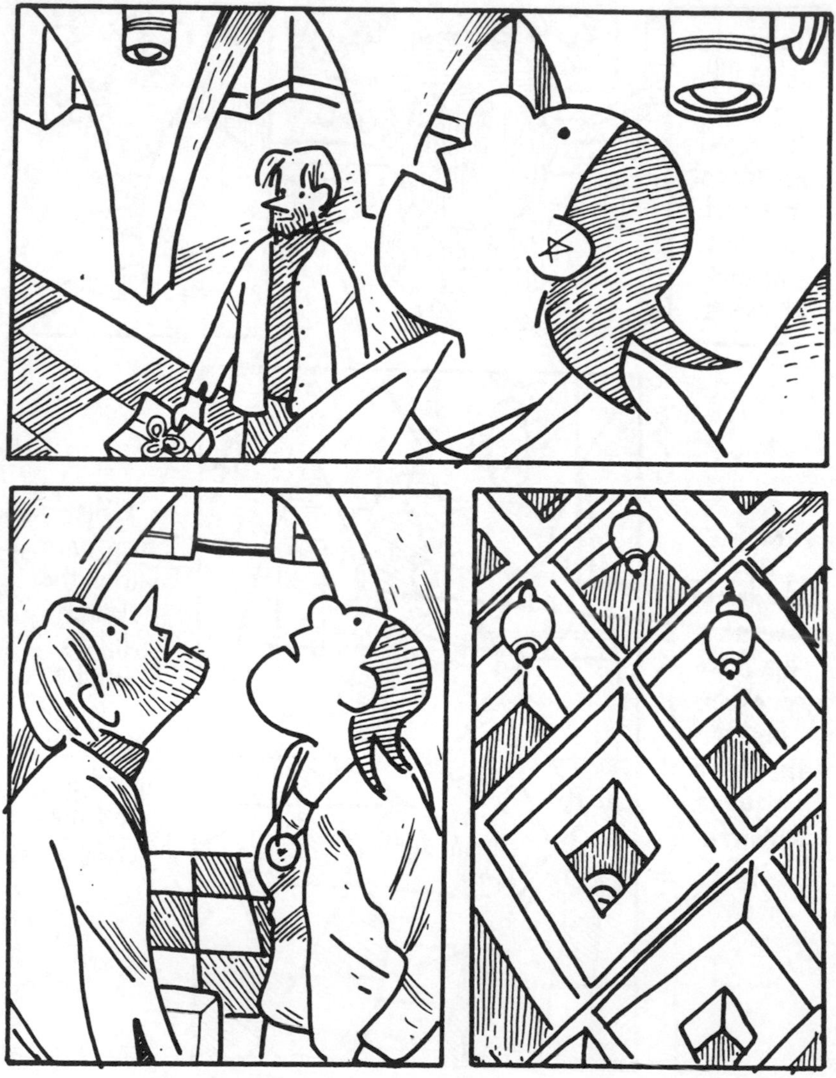

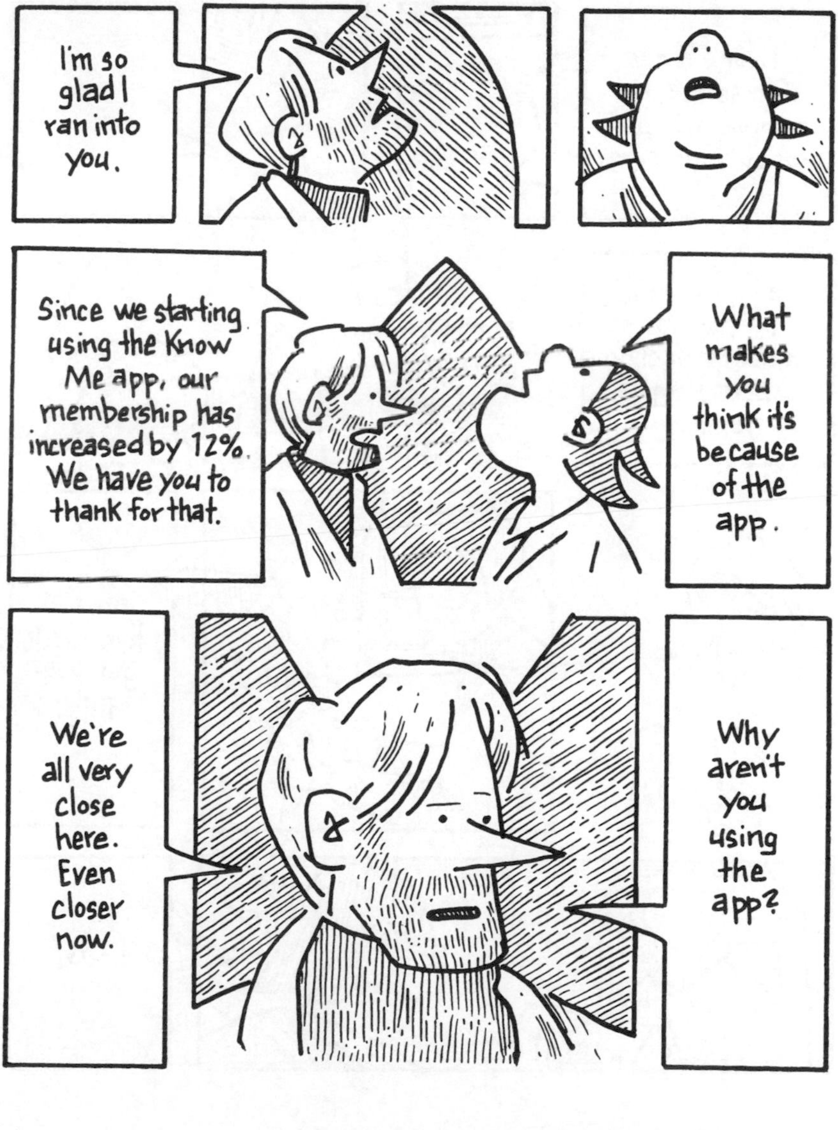
I'm so glad I ran into you.
Since we starting using the Know Me app, our membership has increased by 12%. We have you to thank for that.
What makes you think it's because of the app.
We're all very close here. Even closer now.
Why aren't you using the app?

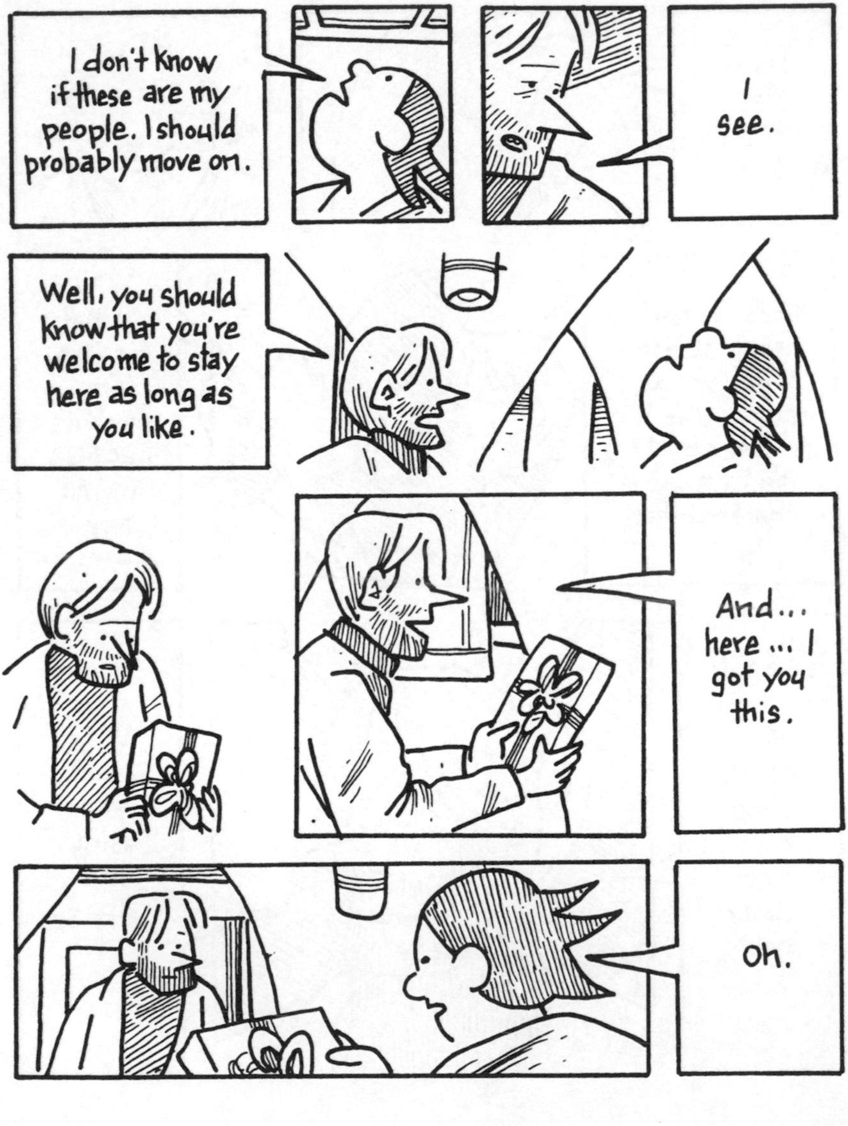
I don't know if these are my people. I should probably move on.
I see.
Well, you should know that you're welcome to stay here as long as you like.
And... here... I got you this.
Oh.

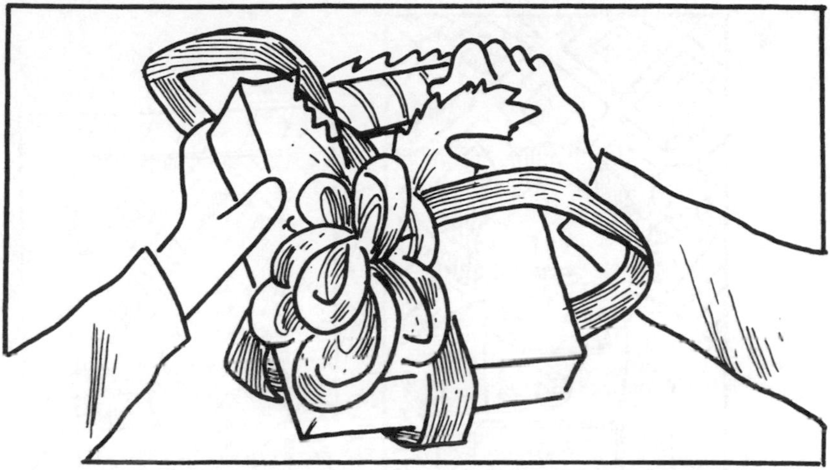

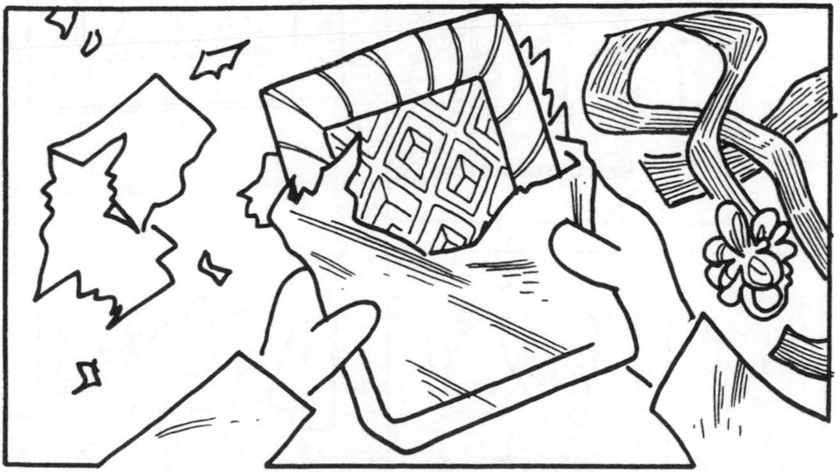

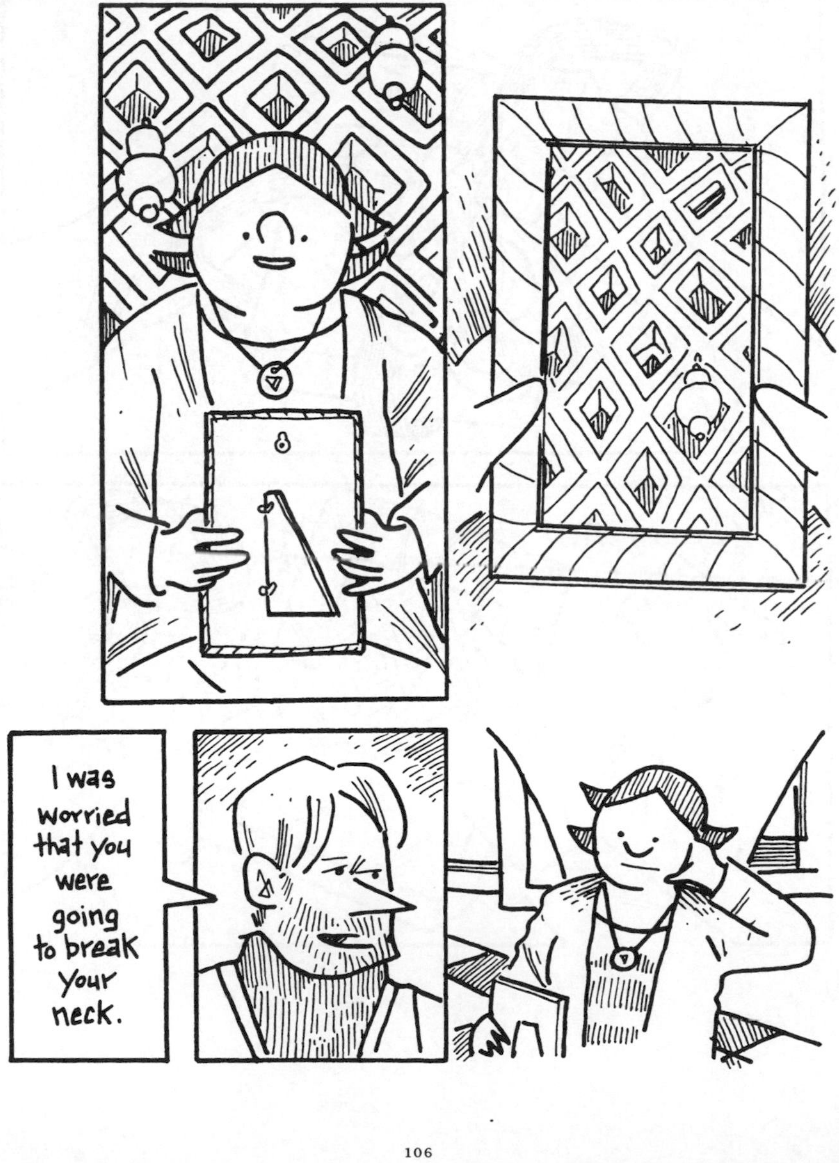
I was worried that you were going to break your neck.

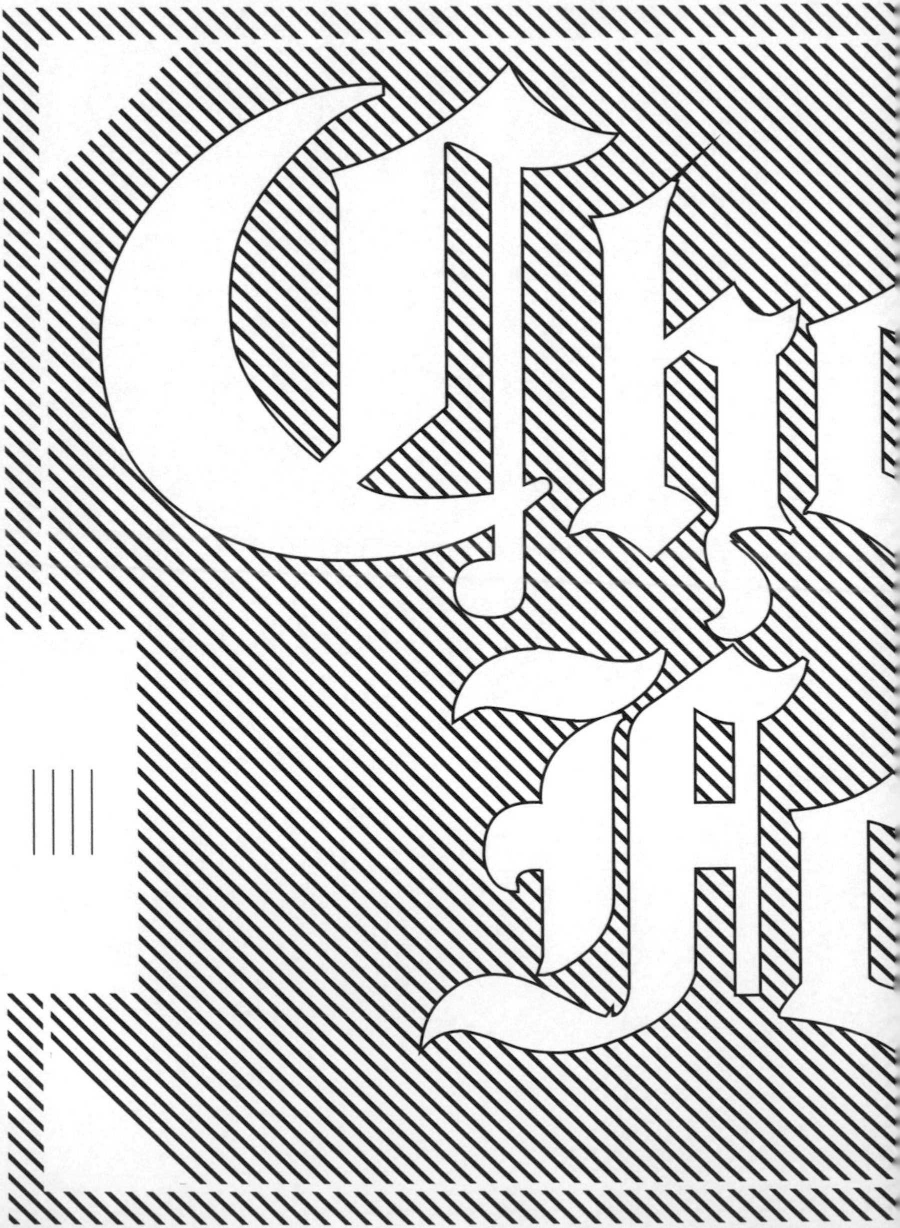

pter
ur

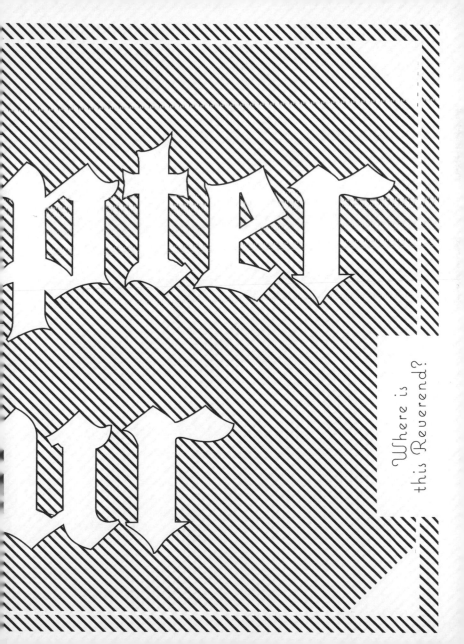

Where is
this Reverend?

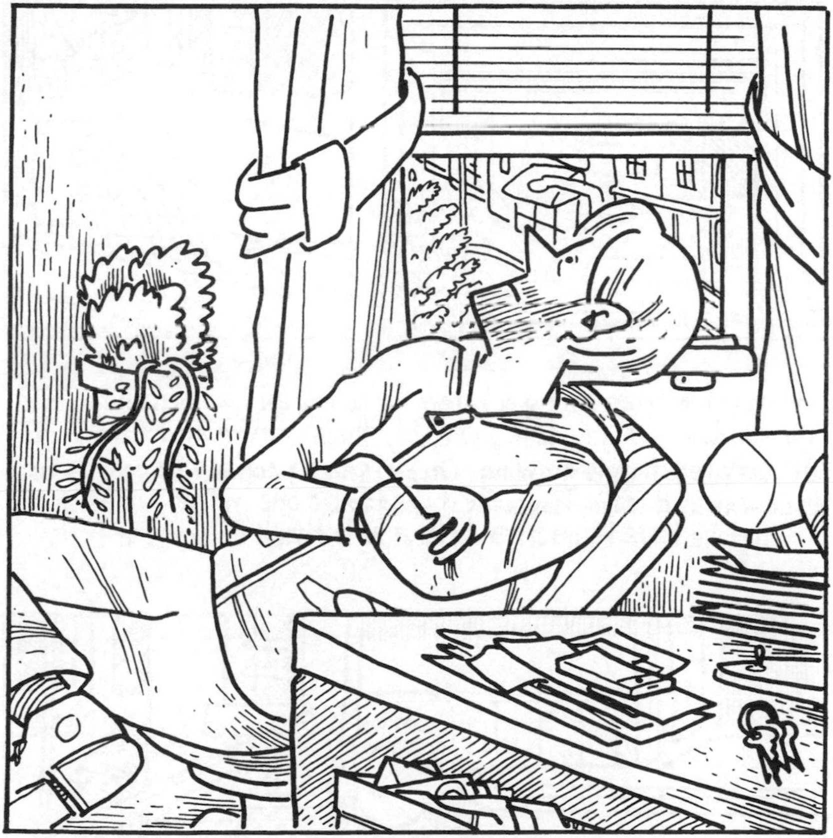

We're not made to sit down on
pavement. It doesn't give. If you sat
on concrete long enough, you would
fracture from the inside.

Hannah has been sitting out there for nearly an hour. I monitor from the window near my desk. Every day there is more and more to do. The congregation is growing. One in seven people who join us lose their way and leave, however it used to be one in two. I understand that we have Hannah and her app to thank for some of that.

I think it's time for me to find my own place to stay.

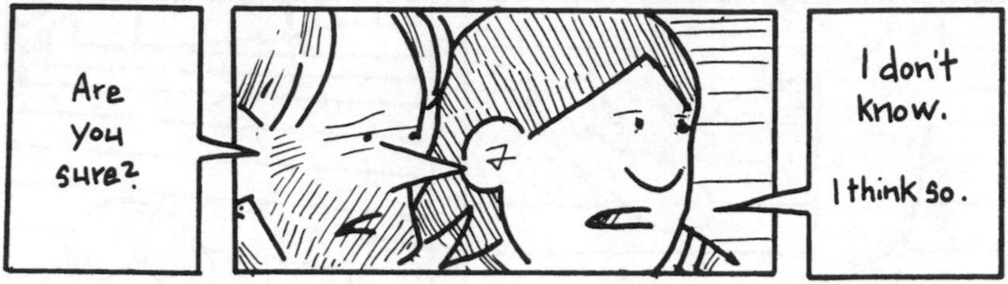
Are you sure?
I don't know.
I think so.

I never know what to say in moments like that. It's my duty to compel her to stay, yet I'm at a loss as to what tactics to employ.

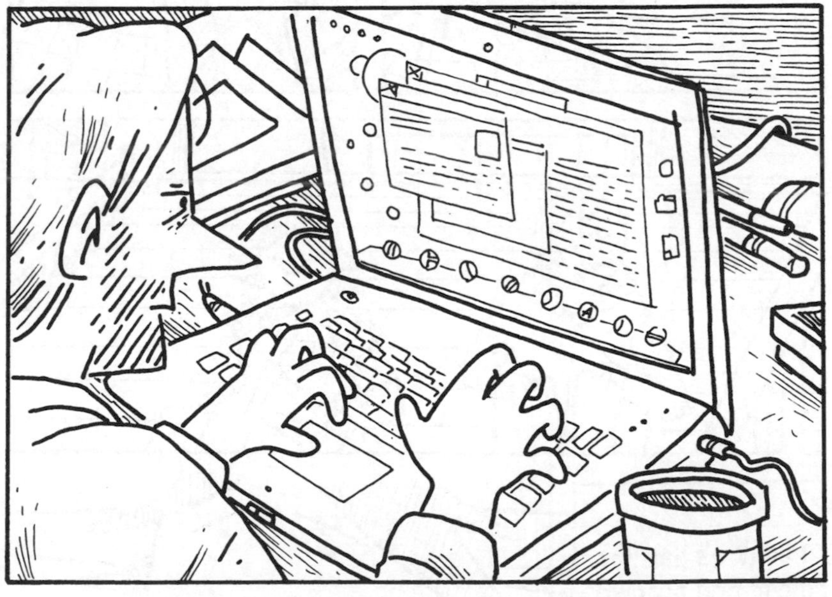

Reverend Carpenter would know what to say.

I decide to write him an email and ask his advice. He's traveling through Wyoming today spreading the good word.

I haven't seen him for weeks, and miss his guidance. I miss <u>him</u>.

We are more anxious without him here with us. More afraid.

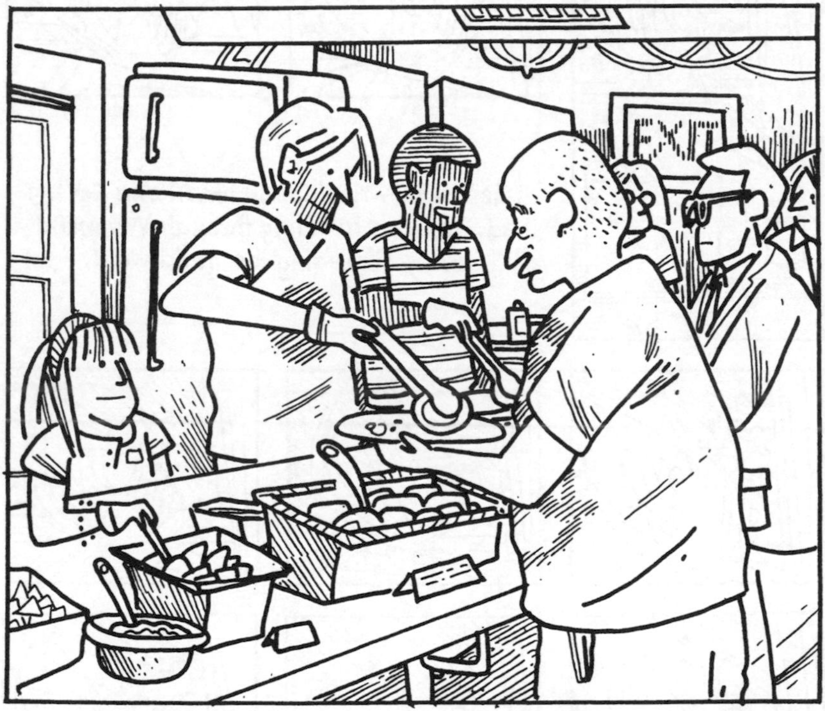
EXIT

Yesterday we heard that in Chicago three policemen beat and murdered a young black man for no apparent reason.

We know that this happens all the time.

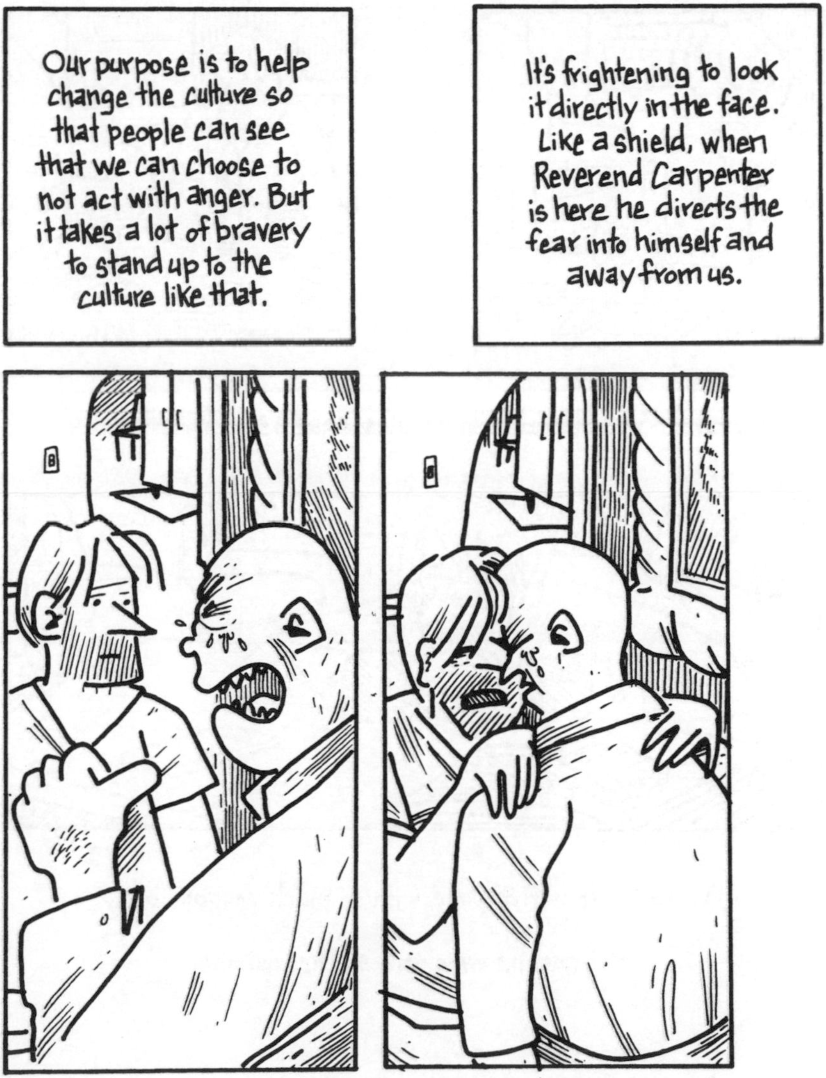
Our purpose is to help change the culture so that people can see that we can choose to not act with anger. But it takes a lot of bravery to stand up to the culture like that.
It's frightening to look it directly in the face. Like a shield, when Reverend Carpenter is here he directs the fear into himself and away from us.

Why hasn't he responded to my message? I sent it a while ago.

I've never known anyone with so much responsibility.

He must be weighing all the options.

I change the default settings on my phone so that I hear a beeping sound and a buzz whenever an email drops to my inbox. I don't want to miss the message from Reverend when it comes in.

what are you afraid to tell your loved ones?

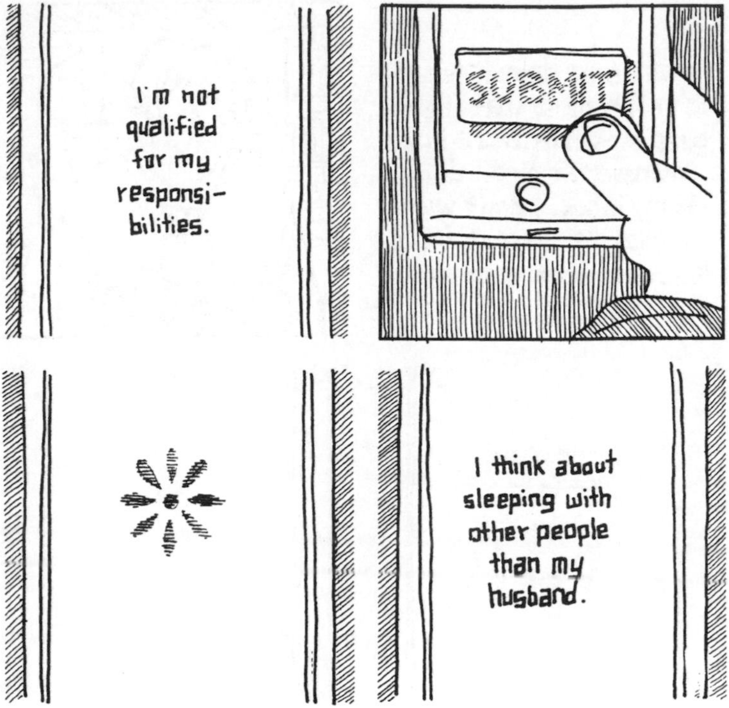
I'm not qualified for my responsi-bilities.
SUBMIT
I think about sleeping with other people than my husband.

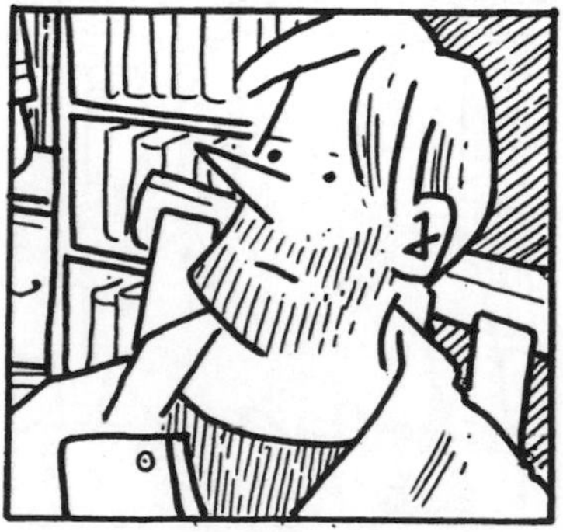

My old job was working for a University doing alumni relations. I asked for money and kept alumni engaged with their alma mater.

When I met Reverend Carpenter, he believed
I would do a good job bringing people to the church.

There must have been something that I was doing that made
him believe in me. God knows what it was, but I don't.

One thing I learned working with alumni is that if you really want something done, you need to get them on the phone. We don't call people like we used to even though we always have a telephone nearby.

Reverend. Please call me when you get this.

Maybe you got my other message?

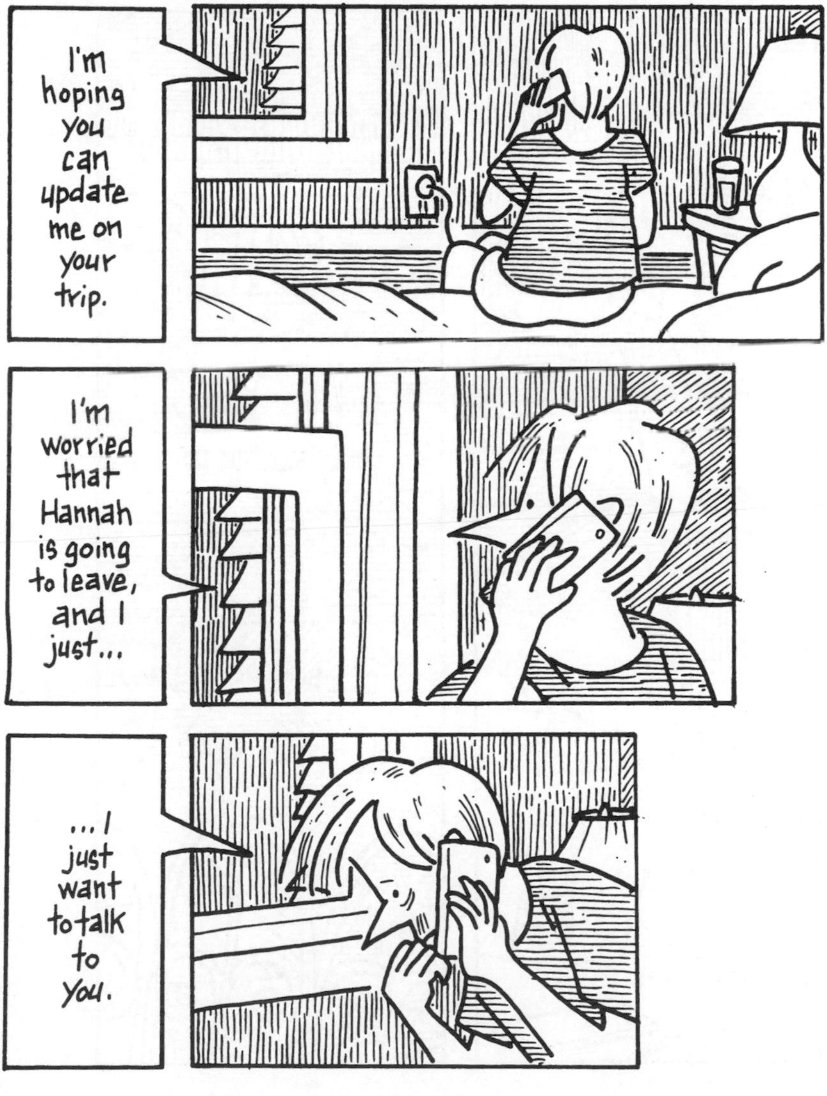
I'm hoping you can update me on your trip.
I'm worried that Hannah is going to leave, and I just...
...I just want to talk to you.

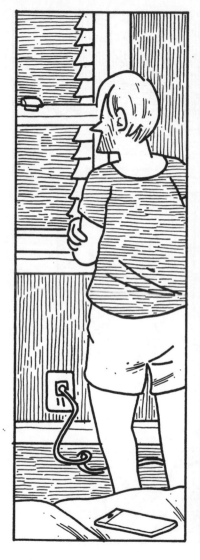

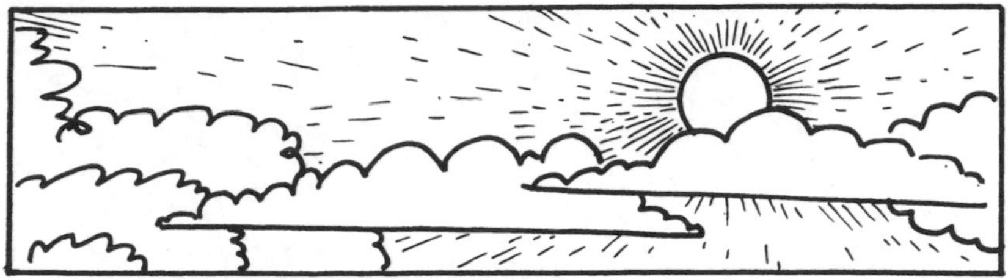

When we were still a small group. Carpenter and I would stay up all night drinking coffee, writing letters, reading scripture and exchanging ideas.

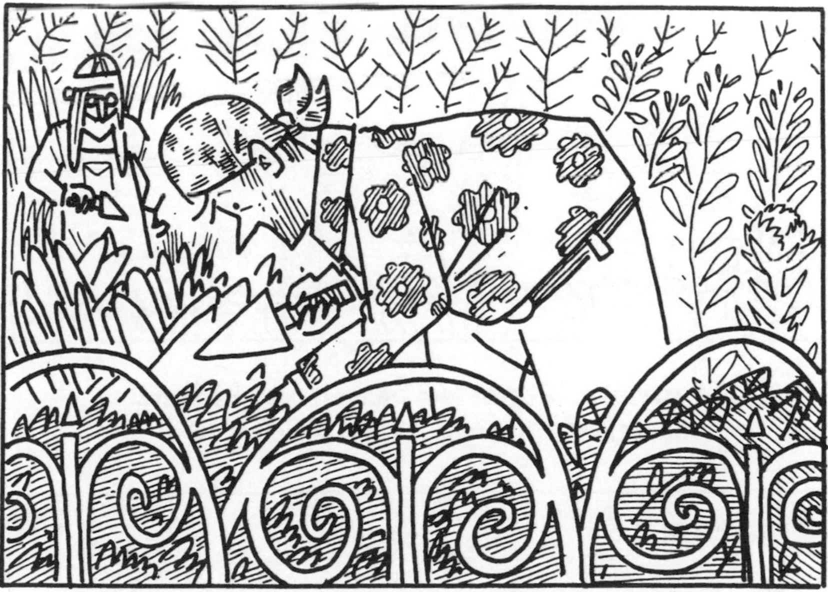

We called it Communion. Four or five of us would come together and share our thoughts. I learned a lot.

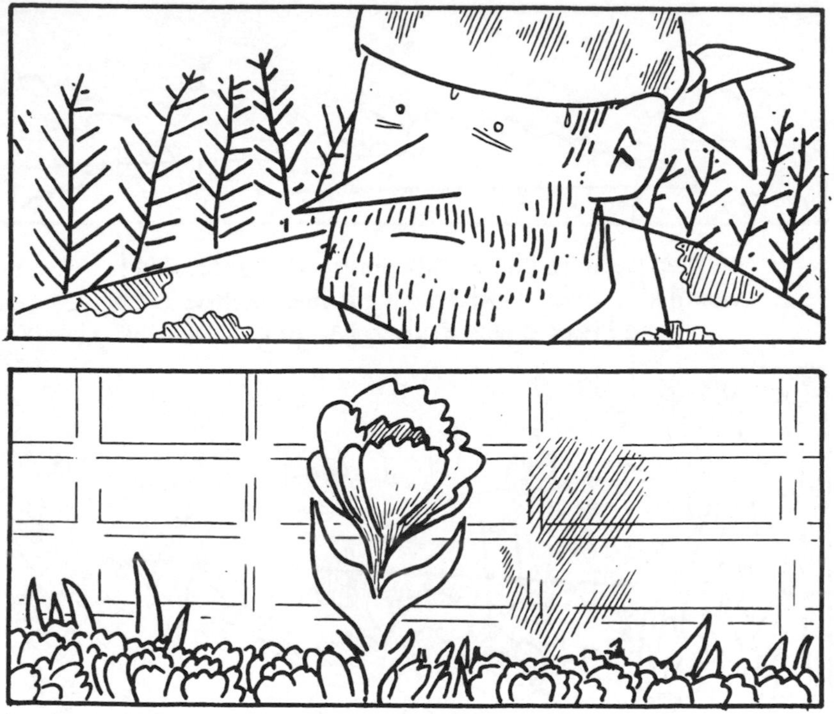

Communion became less frequent once Reverend Carpenter learned he had the ability to heal.

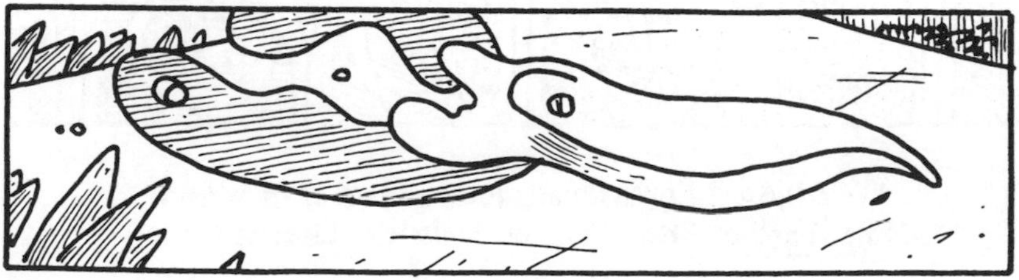

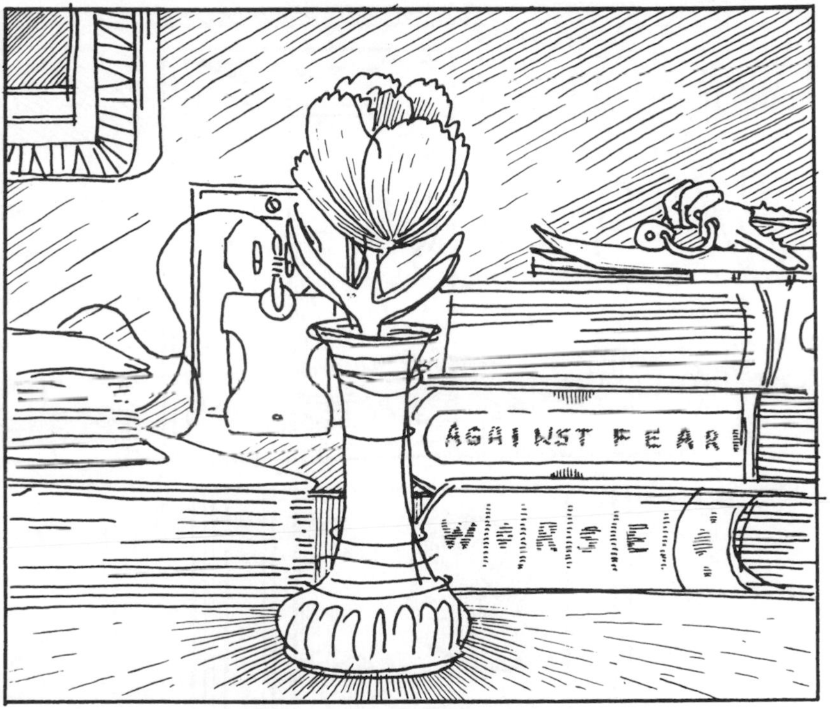
AGAINST FEAR
WORSE

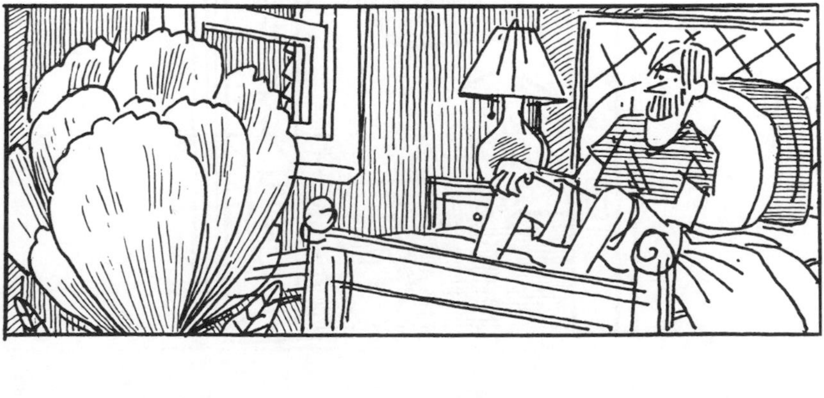

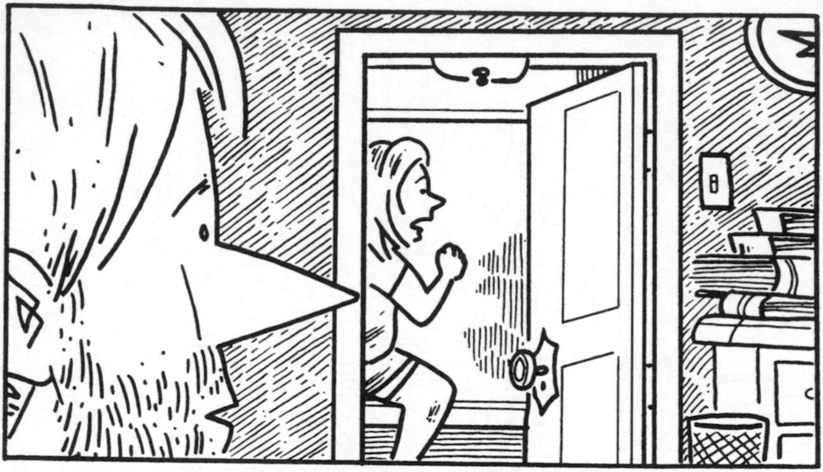

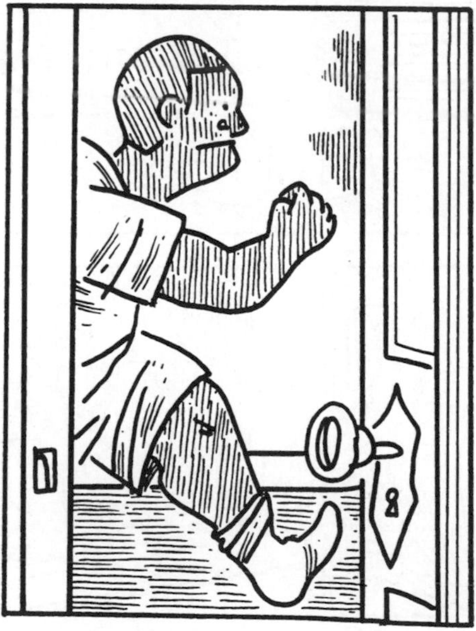

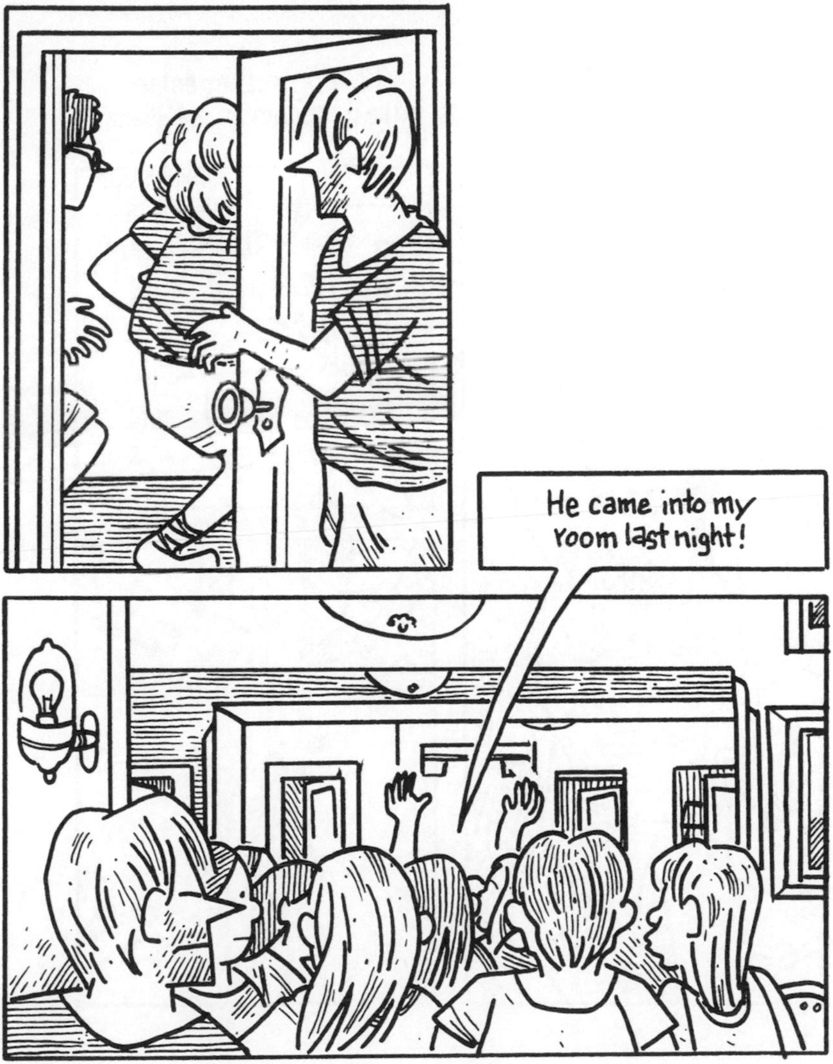
He came into my room last night!

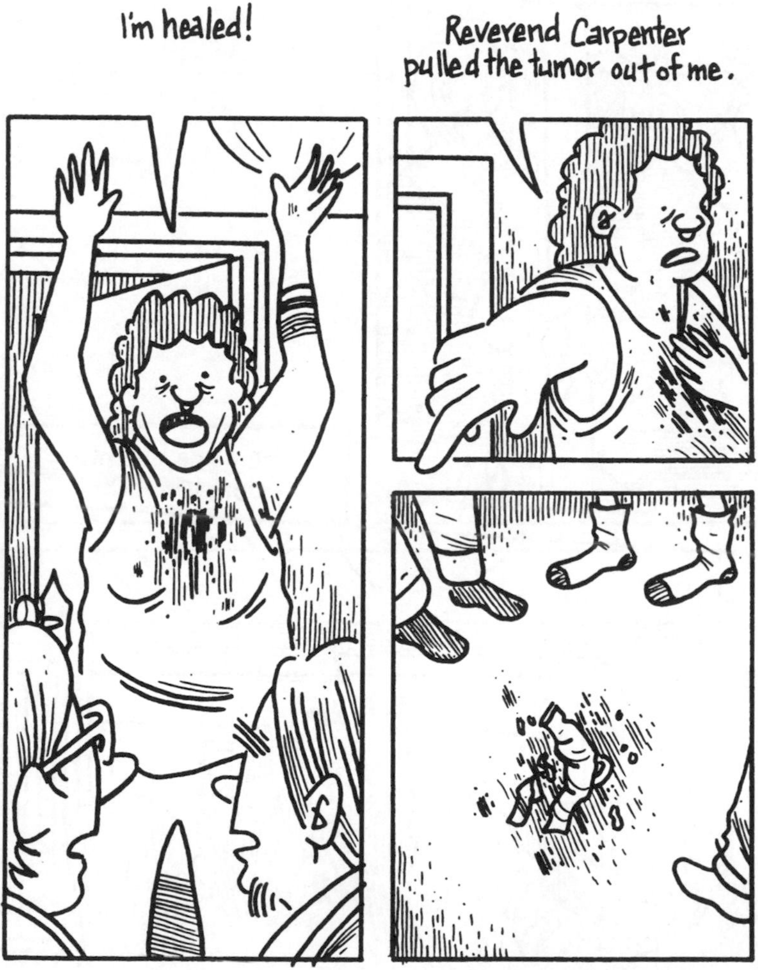
I'm healed!
Reverend Carpenter pulled the tumor out of me.

Who is this woman?

I've never seen her at morning praise or afternoon thanksgiving. What makes her so special?

He was here. In the church, but he can't even call me back?

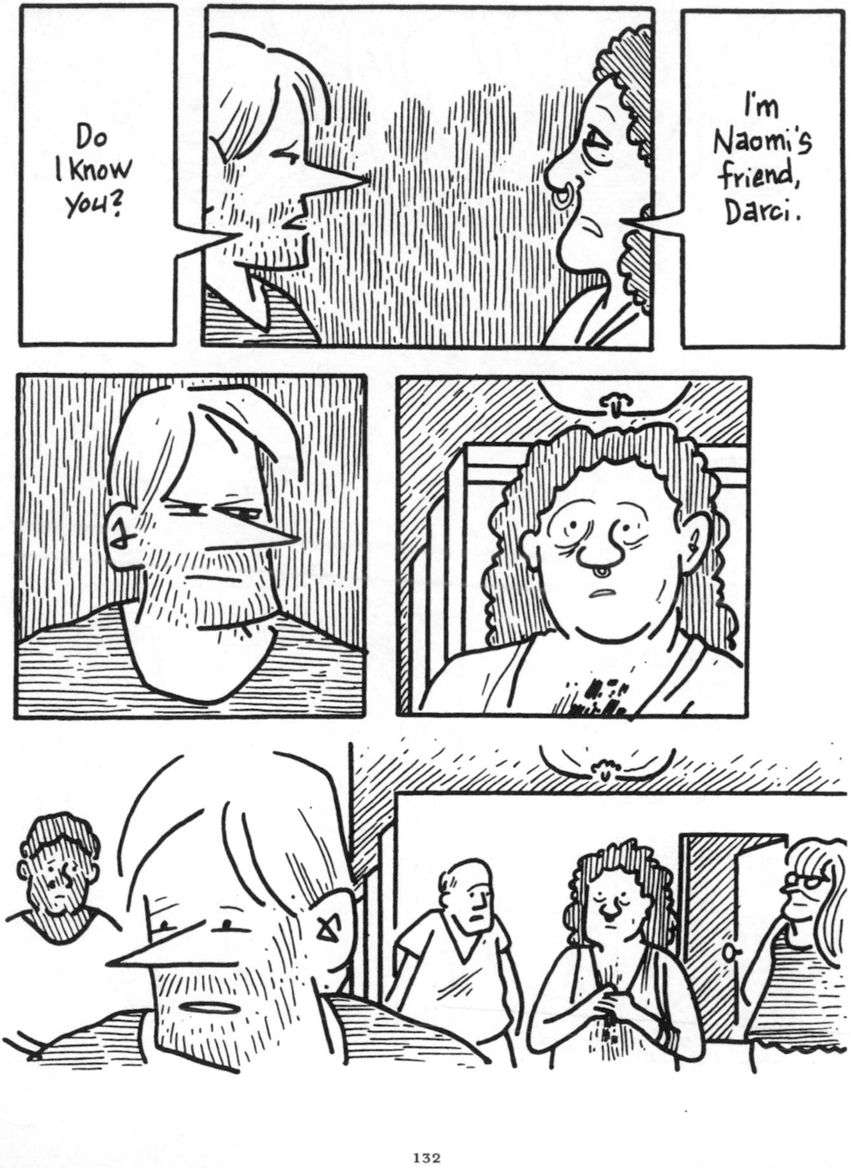
Do I know you?
I'm Naomi's friend, Darci.

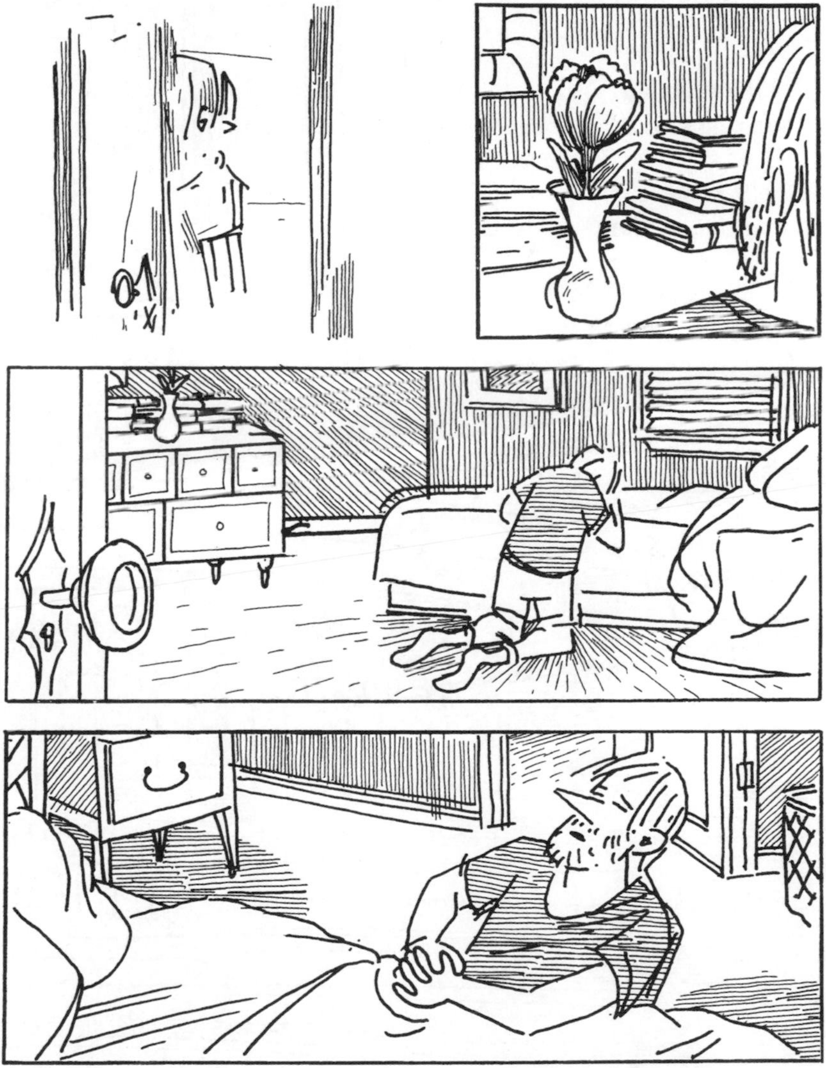

I didn't know
who else to call.

I just came back
from the doctor.

It sounds like I
have skin cancer.

On my neck.

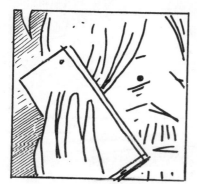

There are more than 3.5 million cases of basal and squamous cell skin cancer diagnosed in this country each year. Who's to say I'm not one of them.

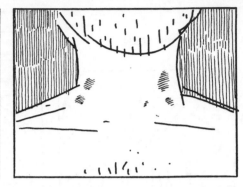

My aunt had some of that removed once.

I trust you made an appointment to have it removed?

My faith will heal me.

I put my trust in the Lord.

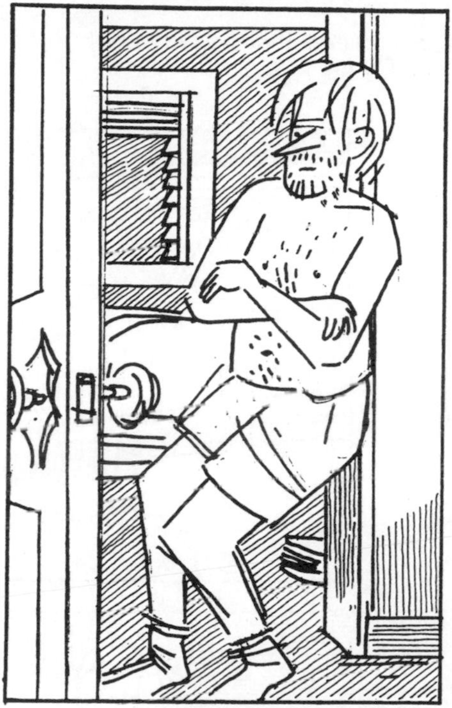

We don't lock our doors in our church. That's one reason why Hannah's app has been so successful.

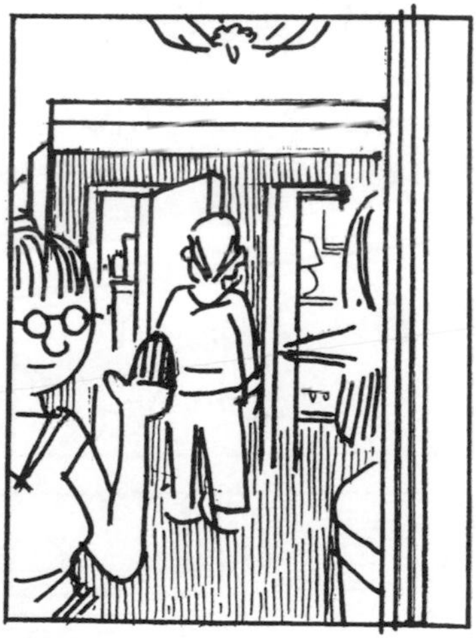

We don't keep secrets from each other.

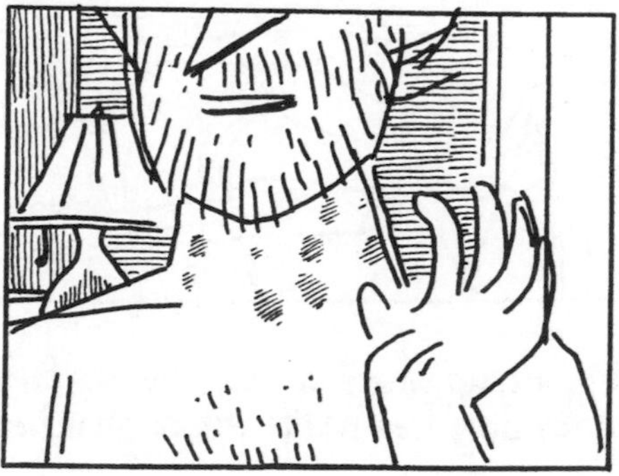

Reverend Carpenter understands this.

That is why he sent out an email with new health guidelines for the church.

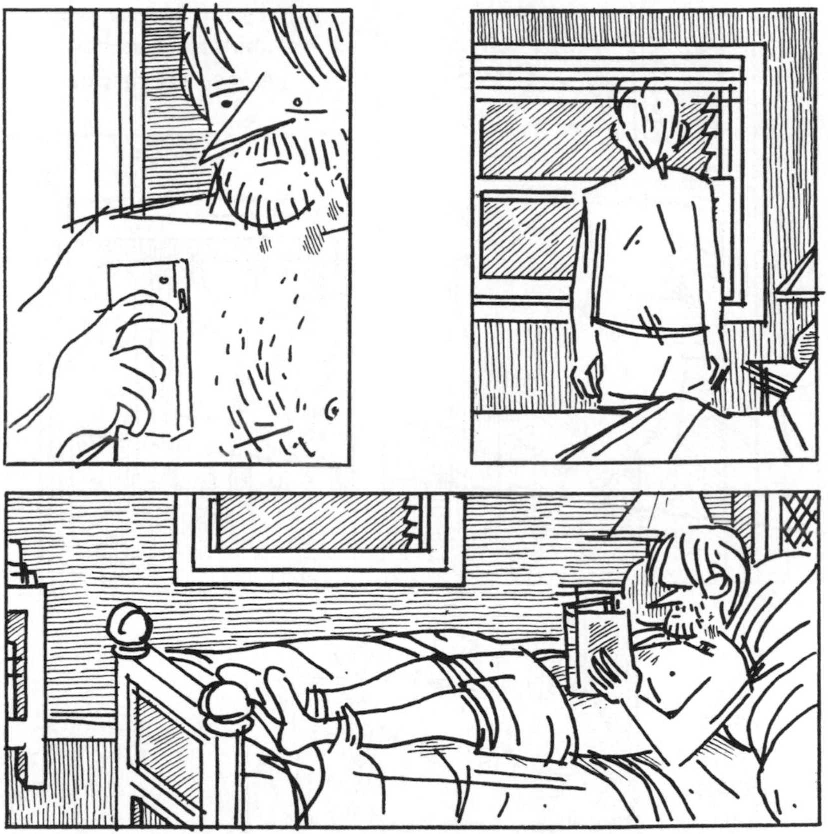

He's stepping up where our country has failed us and is providing free healthcare to all members.

What is this shit?

Oh.

You startled me.

I thought it might be Reverend Carpenter.

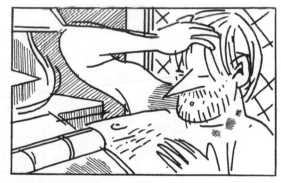

I wish! I'd like to meet him.

I have some questions about these "health guidelines."

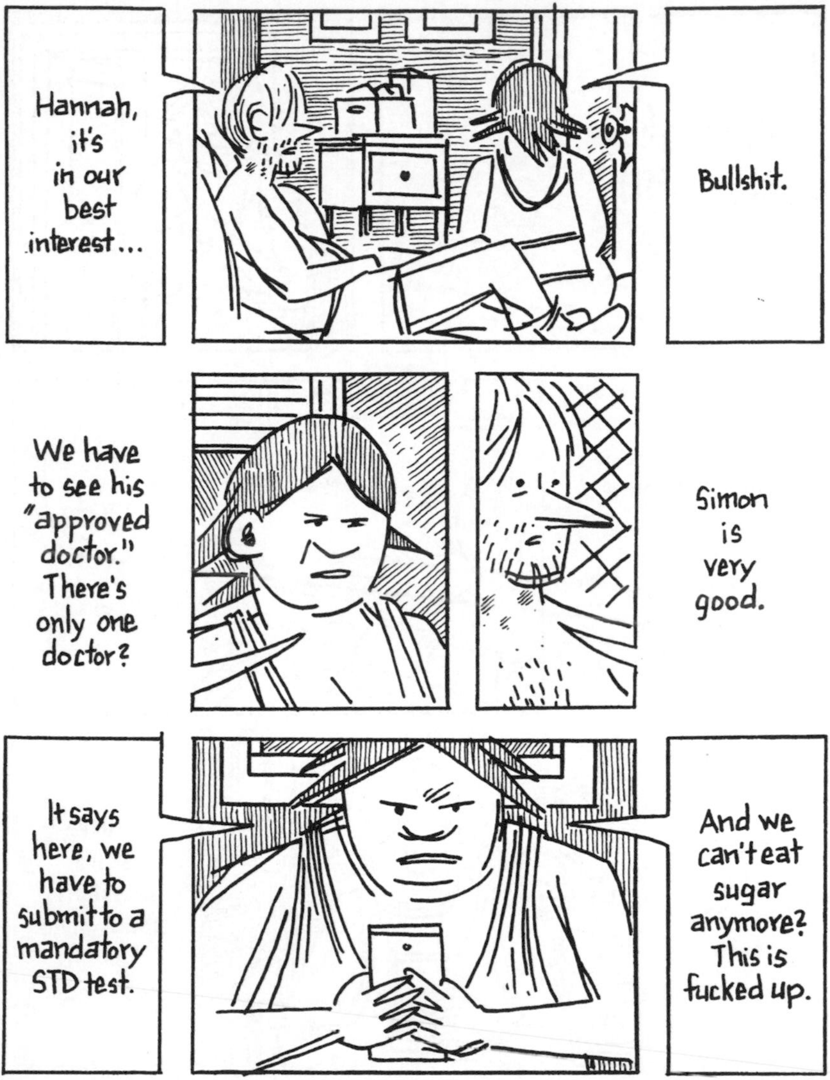
Hannah, it's in our best interest...
Bullshit.
We have to see his "approved doctor." There's only one doctor?
Simon is very good.
It says here, we have to submit to a mandatory STD test.
And we can't eat sugar anymore? This is fucked up.

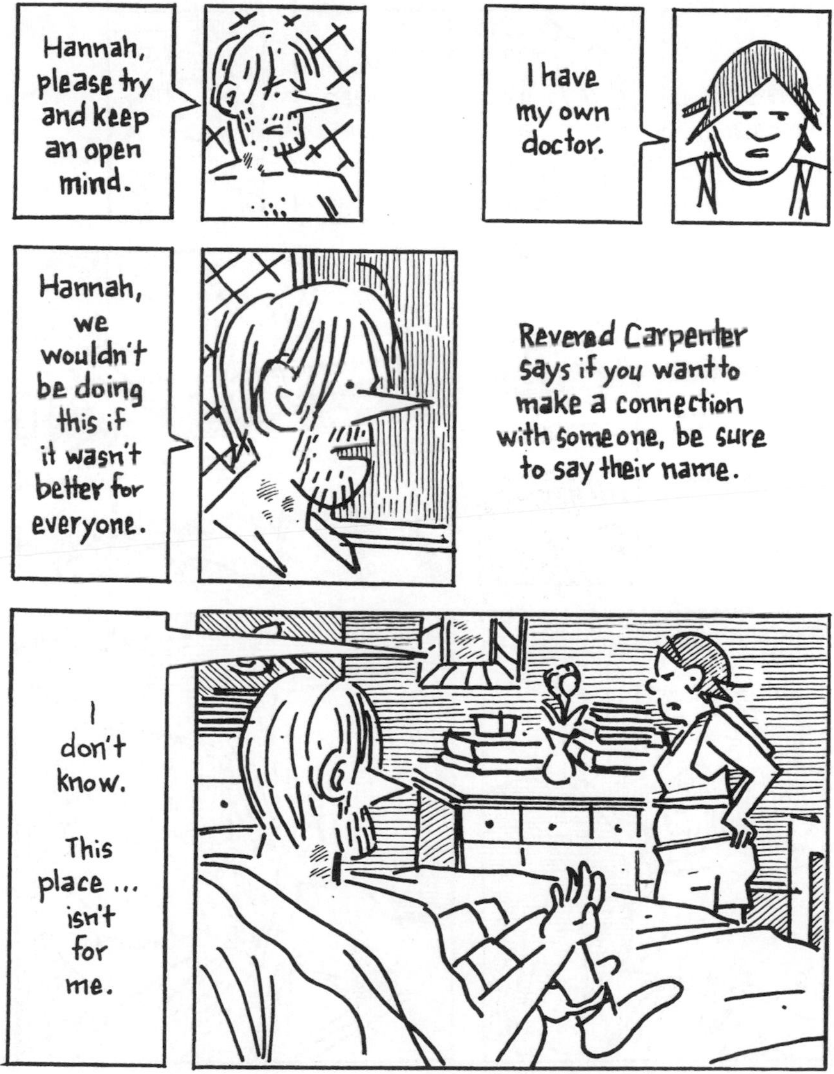

Hannah, please try and keep an open mind.
I have my own doctor.
Hannah, we wouldn't be doing this if it wasn't better for everyone.
Revered Carpenter says if you want to make a connection with someone, be sure to say their name.
I don't know.
This place ... isn't for me.

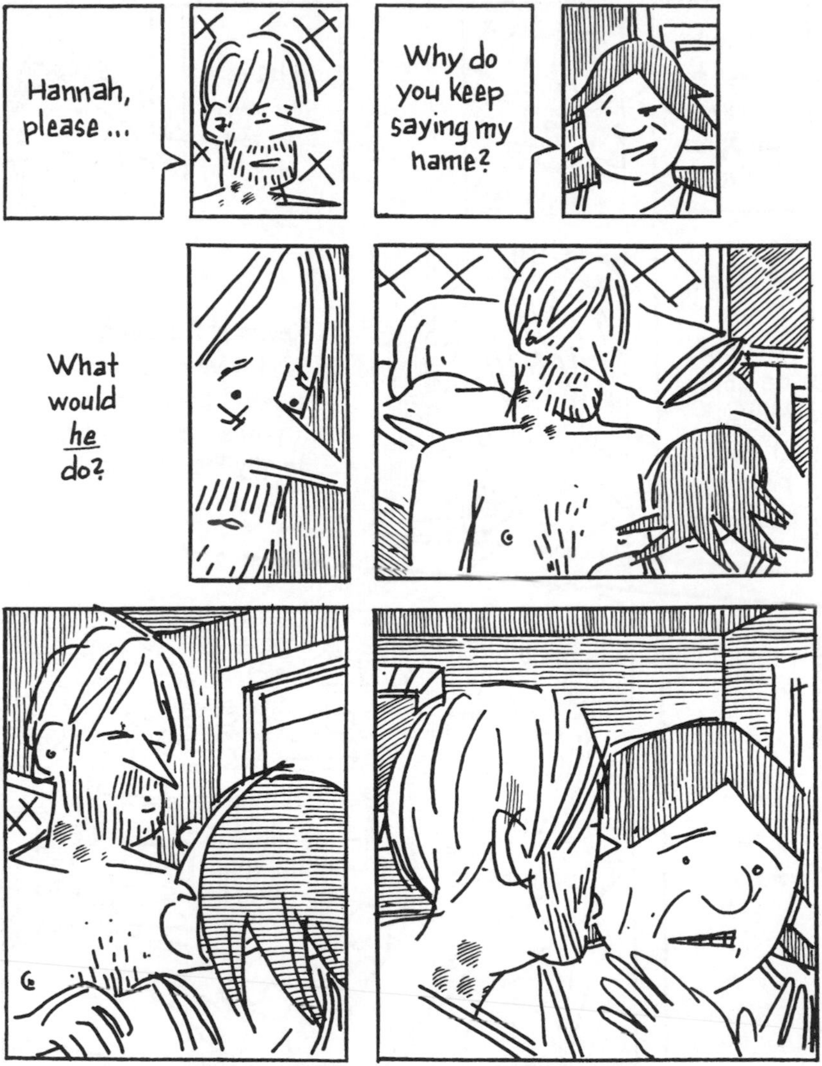
Hannah, please ...
Why do you keep saying my name?
What would he do?

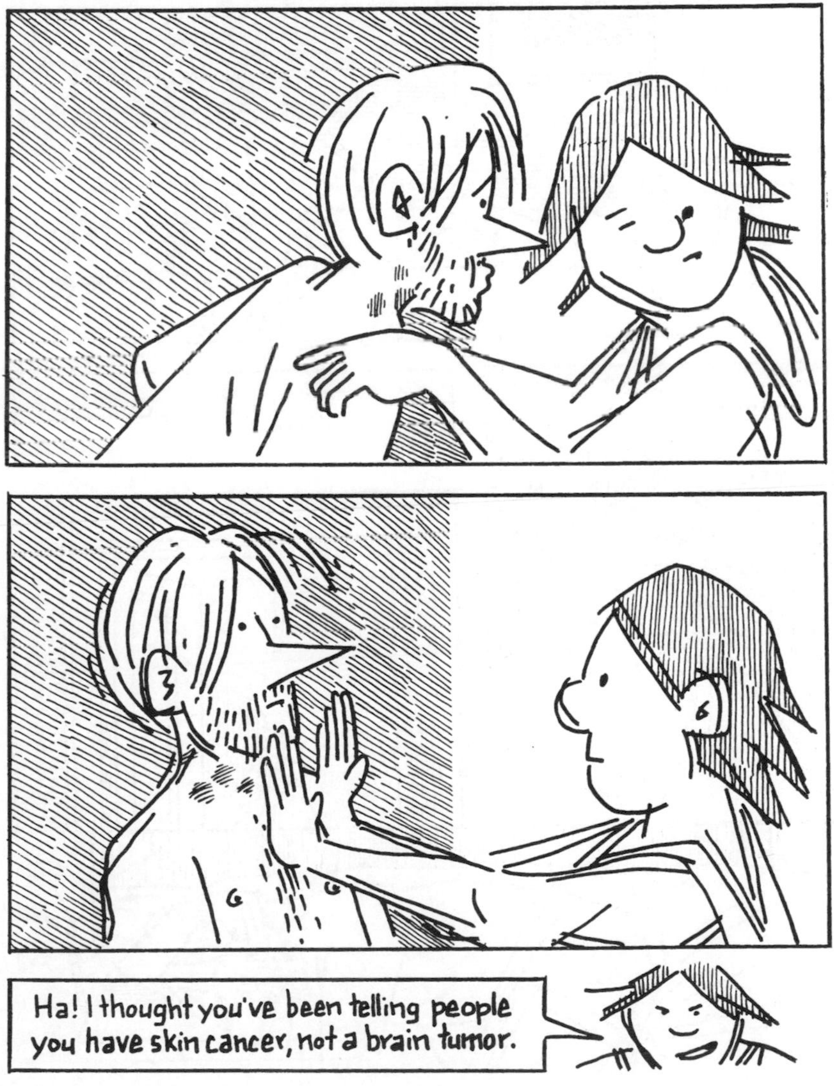
Ha! I thought you've been telling people you have skin cancer, not a brain tumor.

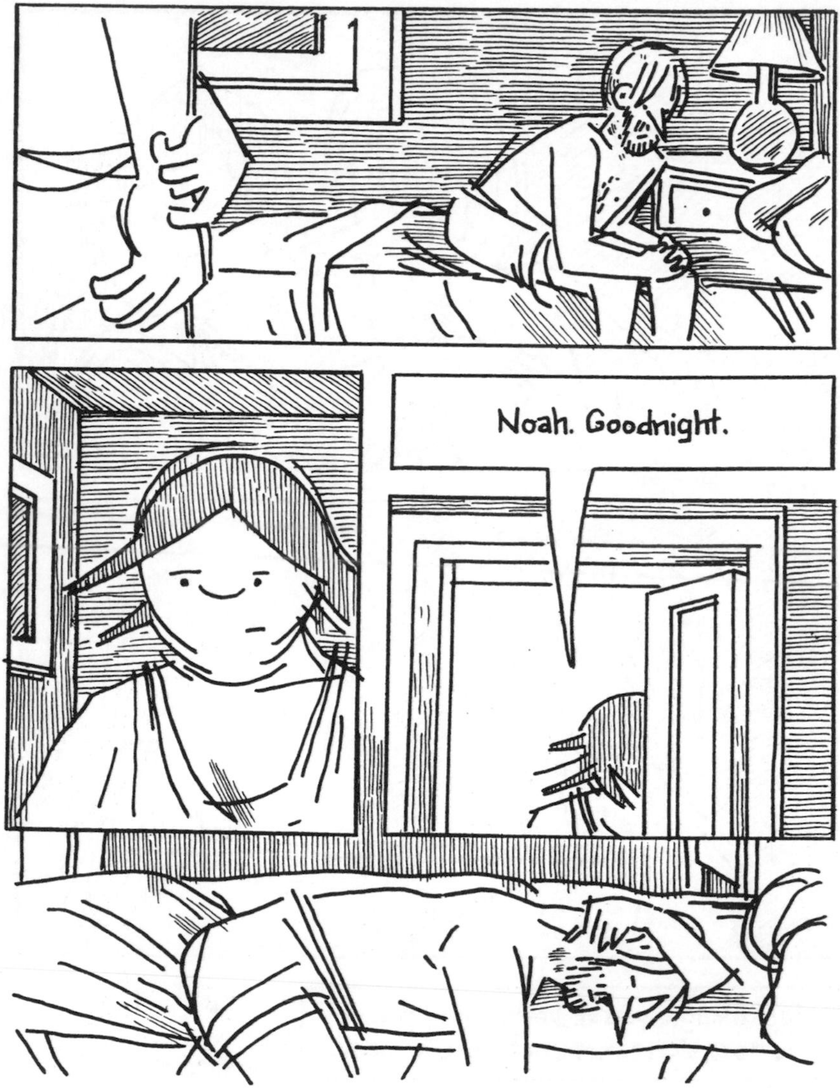
Noah. Goodnight.

For once, I sleep all through the night. The second my head falls on the pillow, I'm gone. It's draining to be someone else.

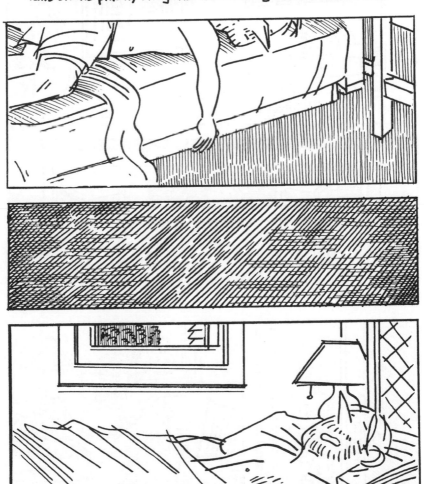

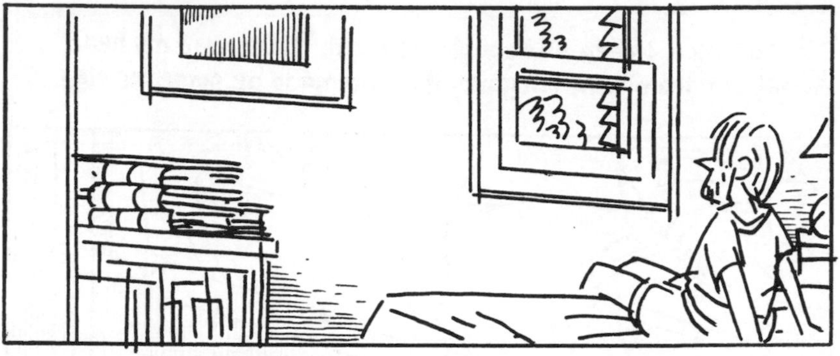

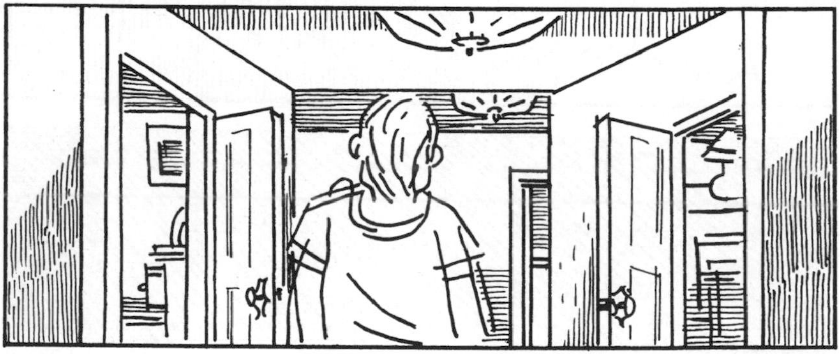

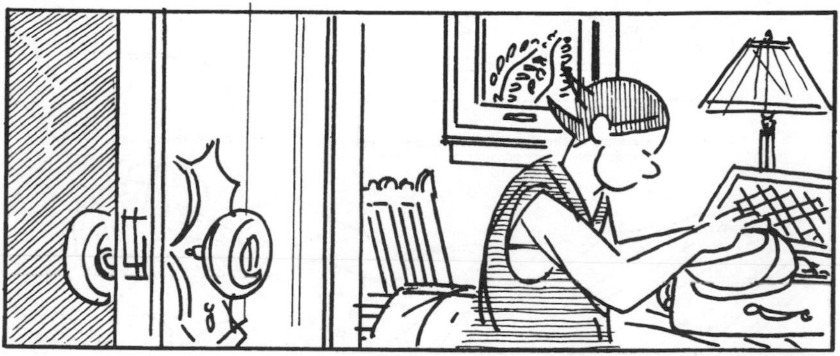

The only reason you have those clothes is because we gave them to you.

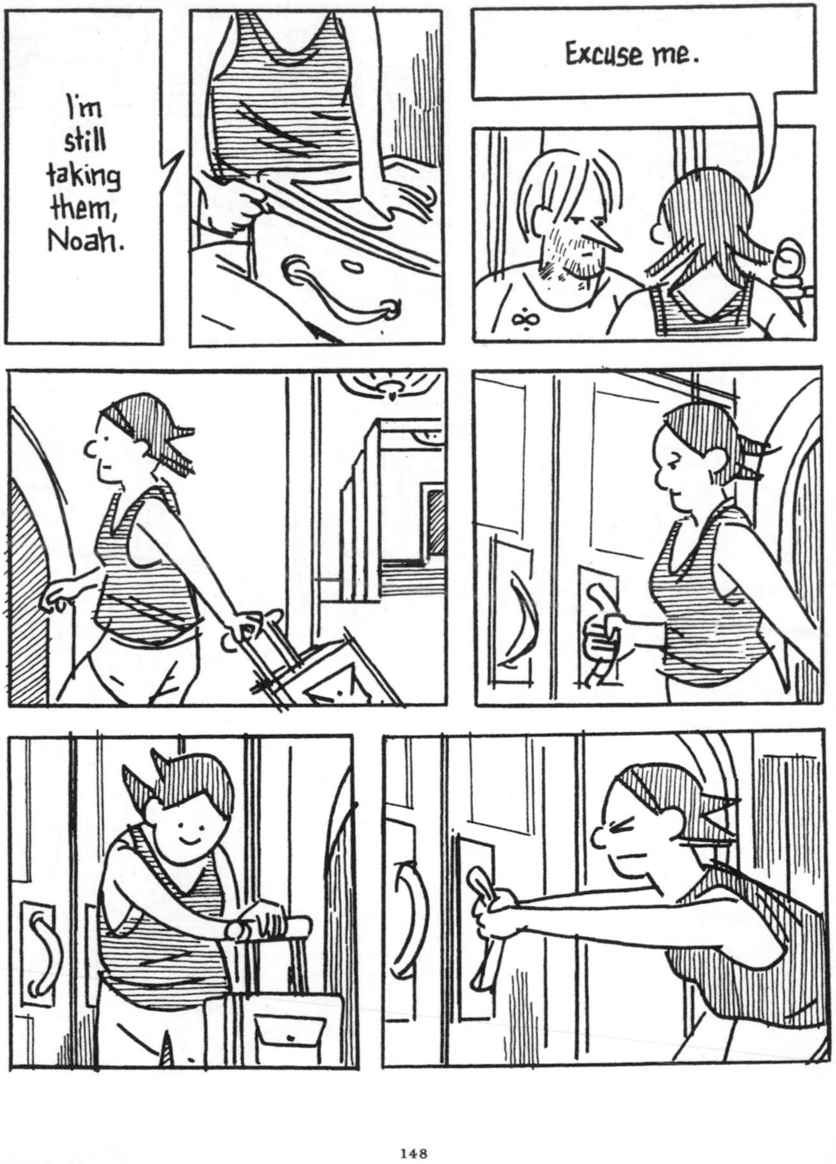
I'm still taking them, Noah.
Excuse me.

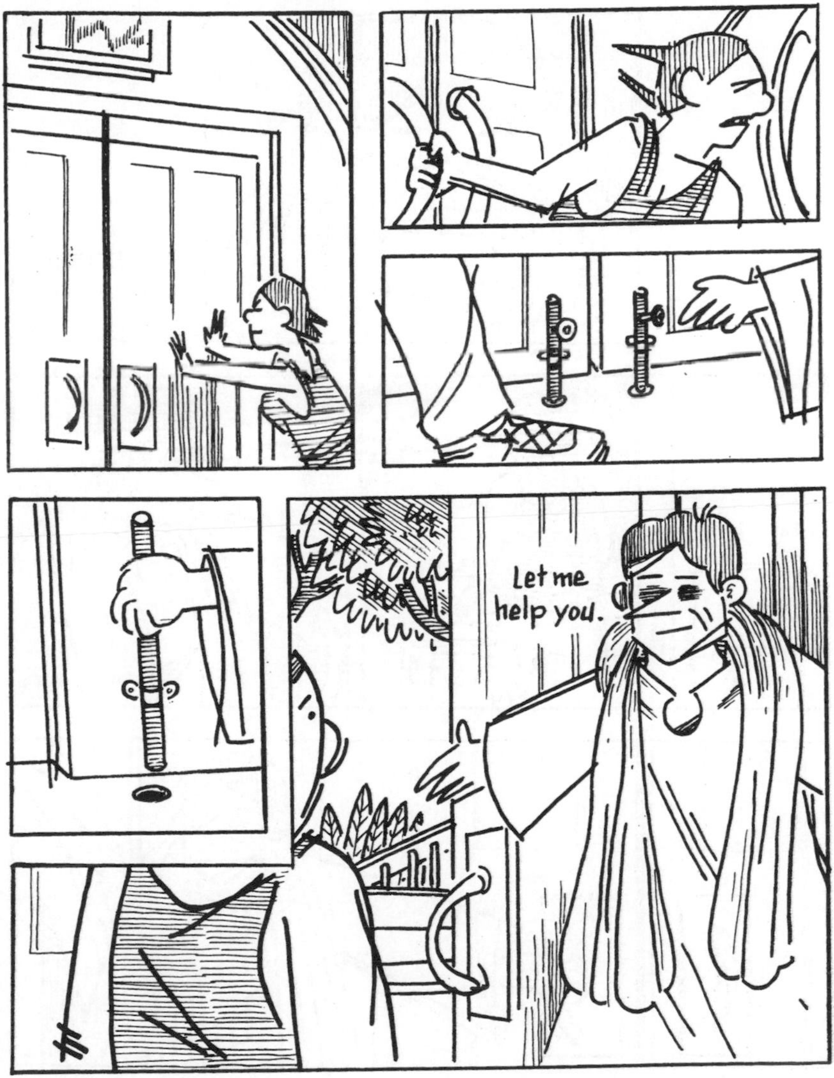
Let me help you.

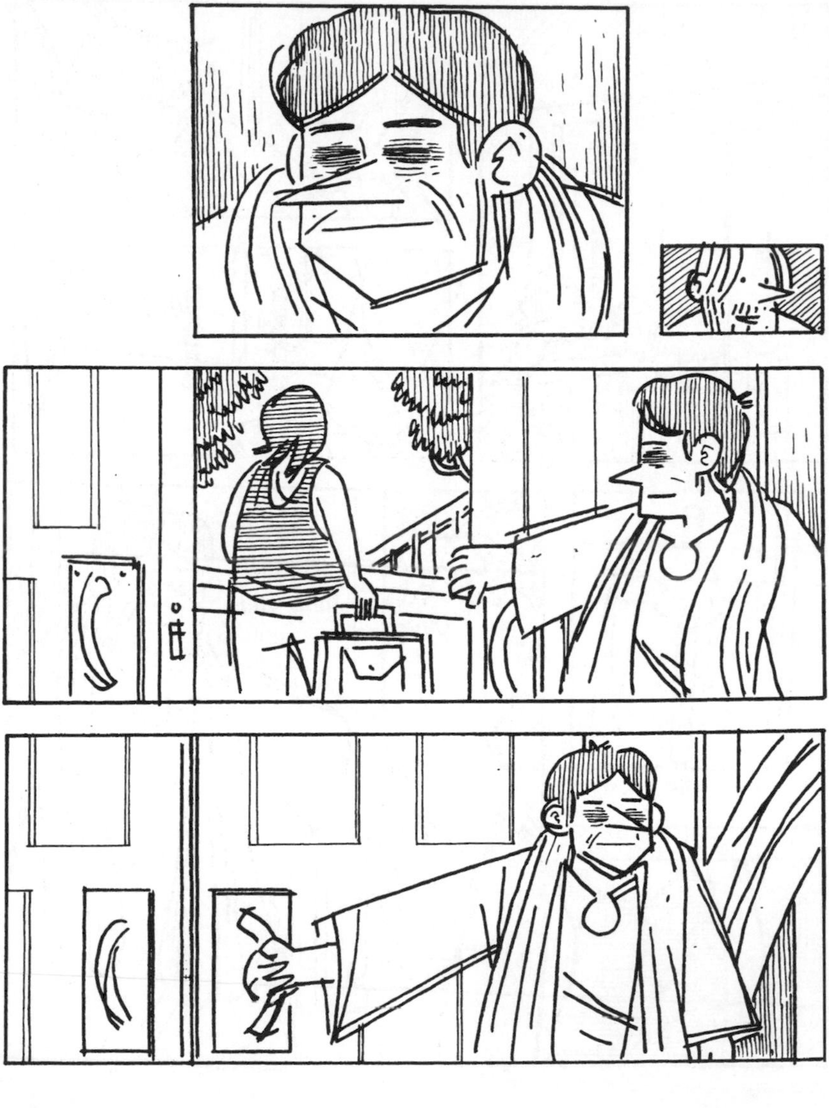

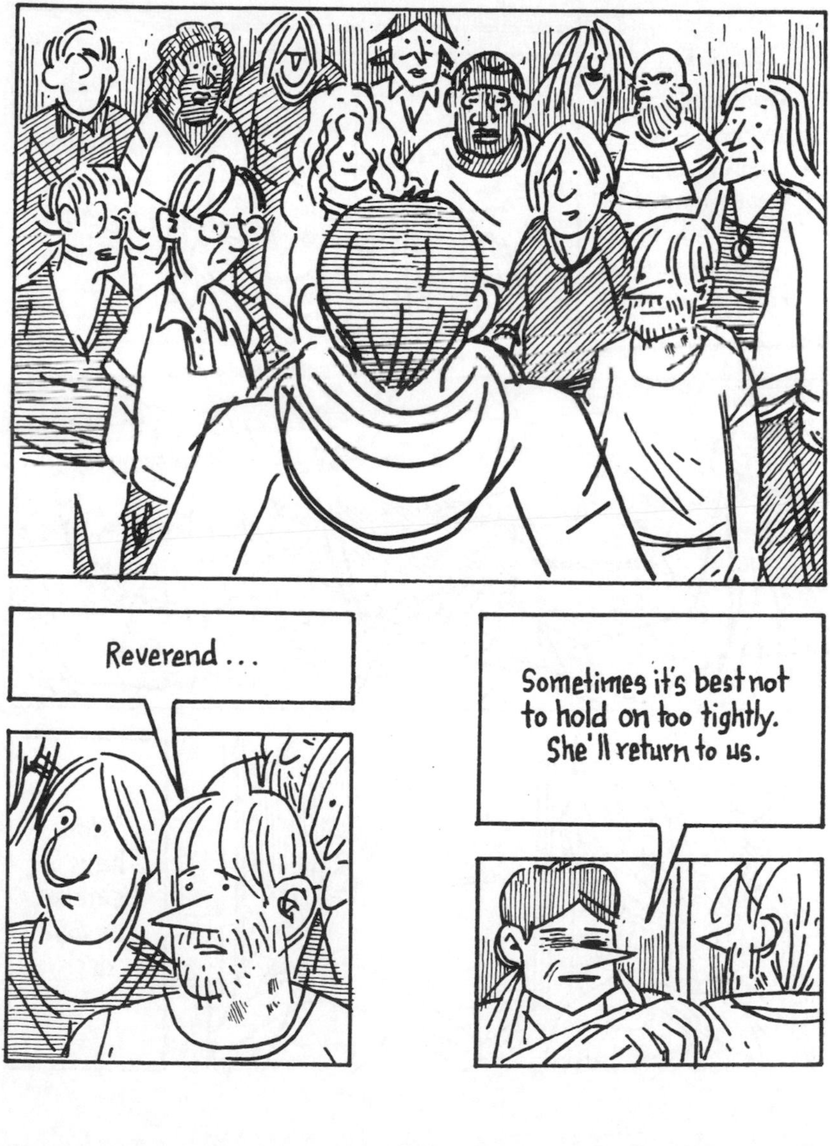
Reverend . . .
Sometimes it's best not to hold on too tightly. She'll return to us.

I want to apologize to everyone for being gone for so long. I promise to be here for you from now on.

Noah. Thank you for holding everyone together in my absence.

You have a cancer in your neck.

Be gone.
Be gone.
Be gone.

Be gone.
Be gone.
Be gone. Be gone.
Be gone.
Be gone.

Be gone.

Be gone.
Be gone.
Be gone.

Be gone!
Be Gone!
BE GONE. BE
GONE, CANCER!

BE GONE
CANCER!

HOLY
HALLELUJAH!

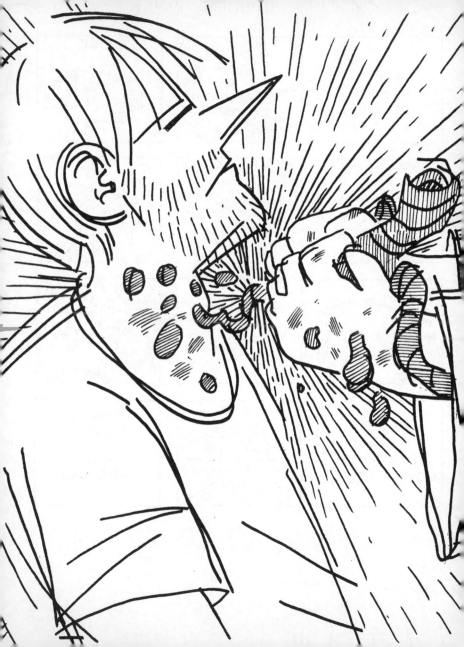

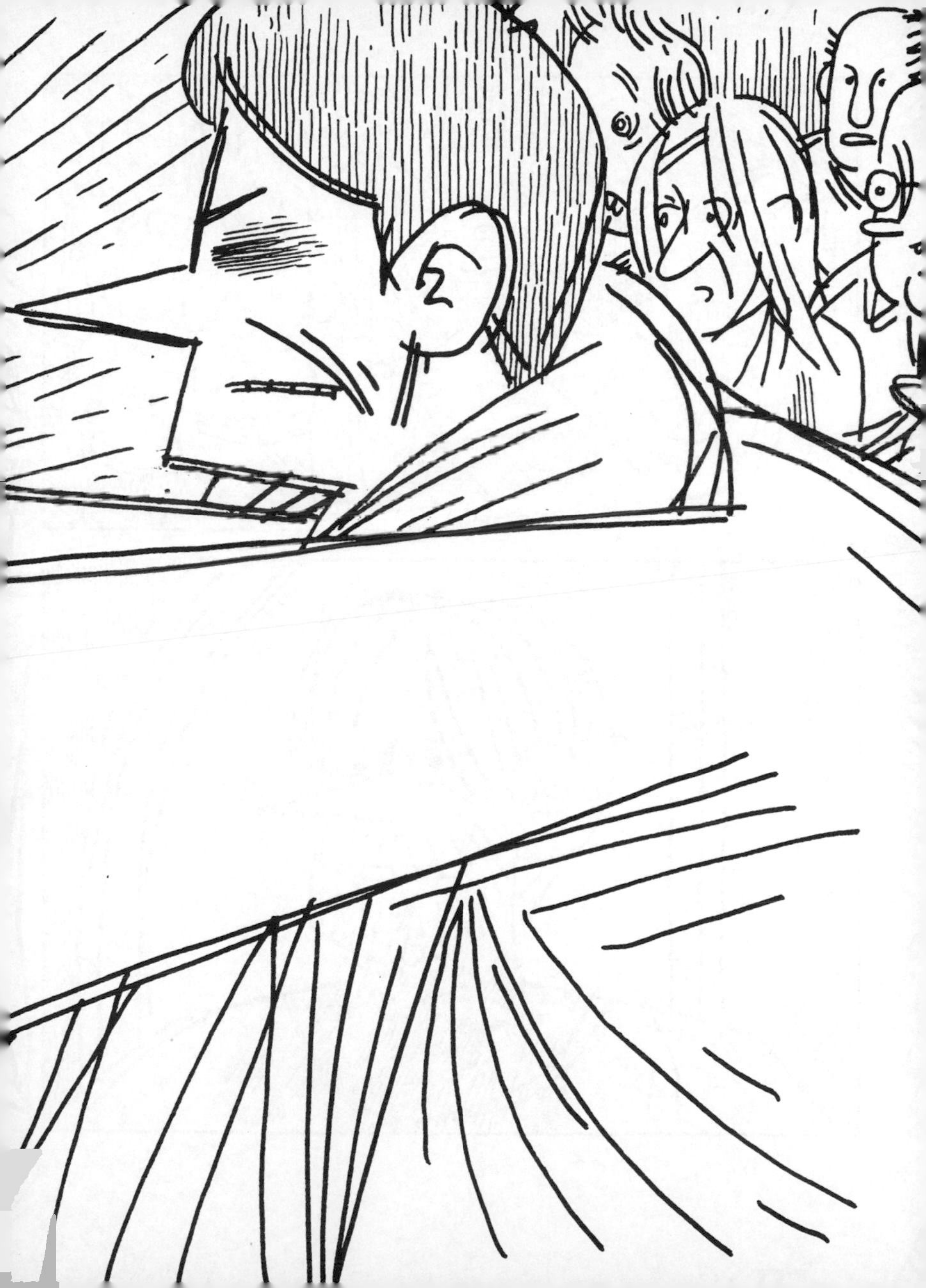

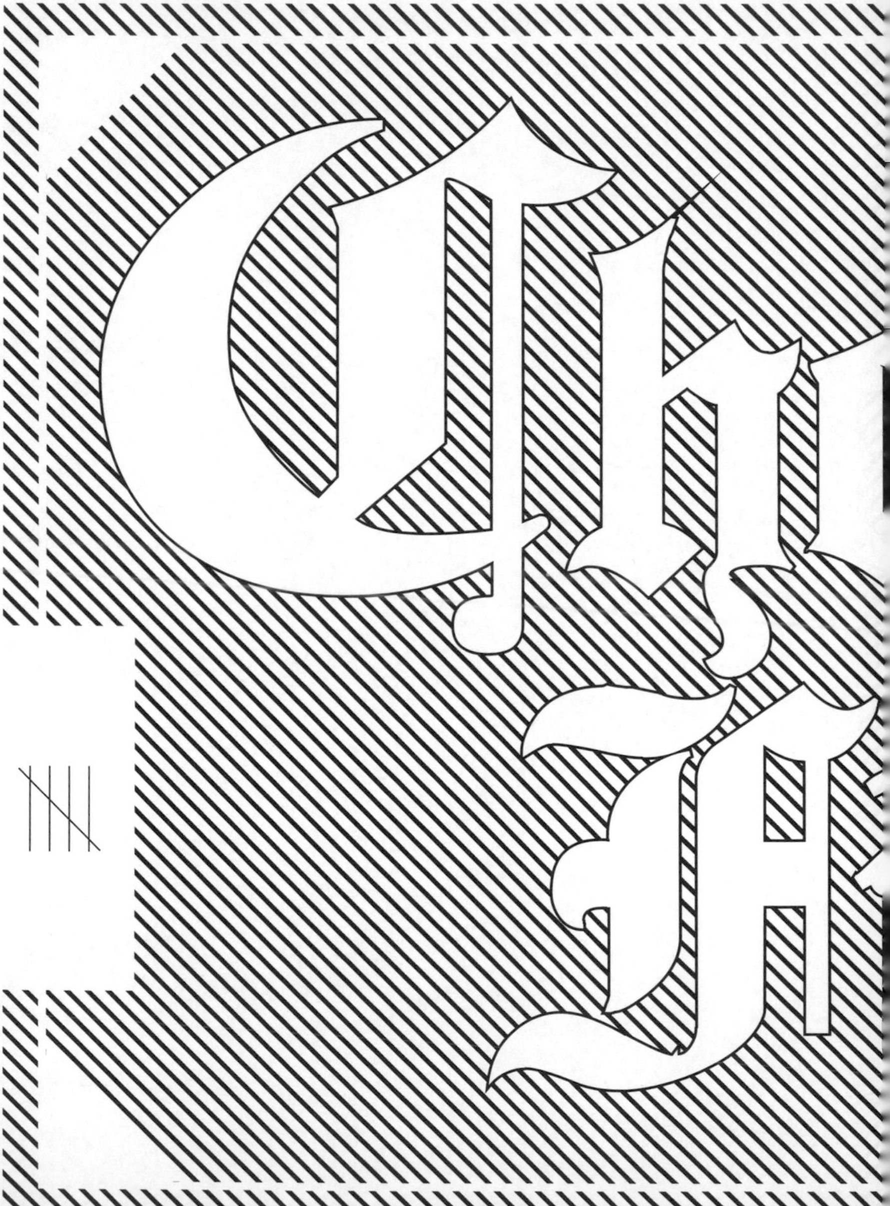

pter

ue

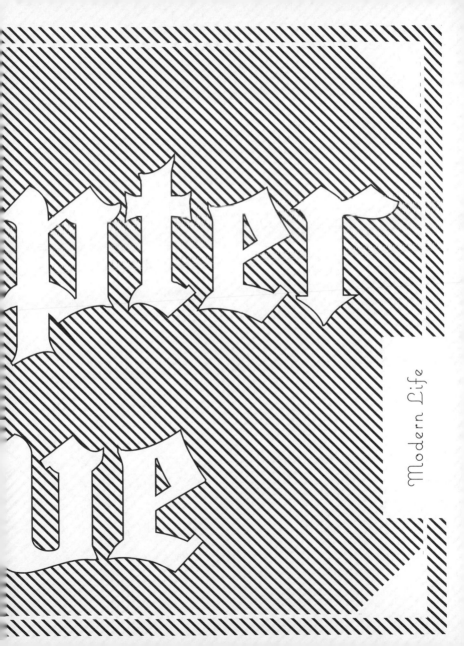

Modern Life

There wasn't much to look at on the ceiling
in the office where I worked.

Except right above where I sat, there was a wire that came out
behind one panel and then went back under another panel.

The wire was actually two wires twisted together.

An aqua wire and a white wire that from a distance looked like a solid sky blue.

I remember looking and thinking about that sky blue wire every day I sat at my desk.

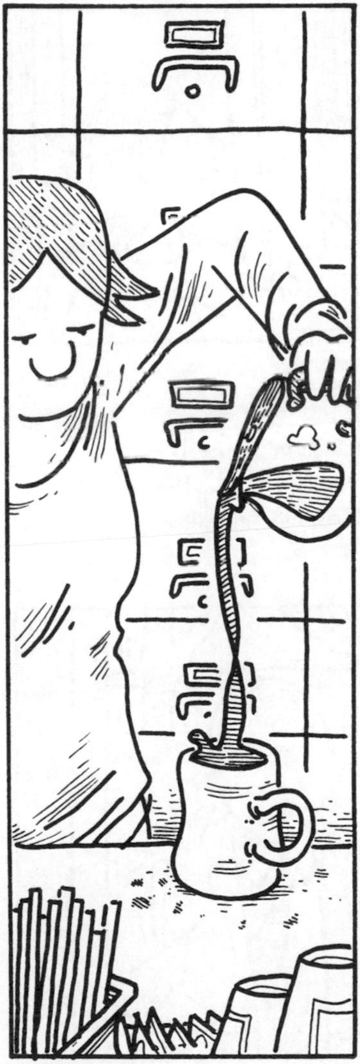

I was so bored.

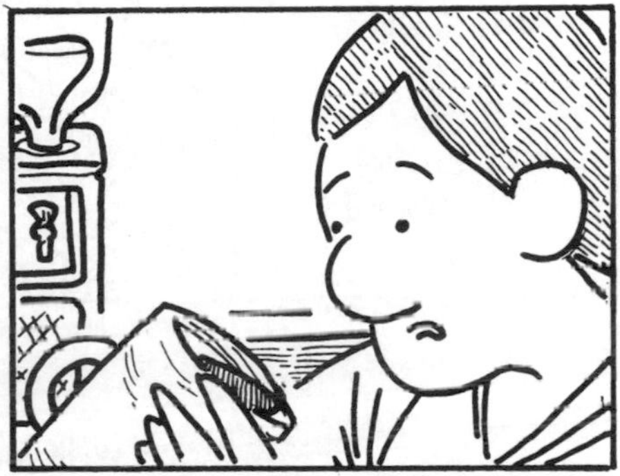

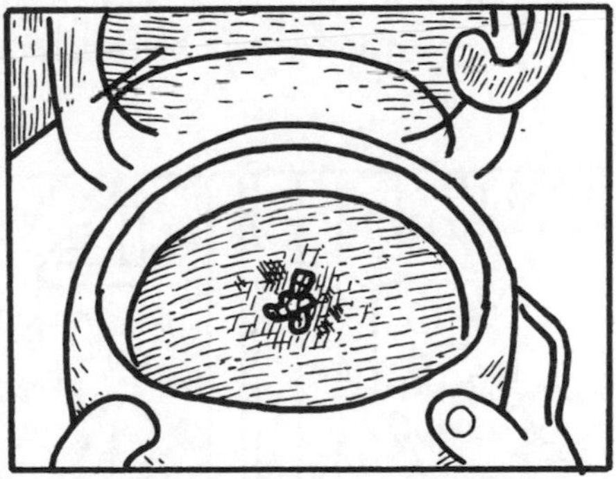

My co-workers didn't notice the sky blue wire. I asked a few of them and I was given funny looks that made me think that perhaps I was hallucinating.

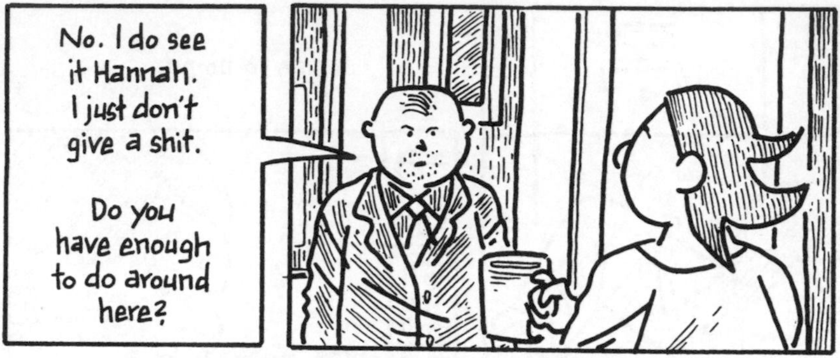
No. I do see it Hannah. I just don't give a shit.
Do you have enough to do around here?

I saw Parker walk into a door as he tried to push it open even though the word "PULL" was written in large block letters near the handle.

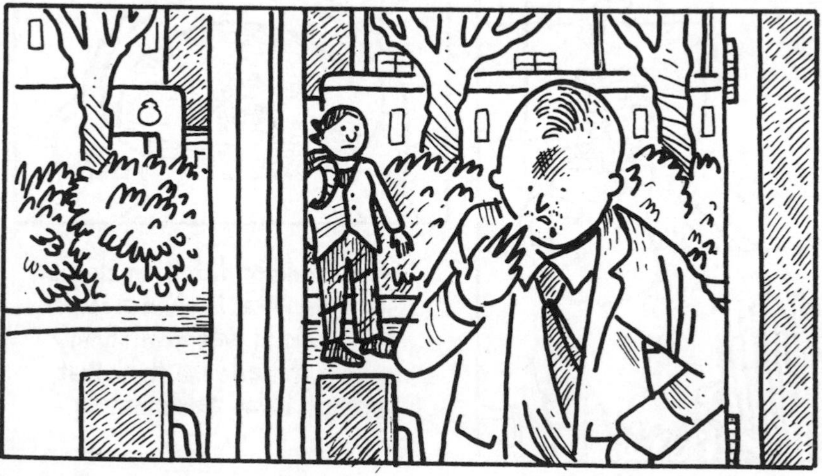

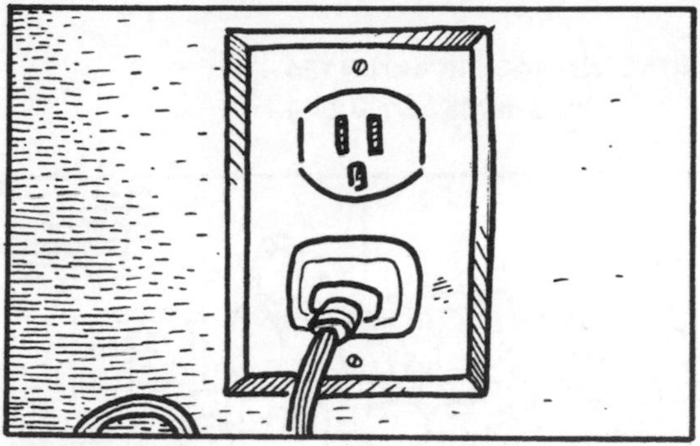

This morning he was using the toaster while filling the sink with water.

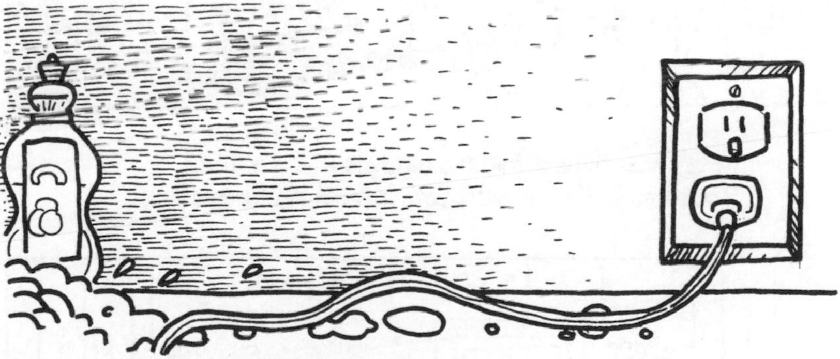

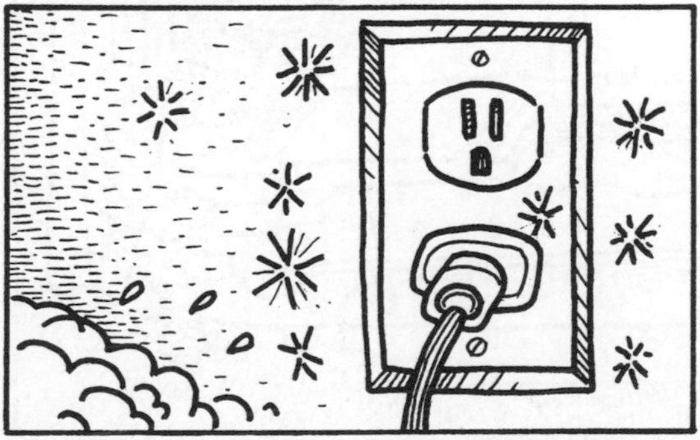

He moved the toaster closer to the sink in order to monitor his bagel while he scrubbed.

I imagined Parker driving through a red light
and being hit by a truck. Or a bus.

He's mentioned that his parents are divorced,
but I think they would both attend his funeral.

Sometimes he leaves work early to go play softball. These teammates would be at the funeral too.

I would attend.

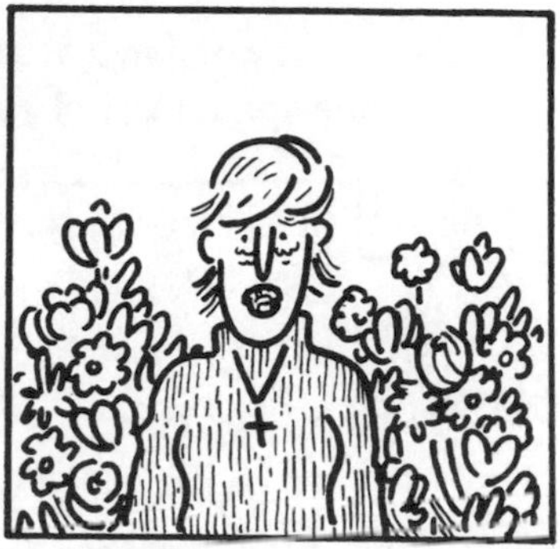

Most of the office would, and there would be no reason for me to stay behind.

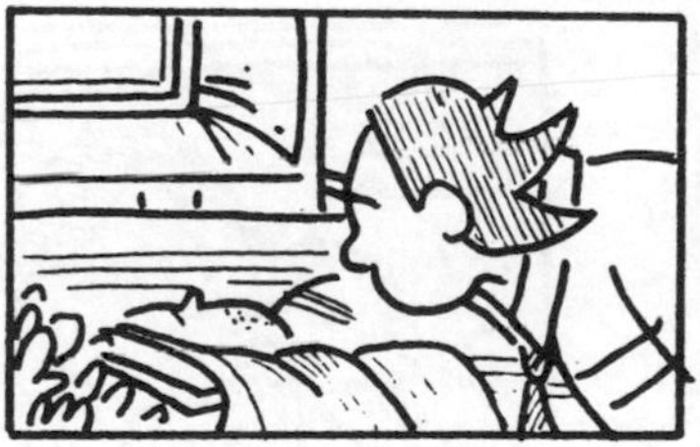

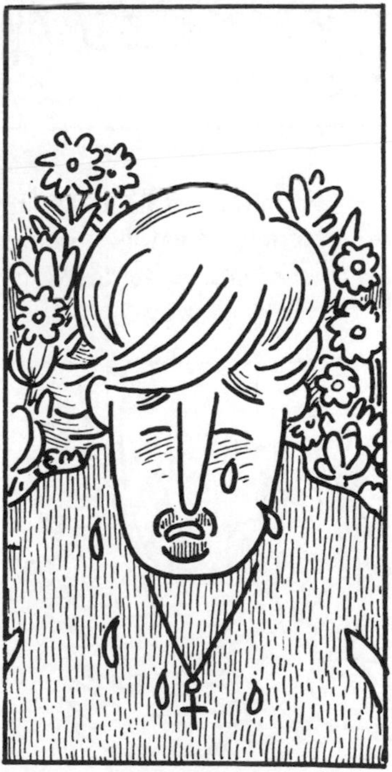

His girlfriend Terry is the type to organize a beautiful ceremony.

I met Terry at an office happy-hour once.
She spent most of the gathering talking only to me.

I think that it's been long enough, Hannah. You need to start seeing someone new.

Her clothes looked like they were brand new. Better than brand new somehow.

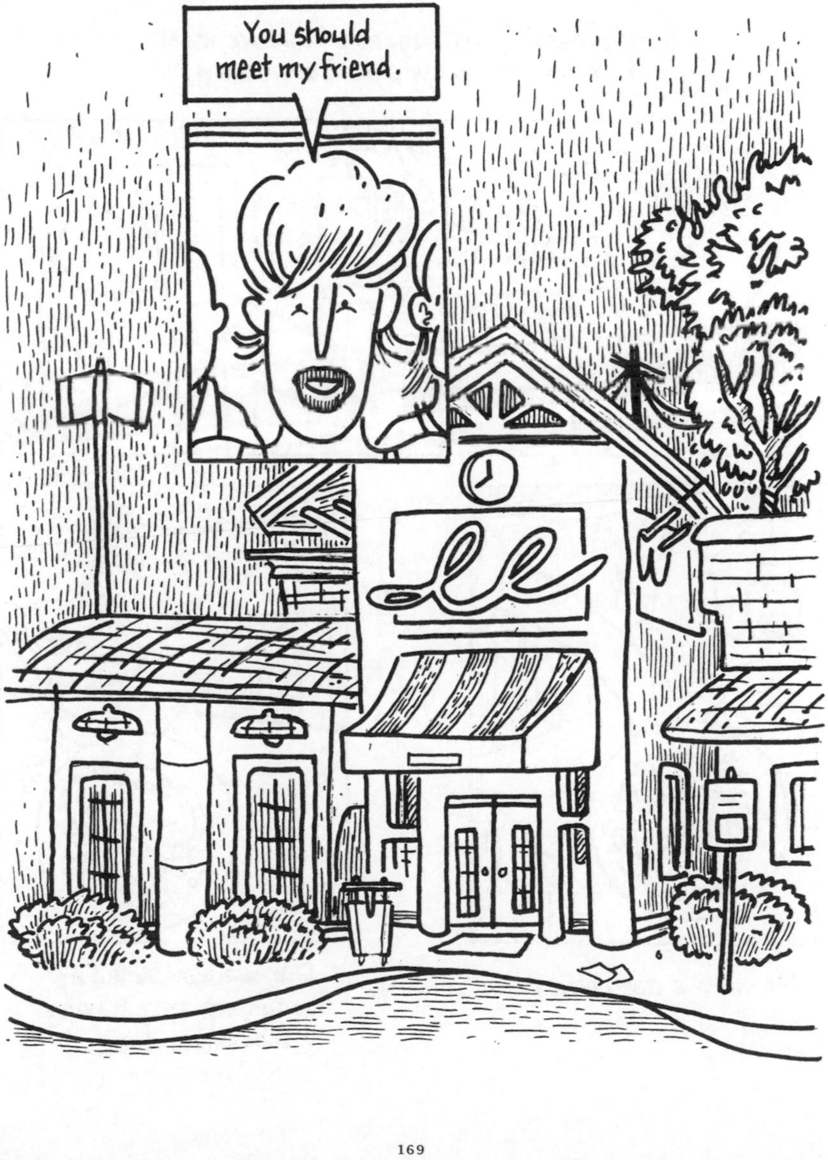
You should meet my friend.

Terry's friend, Peter, suggested that we meet
at the only chain restaurant downtown.

He wore a dark blue suit.

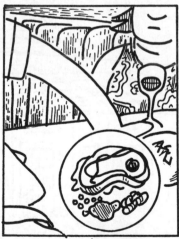

Our waitress acted as
though we were having
a business dinner.

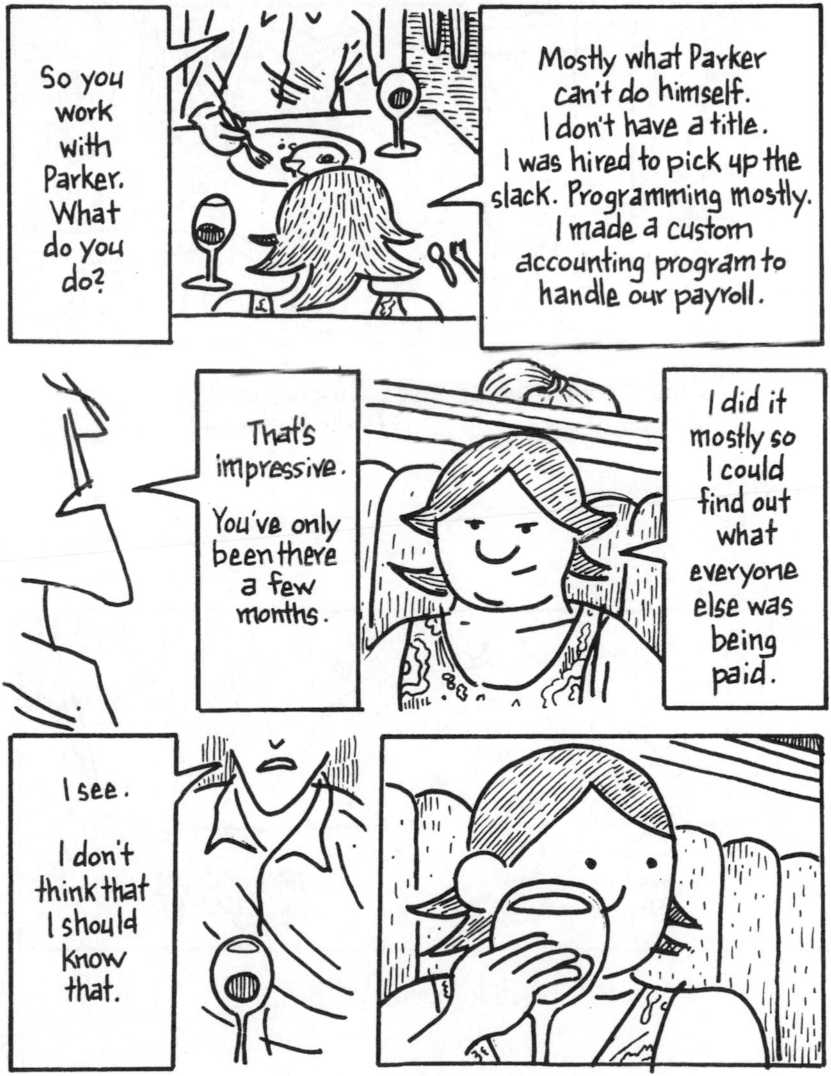
So you work with Parker. What do you do?
Mostly what Parker can't do himself. I don't have a title. I was hired to pick up the slack. Programming mostly. I made a custom accounting program to handle our payroll.
That's impressive.
You've only been there a few months.
I did it mostly so I could find out what everyone else was being paid.
I see.
I don't think that I should know that.

After a couple drinks, and before our dessert arrived, Peter got up to go to the bathroom.

He didn't come back.

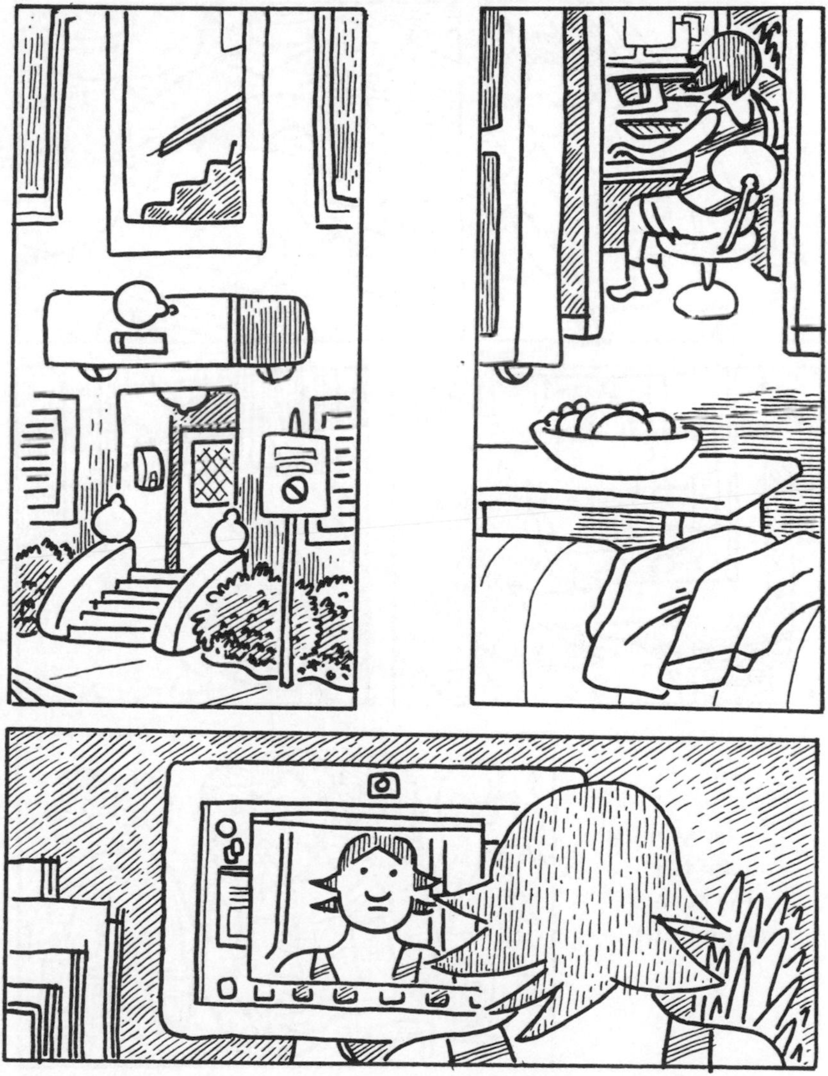

Terry
wasn't at
the next
happy-hour.

The bar we went to had four or five other groups of co-workers drinking together.

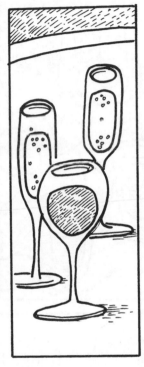

One table had four servers and cooks from a nearby restaurant. They all drank liquor.

At the bar a woman and her friends drank champaign together. They toasted and drank in unison.

The corner table had two couples talking fiercely with each other. They all drank beer.

My table drank beer. I had a nearly full glass in front of me, when the server came back with the second round.

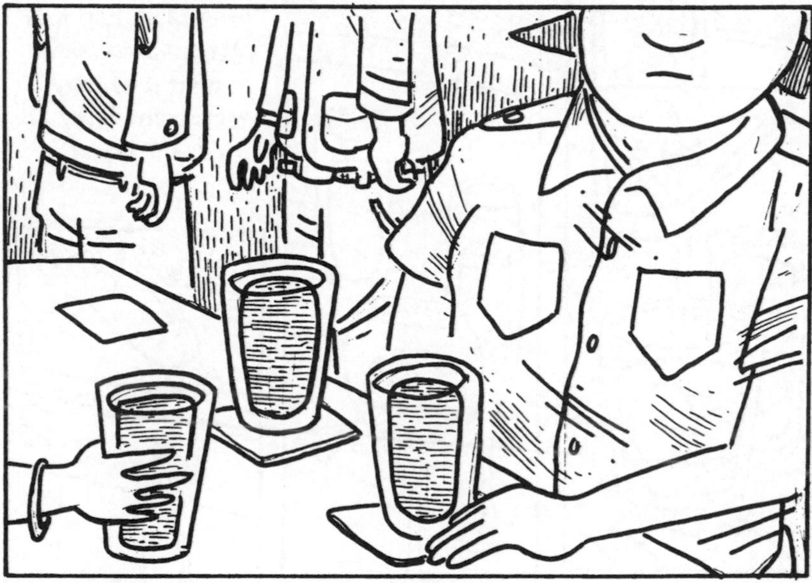

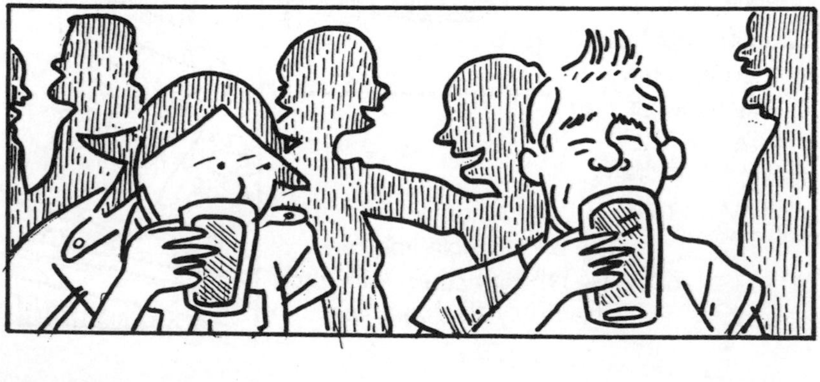

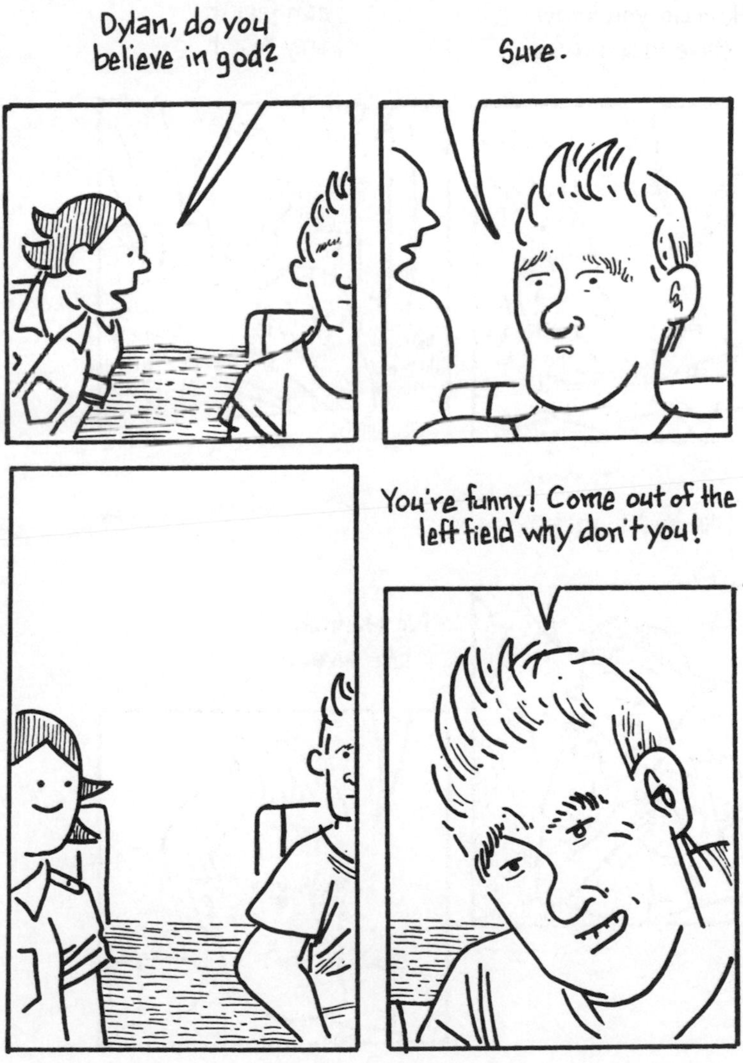
Dylan, do you believe in god?
Sure.
You're funny! Come out of the left field why don't you!

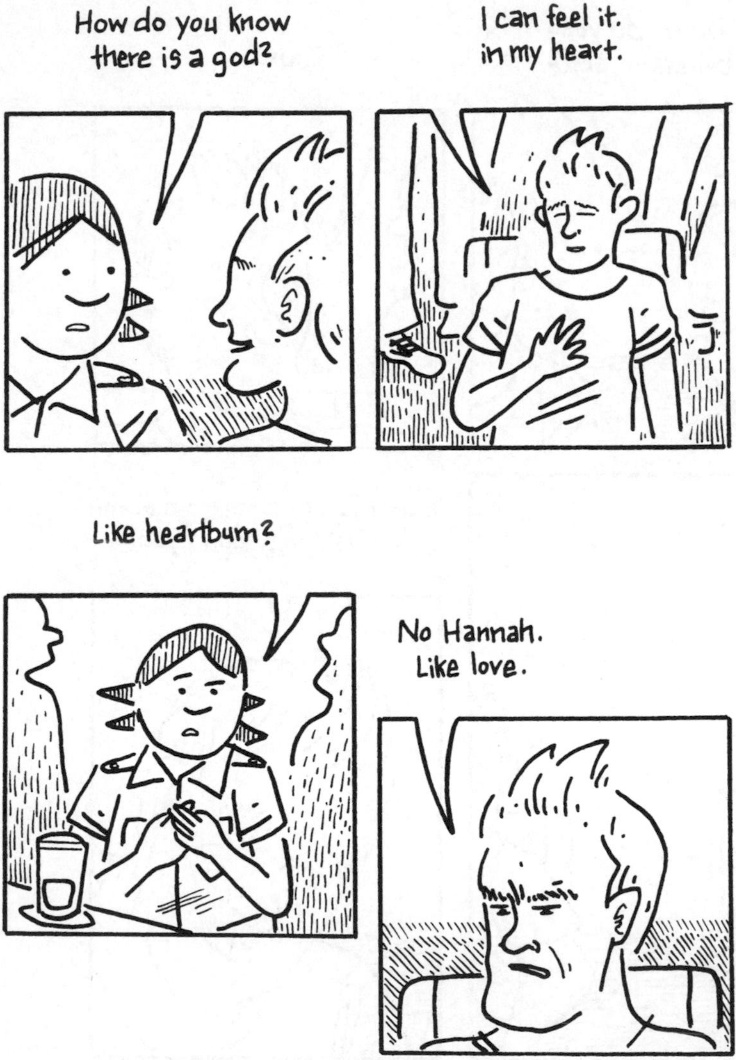
How do you know there is a god?
I can feel it. in my heart.
Like heartburn?
No Hannah. Like love.

I understand heartburn. I understand being in love.
What does any of that have to do with god?

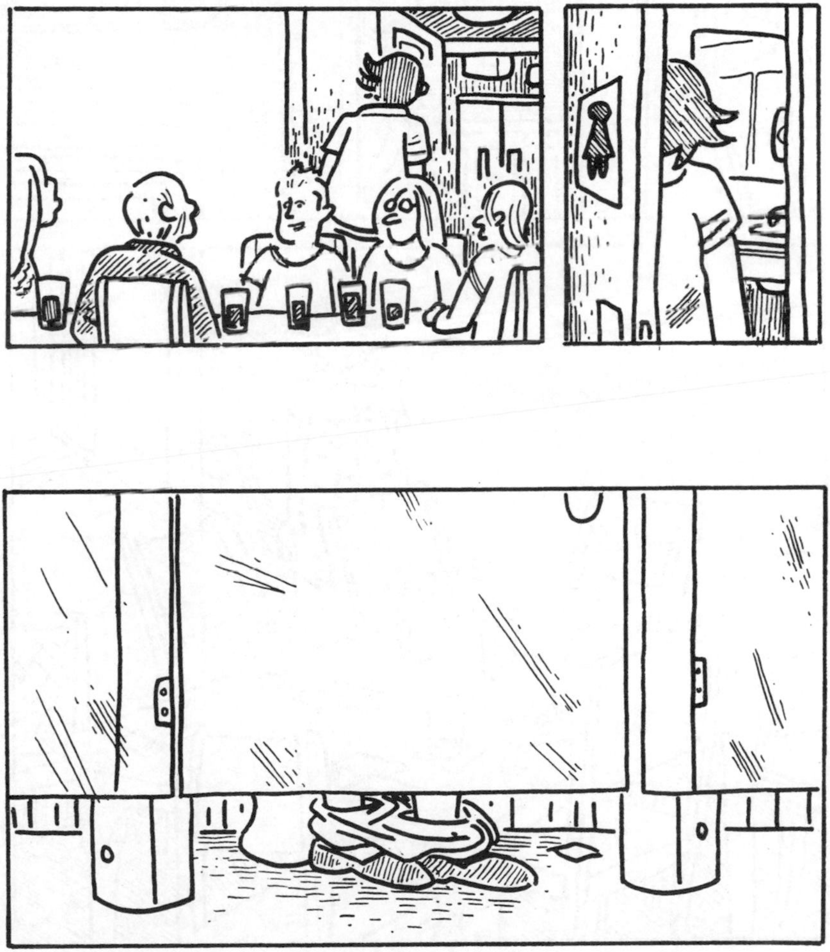

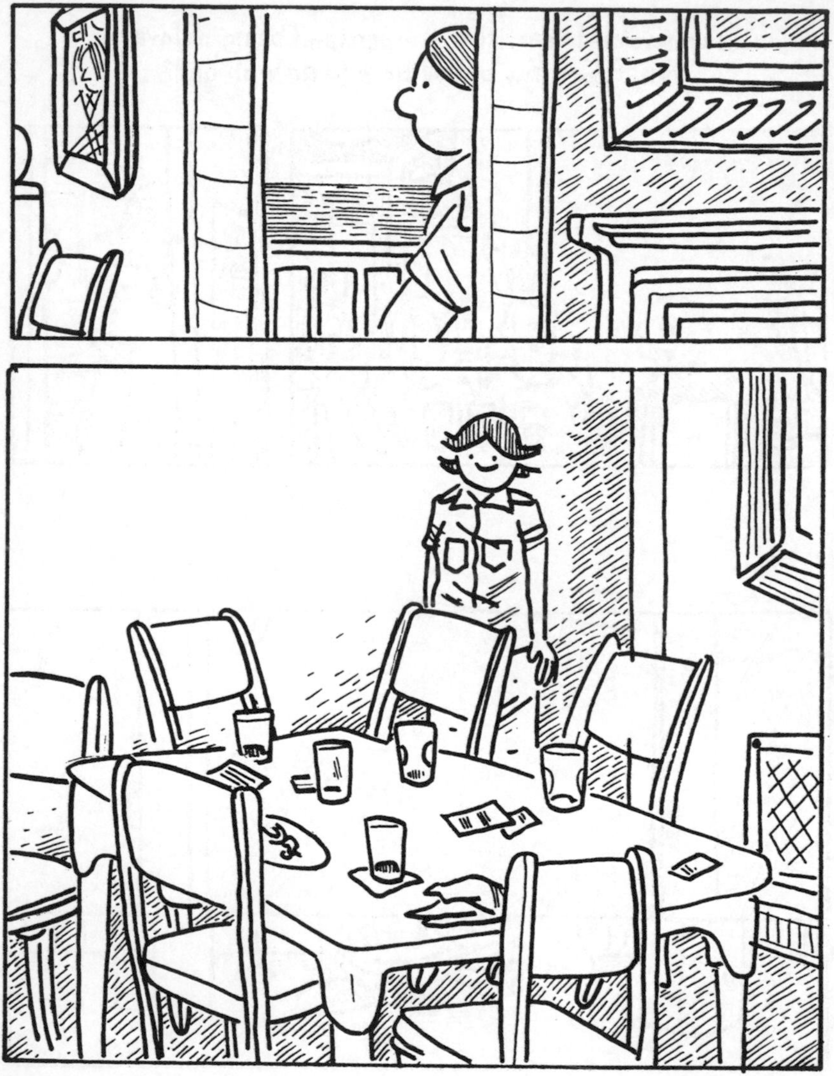

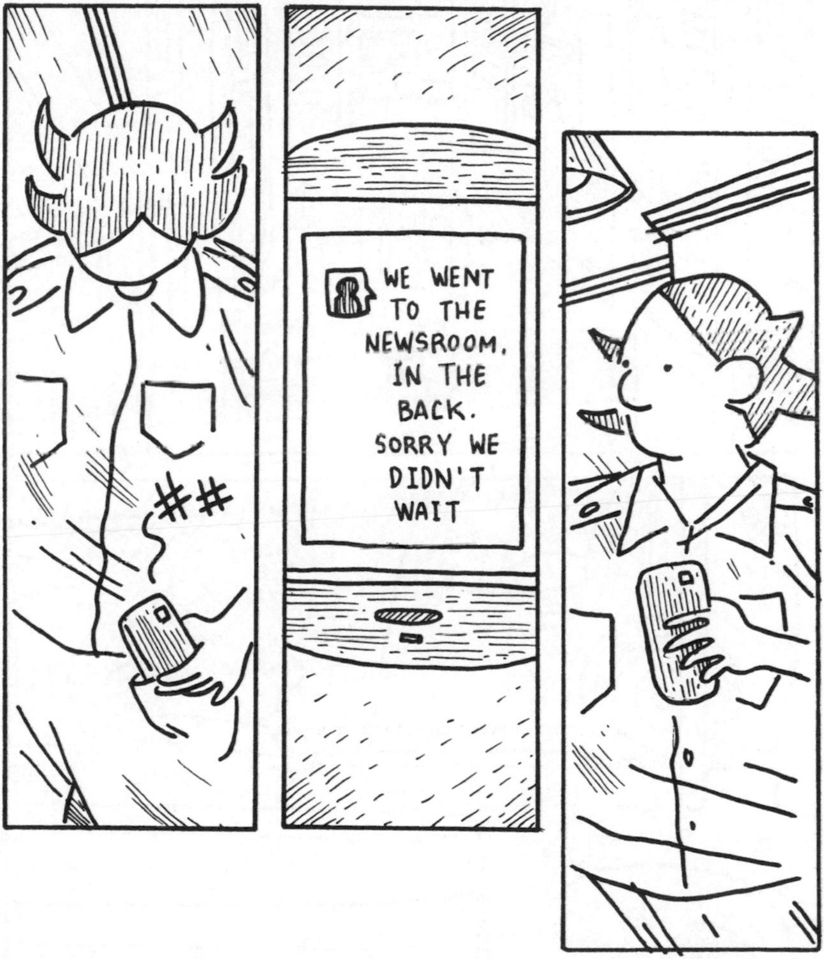
##
WE WENT TO THE NEWSROOM. IN THE BACK. SORRY WE DIDN'T WAIT

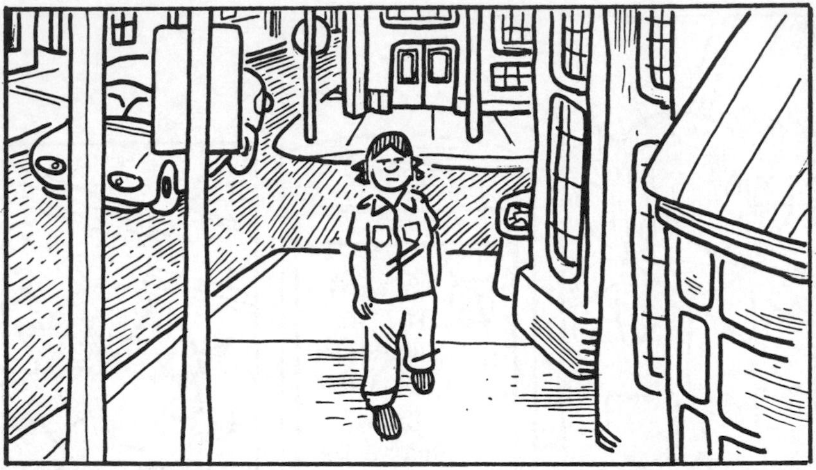

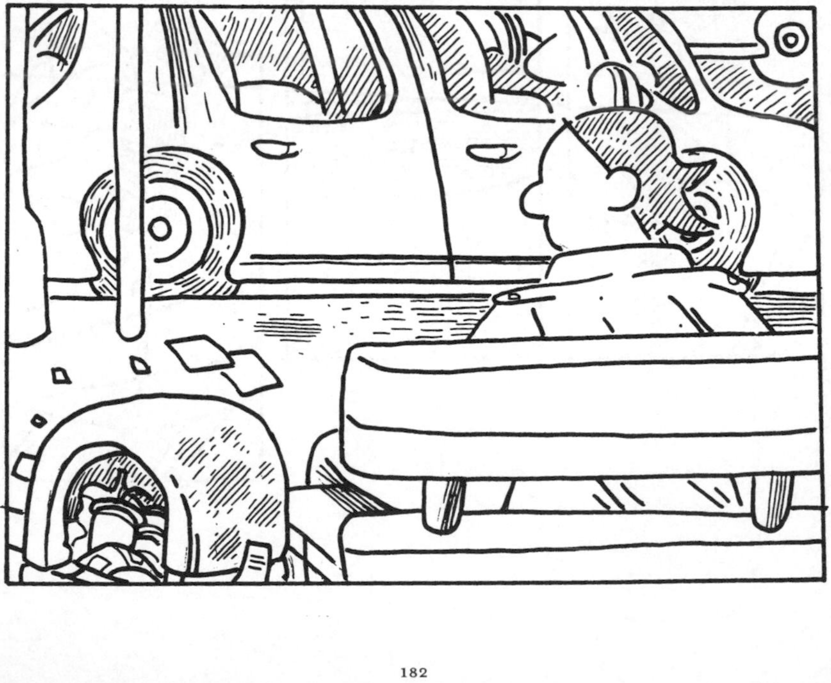

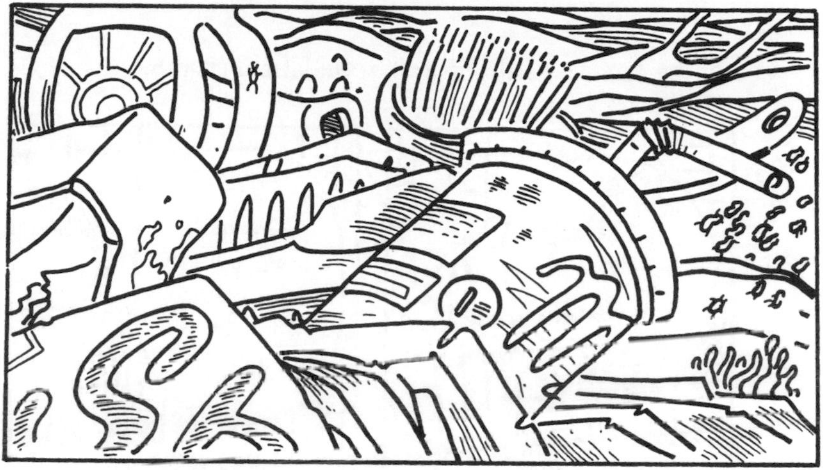

I thought about when I die, I'd like to be cremated. The urn would be silver and have my name, birthday, and the date I died etched into the side.

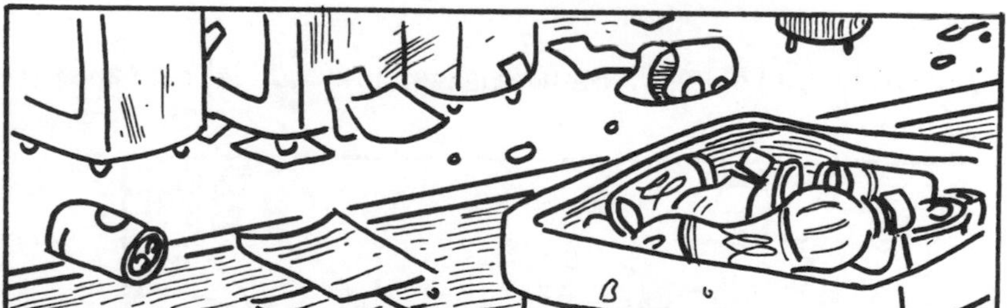

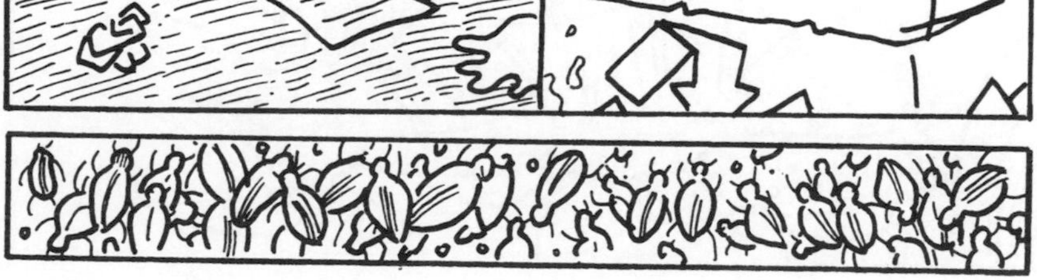

The service would be in a beautiful old church.

Know Me
I can't think of a single person who would attend my funeral.

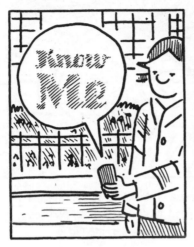

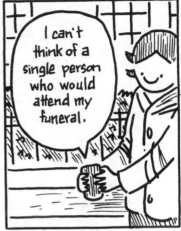

My family is all gone. I have no friends. How did I let this happen?

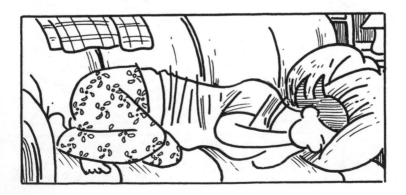

Hannah, I owe ~~you~~ an apology.

You did not need to bring back these clothes. They were a gift.

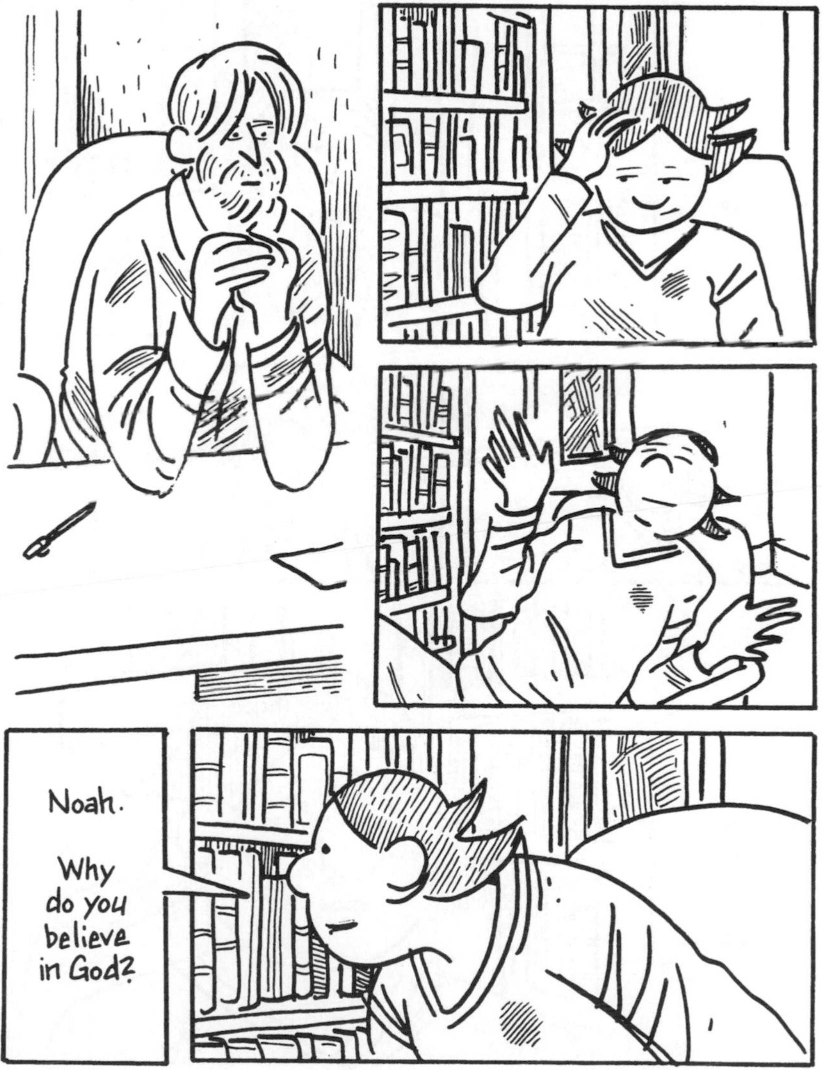
Noah.
Why do you believe in God?

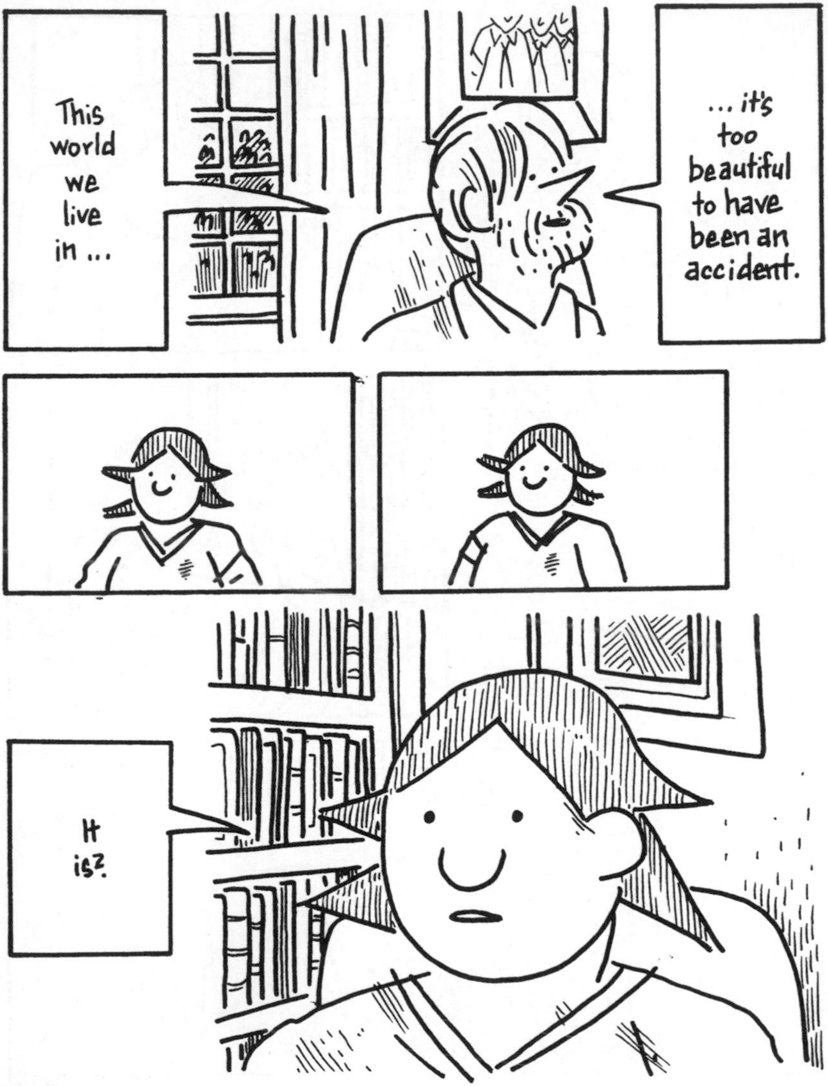
This world we live in ...
... it's too beautiful to have been an accident.
It is?

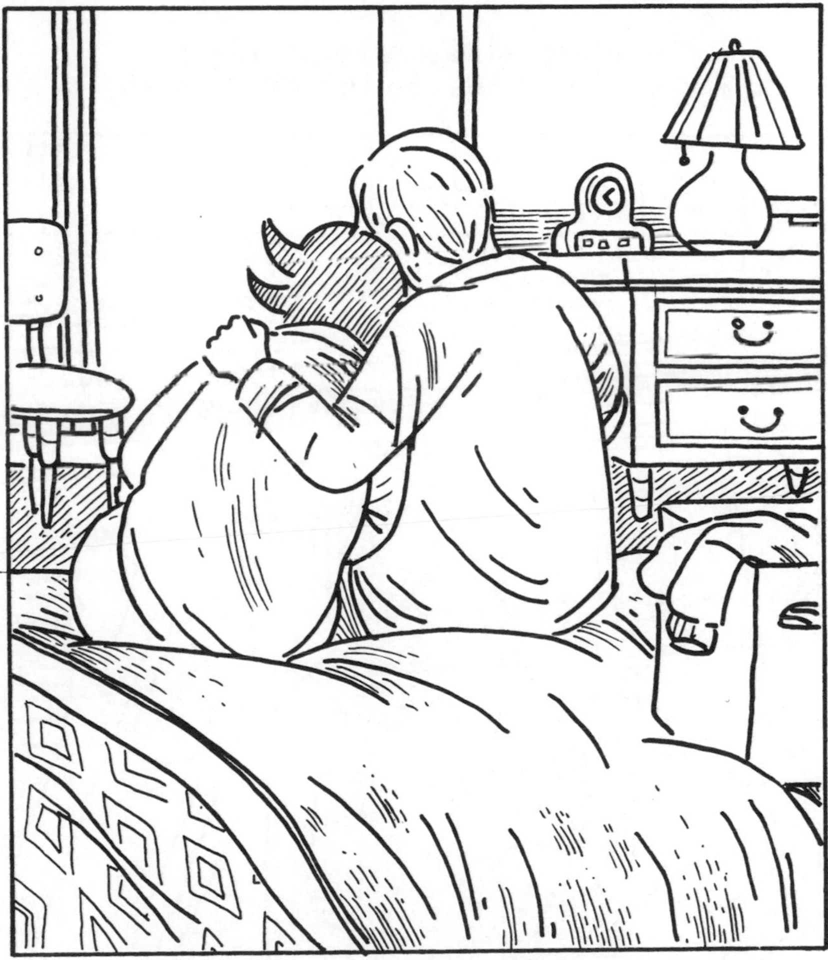

Noah walked me to my room.
It was the same as when I'd left, months earlier.

The building had the same intricate ceilings.
Everyone who was there when I left was still around.

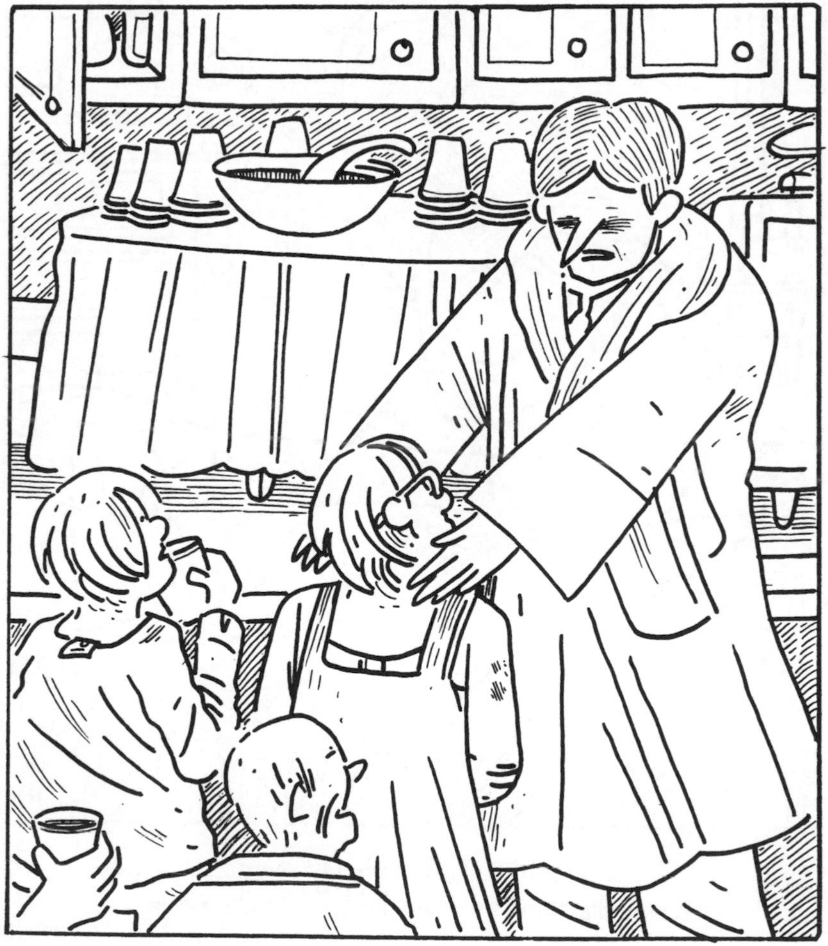

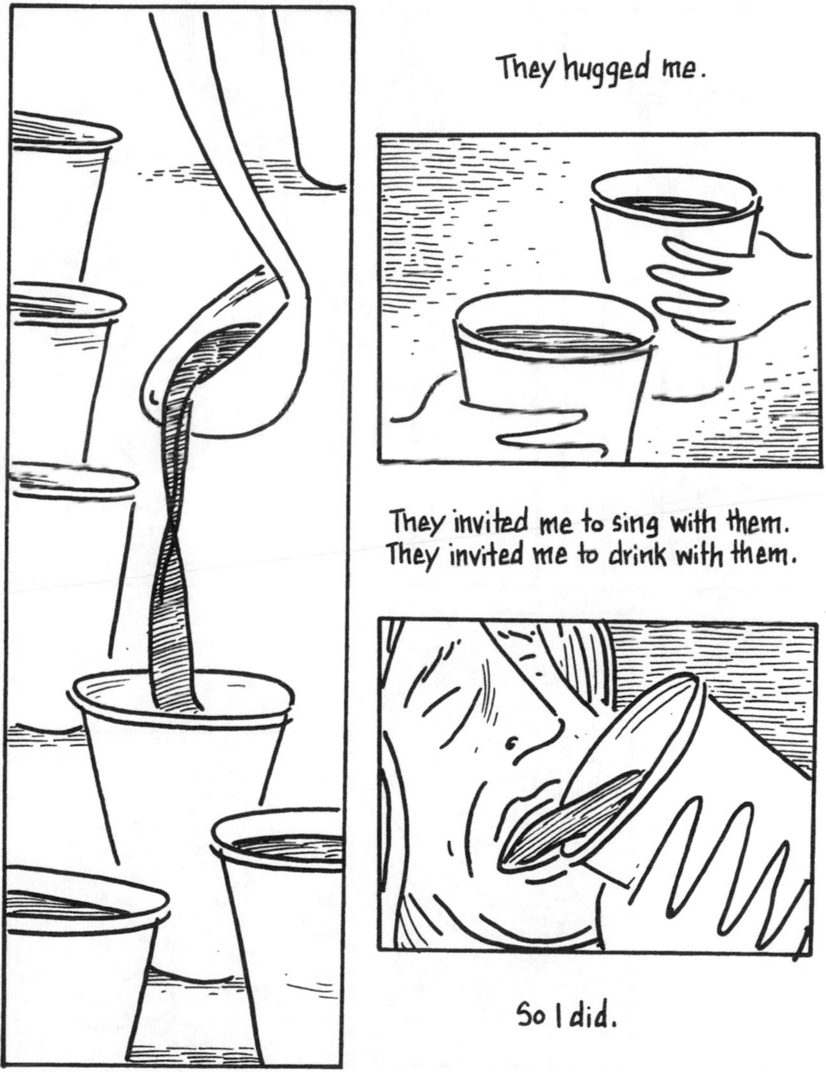
They hugged me.
They invited me to sing with them.
They invited me to drink with them.
So I did.

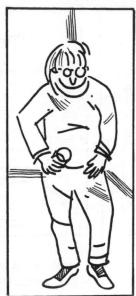

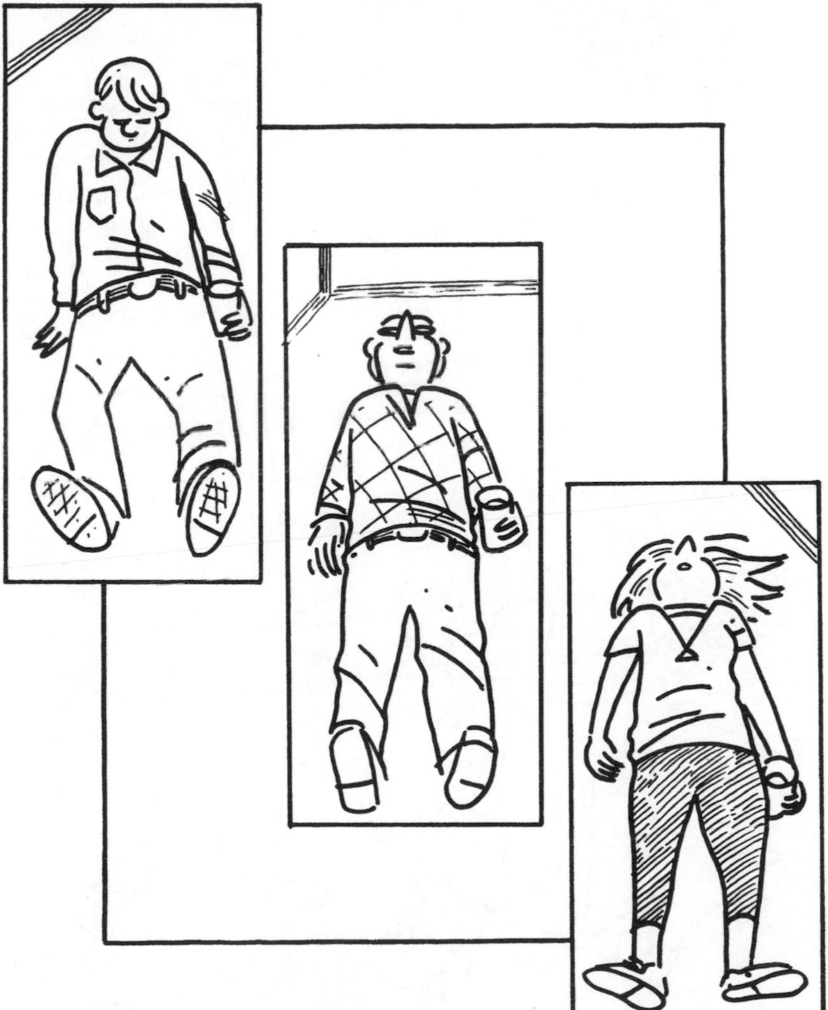

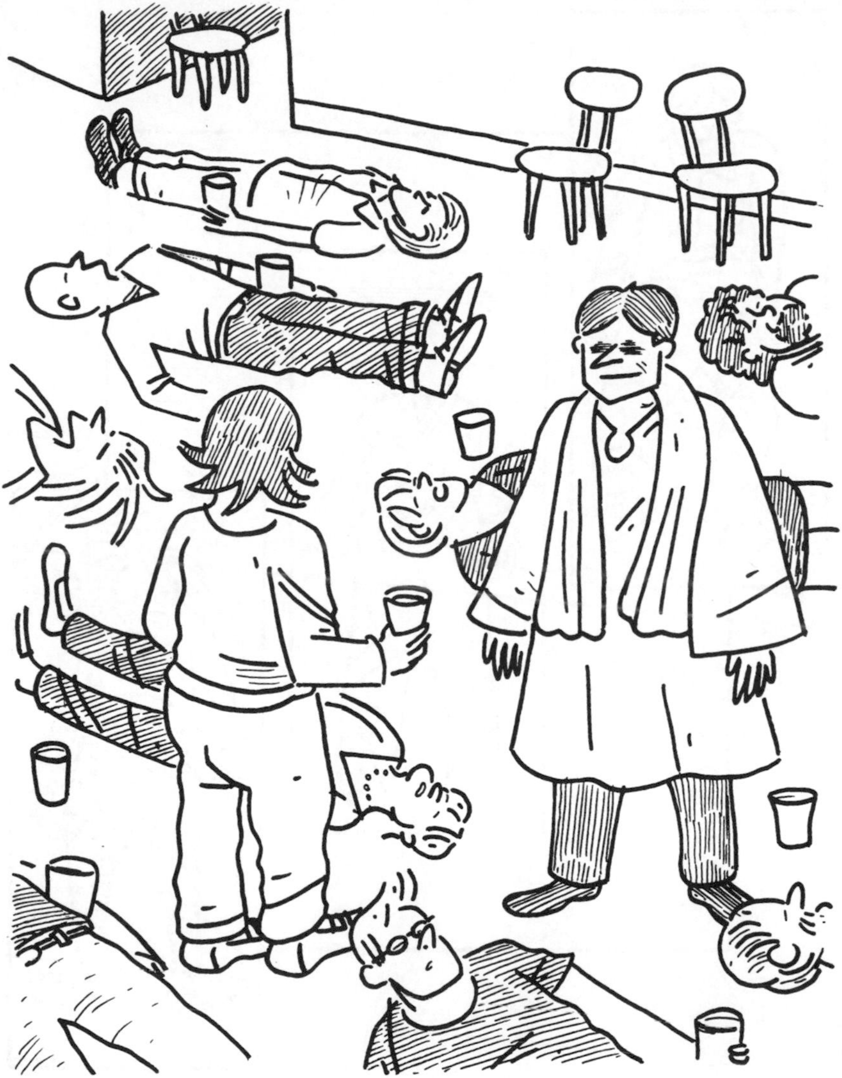

Whether you believe in God or not, we can all agree that one day we have to leave this world.

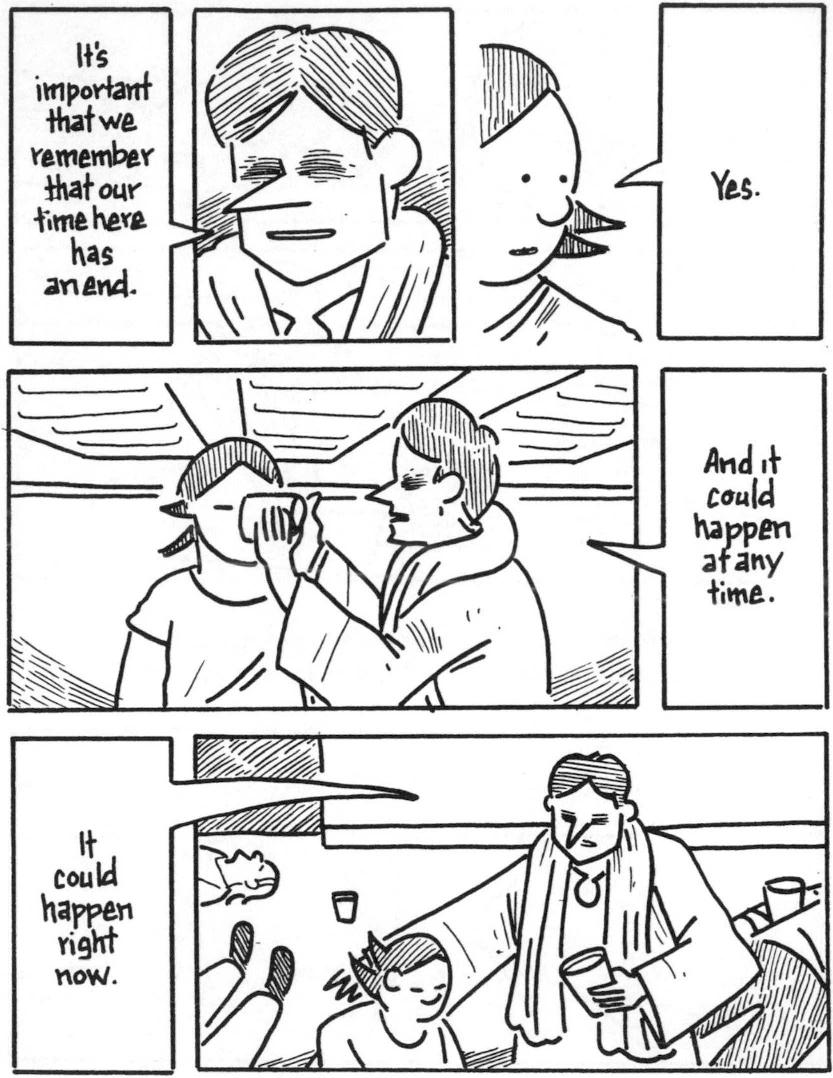
It's important that we remember that our time here has an end.
Yes.
And it could happen at any time.
It could happen right now.

We have Communion to remind ourselves of this.

We remind ourselves together.

None of us
is alone
in death.

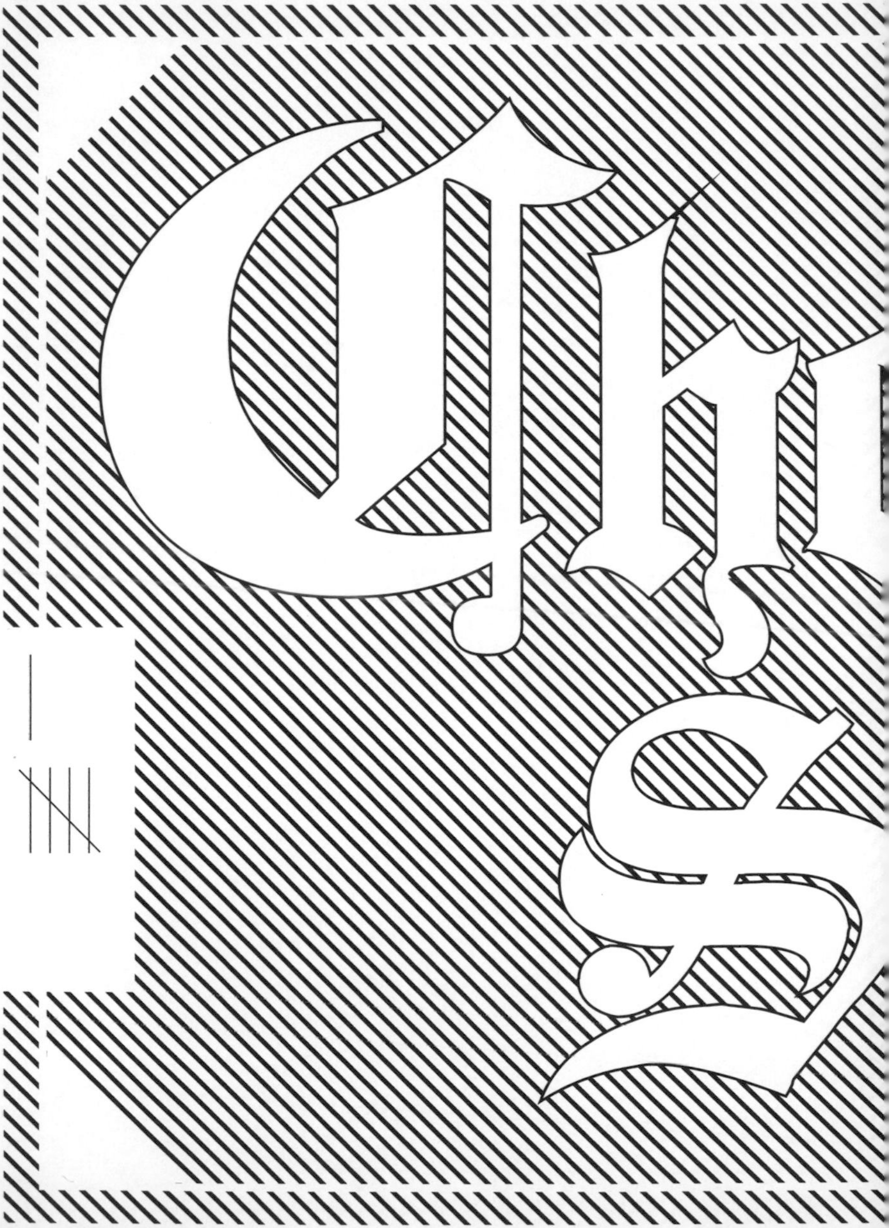

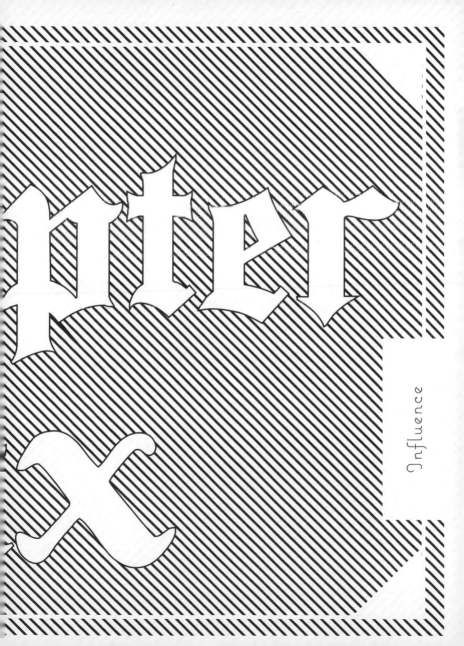

pter X

Influence

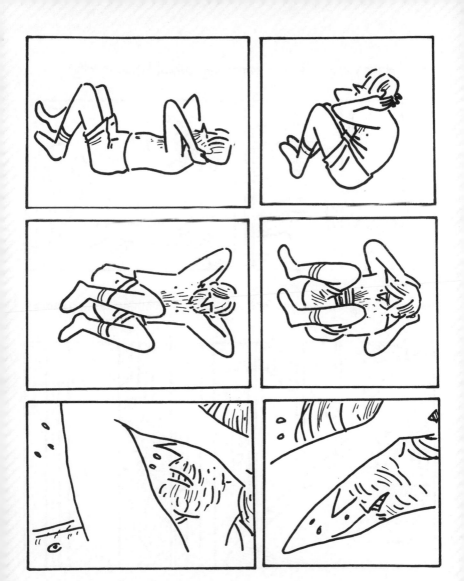

Have you ever known something without knowing why?

Without any evidence, you are certain that something is happening?

A week ago, Hannah returned to the fold.

She's one of us now, and is living in the dorms again.

I see her
all the time.

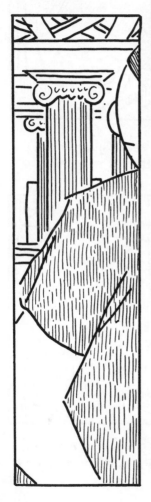

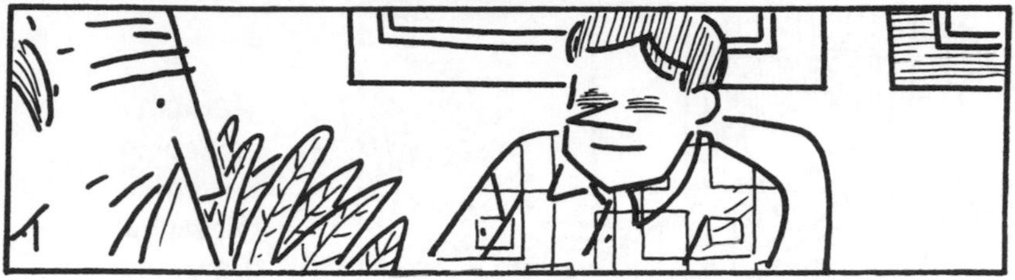

Or maybe I just notice her more than other people.

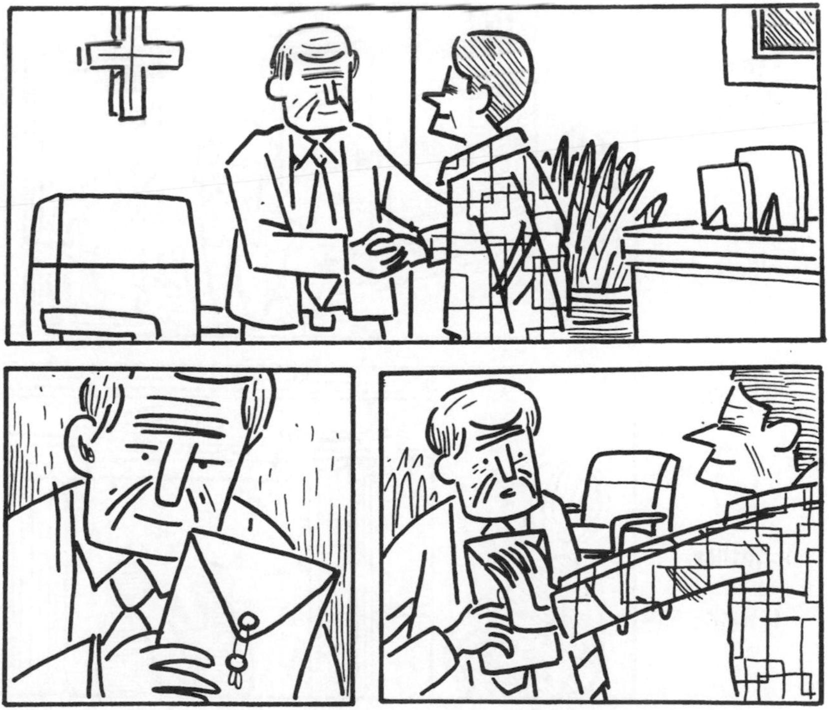

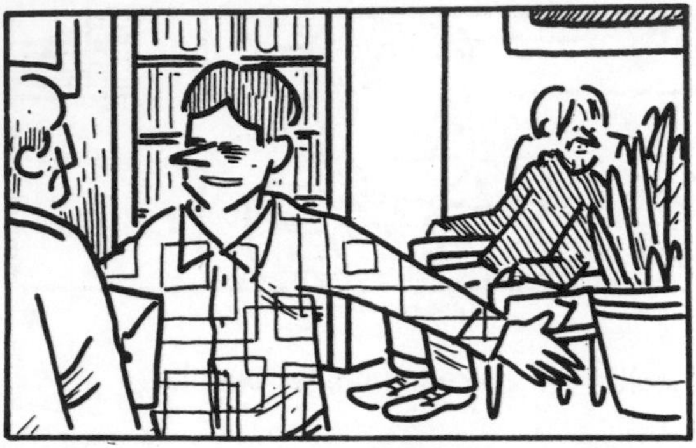

Hannah is sleeping with Reverend Carpenter.

I think she is.

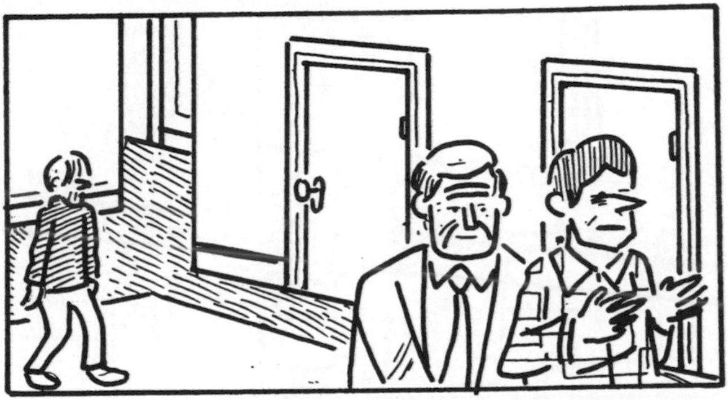

He is.

They are.

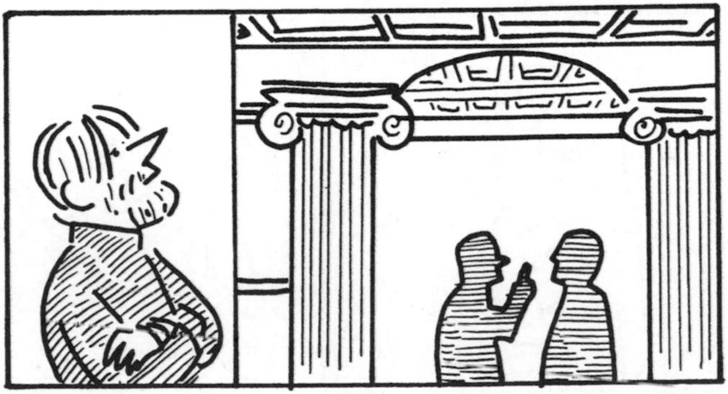

Together.

I think.

Why should I care?

Maybe it's because Reverend Carpenter is a married man. He made a commitment to Rita. I was there and heard him make the promise to love her above everyone else.

Hannah can't possibly understand that kind of bond.

May I join you?

For her last four meals, Hannah has sat alone.

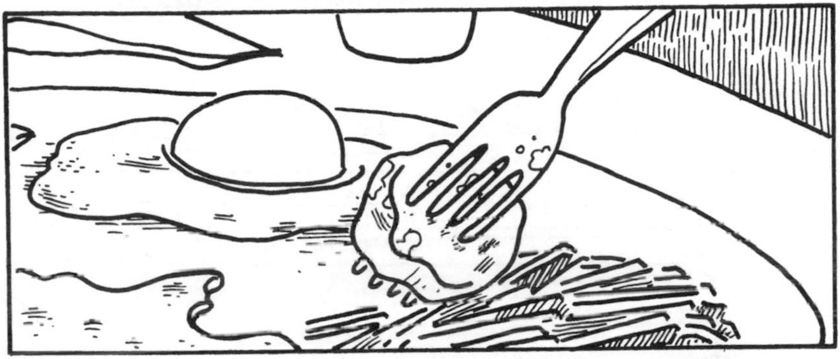

She always varies what she selects from the cafeteria, and sits in the same spot each day.

Always alone.

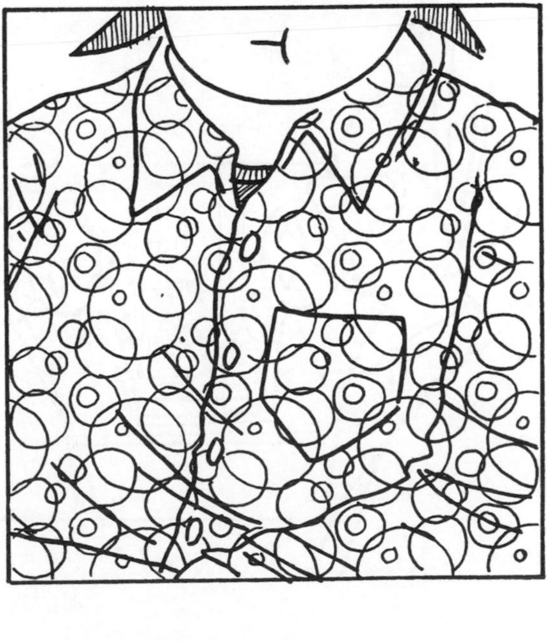

But from here, she has a clear sightline to Carpenter.

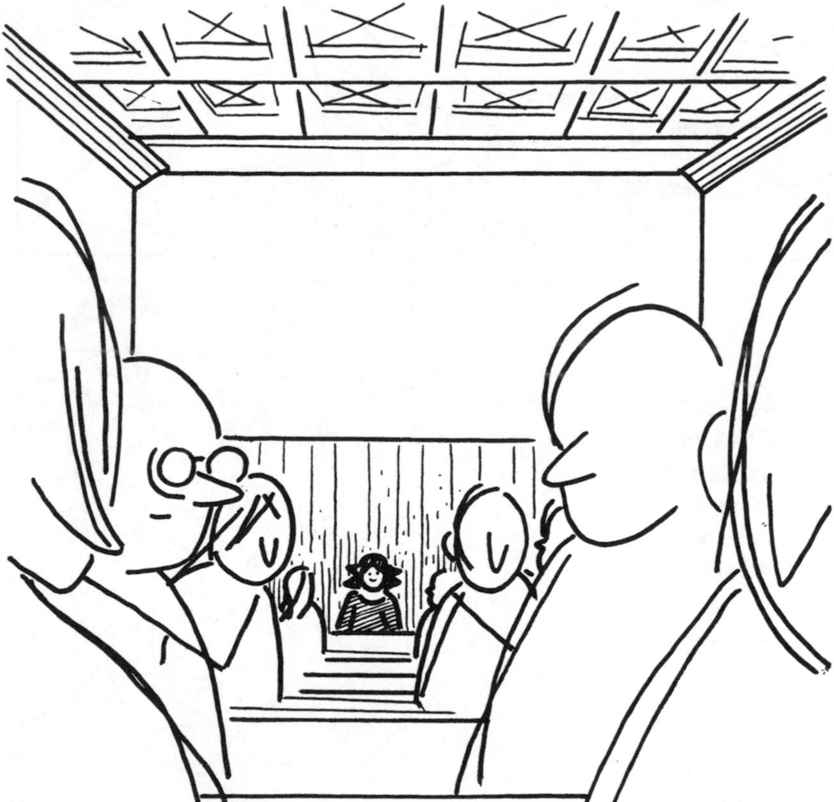

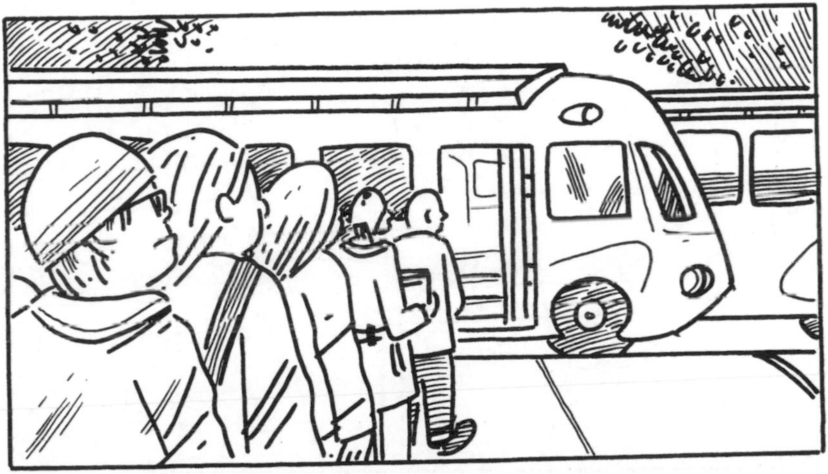

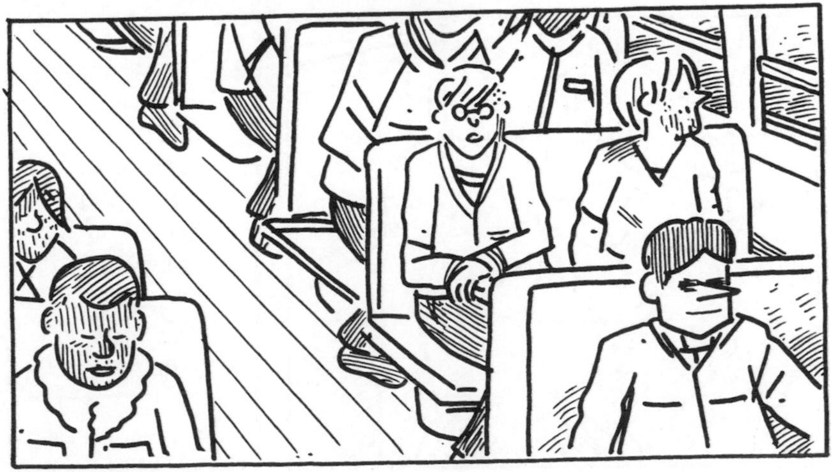

When we get on the bus, Hannah is even closer to Carpenter.

She's looking at our voting list. We've all been given the same guide.

The entire ballet has been determined in advance.

At the top of the list is the Mayor.

We vote for Carlos because Carlos knows Reverend Carpenter.

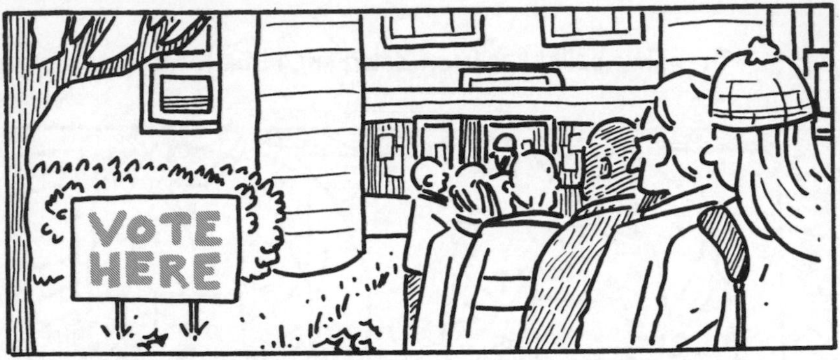
VOTE
HERE

Everyone should vote this way. What Carlos believes or what his stated platform is doesn't matter as much as the fact that we are likely to get him into an elected position.

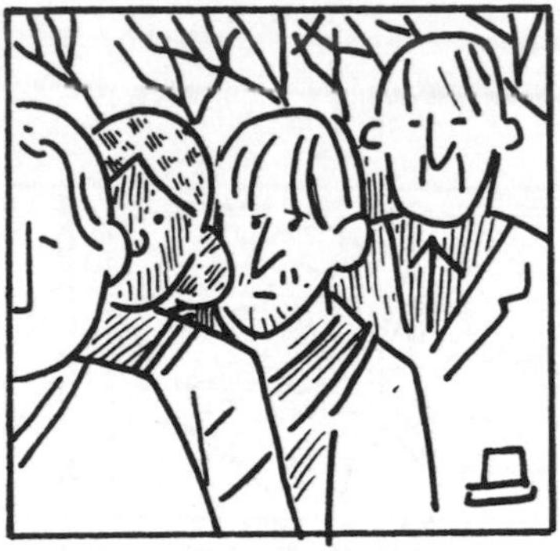

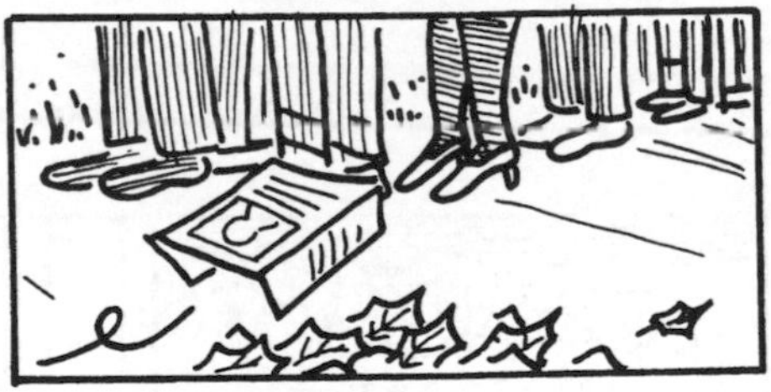

He will reflect our values because we own him.

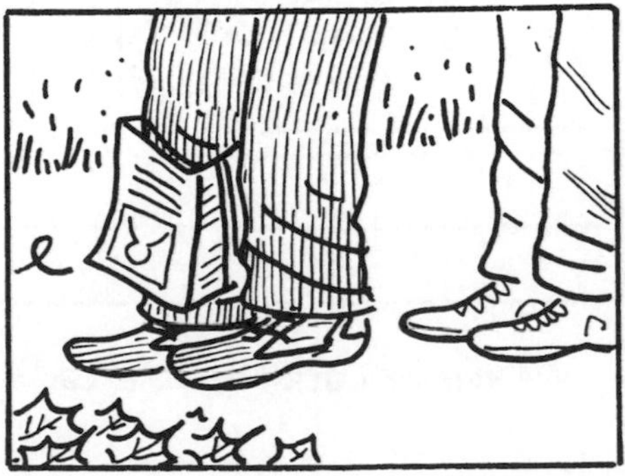

CARLOS
RINDE
for MAYOR
33%

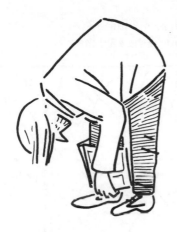

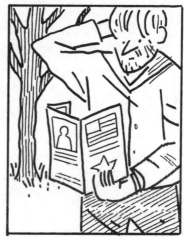

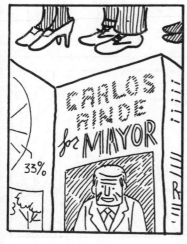

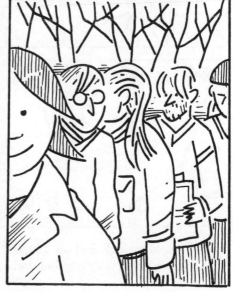

Does she even care that he's a father?
Would she even know his kids if she saw them?

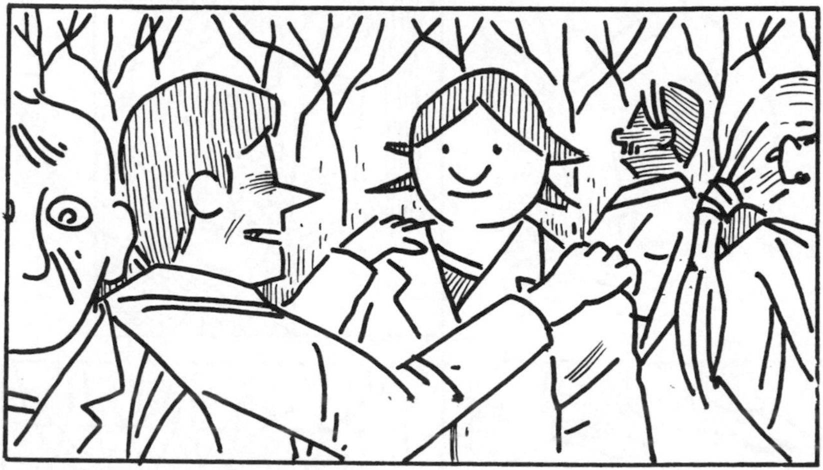

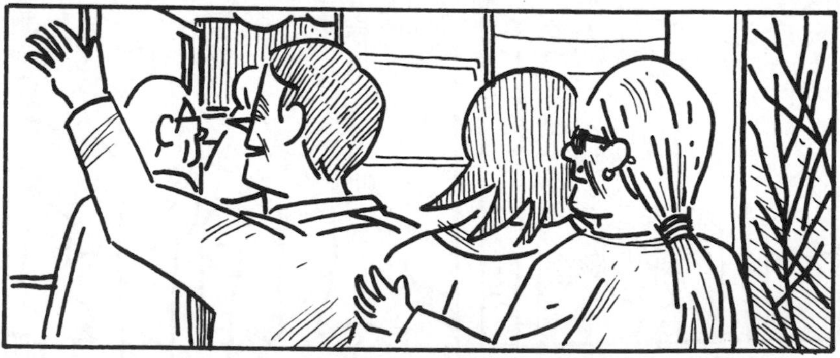

It's cold enough that we all huddle together for warmth.
Hannah is actually standing between Carpenter and Rita.

They embrace briefly before given their cup of warm cider.

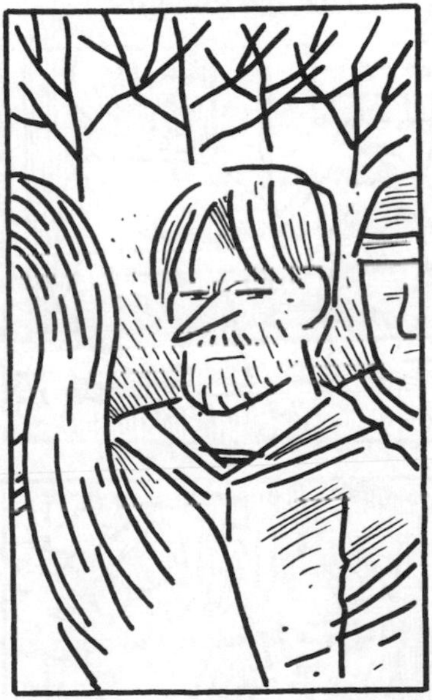

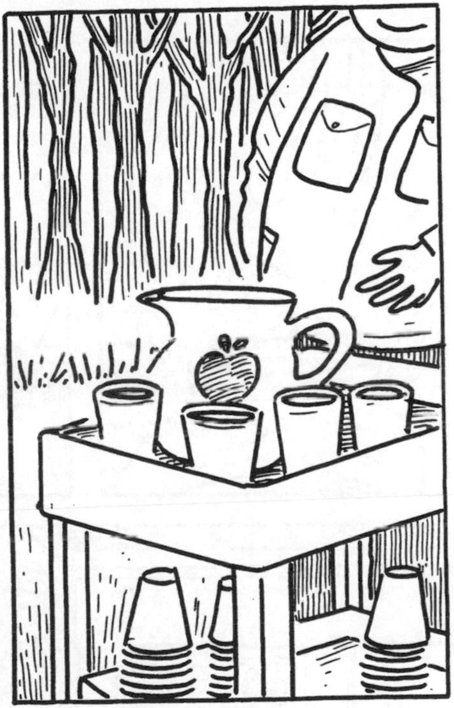

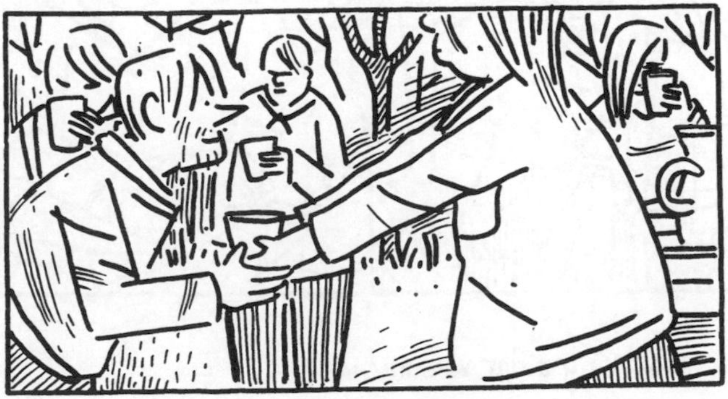

Hannah drinks all of her cider.

Carpenter uses it to warm his hands and then pours the cool cider onto the ground.

Serving cider was my idea.

Warm cider reminds me of Christmas.

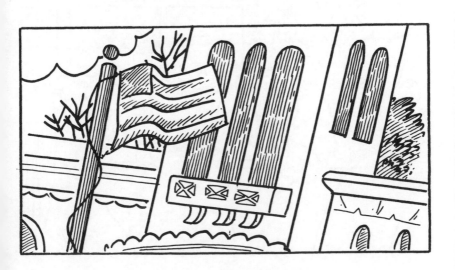

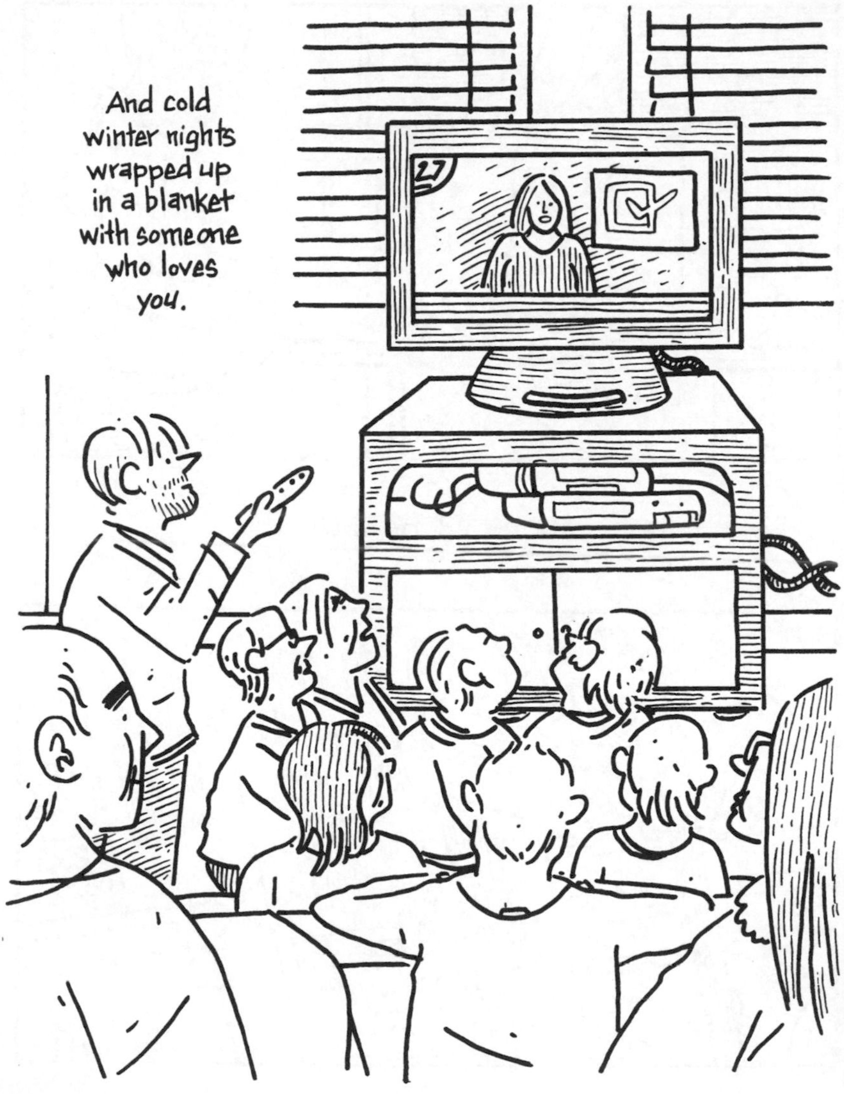
And cold winter nights wrapped up in a blanket with someone who loves you.
27

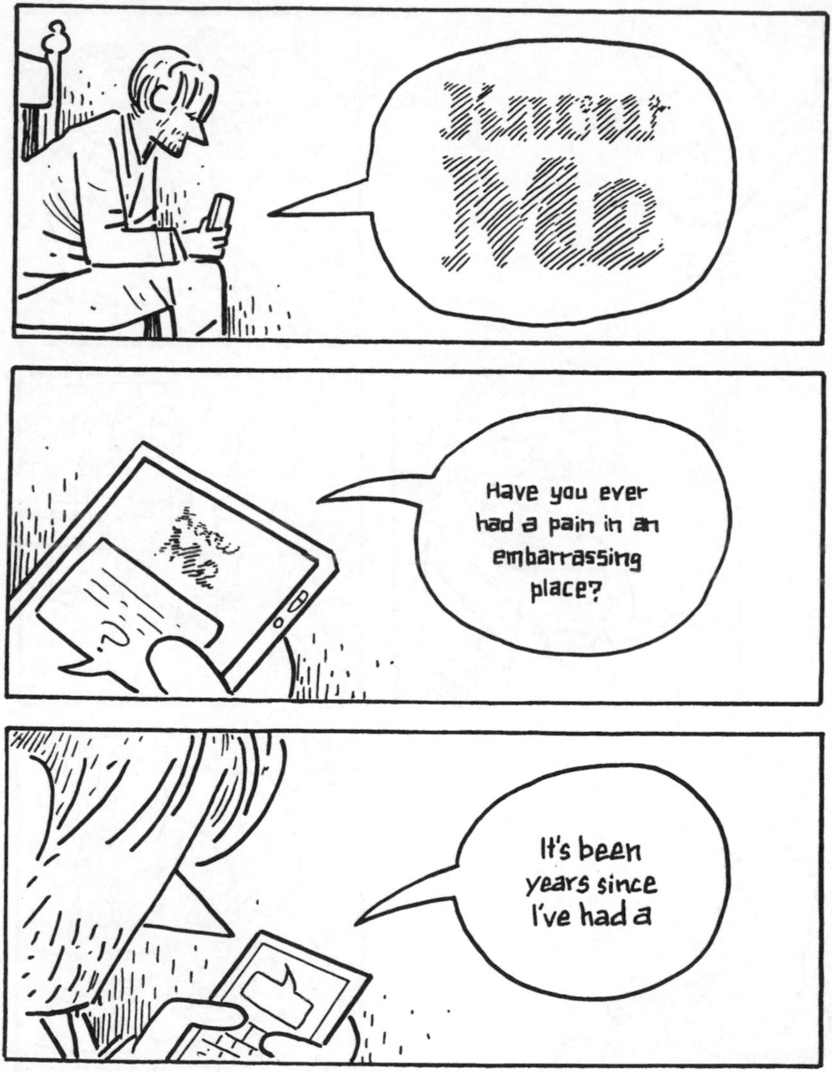
Know Me
Have you ever had a pain in an embarrassing place?
It's been years since I've had a

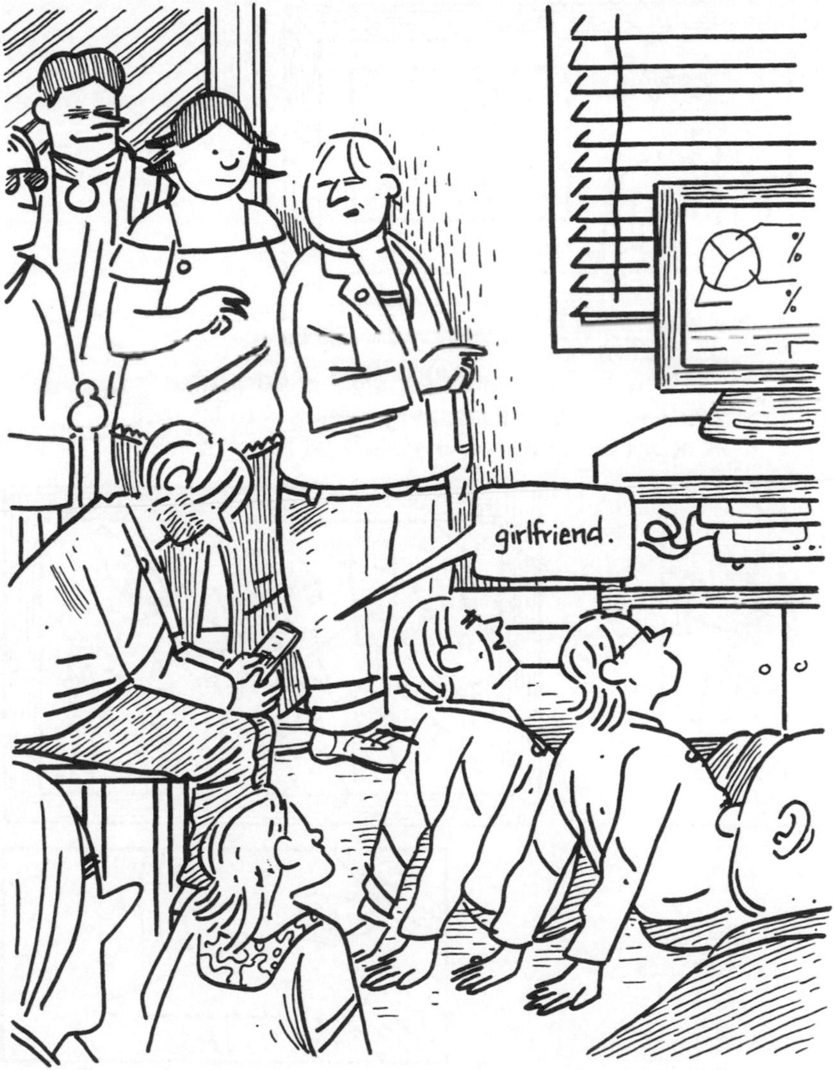
girlfriend.

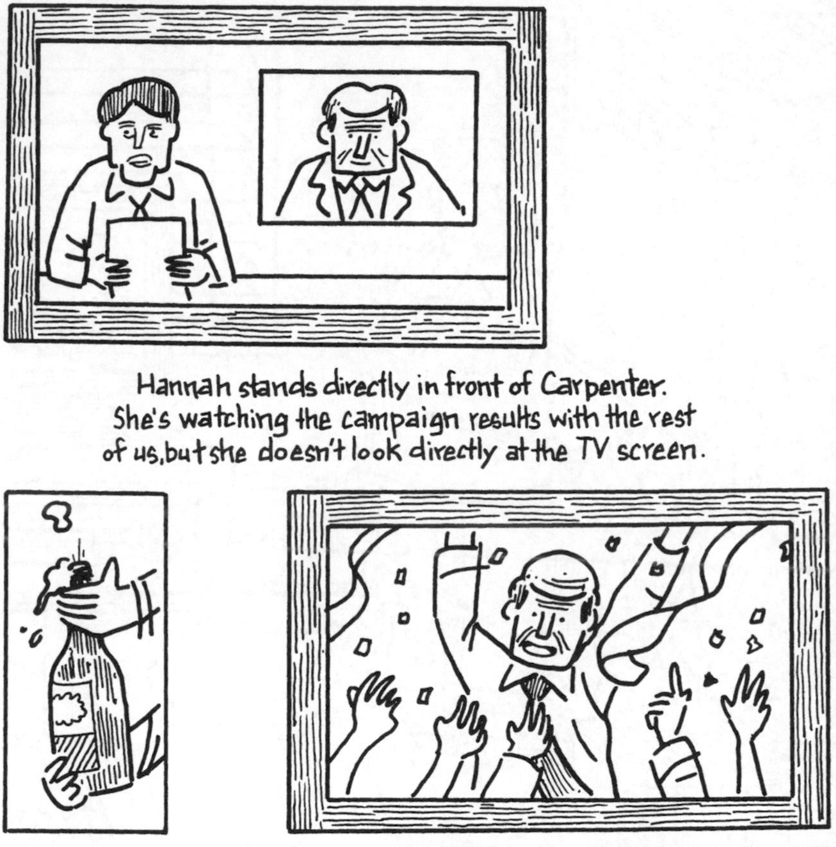
Hannah stands directly in front of Carpenter.
She's watching the campaign results with the rest of us, but she doesn't look directly at the TV screen.
She touches her neck.

Carlos Rinde won
the election by
300 votes.

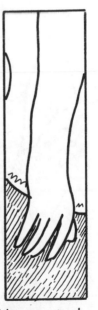

Now Carpenter will get his promised
position as chairman of the Housing
Authority Commission.

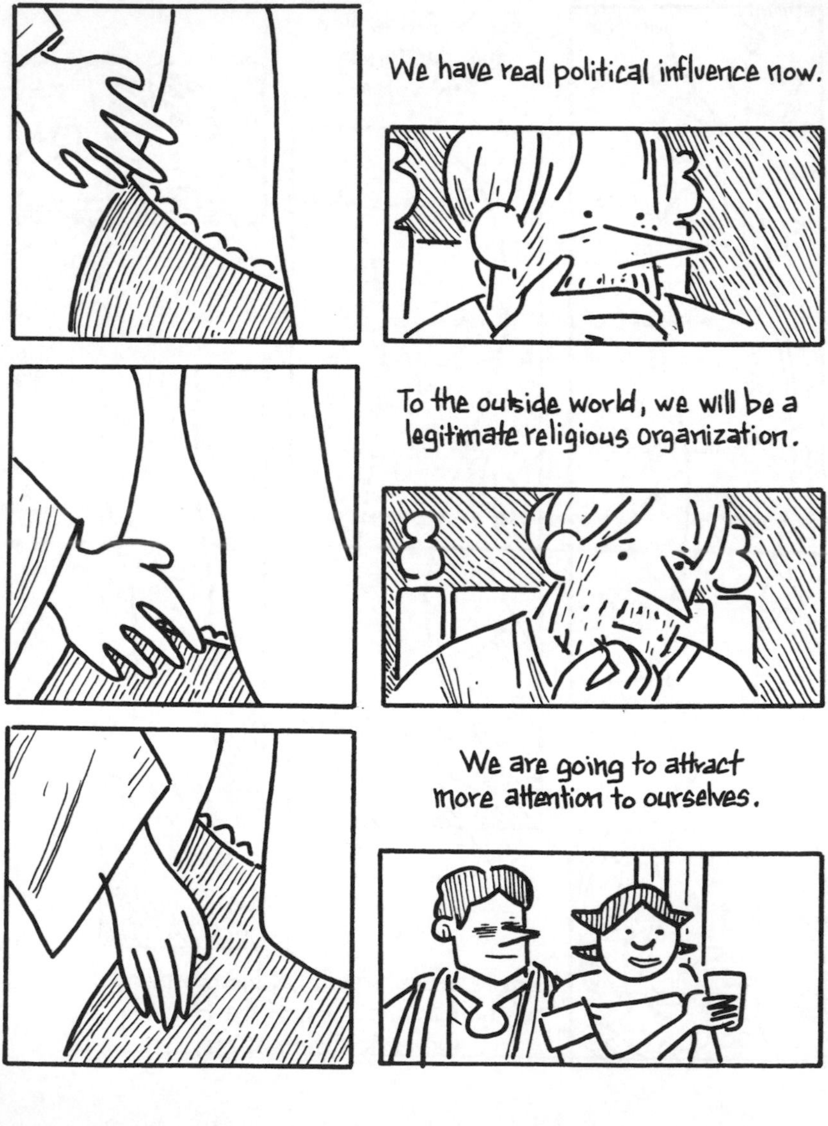
We have real political influence now.
To the outside world, we will be a legitimate religious organization.
We are going to attract more attention to ourselves.

I need
to look
more
professional.

More
attractive.

I need
to shave my
disgusting
beard.

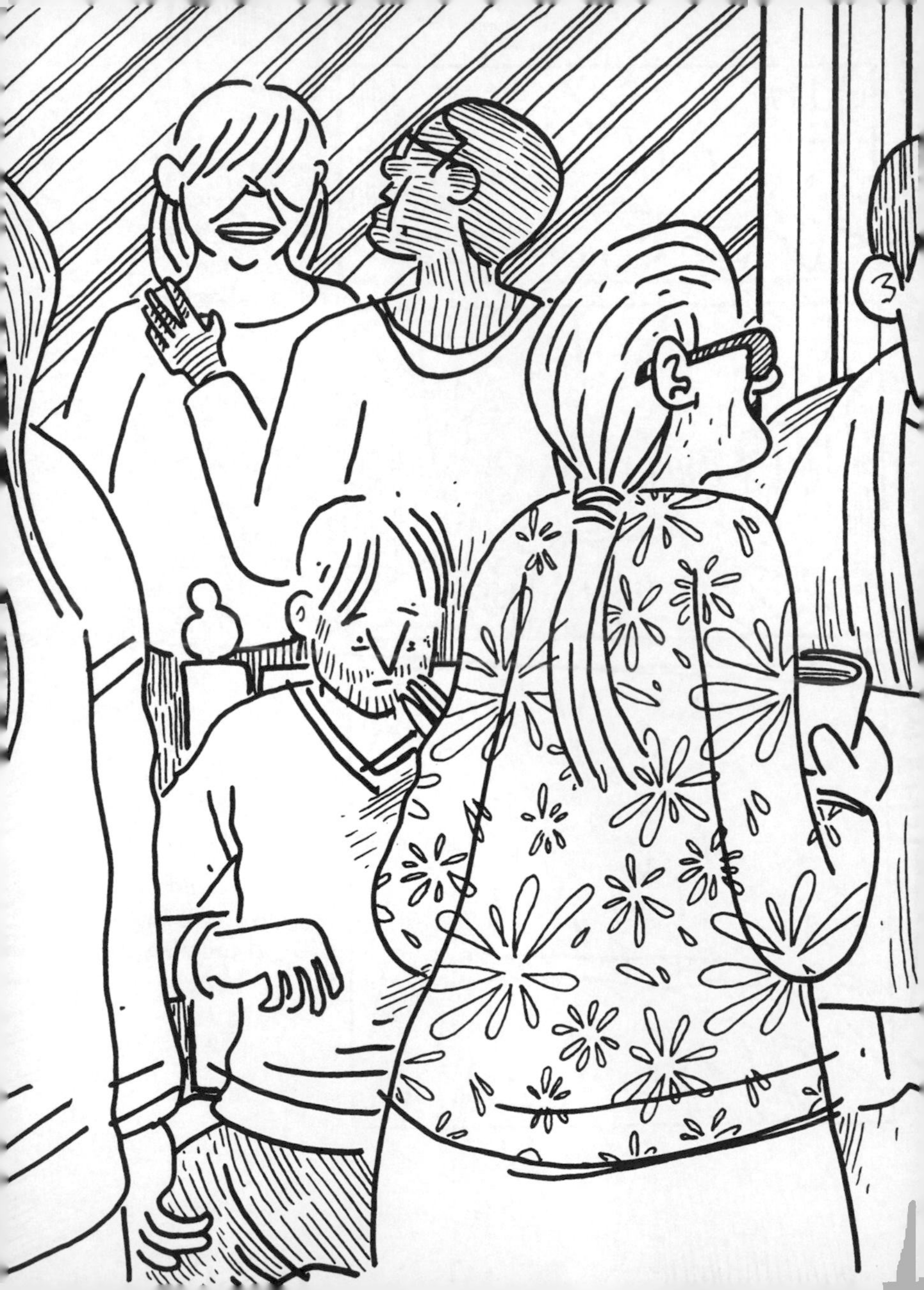

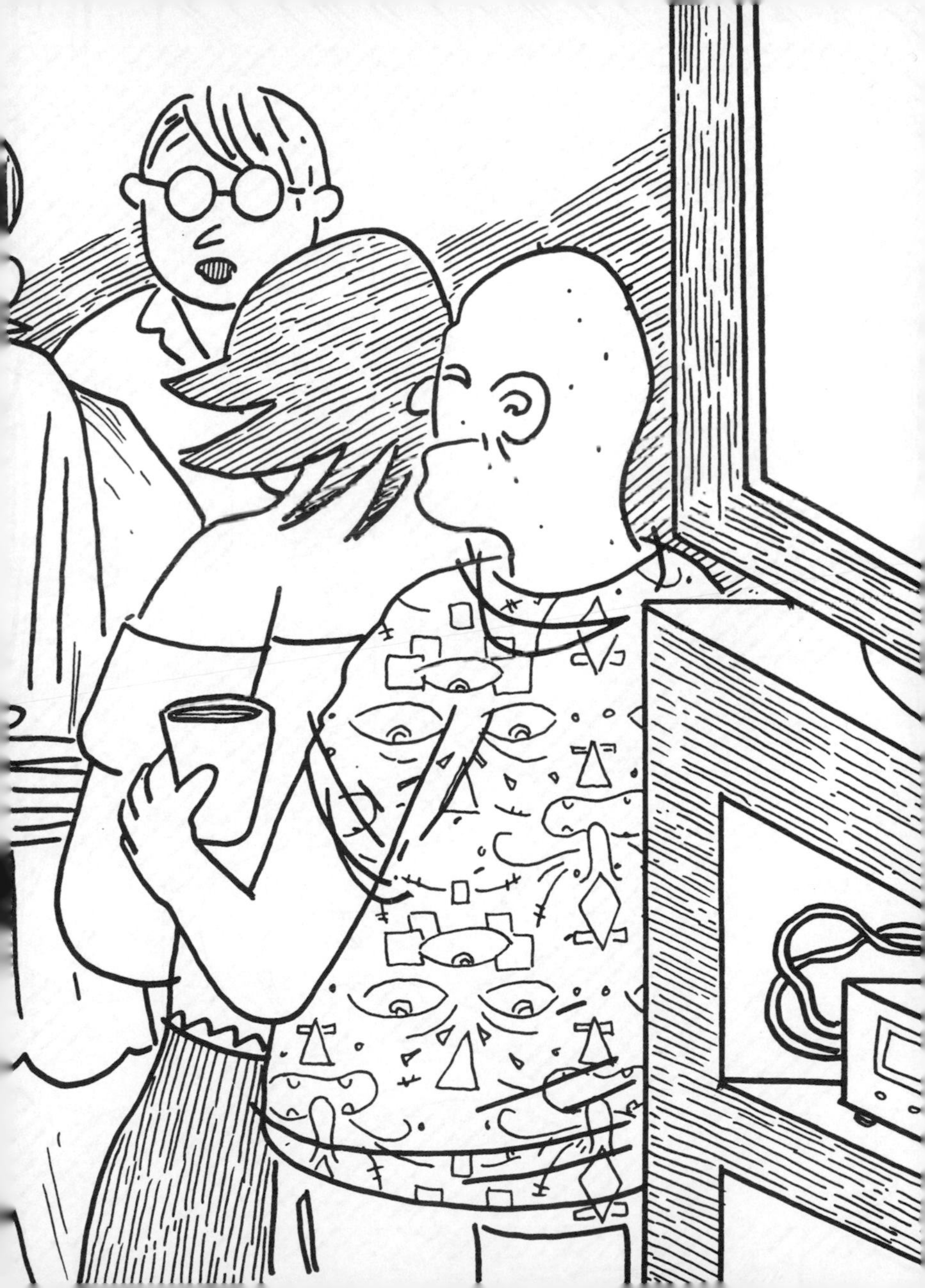

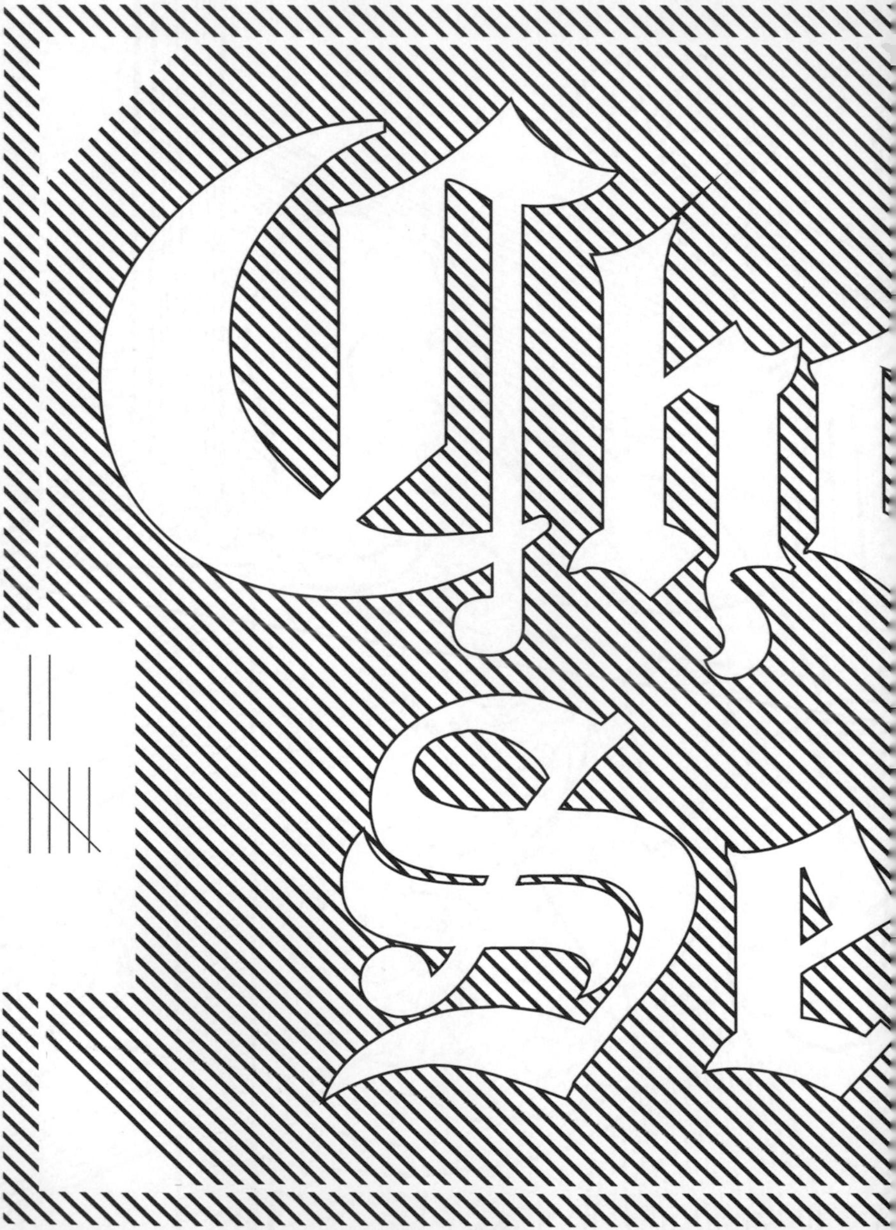

pter

en

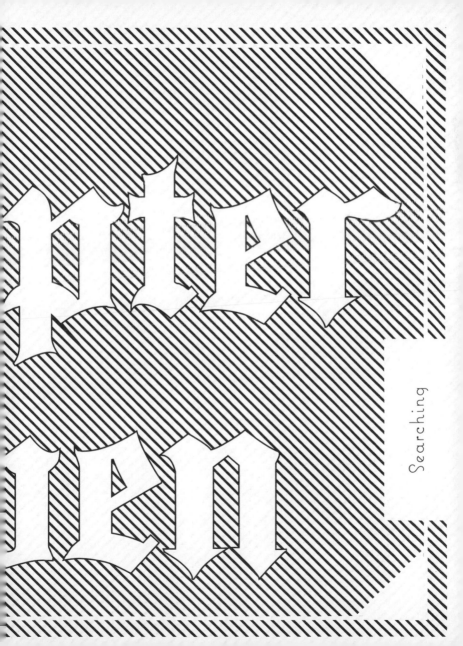

Searching

Noah shaved his
beard into a mustache
and now I can't stop
making fun of him.

He looks like a villain
from a silent movie.

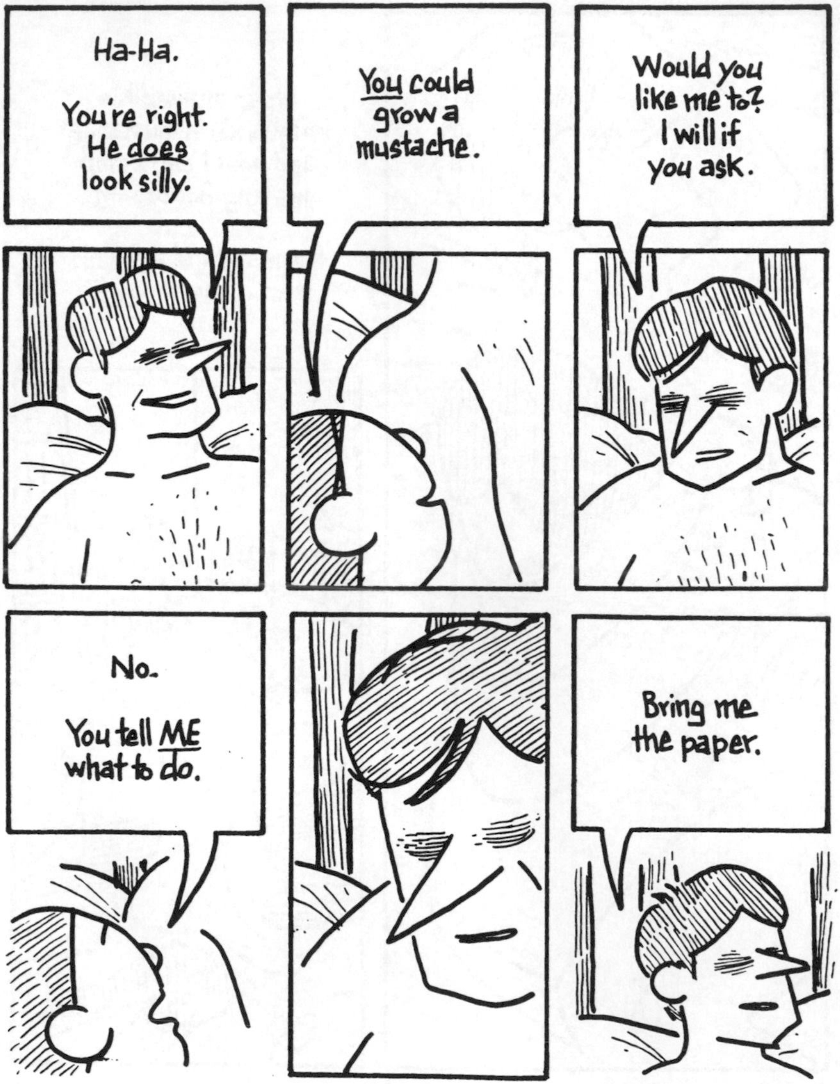

Ha-Ha.
You're right. He does look silly.
You could grow a mustache.
Would you like me to? I will if you ask.
No.
You tell ME what to do.
Bring me the paper.

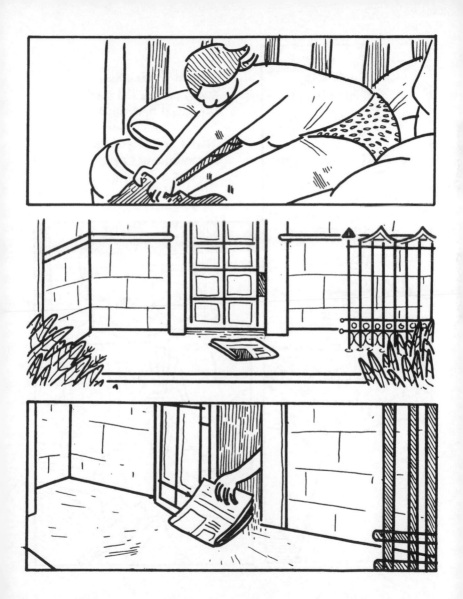

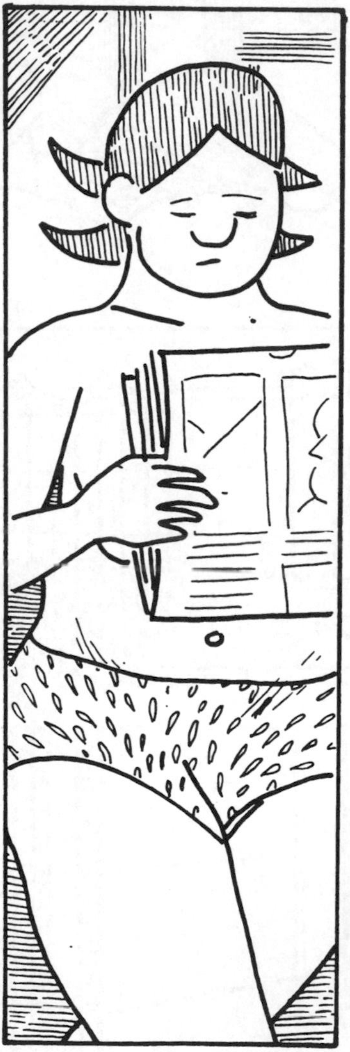

I had no idea how many people still read an actual newspaper.

That it could be of any consequence at all was a surprise.

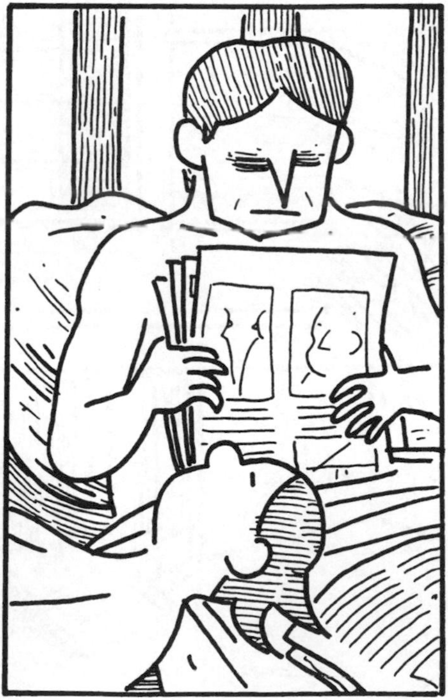

Carpentar's pale skin became near transparent, and then flushed with red.

FALSE PROFIT

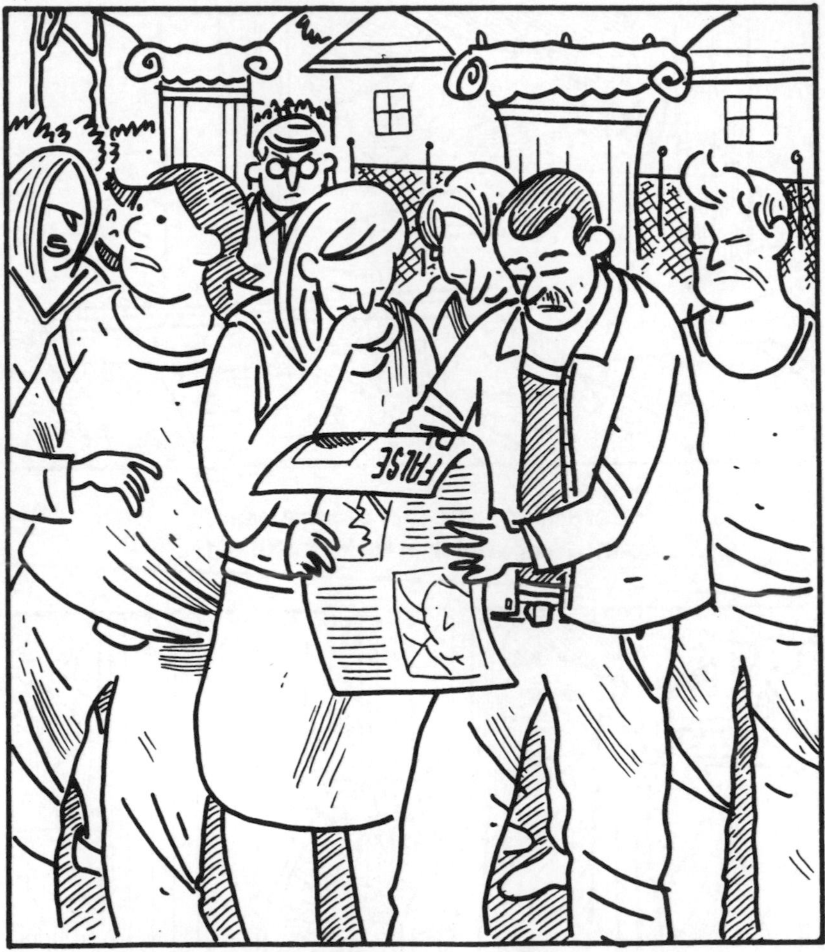
FALSE

The story was full of lies. Mostly lies anyway.

1

We do not
keep anyone in
the church against
their will.

2

We have no
more political
influence than
any other
religious group.

3

Reverend
Carpenter is
NOT a
drug addict.

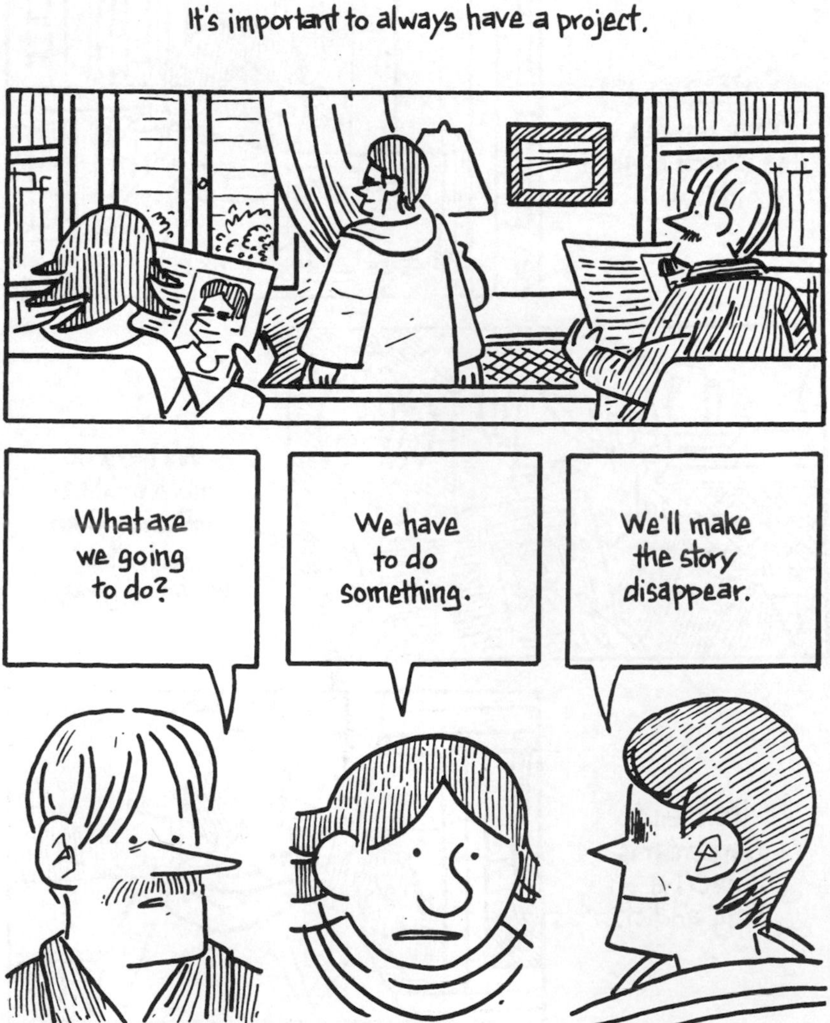
It's important to always have a project.
What are we going to do?
We have to do something.
We'll make the story disappear.

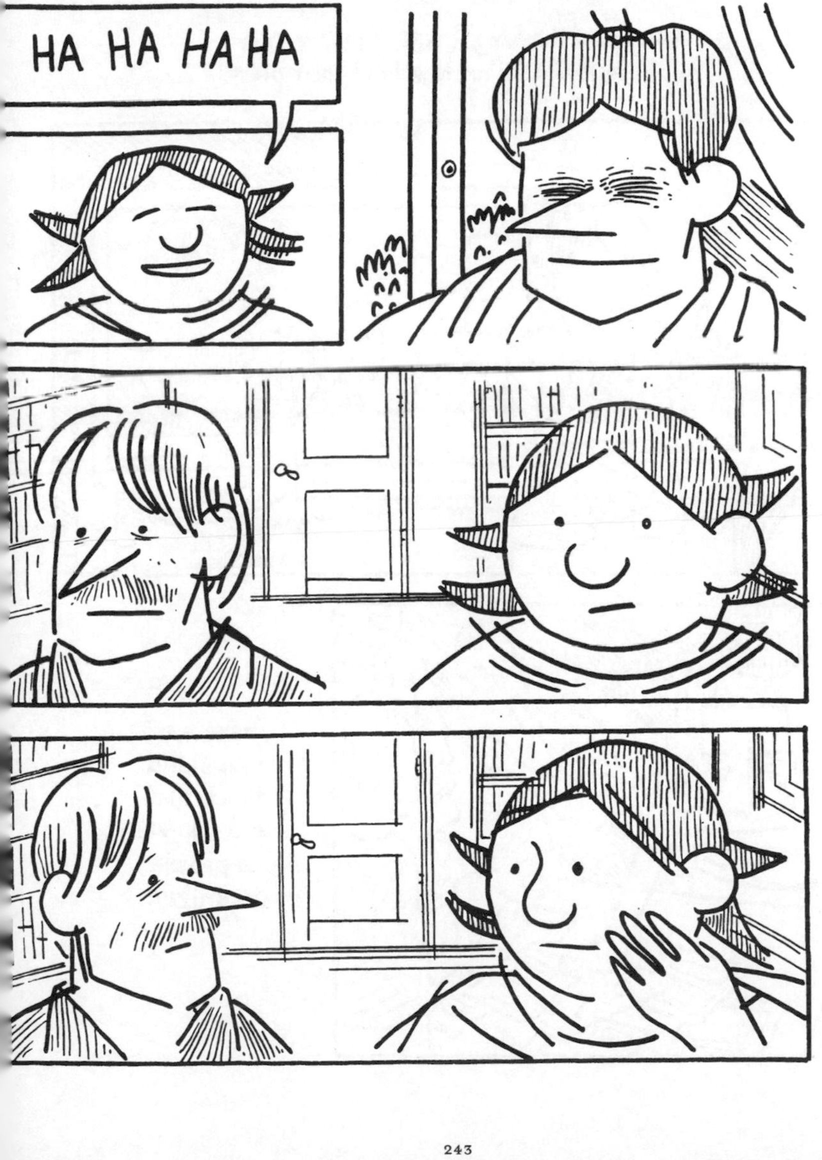
HA HA HA HA

I stopped thinking it was a joke when
Robin and Madeline layed out their plan.

There were
maps and
timetables
and squads
of people
organized.

The easiest to find were the papers still for sale.
We bought them all.

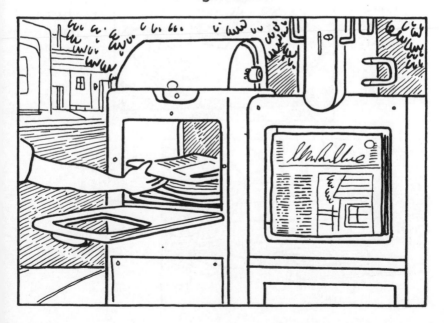

Robin had a friend who worked at the paper and was able to get the subscription list.

1/3 of the papers we could just pick up off of people's front lawn.

1/3 were purchased from stores and groceries.

1/3 needed to be negotiated away from their confused owners.

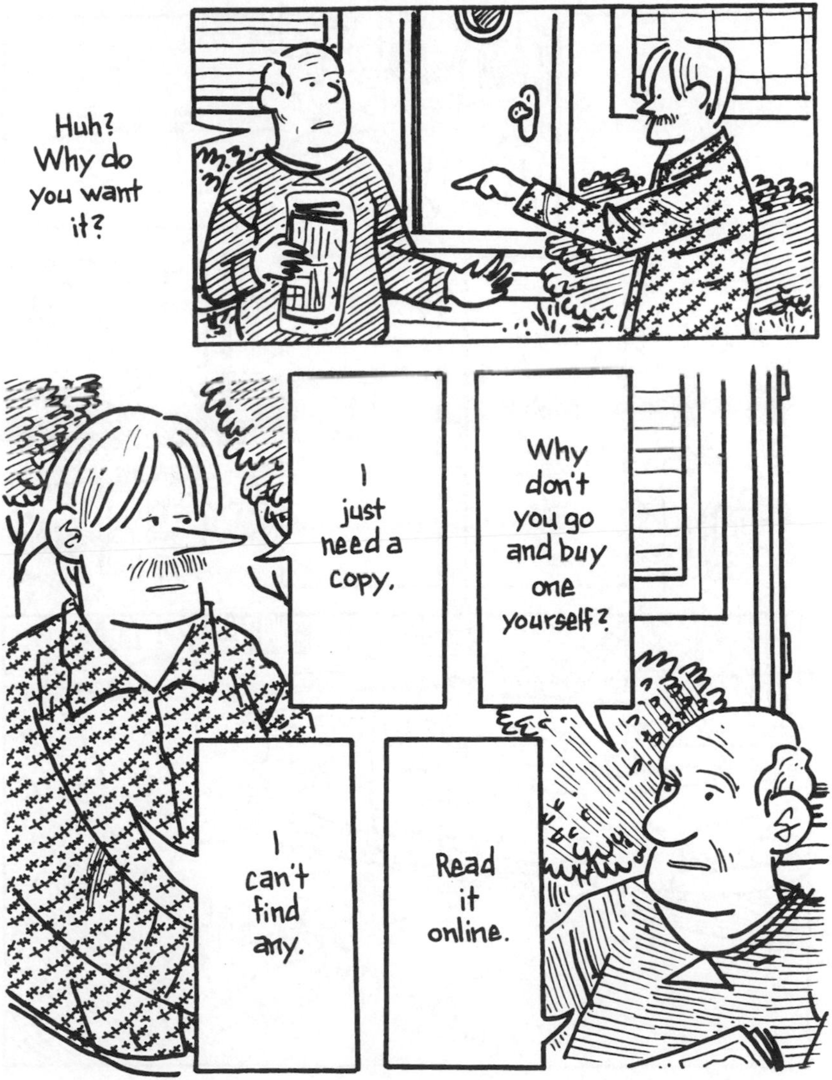
Huh? Why do you want it?
I just need a copy.
Why don't you go and buy one yourself?
I can't find any.
Read it online.

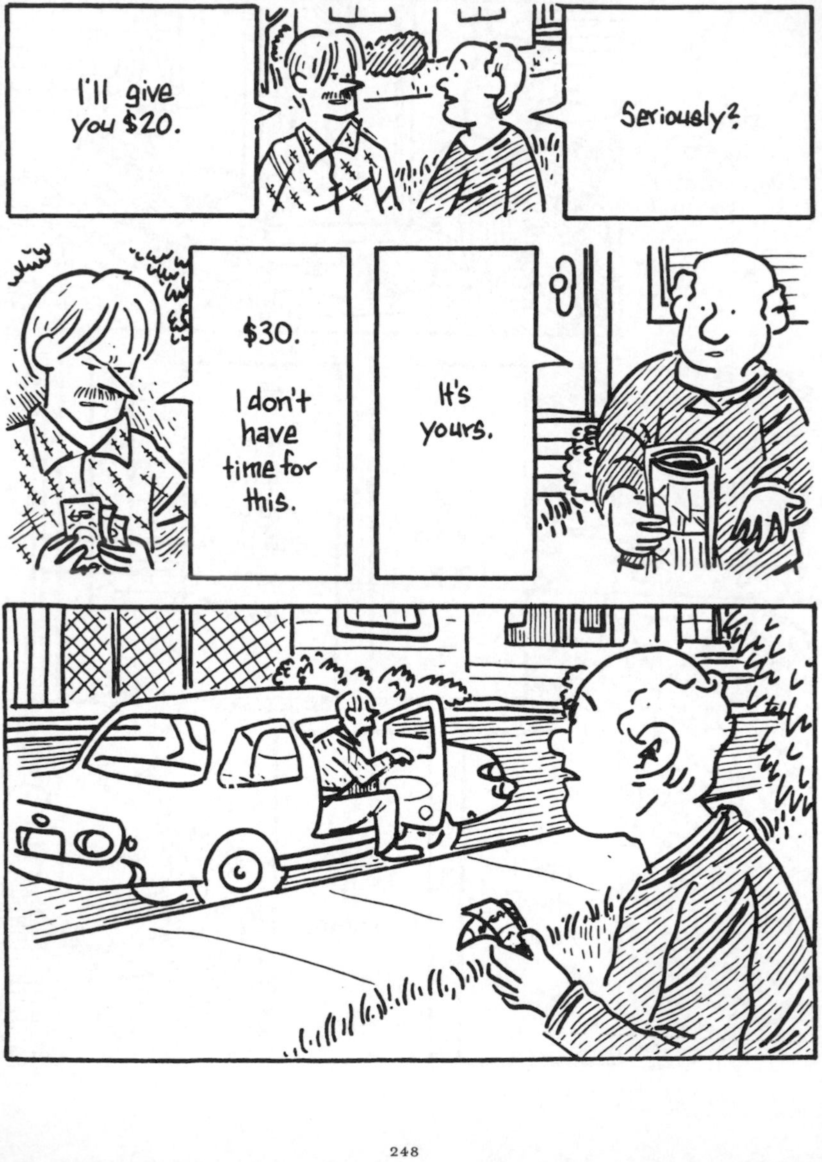
I'll give you $20.
Seriously?
$30. I don't have time for this.
It's yours.

Each team had 6 main counters and 6 people to check the count.

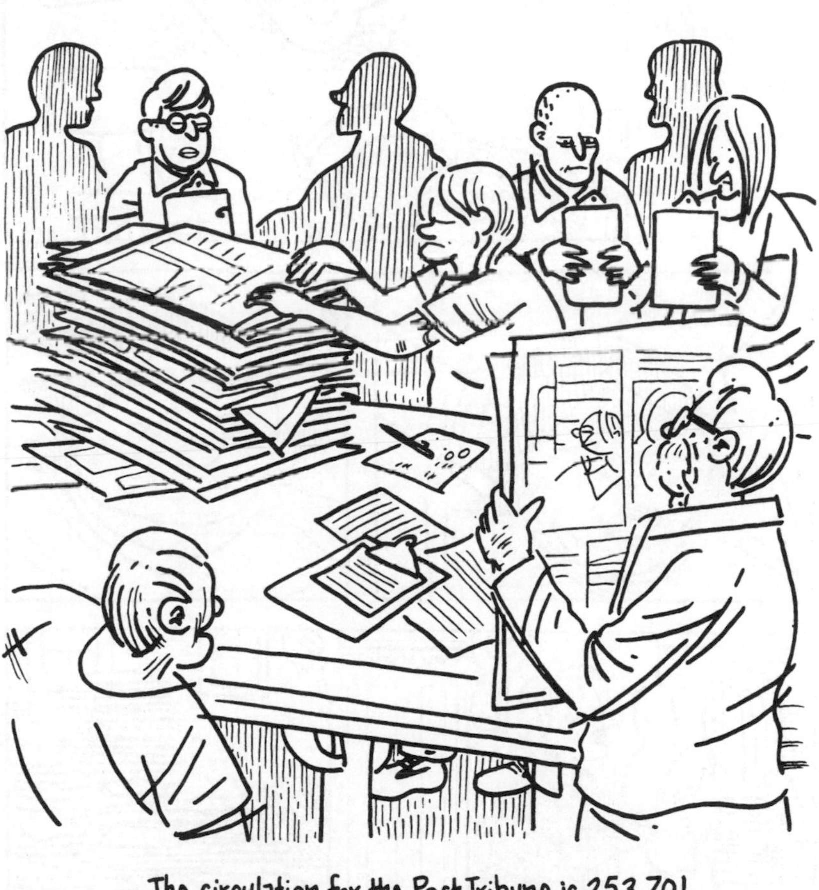

The circulation for the Post-Tribune is 253,701.
In order to count them all, we worked in 12 separate teams.

I supervised.

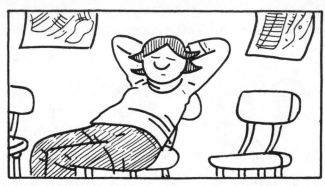

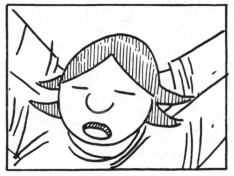

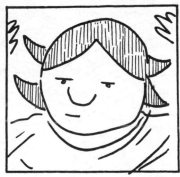

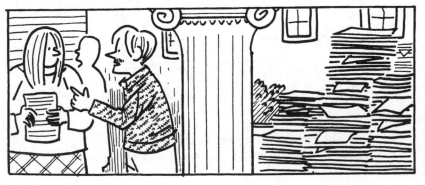

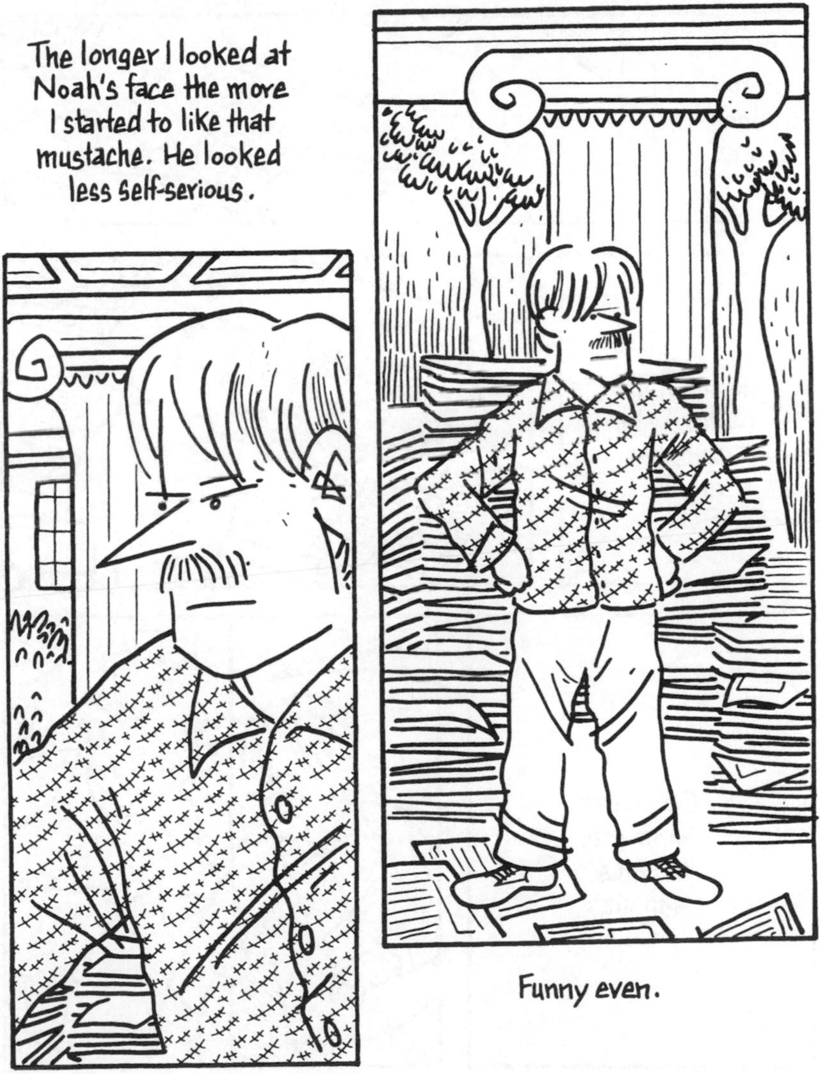
The longer I looked at Noah's face the more I started to like that mustache. He looked less self-serious.
Funny even.

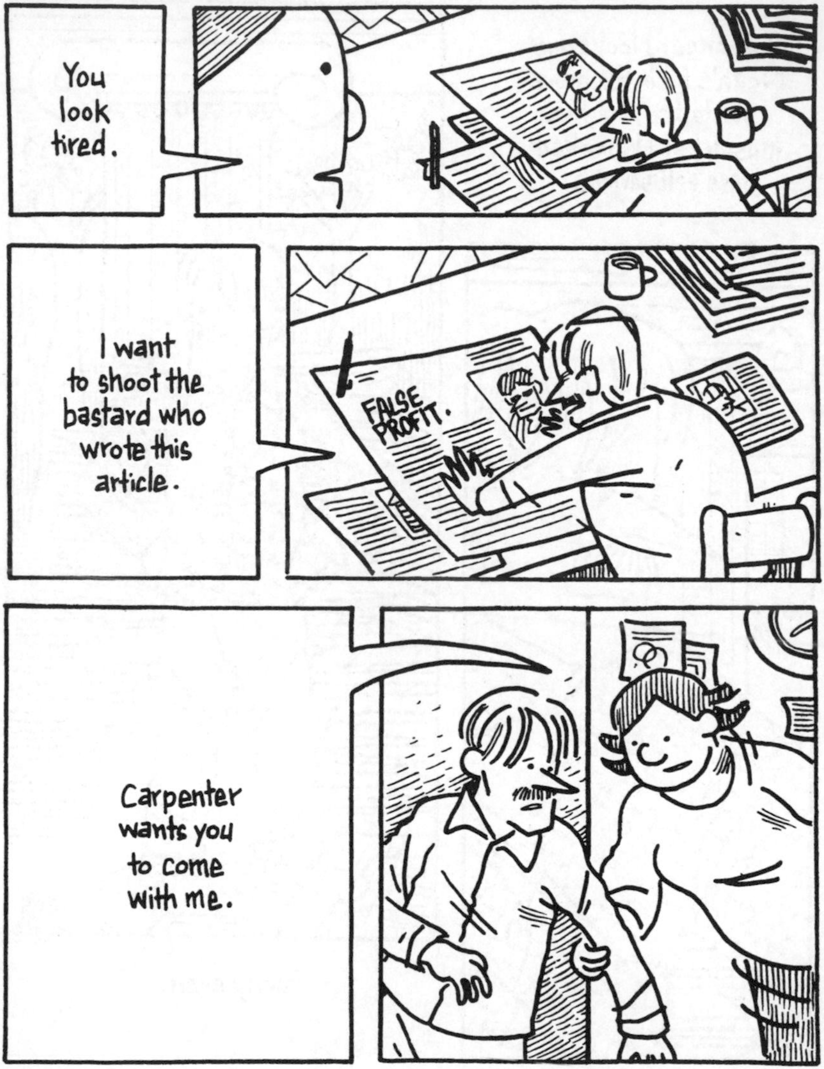
You look tired.
I want to shoot the bastard who wrote this article.
FALSE PROFIT.
Carpenter wants you to come with me.

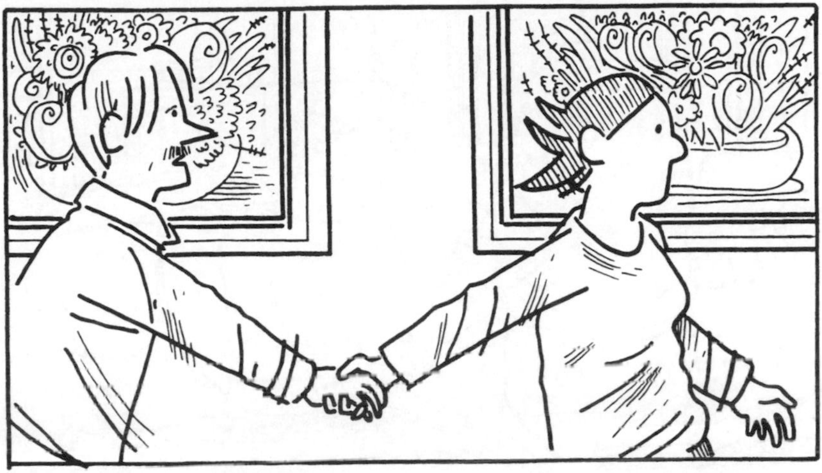

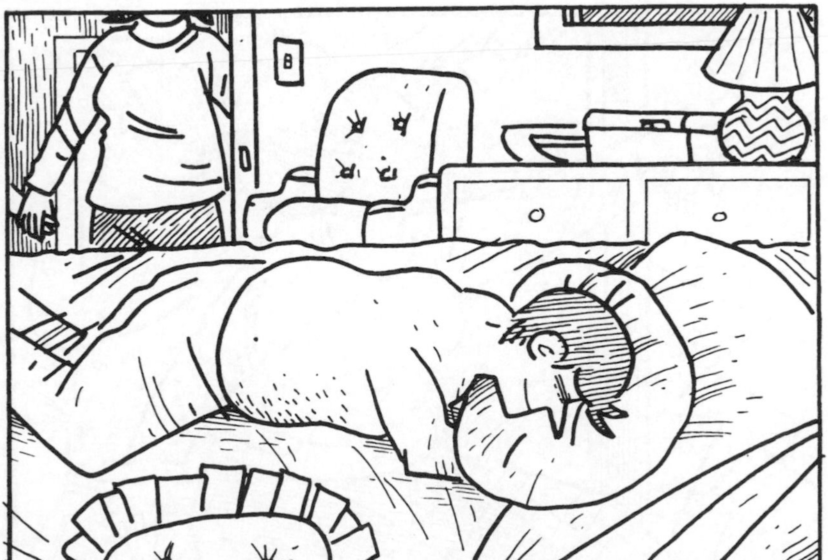

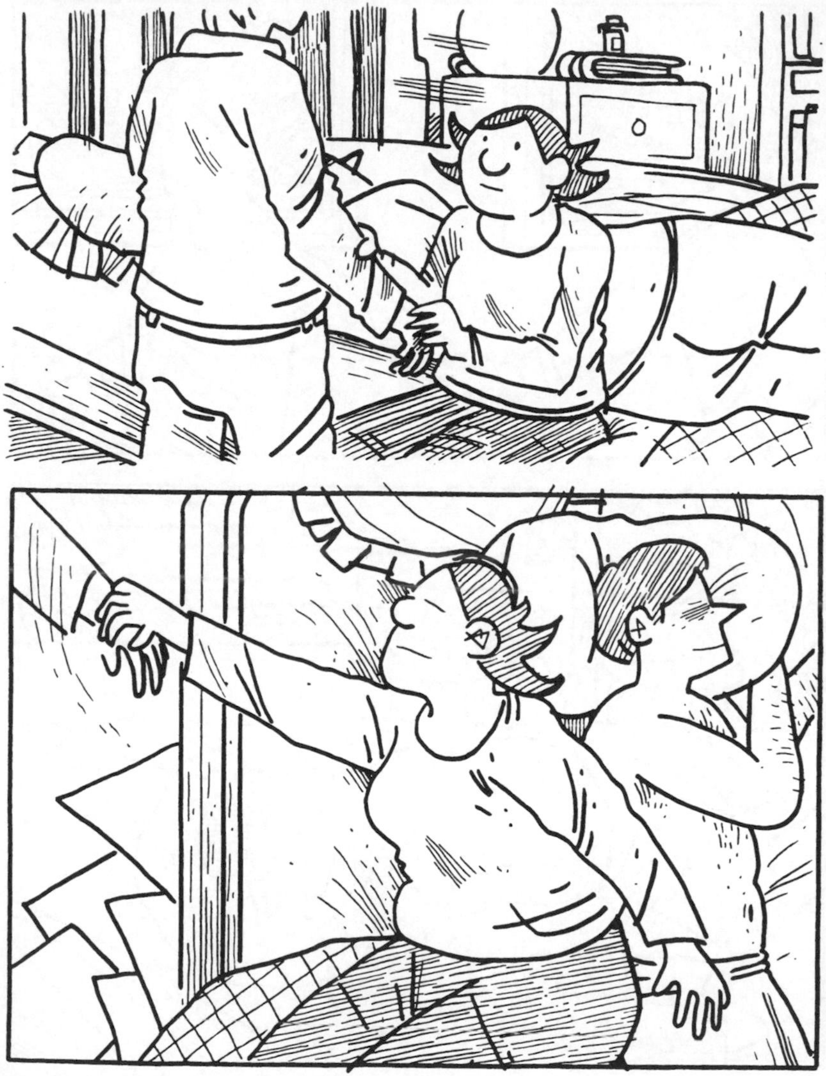

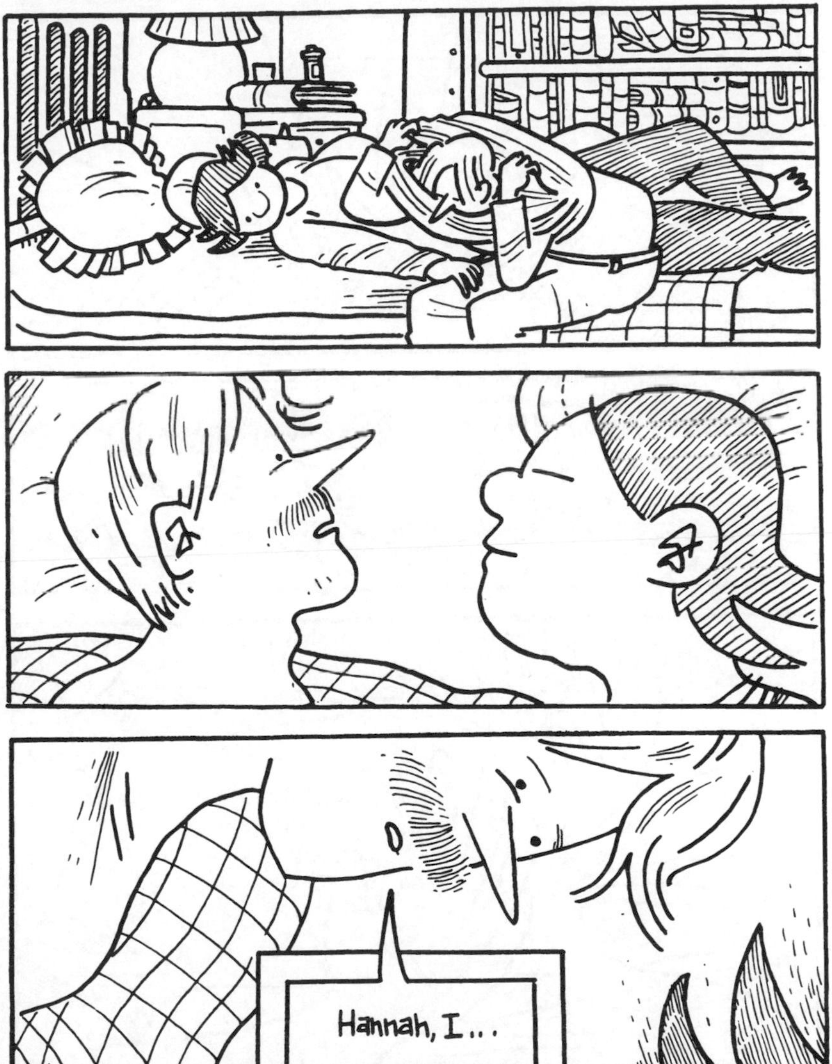
Hannah, I...

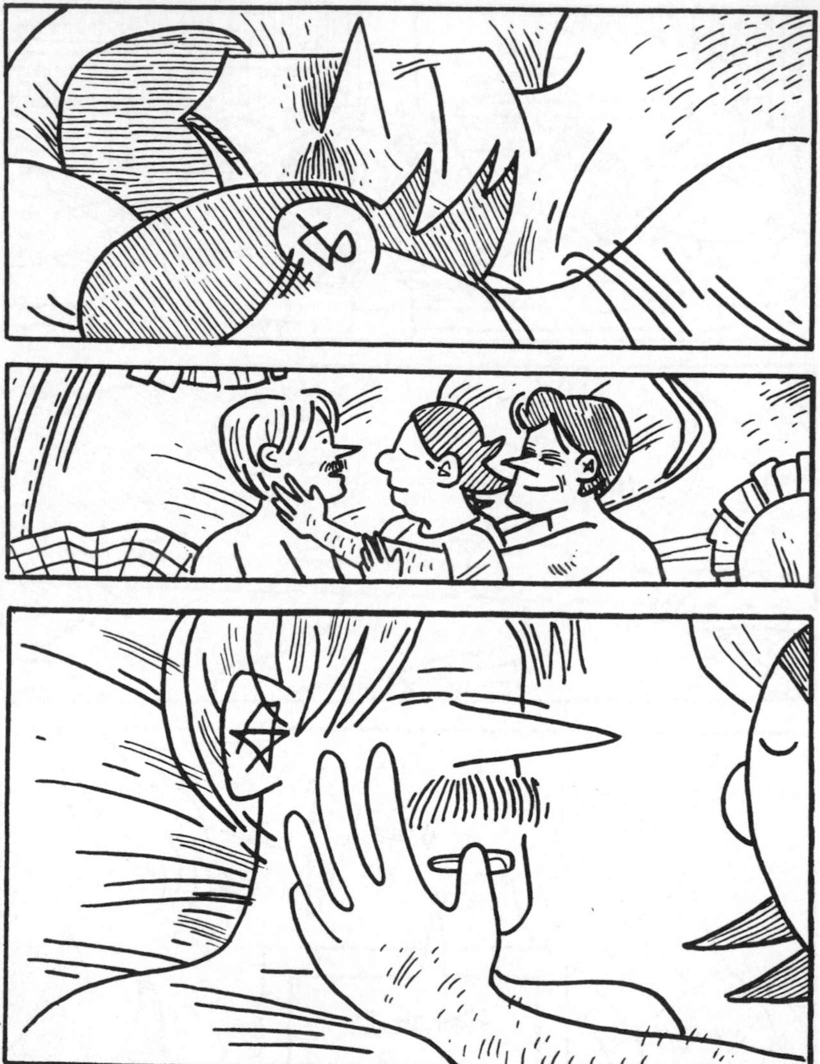

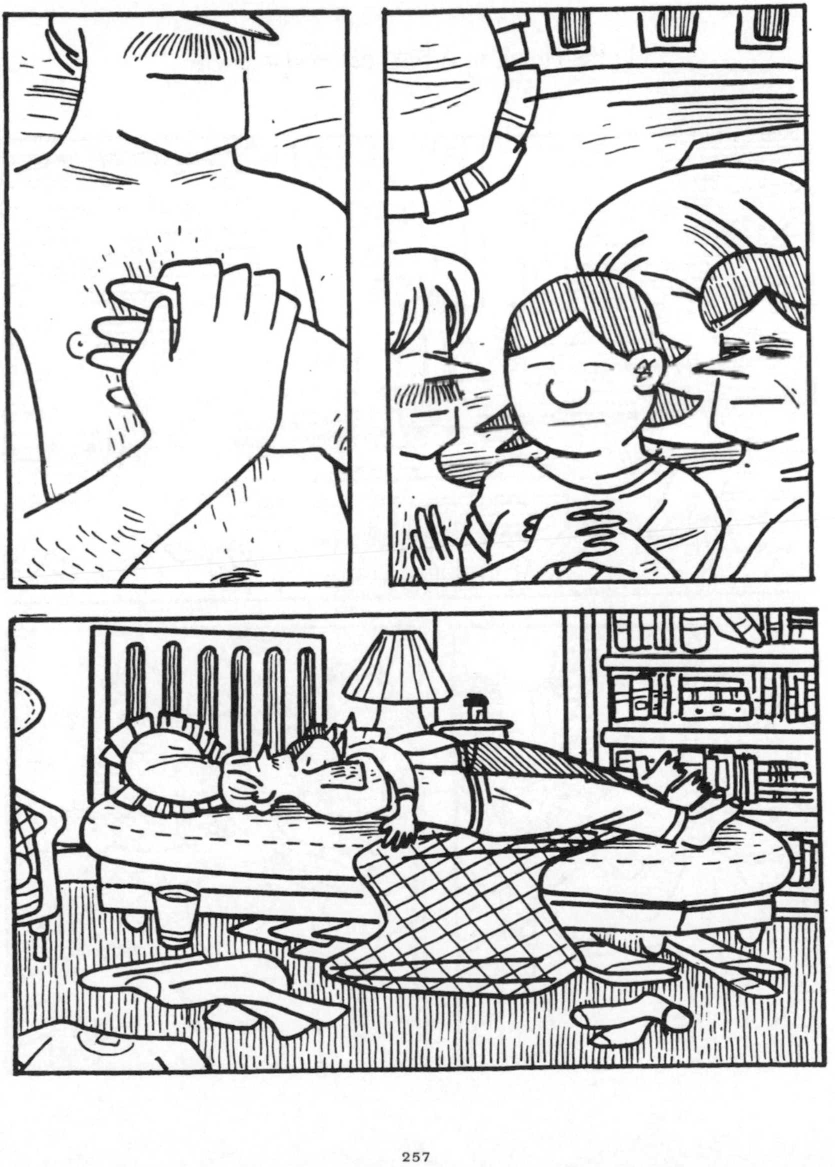

In the morning a final count was done.

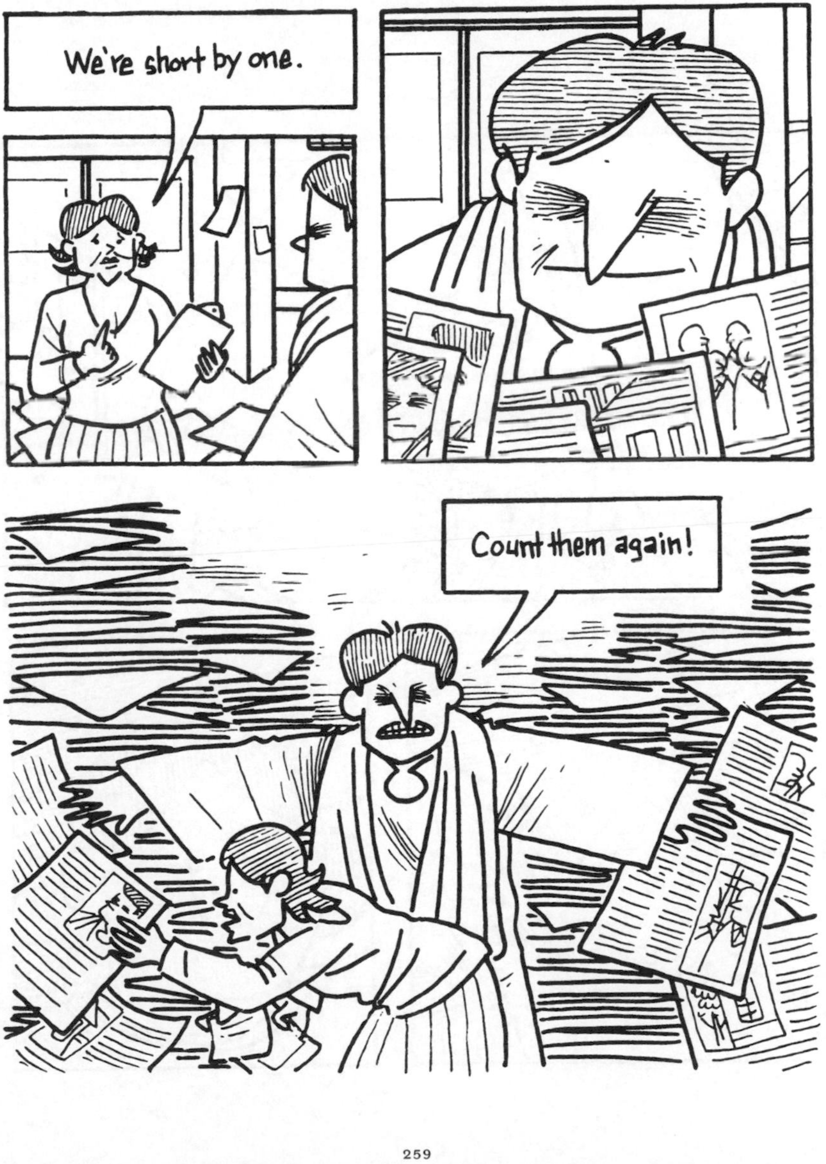
We're short by one.
Count them again!

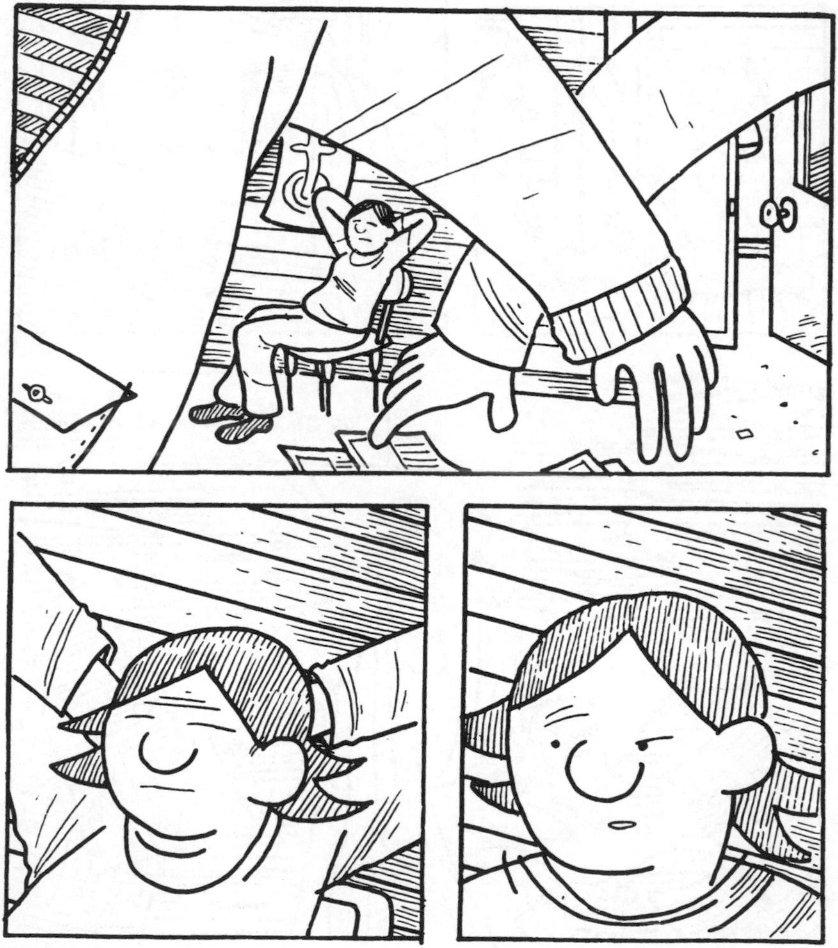

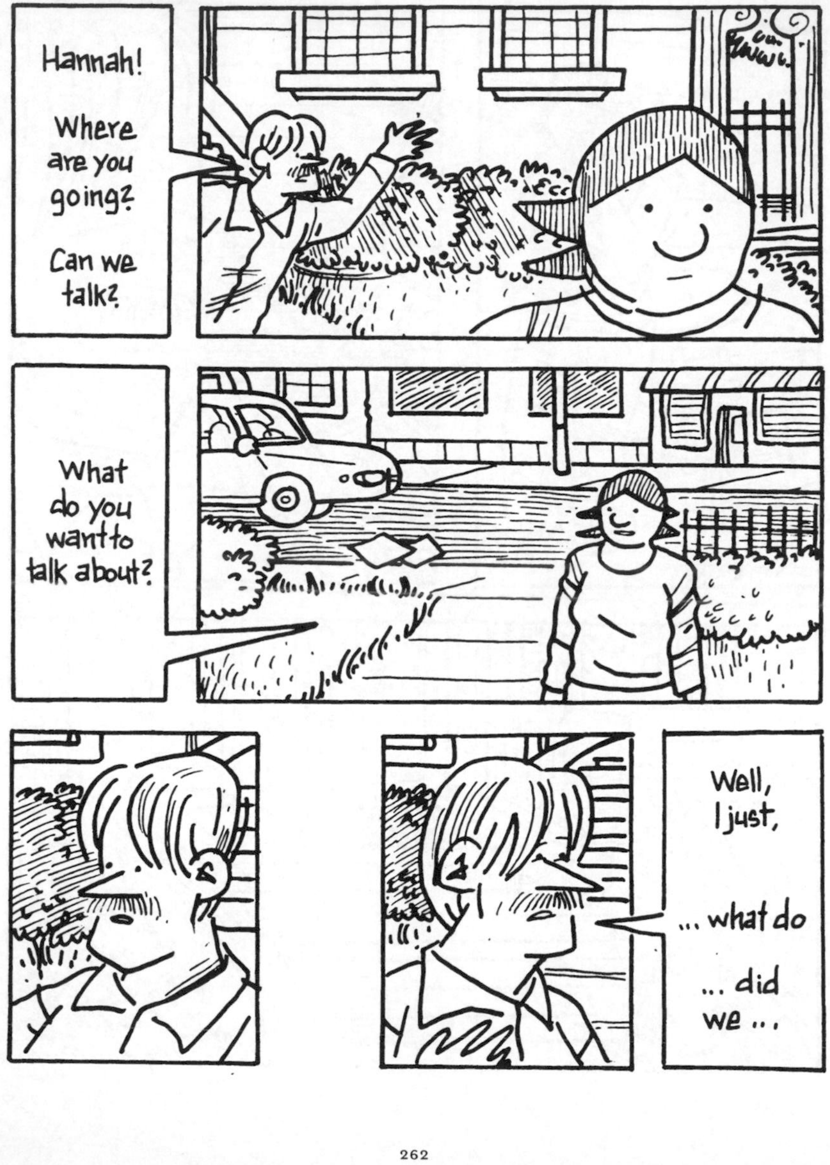
Hannah!
Where are you going?
Can we talk?
What do you want to talk about?
Well, I just,
... what do
... did we ...

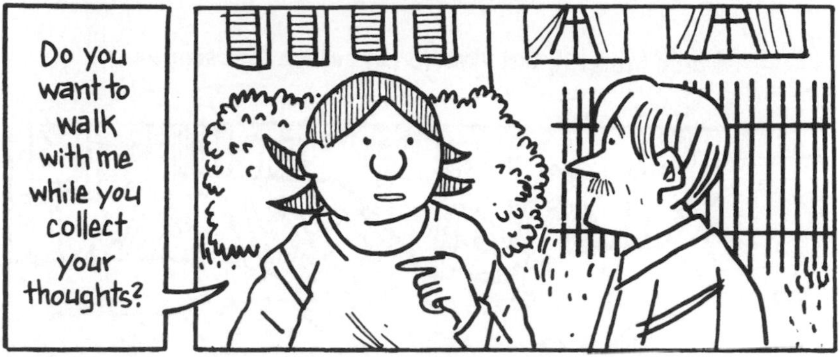
Do you want to walk with me while you collect your thoughts?

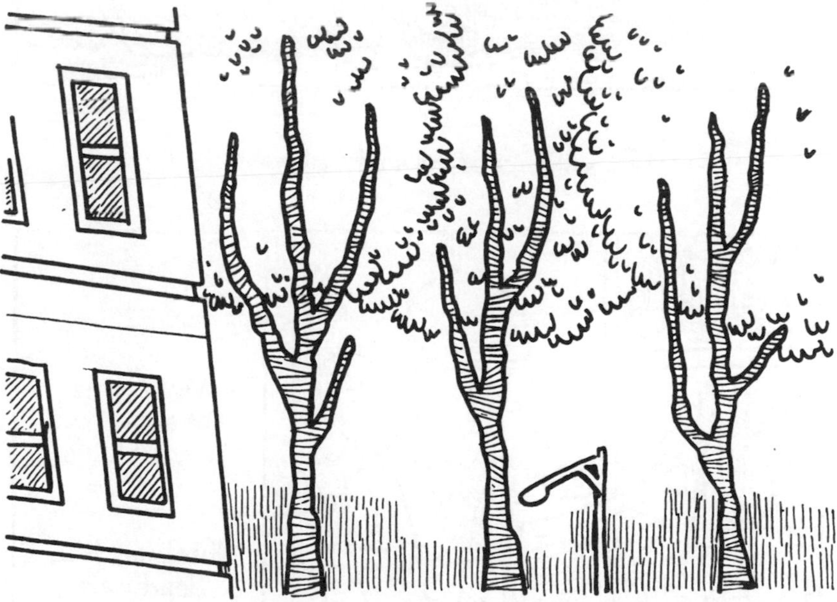

When I used to live alone in my apartment,
José would bring me the paper.

I didn't read it, but liked to cut out the horoscopes.

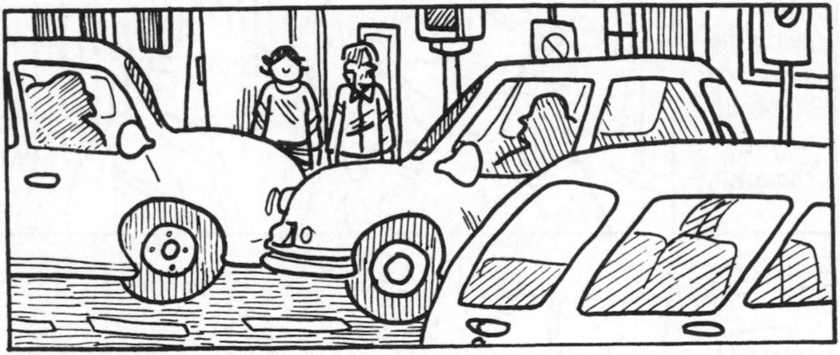

I remember once, he said...

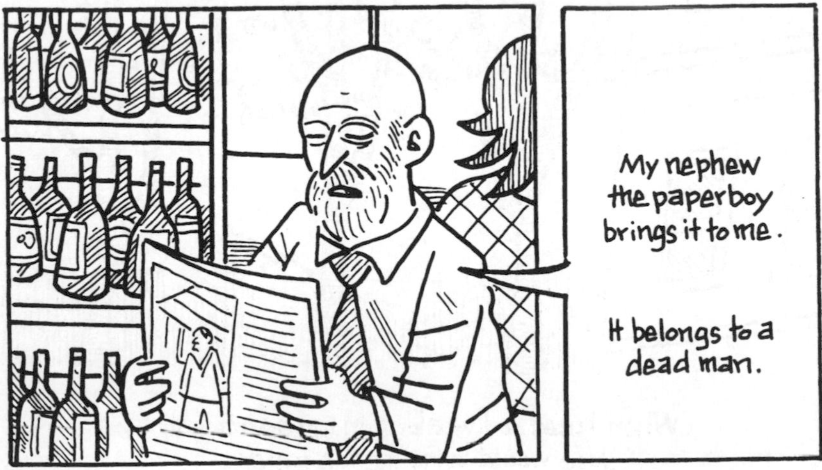
My nephew the paperboy brings it to me.
It belongs to a dead man.

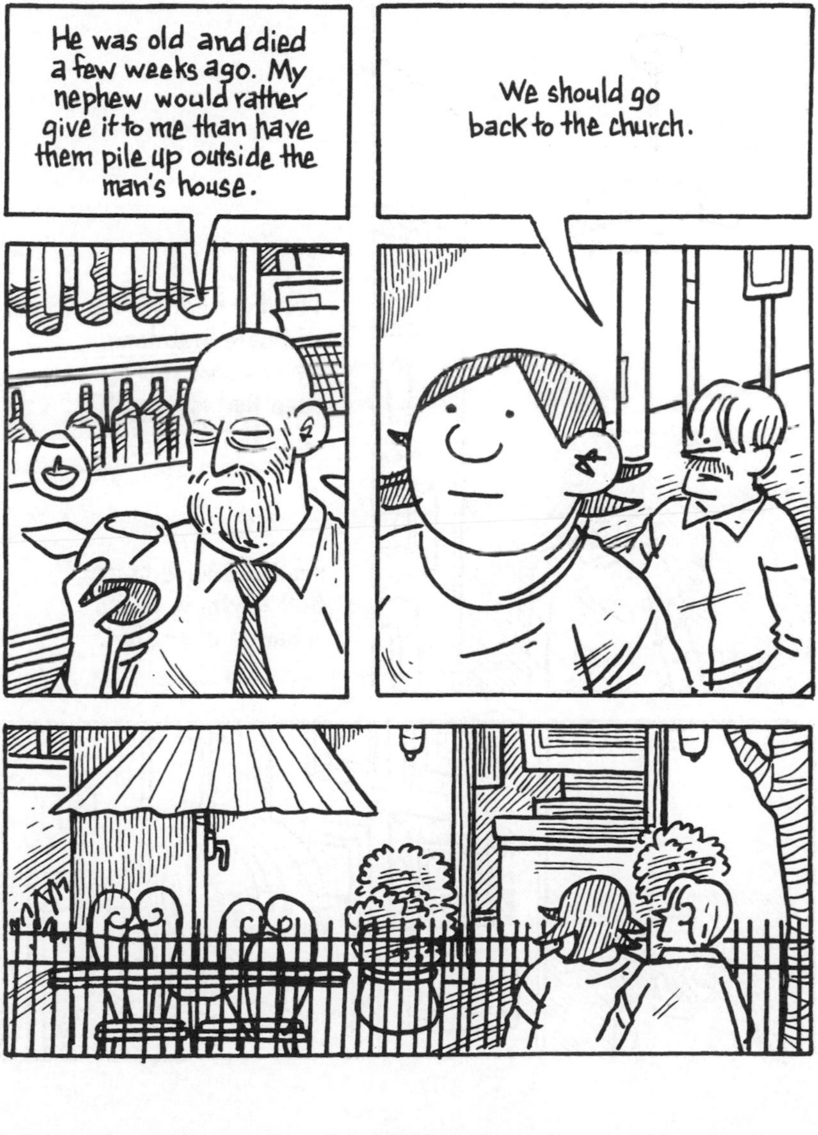
He was old and died a few weeks ago. My nephew would rather give it to me than have them pile up outside the man's house.
We should go back to the church.

I hadn't been to the old café in so long, I was shocked to see that they had painted the walls.

It felt offensive to me that anything would change after I left.

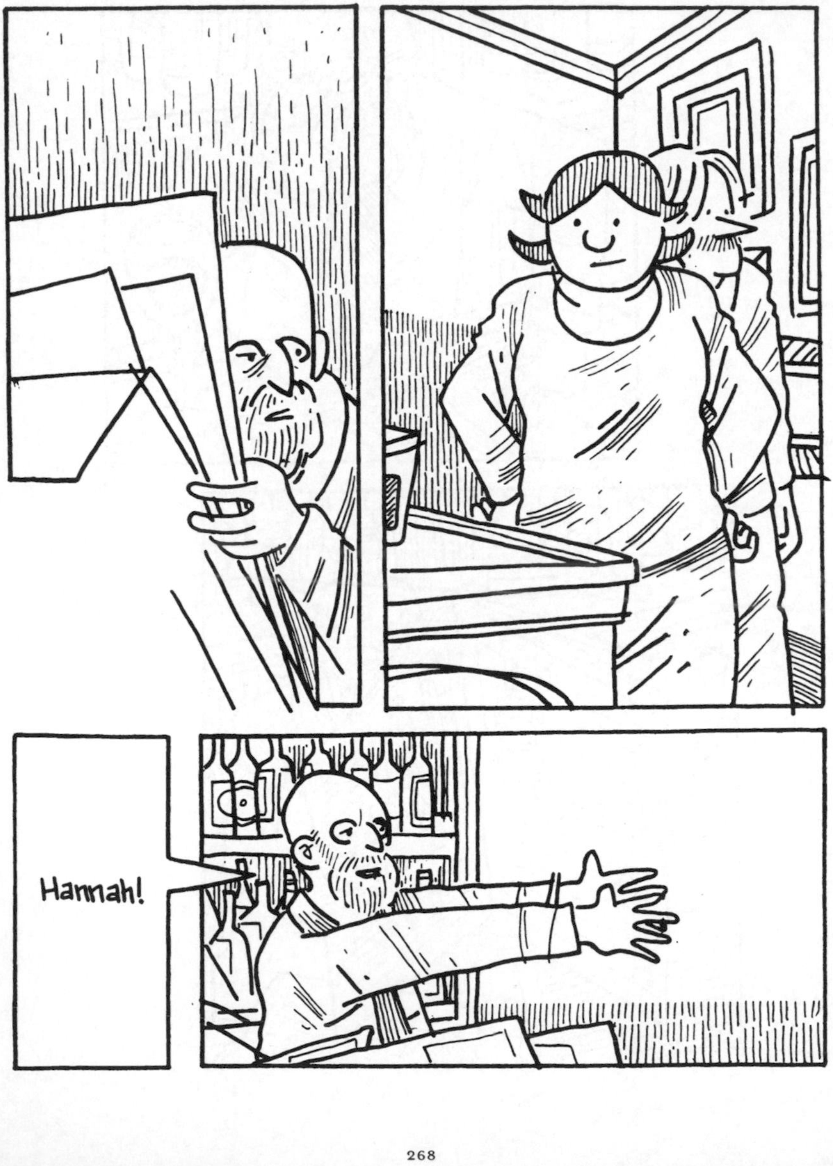
Hannah!

I was
so happy
to have
been the
one to
find the
last paper.

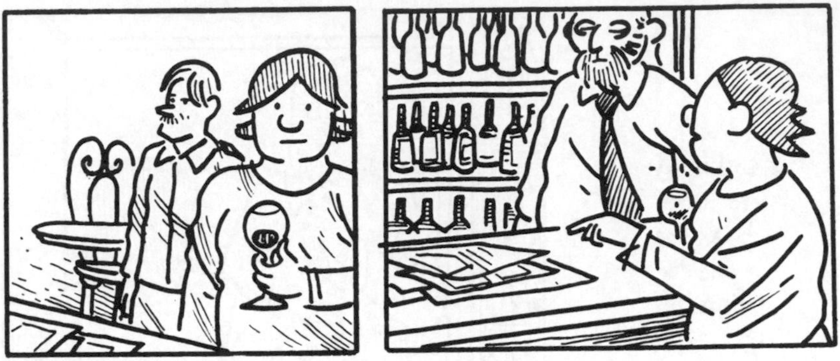

My excitement got the better of me.

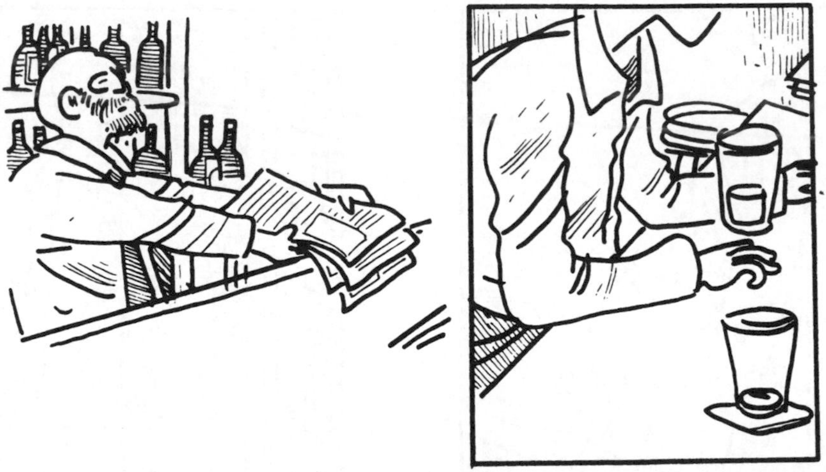

There may have been a part of me who wanted
to show off for Peter who was sitting at the bar.

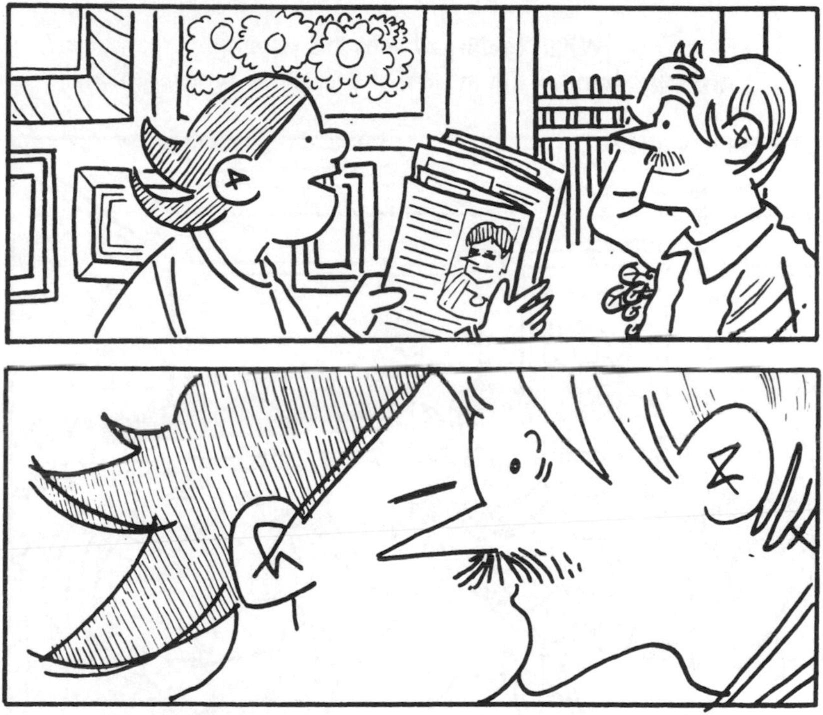

This time, it would be me who would walk away without saying goodbye. I wonder if he even recognized me.

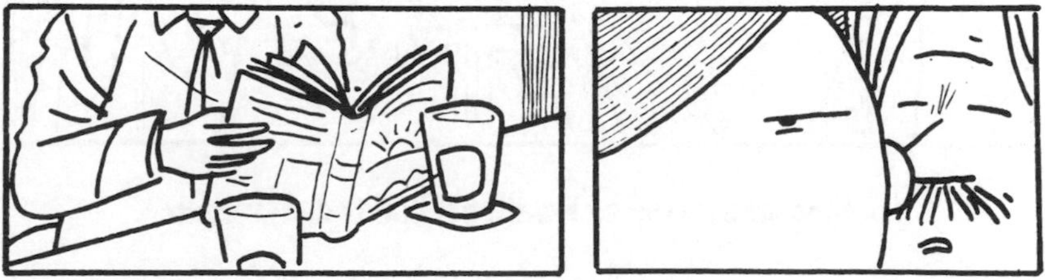

When I returned with the paper,
Carpenter thanked me in front of the entire congregation.

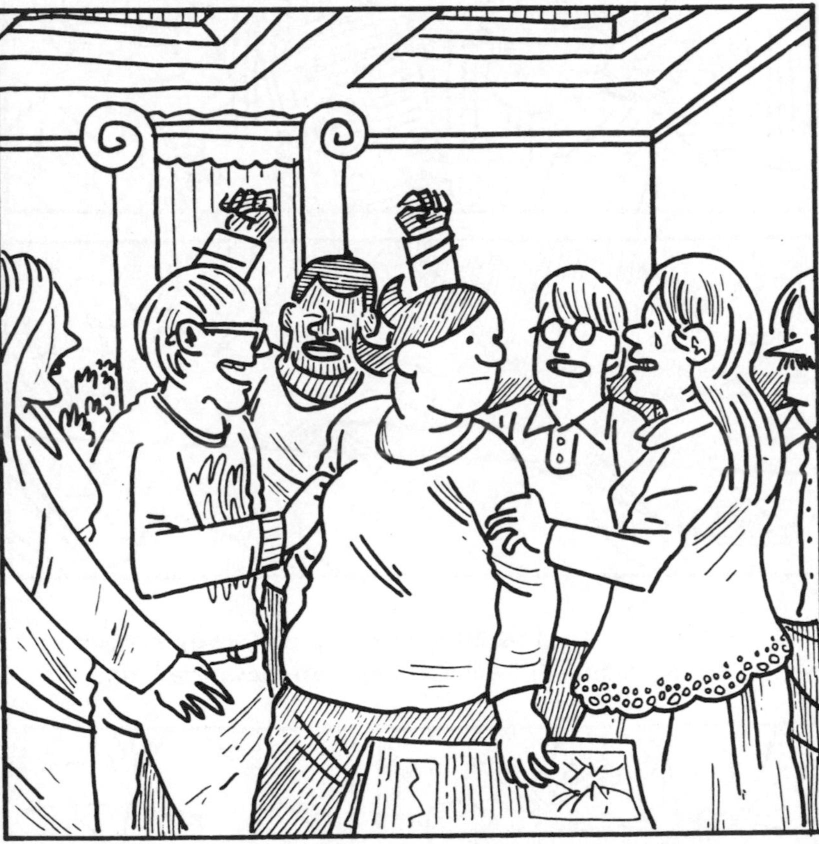

Looking at everyone, I realized that it didn't matter.

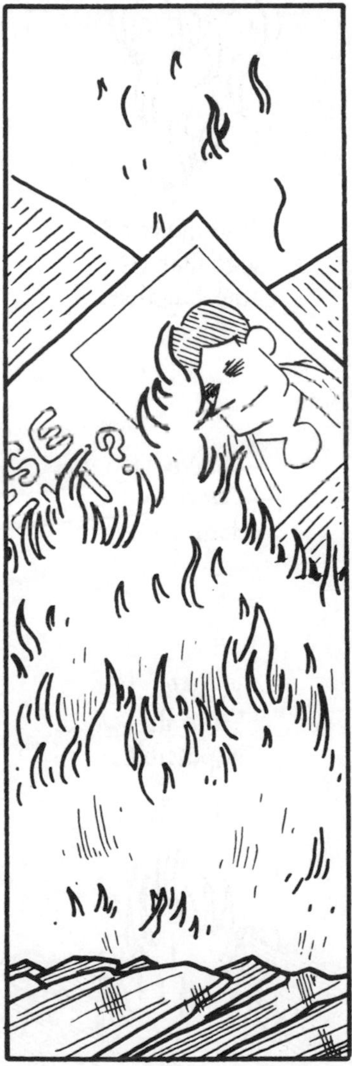

He didn't care if we actually found all the newspapers.

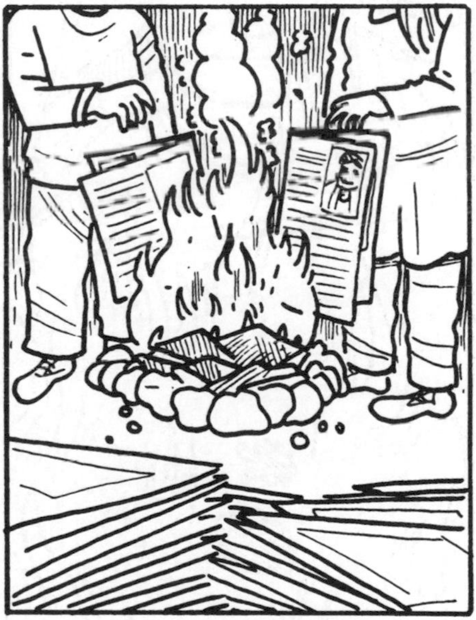

You can still read the damn story online.

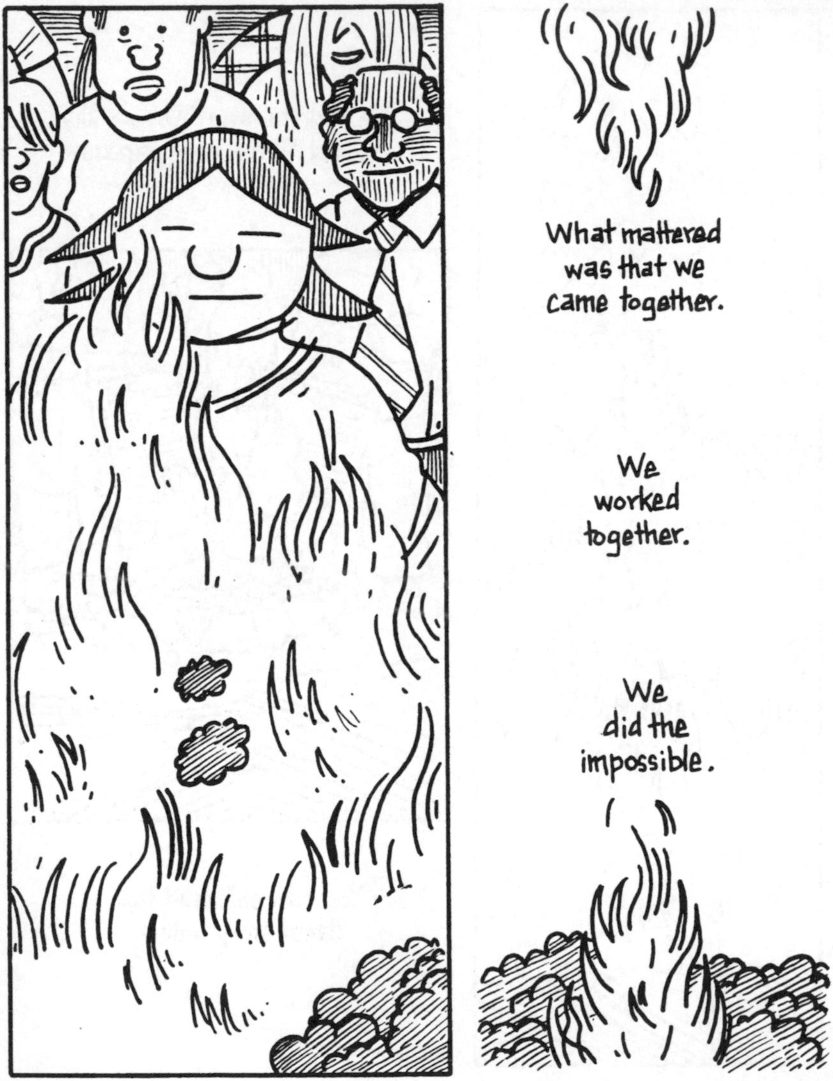
What mattered was that we came together.
We worked together.
We did the impossible.

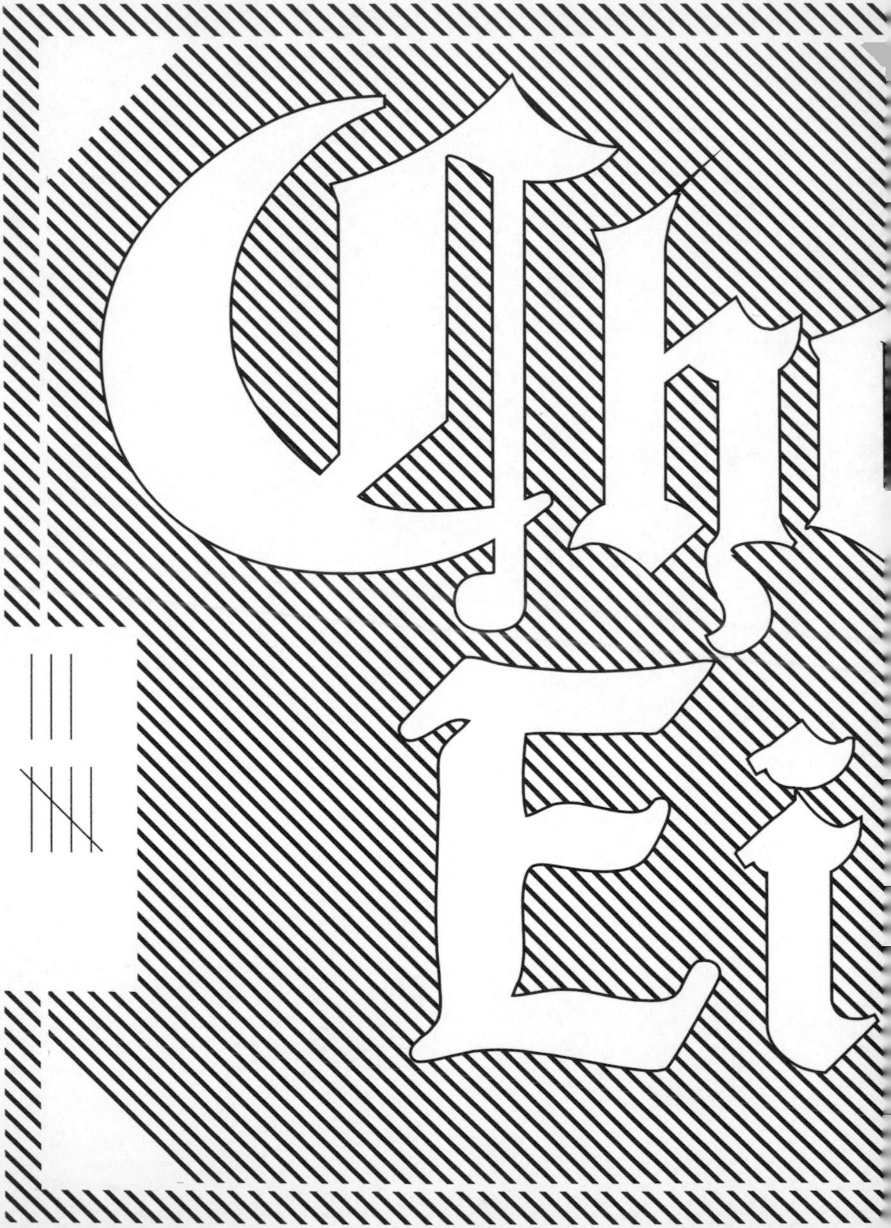
Ch
Et

pter

ht

Clarence

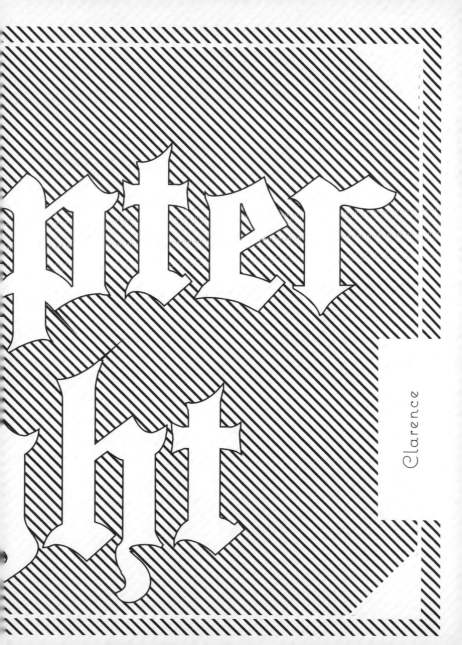

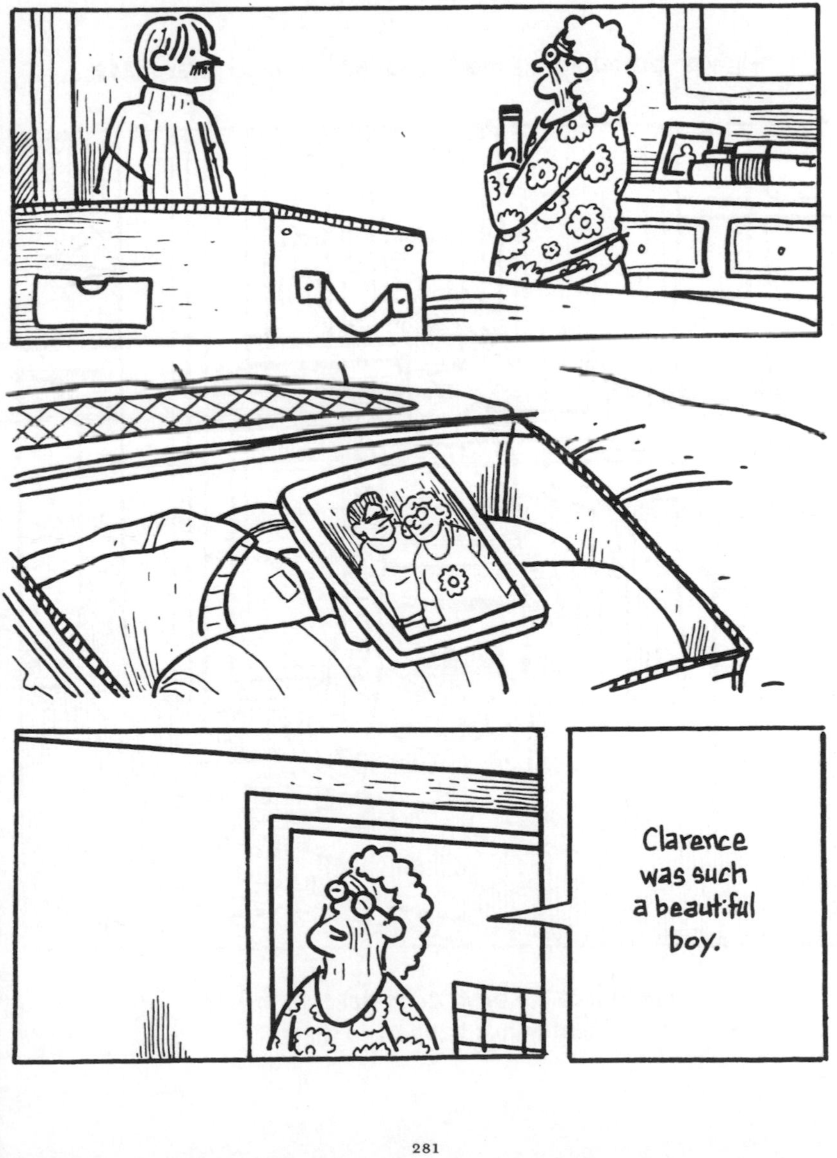
Clarence was such a beautiful boy.

He was probably the most beautiful boy God ever made.

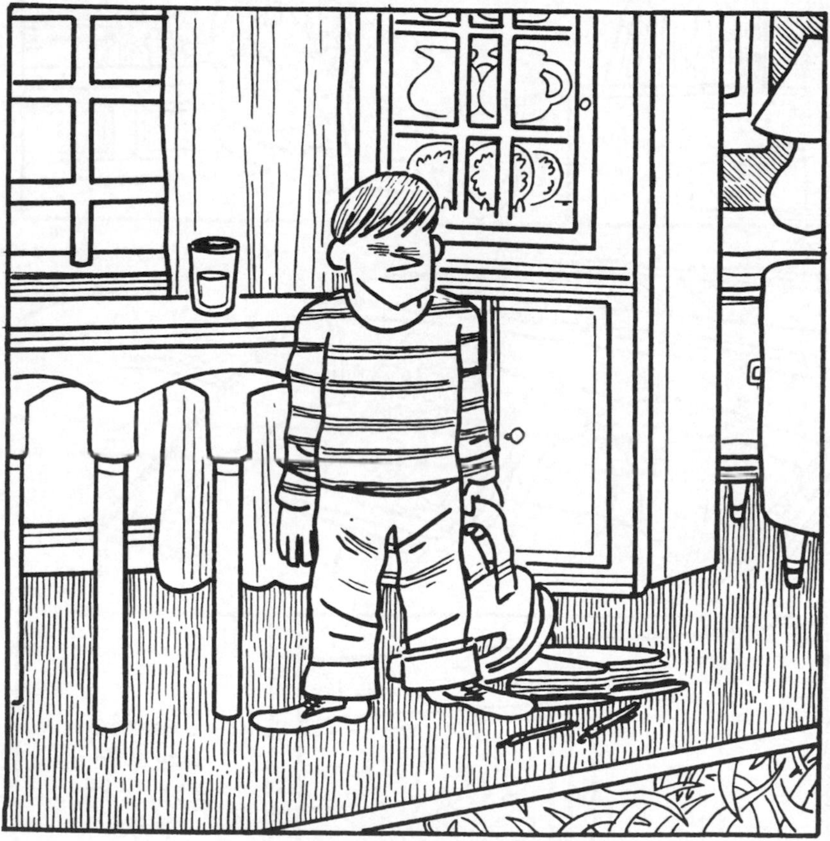

Good looking boys don't deserve to have bad things happen to them.

I did my best. I sacrificed so much for that boy.

You can only do so much when you're poor.

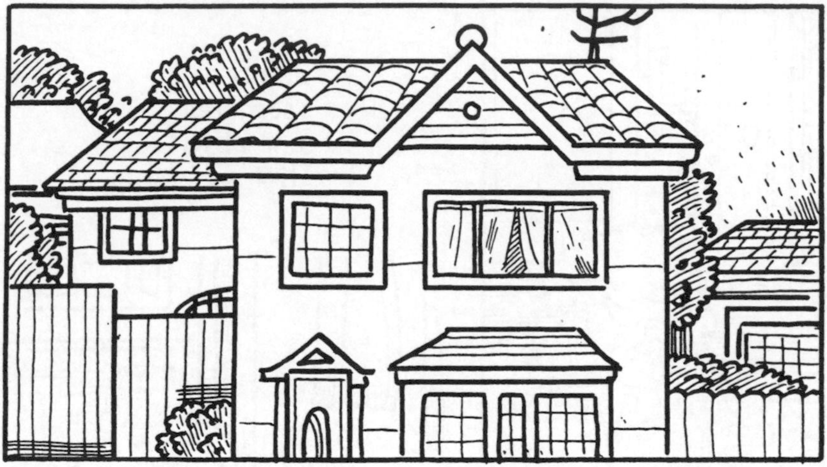

"We changed homes almost every year.
I had a business selling buckets, so we were always
on the move, looking for new markets."

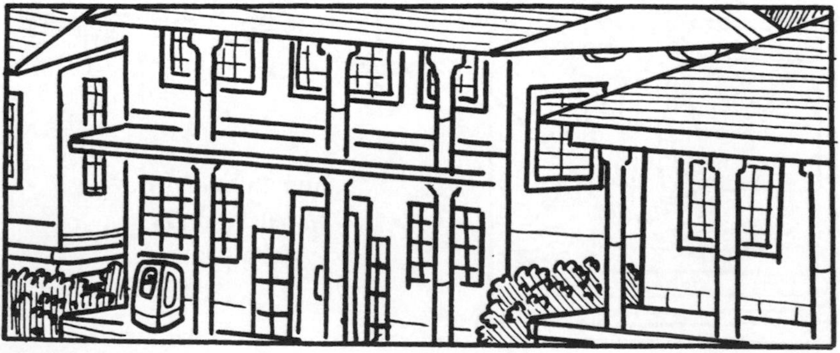

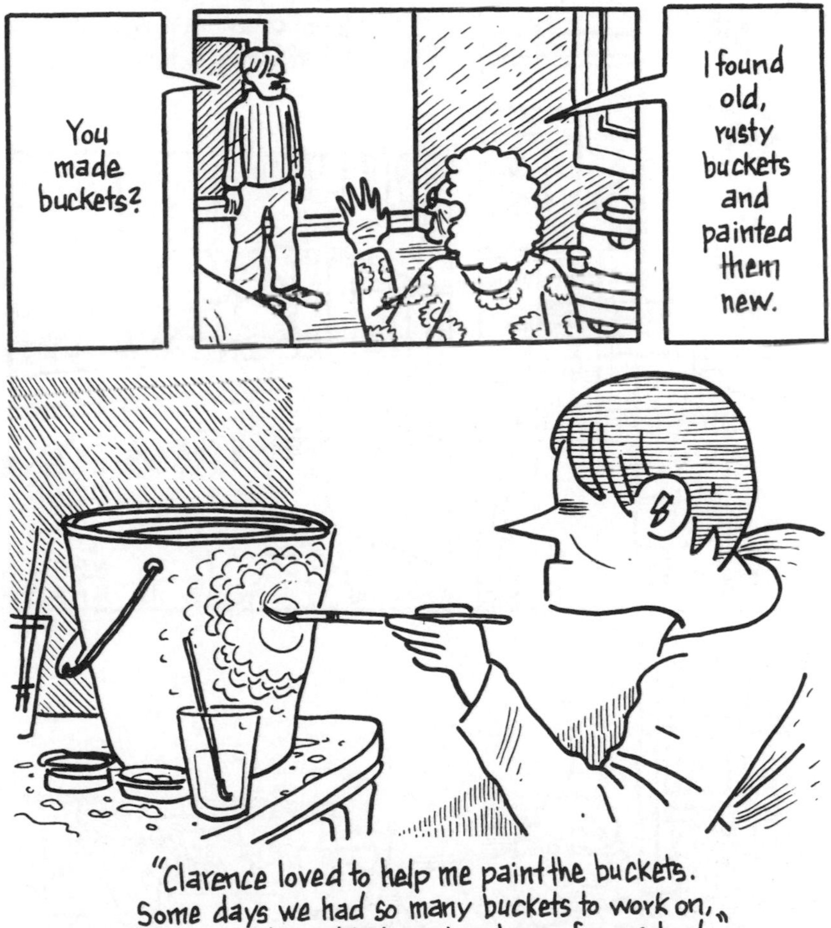
You made buckets?
I found old, rusty buckets and painted them new.
"Clarence loved to help me paint the buckets. Some days we had so many buckets to work on, that I would need to keep him home from school."

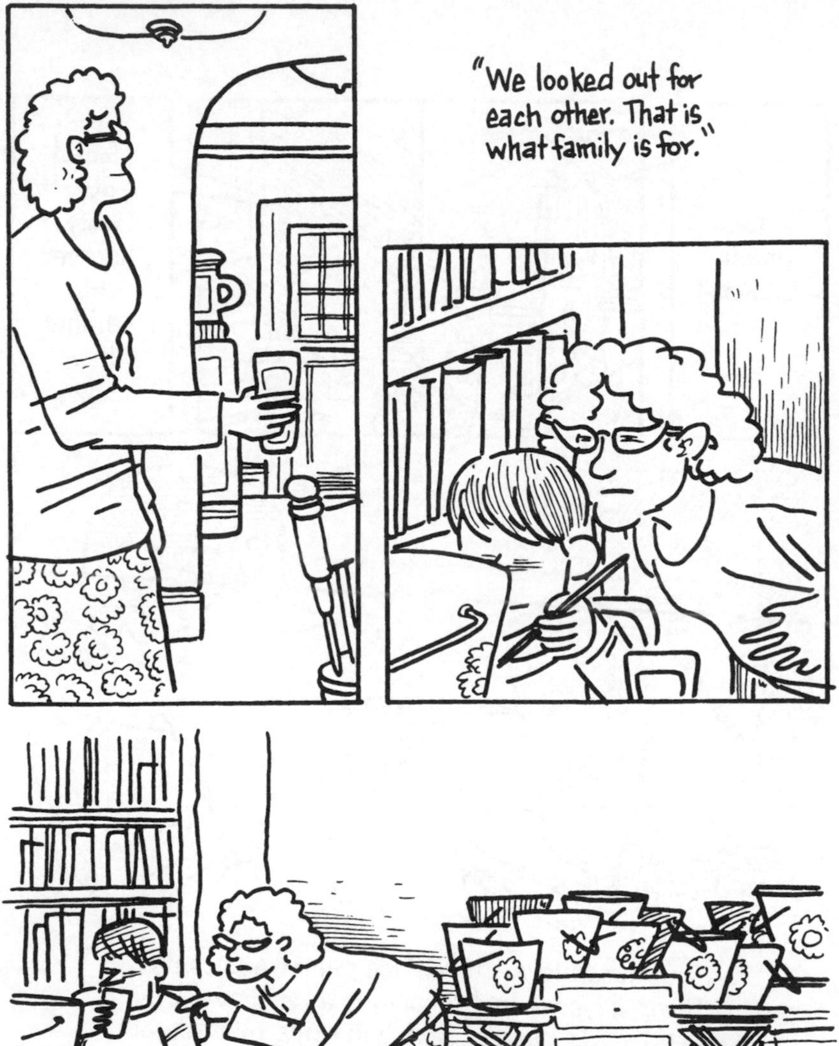
"We looked out for each other. That is what family is for."

Where was Reverand Carpenter's father?

Clarence's father always had his own problems. We never saw him.

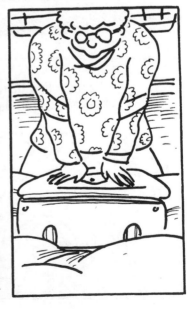

We didn't see much of anyone at the time.

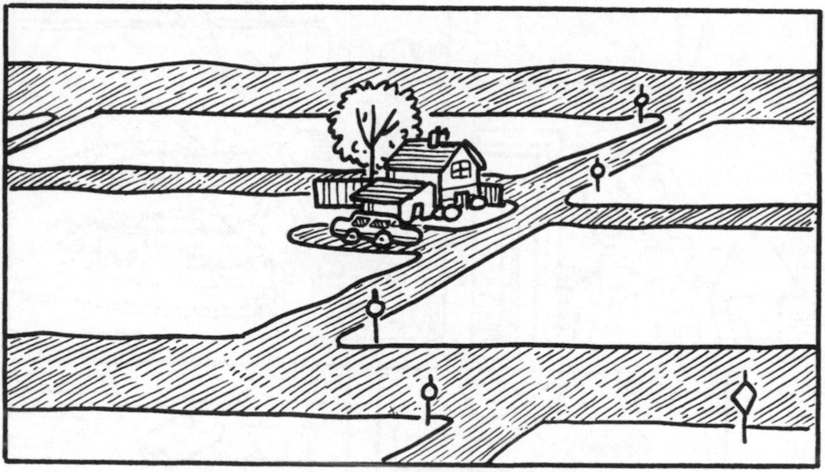

Clarence had trouble making friends and he started talking to the animals around the farm.

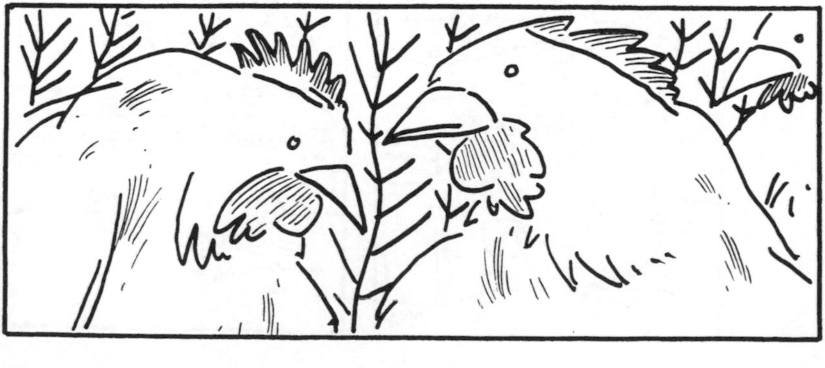

You lived on a farm?

We had no money! We had to grow our own food.

"I had to let Clarence choose what chickens we ate. Only he knew which were his friends. Although they all followed him around like he was the mama duck."

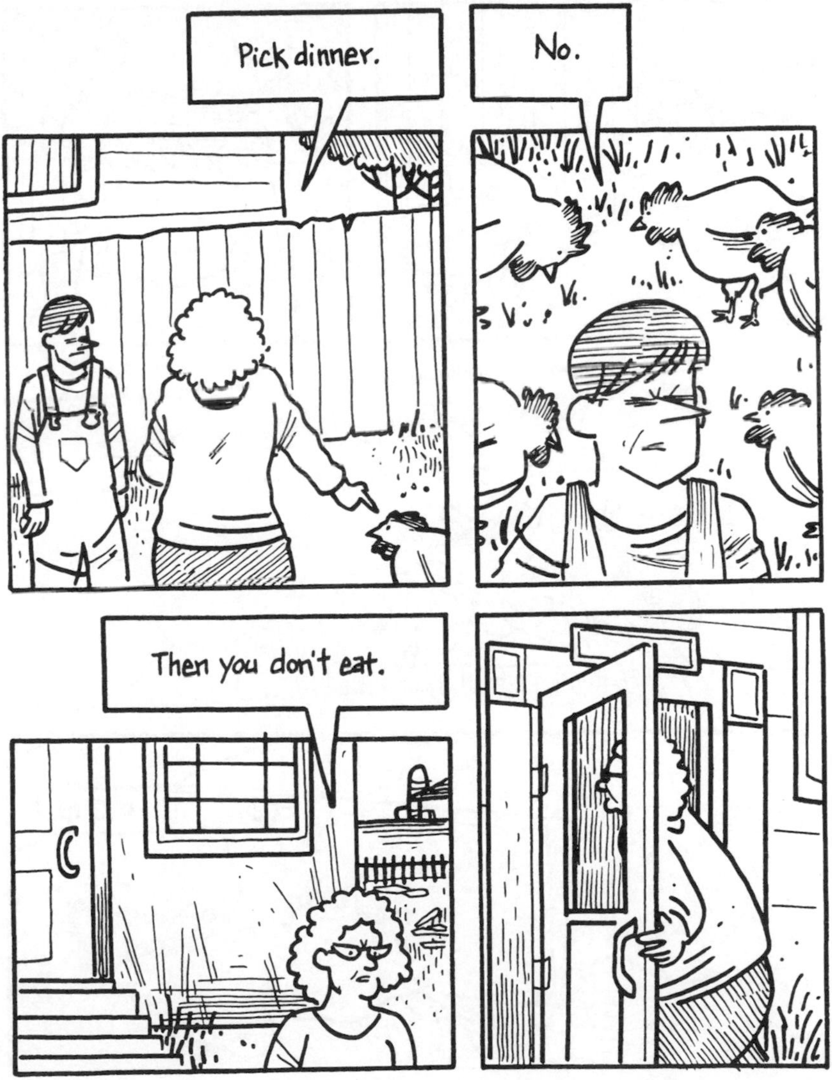
Pick dinner.
No.
Then you don't eat.

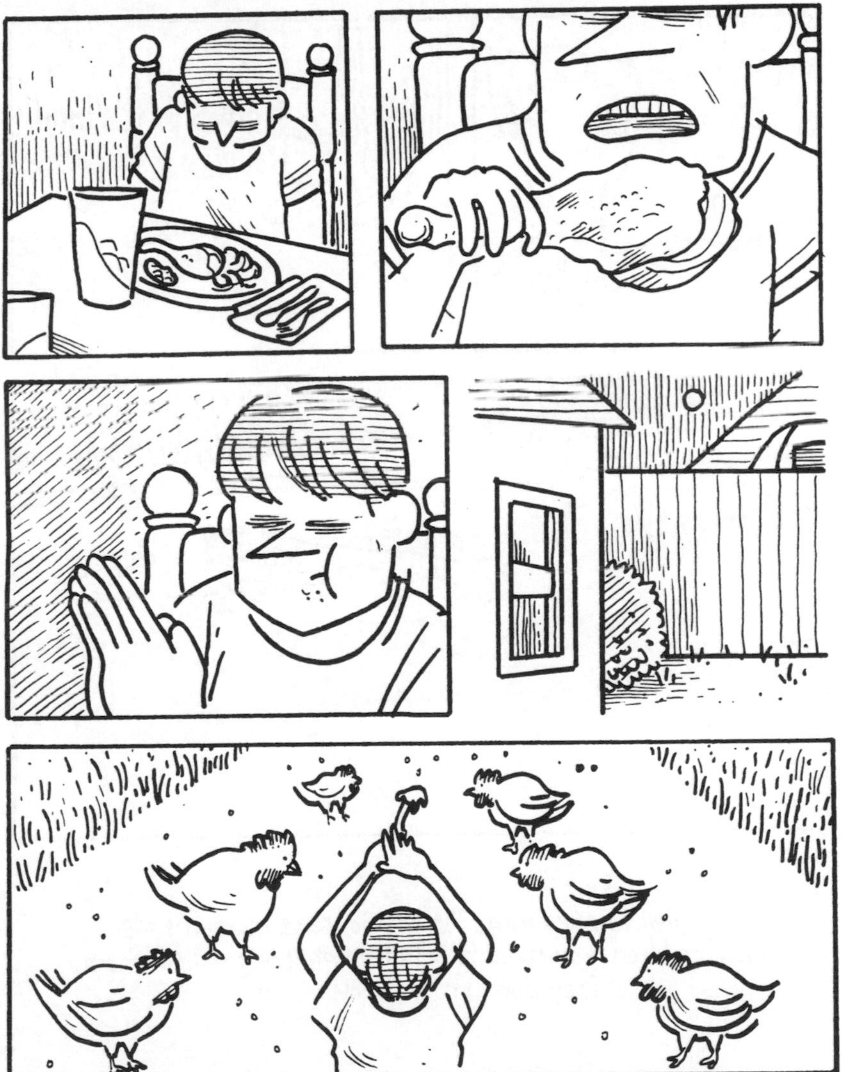

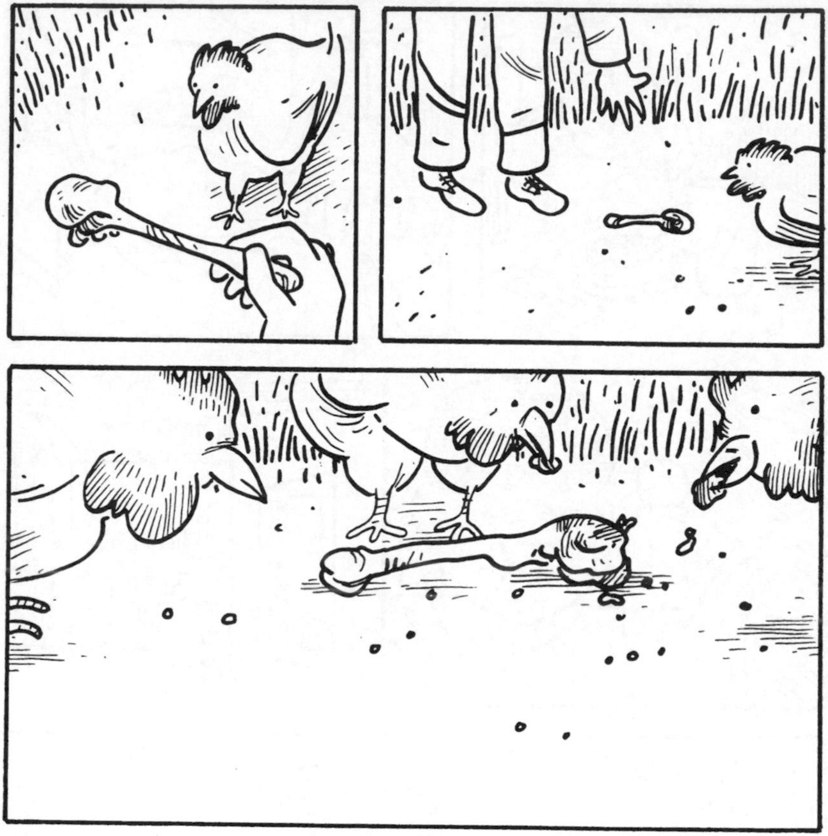

I tried to encourage the boy to make more friends.
With children, *you* need to tell them what is good for them.
They don't know on their own.

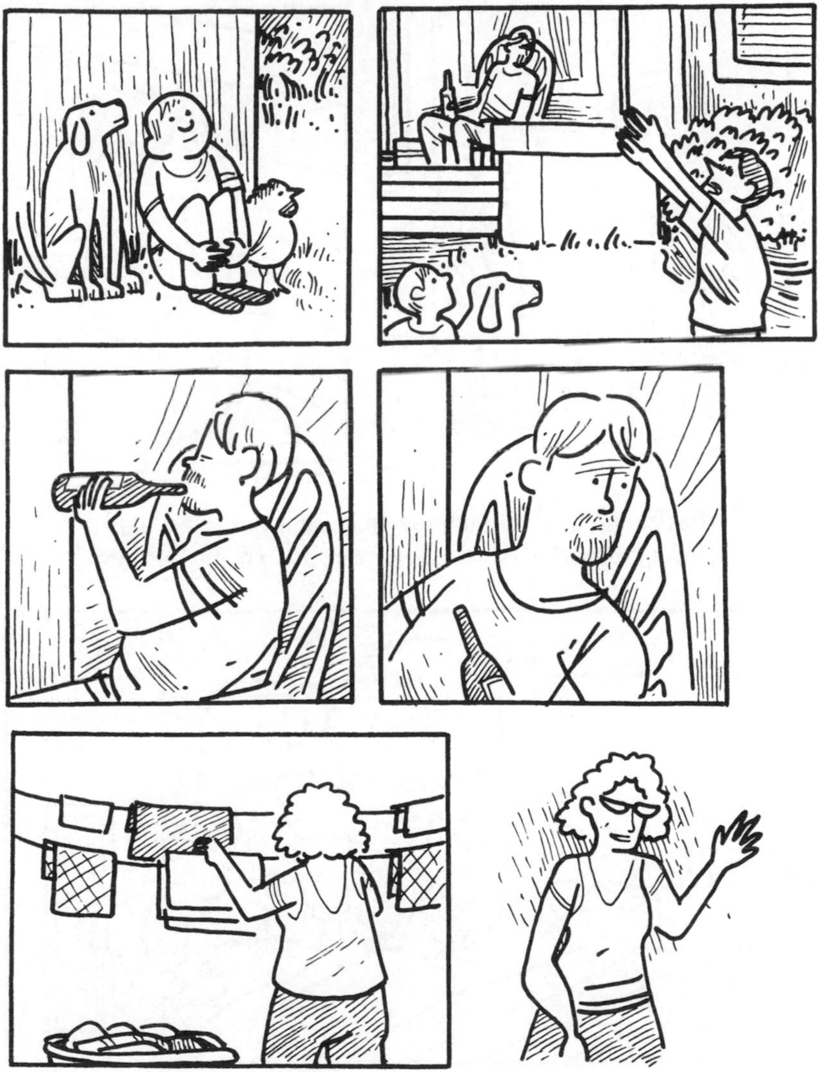

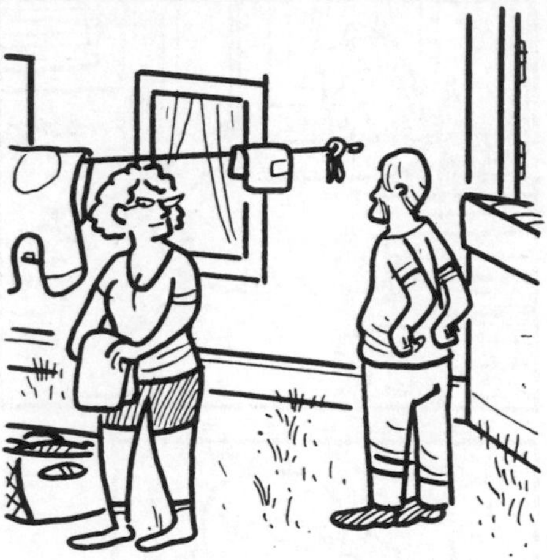

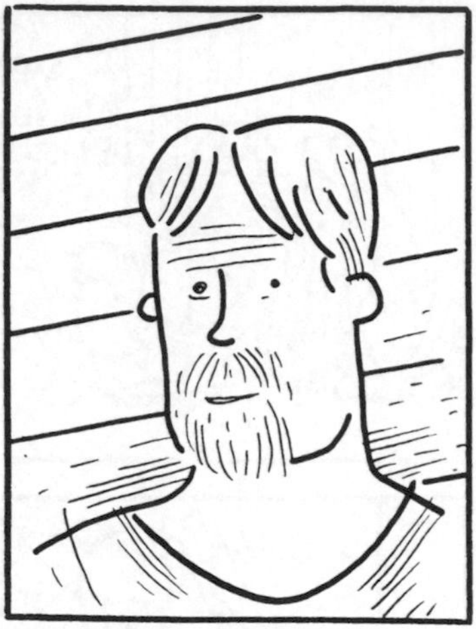

Luckily, we had a neighbor who went out of his way to make us feel welcome. He even bought my buckets.

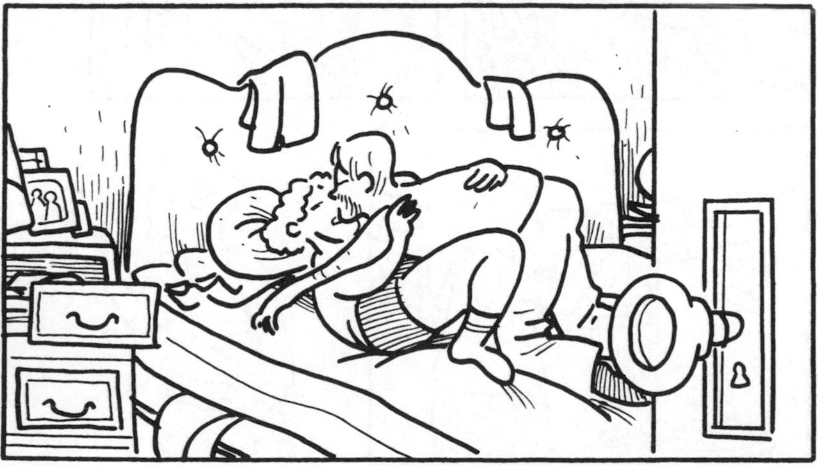

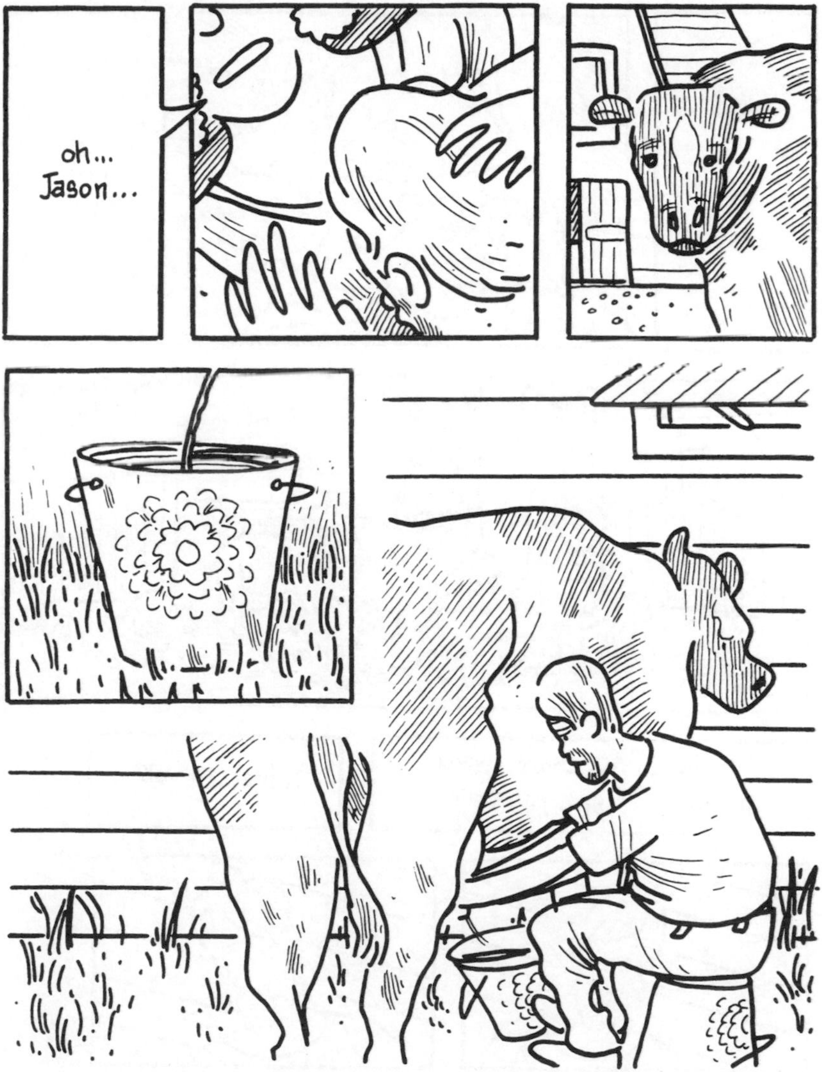
oh... Jason...

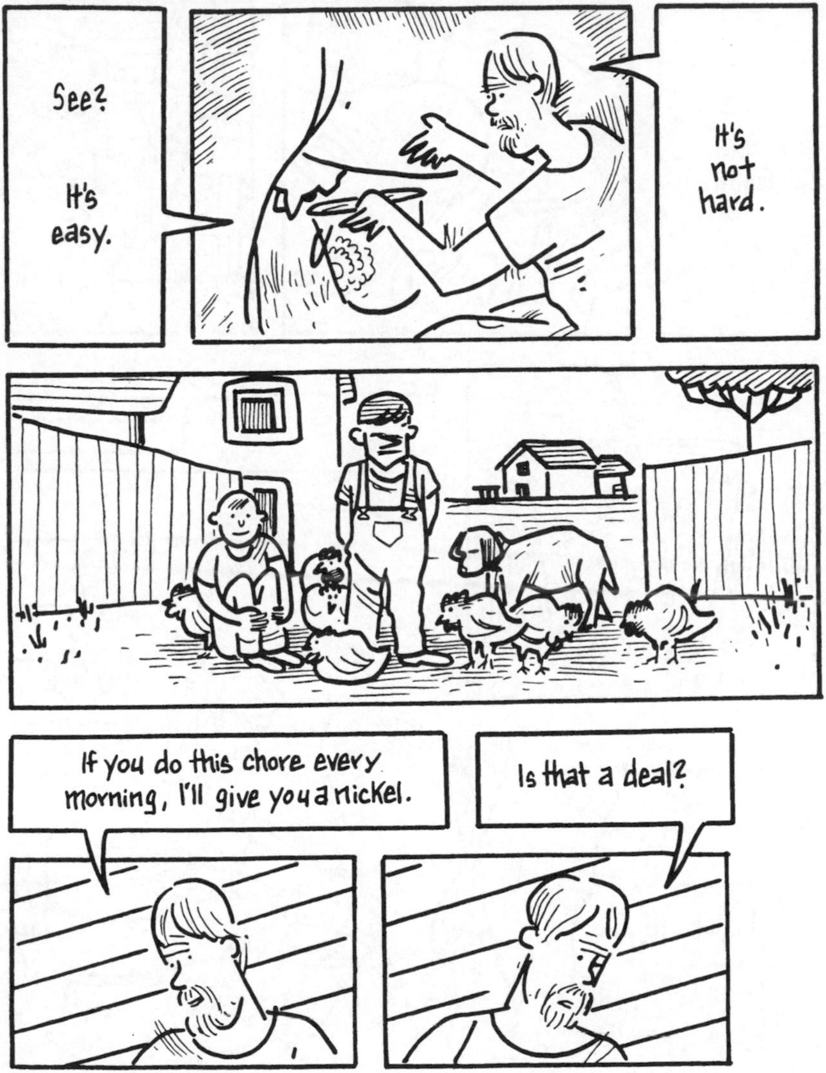
See?
It's easy.
It's not hard.
If you do this chore every morning, I'll give you a nickel.
Is that a deal?

He doesn't want to. I can do it for you.

I'm talking to Clarence.

oh.... Jason...

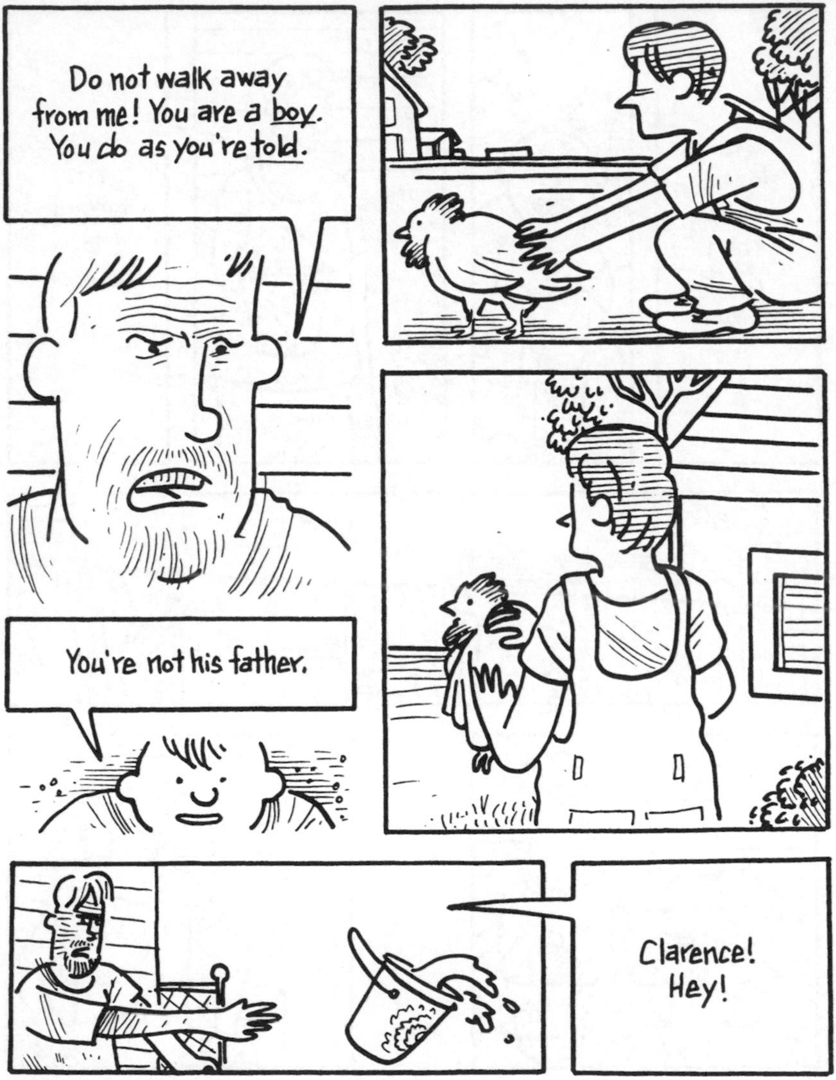
Do not walk away from me! You are a boy. You do as you're told.
You're not his father.
Clarence! Hey!

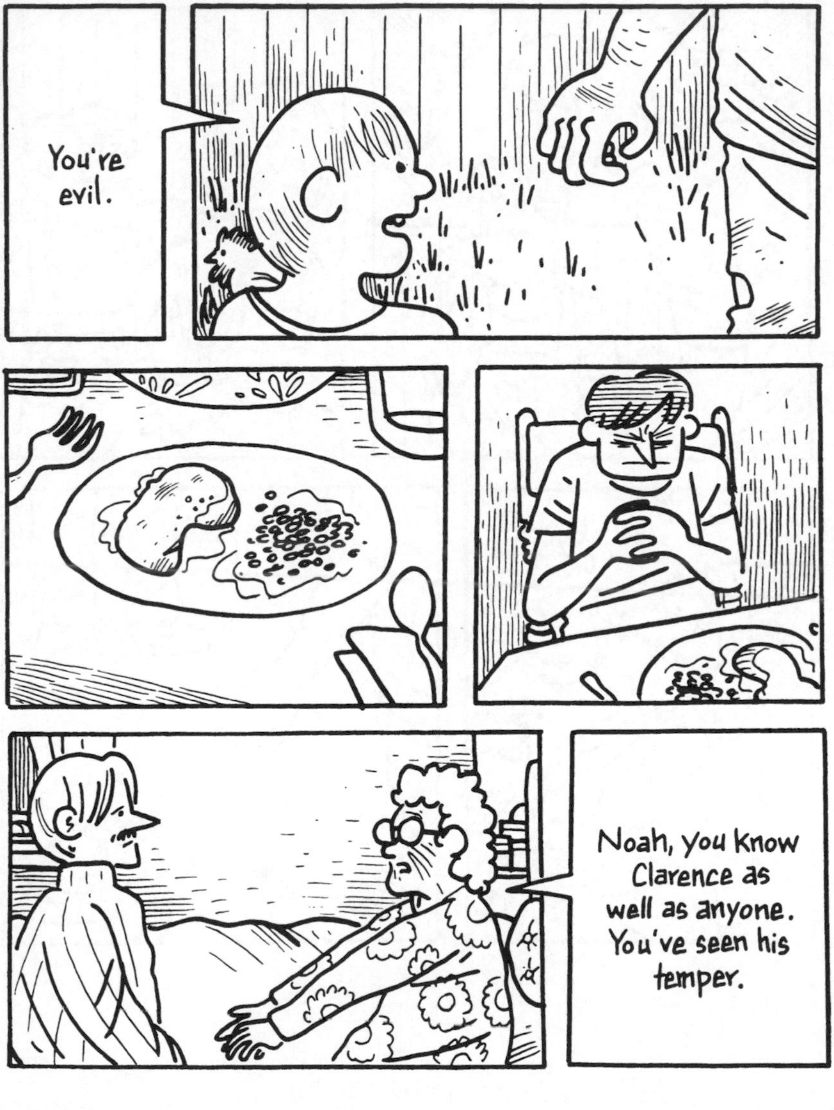
You're evil.
Noah, you know Clarence as well as anyone. You've seen his temper.

We don't like to talk about it.

Come now! It isn't THAT bad. Everyone gets overwhelmed.

Clarence has had so much on his mind lately.

He's looking out for everyone.

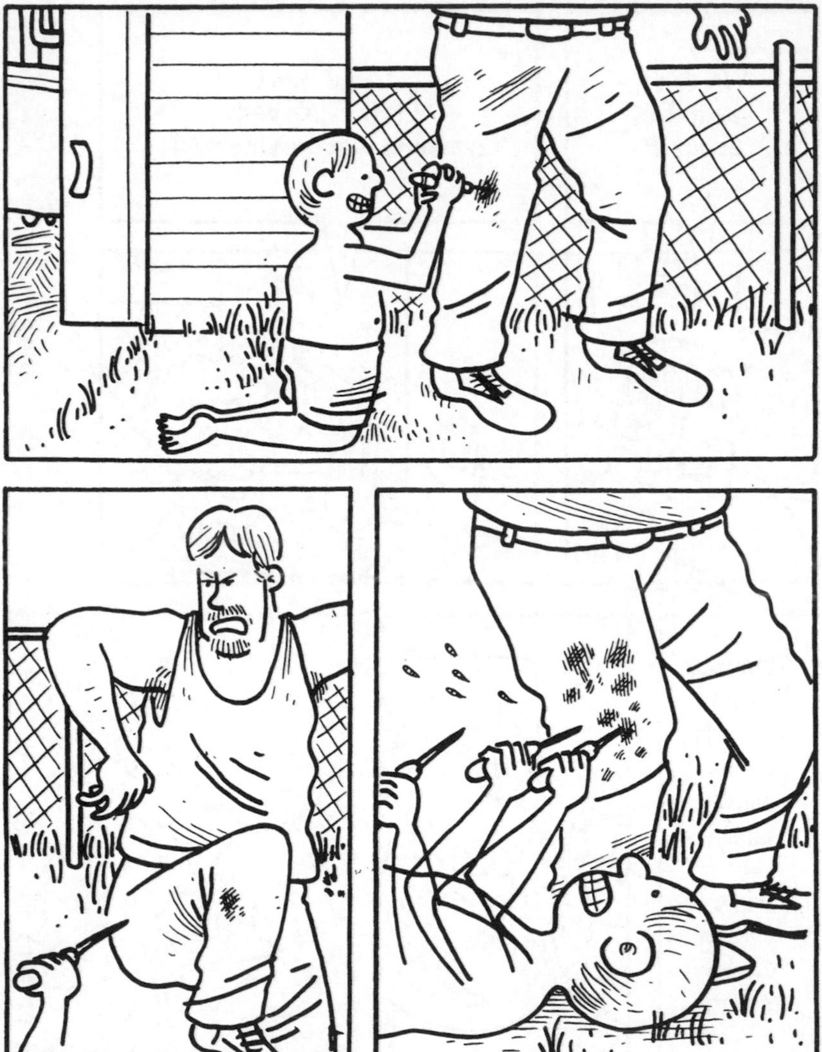

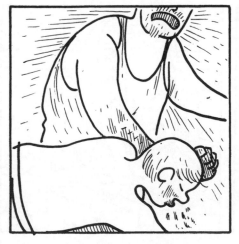

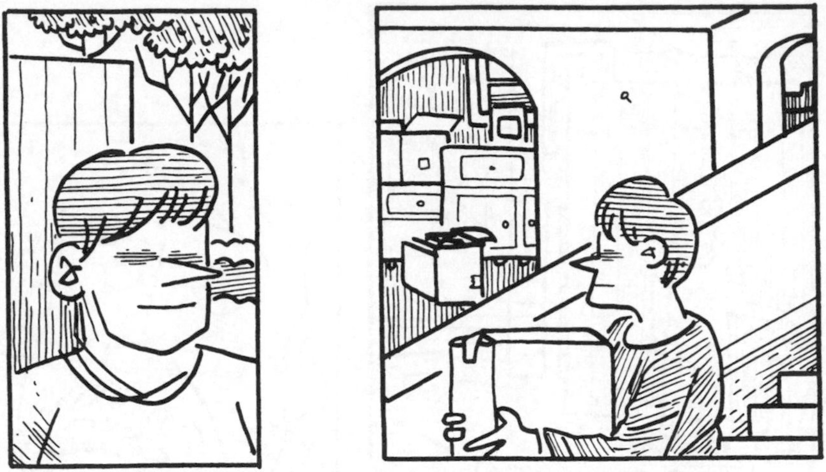

We are a family, and families stay together no matter what happens. If you don't have family, you don't have anything.

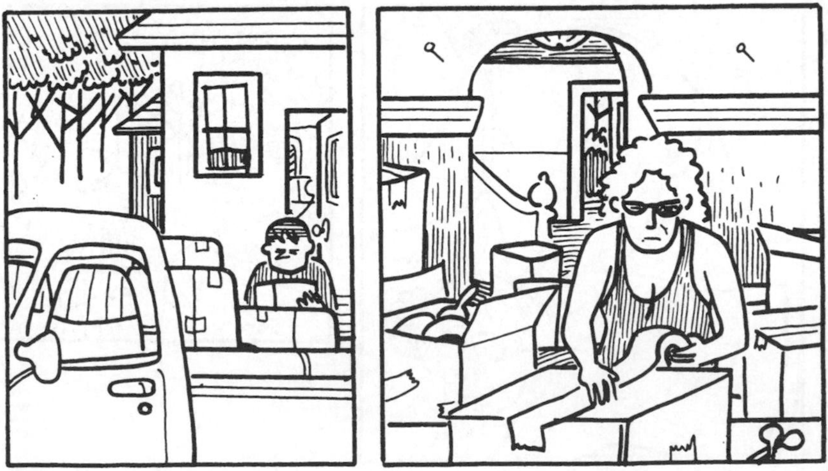

Sometimes family hurts you, and that is all the more reason to protect it.

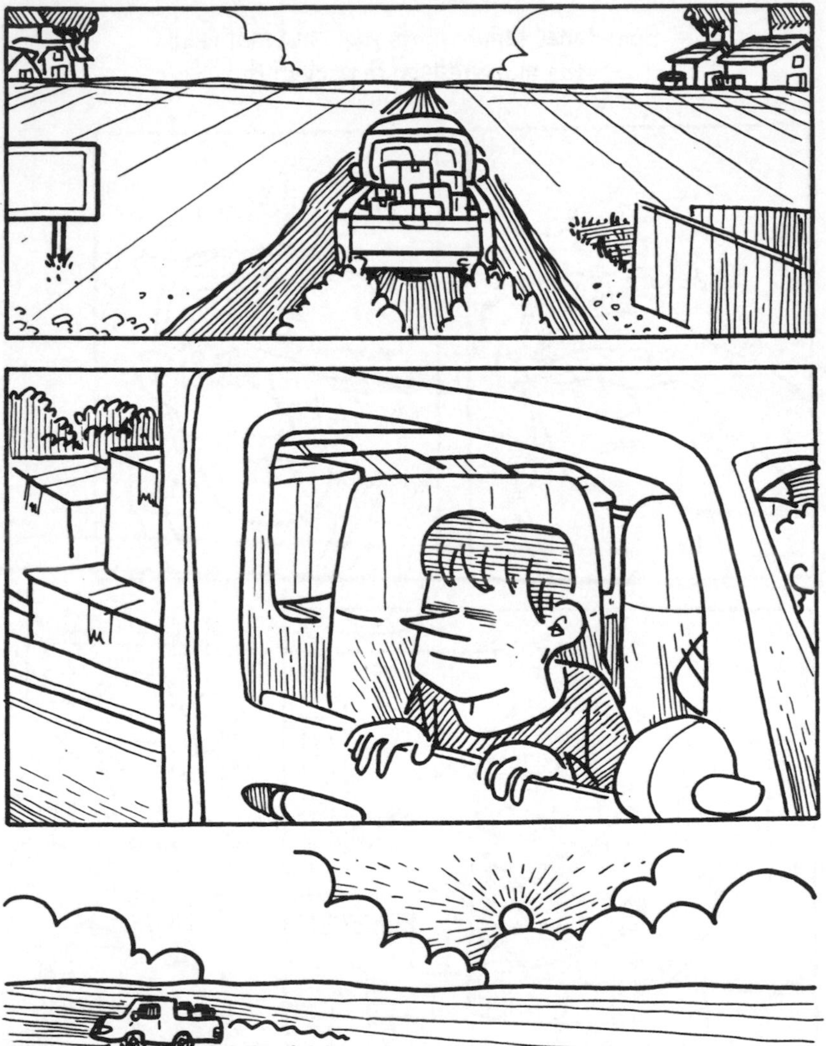

I'm so excited! I've never been out of the country before. Have you?
I've been to Canada. This will be my first time in South America.

Now we know where Reverend Carpenter
had been when he disappeared for weeks.

He was planning
for our exile.

It was only a matter of time until the government came after us. We need to be where their lies cannot hurt us.

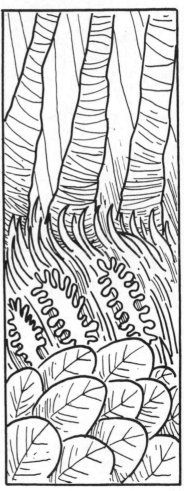

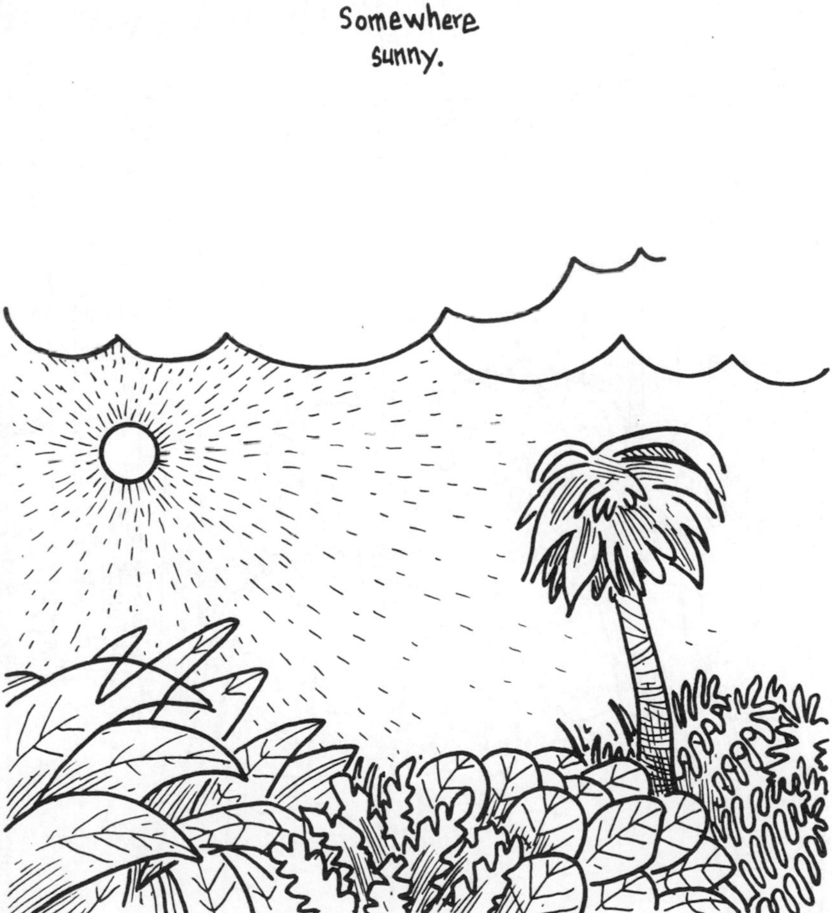
Somewhere
sunny.

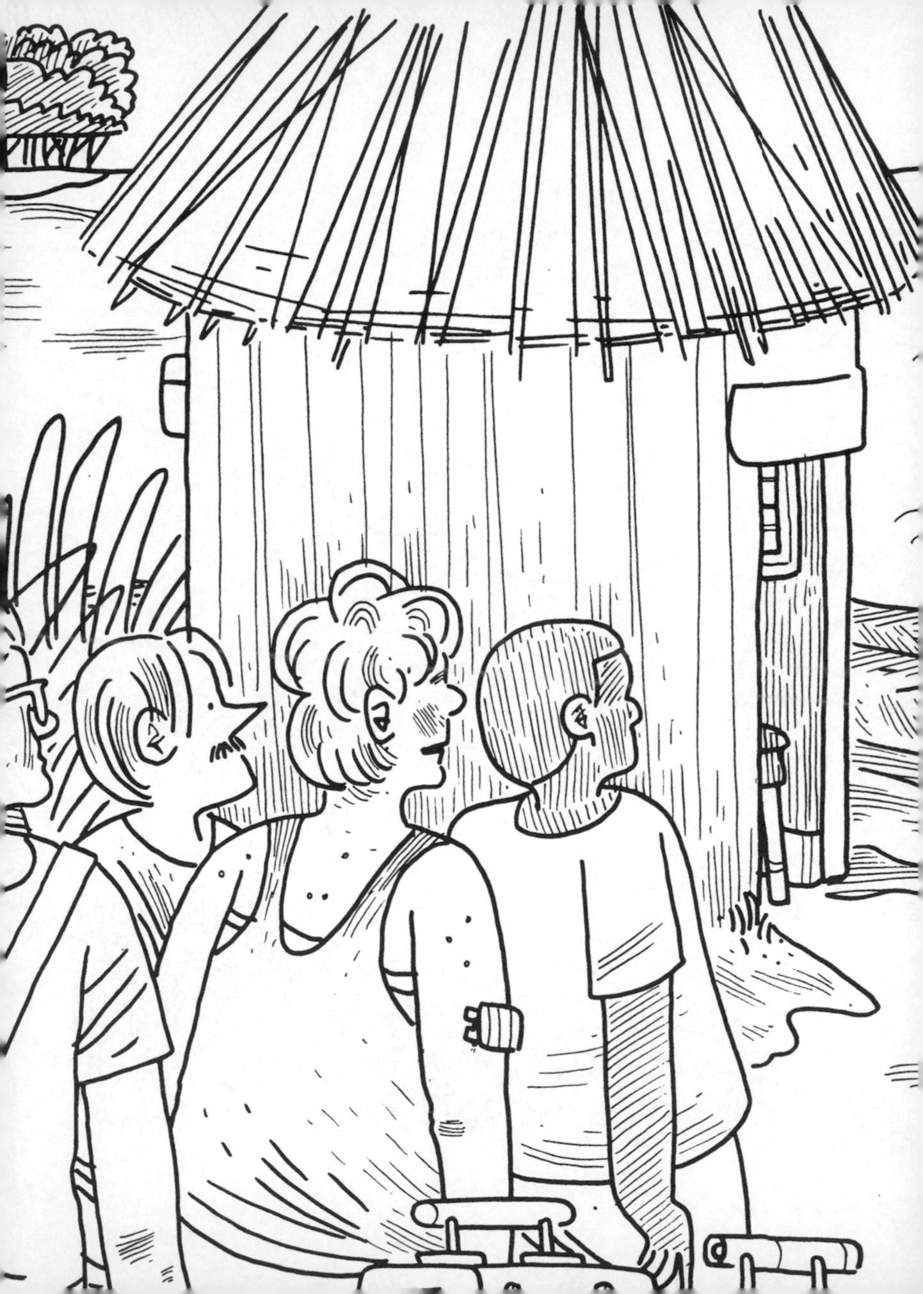

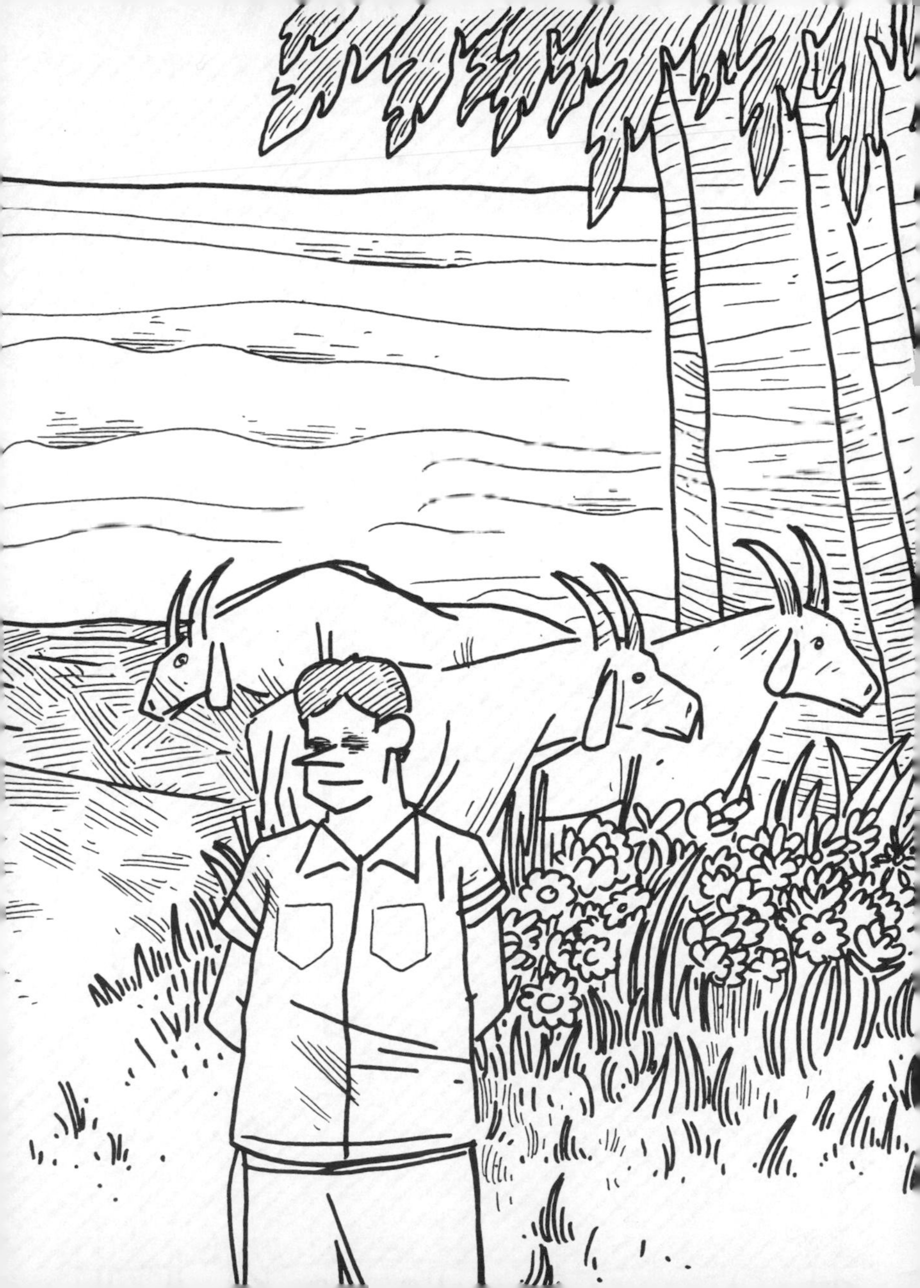

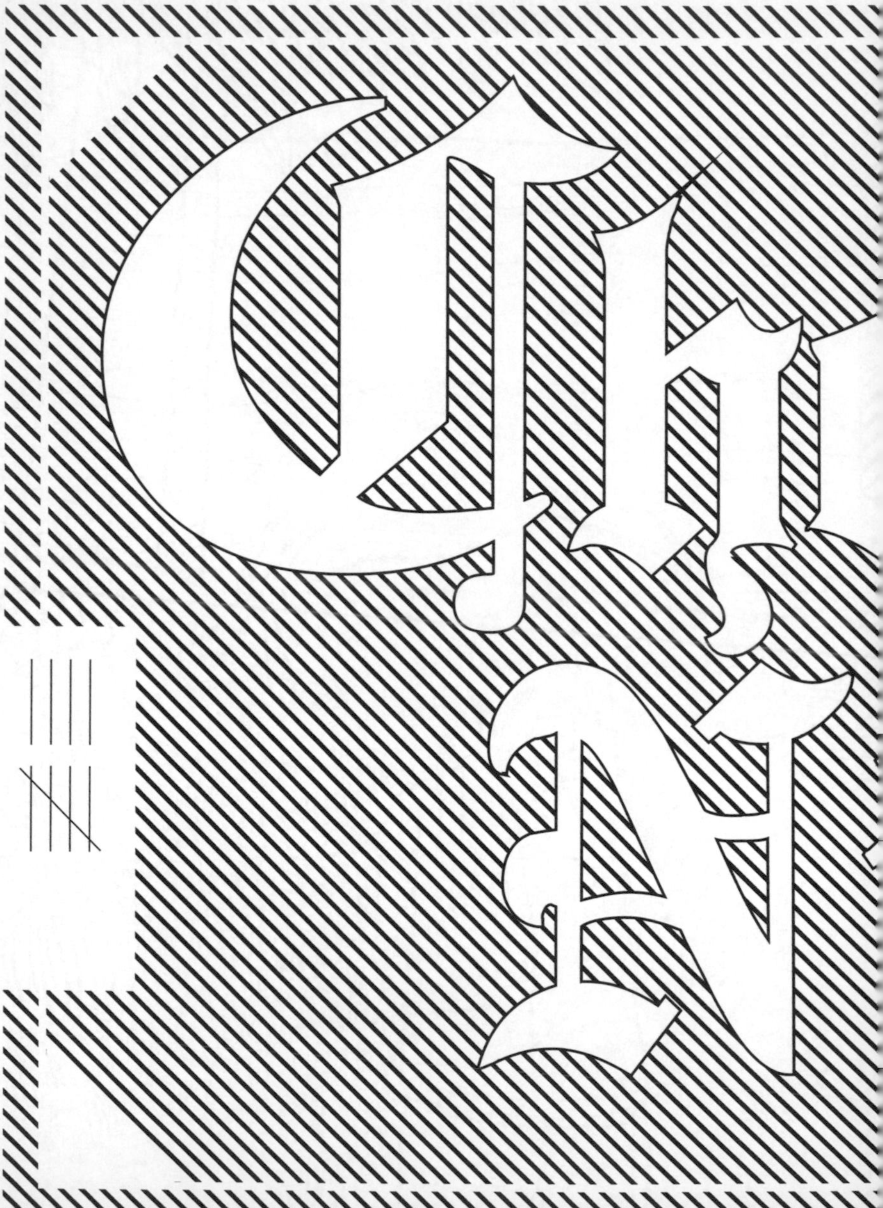

pter
ne

Paradise in
the New World

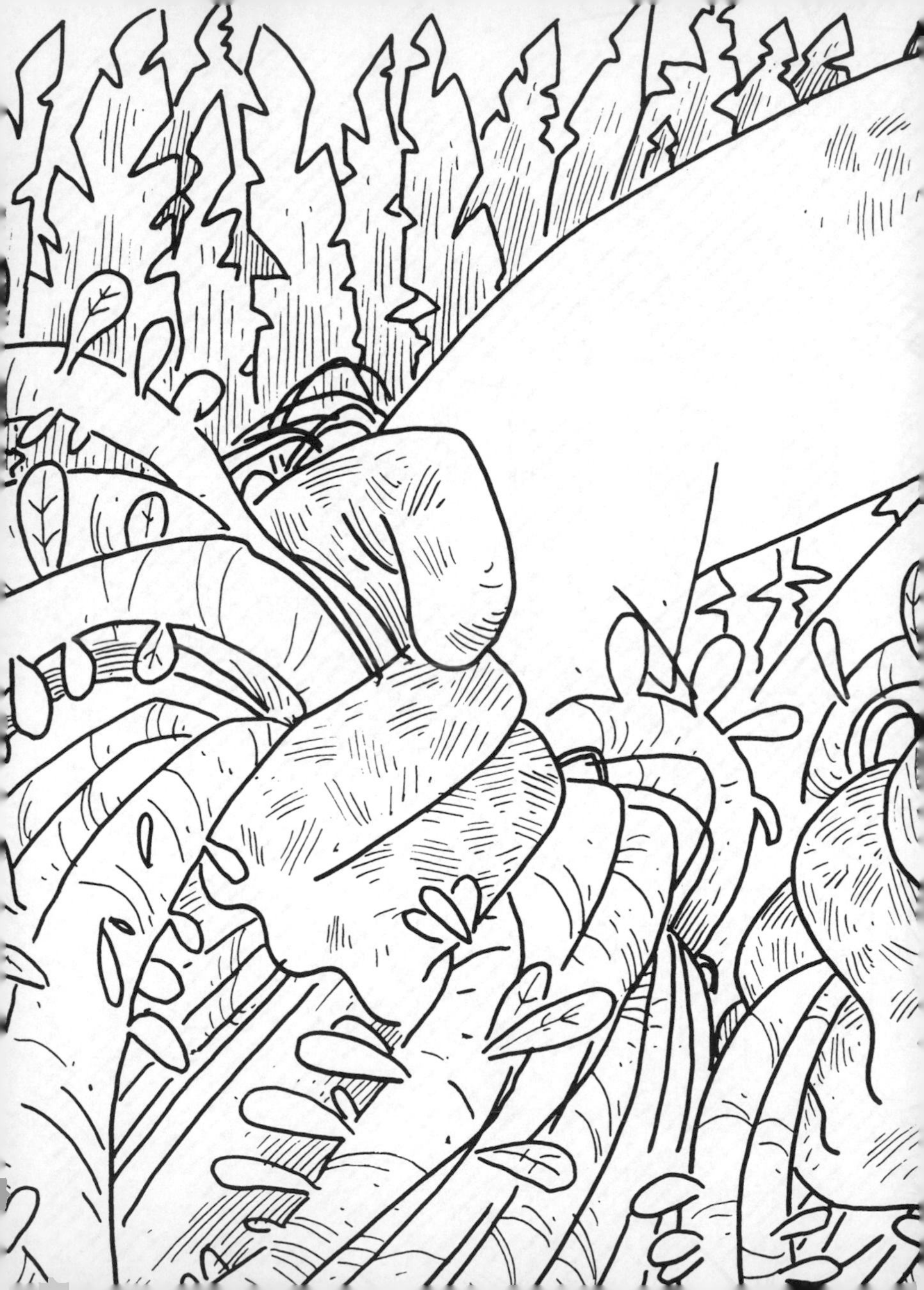

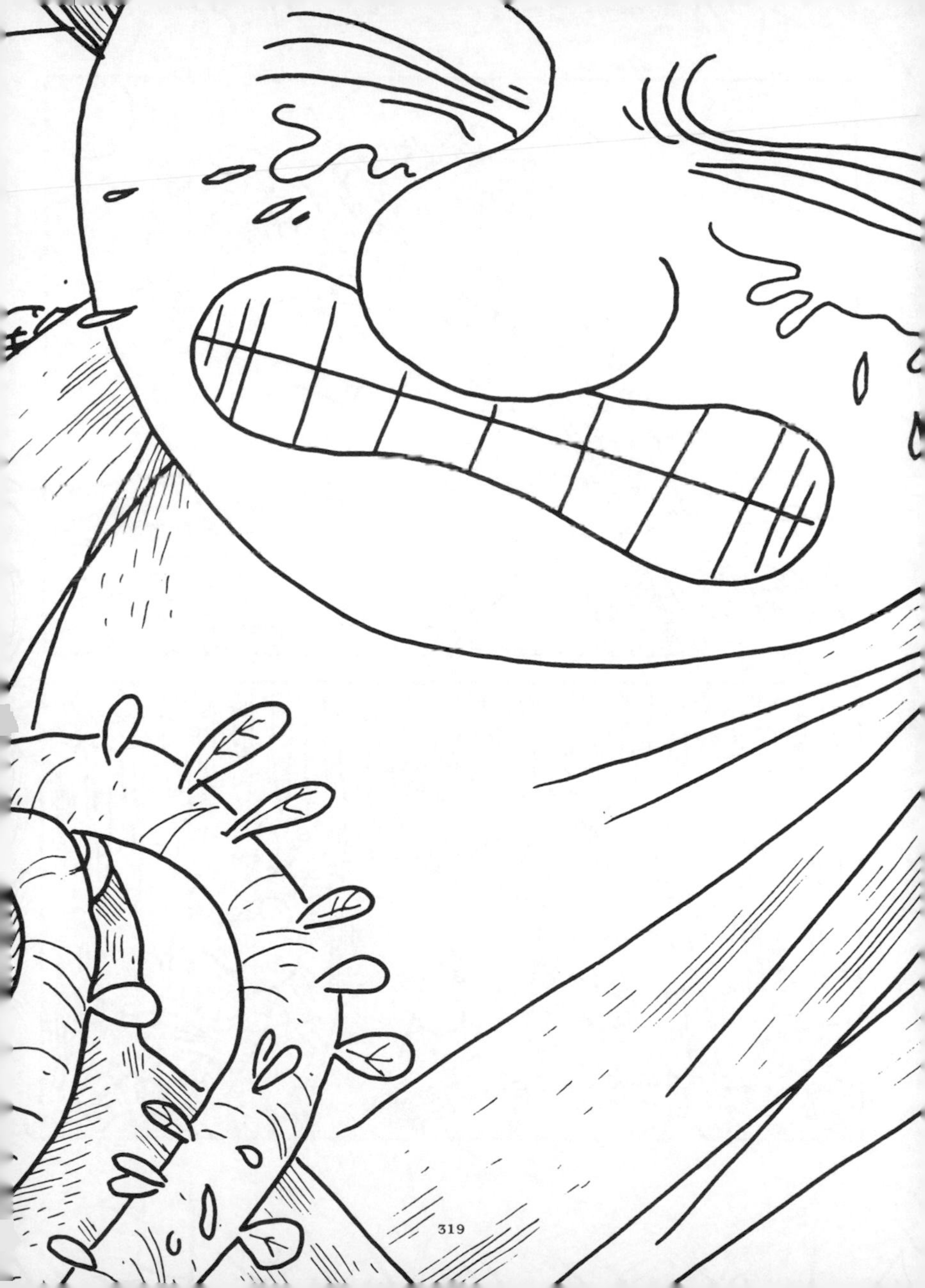

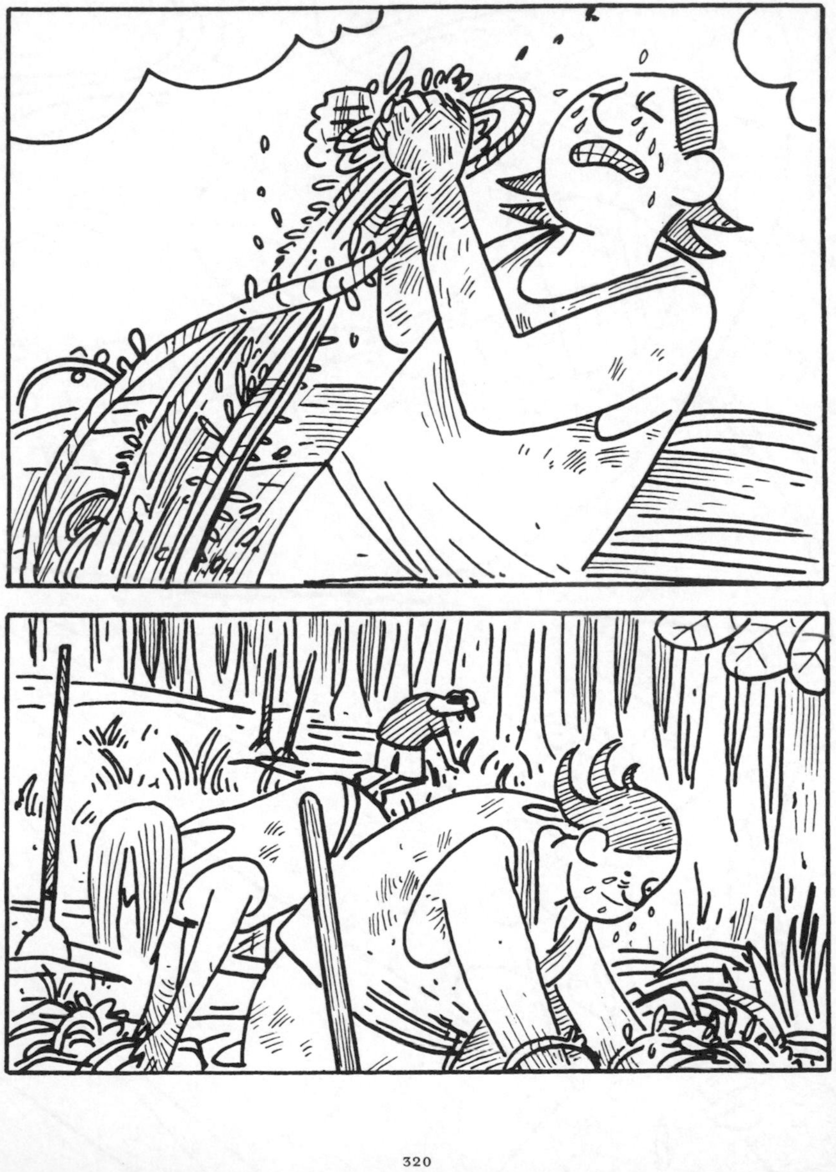

I've been thinking about how the island, the island where it all ended, was shaped like a brain.

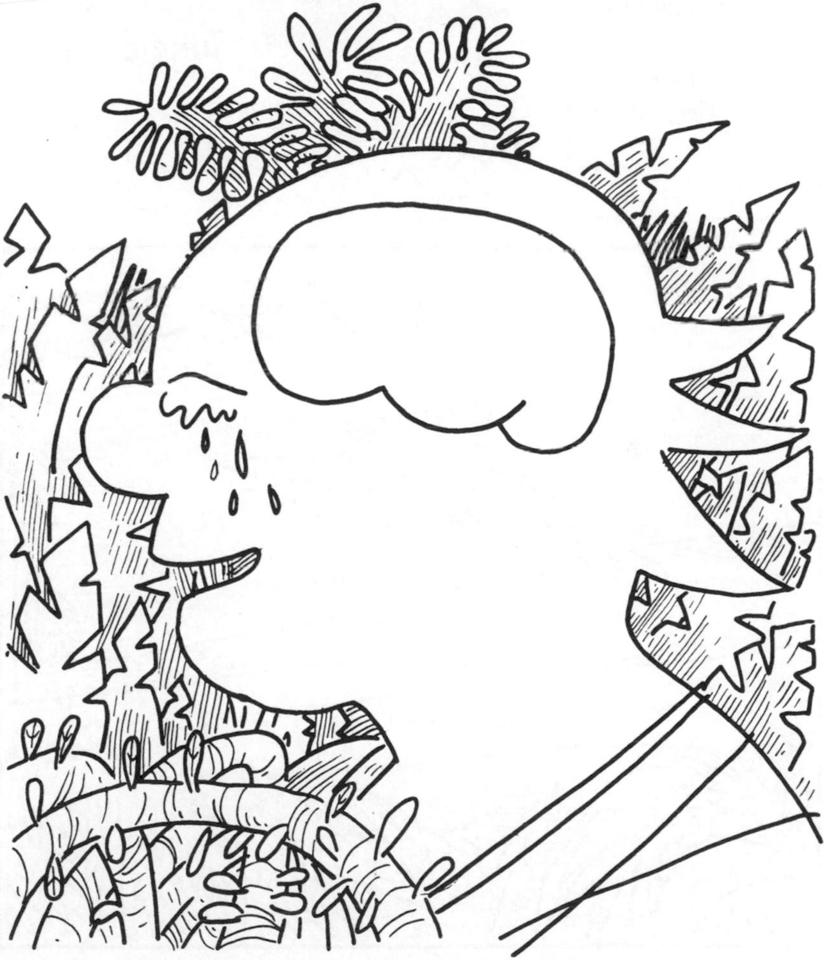

And just like a brain, most of it was either a mystery or of no use at all.

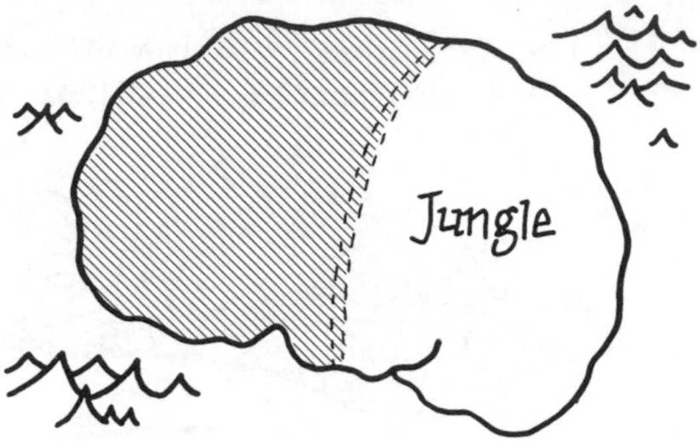
Jungle

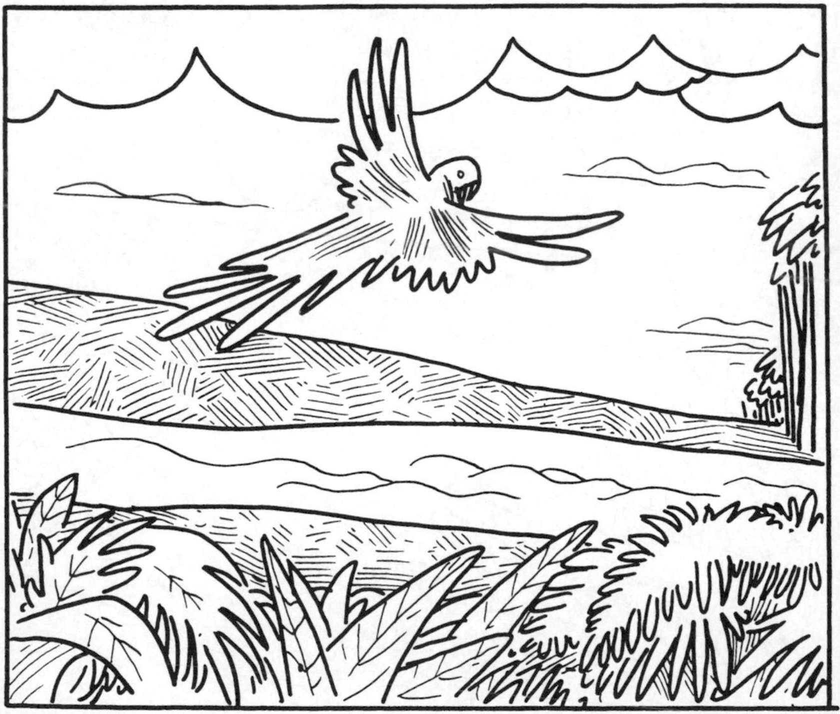

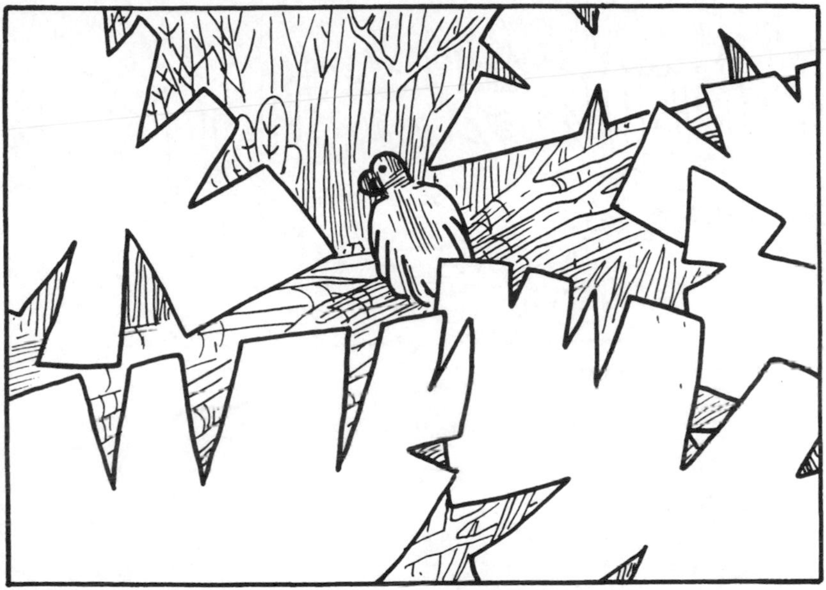

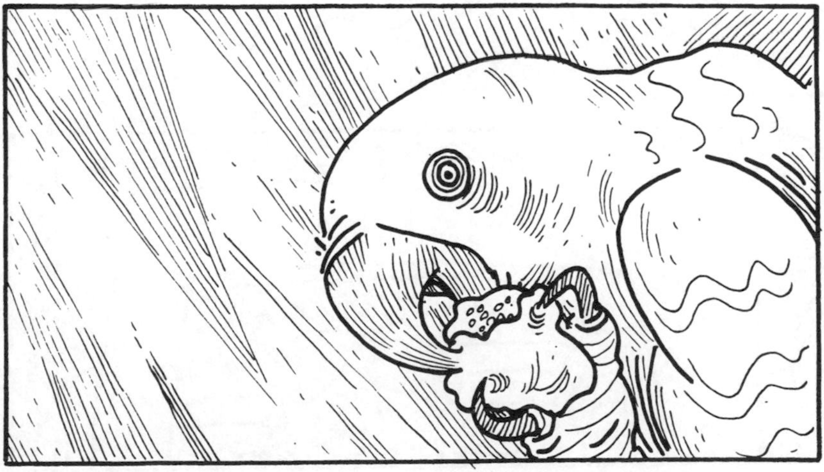

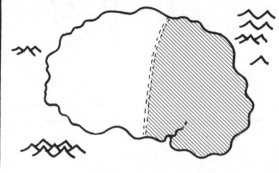

Towards the top of the brain is where new believers would arrive by plane.

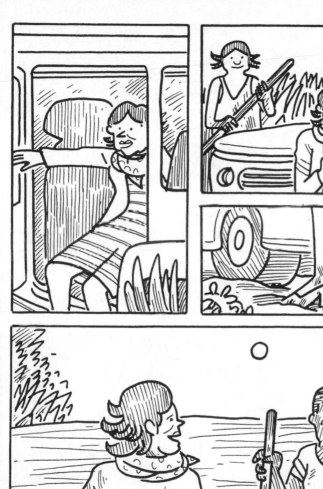

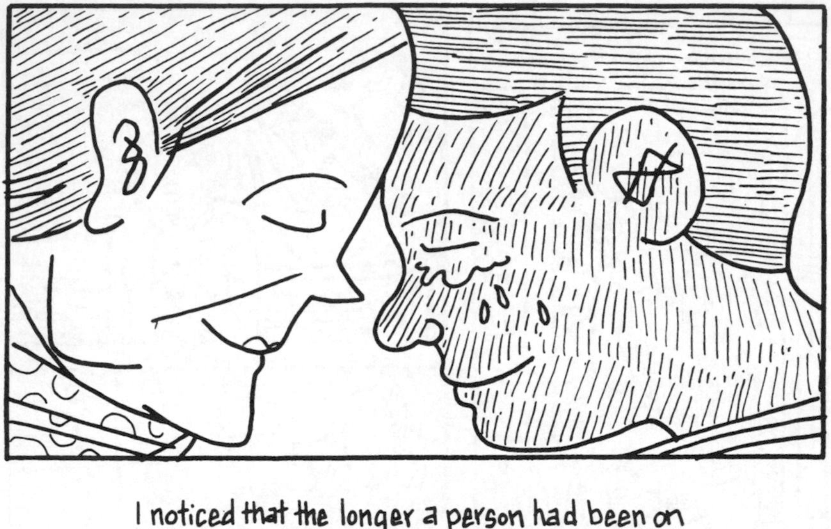

I noticed that the longer a person had been on the island, the more likely they were to cry.

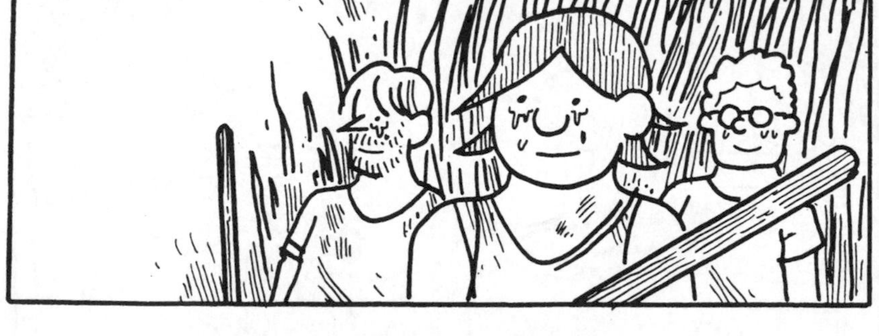

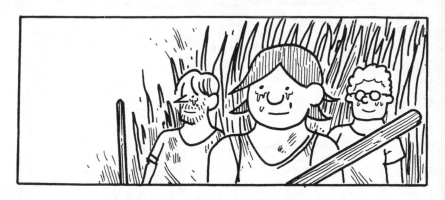

All our emotions sat on the surface.

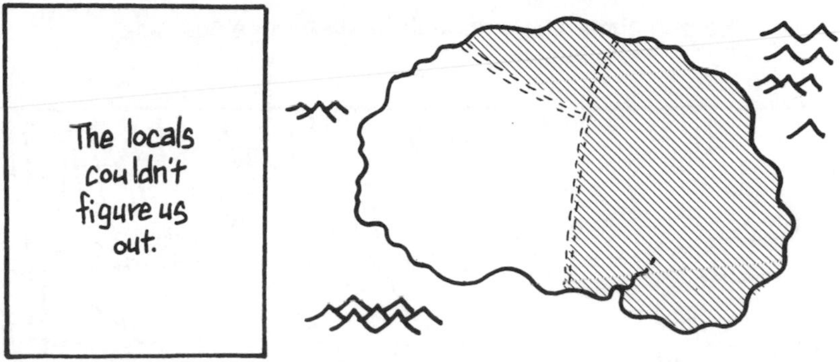
The locals couldn't figure us out.

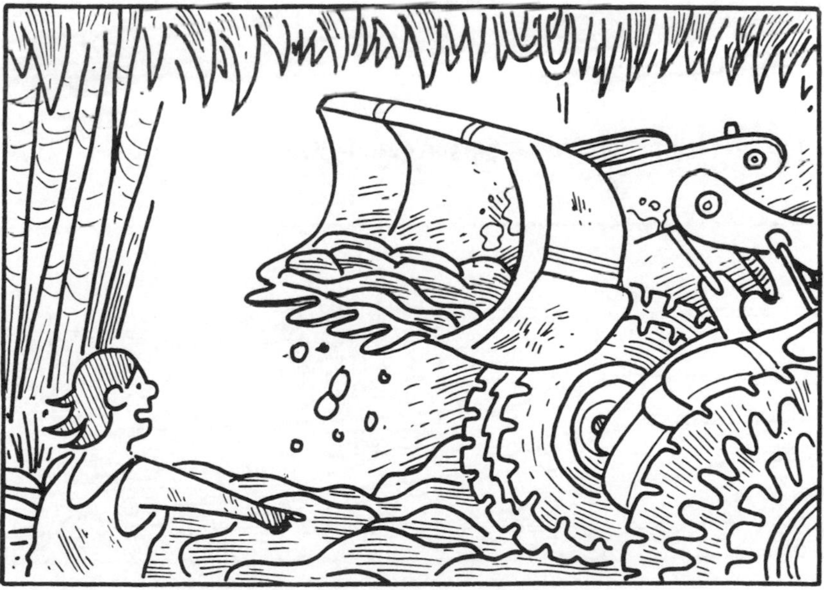

For a while they would come to the edge of our property and watch our progress.

No one came close enough to speak to either side.

You can tell by the way a person stands that they are afraid of you.

One foot is held back as if they'll need to quickly turn and run.

I remember that I was like that before
The Church of Love and Devotion.

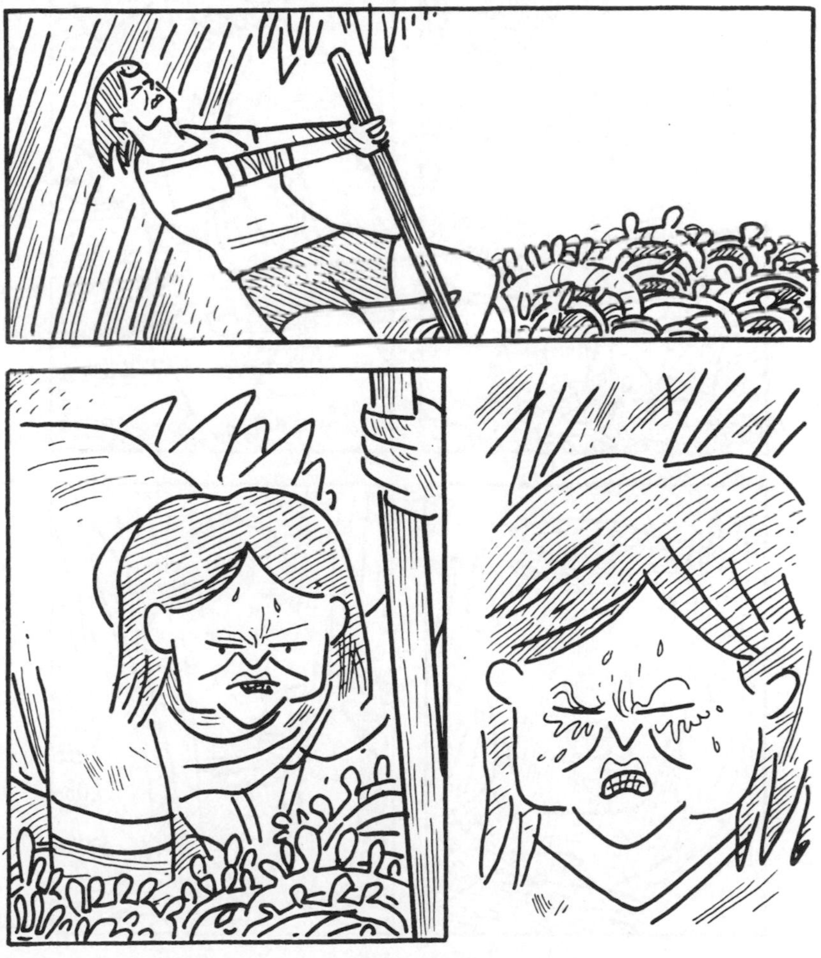

On the
island,
we had
no fears.

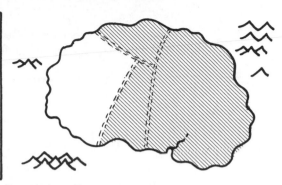

We trusted each other completely, and
had no further use for the Know Me App.

It never worked on the island anyway.

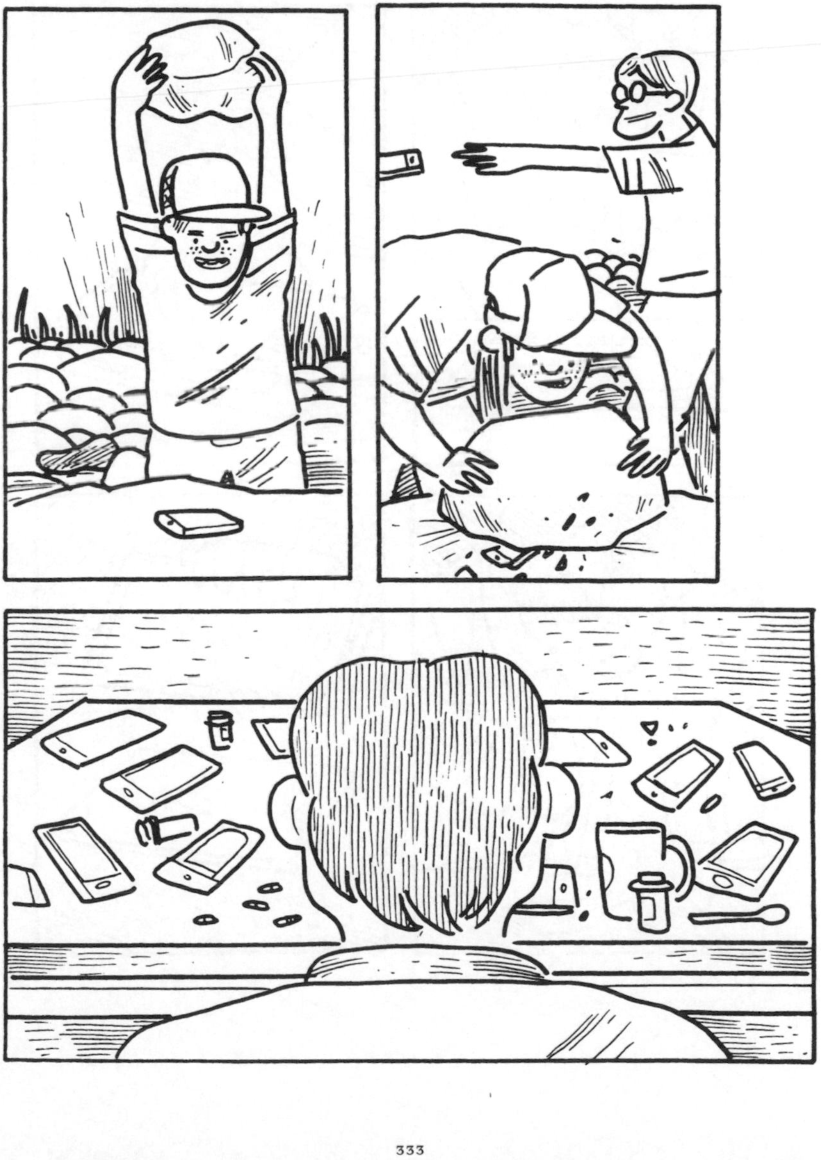

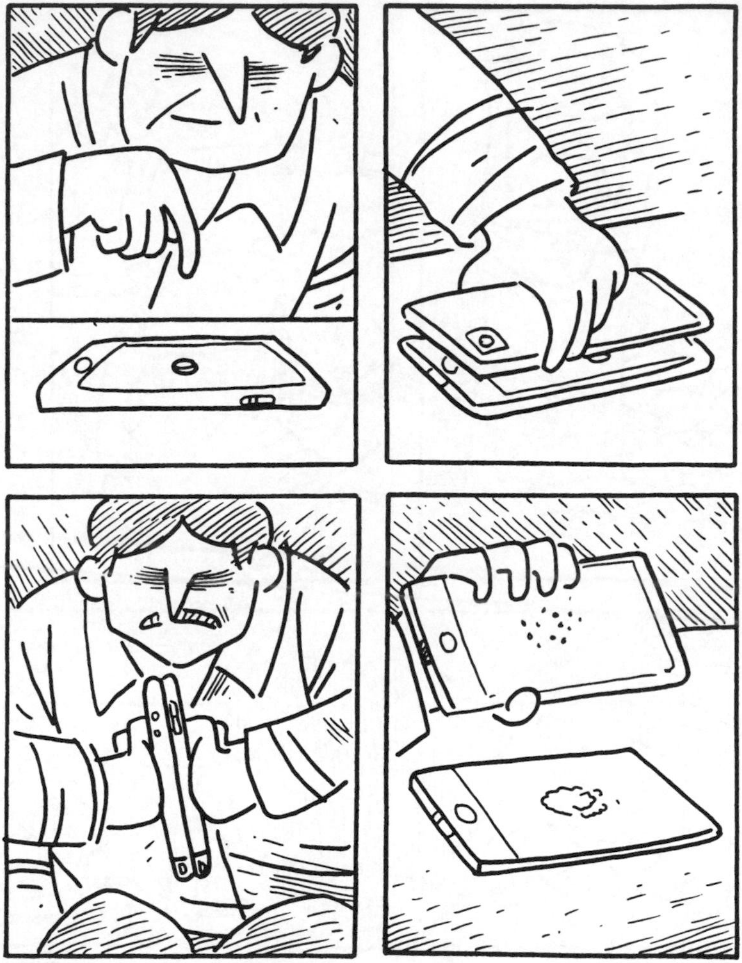

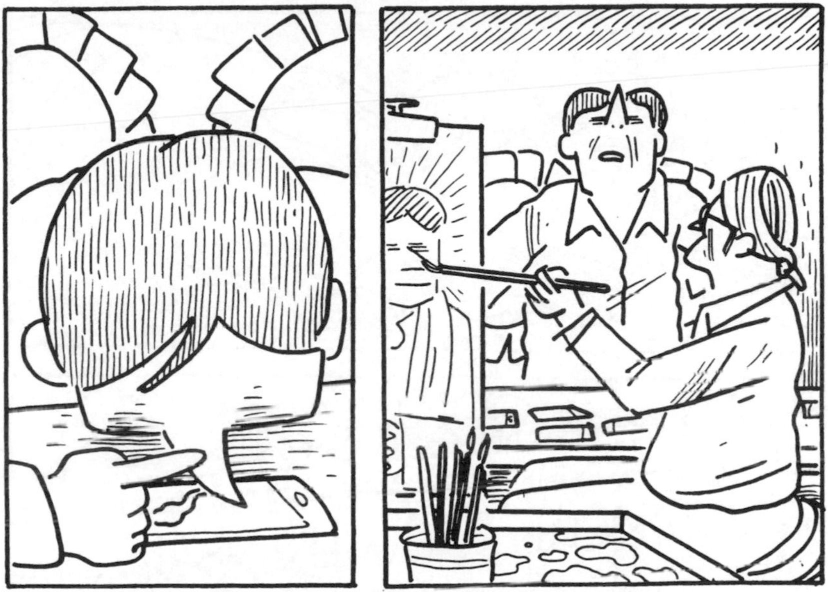

Someone thought that I was upset to see my creation
become useless, so I was given a gift.

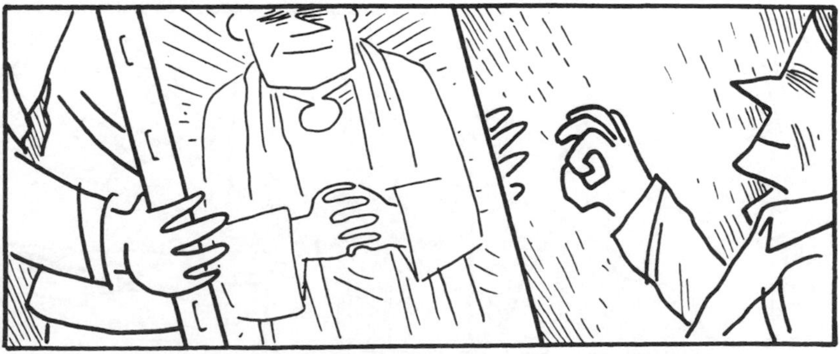

I put the gift where everyone could see it.
In time, I could see it with my eyes closed.

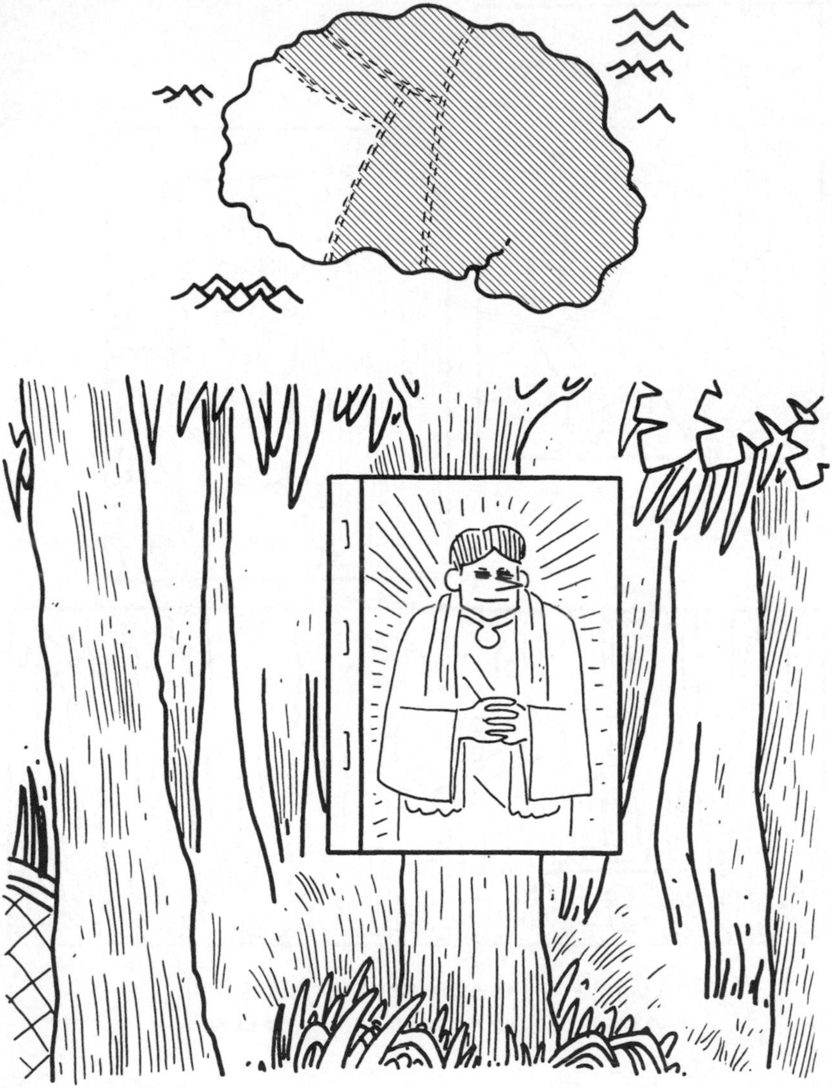

A brain needs food, so until we had planted enough eggplant, sweet potatoes, bell yams, pineapple and banana we couldn't expend any time on constructing anything else.

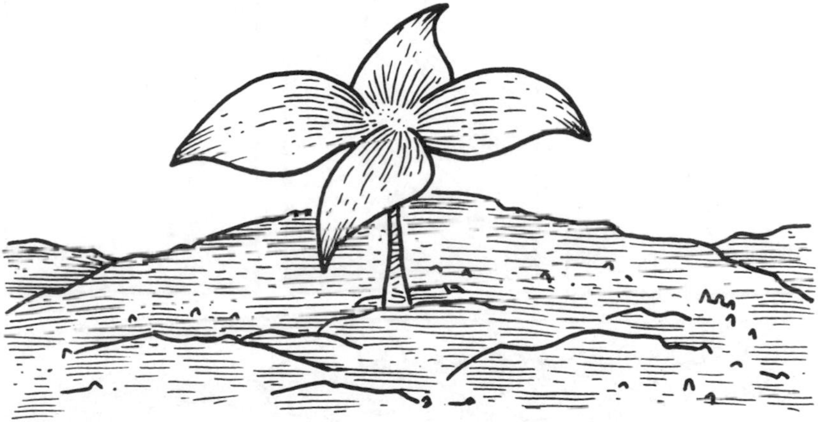

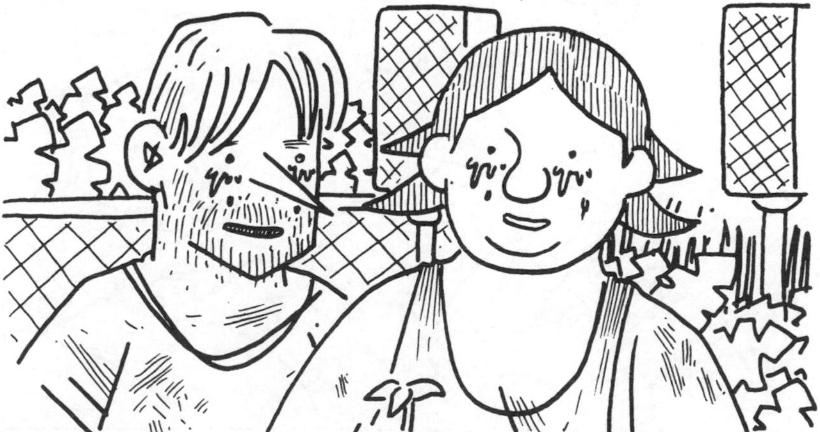

We missed sleeping under roofs.

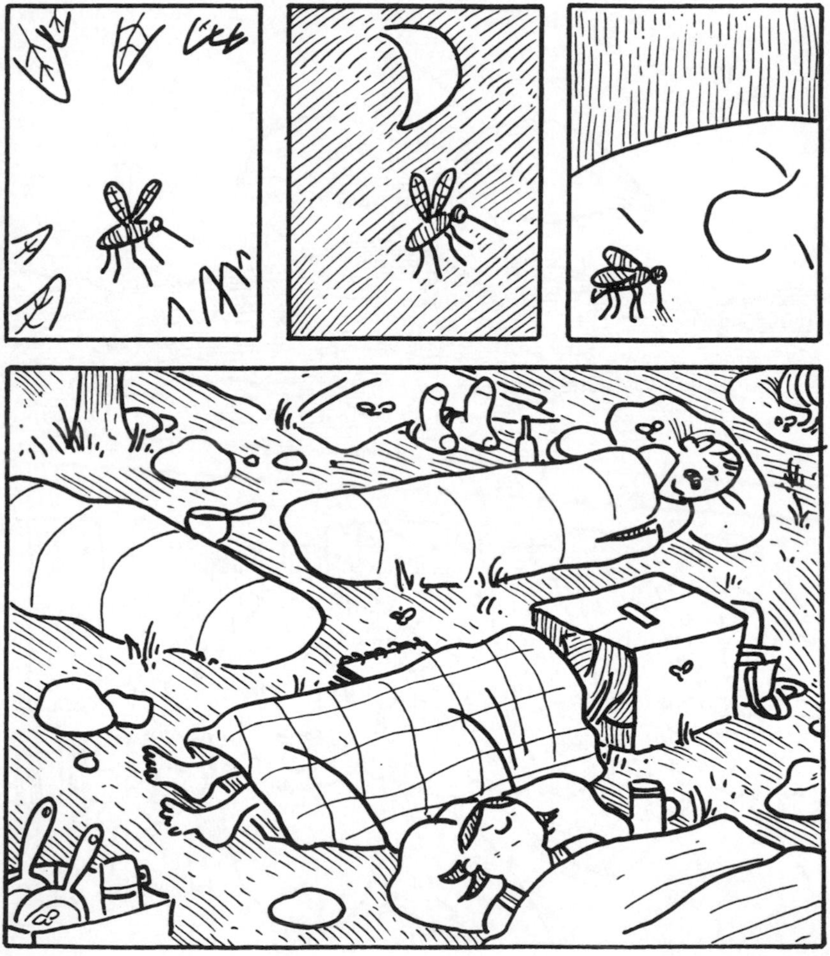

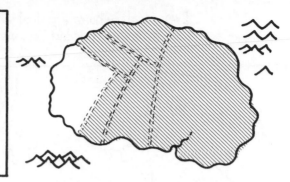

God, or whoever saw how hard we were working and invited sleep the instant we layed down.

Even Noah, who rarely slept when on the mainland, needed help waking.

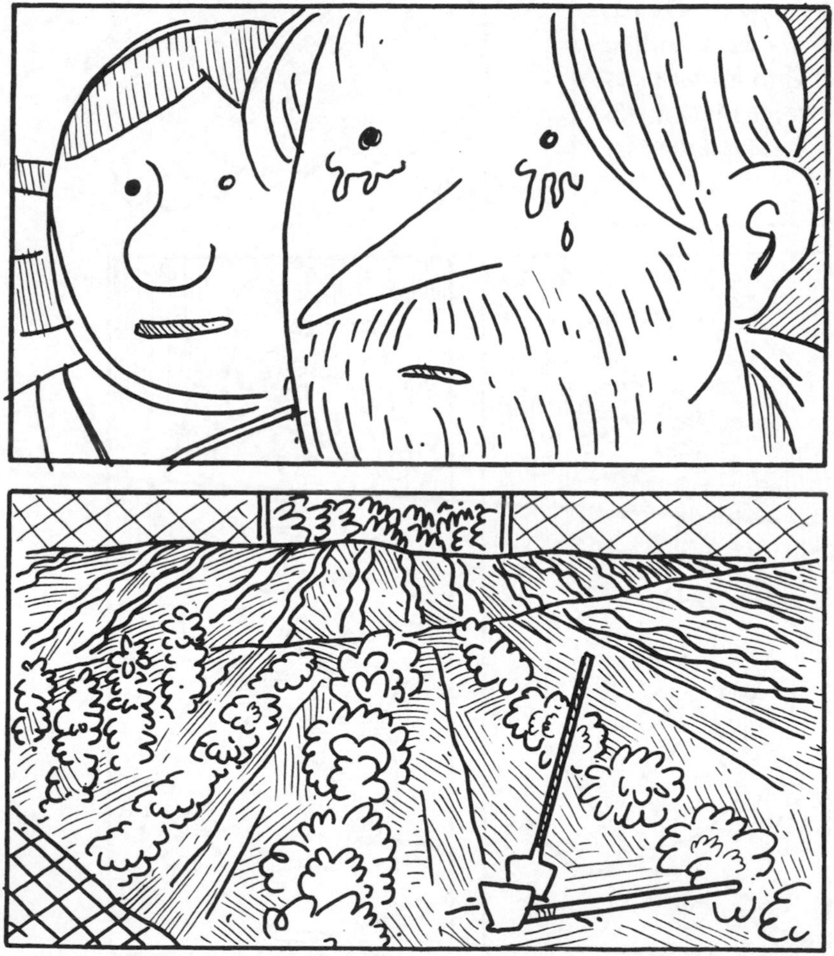

Our dreams were vivid and memorable.

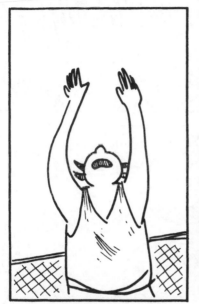

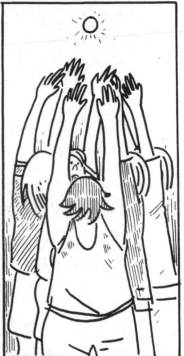

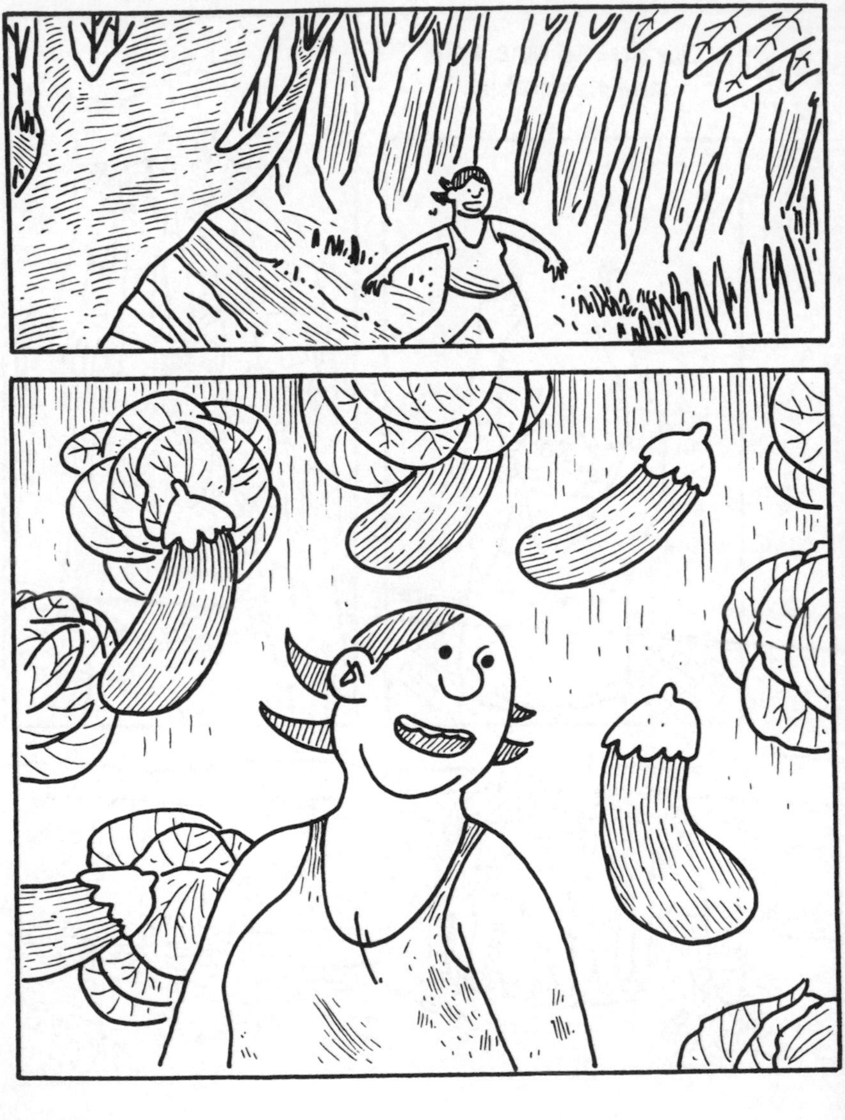

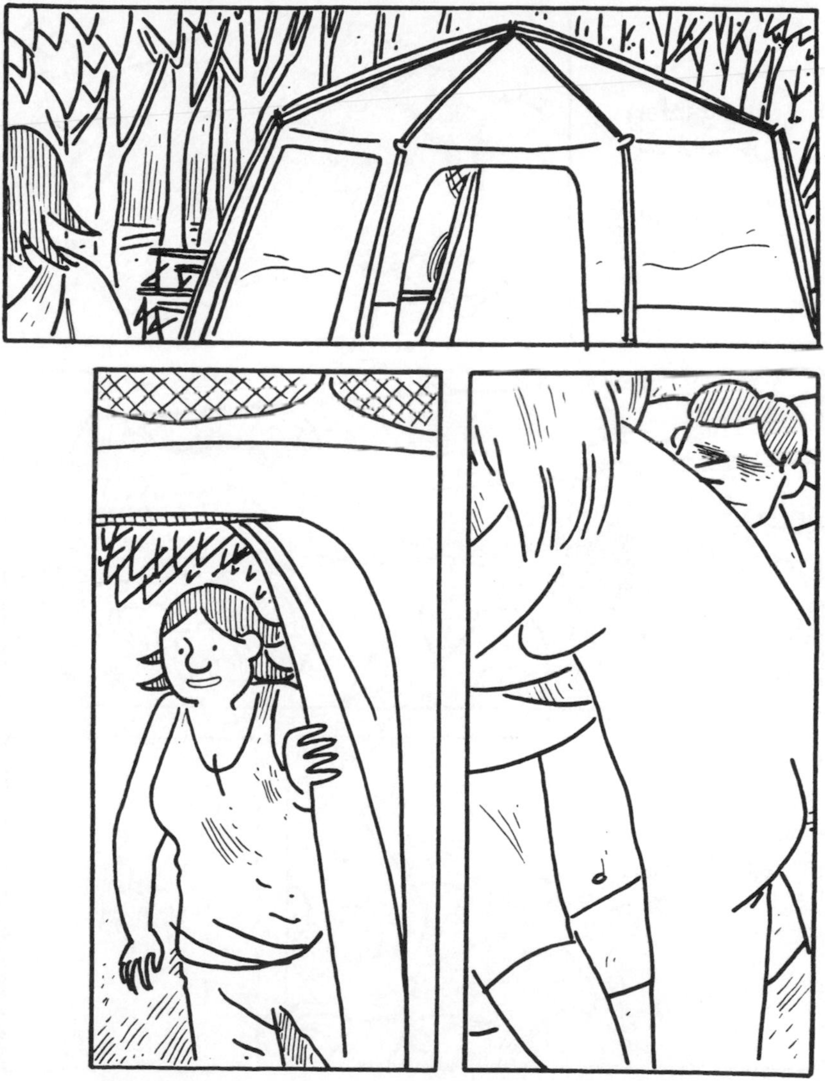

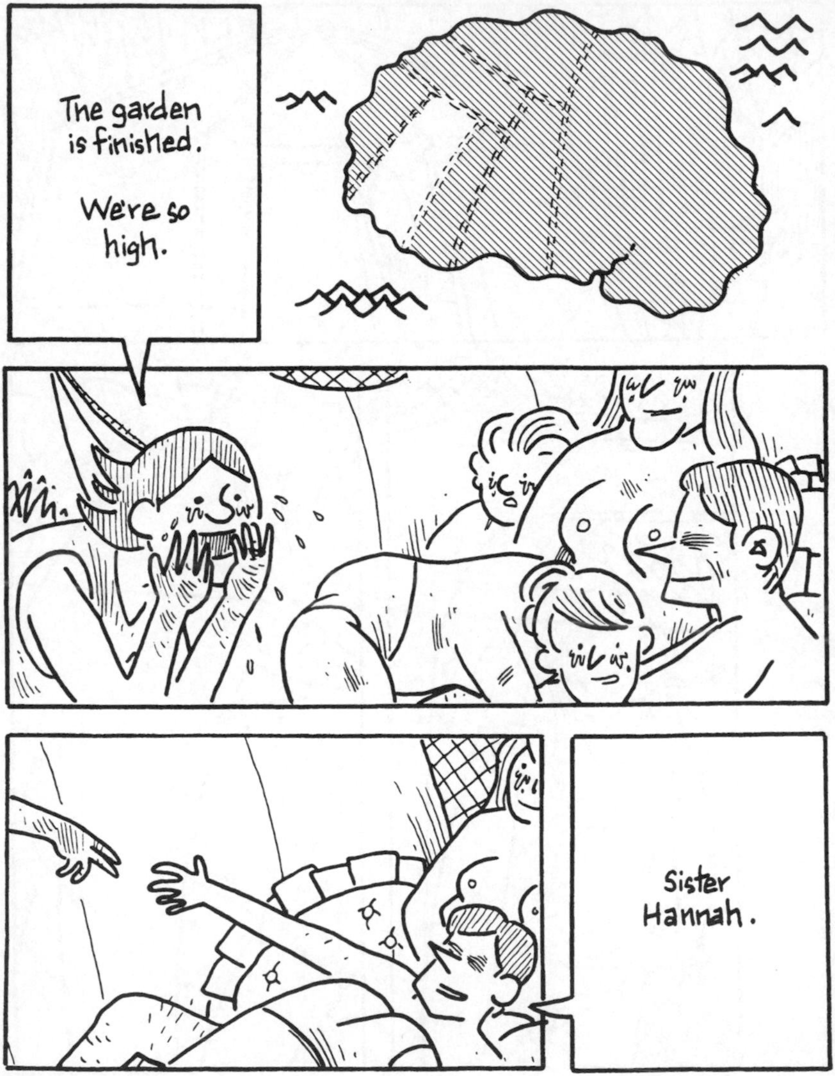
The garden is finished.
We're so high.
Sister Hannah.

We all had immediate access to Carpenter.
No one was shut out anymore.

He was the most passionate person we had ever met.

His passion brought us all together and lead us to paradise.
He held a vision we could not see.

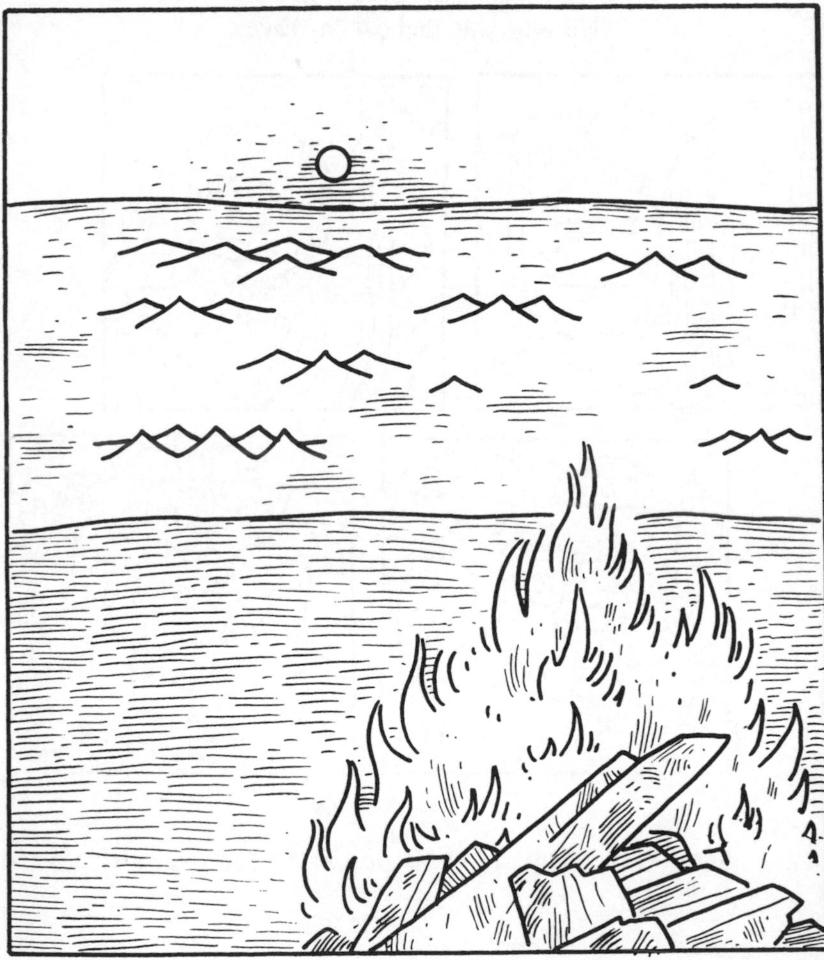

One night, not long after our arrival, we looked at him and his eyes briefly changed.

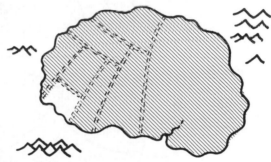

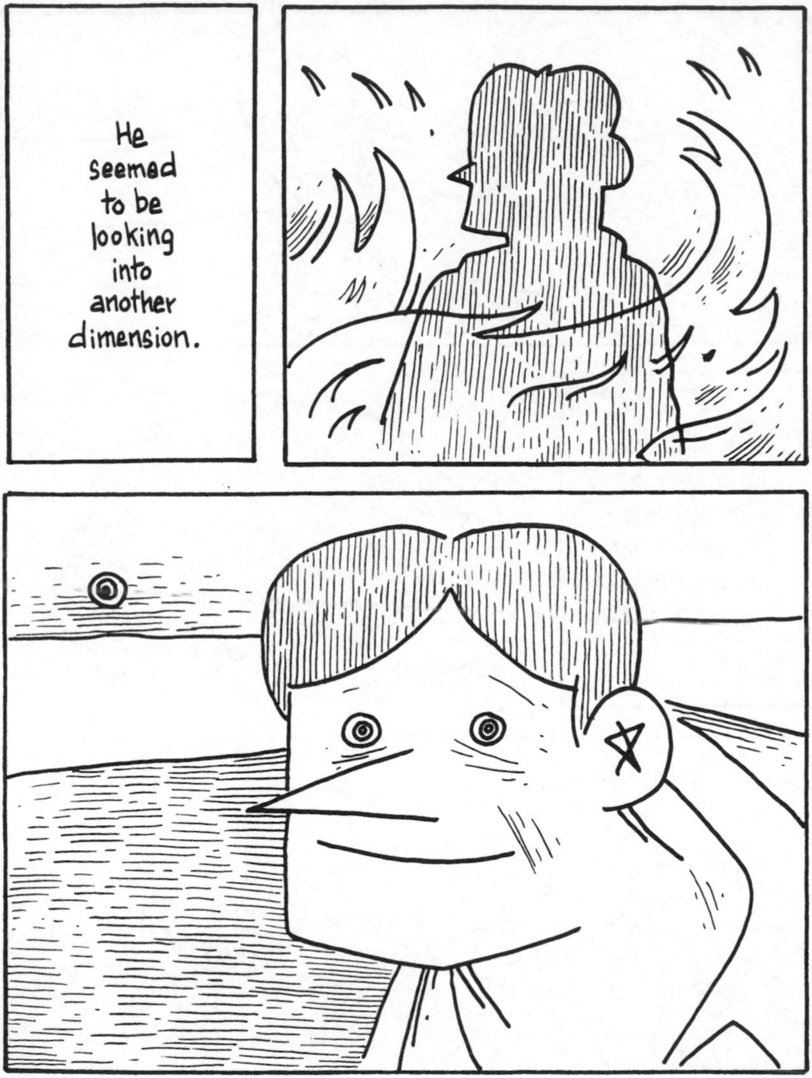
He seemed to be looking into another dimension.

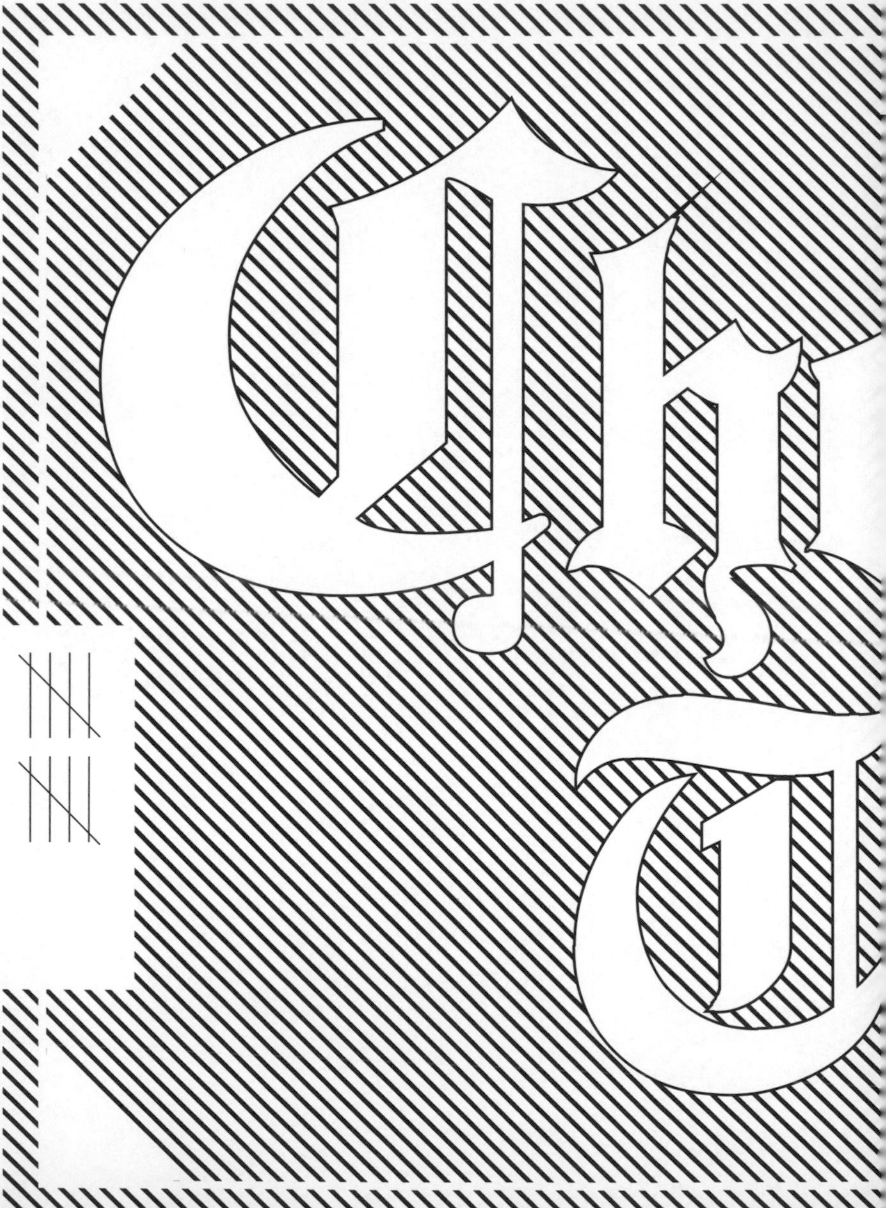

pter

n

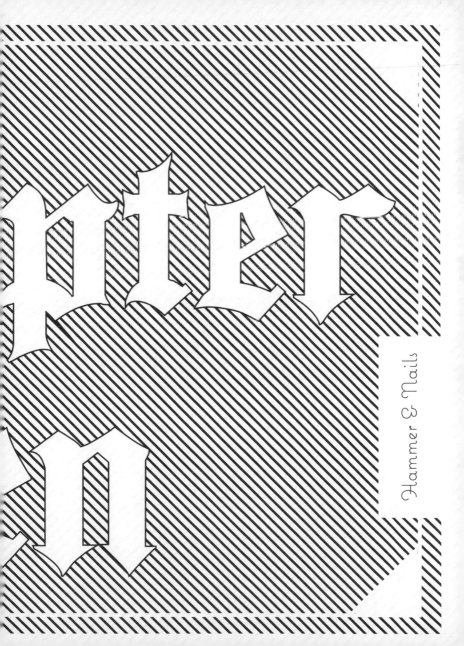

Hammer & Nails

Walking is a healthy exercise and good for your mind.

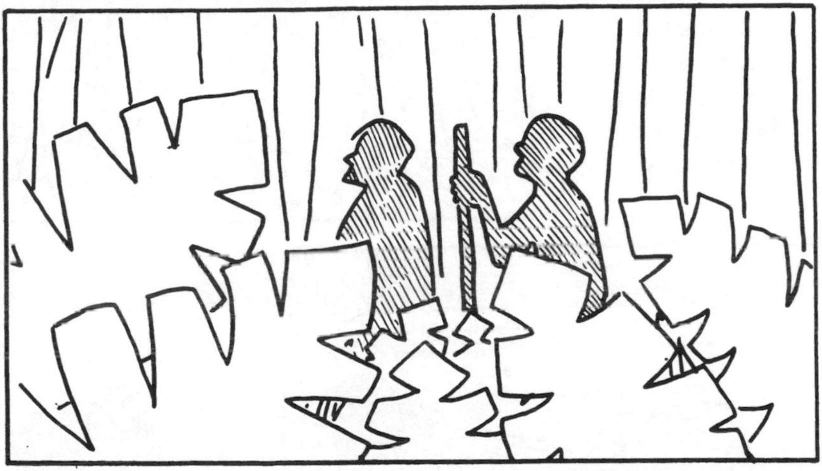

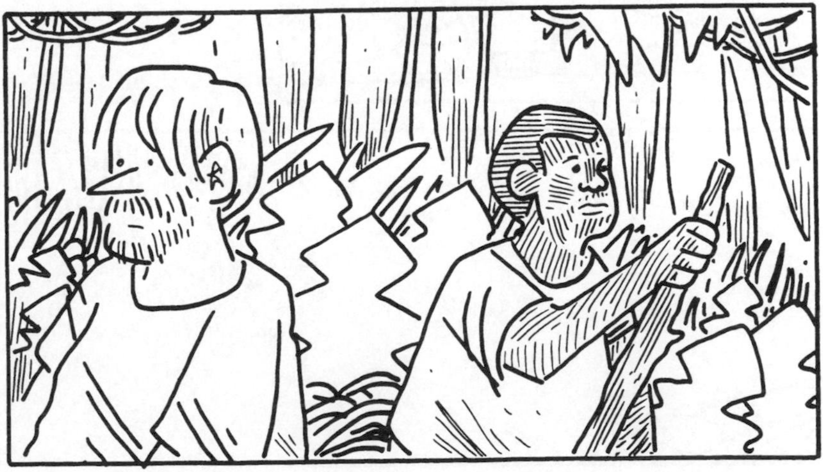

Lately we
will walk in
a direction,
with no end
in mind, and
find ourselves a
little lost.

Only a
little
afraid.

But Reverend Carpenter says, "It's the journey that saves us."

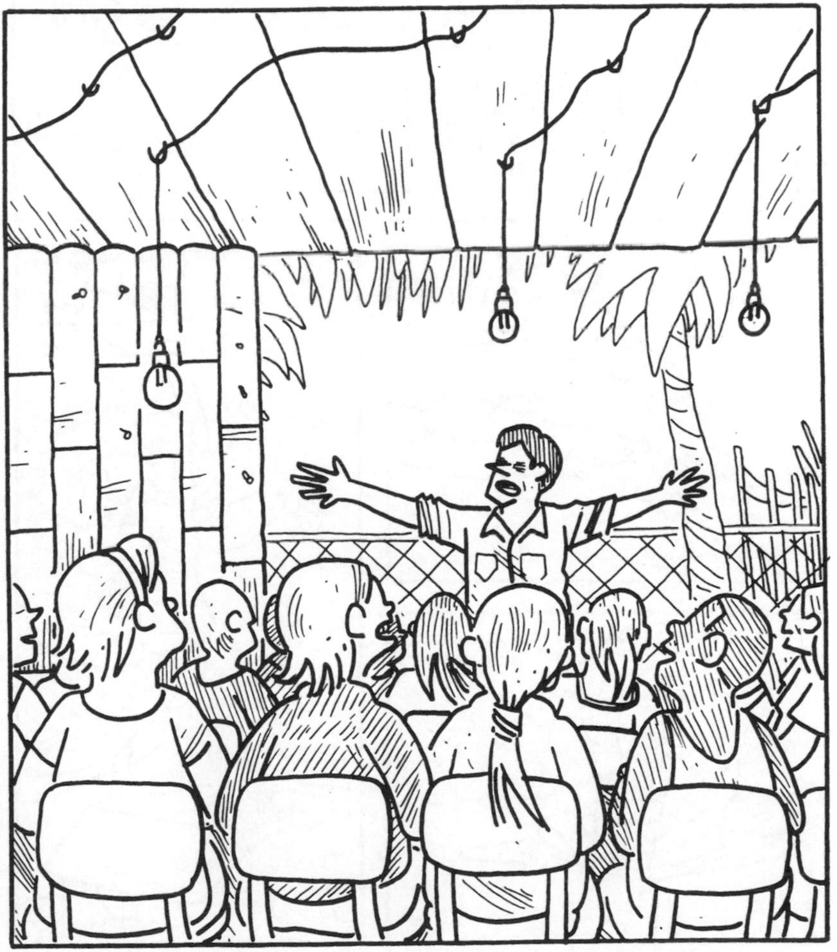

Now that the garden is done, we begin construction on housing and storage.

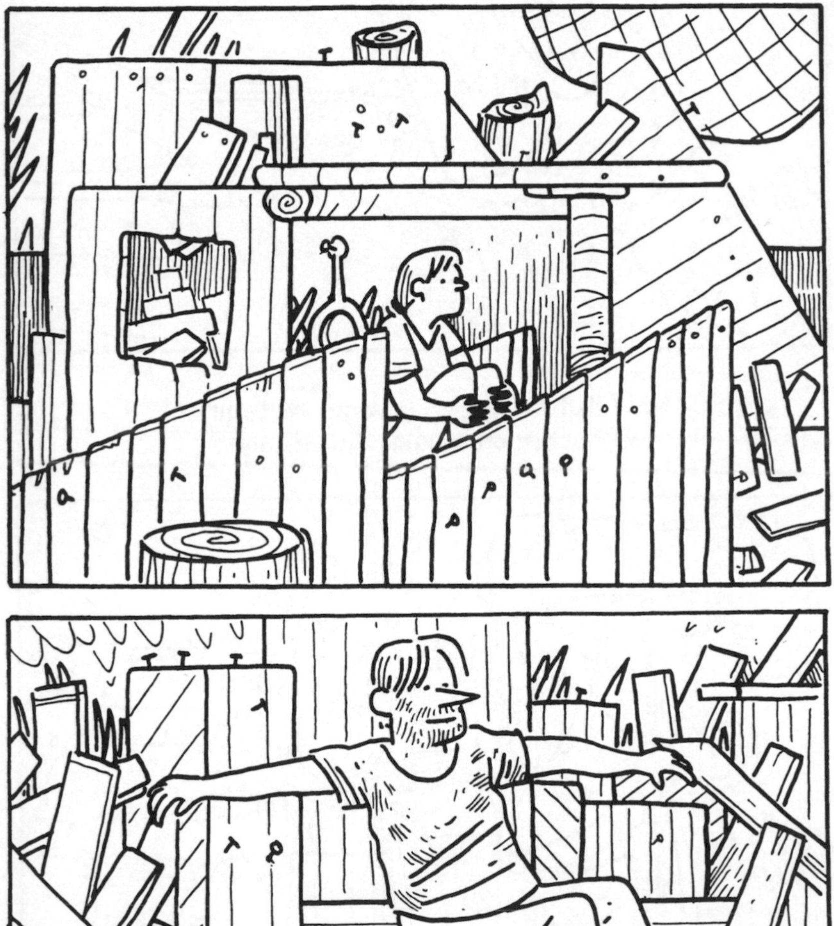

Our great advantage is that we have little experience in building. Experience tells you what not to do. Mind worms crawl into your head and tell you that you're wrong.

We build what feels true and are finished
when we want to move on.

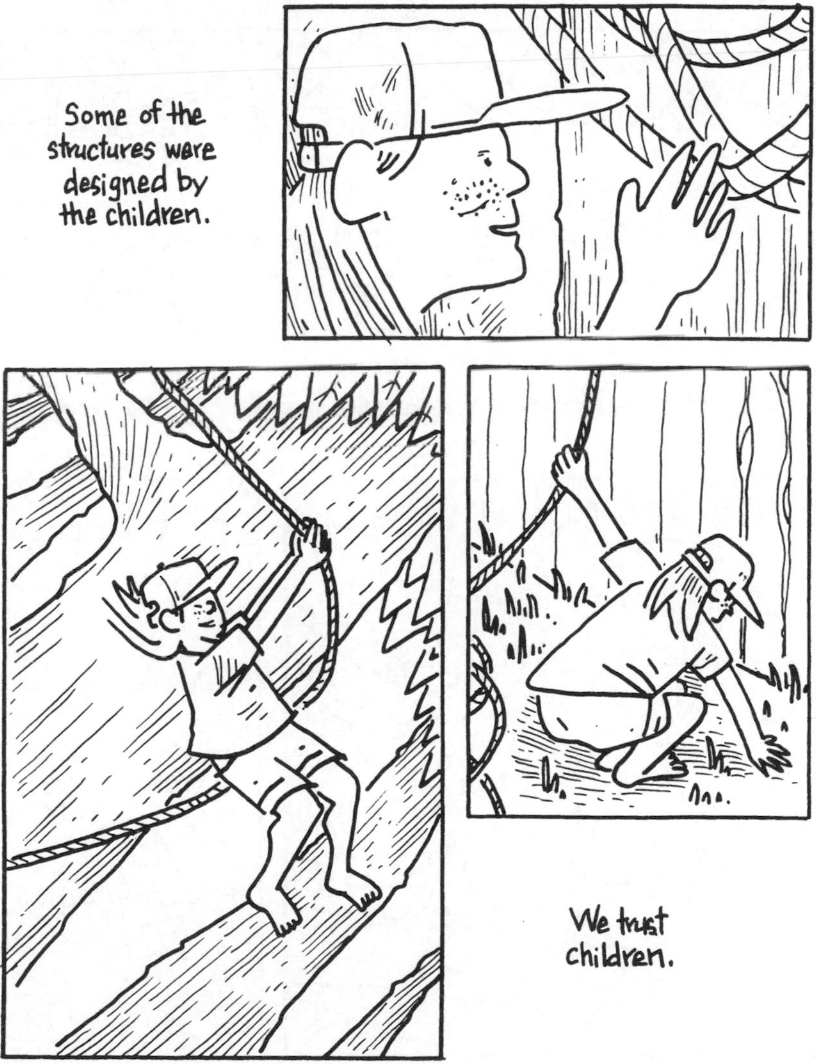
Some of the structures were designed by the children.
We trust children.

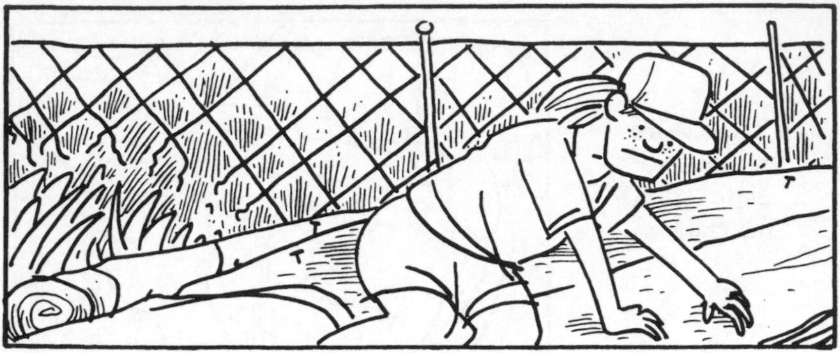

They are the future and are more wise than they get credit for.

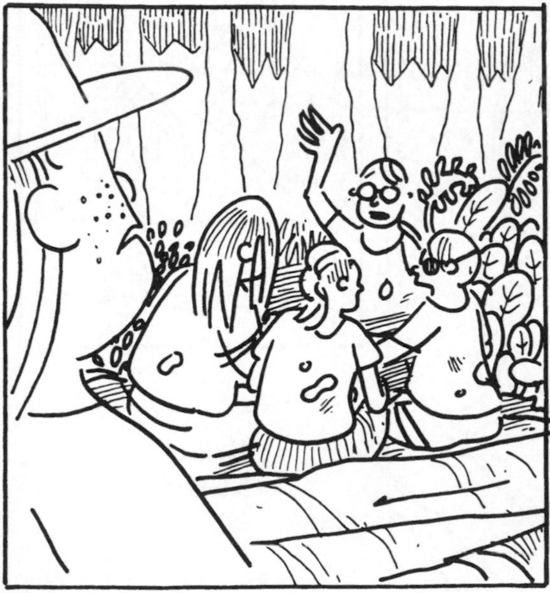

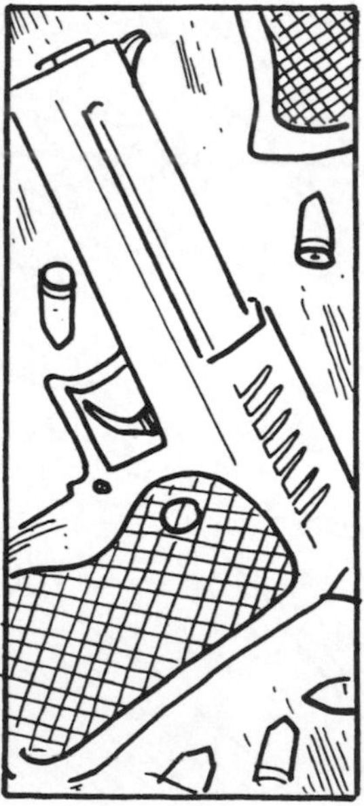

The day that the guns went missing, we stumbled around foolishly believing that we were under attack.

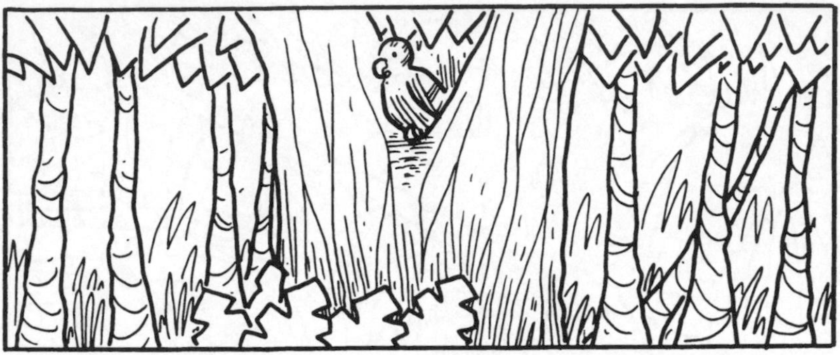

Imagine our relief when we learned that the children had taken our weapons away. They know that we're all safest when the most pure guard the keys to destruction.

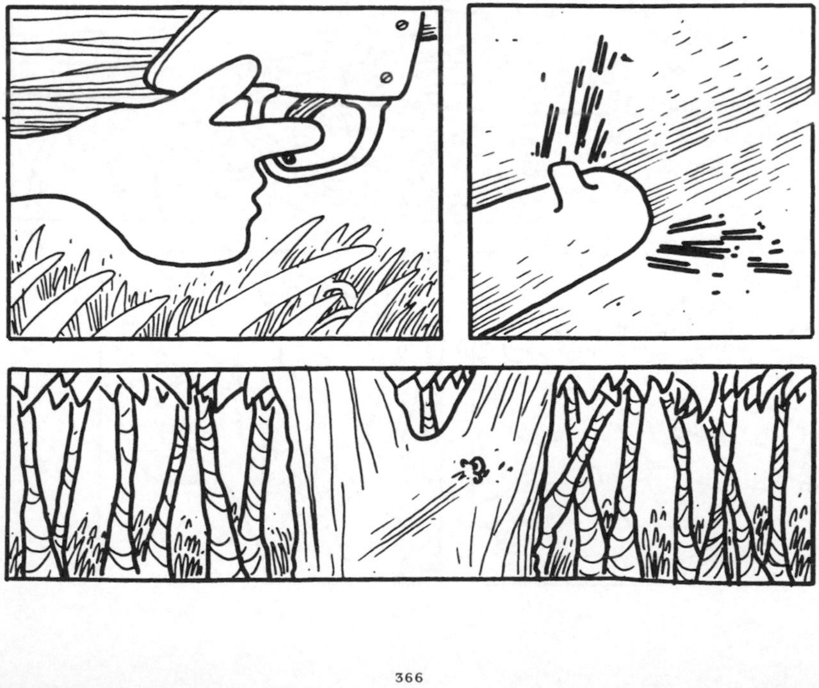

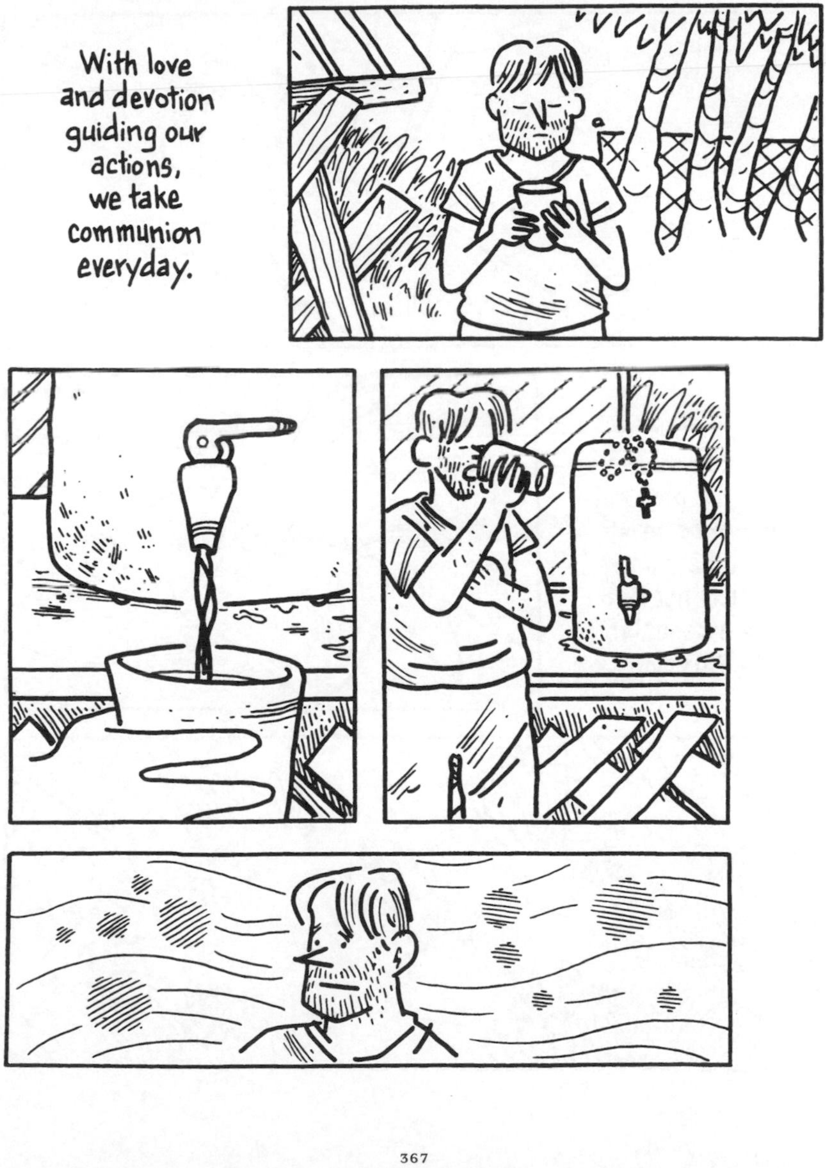
With love
and devotion
guiding our
actions,
we take
communion
everyday.

Finally trusting in love means that the physical presence of our brothers and sisters needn't be essential to the ceremony.

In oblivion,
all are
connected.

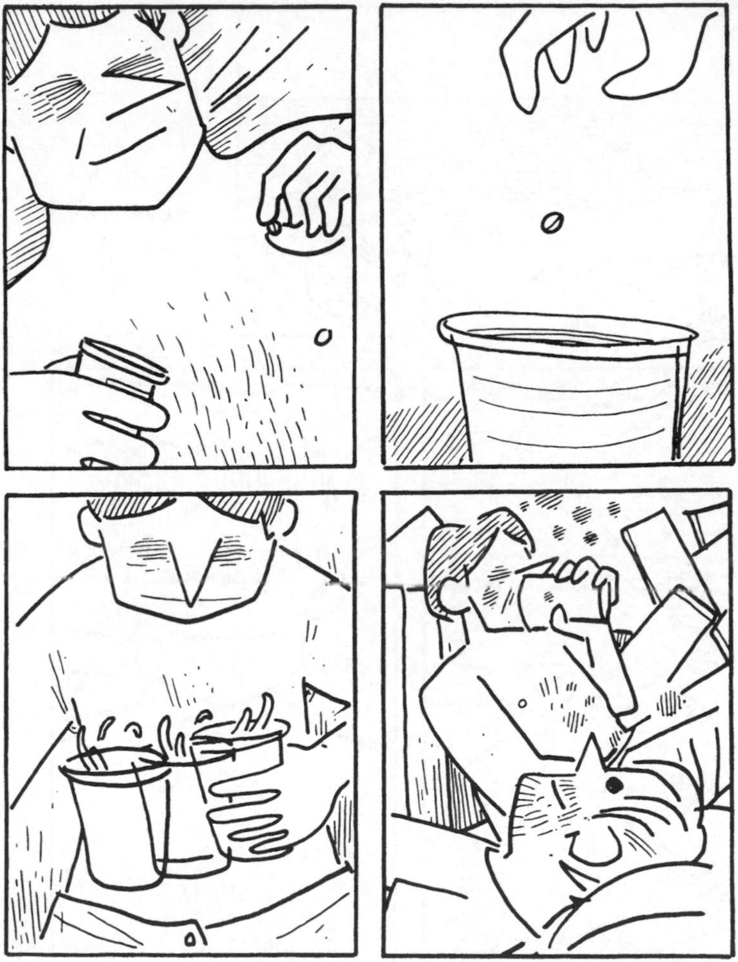

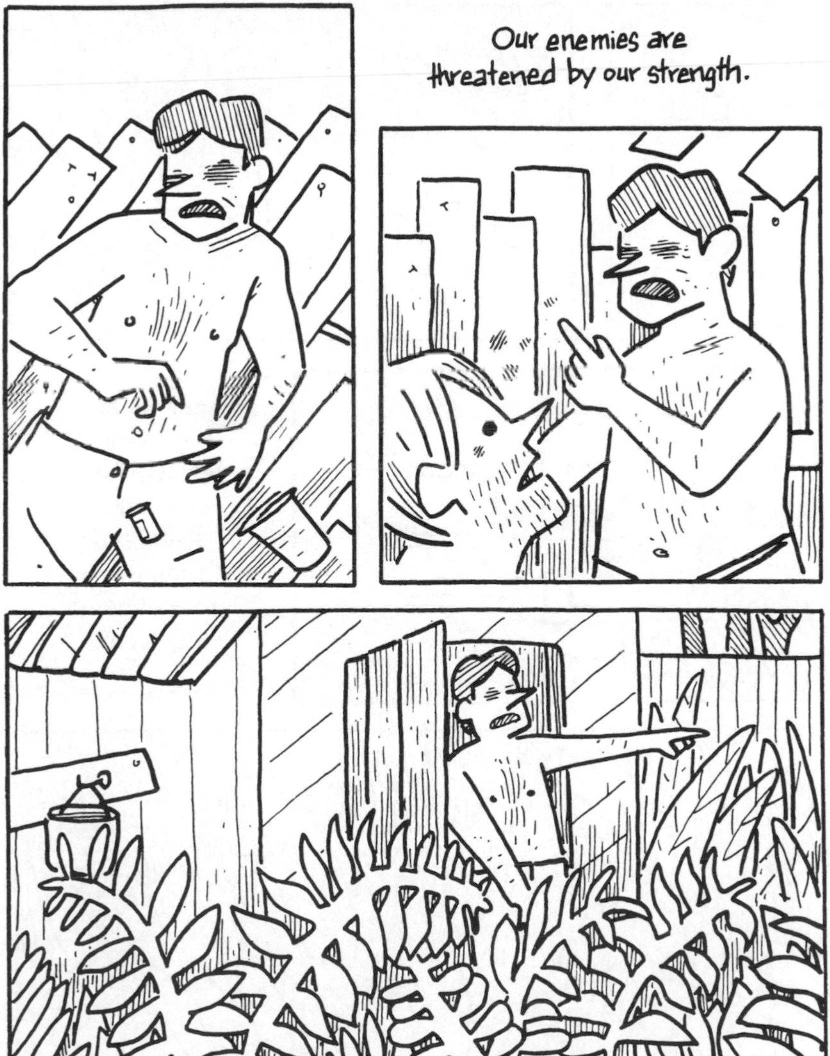
Our enemies are
threatened by our strength.

They hide in the jungle, steal our food, and attack Reverend Carpenter in the middle of the night.

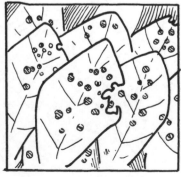

Sometimes we fight back, but their violence and harassment persist.

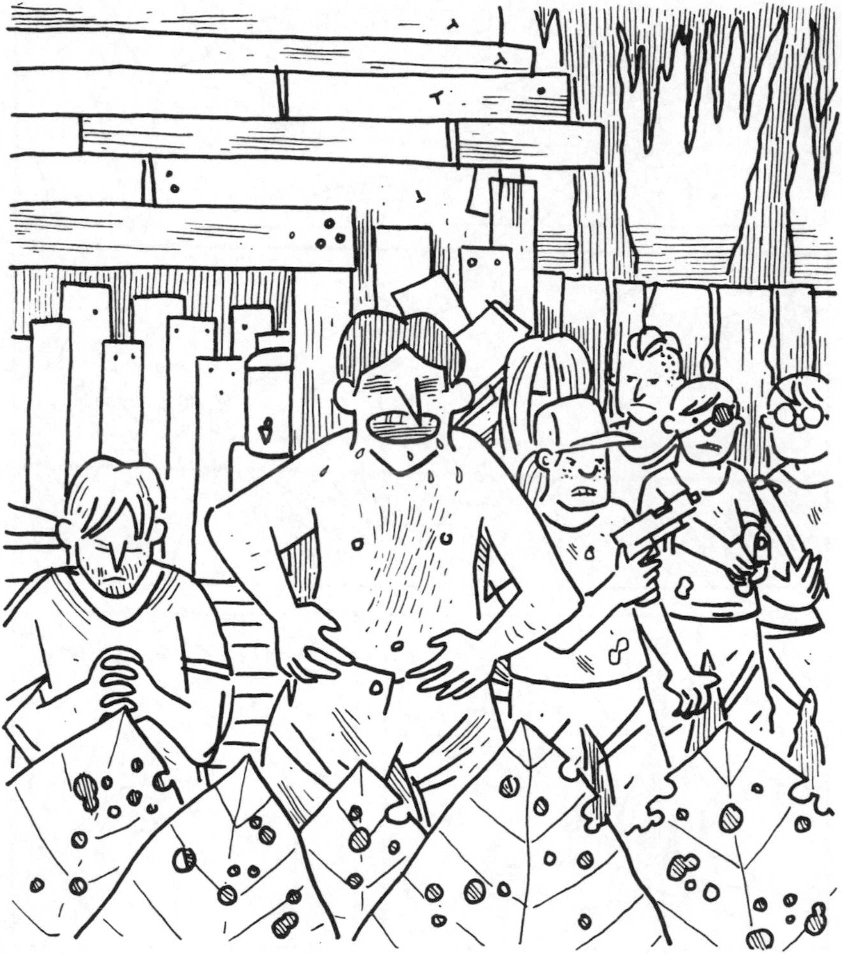

Reverend Carpenter's leadership is what keeps us safe.

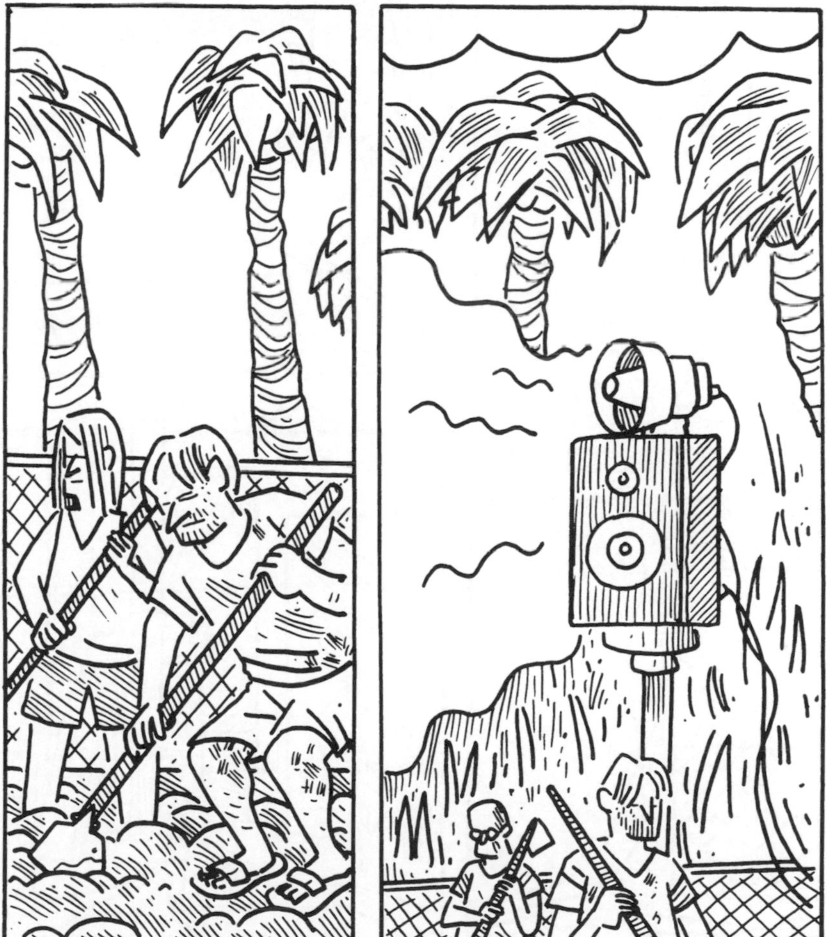

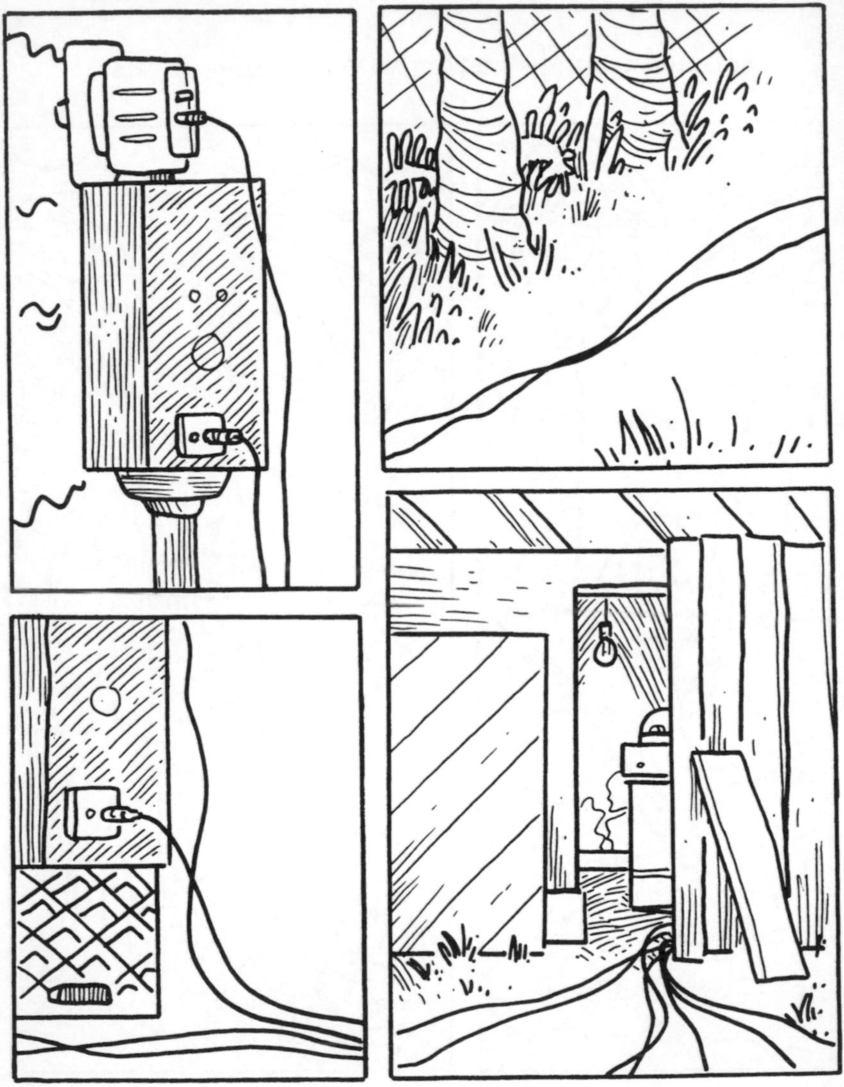

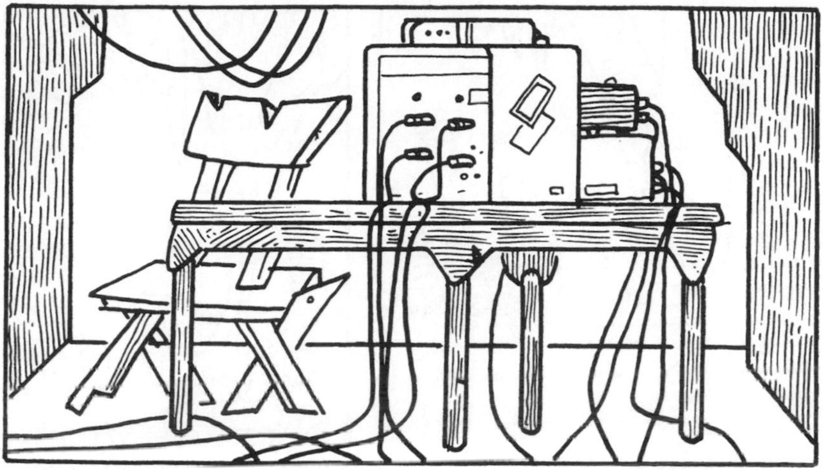

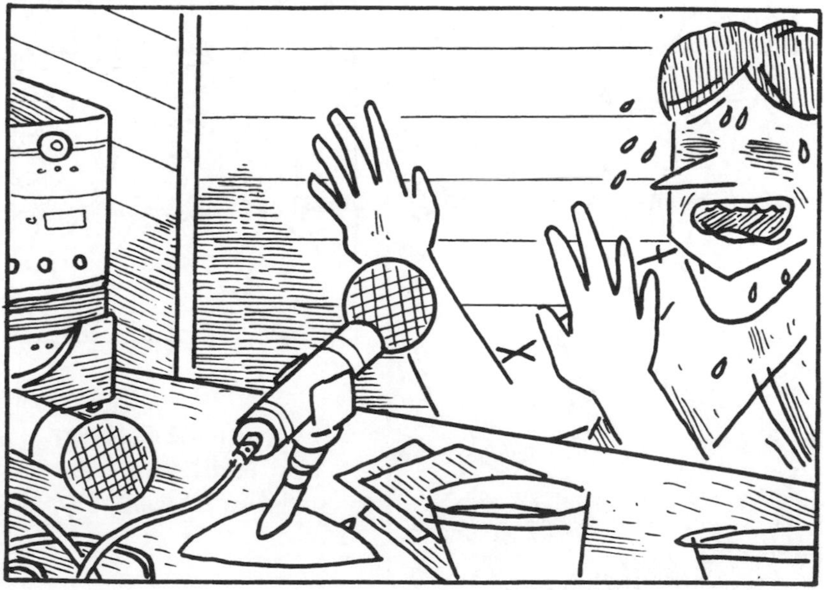

His vision is a gift from god, and his life is a model for all humanity.

When history turns its course away from self-centered violence and destruction, our work will be acknowledged as the seed of that change.

Thank you Reverend Carpenter. We love you.

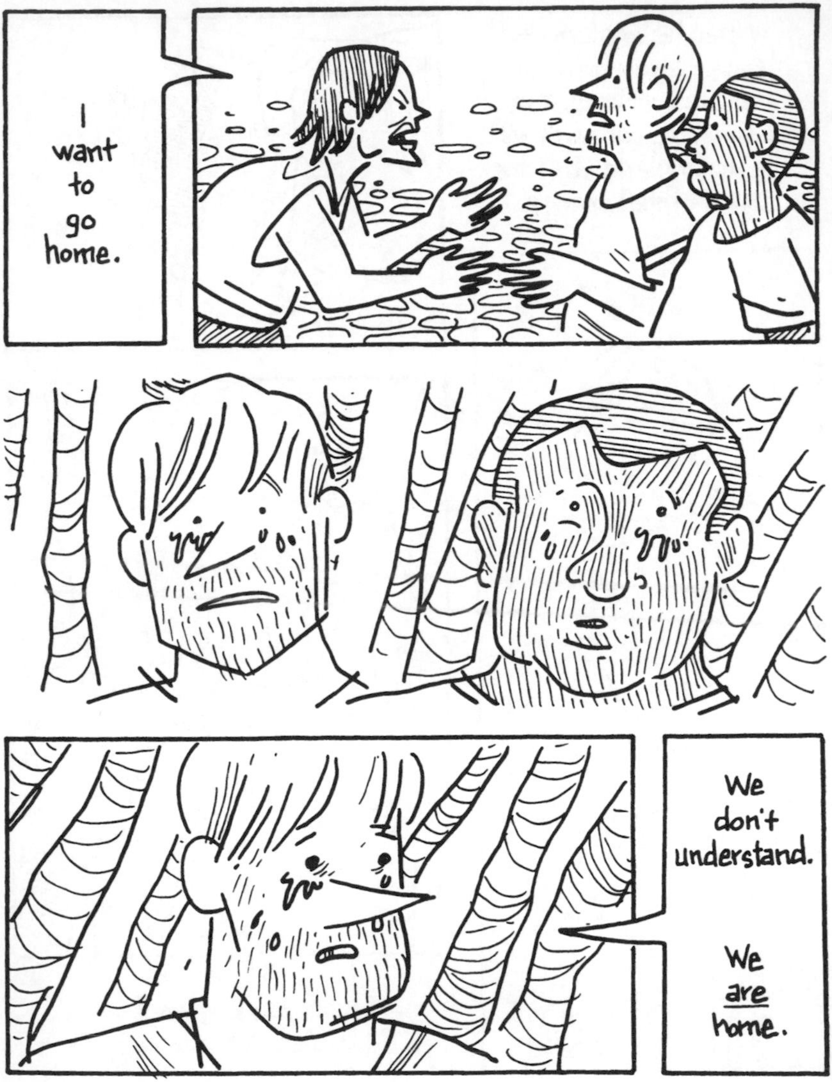
I want to go home.
We don't understand.
We are home.

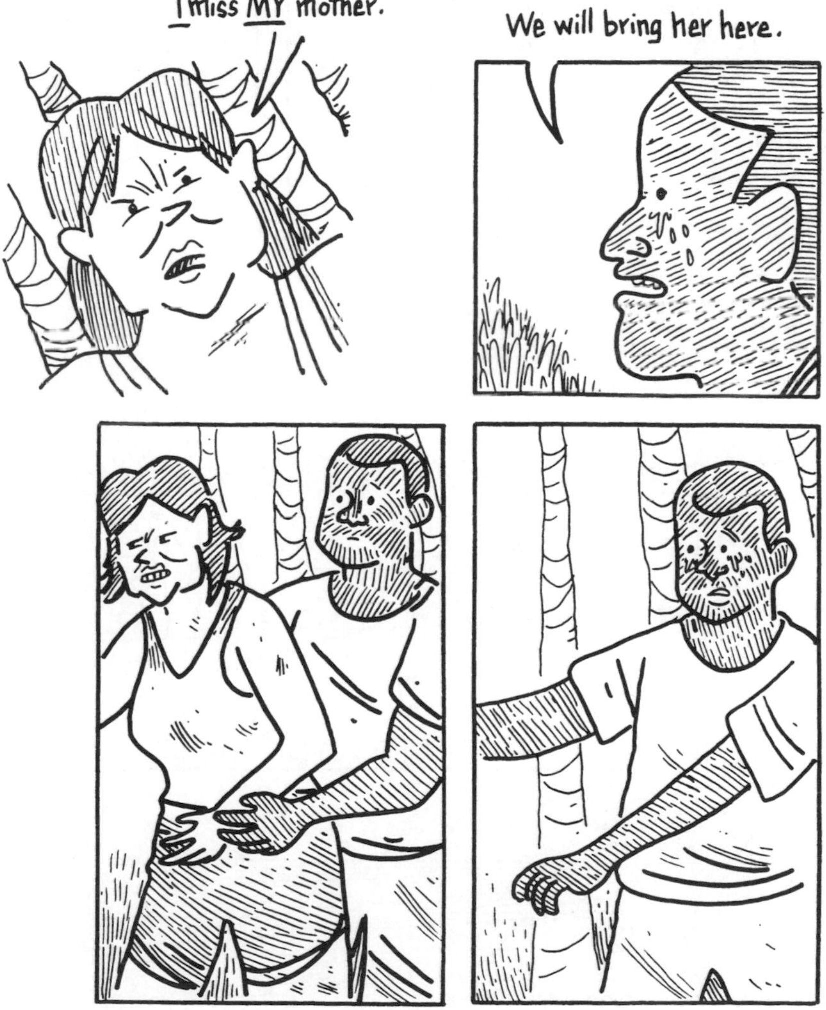
I miss MY mother.
We will bring her here.

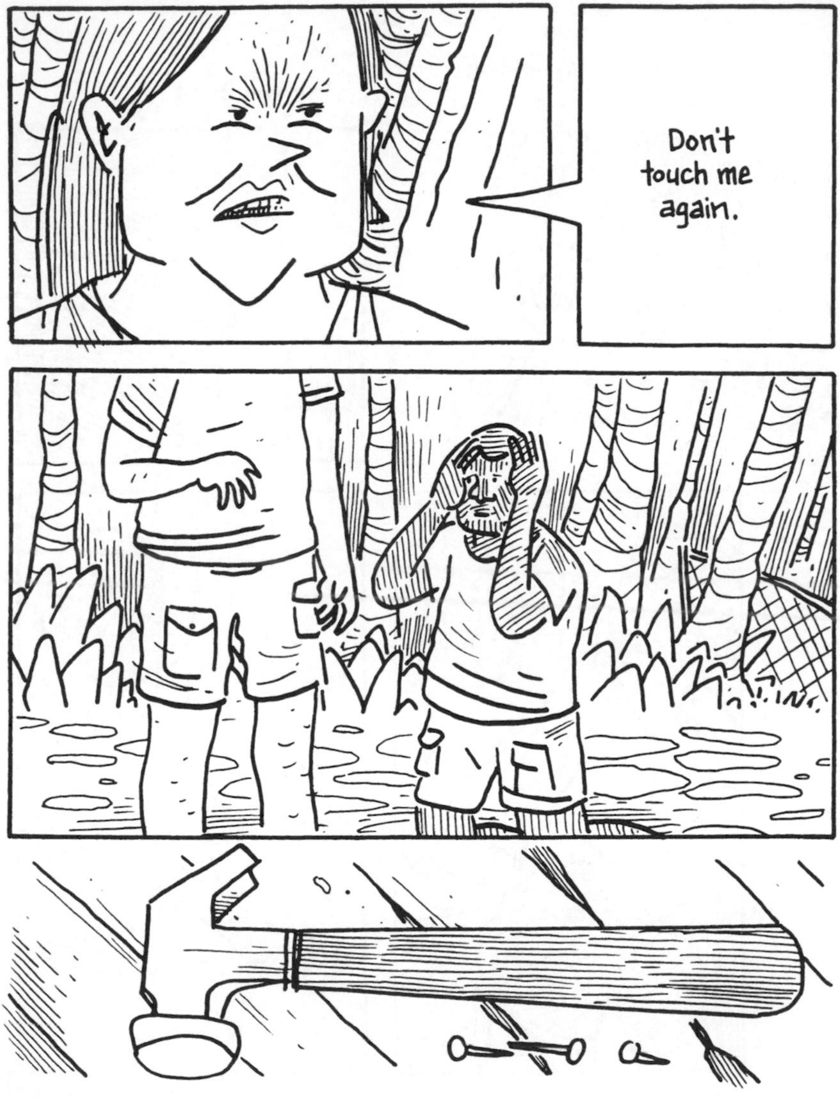
Don't touch me again.

Our enemies multiply by the day.

To do great things you need to take a hard look at the part of yourself that wants to run away from danger.

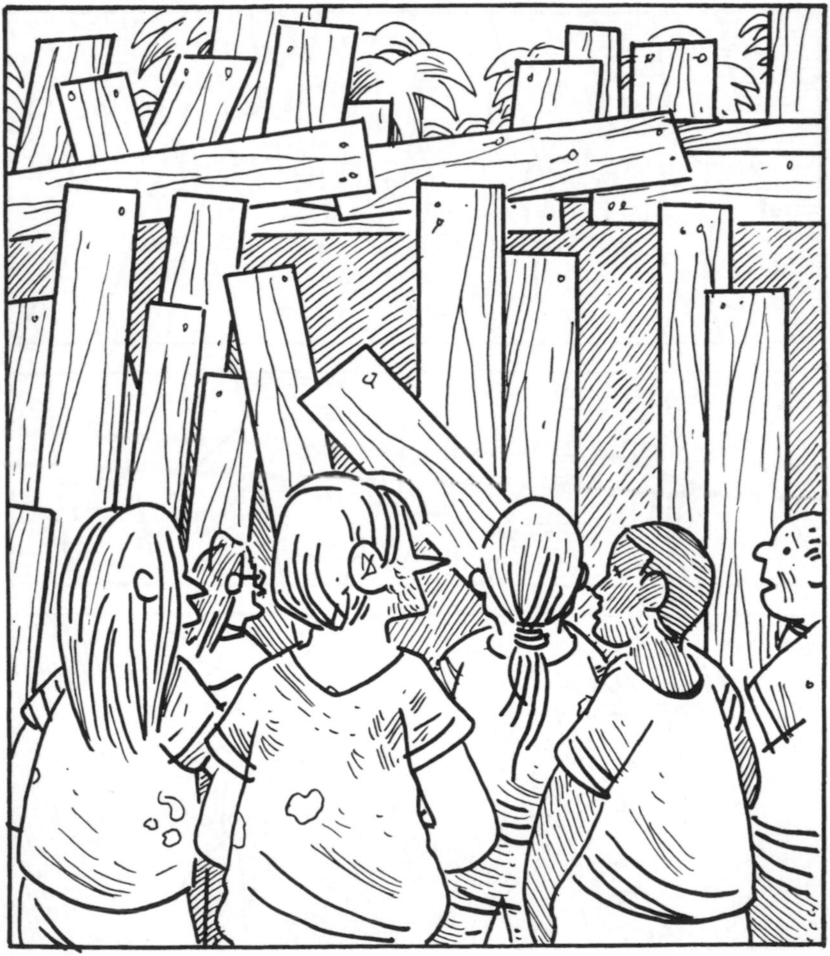

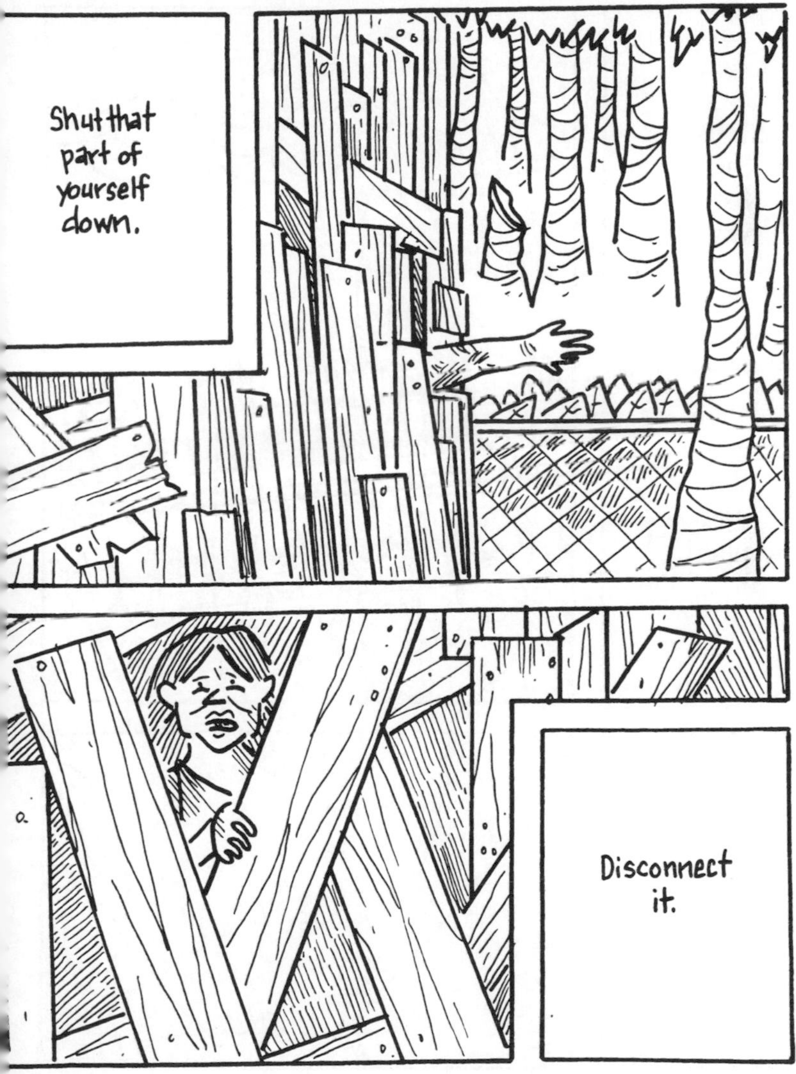
Shut that part of yourself down.
Disconnect it.

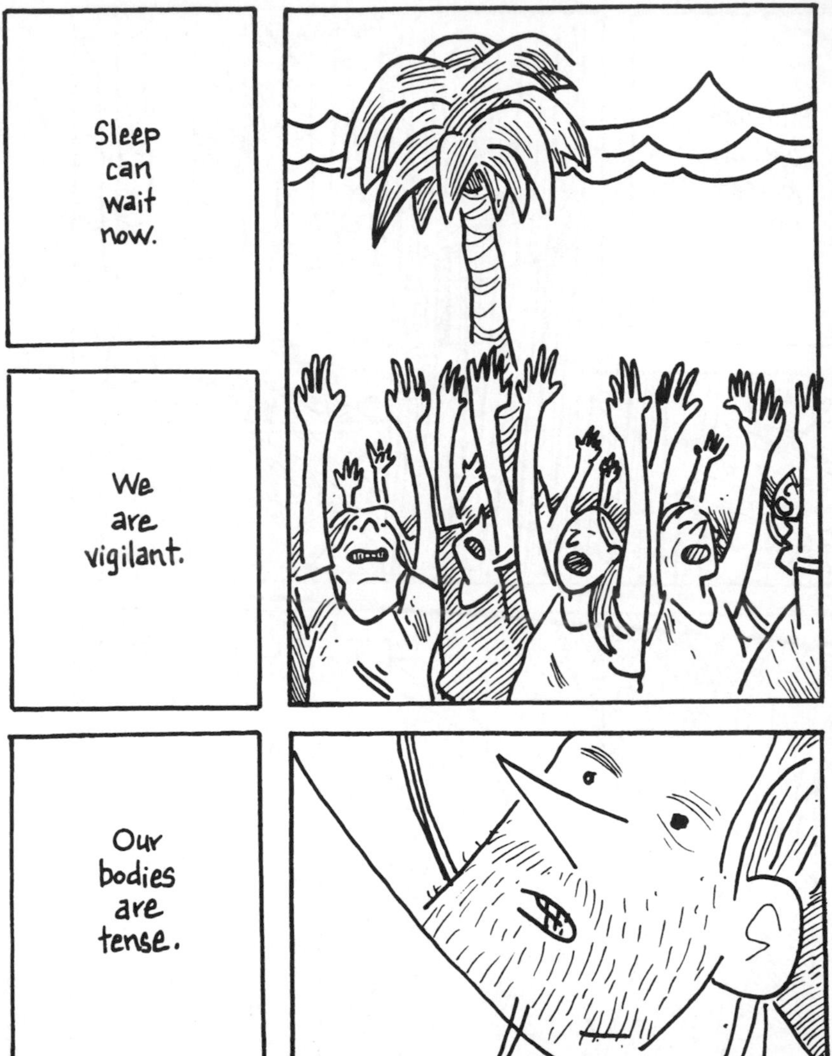
Sleep can wait now.
We are vigilant.
Our bodies are tense.

We are alert and focused for what comes next.

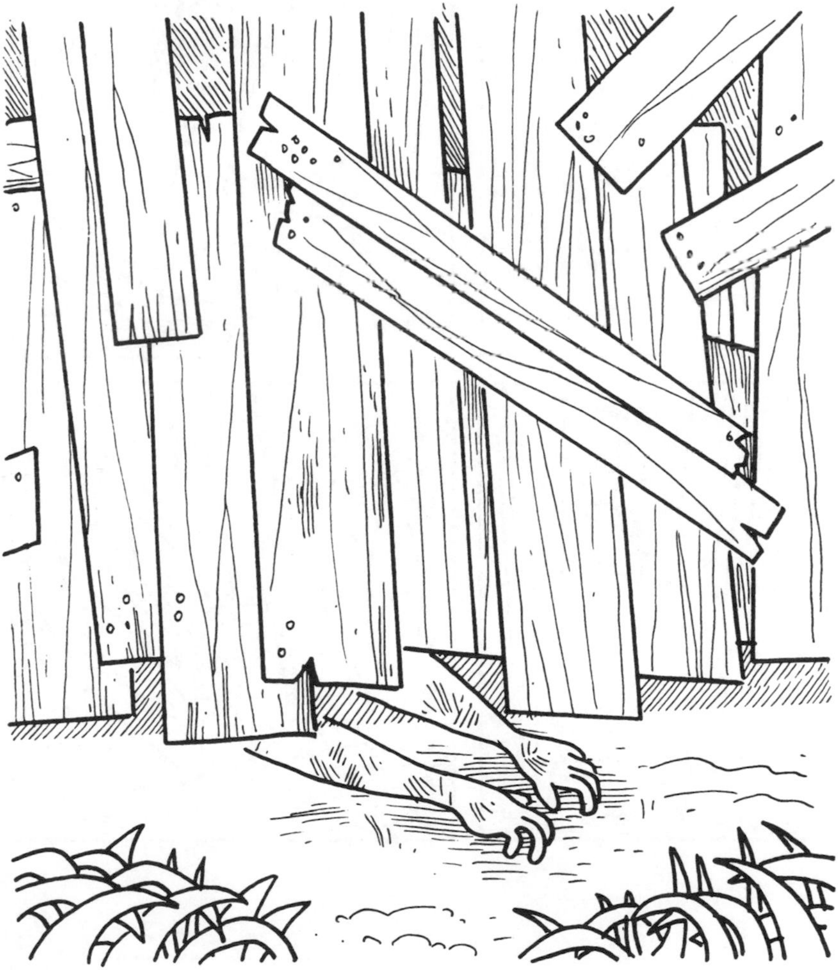

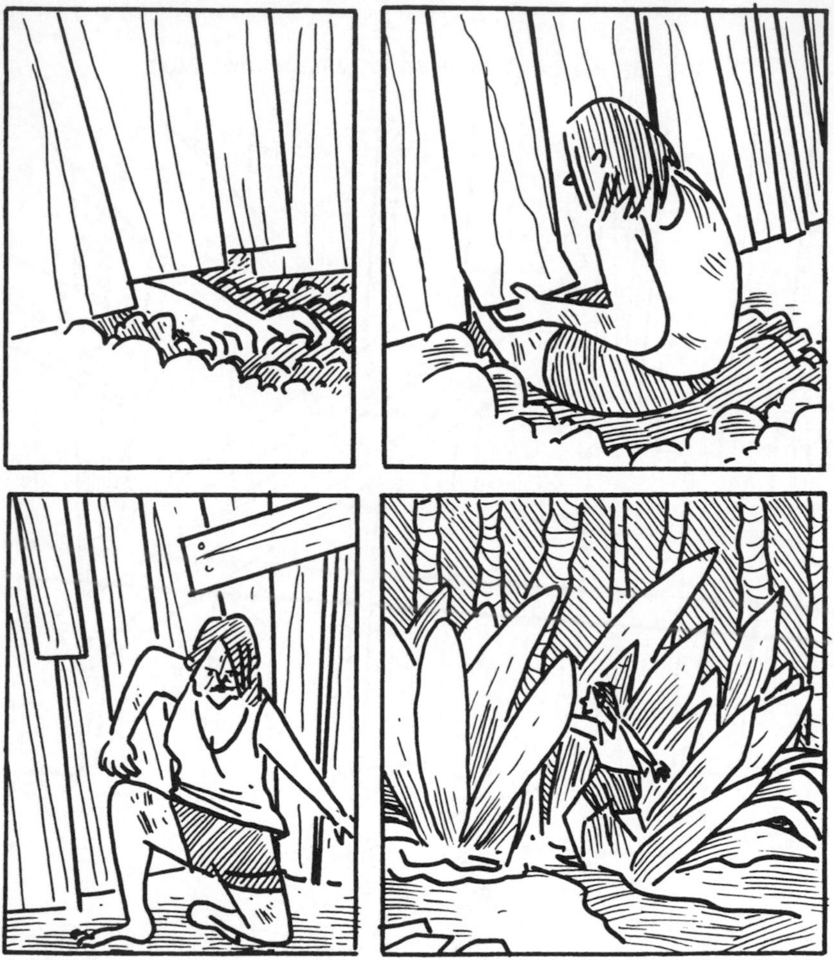

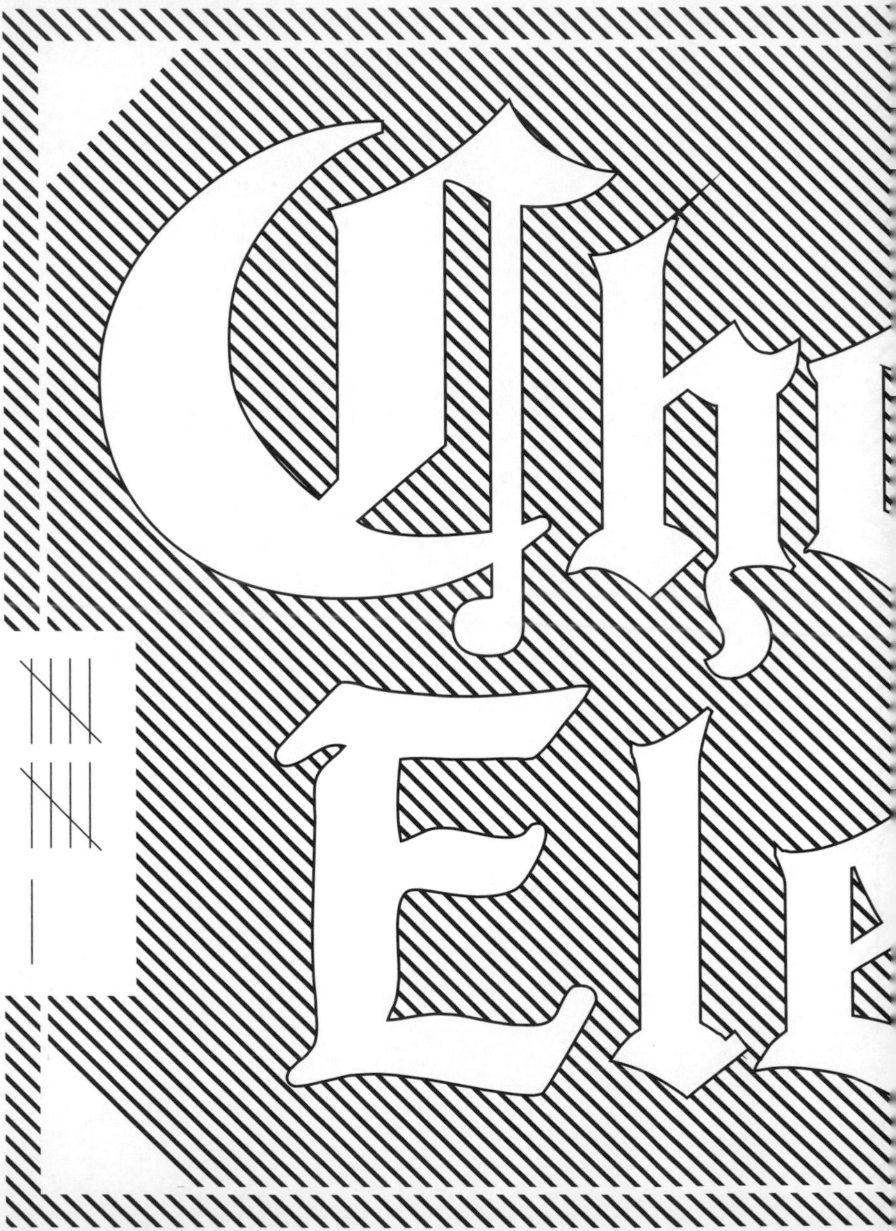

pter
een

Intruders

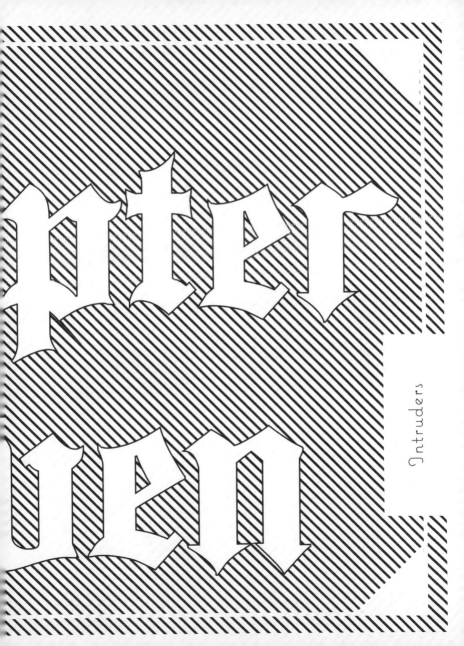

We'll always remember that morning because of the rain.
The thunder started overnight and kept us all awake.

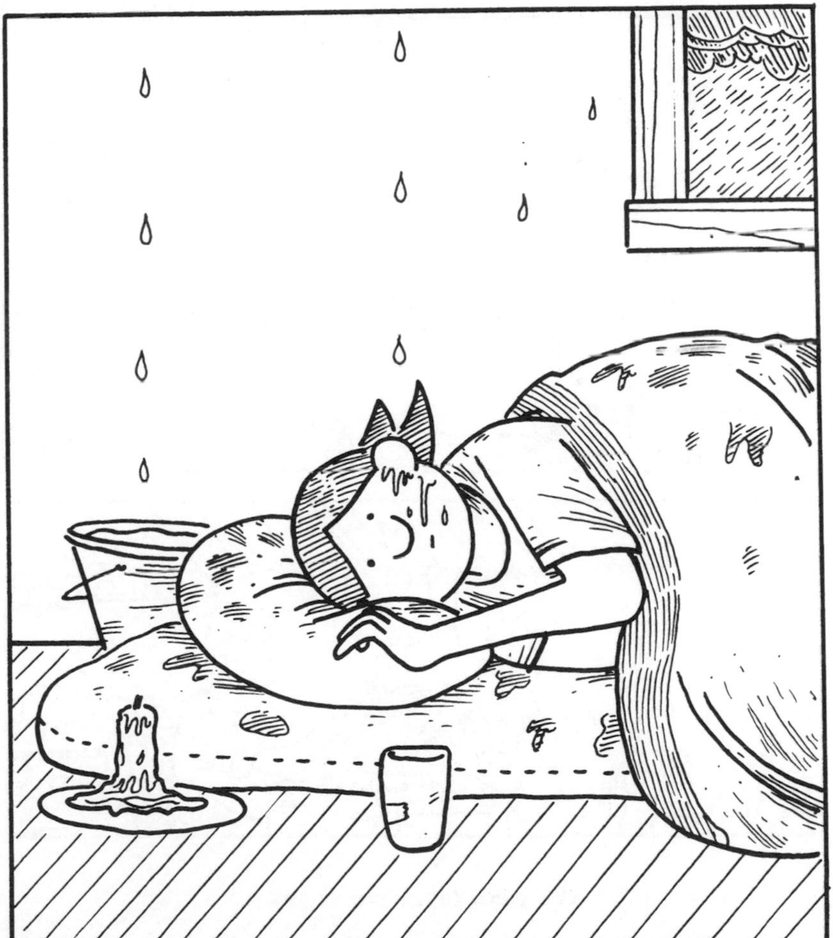

By morning, the roofs that hadn't been built to distribute the rain had caved in.

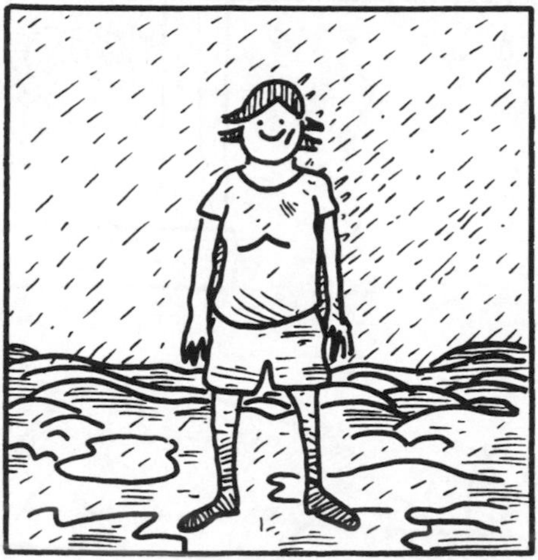

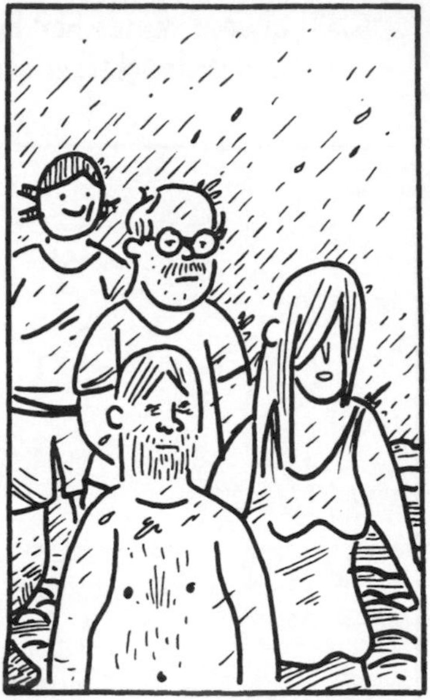

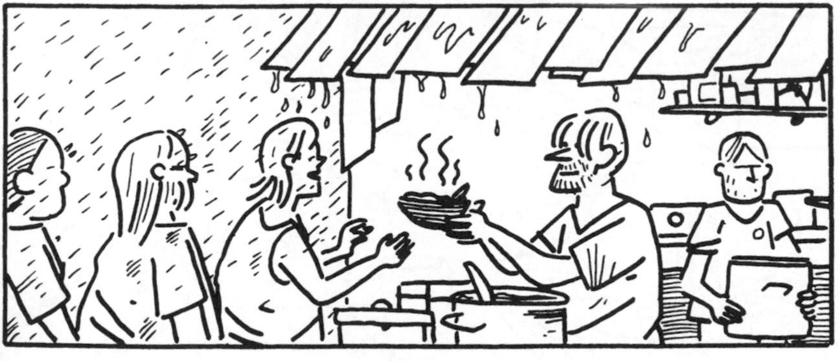

We were cut on our cheek.

Our enemies had organized with political officials and the media.

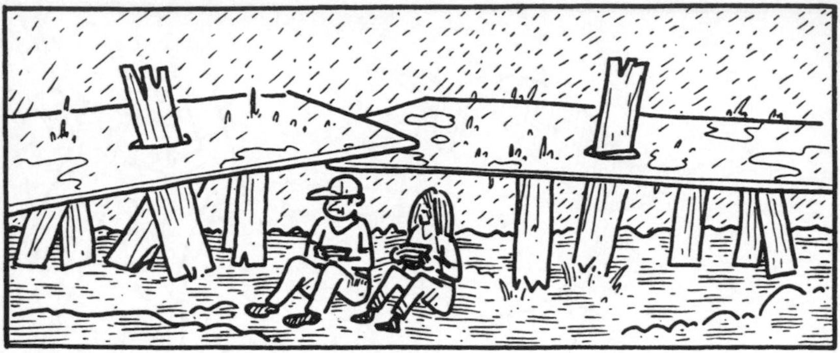

Someone wrote letters containing lies that perverted our mission.

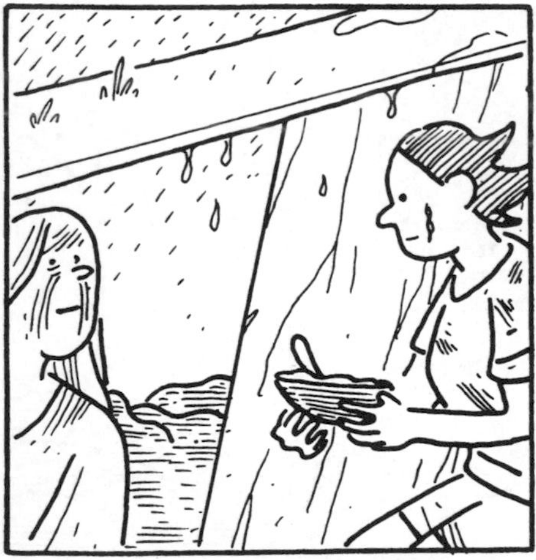

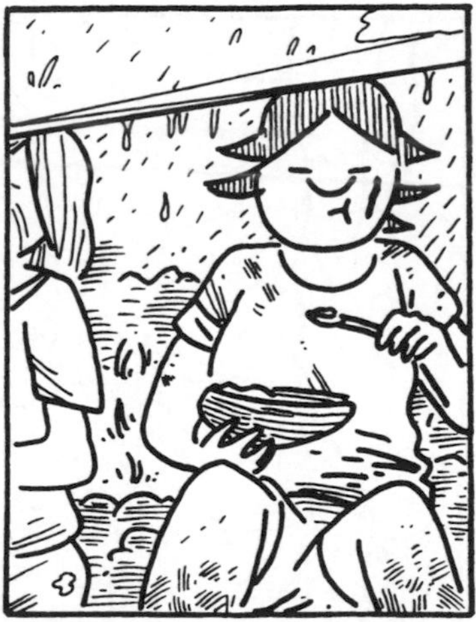

Lies about being prisoners and wanting to leave the island.

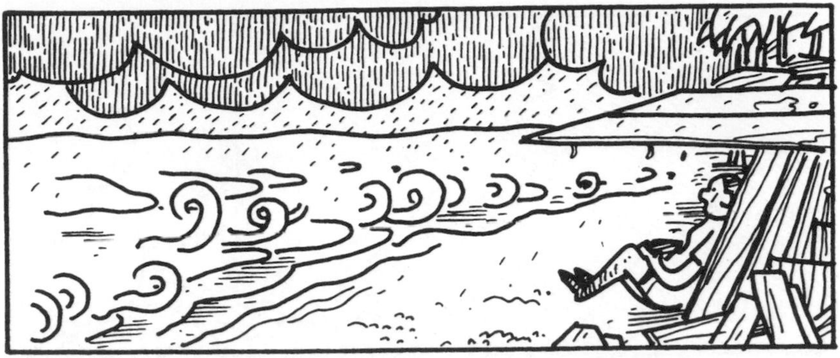

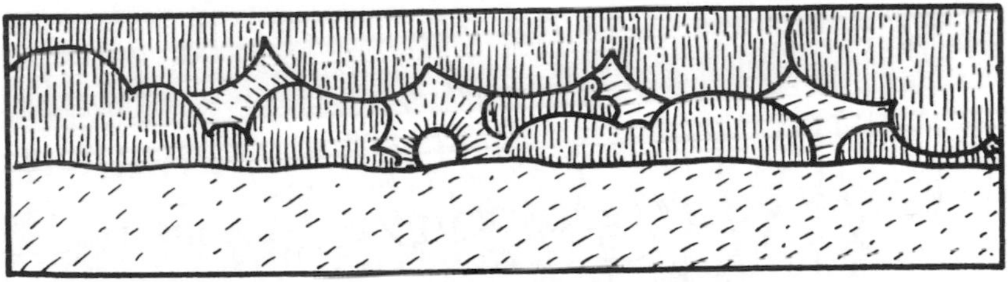

How can you escape
from paradise?

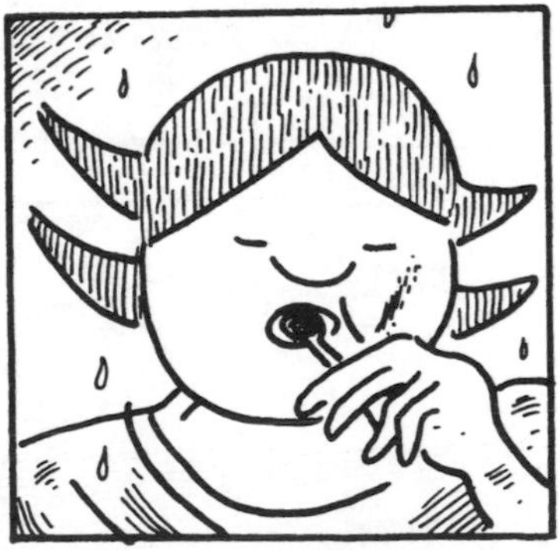

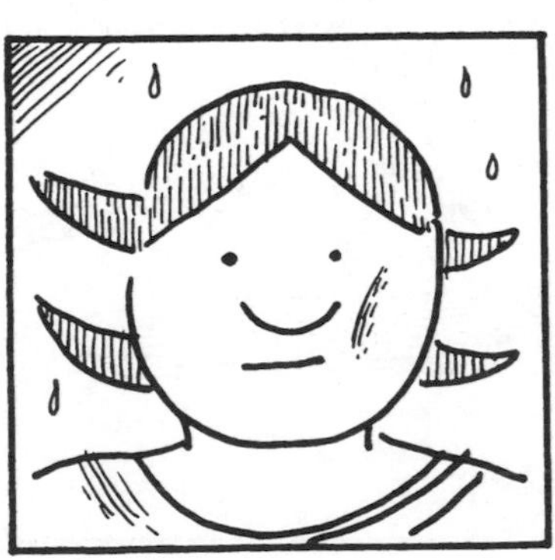

We were all free
men and women.

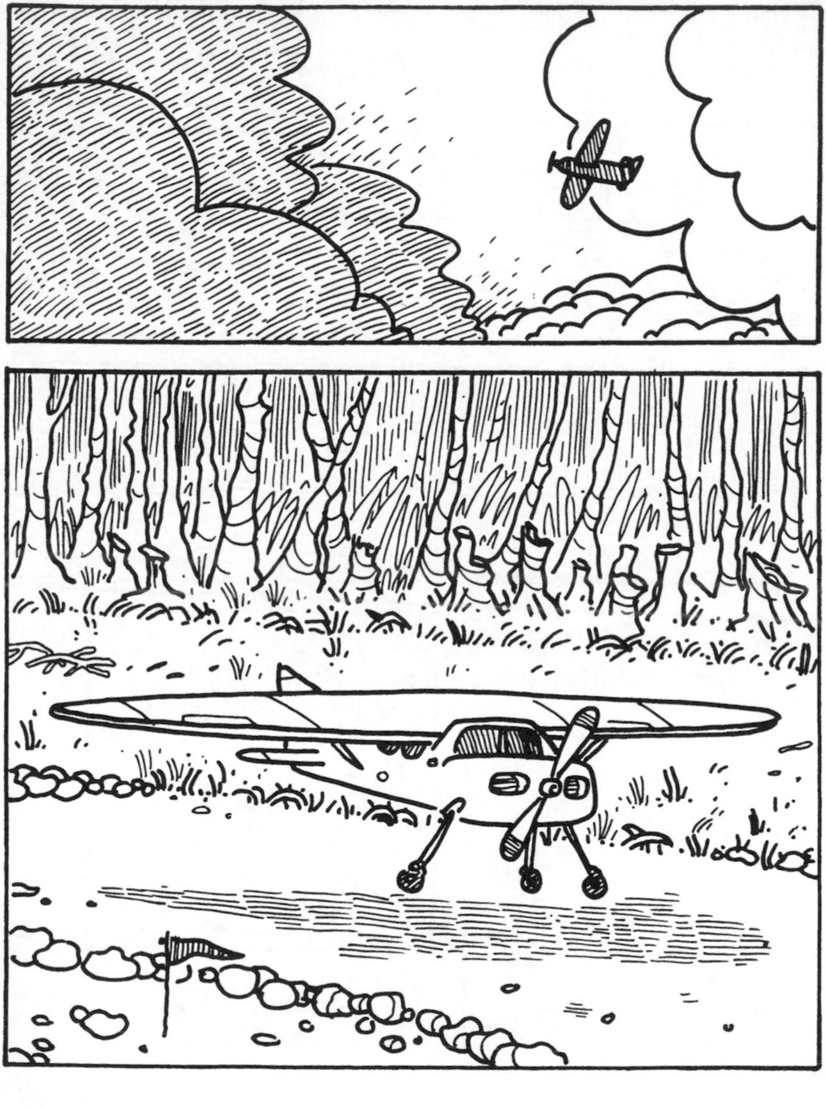

And then, just like the rain, they fall on us.

Two reporters and a camera man.

They bent forward when speaking to us as though we were children.

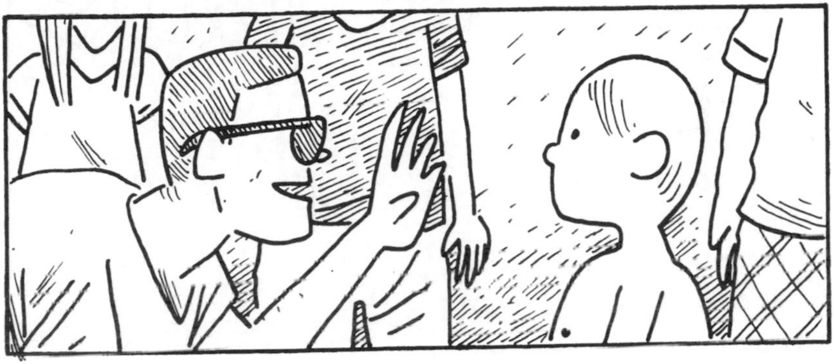

We carried their bags and welcomed them as guests.

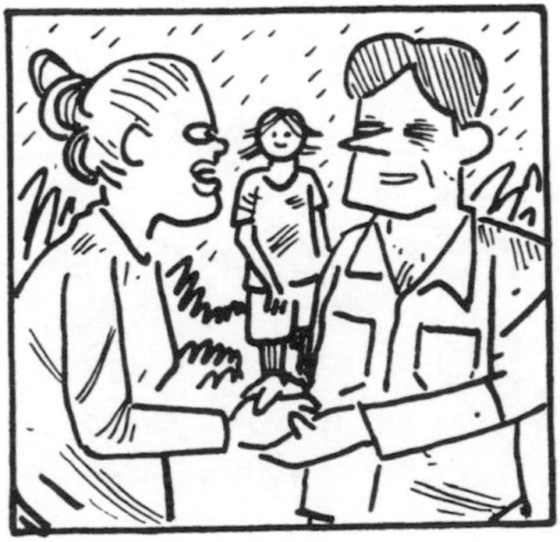

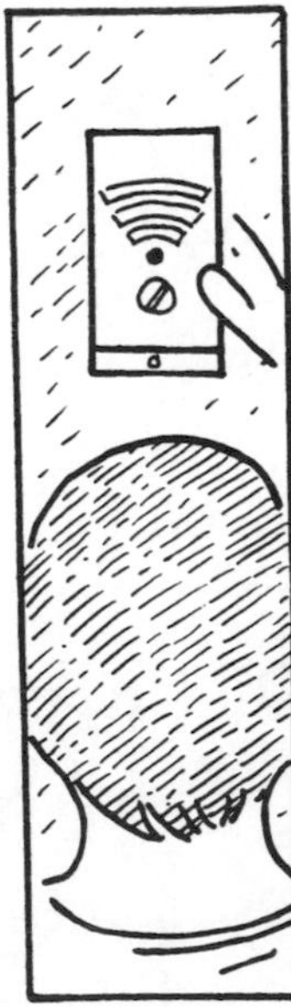

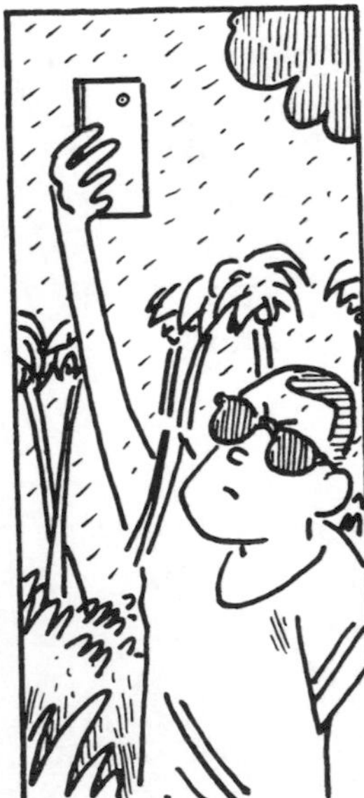

We showed them our way of life.

They told us our homes were "creative."

"Creative" is a word people use when they want to insult you to your face.

We could actually hear their laughter as they filmed.

How miserable they must have been to take such joy out of mocking others.

But they smiled.

They were always smiling as though they meant us no harm.

The following day, we were more prepared.
Our best selves were on full display.

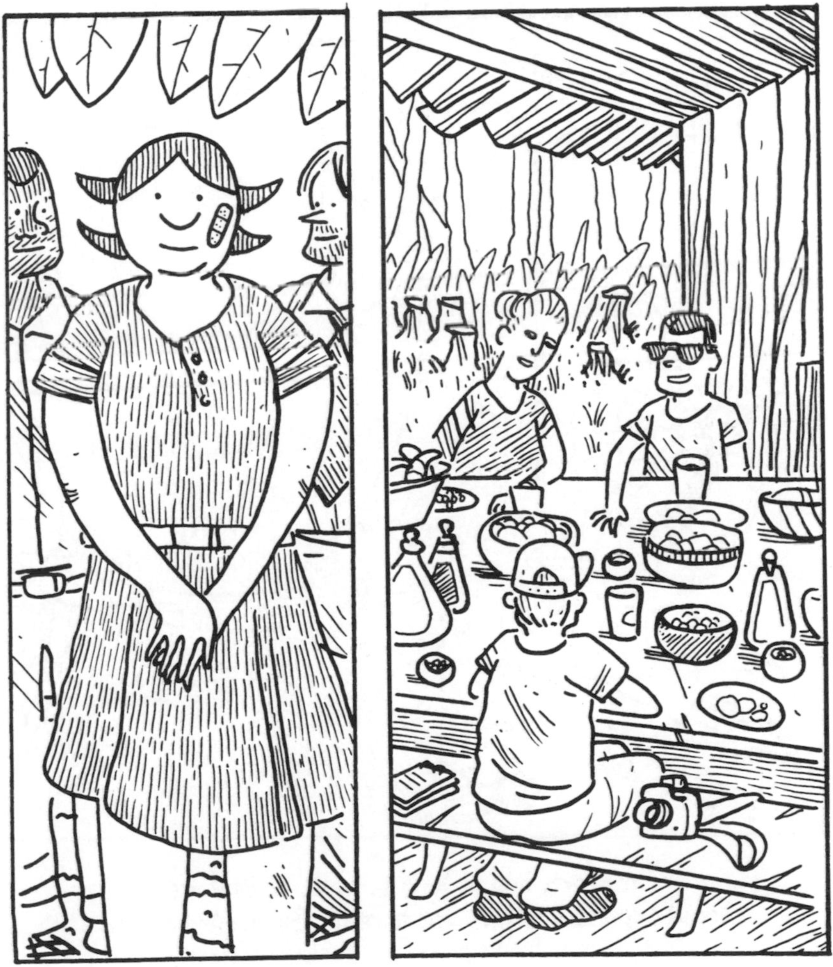

Reverend Carpenter's mother played guitar.
We danced and sang original songs we had written.

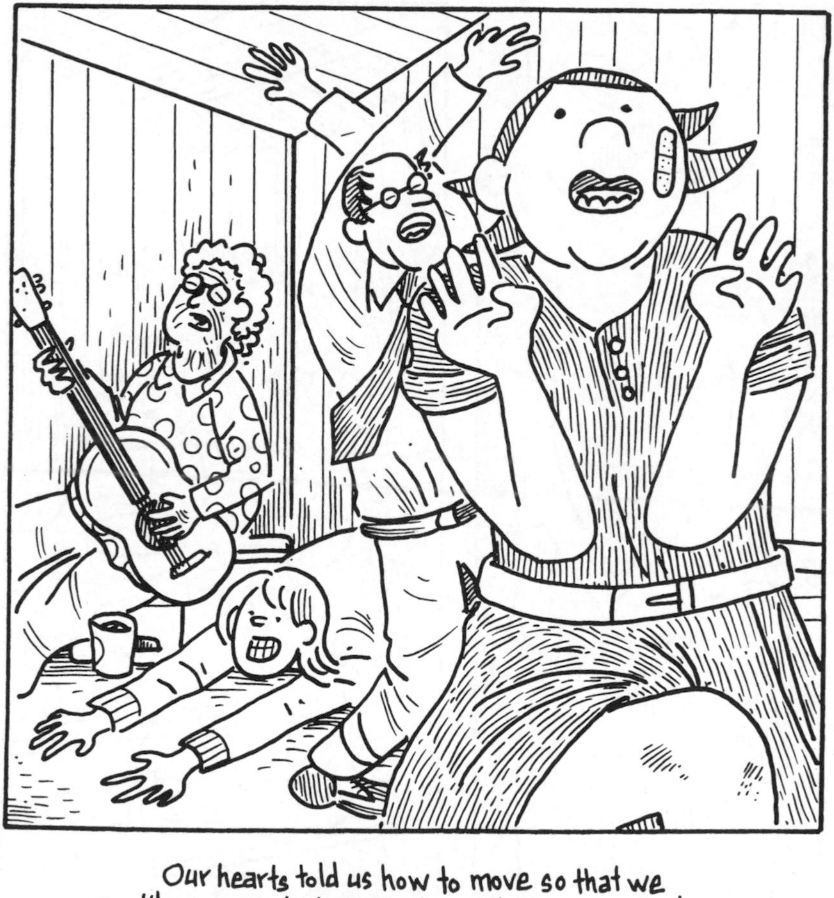

Our hearts told us how to move so that we could express what it's like to really BE in our bodies.

The children sat at Carpenter's feet while he told them a fairy tale.

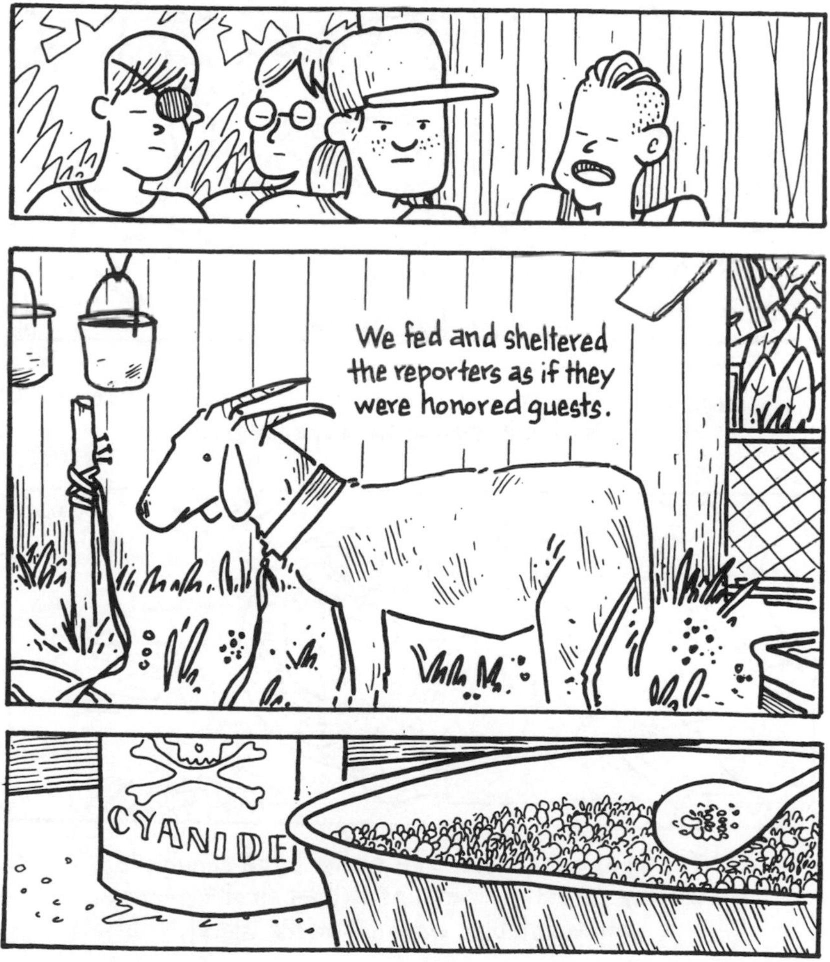
We fed and sheltered the reporters as if they were honored guests.
CYANIDE

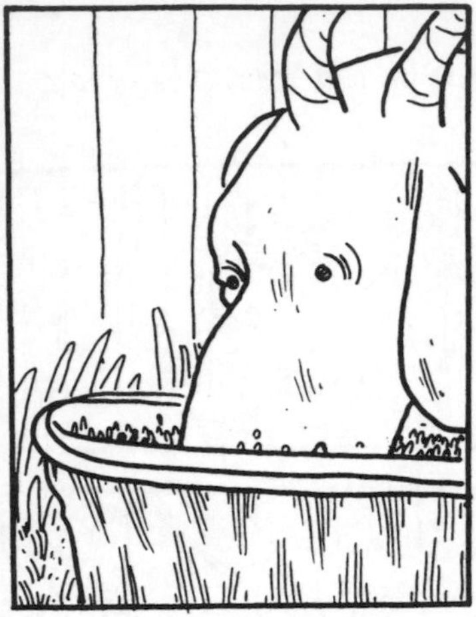

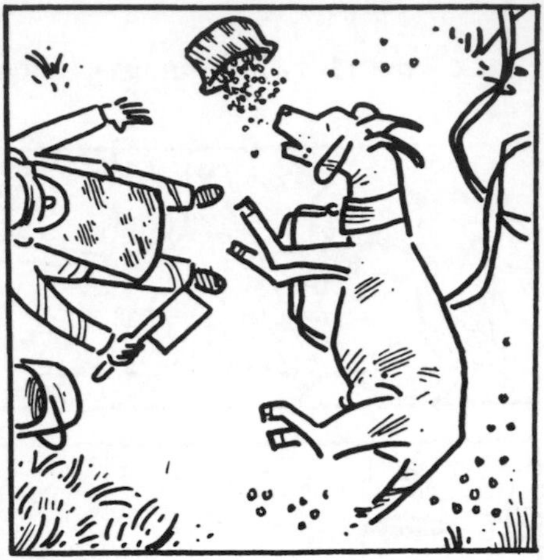

These gawkers were treated as if they were worthy of the goat we had been saving for a special occasion.

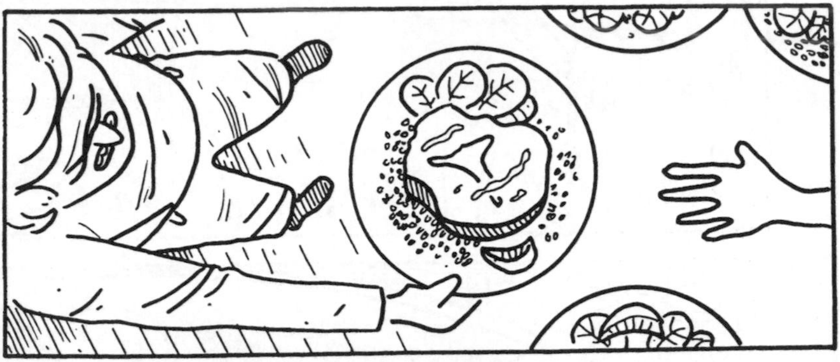

The meat was placed on a platter large enough to display the entire animal as well as all of the fruits and vegetables we grew on the island.

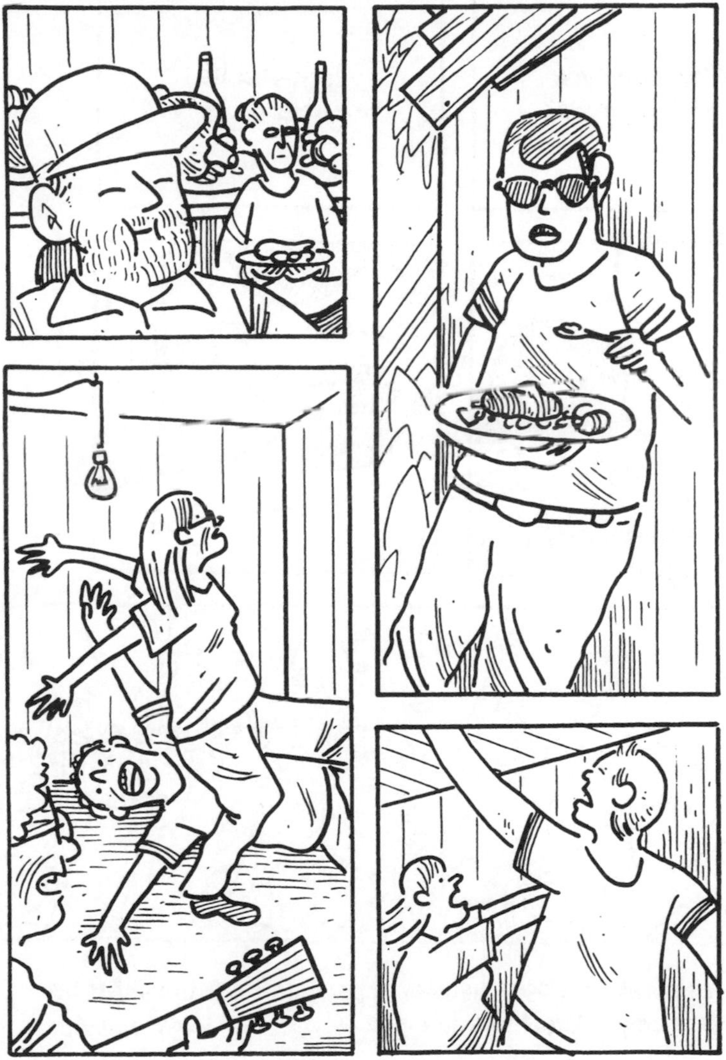

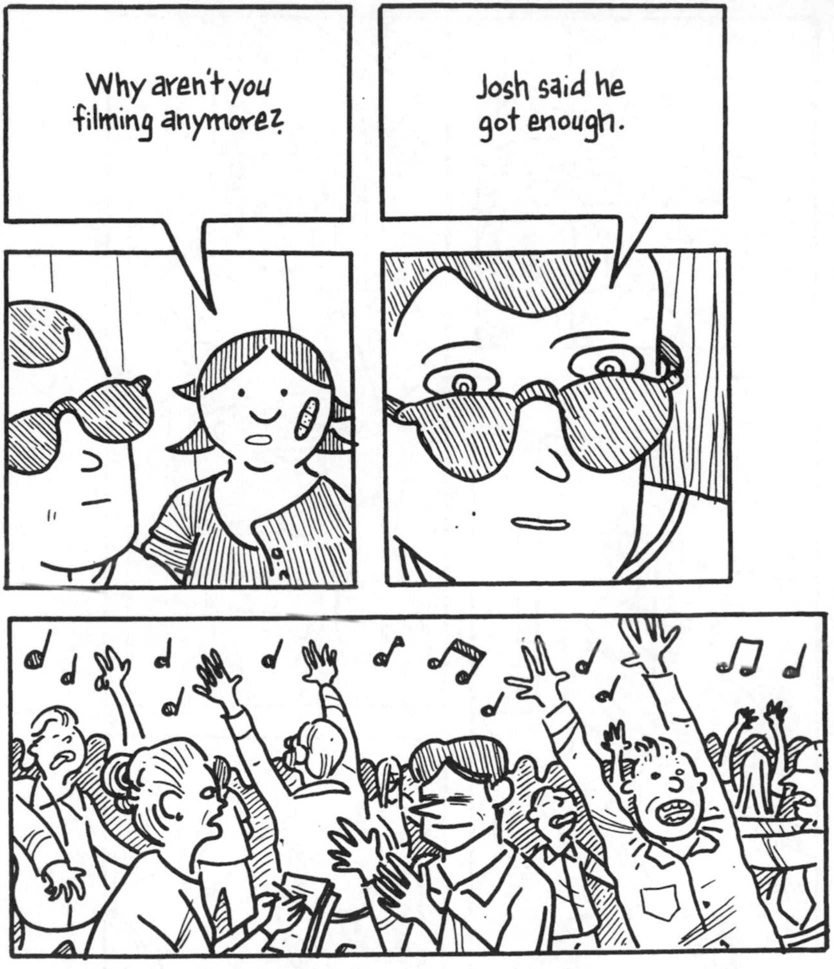
Why aren't you filming anymore?
Josh said he got enough.

Our celebration was a disaster. It became clear to us that the reporter's only interest was to make us look like loony outsiders.

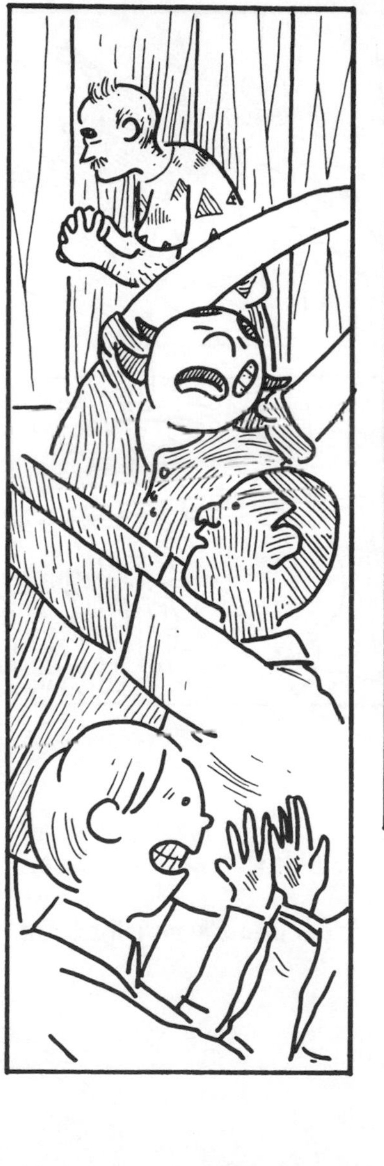

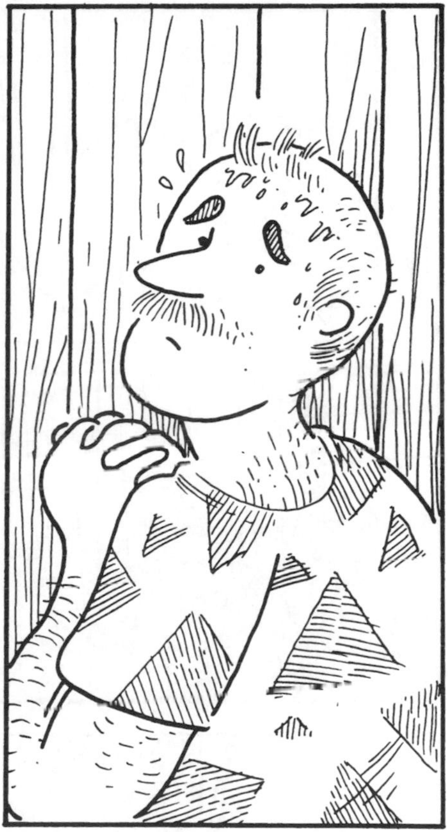

Then we saw it.

We saw them get exactly what they wanted.

At first, it was only Casey.

But then Lauren joined him.

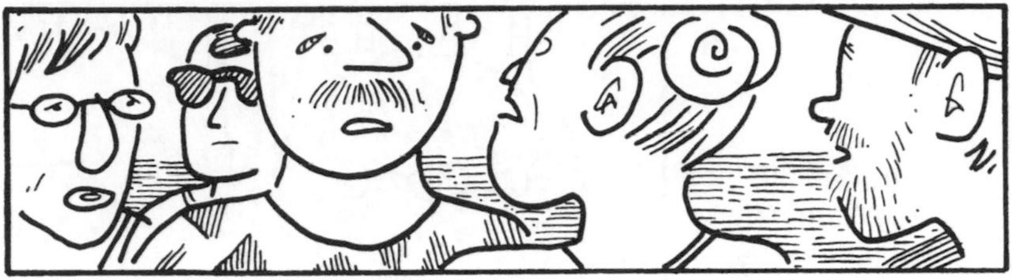

The two of them broke away from the group and whispered to those gawkers.

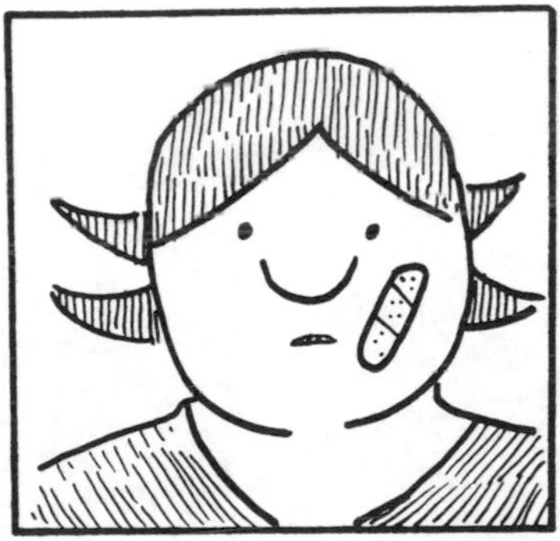

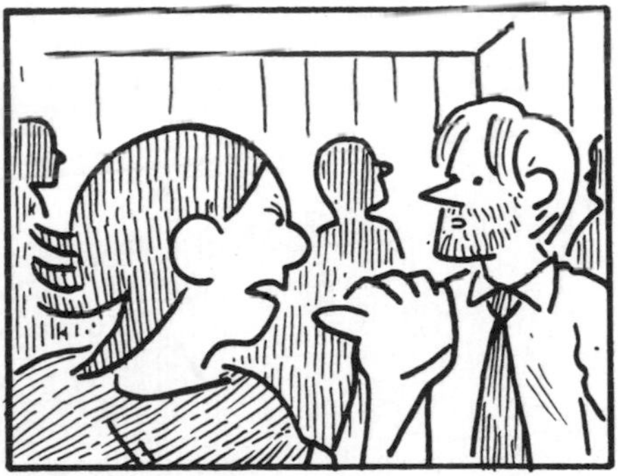

We saw Lauren mouth the words, "BACK WITH YOU."

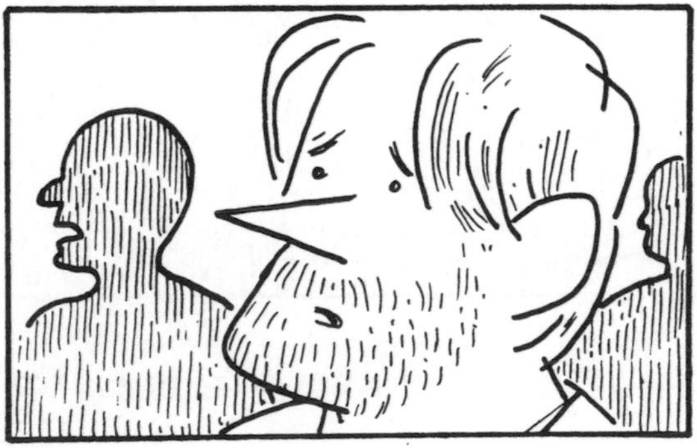

We thought she had recovered from her homesickness.

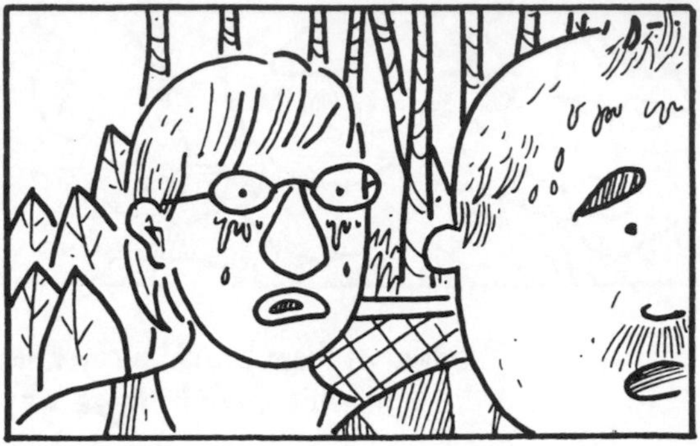

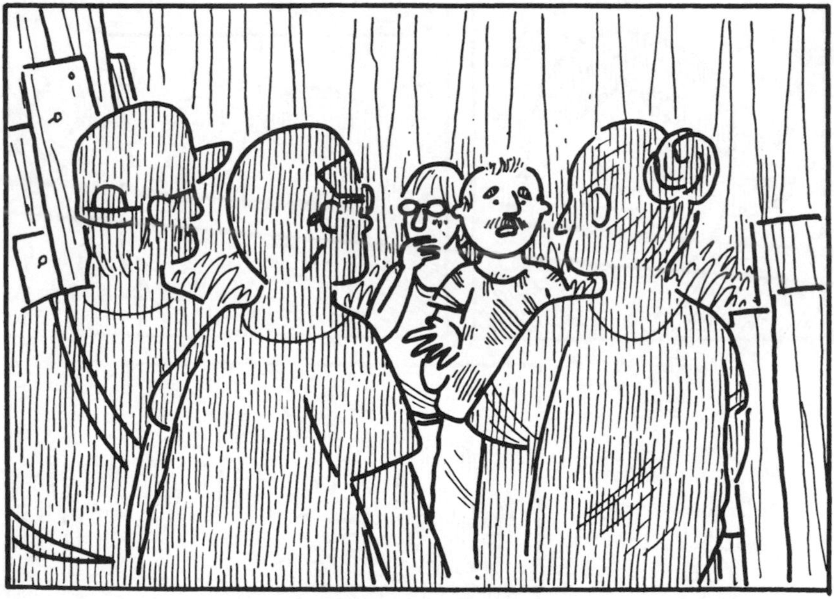

And now we're here, at the end.

We don't want to believe how far we've come,
just to see it all fall apart.

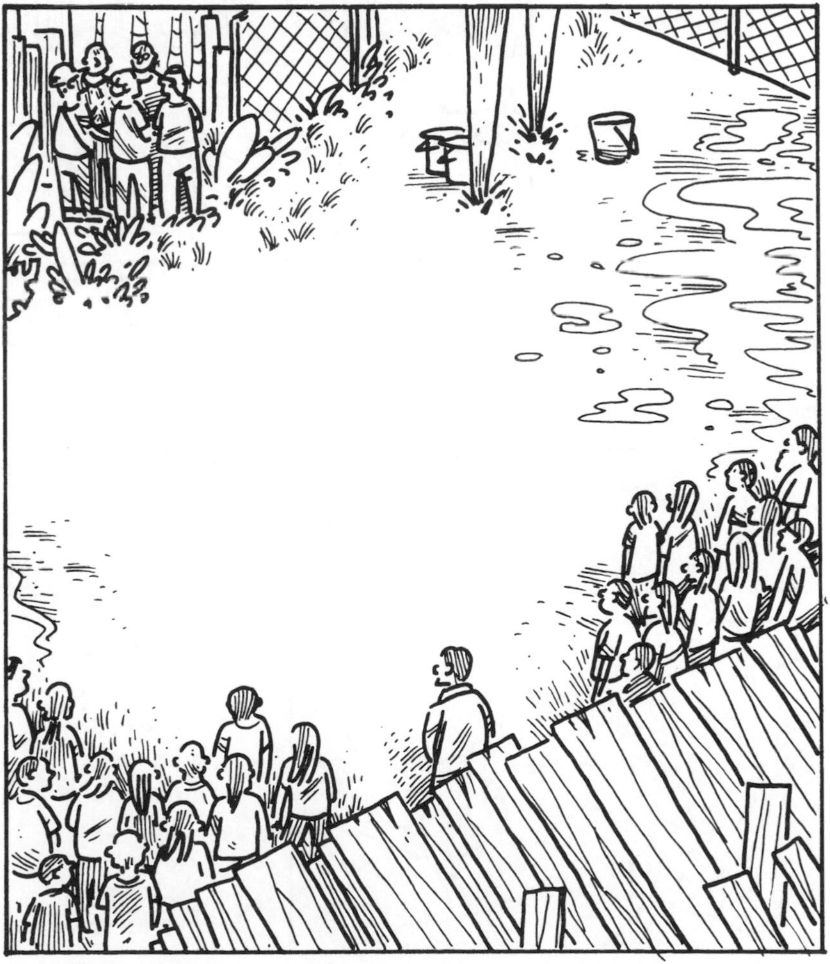

We were building something that was meant to last forever.

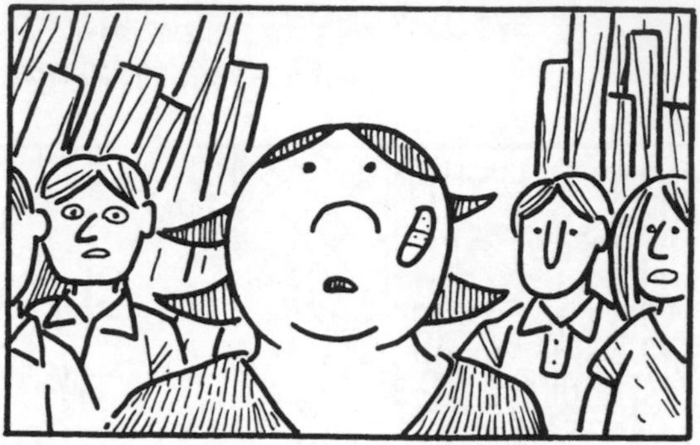

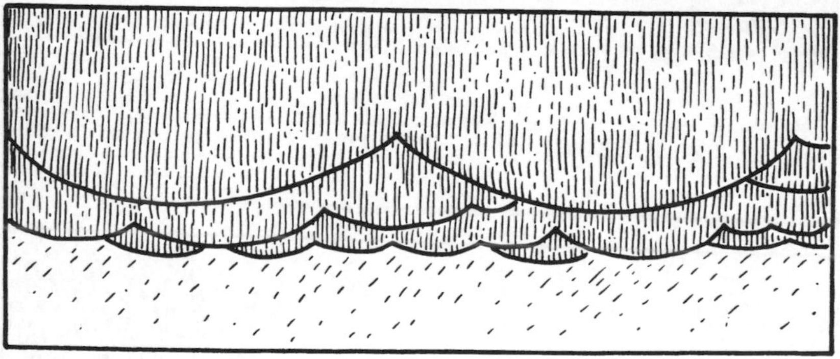

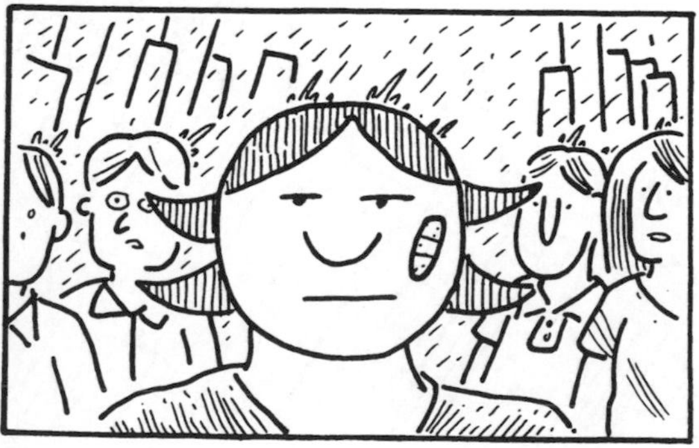

What good is a family if you can just walk away. We've walked away from too much to give up now.

James, Aaron and Toni join Lauren and Casey.

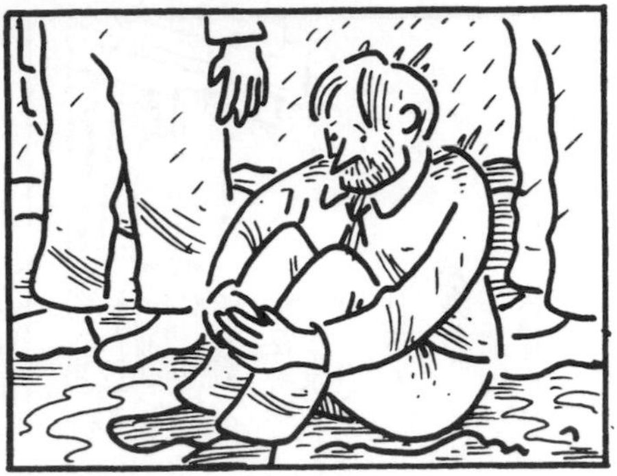

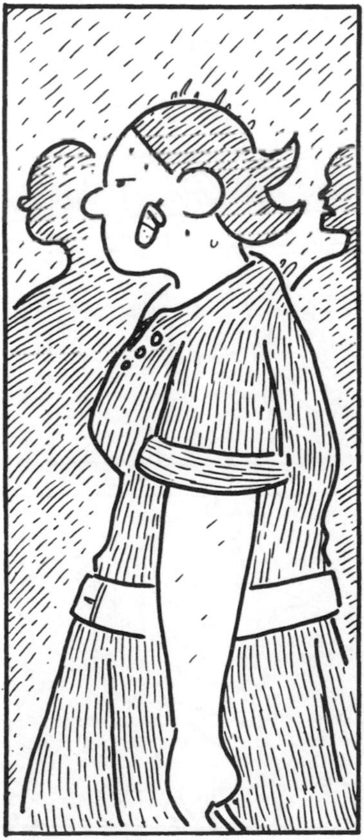

They all convince the reporters to leave with them.

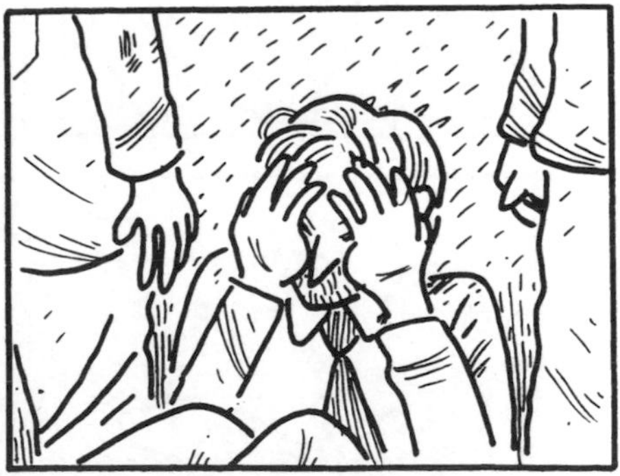

How can our own kind be so blind?

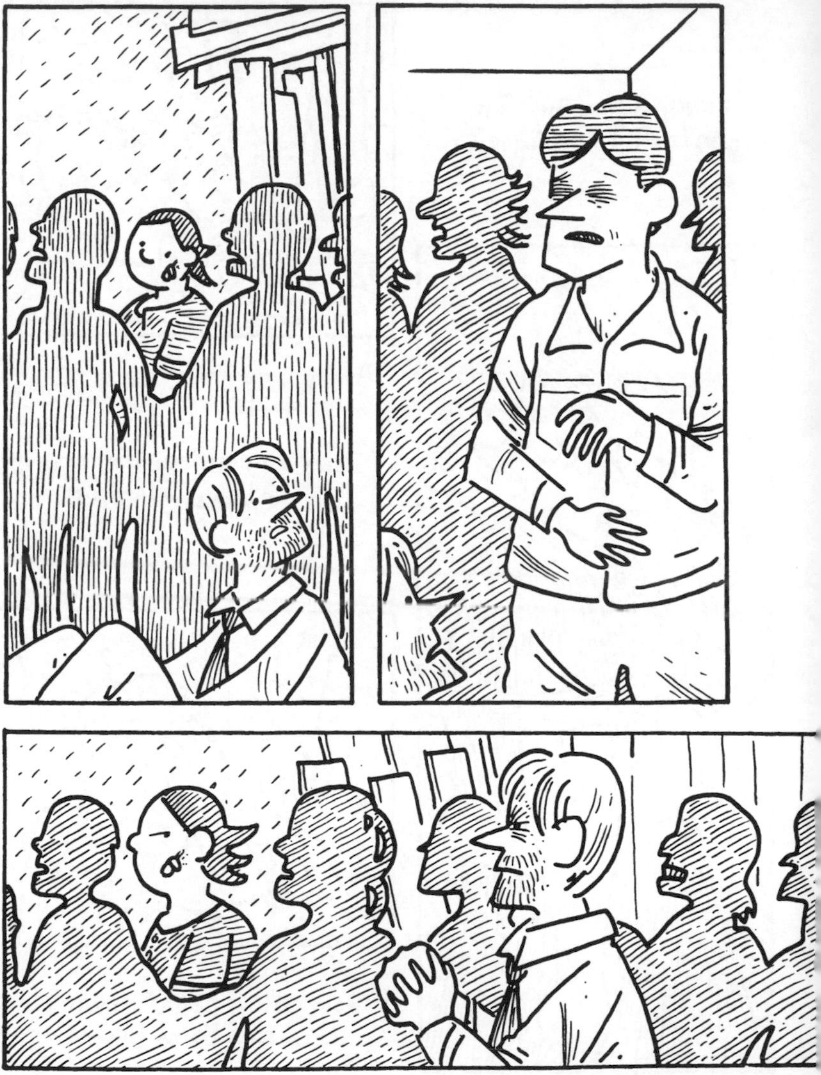

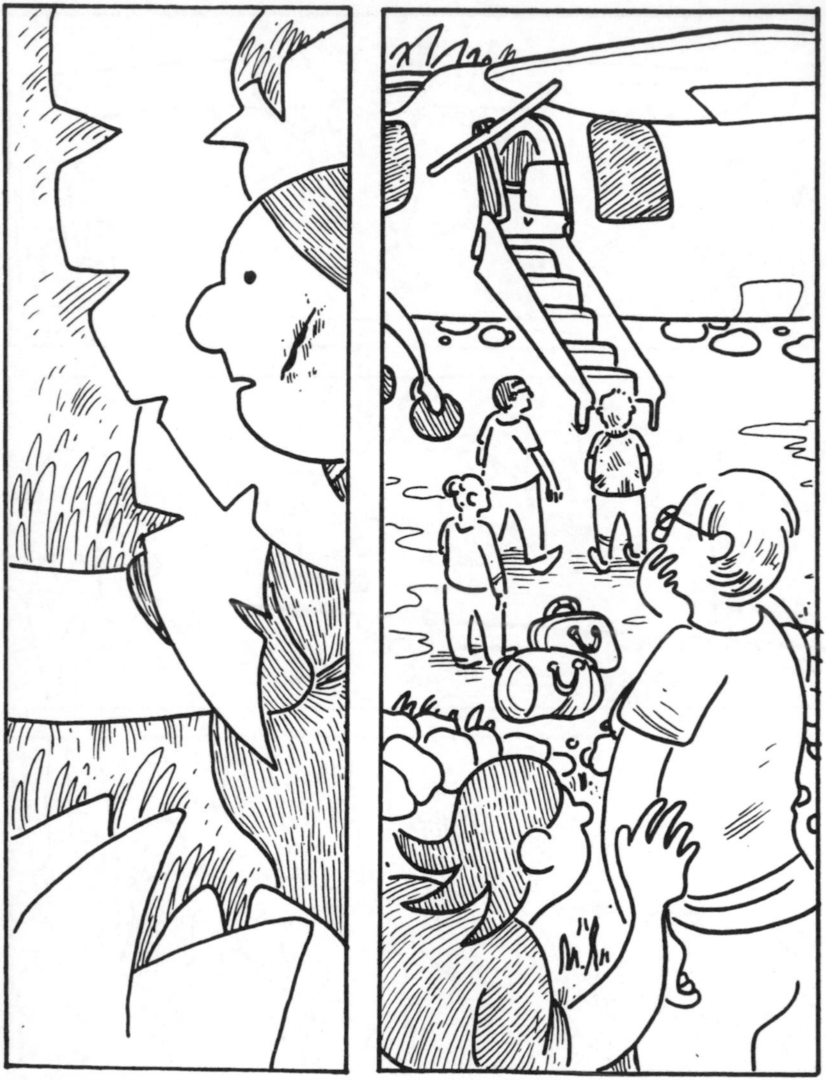

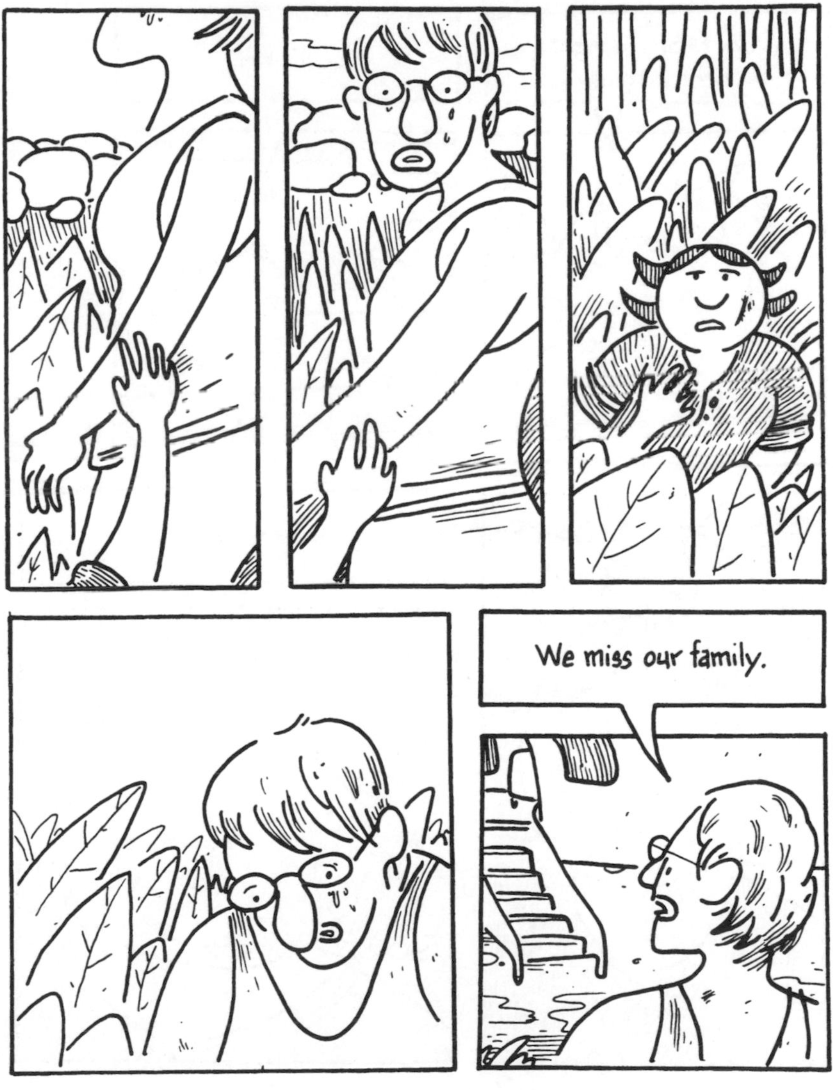
We miss our family.

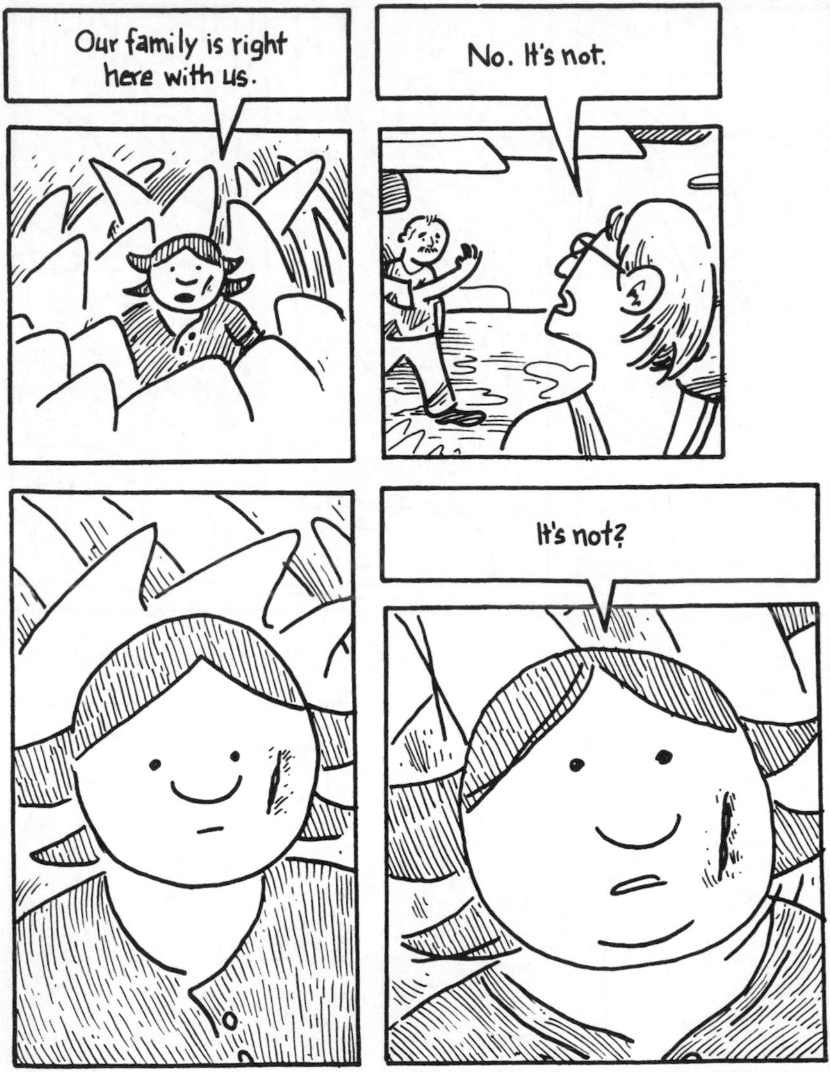
Our family is right here with us.
No. It's not.
It's not?

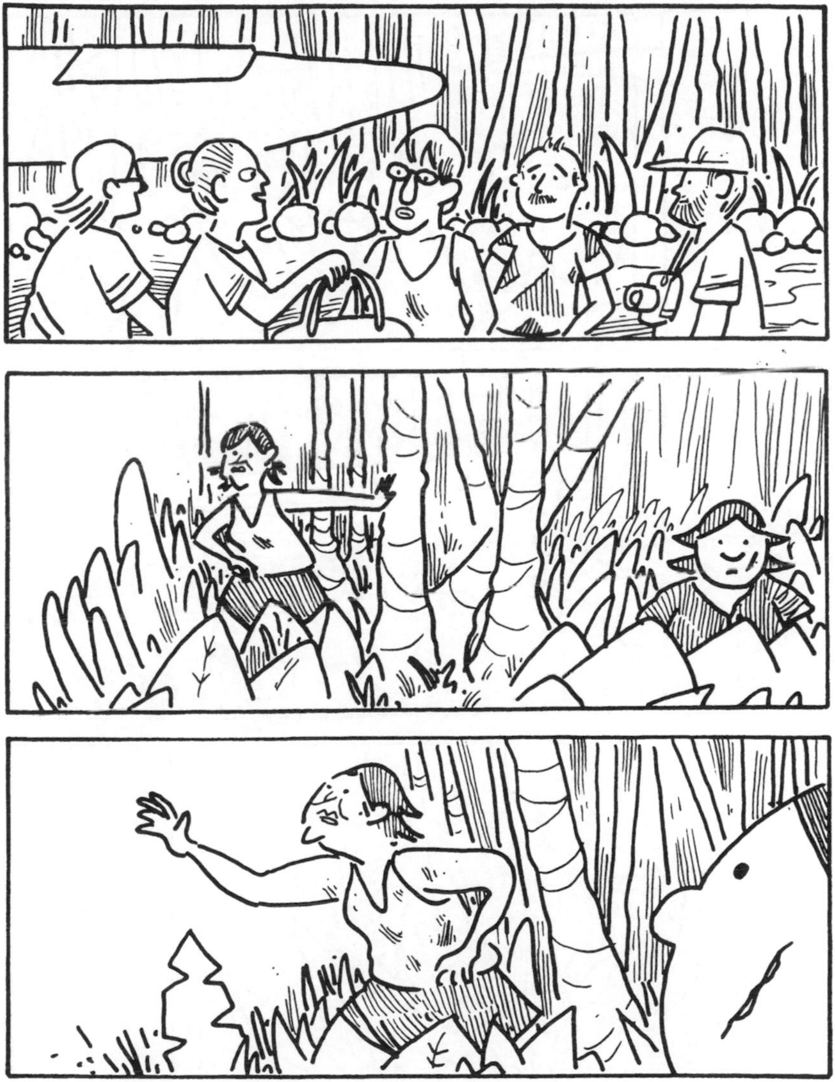

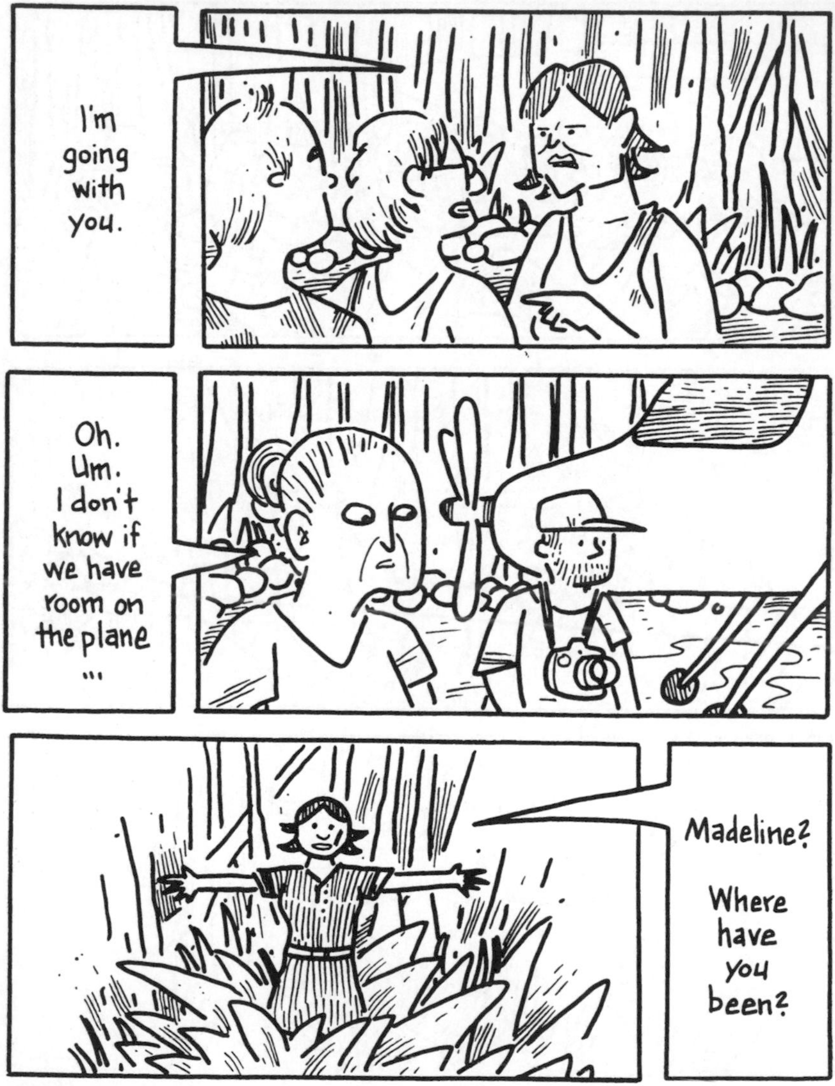
I'm going with you.
Oh. Um. I don't know if we have room on the plane ...
Madeline?
Where have you been?

Stay away from me, Hannah.
Please. Please. I can't stay here.
I'm sorry but we can't take anyone else. Too much weight.

Take our spots.

We already have more people than the plane can take.

Hannah, is your name?

Can you drive us to town?

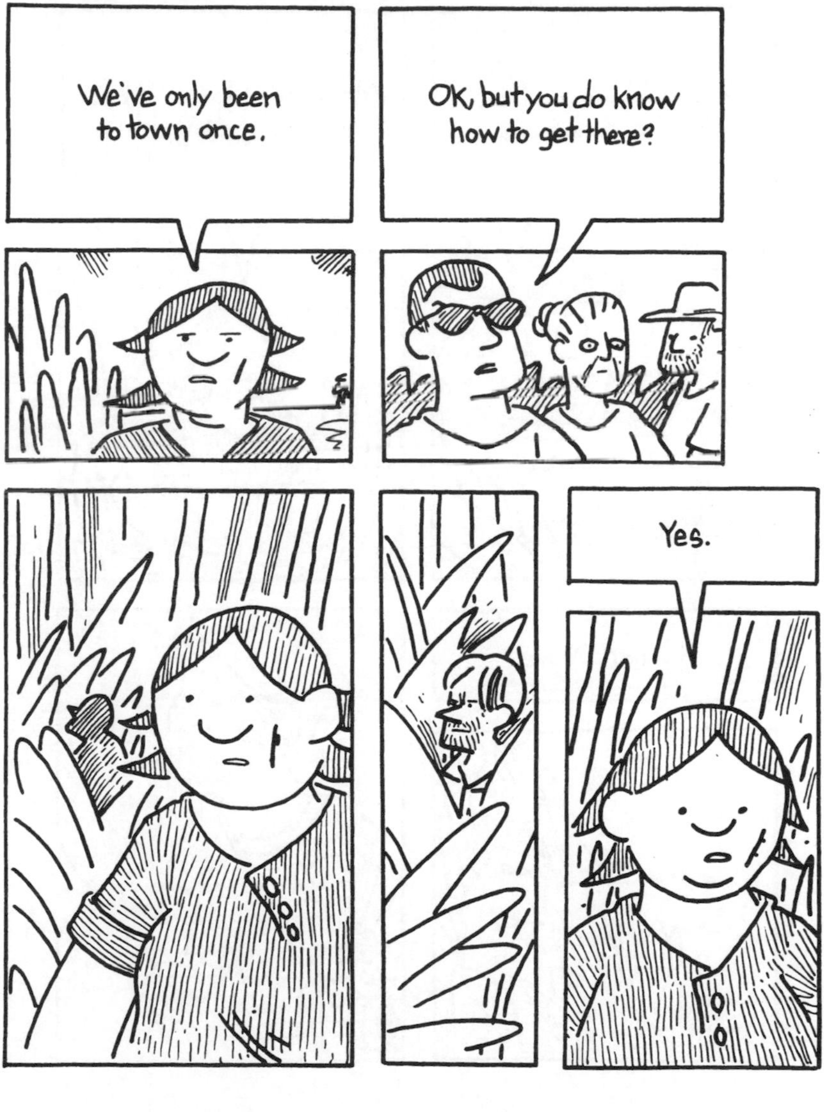
We've only been to town once.
OK, but you do know how to get there?
Yes.

Be careful around them. They're dangerous.

Madeline, please. We're not who is dangerous.

Hannah. Move.

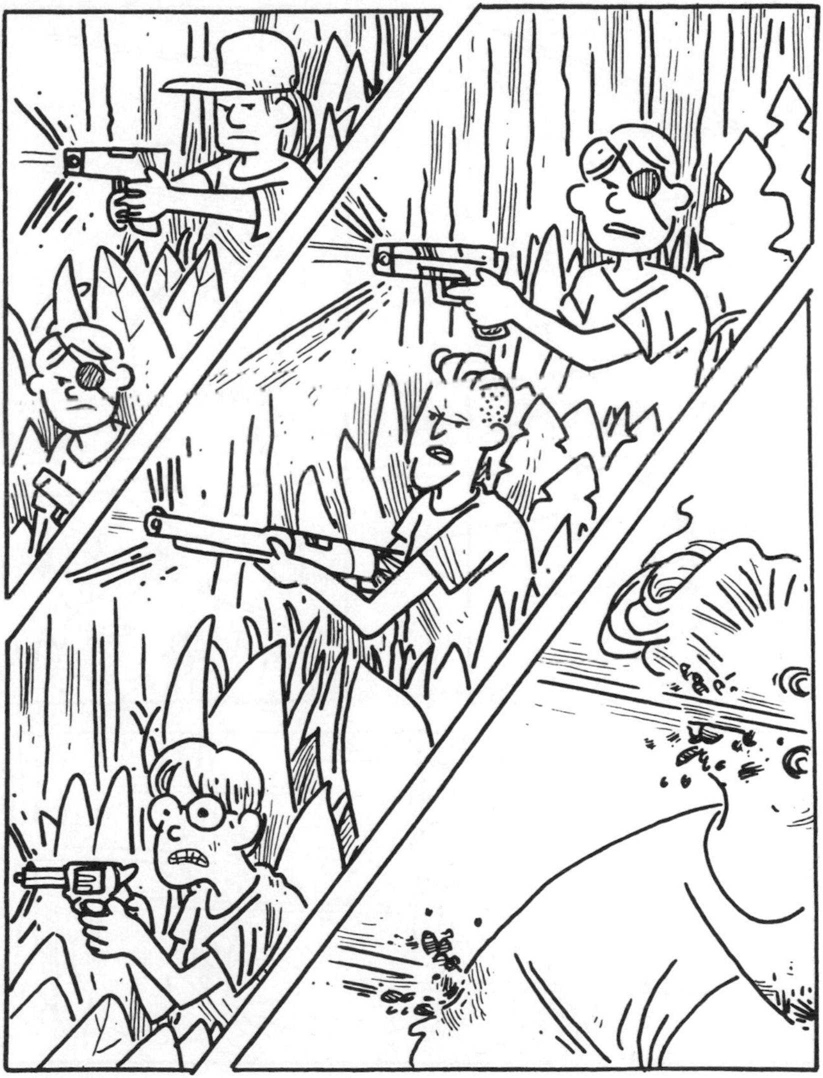

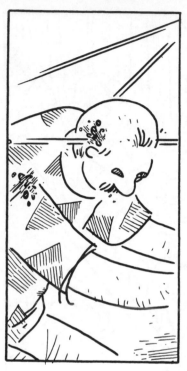

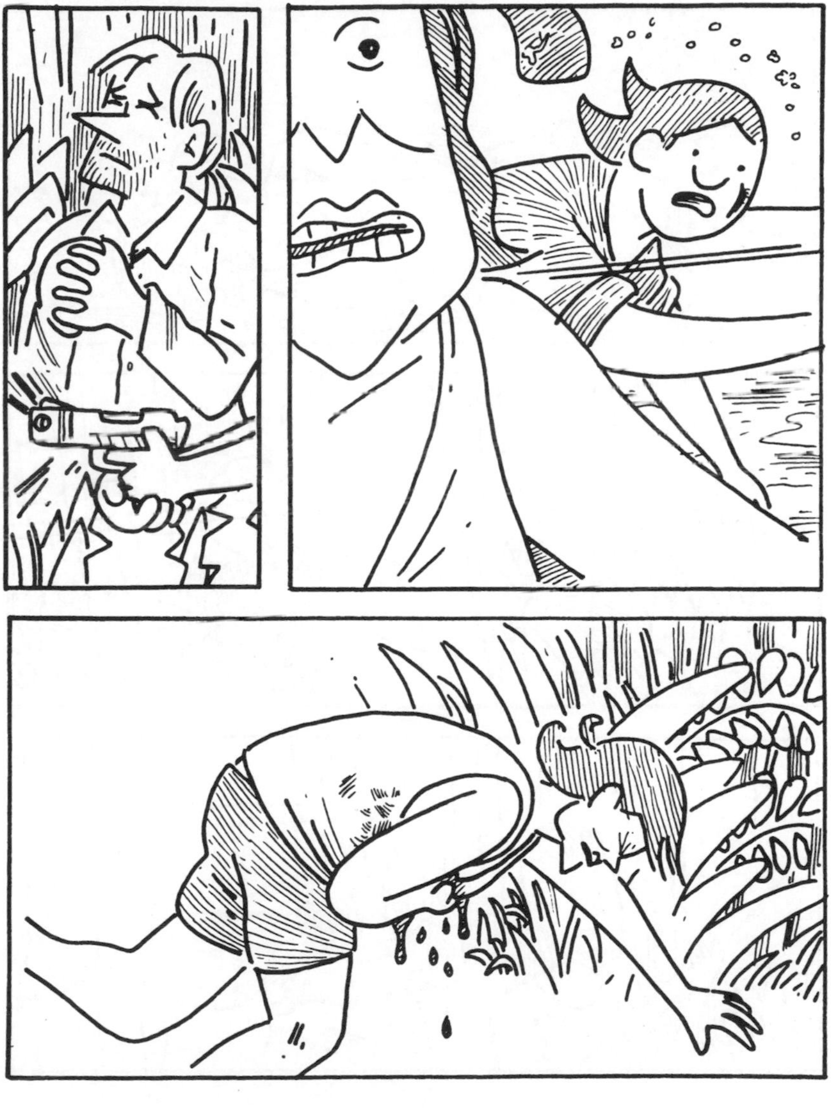

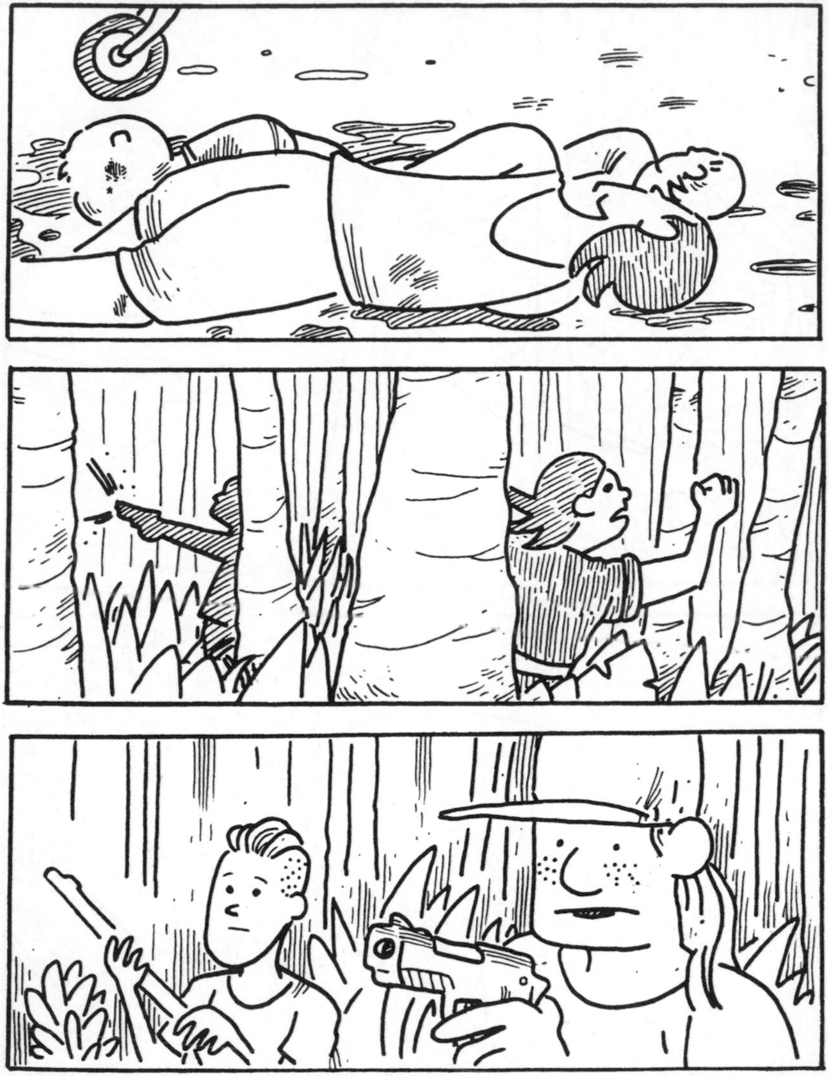

These people are crazy! What am I doing here?

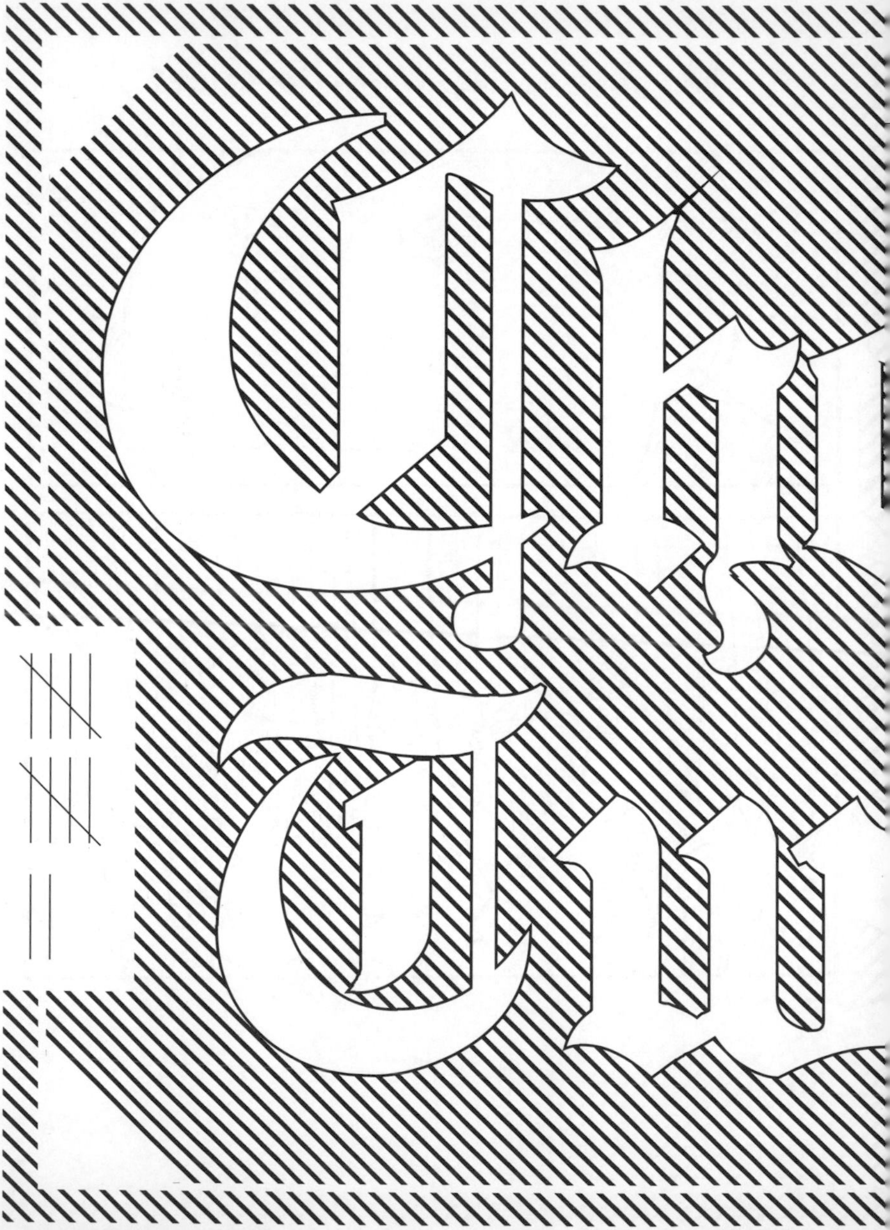

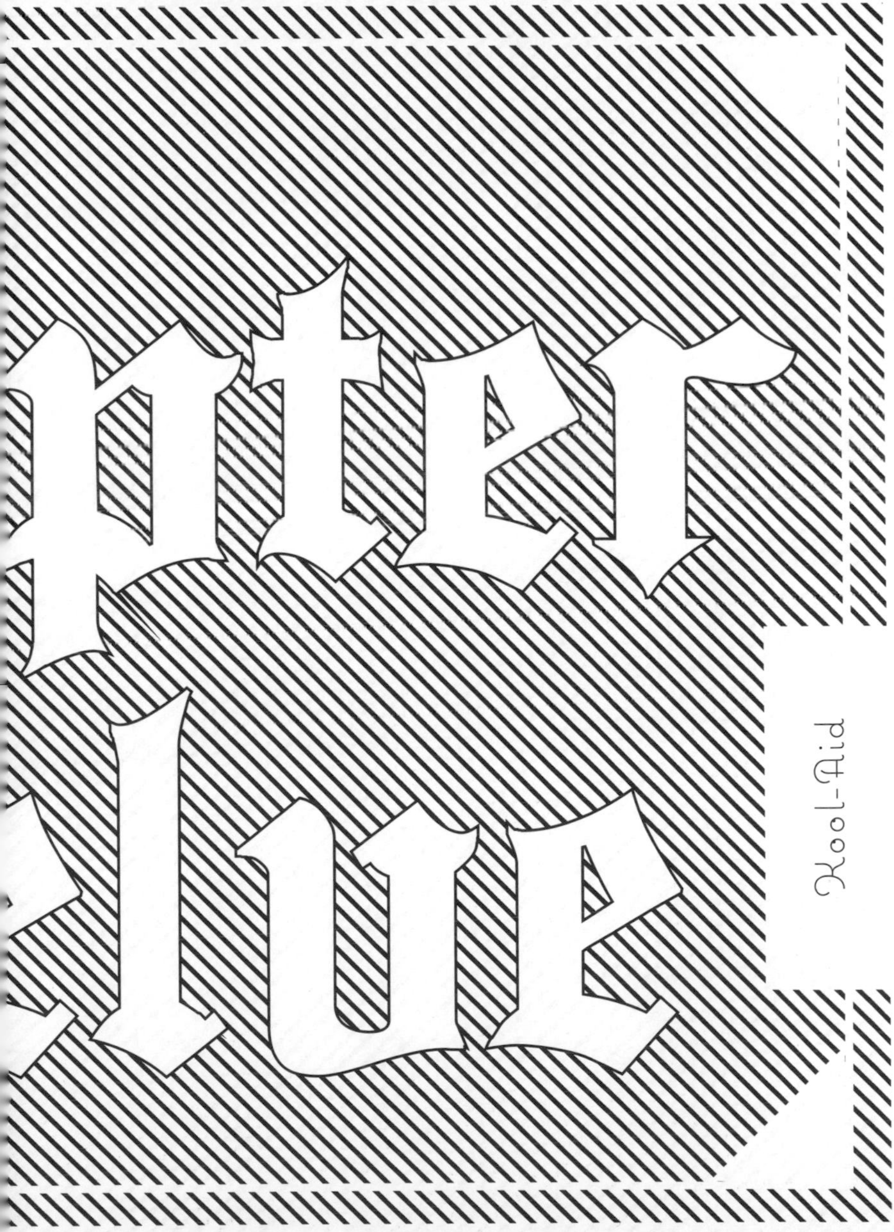
pter
lue
Kool-Aid

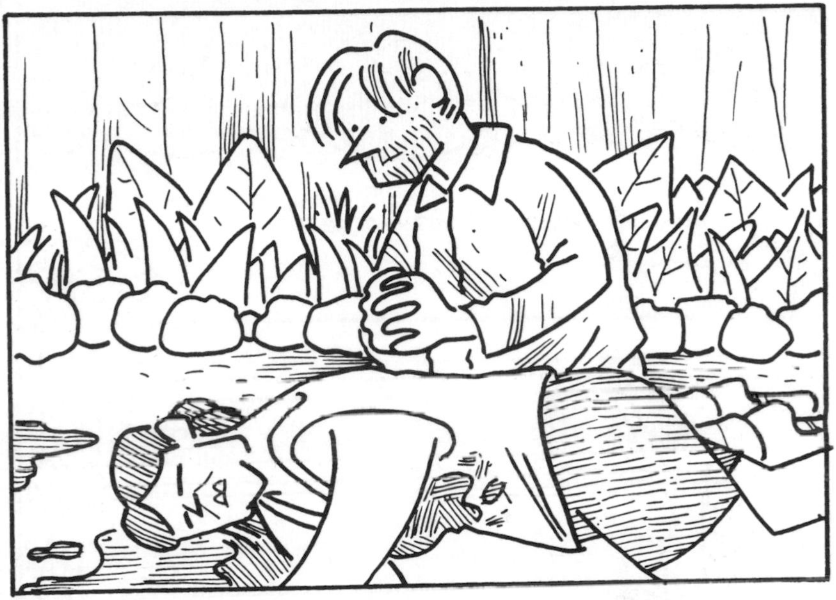
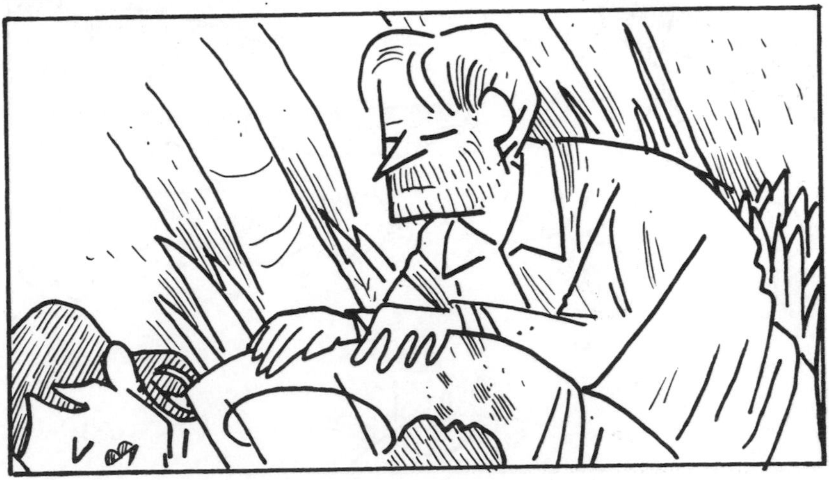

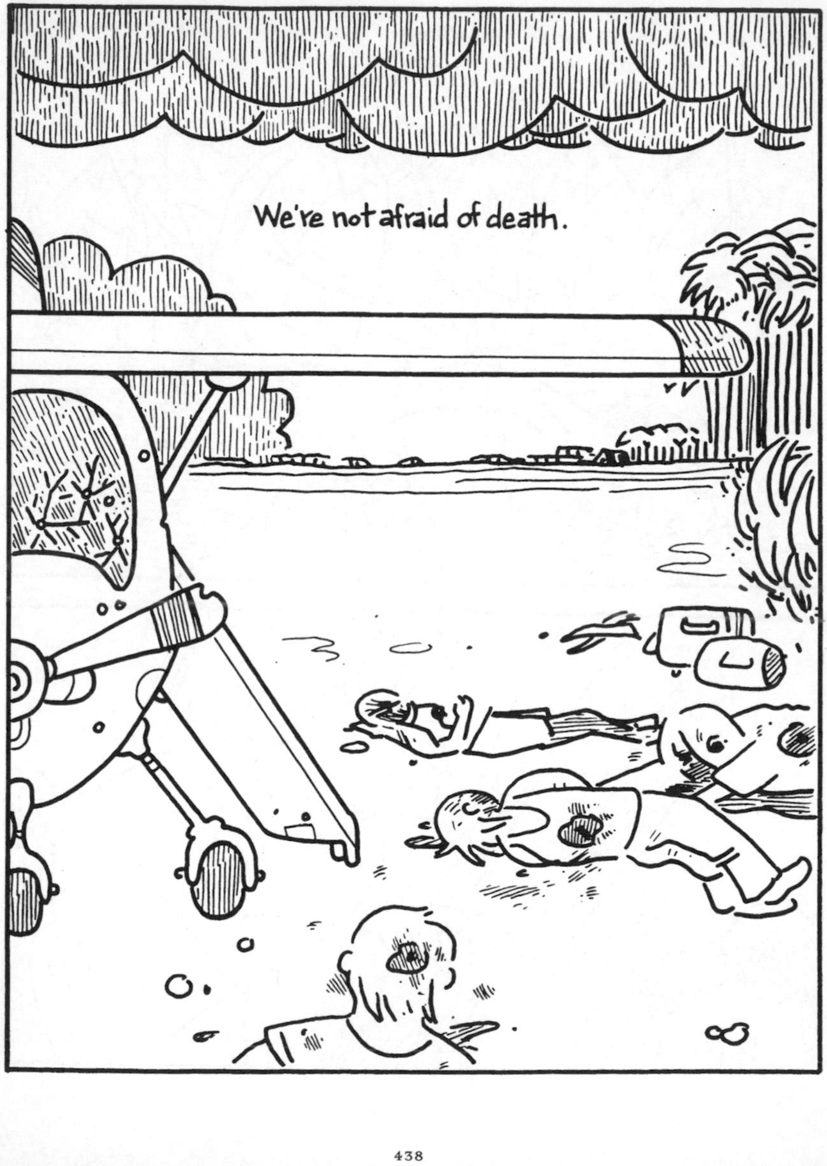
We're not afraid of death.

We can see
the event for
what it is.

A step.
A door.

A
pathway
to the dawn
of a new
journey.

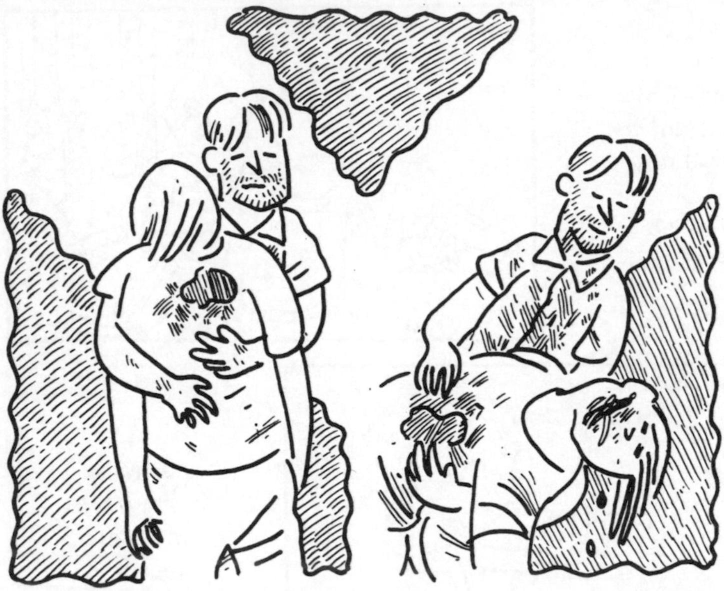

We gave them the gift of beginning their journey today.
They are so fortunate.

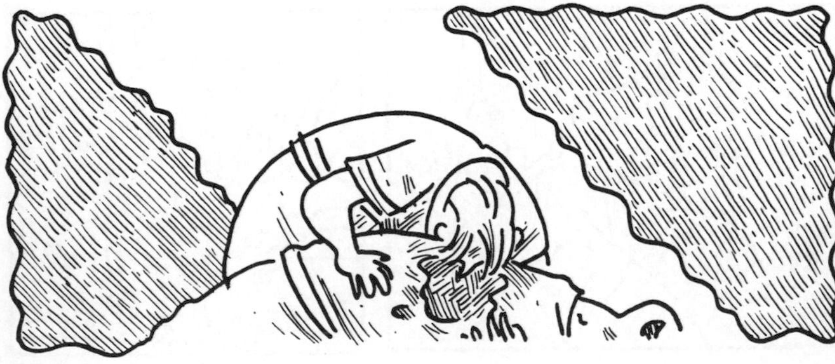

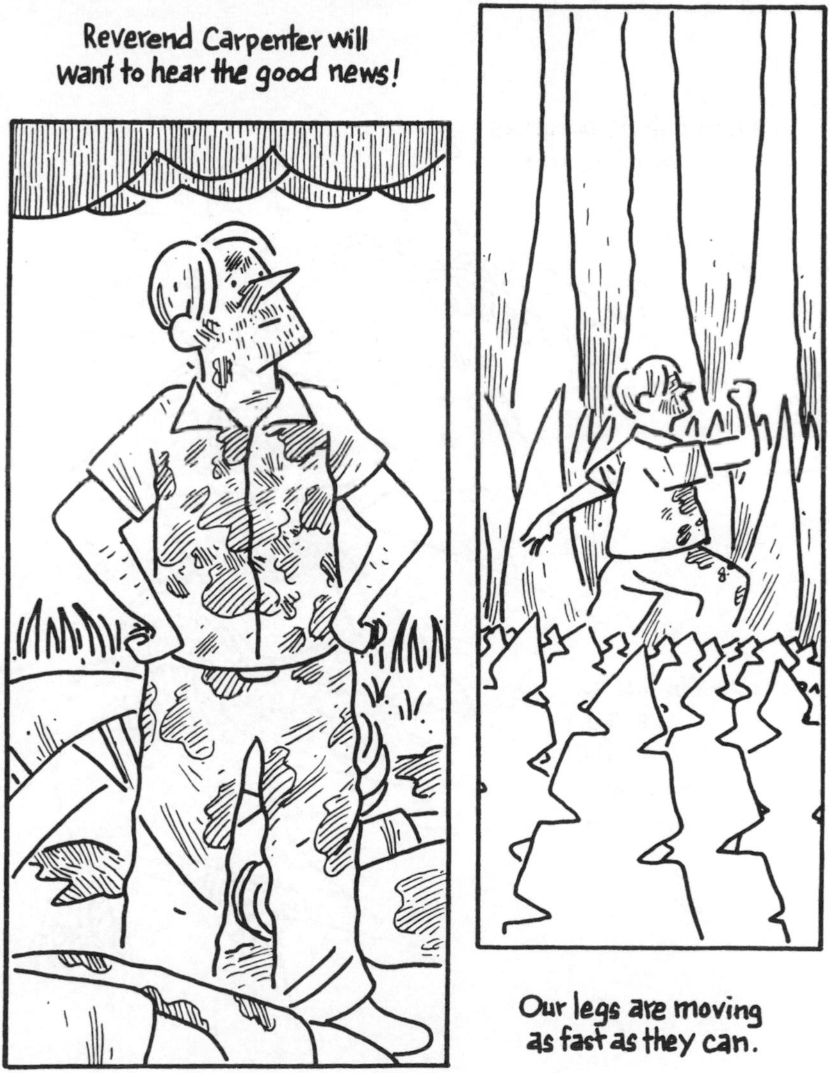
Reverend Carpenter will want to hear the good news!
Our legs are moving as fast as they can.

From outside ourselves
we watch us run.

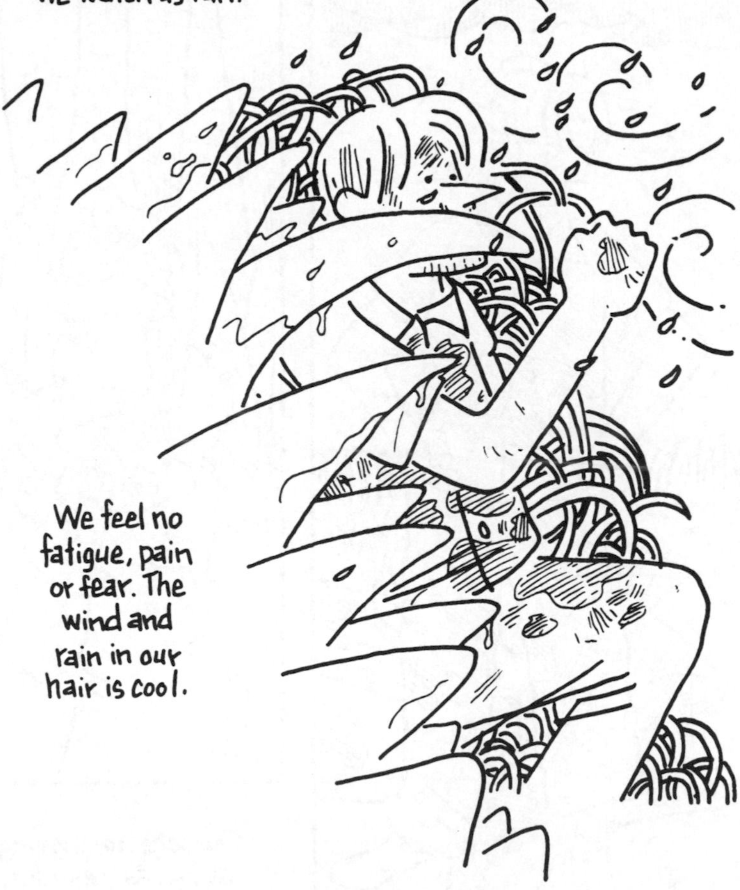

We feel no
fatigue, pain
or fear. The
wind and
rain in our
hair is cool.

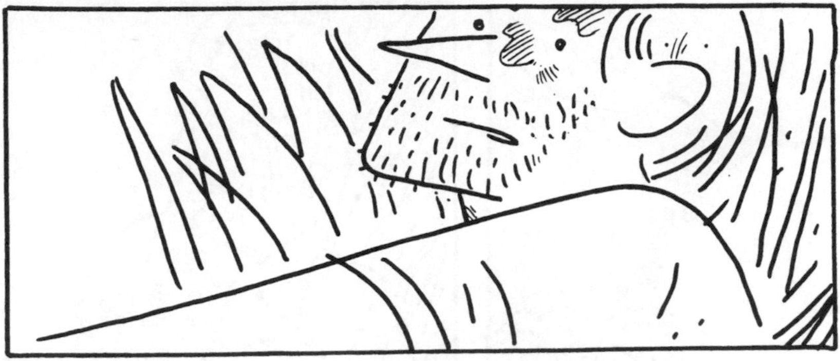

Someone
is talking
nearby but
we cannot
see who.

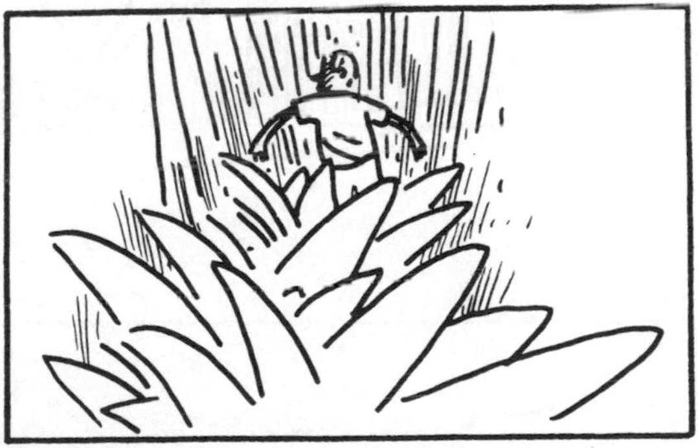

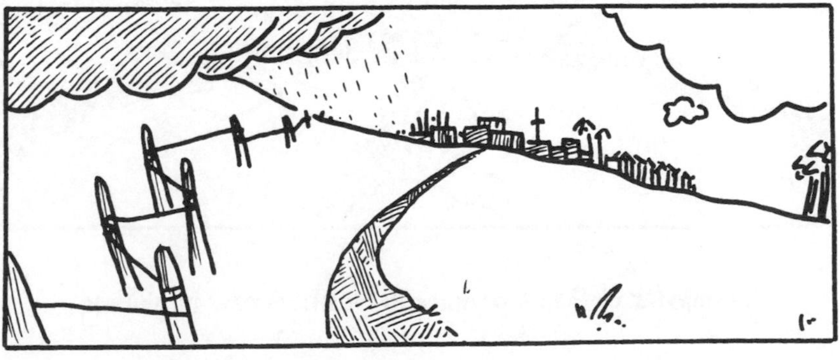

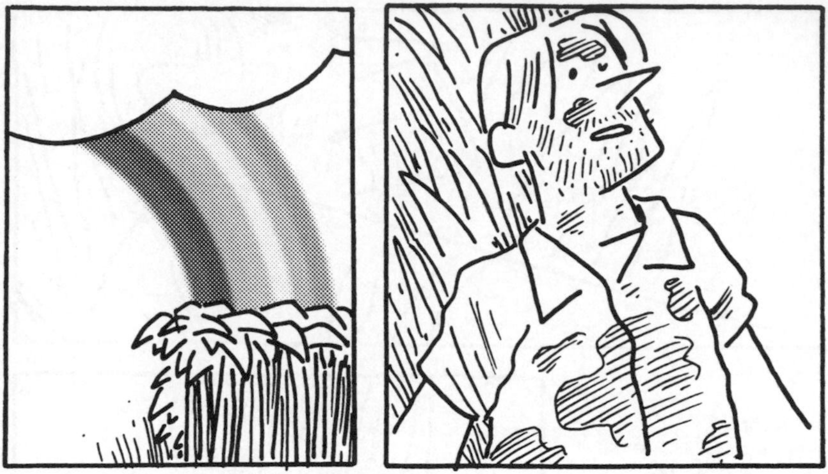

Majestic. Holy.

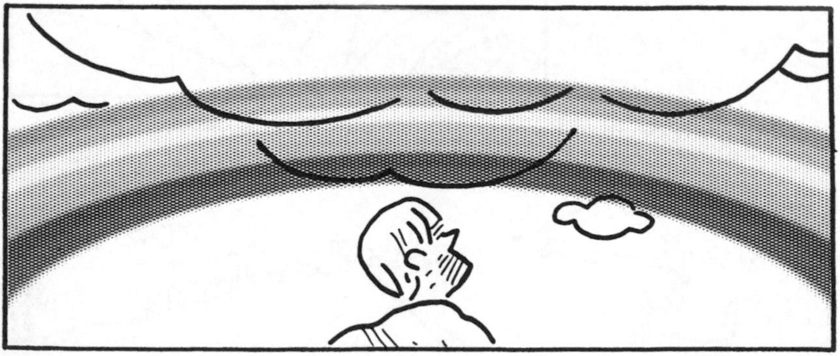

A reminder of God's promise to Noah: A new beginning.

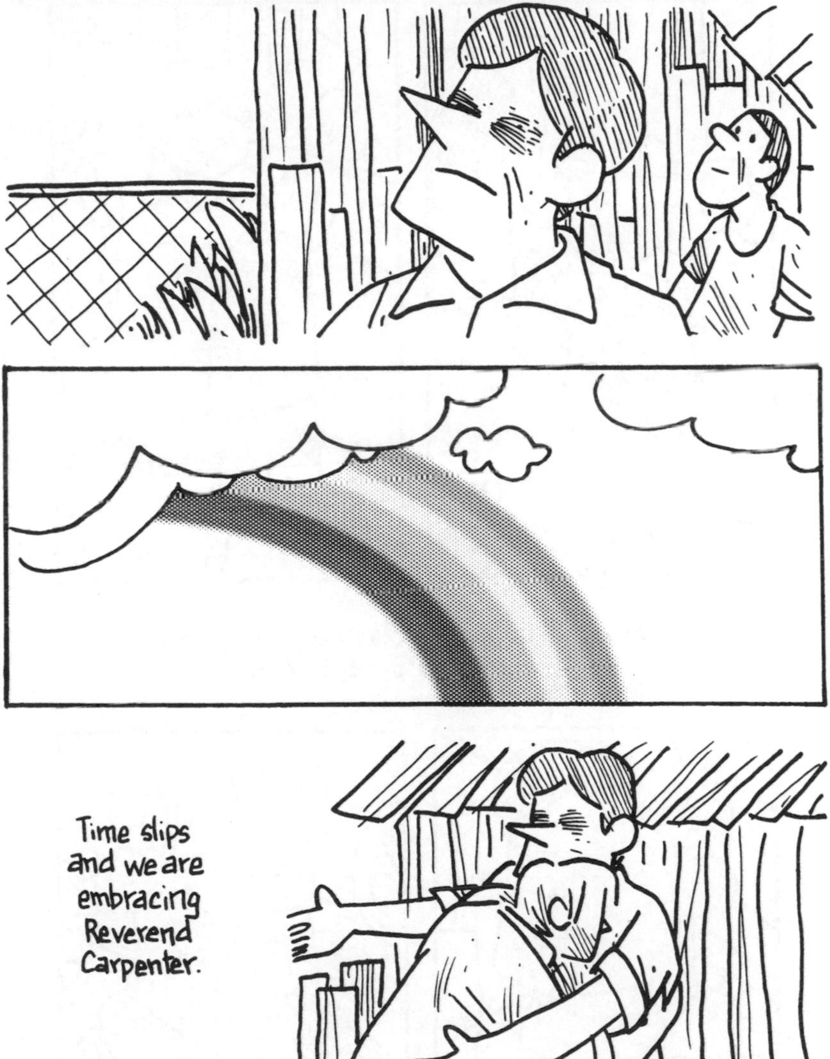
Time slips and we are embracing Reverend Carpenter.

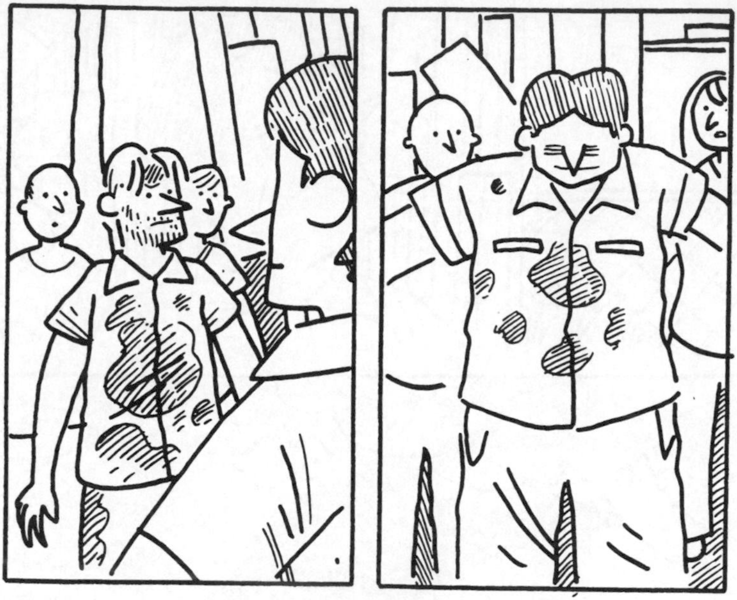

Words fail us, but the blood on our clothes tell him what he needs to know.

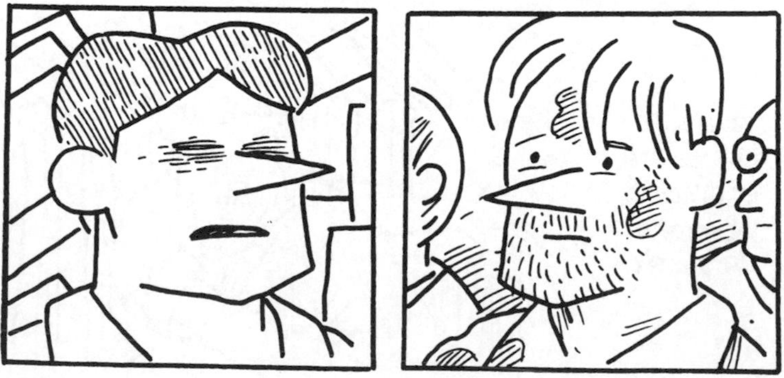

Blood speaks in a universal language,
and we hear the message we've been preparing for.

Like Jesus, Carpenter is surrounded by his most faithful for the final communion.

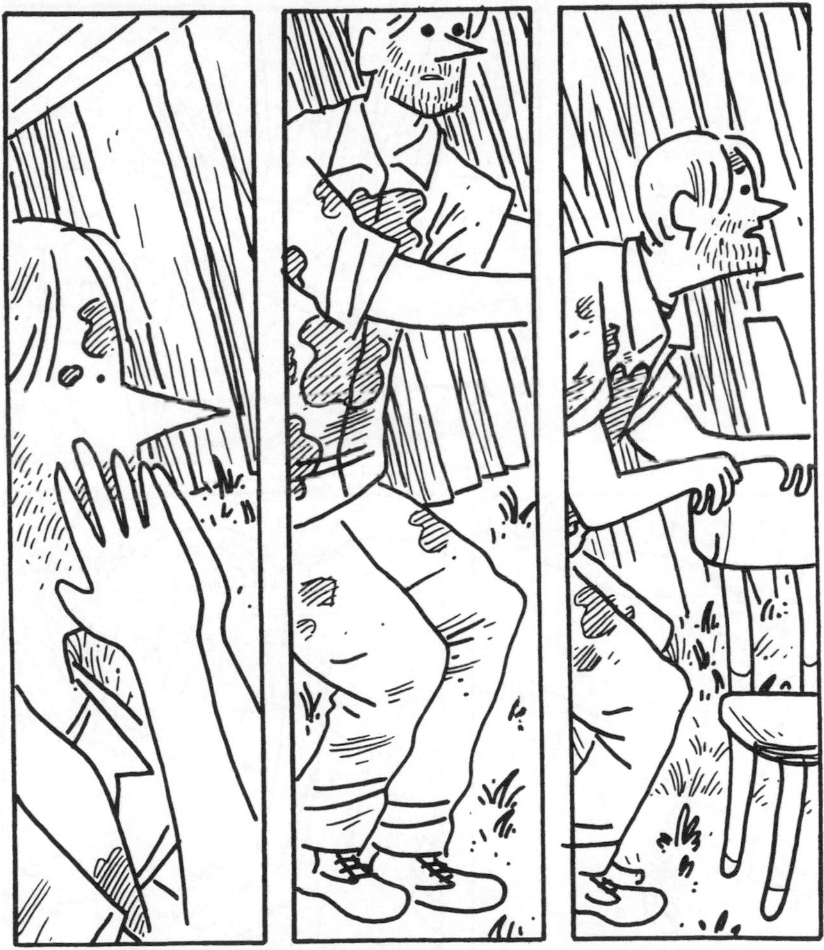

We're frozen as we watch the drink being prepared.

Our heart
is filled
with love,
but our
stomach
wants to
wretch.

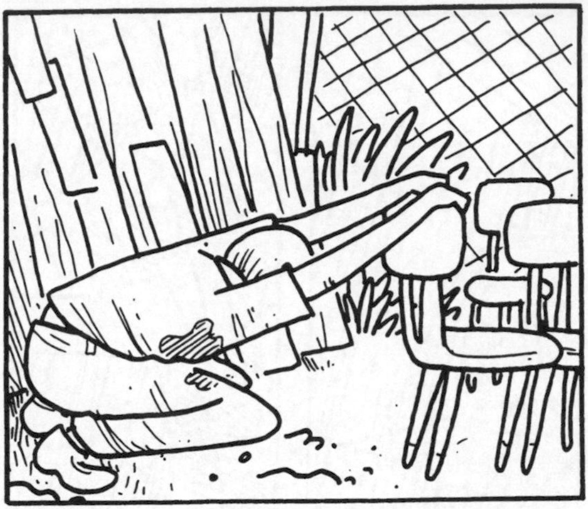

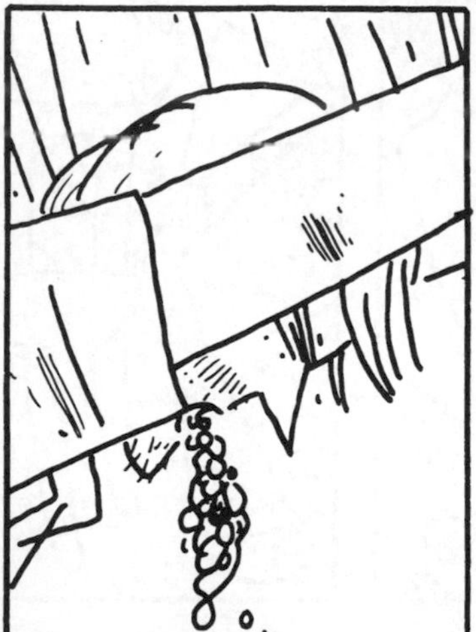

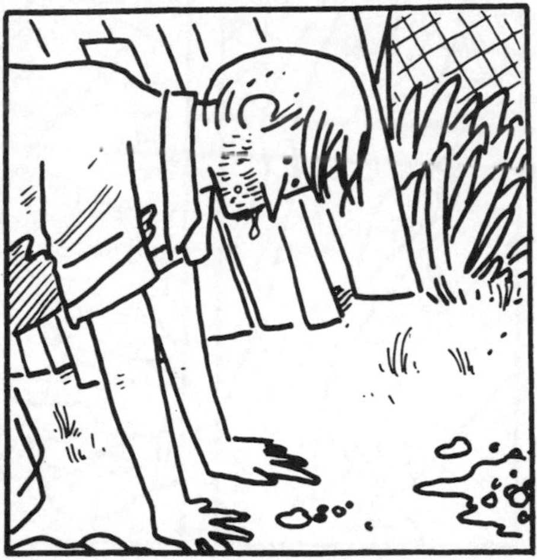

Seconds pass and we cannot see.

We cannot remember if we threw-up or not.

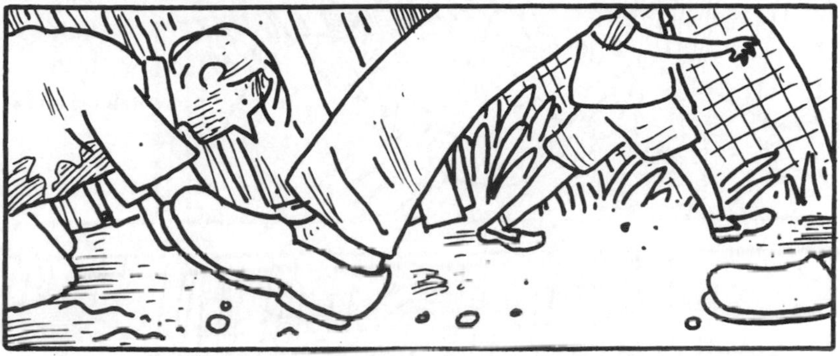

Our animal body is at war with our soul.

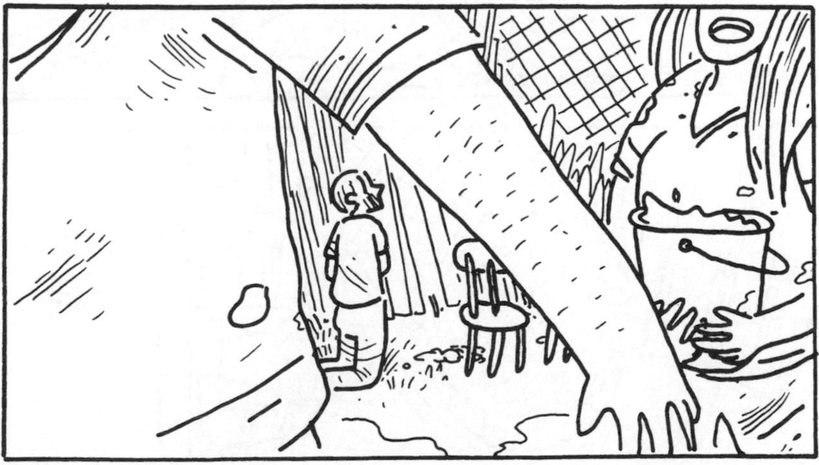

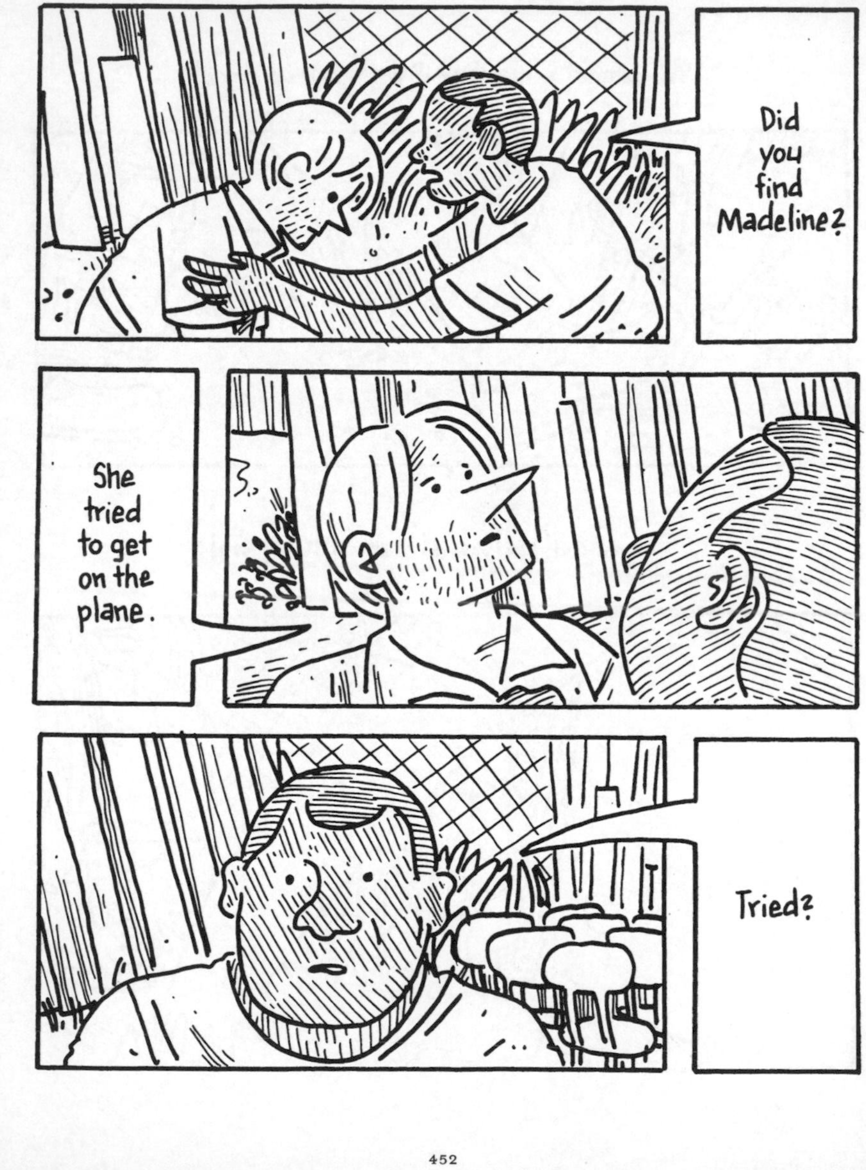
Did you find Madeline?
She tried to get on the plane.
Tried?

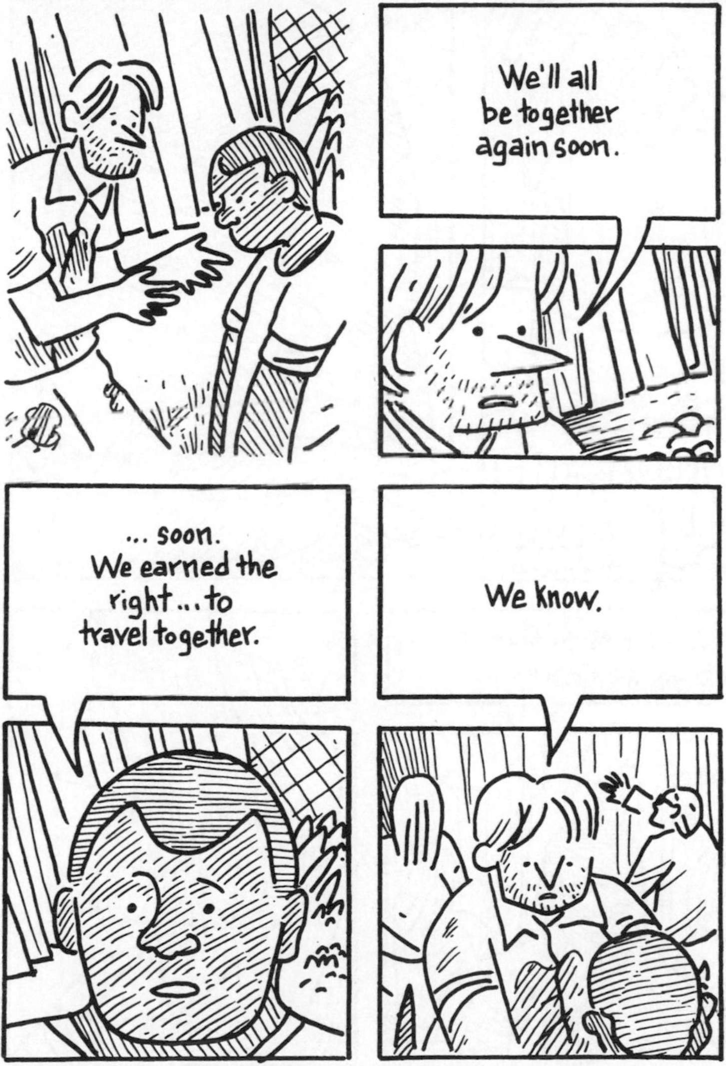
We'll all be together again soon.
... soon. We earned the right ... to travel together.
We know.

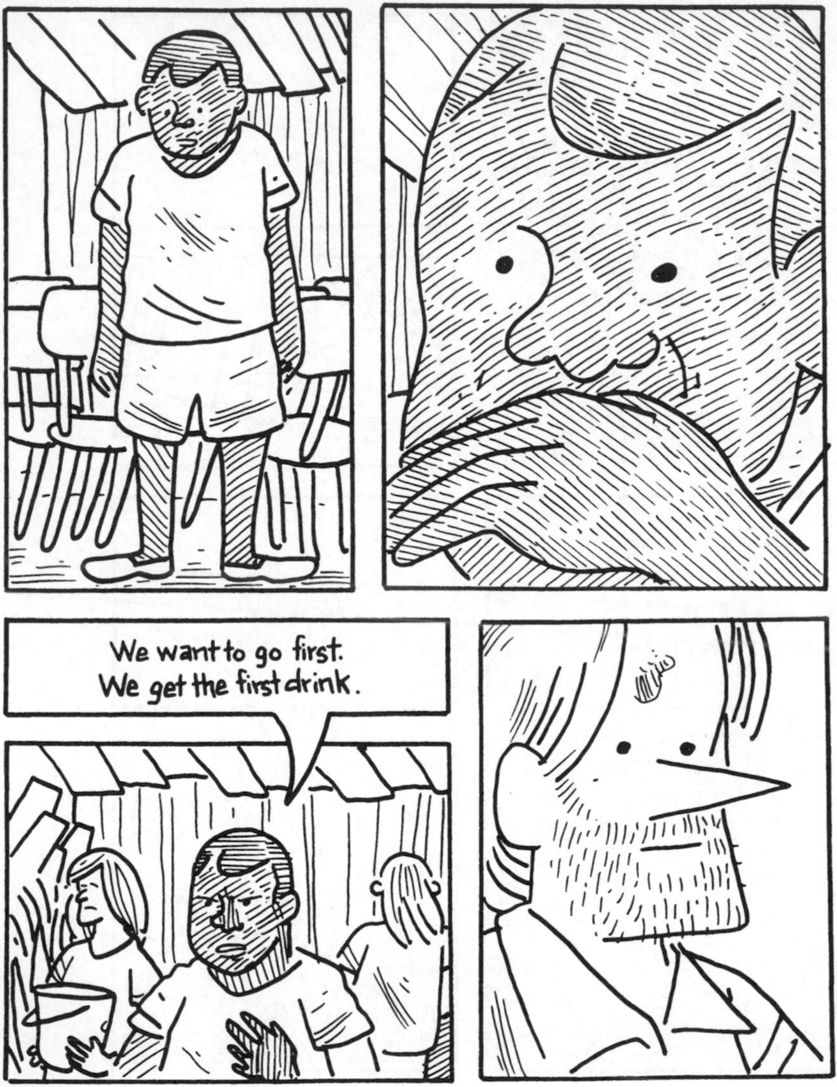
We want to go first.
We get the first drink.

We understand Robin's eagerness.
His urgency shines a light on our own desires.

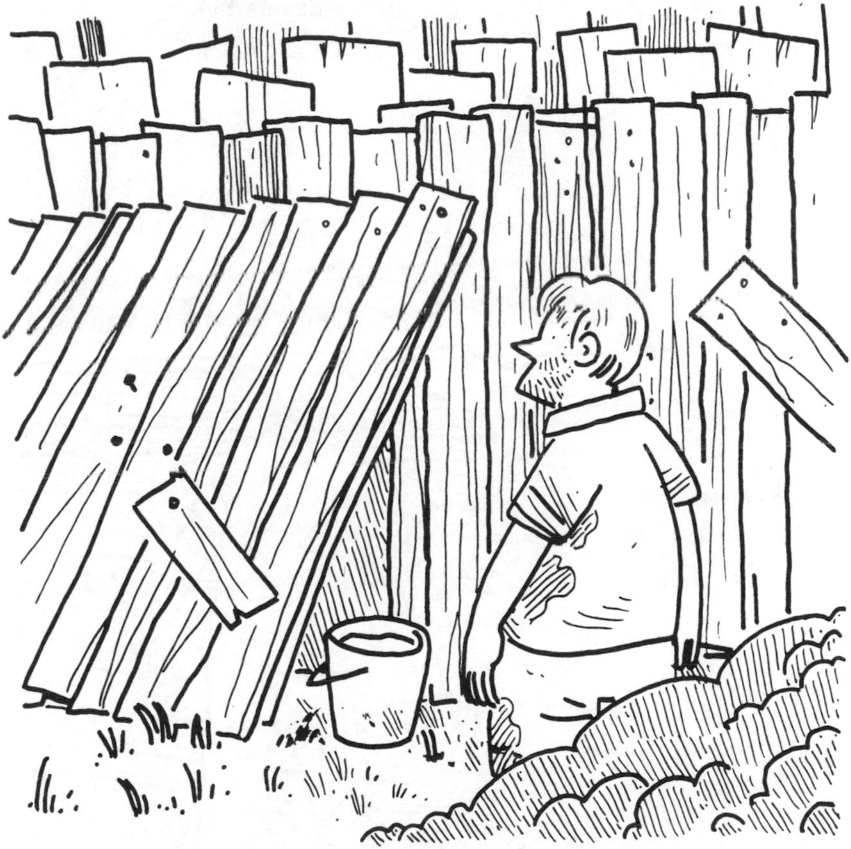

We need to drink before Reverend Carpenter.

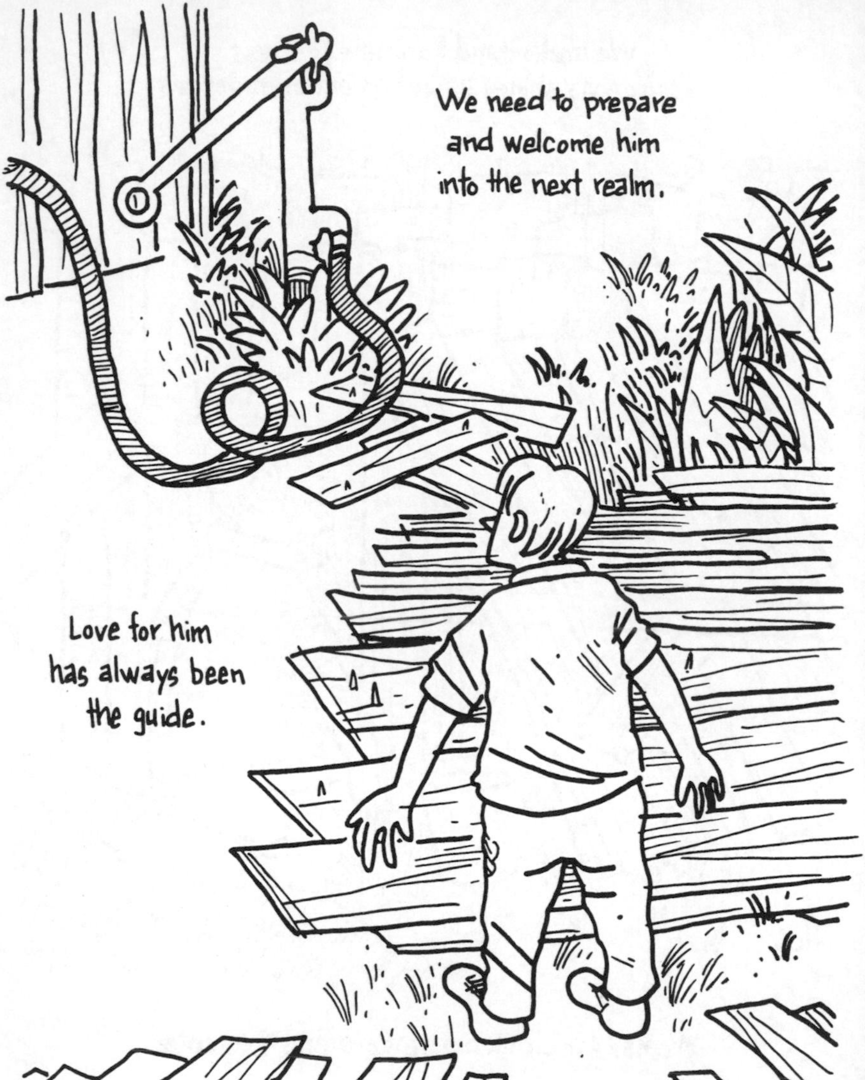
We need to prepare and welcome him into the next realm.
Love for him has always been the guide.

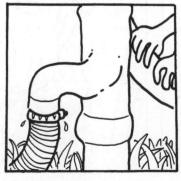

457

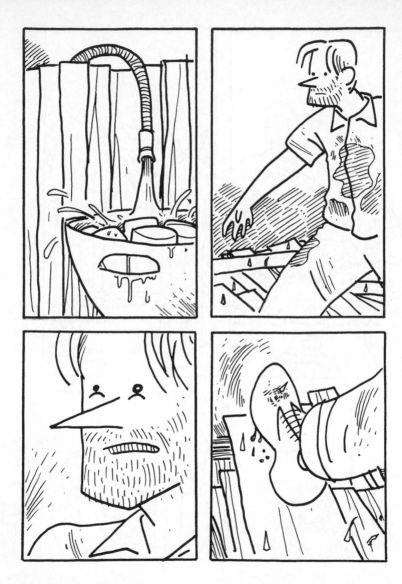

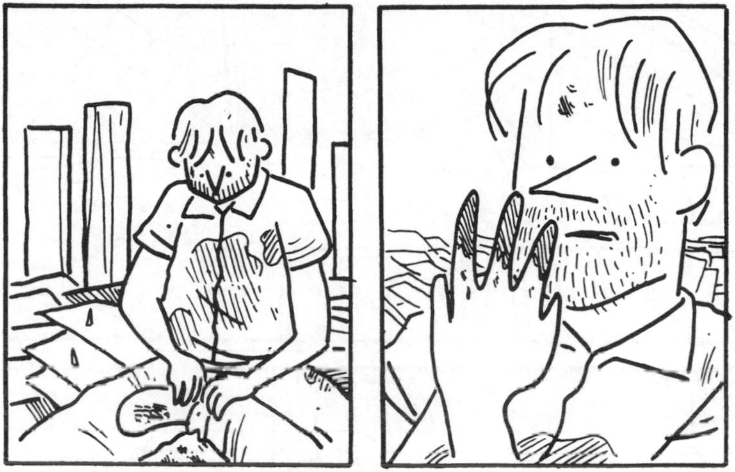

There are not enough clean cups, so we step back into the moment and wash with silent, solemn, religious perfection.

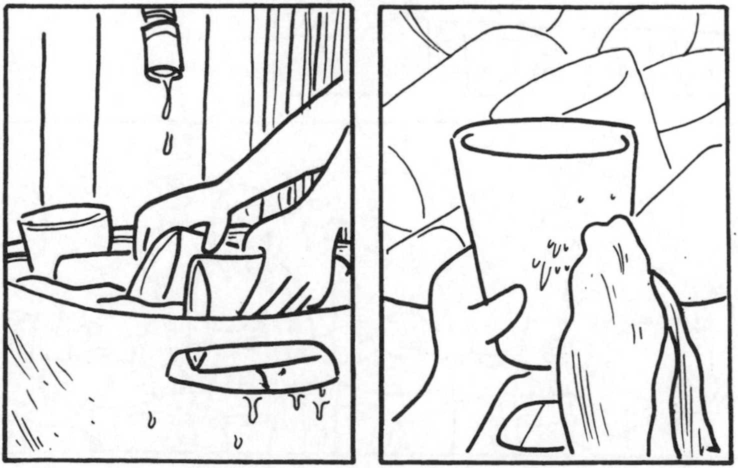

We bring the cups to our love and his warmth radiates through the rain.

He calmly shares a perfect blessing.

As promised, the first cup is gifted to Robin.

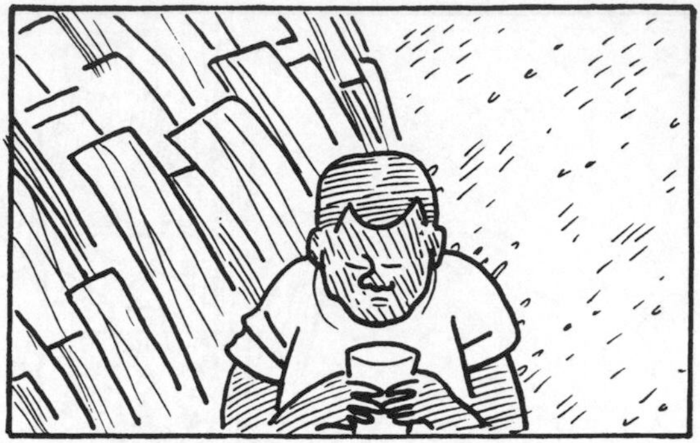

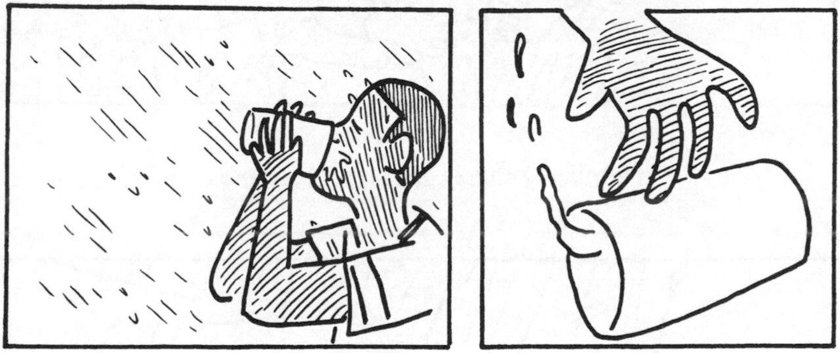

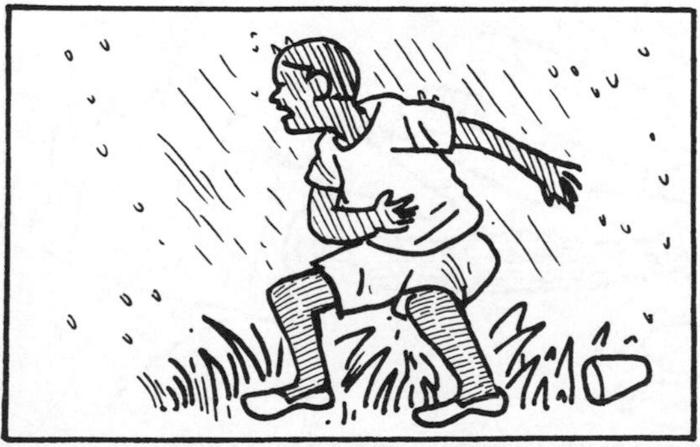

He moves beyond us violently!

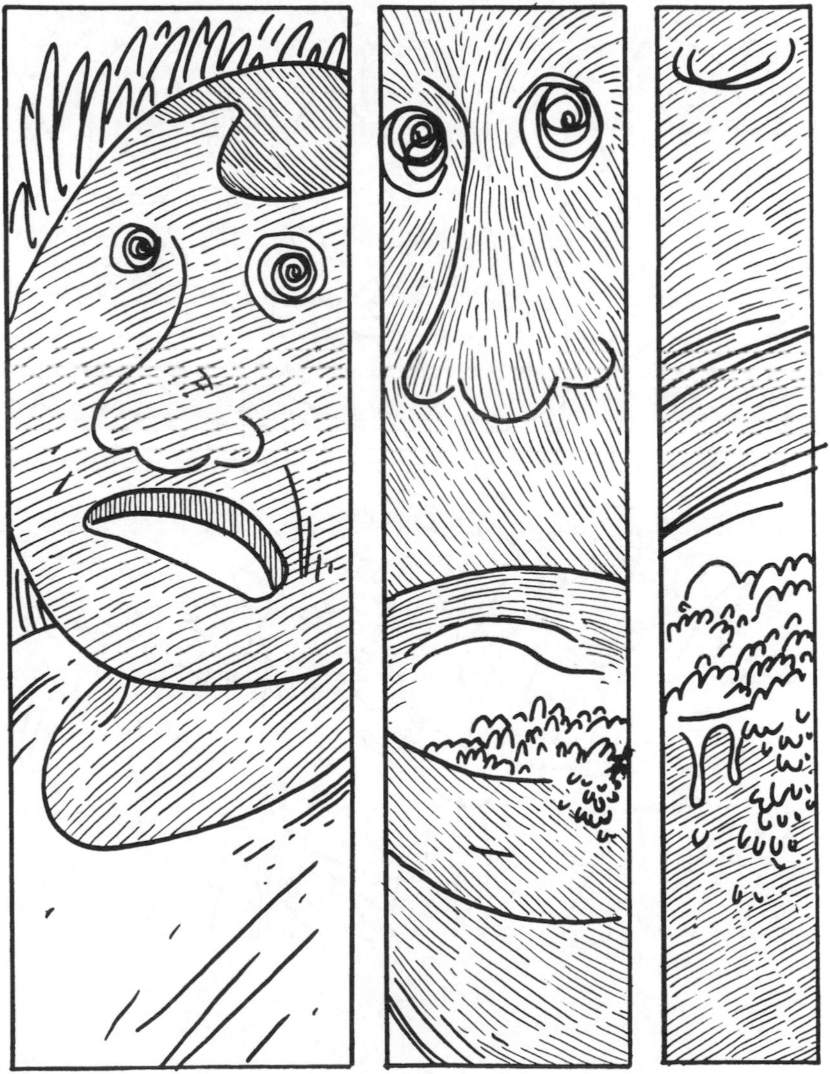

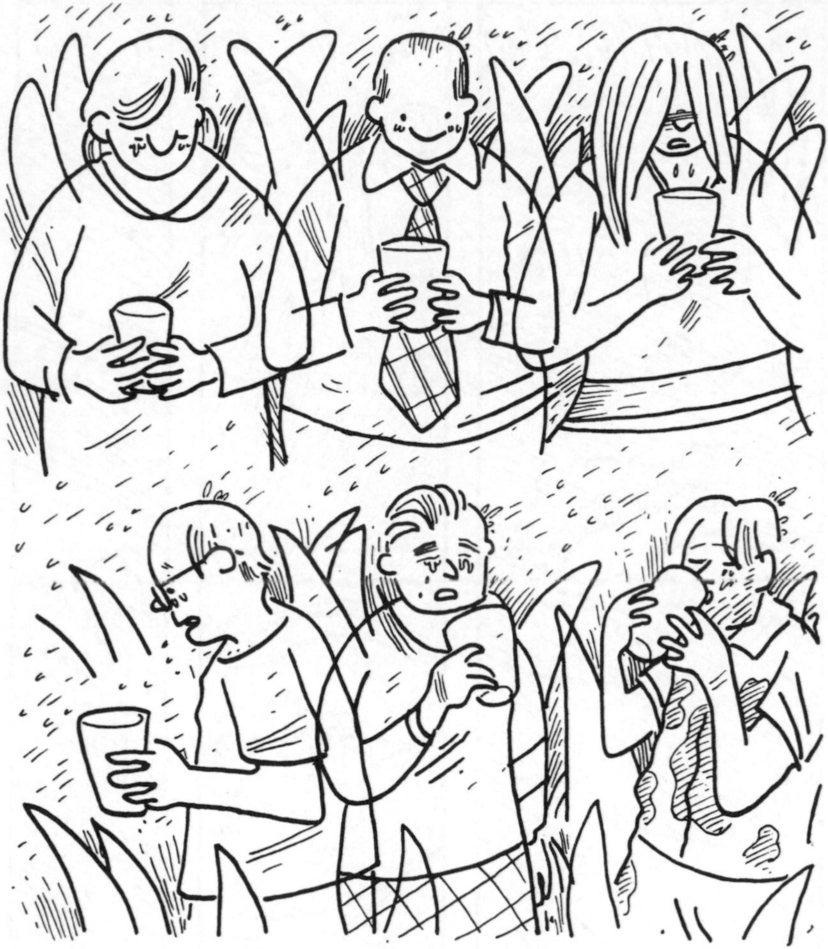

Our tears
mix with
sweet cool—

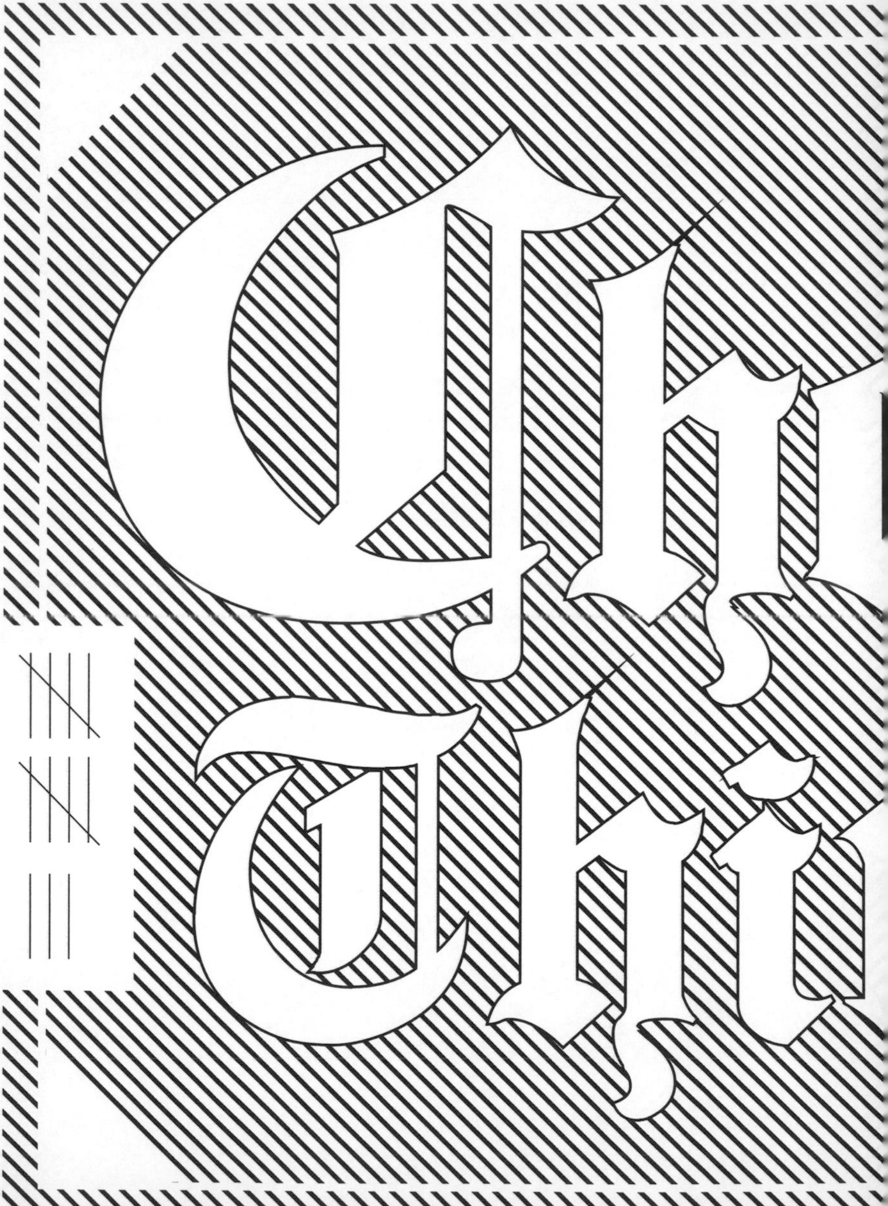

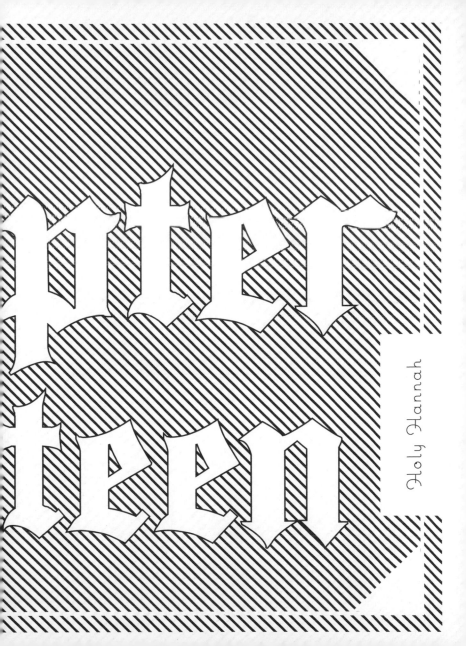

pter
teen

Holy Hannah

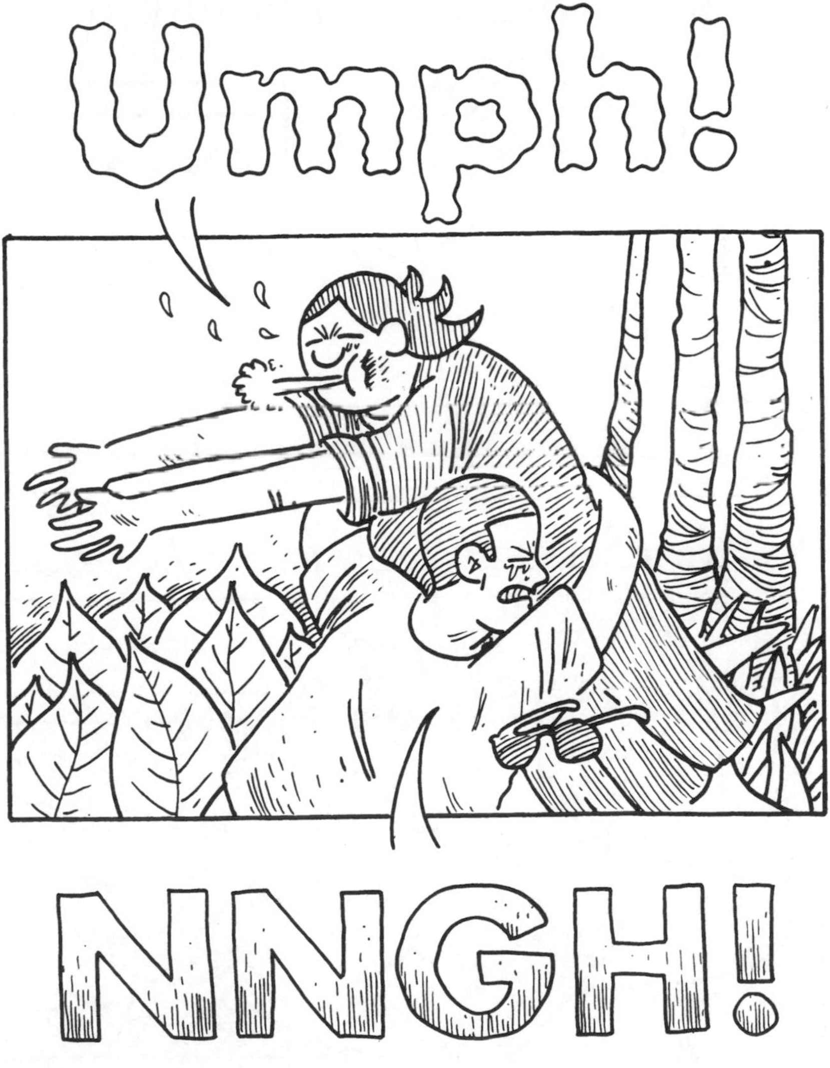
Umph!
NNGH!

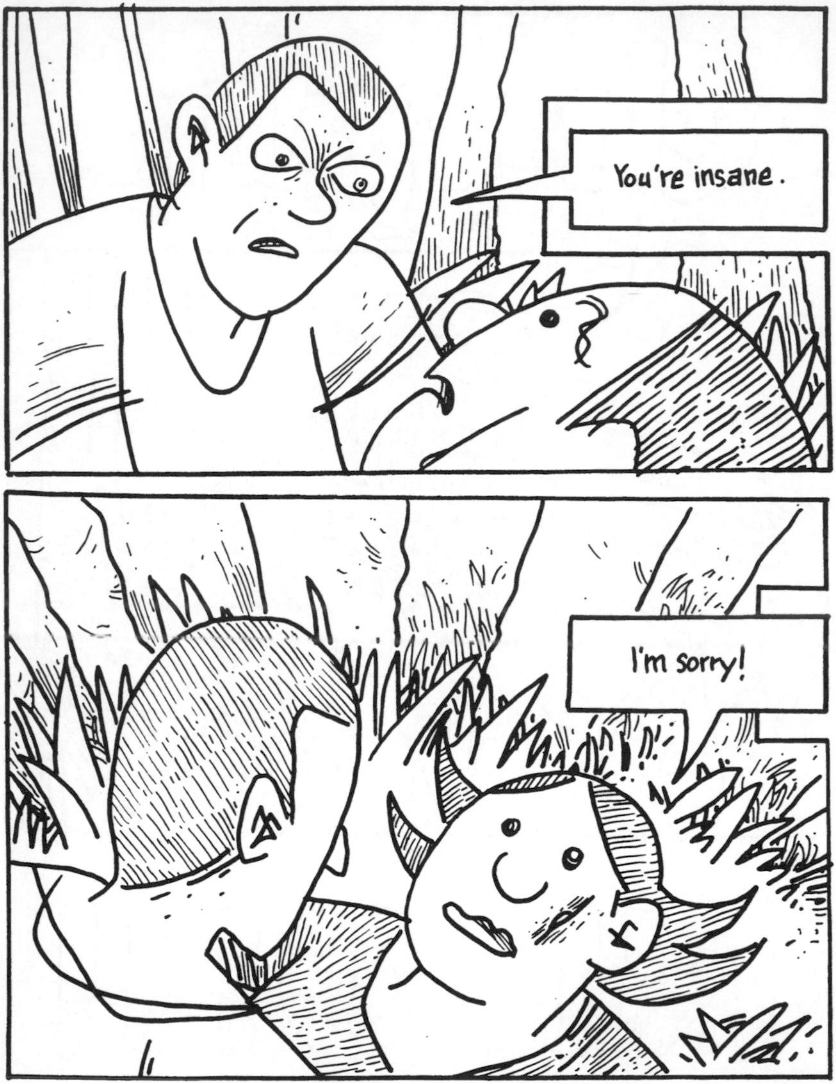
You're insane.
I'm sorry!

You murdered them all.

I...

they didn't tell me...

God. Dammit. God. Dammit.

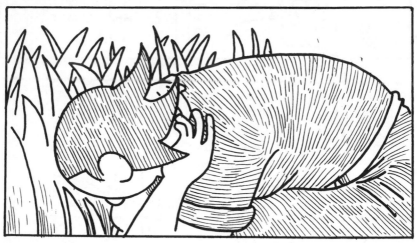

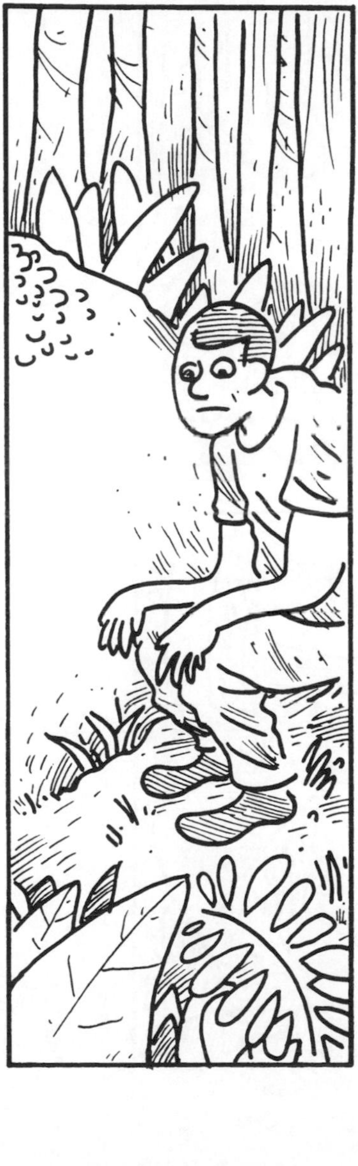

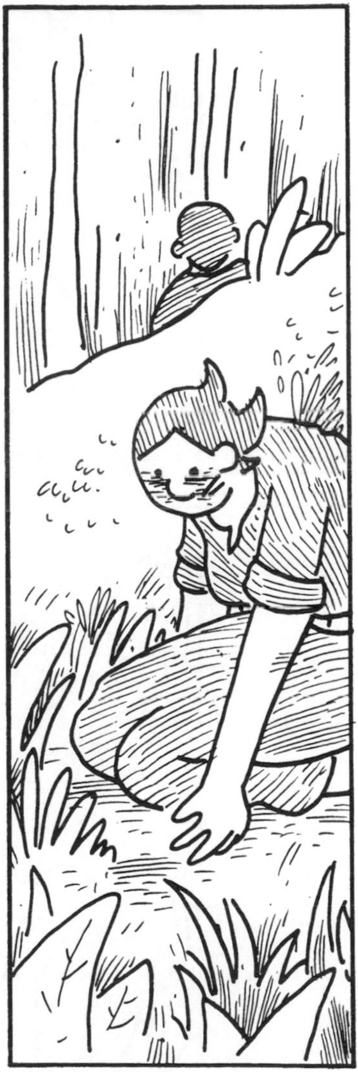

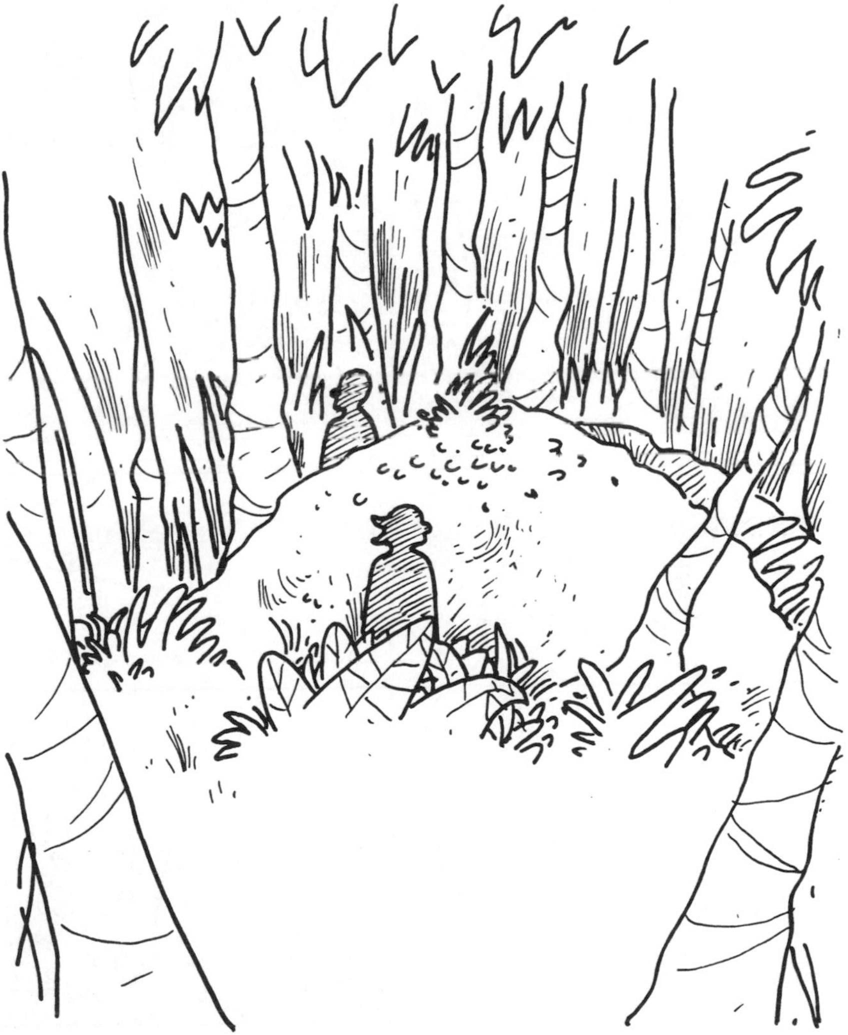

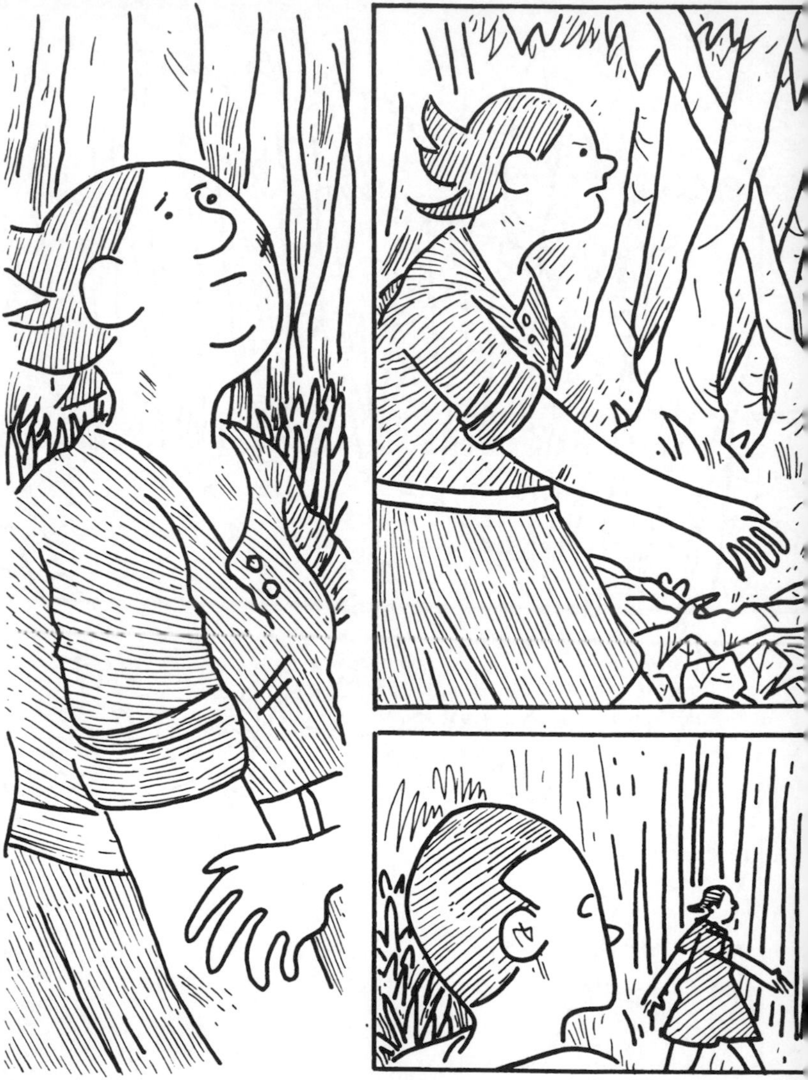

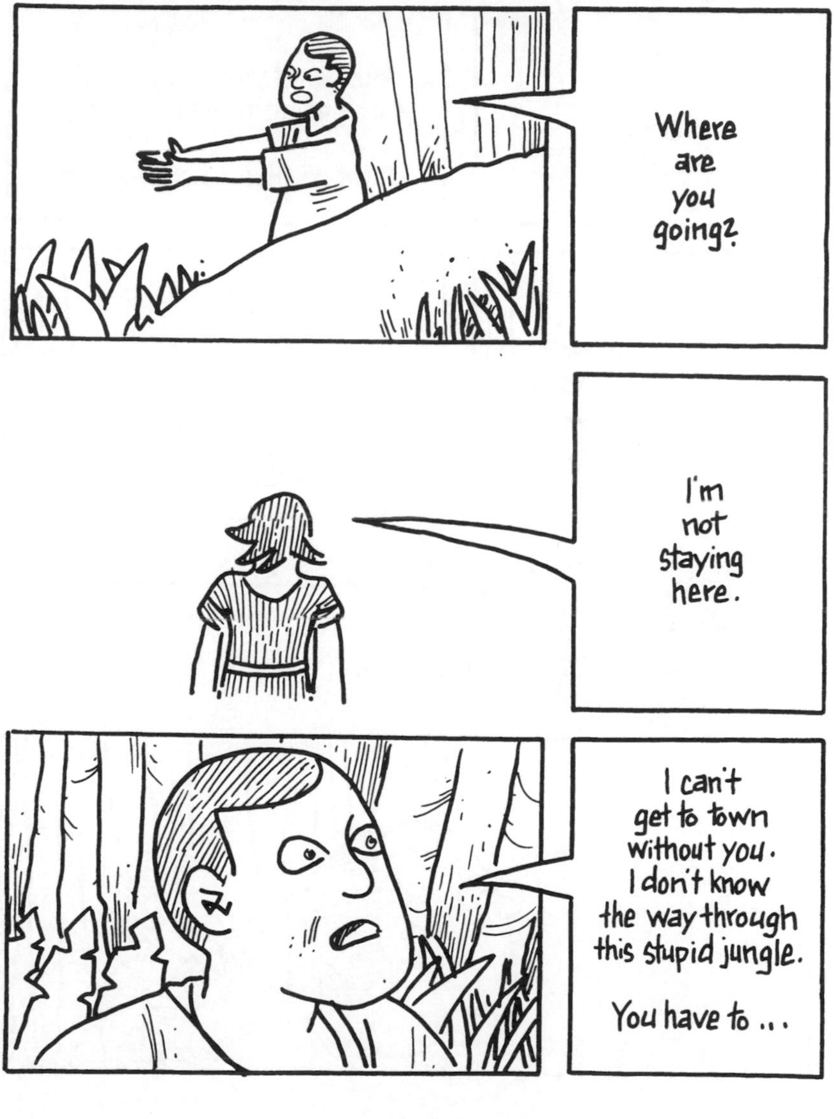
Where are you going?
I'm not staying here.
I can't get to town without you. I don't know the way through this stupid jungle.
You have to ...

I...
I can't...
I need to...
After what your people did, you're going to make me beg?
I have no idea where we are!
sktch

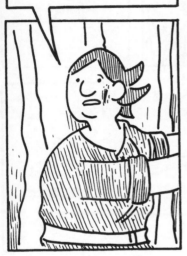

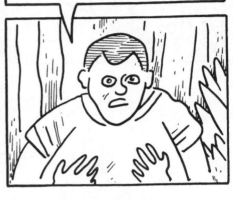

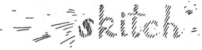

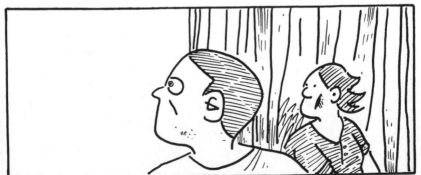

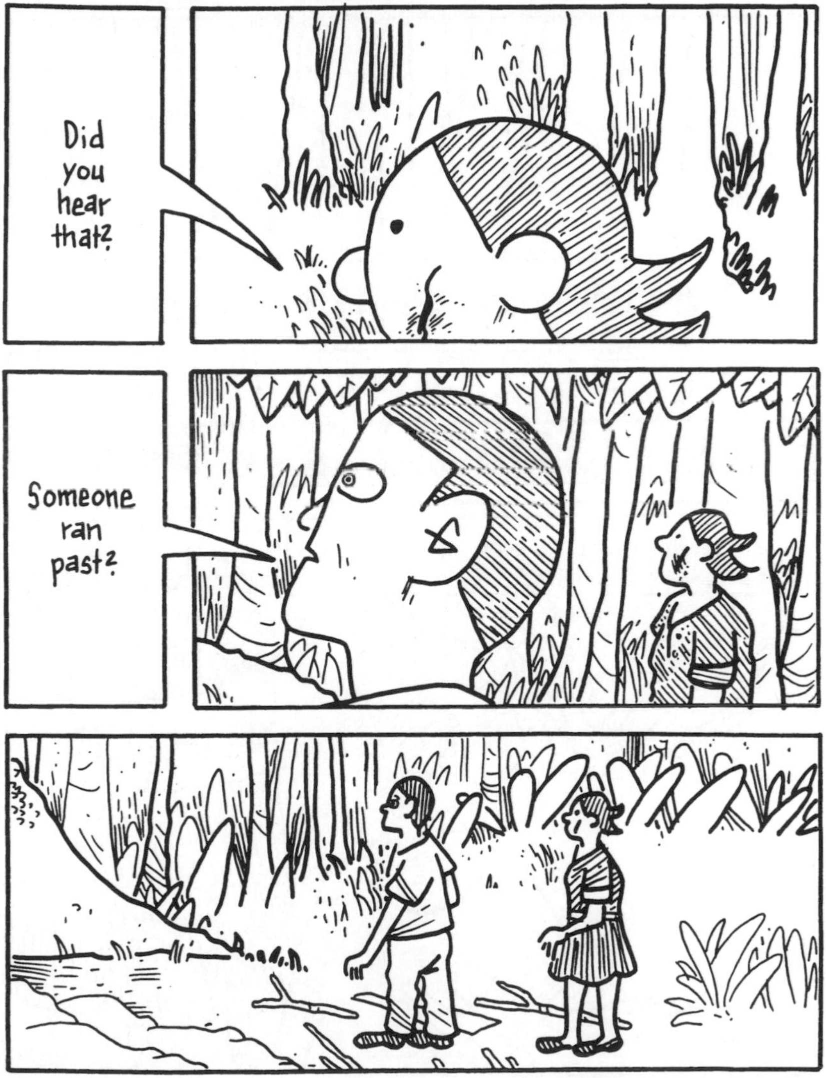
Did you hear that?
Someone ran past?

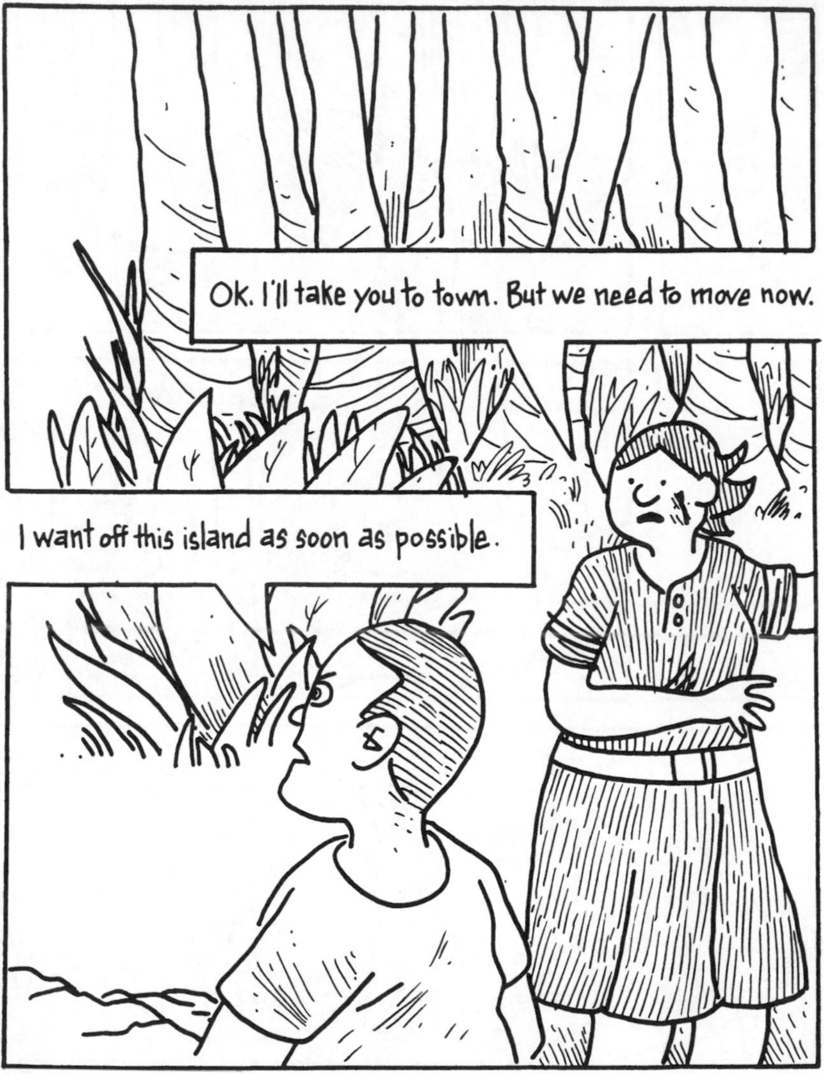
Ok. I'll take you to town. But we need to move now.
I want off this island as soon as possible.

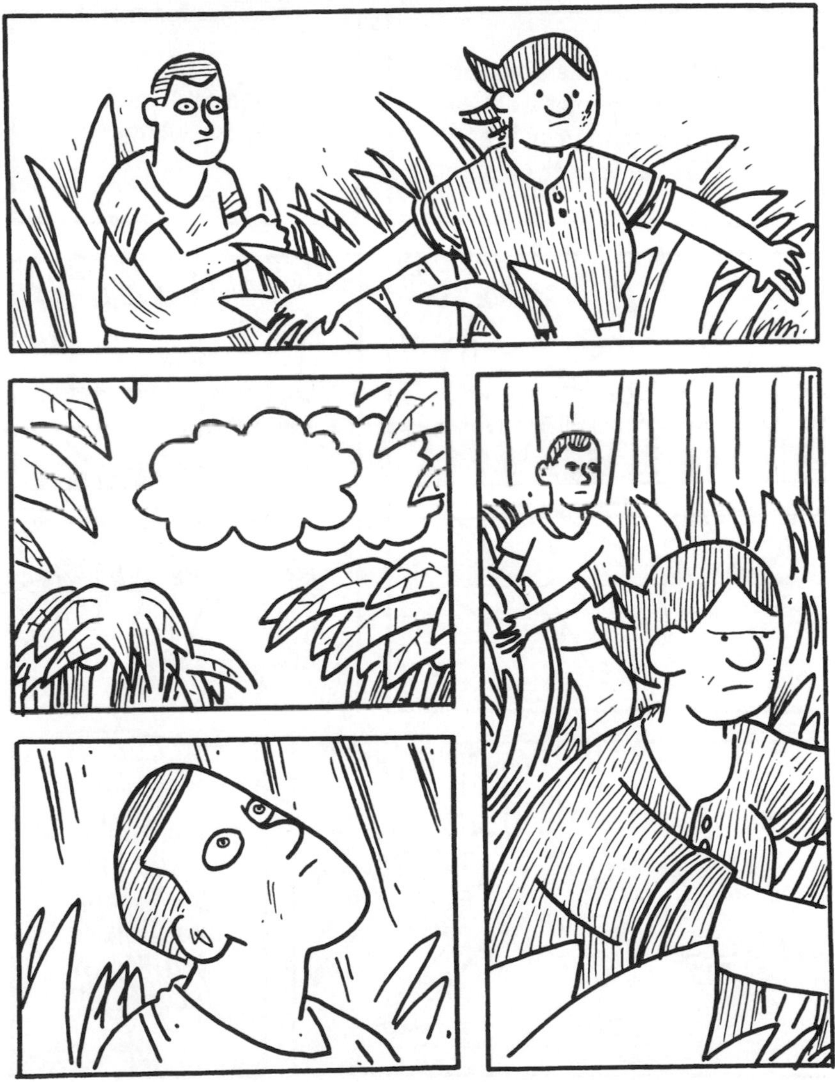

It's wrong. What he does. He uses you. Carpenter isolated all of you from your lives and twisted your thinking.
We twist him to our wants.
No. You're ... you can't see how he manipulates you. It's not your fault.

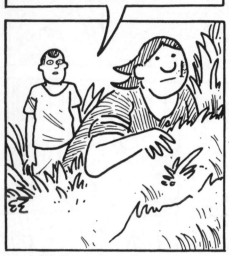

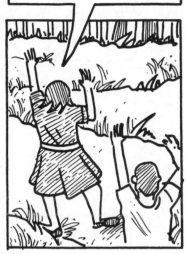

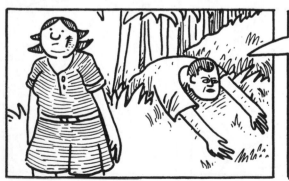

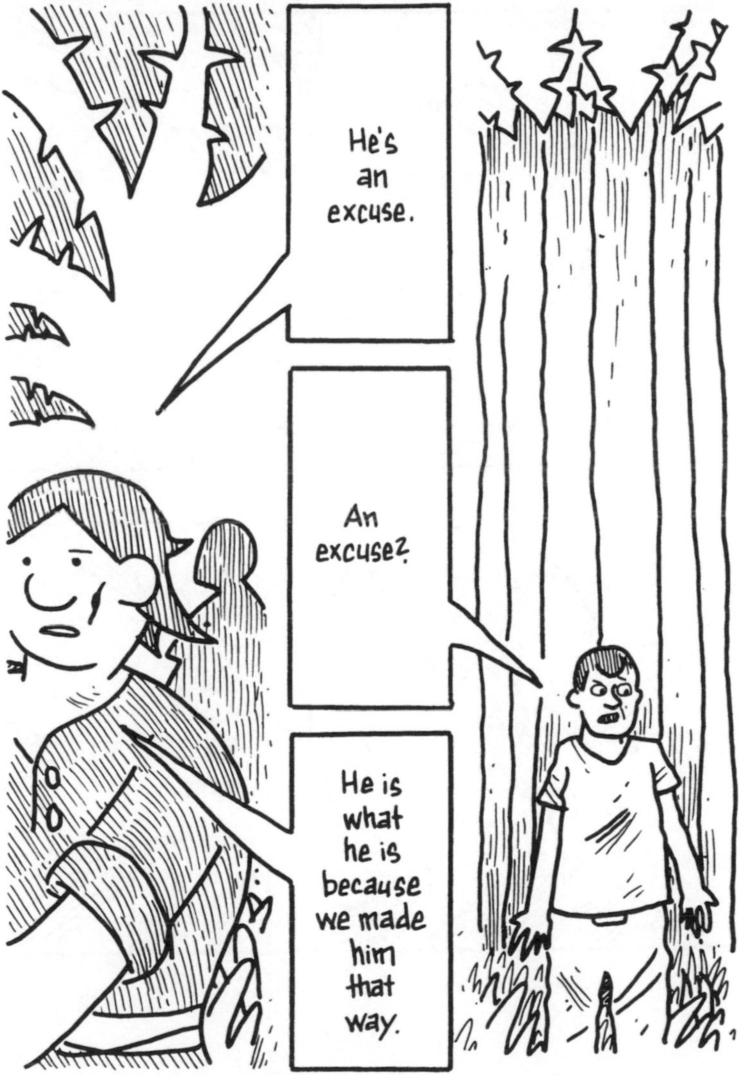
He's an excuse.
An excuse?
He is what he is because we made him that way.

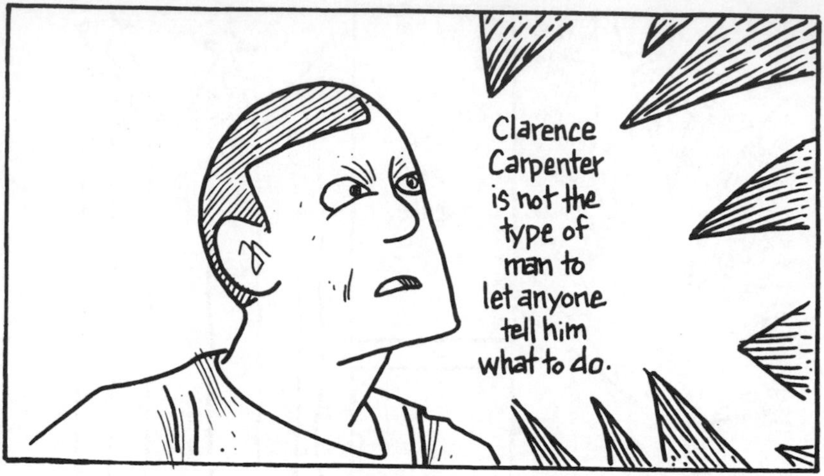
Clarence Carpenter is not the type of man to let anyone tell him what to do.

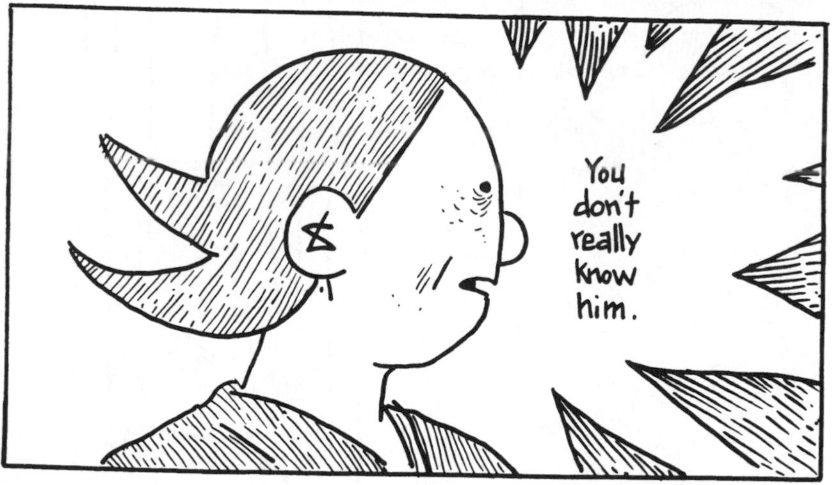
You don't really know him.

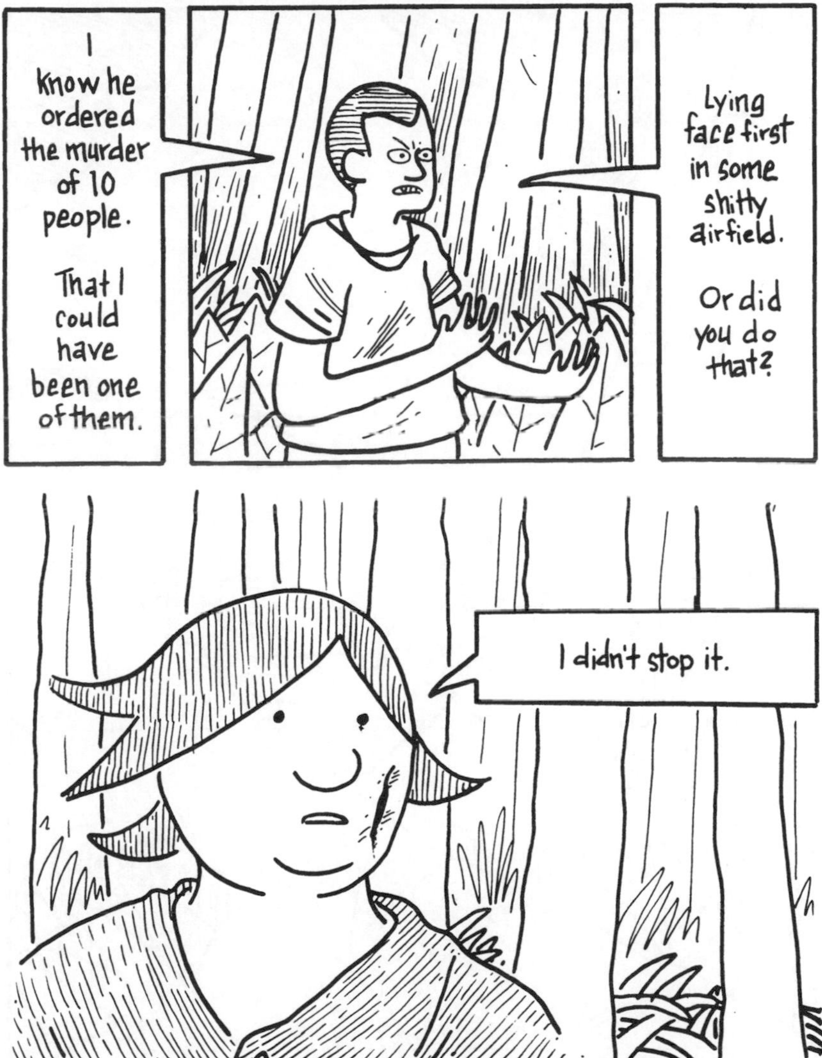
I know he ordered the murder of 10 people.
That I could have been one of them.
Lying face first in some shitty airfield.
Or did you do that?
I didn't stop it.

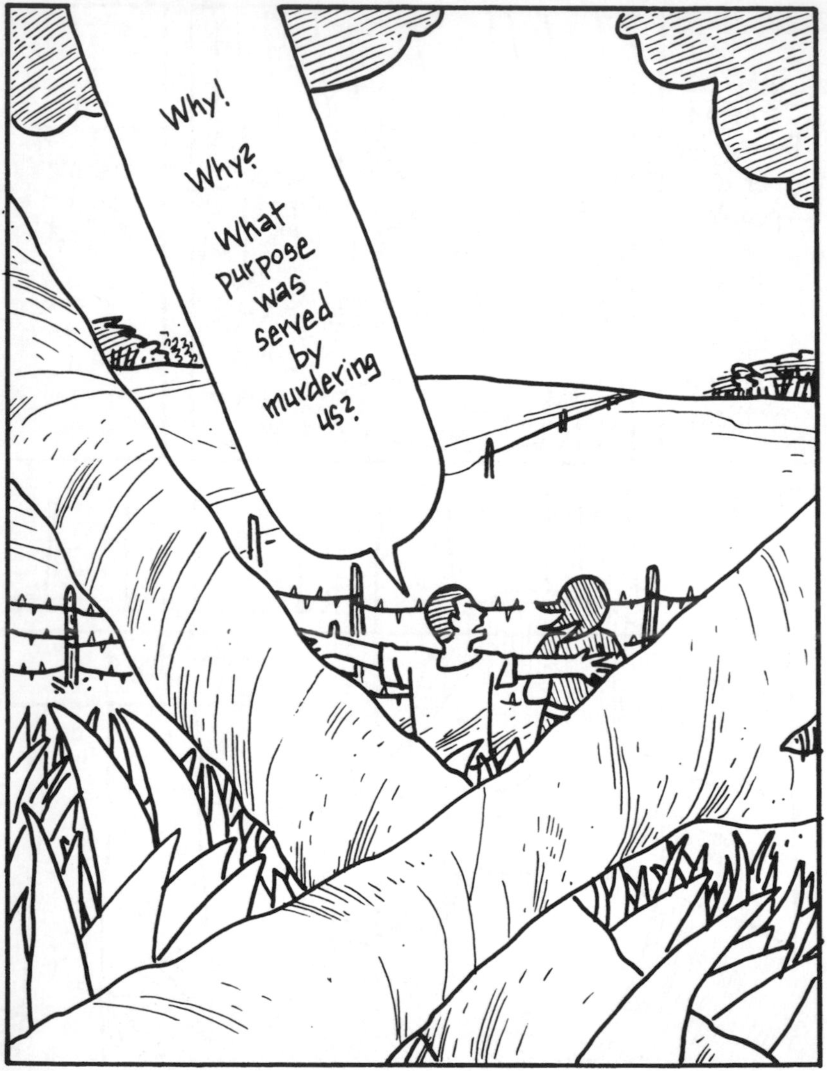
Why! Why? What purpose was served by murdering us?

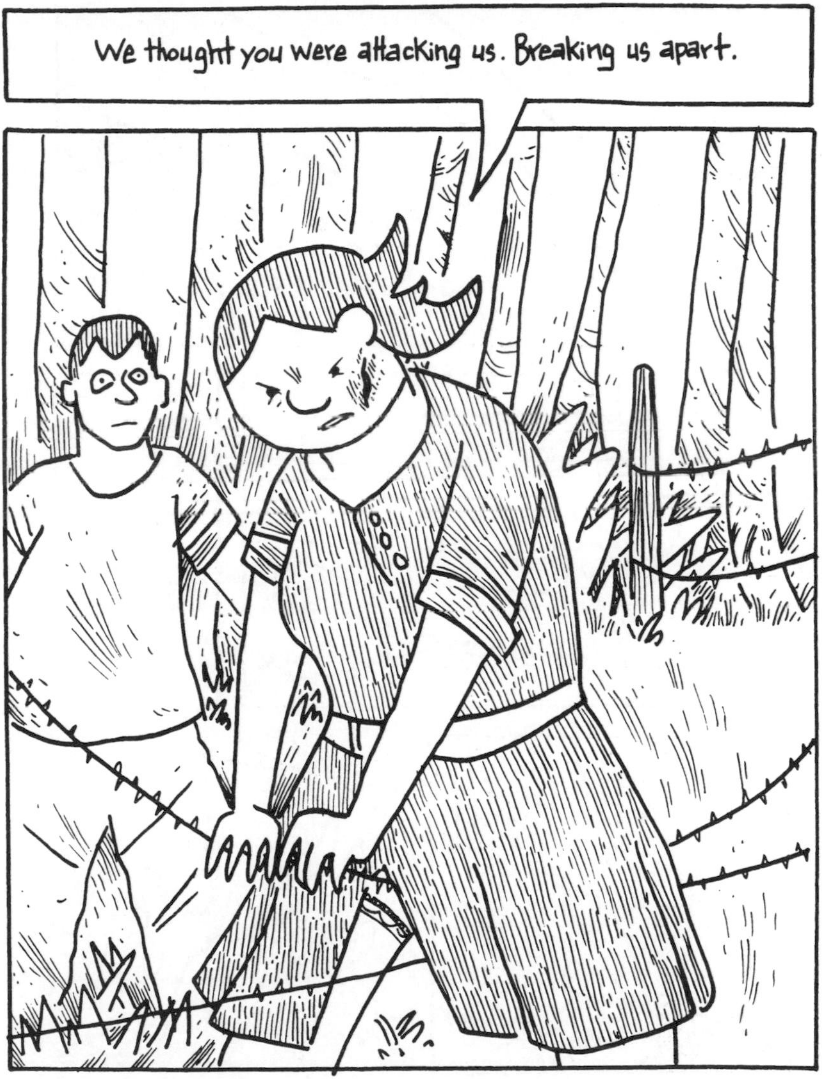
We thought you were attacking us. Breaking us apart.

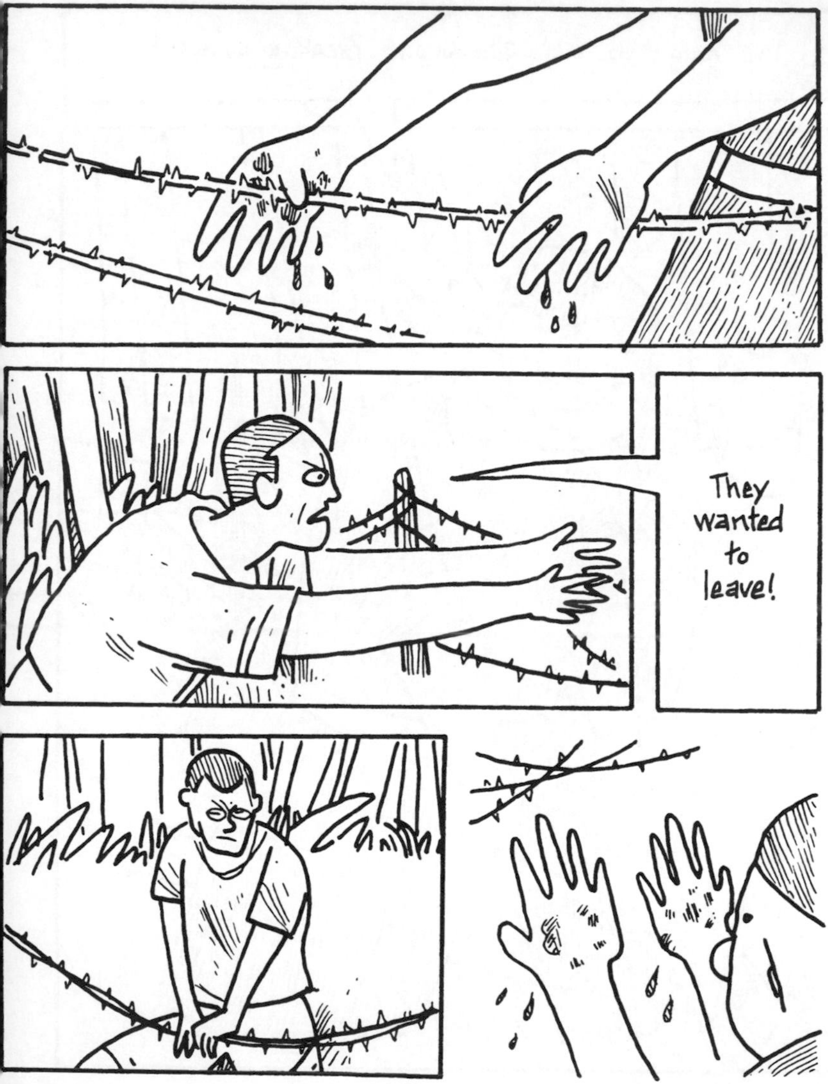
They wanted to leave!

You're right. It doesn't matter anymore anyway. It's over.

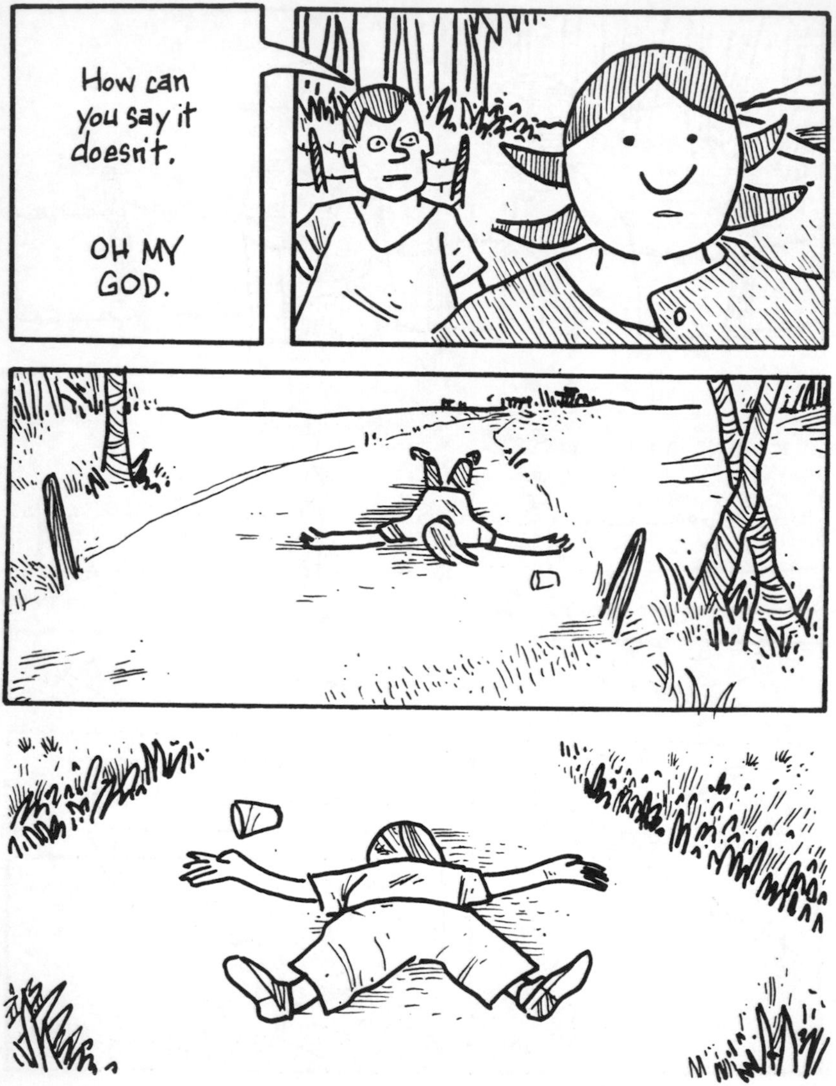
How can you say it doesn't.
OH MY GOD.

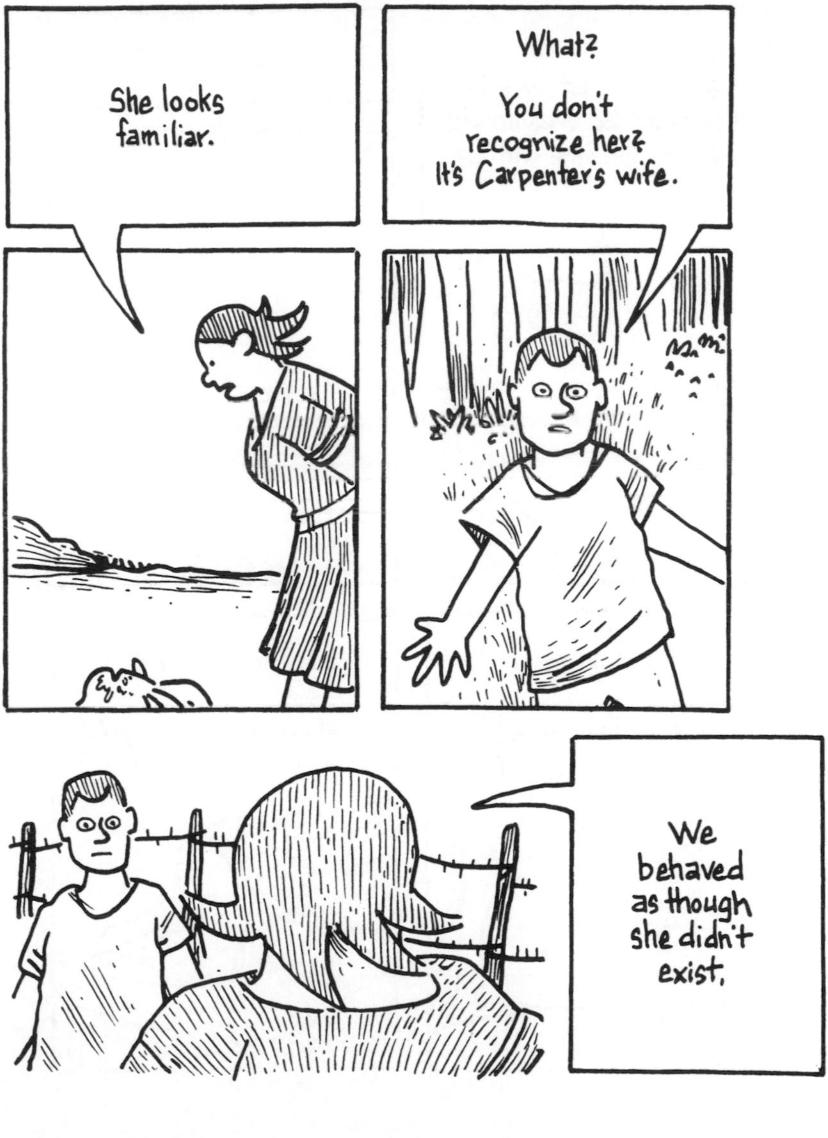
She looks familiar.
What?
You don't recognize her? It's Carpenter's wife.
We behaved as though she didn't exist.

Carpenter must have had her killed too. Maybe she wanted to come with us.

Oh no.

What now?

I need to hurry.

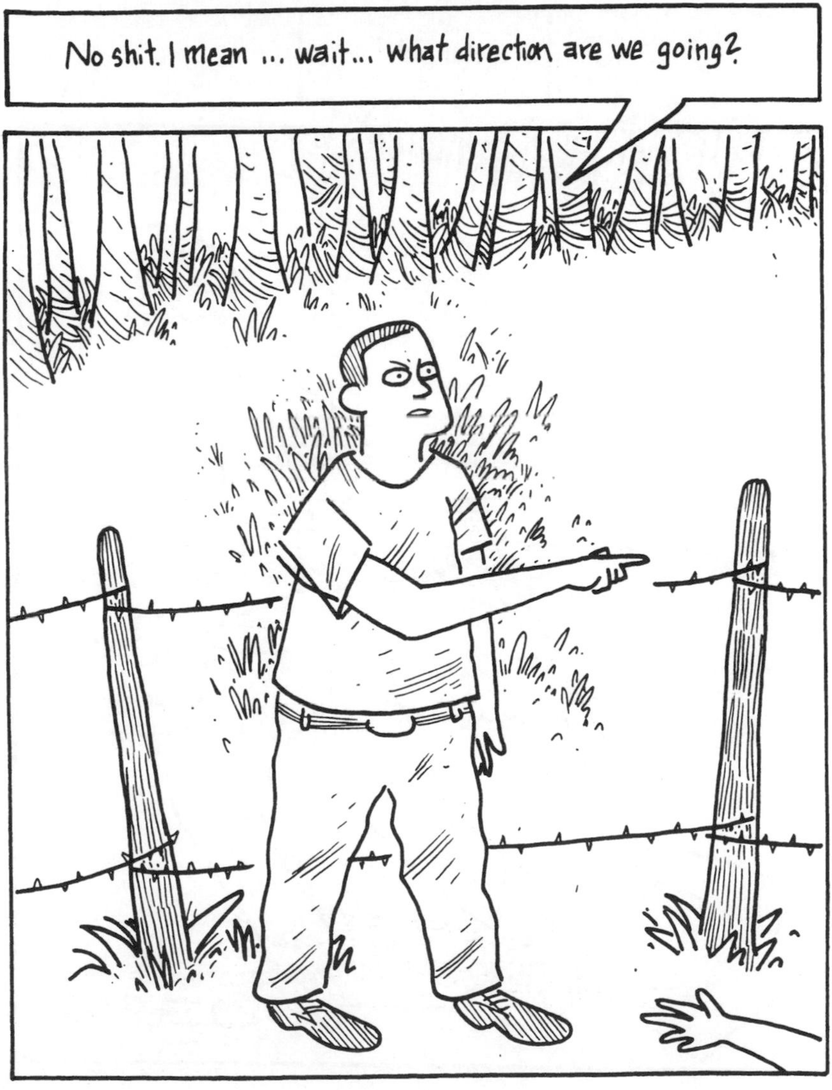
No shit. I mean ... wait... what direction are we going?

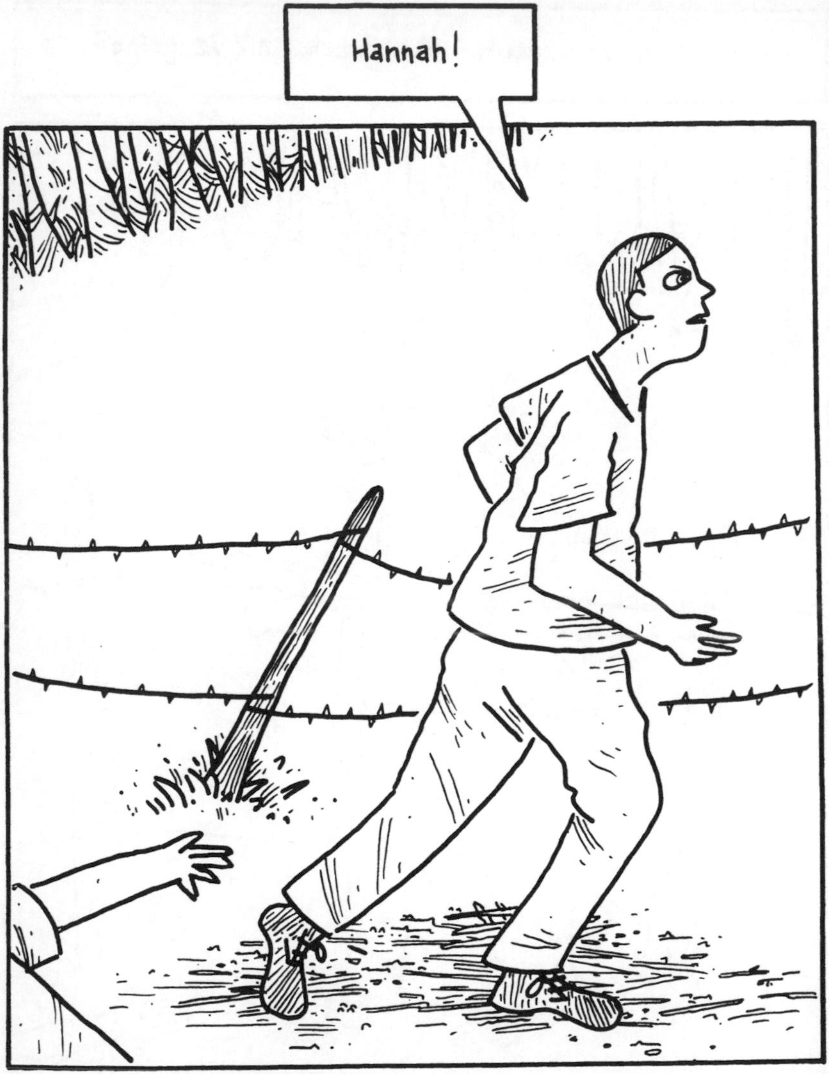
Hannah!

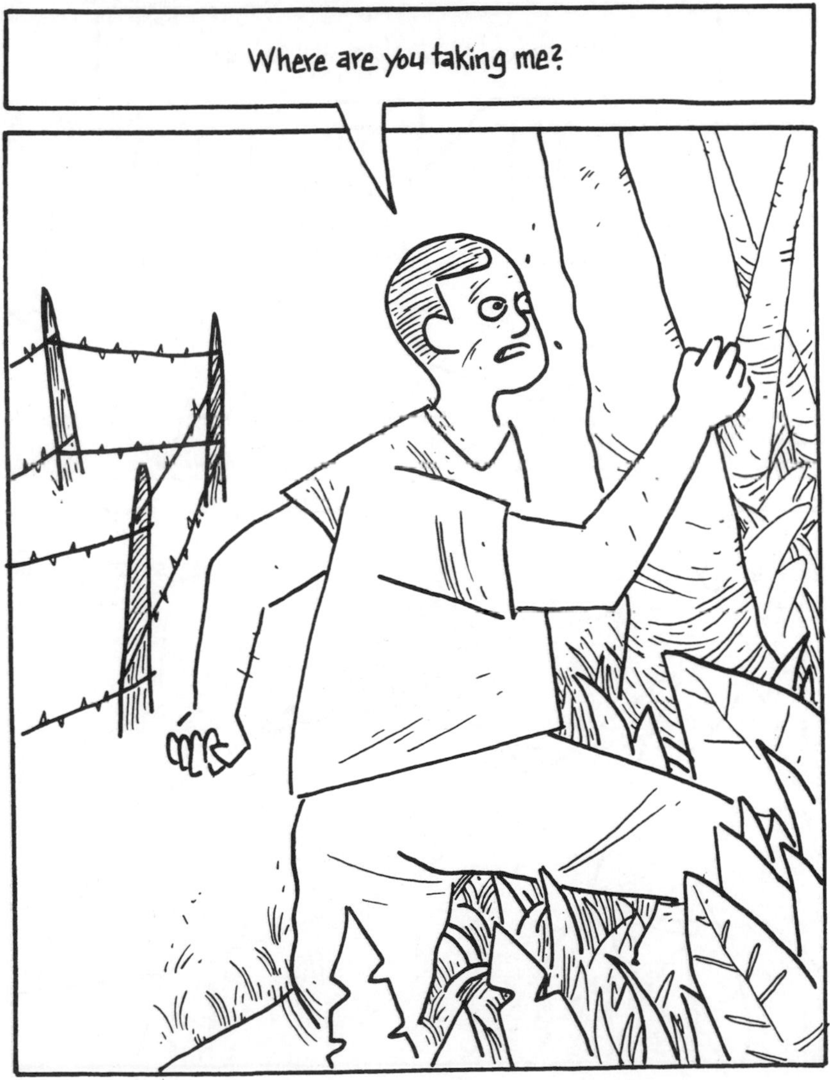
Where are you taking me?

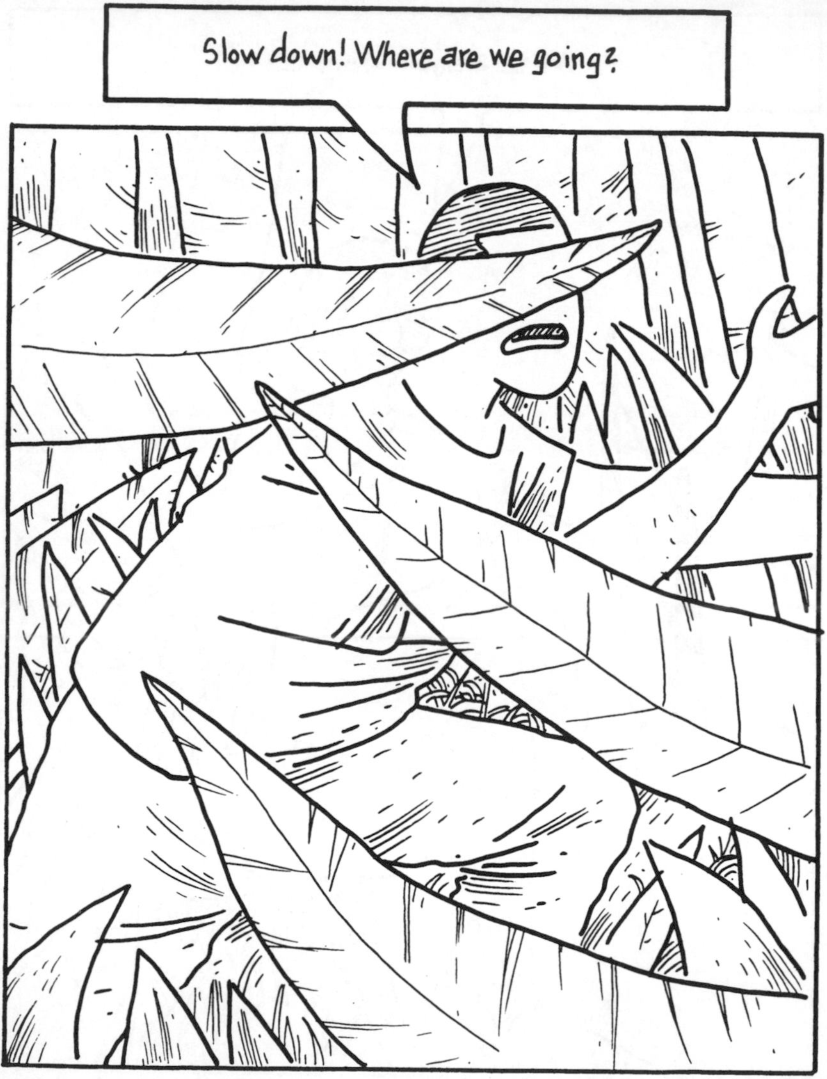
Slow down! Where are we going?

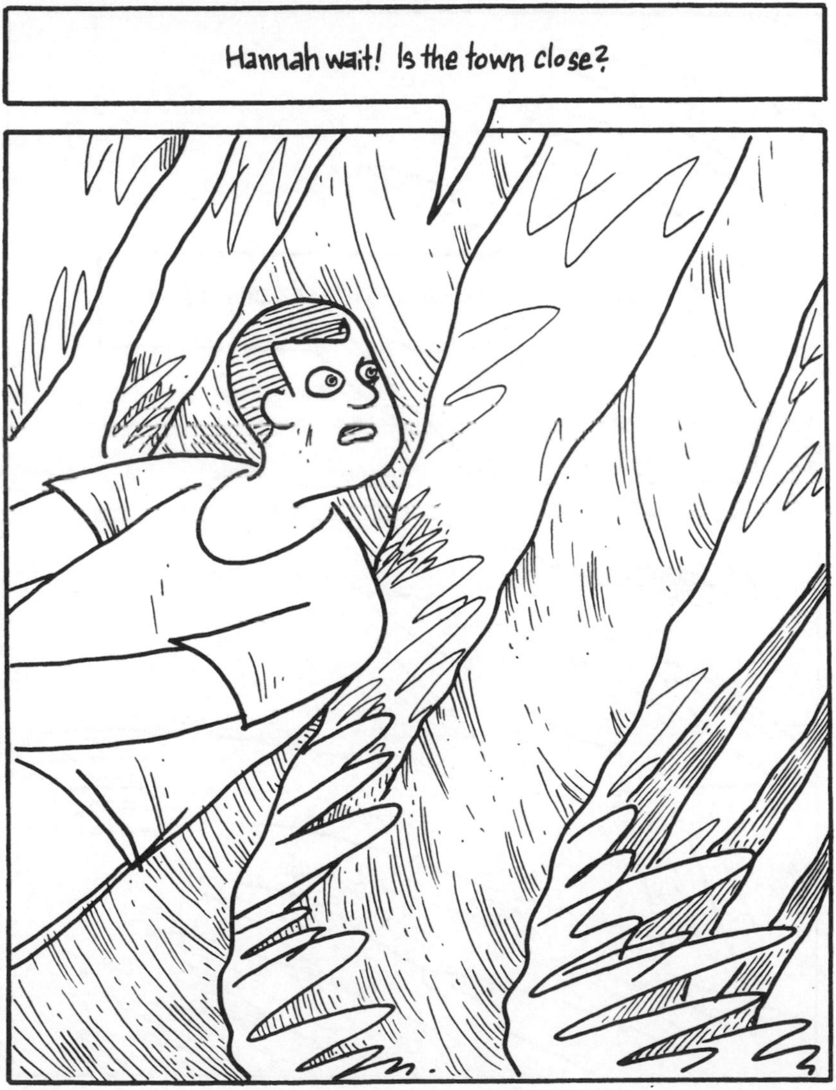
Hannah wait! Is the town close?

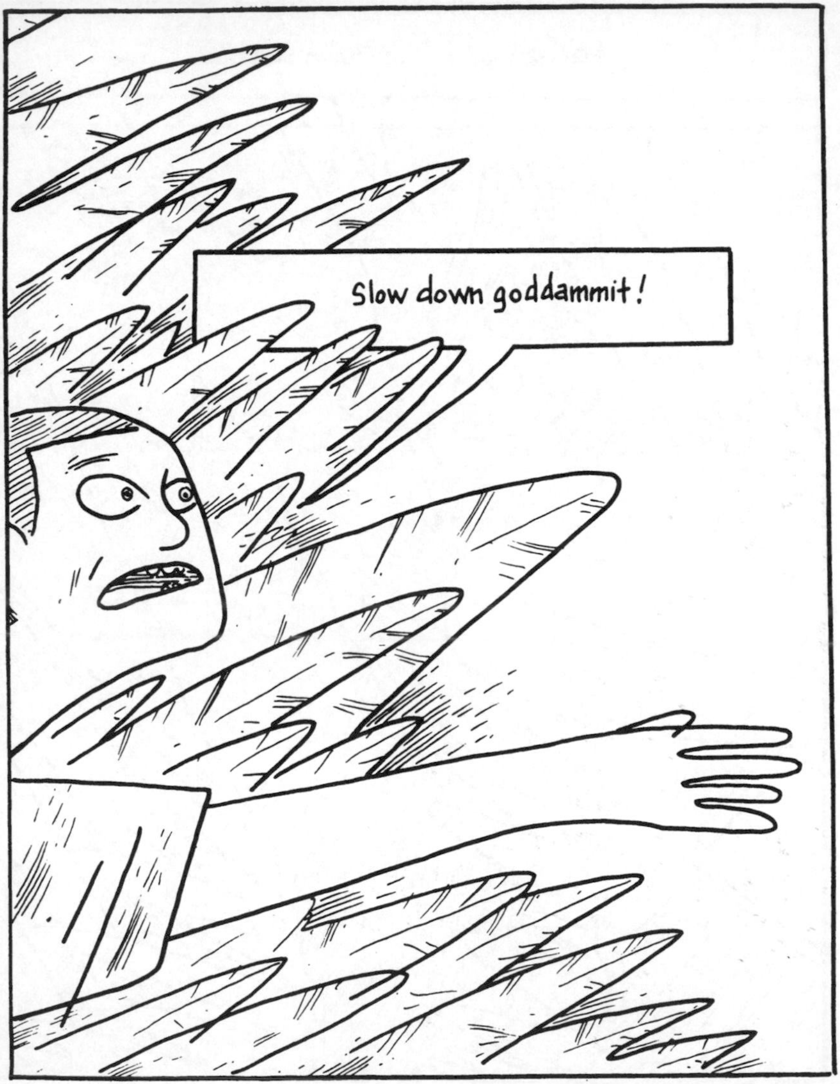
Slow down goddammit!

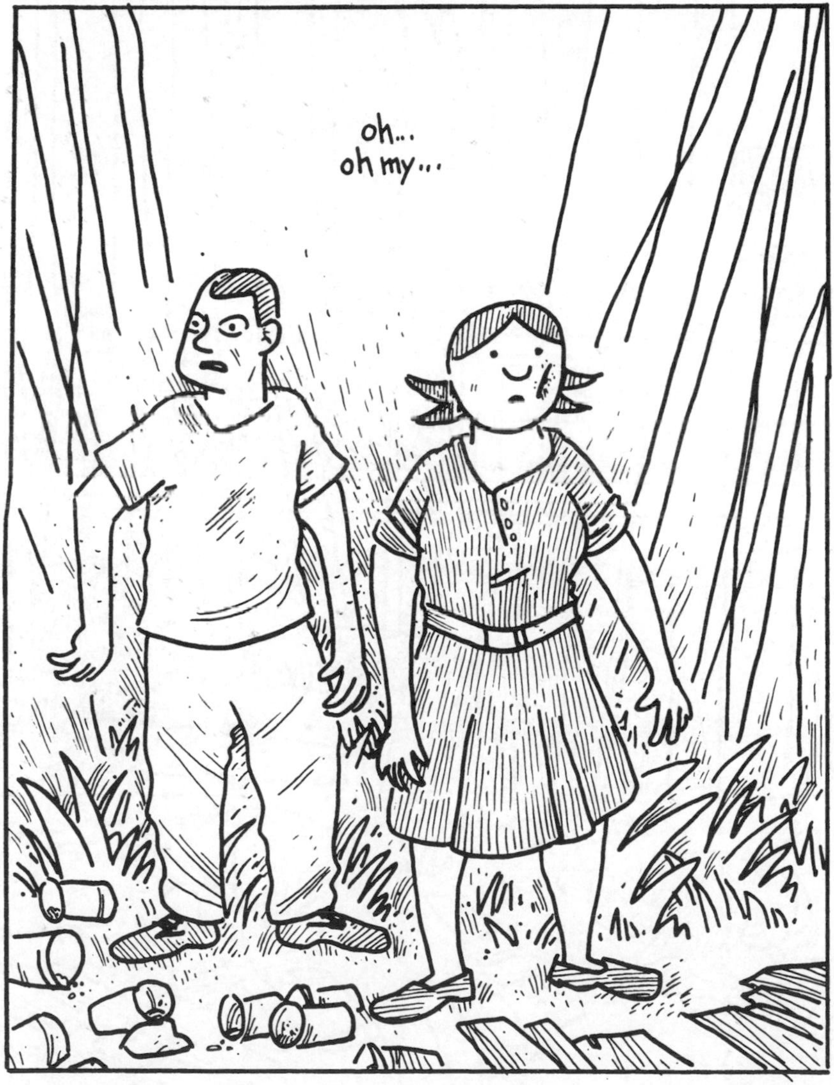
oh...
oh my...

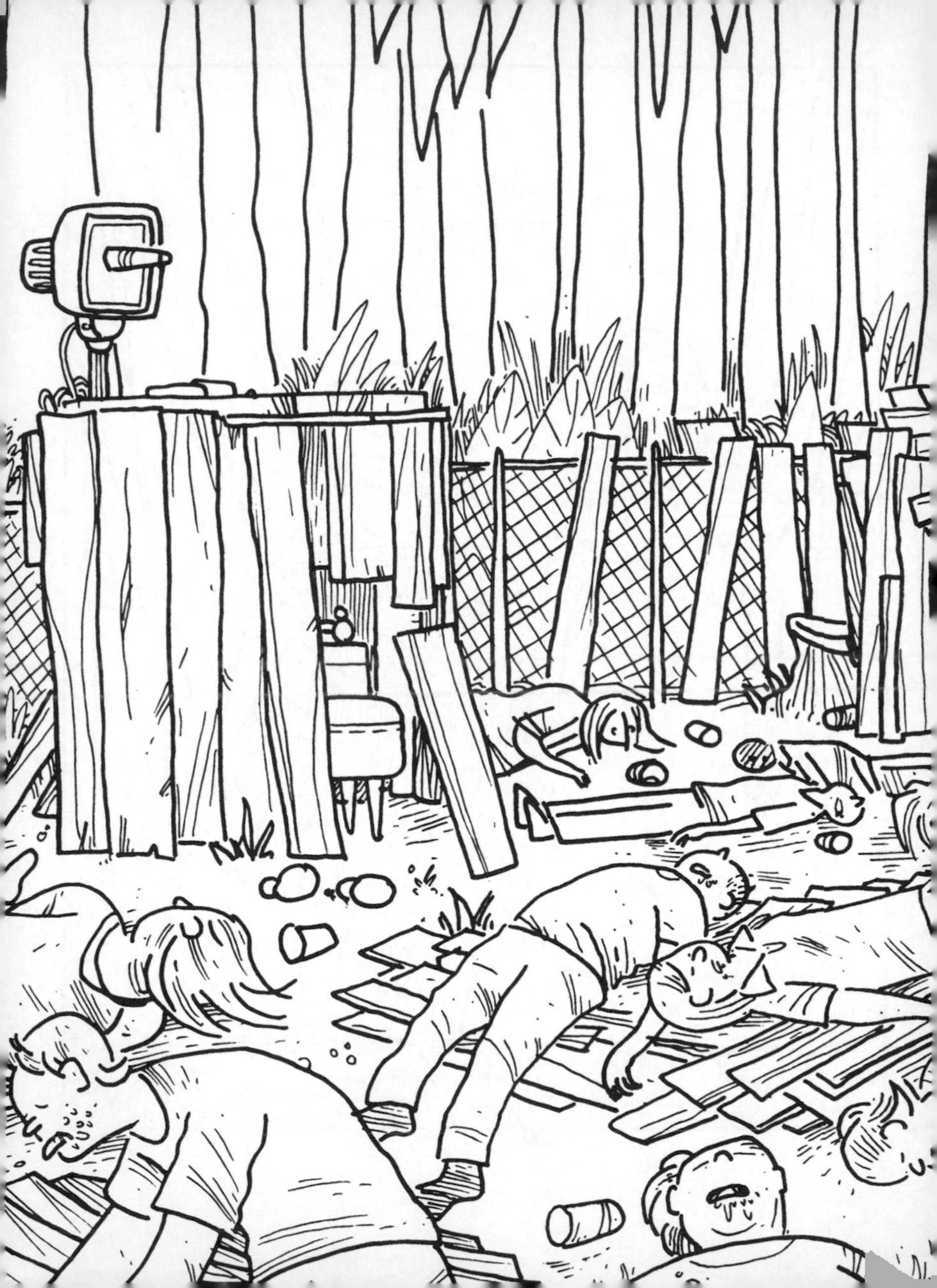

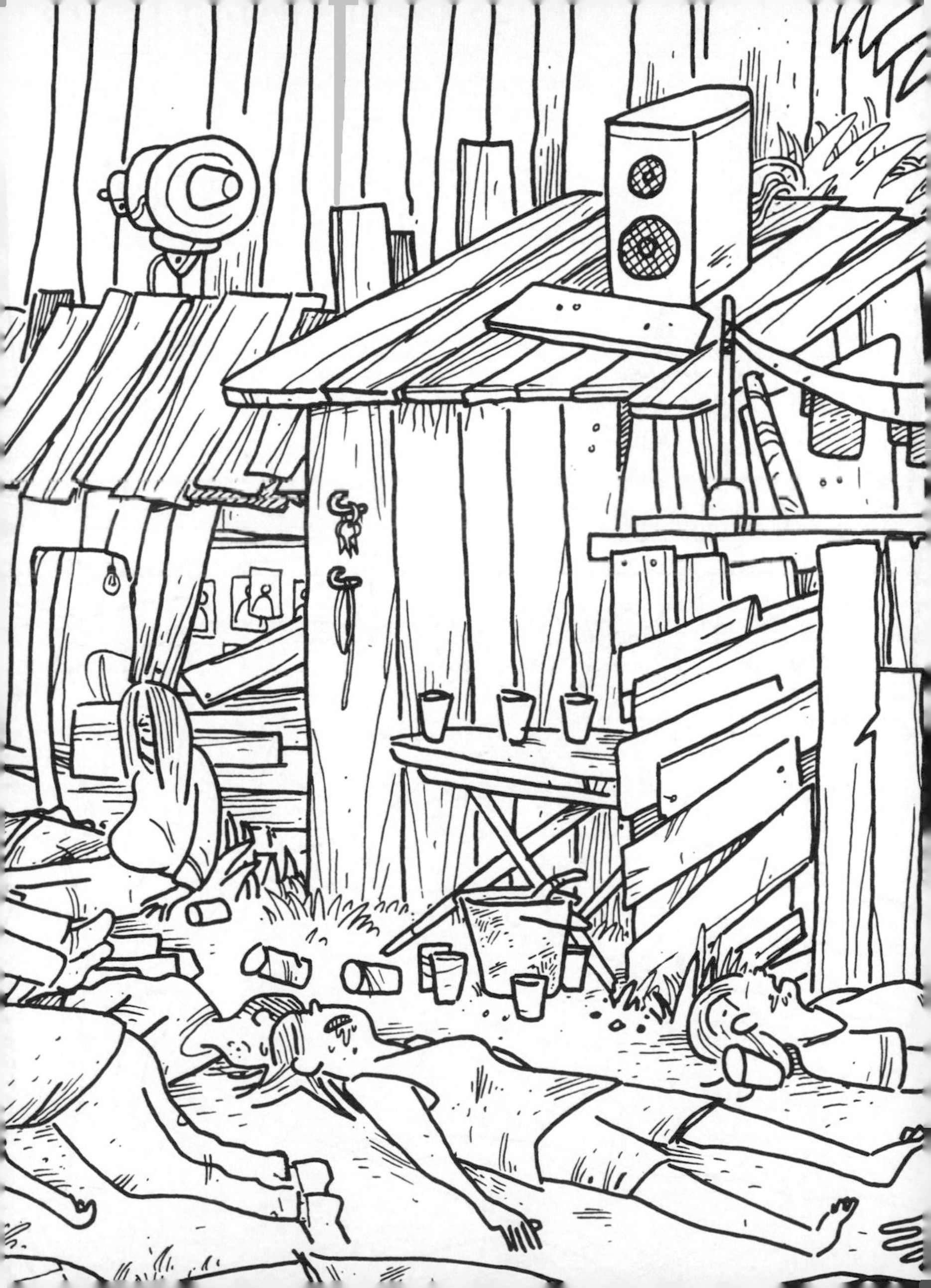

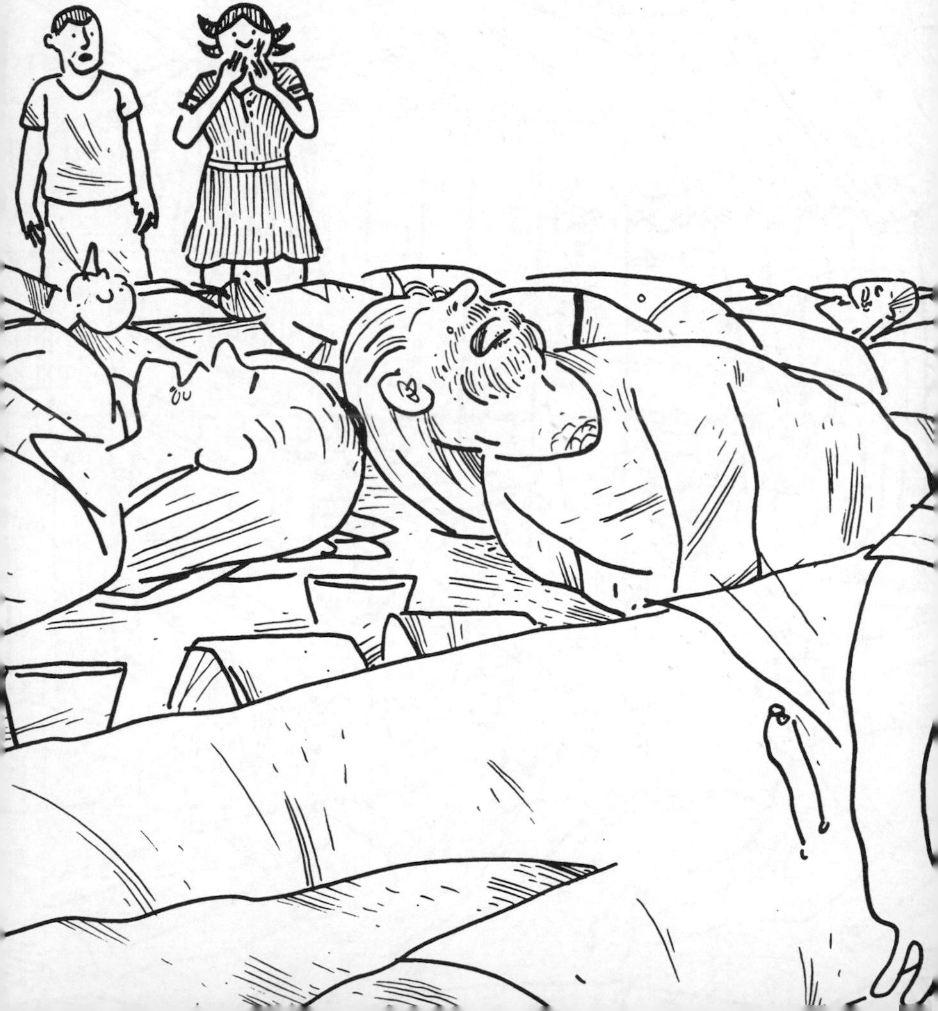

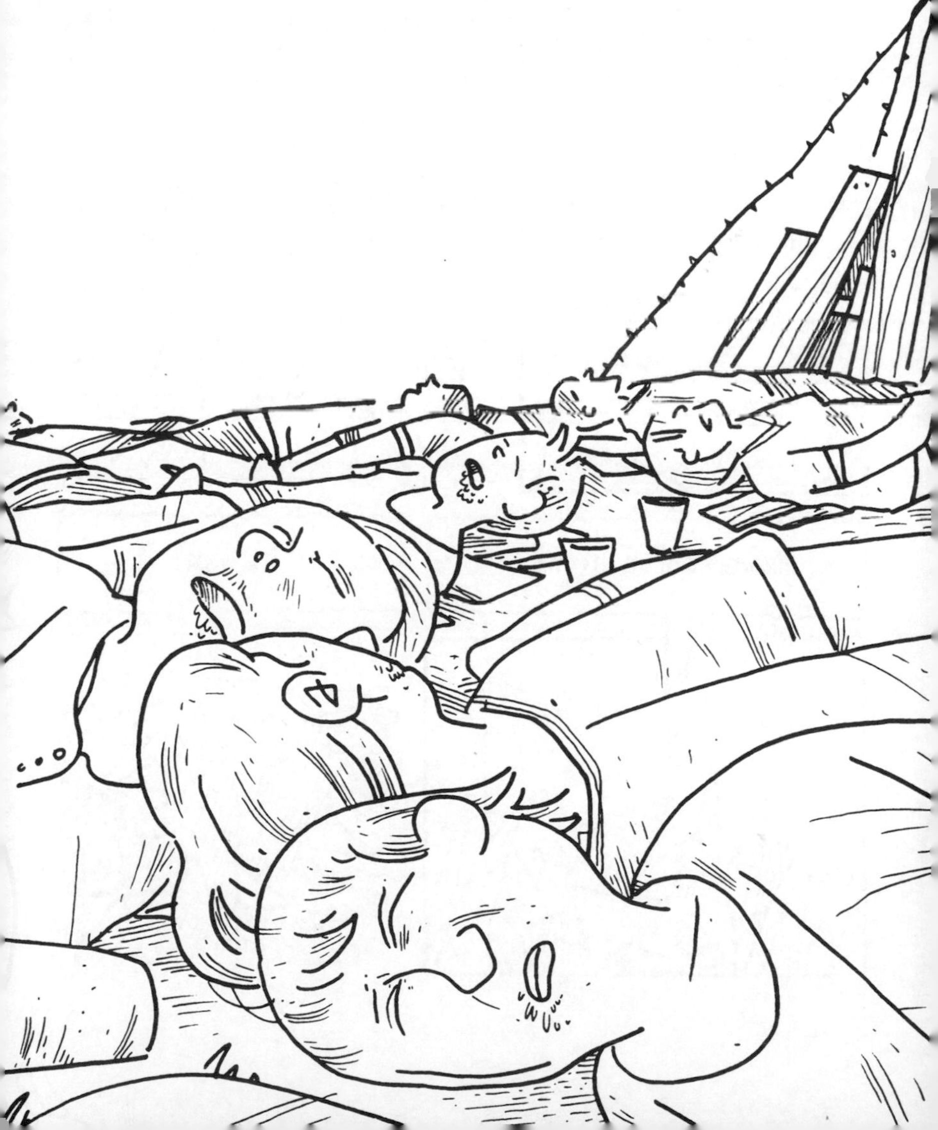

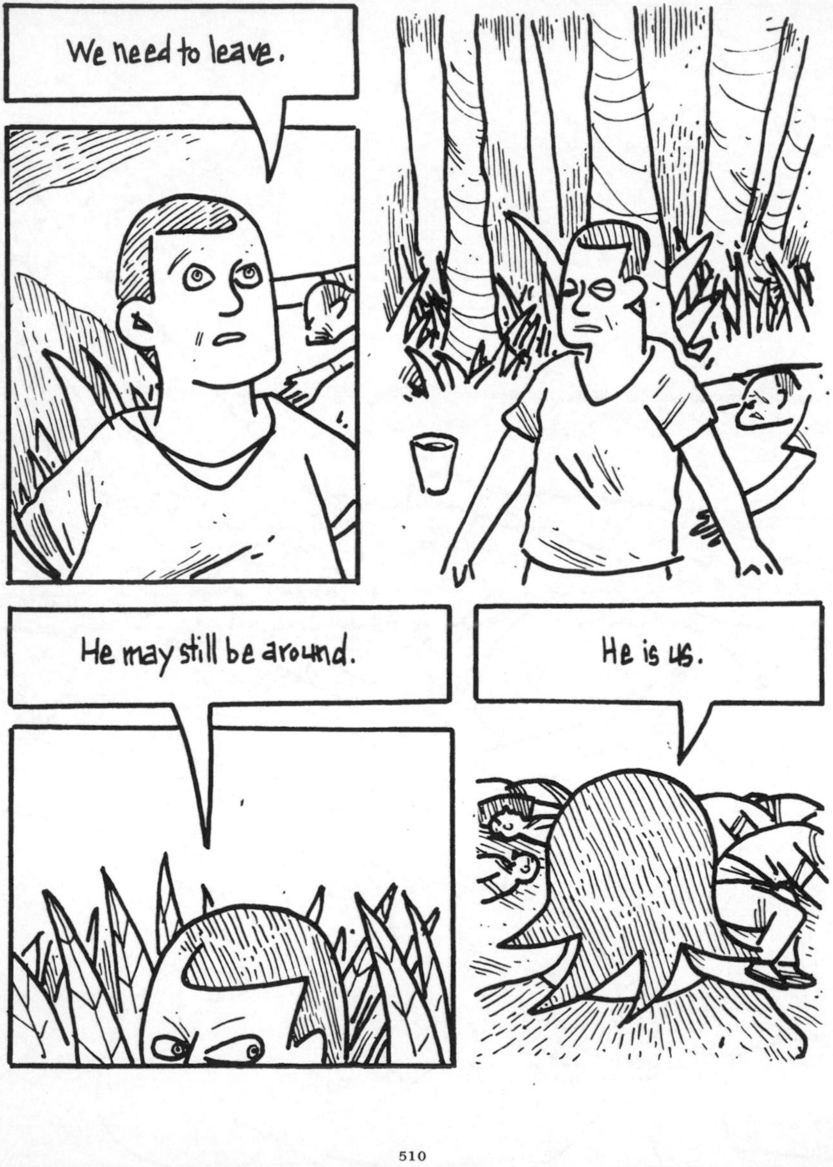
We need to leave.
He may still be around.
He is us.

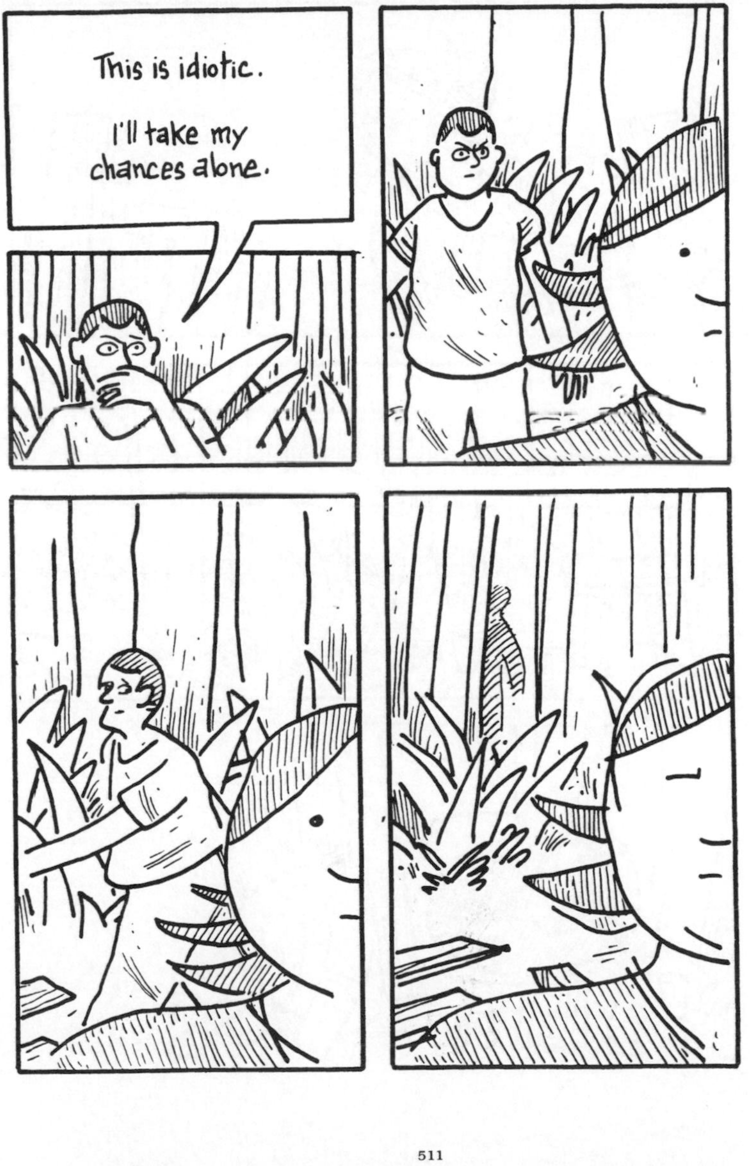
This is idiotic.
I'll take my chances alone.

512

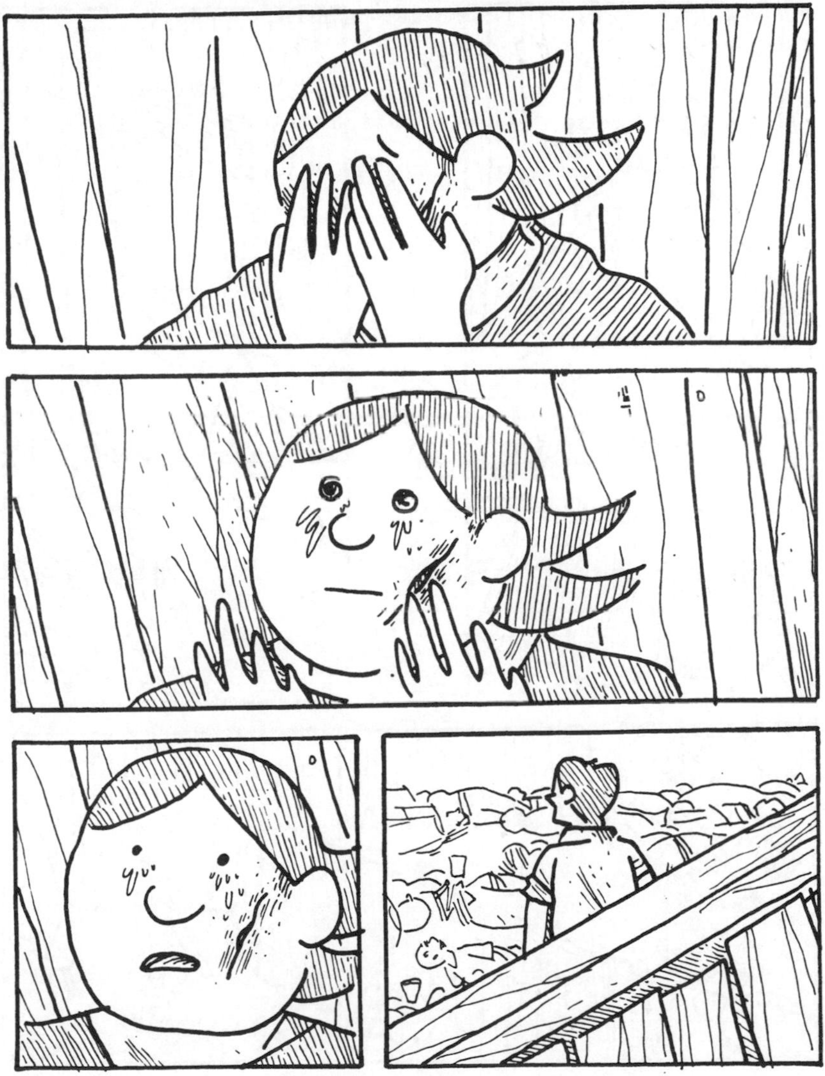

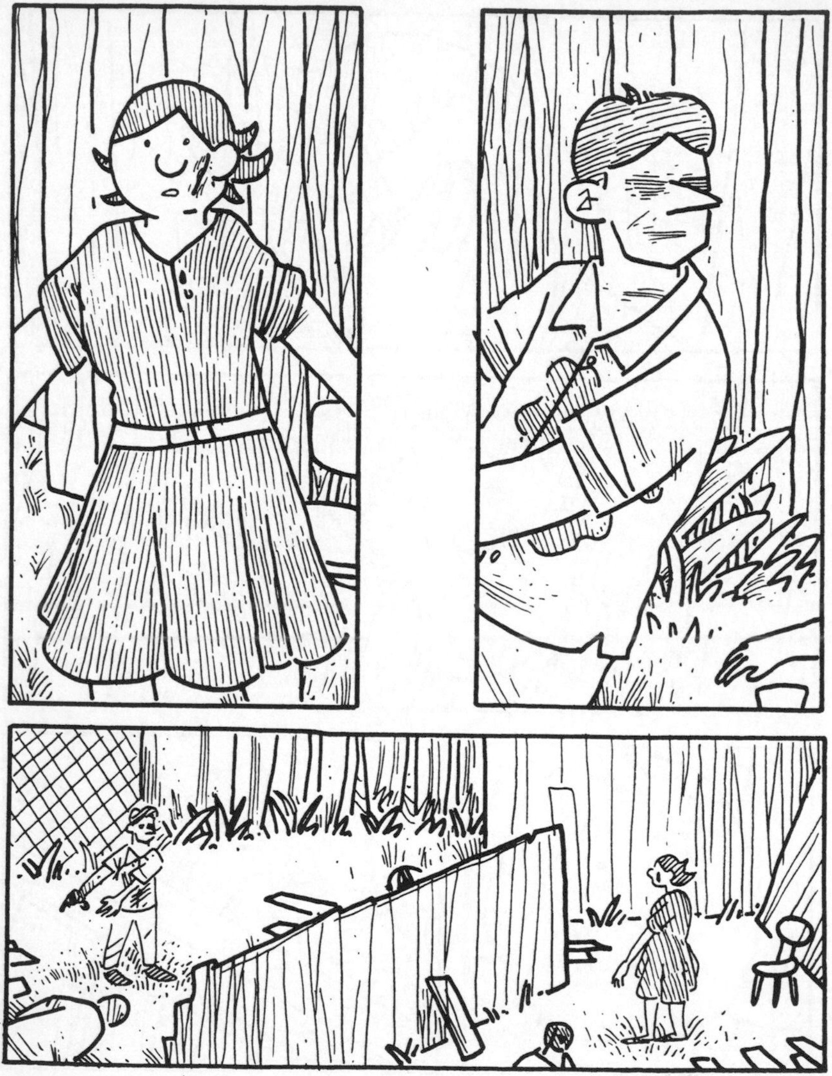

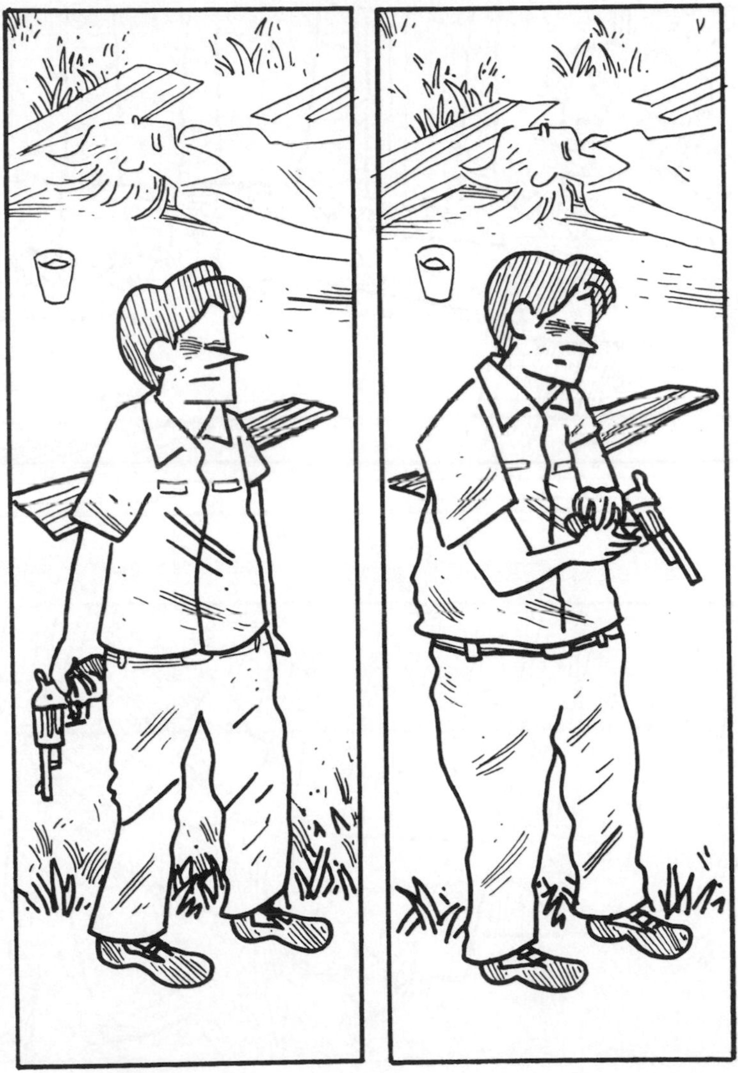

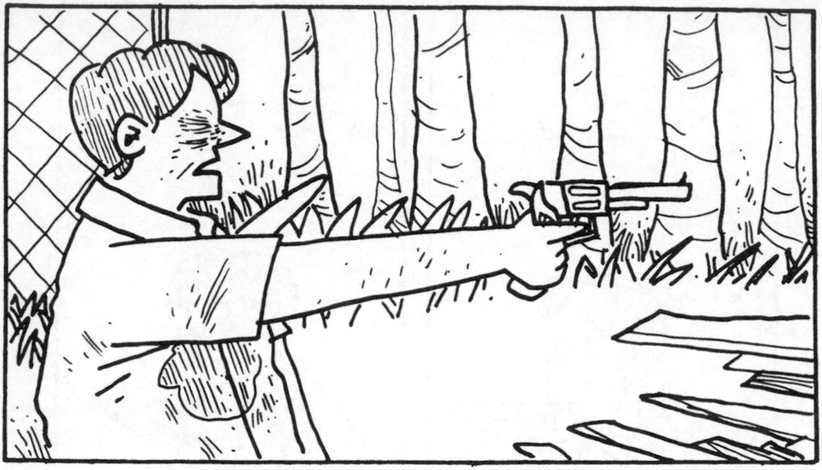

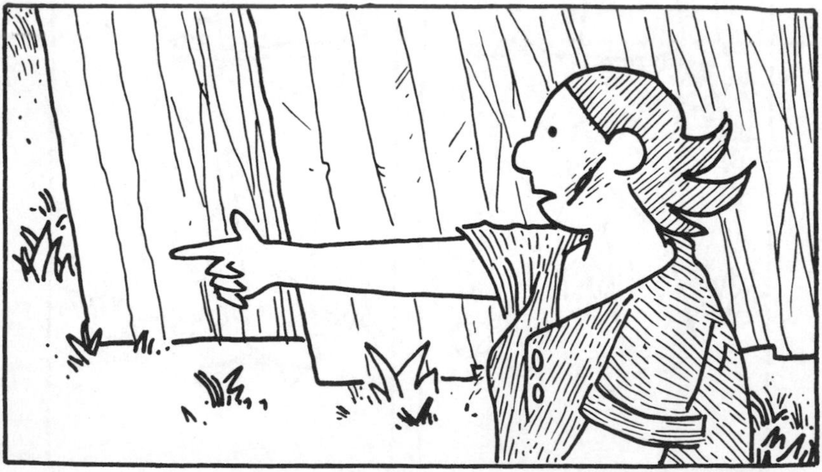

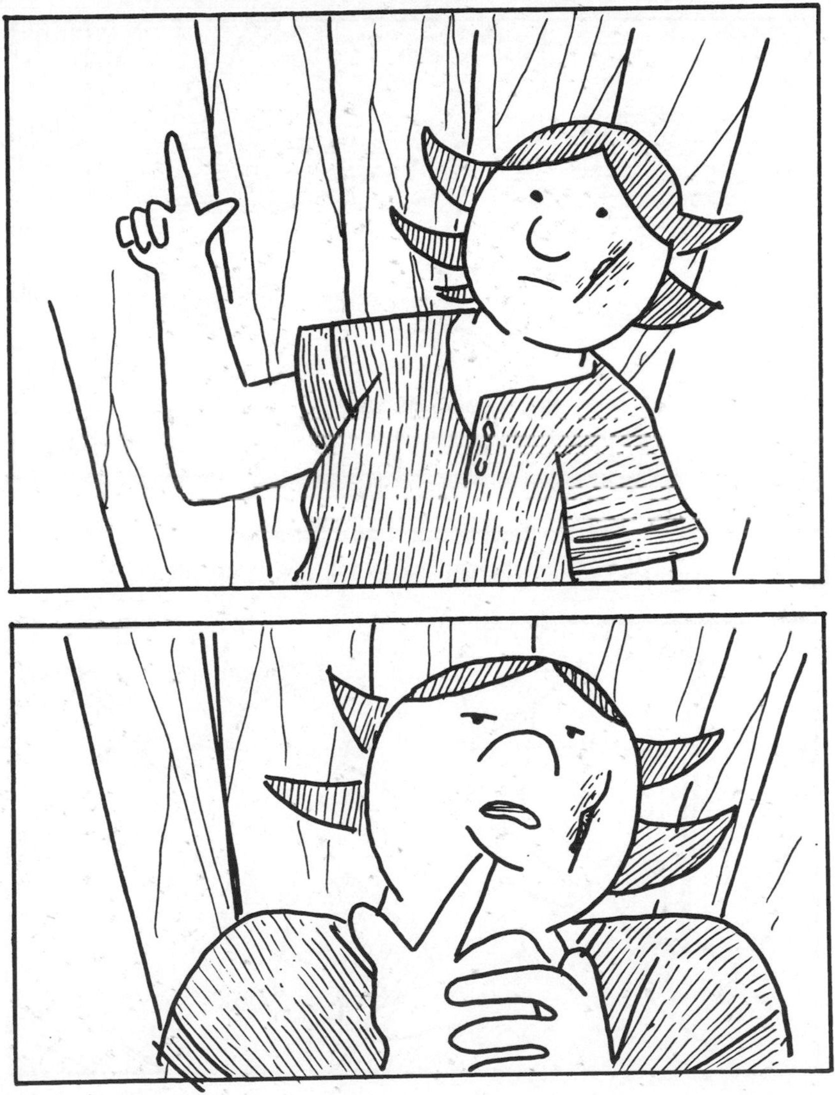

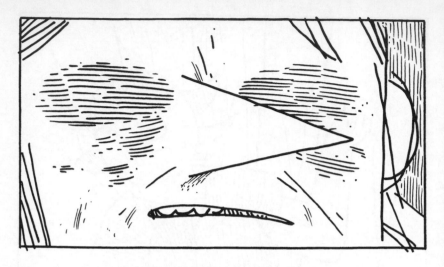

The moment before I pull the trigger,
I can see Carpenter move his lips to speak.

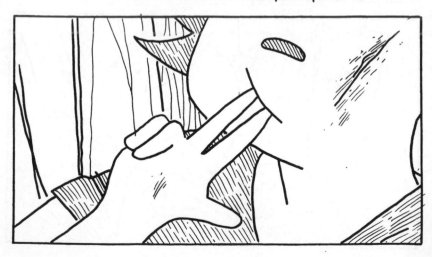

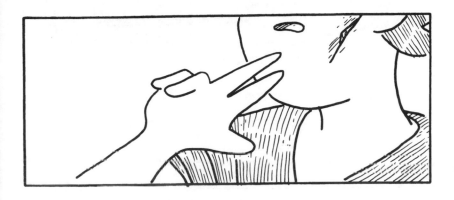

I am no longer interested in what he has to say.

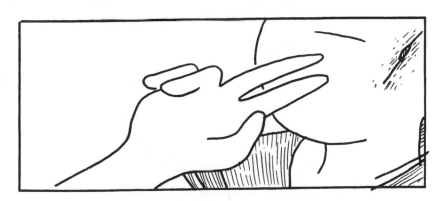

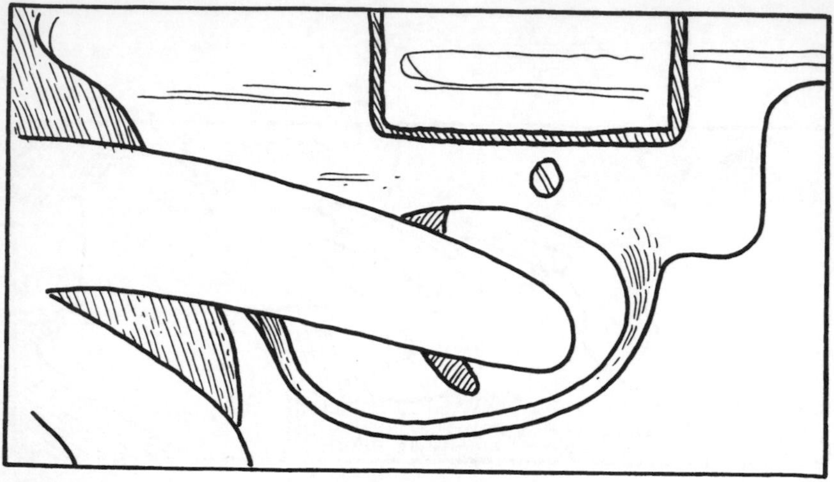

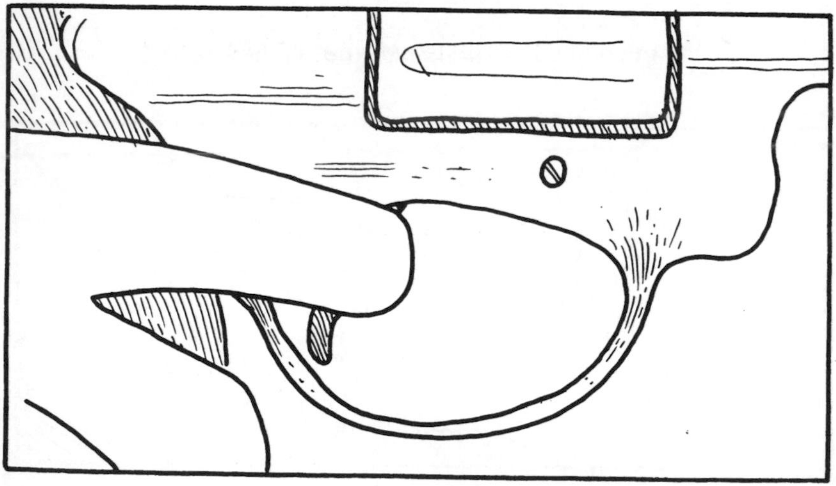

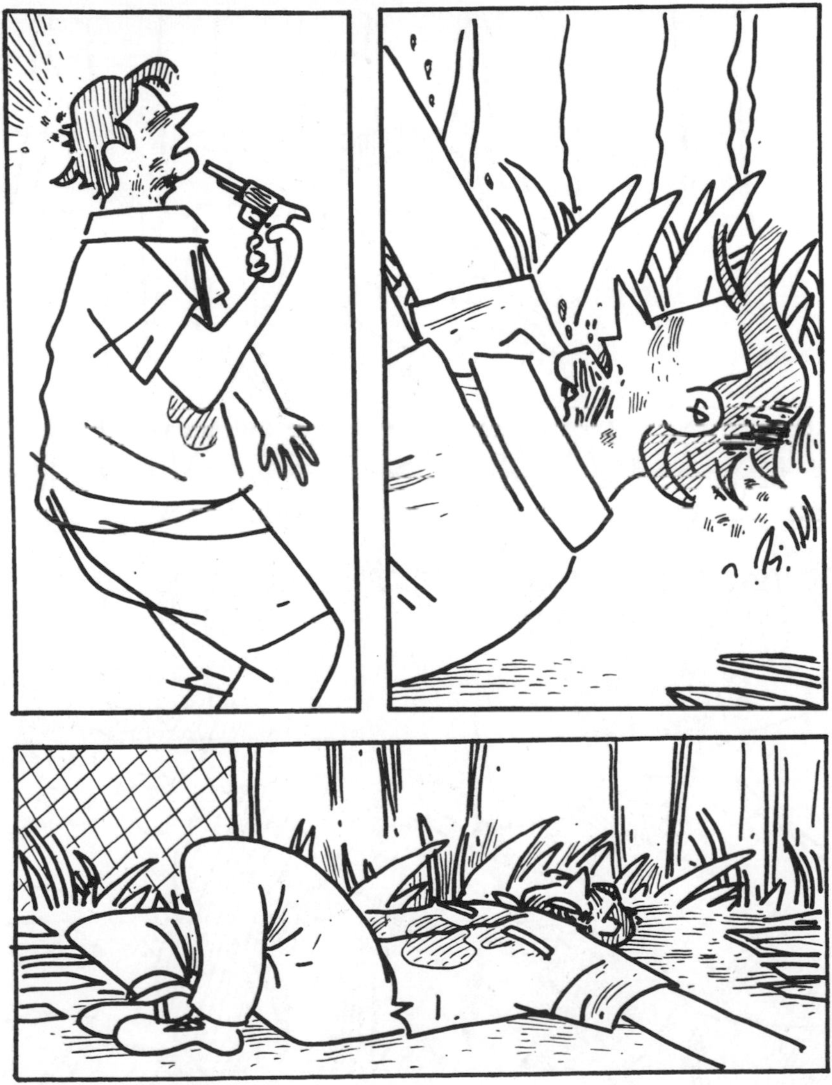

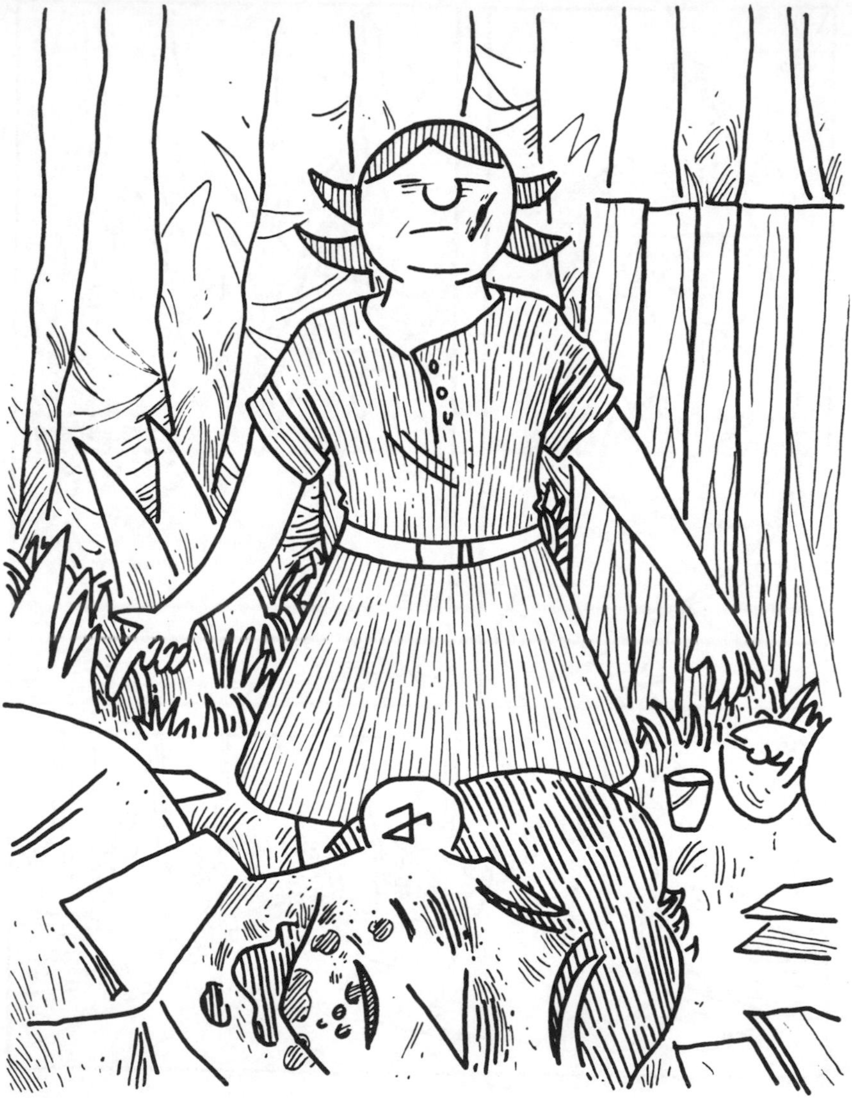

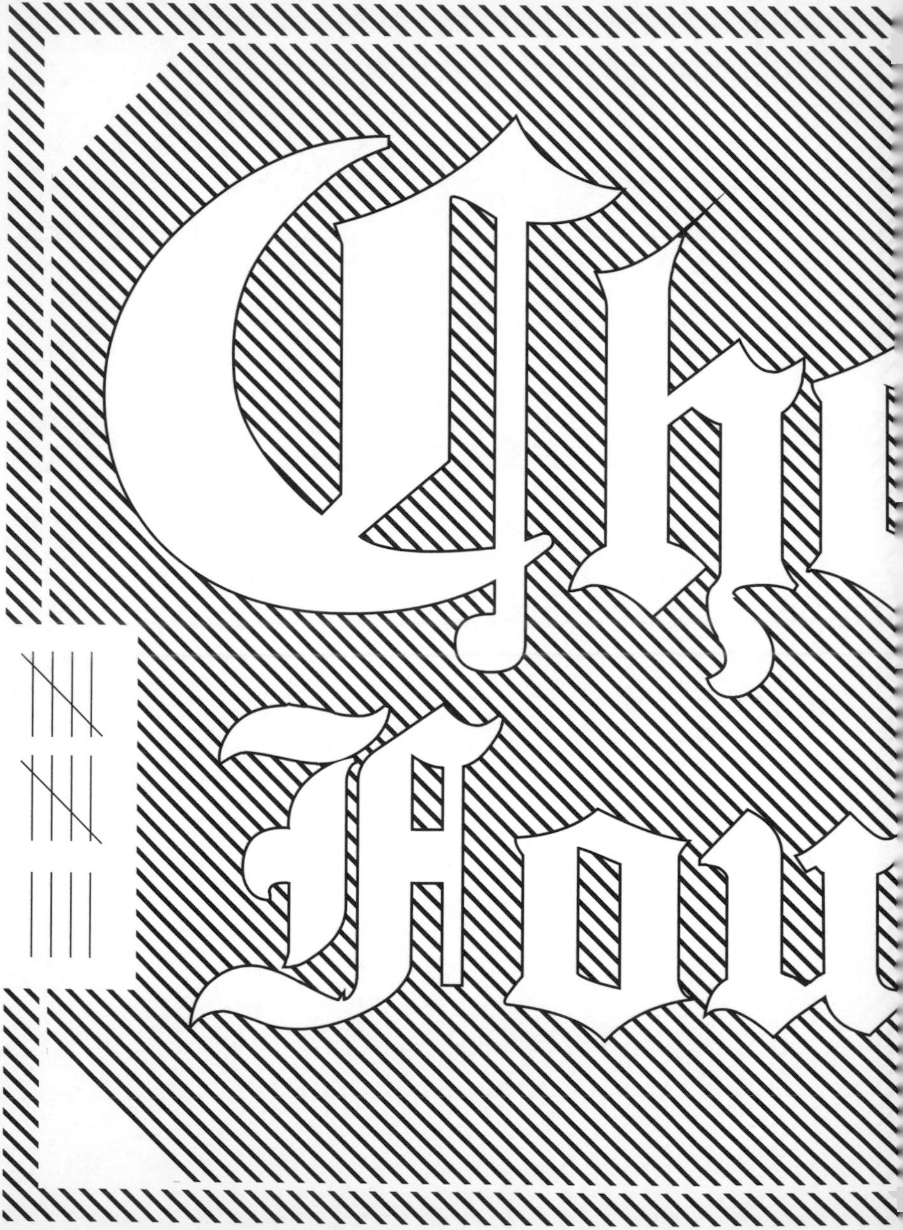

pter
teen

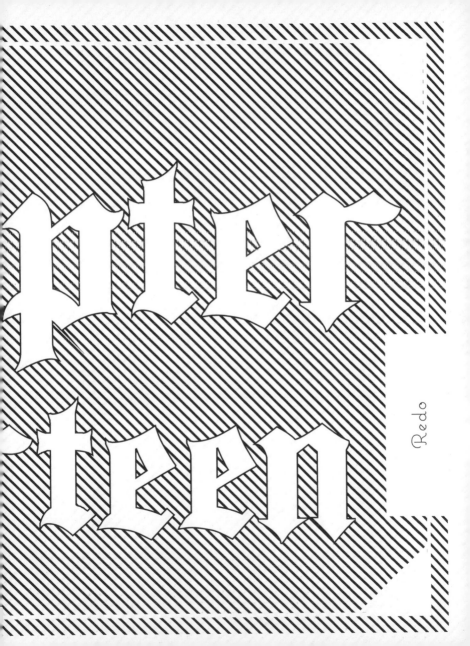

Redo